Introduction to Law in Canada

John Fairlie & Philip Sworden

emond

Toronto, Canada
2014

Emond Montgomery Publications Limited
60 Shaftesbury Avenue
Toronto ON M4T 1A3
http://www.emond.ca/highered

Printed in Canada.
Reprinted July 2015.

We acknowledge the financial support of the Government of Canada.
Nous reconnaissons l'appui financier du gouvernement du Canada.   **Canadä**

Publisher: Mike Thompson
Acquisitions editor: Bernard Sandler
Senior developmental editor: Sarah Gleadow
Developmental editor: Jamie Bush
Director, editorial and production: Jim Lyons
Production editor: Andrew Gordon
Proofreader: Nancy Ennis
Permissions editor: Monika Schurmann
Text designer and typesetter: Shani Sohn
Indexer: Paula Pike
Maps: VISU*TronX*
Cover image: © Michel Loiselle | Dreamstime.com

Library and Archives Canada Cataloguing in Publication

Fairlie, John, author
    Introduction to law in Canada / John Fairlie, Philip Sworden.

Includes index.
ISBN 978-1-55239-375-8 (pbk.)

    1. Law—Canada—Textbooks.   I. Sworden, Philip James, 1950-, author   II. Title.

KE444.F33 2014   349.71   C2013-907788-X
KF385.ZA2F33 2014

*To my wife, Christine, who patiently bore my long absences
while I worked in my study on this project.*

—JF

To my son Greg. I love you past infinity.

—PS

Brief Contents

Contents

PART I
Theory and Context

PART II
Law and the Canadian Constitution

6 The Executive: The Second Branch of Government 147

7 The Judiciary: The Third Branch of Government 169

8 Civil Liberties 217

PART III
Private Law and Public Law

Preface

There are many textbooks introducing the study of law in Canada. Our goal in writing *Introduction to Law in Canada* was not only to provide a theoretical basis for understanding the law and its development in the Canadian context, but also to provide a comprehensive overview of all key aspects of the Canadian legal system—from its constitutional underpinnings and the machinery by which laws are made and enforced, to specific areas of regulation like contracts, property, and criminal law, among others.

We wrote this text from a pan-Canadian perspective, imagining how readers from all parts of Canada would interpret its relevance, and not just those from its most populous regions. When citing statutory or case law, for example, we have tried to be as representative as possible. And in our discussion of the division of powers under the Constitution, the territories are included alongside the provinces in our explanations of the relevant principles.

We also wanted our writing to reflect Canada's social and multicultural diversity. For example: we include a chapter specifically dedicated to comparative law, looking at the different legal systems around the world and placing our system in that larger context; we describe how we are a bijural nation and how we have been influenced by both the common law and the civil law traditions; we look at how Aboriginal peoples are part of our legal heritage; and we examine how the *Canadian Charter of Rights and Freedoms* has shaped equality and other rights.

At the same time, we have tried to be mindful that law is a tool for the regulation of individuals and societies; there is a very practical side to the study of law. We have attempted to walk a fine line between introducing the law in a way that is accessible and describing it in sufficient detail to be useful. Part I covers theory and context. Part II examines the Canadian Constitution, including: how legislative power is divided between our federal, provincial, and territorial governments; how executive power is used to administer the law; how judicial power is distributed through our system of courts and the significance of the Supreme Court of Canada; and, finally, how civil liberties and the guarantee of rights and freedoms under the Charter influence our laws.

In Part III, our coverage of specific areas is divided between private and public law. We describe a wide array of subjects in enough detail to allow readers to take the next steps in their studies, with confidence in the grounding they have received and wherever their career paths take them. Part IV concludes by looking at legal professionals and their ethical obligations to the public and others, and by examining access to justice and law reform.

It is our hope that this text will serve as a useful guide for all students of law—including those in paralegal programs, business, justice studies, criminology, security and policing, border services, social work, history, and political science—and for anyone else who is interested in learning how the law operates in Canada.

Finally, we would like to thank the staff at Emond Montgomery for helping us put this book together—in particular, Jamie Bush, who worked with us through the initial drafts; Jim Lyons, who oversaw the final stages of this project; and Sarah Gleadow, who provided us with invaluable editorial assistance throughout. Our gratitude goes out to them all.

John Fairlie
Vancouver, British Columbia

Philip Sworden
Burlington, Ontario

February 2014

About the Authors

John Fairlie, BMus, LLB, LLM, is chair of the School of Legal Studies at Capilano University in North Vancouver. He was the lead developer of Capilano's Bachelor of Legal Studies (Paralegal) degree, which launched in 2010. He has taught a range of law courses, including Introduction to Law, Jurisprudence, Torts, Contracts, Property, Family, Company, Business, Criminal, Evidence, and Legal Research.

John is also the author of a book on legal research, *How to Find Canadian Law*, first published in 1999.

He has taught previously in the School of Criminology at Simon Fraser University and in the School of Business at the British Columbia Institute of Technology. His other pursuits have included working as a legal writer and co-running a small importing business.

Philip Sworden, BA, MA, LLB, PhD, is a professor in The Business School at Humber College Institute of Technology and Advanced Learning in Toronto and a former coordinator of Humber's Paralegal Education Diploma Program. He was instrumental in the development of Humber's Bachelor of Applied Arts (Paralegal Studies) degree program and co-designed its four-year curriculum. He currently teaches Legal History in that program.

Prior to *An Introduction to Law in Canada*, Philip has published *An Introduction to Canadian Law*, 2d ed (2006) and *Dimensions of Law: Canadian and International Law in the 21st Century* (2004) with Emond Montgomery. His passion for history has inspired publications including an essay in *Inside the Law: Canadian Law Firms in Historical Perspective* (volume 7, 1996) and legal history articles in *Business History Review*, *Research in Economic History*, and *The Law Society of Upper Canada Gazette*.

Philip has taught at McMaster University, Osgoode Hall Law School, Nipissing University, and Laurentian University. He is a co-recipient of the College Innovation of the Year Award and a recipient of Humber's Distinguished Faculty Award.

PART I
Theory and Context

1 What Is Law?

The bronze statue of Lady Justice atop the dome of the Old Bailey courthouse in London, England is one of the most iconic in the world.

> Few questions concerning human society have been asked with such persistence and answered by serious thinkers in so many diverse, strange, and even paradoxical ways as the question "What is law?"
>
> HLA Hart, *The Concept of Law*, 2d ed (Oxford: Oxford University Press, 1994) at 1

Introduction

This chapter provides some basic definitions of the law, then considers the law in relation to moral and ethical rules, to models of justice, and to religion. We then consider some prominent theories of law, including natural law, legal positivism, and legal realism, before proceeding to explain the concept of the rule of law. We outline the different divisions of the law, and conclude by discussing some important aspects of legal terminology.

Exploring these concepts will raise questions that cannot always be answered. This is a valuable lesson in itself; one of the things your legal studies will teach you is that absolutes and certainties are not always available. Learning the limitations of the law can be challenging. But you will discover that, despite its uncertainties, the law is an endlessly rich and fascinating field with the potential to engage you for a lifetime.

How Law Is Commonly Defined

Is the law simply what we say it is? Or is there more to it than that? Is it subject to higher standards? And do our rules have to meet these standards in order to qualify as law? For example, if our Parliament passed a law providing that all green-eyed babies must be given up for medical stem cell research, would that law be valid? Why or why not?

We will return to these questions later in the chapter, in connection with various conceptions of justice and theories of law. For now, though, we need a basic definition of law to help us get our bearings. There are many definitions of the law (see Box 1.1). For our purposes, the law can be defined as *a system of enforceable rules that governs the relationship between the individual members of a society and between those members and the society itself.* The law allows us to live in communities safely and to balance the needs of the individual with the needs of the community.

Types of Rules

The *rules* that make up the law can be divided into many categories. A good place to start is to say that there are three types of rules:

1. *General norms or standards of behaviour.* These rules usually prohibit certain activities, such as murder or careless driving.
2. *Condition rules.* These rules establish conditions or requirements that must be met before certain activities can be carried out. Licensing requirements for conducting a business, for getting married, or for driving a car are examples of these rules.
3. *Power-conferring rules.* These rules allow you to define your own legal relationship within certain contexts. The main examples of power-conferring rules are those relating to the law of contract—they allow you to set the terms and conditions that govern your relationship with another person, such as when purchasing or selling property, and in business transactions generally. Other examples of power-conferring rules include those relating to wills, which allow you to control how your property is distributed after you die.

Structure of Rules

Whatever the type of rule involved, the *form* of the rules is relatively standard:

If A, B, and/or C, then X

A, B, and C are elements (or conditions) that must be present for X (the legal result) to occur. Many legal rules involve three elements: A, B, and C. But some rules may have more elements, some fewer. The more complex rules may involve sub-elements.

If the elements are joined by "and" (A, B, *and* C), it is called a "conjunctive" list. This means that all elements must be satisfied or proved in order for the legal result to occur. If the elements are joined by "or" (A, B, *or* C), it is a "disjunctive" list. In this case, only one of the elements must be satisfied or proved in order for the legal result to occur. (Sometimes the elements may be part of a "hybrid" list, part conjunctive and part disjunctive.)

The crime of murder, seen from a conveniently simplified perspective, is structured in the conjunctive form. If an accused engages in behaviour (element A: the *actus reus* element) that causes the death of the victim (element B: the causation element), and if the accused means to cause the death (element C: the *mens rea* element), then the accused is guilty of murder and subject to punishment (X: the legal result).

Now let's look at a motor vehicle accident case, again from a simplified perspective and also based on a conjunctive list of elements. If a defendant's driving falls below the standard of a "reasonable motorist" (element A: the standard of care element), and this causes a loss to the plaintiff (element B: the causation element), and the loss is a compensable form of injury (element C: the damages element), then the defendant is liable in negligence and obliged to pay damages to the plaintiff (X: the legal result).

Legal claims are based on these underlying rules, regardless of their type or precise form. To succeed with a claim—that is, to obtain a legal result—you must establish all the required elements and sub-elements of the case. This is true whether you are a prosecutor in a criminal case or a plaintiff in a civil case.

Definitions of Law

The more laws and restrictions there are, the poorer people become. … The more rules and regulations, the more thieves and robbers.

Laozi (ca. 6th century BCE), *Tao Te Ching*

[L]aws were invented for the safety of citizens, the preservation of States, and the tranquility and happiness of human life. …

Marcus Tullius Cicero (106–43 BCE),
De Legibus or *On the Laws*

Law … is nothing else than an ordinance of reason for the common good, made by him who has care of the community, and promulgated.

Thomas Aquinas (1225–1274), *Summa Theologica*

Law … is the perfection of reason.

Edward Coke (1552–1634),
Institutes of the Laws of England

No enactment of man can be considered law unless it conforms to the law of God.

William Blackstone (1723–1780),
Commentaries on the Laws of England

[L]aw [may be thought of] as a set of rules which are generally obeyed and enforced within a politically organized society.

Graham Stephenson & Peter Shears,
James' Introduction to English Law, 13th ed
(London: Butterworths, 1996) at 6

How Law Relates to Other Rules

One thing that distinguishes the law from other kinds of rules is its enforceability. This enforcement occurs by way of state-sanctioned mechanisms or institutions such as the following: police forces, regulatory agencies (such as those that license certain activities), and court systems. The state does not enforce other kinds of rules—ethical or religious codes, abstract principles of justice—until they have been incorporated into or recognized as law.

Law, Morality, and Ethics

Most of us have a sense of right and wrong. And many of us are in general agreement about what is moral or immoral, ethical or unethical. Despite this common ground, ethical and moral disagreements frequently arise. What seems immoral to one person may be acceptable to another. For example, is it acceptable to lie? Never? Sometimes, depending on the circumstances? Always?

We can define **morality** as a system of values or principles concerning what is right or wrong with respect to human behaviour. Morality can be viewed from two perspectives:

1. descriptive, or
2. normative.

When we consider morality from a *descriptive* perspective, we are simply observing what a particular community believes to be right or wrong. We are offering no judgments or endorsements of these beliefs. We are describing things as they are.

When we approach a moral system from a *normative* perspective, we believe it to have an objective truth, or to set an ideal standard. We accept it and are invested in it. A moral code viewed in this light tells us how we should behave. Conduct that offends the code is considered immoral.

Ethics also deals with standards of human behaviour—with what is right or wrong, good or bad. And ethics, like morality, can be approached from either a descriptive or a normative point of view. There are many branches and sub-branches of ethics. One of these is *meta-ethics*. This area deals with basic questions such as how we determine what is good or bad and the nature of behavioural standards.

There is no generally accepted distinction between morality and ethics. But most people do tend to distinguish the two. One view is that morality focuses on personal character and behaviour, whereas ethics focuses on standards of behaviour in defined social settings, within specific groups of individuals. The word *ethics* is frequently used in professional contexts to describe standards of conduct. Most professions, including the legal profession, have codes of ethics. Members who offend these codes may be disciplined by their governing bodies. We will examine codes of ethics in the legal profession in more detail in Chapter 15.

What about the relationship between law and ethics? Earl Warren (1891–1974), a former American chief justice, said the following: "In civilized life, law floats in a sea of ethics."[1] In other words, a civilized society contains many ethical rules and standards; they vary according to context and do not have the status of law. They do, however, underlie the society's laws, which are applicable to everyone and are enforceable by the state. And both the law and the myriad ethical rules and standards are rooted in a common value system.

Law and Justice

A Roman statesman once said the following regarding justice: "Let justice be done, though the heavens fall." What does this mean? It means that justice must prevail regardless of the consequences. But what is justice? Where does it come from? Are conceptions of justice fixed or can they change? The answer to these questions depends, of course, on how we define justice (see Box 1.2).

In popular culture, justice is most often associated with criminal justice. *Where's the justice* when a person commits a serious crime and is freed on a technicality? *Where's the justice* when a person commits murder but only serves jail time? Such questions, often raised by the news media, reflect the view that our criminal laws place too much emphasis on the rights of criminals and process, and that sentencing is generally too lenient. But the concept of justice transcends criminal law; many theories of justice have a wider scope. Here, we are mainly concerned with theories of justice that are closely tied to law.

Justice can be considered in two ways:

1. as an end itself, or
2. as an instrument, or a means to an end.

Proponents of justice as an end in itself take what is called a **deontological** (from the Greek *deon*, meaning "obligation, duty") approach. This approach is non-consequentialist and rule-based; it holds that certain rights and responsibilities are fundamental and universal and that justice consists in upholding them. These standards are objectively good and true and require no analysis of social consequences or outcomes for their justification; they are an end in themselves.

Proponents of justice as a means to an end (an instrument) take what we call the **instrumentalist** approach. A desired social end might be, for example, a safer community or the

---

1 Earl Warren, Address (Speech delivered at the Louis Marshall Award Dinner of the Jewish Theological Seminary, Americana Hotel, New York City, 11 November 1962).

BOX 1.2

Definitions of Justice

What I say is that "just" or "right" means nothing but what is in the interest of the stronger party.

Plato (429–347 BCE),
The Republic

Revenge is a kind of wild justice; which the more man's nature runs to, the more ought law to weed it out.

Francis Bacon (1561–1626),
"Of Revenge" from *Essays* (1625)

Justice is truth in action.

Benjamin Disraeli (1804–1881),
House of Commons speech, 1851

Injustice anywhere is a threat to justice everywhere.

Martin Luther King (1929–1968),
Letter from Birmingham Jail, Alabama, 1963

Overcoming poverty is not a gesture of charity. It is an act of justice. It is the protection of a fundamental human right, the right to dignity and a decent life.

Nelson Mandela (1918–2013)
(Speech at Trafalgar Square in London, England, 2005)

Everyone knows that law is not the same thing as justice.

SM Waddams,
Introduction to the Study of Law, 7th ed
(Toronto: Carswell, 2010) at 4

---

reduction of poverty. A method of regulation would be a just one, according to this view, if it succeeded in making the community safer or in reducing poverty. This distinction—between deontological and instrumentalist conceptions of justice—offers us a general organizing principle, and a context in which to discuss three established and commonly cited models of justice: corrective justice, retributive justice, and distributive justice.

Corrective Justice

The concept of justice most closely attached to the deontological approach—that is, taking justice as an end in itself—is **corrective justice**. Central to the notion of corrective justice is the belief that a person has a moral responsibility for the harm he causes another, and that the loss must be rectified or corrected. (Corrective justice is also known as *rectificatory justice*.) Responsibility here is defined by the relationship between the causer and the injured, and there is no regard to consequences beyond the required rectification. The rectification (or correction) itself represents justice.

THEORY AND ORIGINS: ARISTOTLE

Most discussions of corrective justice begin with Aristotle (384–322 BCE) and his *Nicomachean Ethics*.[2] In this work, Aristotle describes two particular forms of justice: distributive justice and corrective justice. His model of distributive justice is concerned with the distribution of wealth in a society; it provides for the distribution of a state's bounty (property and honours, for example) according to merit, and it looks forward to later theories of distributive justice (see below).

Aristotle's account of corrective justice has a different focus and a different starting-point. It presumes that the status quo is good—that the distribution of wealth is acceptable—

---

2 See Aristotle, *Nicomachean Ethics*, translated by David Ross and revised by JL Ackrill & JO Urmson (Oxford: Oxford University Press, 1998) at V 4, 8; Jonathan Barnes, *Aristotle: A Very Short Introduction* (Oxford: Oxford University Press, 2000) at 4-5.

and that the parties to an injury (the wrongdoer and the injured) start from a position of material equality. On that basis, the theory addresses the imbalance that results when one person injures another.

Where one party inflicts injury on another, according to Aristotle, restitution rather than punishment is required. This notion of justice takes it for granted that the injured person's loss is equal to the gain of the person inflicting the injury. The parties were equal before, and now are separated by two "units." Why two units? Aristotle's theory holds that the person who inflicted the injury removed a benefit from the injured party while gaining a benefit herself.

This notion of the offender's gaining a benefit at the victim's expense is central to Aristotle's theory of corrective justice. It applies whether or not the offender receives any *actual* benefit from his action (as he clearly does, for example, in the case of stealing). Aristotle understood that with many injuries (for example, those involving physical harm), the person inflicting injury does not receive an actual gain—for example, a material benefit—from damaging the other person. For the purposes of his theory of corrective justice, however, Aristotle assumed that the offender's gain is equal in value to the victim's loss. In other words, whether the crime involves the theft of $100 cash or a physical injury whose damage is assessed at $100, the person causing the loss is judged to have received a $100 benefit at the expense of the victim.

Justice seeks to restore equality by compensating the injured party at the injurer's expense; it requires the return of the victim's original benefit, so the balance is restored. Both distributive justice and corrective justice are considered important concepts in the field of private law.

Underlying Aristotle's concept of corrective justice is the principle of causal responsibility. The injurer is responsible for causing the victim's injury. But Aristotle recognized that causation alone is not a sufficient principle when trying to assess responsibility. That is because there are degrees of wrongdoing. Wrongdoing may be voluntary or it may be involuntary. Aristotle defined two forms of voluntary wrongdoing:

1. *Deliberately caused harm.* Even where harm is inflicted deliberately, there are degrees of wrongdoing; premeditated harm is worse than harmful action that arises from passion.
2. *Harm caused contrary to reasonable expectation.* Aristotle referred to this as "misadventure" and we now refer to it as *negligence*.

LIMITATIONS OF CORRECTIVE JUSTICE

Enlightenment philosophers as well as modern ones have developed and supplemented Aristotle's ideas about corrective justice. Certain parts of his theory raise doubts and questions. For example, why should we presume that the injurer and the injured start from a position of equality? How do the varying degrees of culpability affect responsibility?

Although corrective justice theory has been refined since Aristotle's time, there is still no consensus about how widely it can be applied and about limits on—and degrees of—culpability. Its relevance to actions causing physical loss seems clear, but it applies less clearly to other kinds of actions. For instance, does corrective justice apply to losses caused by a failure to act (misfeasance)? How far are you responsible—to take a classic misfeasance issue—if you fail to help a drowning stranger in circumstances where there is little or no risk to yourself? Does corrective justice apply to injuries caused indirectly (for example, where someone comes to harm through information they have acquired from you) or to losses that are purely financial?

BOX 1.3

The Image of Justice

The personification of justice as a woman, blindfolded,* and holding scales and a sword, is based on ancient iconography. Her earliest incarnations were the Egyptian goddesses Ma'at and Isis. Later, in the classical era, she appeared as the Greek goddess Themis, and then as the Roman equivalent of Themis: Justitia.

In the modern context, the personification of justice is often referred to as Lady Justice. Her statues are seen outside courthouses, government buildings, universities, and other buildings where order and fairness are central ideals. The blindfold represents impartiality. Her scales signify that she will weigh opposing claims and conflicting evidence. And the sword represents the power she has to enforce her judgments. This icon of justice is associated with the law in general.

*   The statue of Lady Justice in front of the Old Bailey Courthouse, in London (pictured on the opening page of this chapter), does not include a blindfold. Courthouse pamphlets explain that this is because Lady Justice originally did not wear one. The blindfold did not become standard until the 16th century.

CORRECTIVE JUSTICE TODAY

Despite its limitations, corrective justice theory is important in the whole context of the law. A Supreme Court justice has remarked that private law and certainly tort law (a specific area of private law) can be "viewed primarily as a mechanism of compensation. Its underlying organizing structure remains grounded in the principle of corrective justice."[3]

As the justice's words suggest, corrective justice is primarily seen as a justification for ordering compensation in private law disputes. But it also applies to criminal cases, where *restitutionary orders*—based on principles of corrective justice—are possible. Take the example of a person who, in the course of committing a crime, physically or mentally injures a victim or damages his property. If convicted, this person may be ordered, at the time of sentencing, to compensate the victim directly for these losses. The amount payable is based on the victim's actual provable losses. Under section 738 of the *Criminal Code*,[4] the losses may relate to bodily harm, psychological harm, or property damage. Restitutionary orders are in line with the general purposes and principles of sentencing under the *Criminal Code*. These purposes, under section 718 of the Code, include (1) providing reparations for harm done to victims or to the community, and (2) promoting a sense of responsibility in offenders, and acknowledging the harm done to victims and the community.

Retributive Justice

Now let's consider **retributive justice**. If corrective justice is best suited to private law disputes, then retributive justice applies best to criminal law and to the perceived need for punishment. Does it reflect a *deontological* or an *instrumentalist* approach? Retribution can be viewed either as an end in itself—that is, as a self-evidently appropriate response to morally

---

3   See LeBel J in *Whiten v Pilot Insurance Co*, 2002 SCC 18, [2002] 1 SCR 595 at para 152.

4   RSC 1985, c C-46.

wrong behaviour—or as the means to socially worthwhile objectives, such as public safety or appeasement. To the extent that one accepts both views, it is a hybrid theory, with both deontological and instrumentalist aspects.

THEORY AND ORIGINS

The law of retaliation, or *lex talionis*, is often cited as the guiding principle of retributive justice. We are all familiar with such phrases as "an eye for an eye," "measure for measure," and "let the punishment fit the crime." These expressions are based on the idea that the response should be proportional to the wrong. Retaliation, which is linked to revenge, has always been part of human behaviour. Some of the oldest recorded references to *lex talionis* are in the *Code of Hammurabi*, a collection of Babylonian laws compiled around 1750 BCE.

LIMITATIONS OF RETRIBUTIVE JUSTICE

When it comes to administering retributive justice, we are faced with questions of balance and measure. At first glance, it appears that retribution is based on the ideal of an "equal" response—an eye for an eye. In practice, however, retributive codes seem to depart from this ideal. In the *Code of Hammurabi*, for example, the punishment for striking your father is not to be struck yourself, but to lose your hand. Also, the "eye for an eye" rule varied in Babylon according to the social status of the participants. Crimes against those of lesser status called for lesser punishments. Other ancient legal codes, too, seem to depart from the ideal of an equal response. To the modern mind, some of the punishments prescribed by the Old Testament—for example, stoning to death a person who swears—seem to exceed the limits of reasonable retaliation.

The law of retaliation raises questions. When is an equal response the right one? When are greater or lesser consequences appropriate? Whatever the answers, most people today would agree that the Babylonian practice of reducing the penalty because of the victim's "low" social standing is unacceptable. As an instrument for social order, retributive justice also raises questions of cause and effect. When it comes to public safety or crime reduction, are harsh penalties or lenient penalties more effective? Will new penalty regimes result in unintended consequences?

RETRIBUTIVE JUSTICE TODAY

Retributive justice is most relevant to criminal law. However, it can play a role in private law disputes—for example, in breach of contract and tort cases. This doesn't happen often. Private law disputes usually involve careless as opposed to deliberately hurtful conduct. And yet Canadian courts have awarded punitive damages—in other words, damages over and above compensatory damages—in cases where a defendant's behaviour has been particularly offensive. Such awards have both a moral end-in-itself (deontological) purpose and an instrumentalist purpose, as the Supreme Court of Canada (SCC) has made clear. They "give a defendant his or her just desert (retribution)," but they also "deter the defendant and others from similar misconduct in the future (deterrence)," and they "mark the community's collective condemnation (denunciation) of what has happened."[5]

What is the principle that courts use when determining punitive damages? The SCC has dictated that proportionality, based on a number of factors, must be the guiding principle. Key factors include the following:

---

5 *Whiten v Pilot Insurance Co, supra* note 3 at para 94.

- the blameworthiness of the defendant's conduct,
- the vulnerability of the plaintiff,
- the harm caused,
- the need of deterrence, and
- whether the defendant has been guilty of the conduct in the past.[6]

In most civil cases, the SCC's model of reasoned proportionality results in relatively modest punitive damage awards. The case is different in the US courts, which have sometimes allowed extremely large punitive damage awards.

Distributive Justice

THEORY AND ORIGINS

The third form of justice, **distributive justice**, is concerned with the way assets and entitlements are shared among members of a society. As we have seen, Aristotle set out certain premises of distributive justice. But Aristotle's treatment of the subject is sketchy.

One of the most significant modern commentators on the subject of distributive justice, and on the subject of justice generally, is John Rawls. In *A Theory of Justice*, he expresses his general conception of justice as follows:

> All social values [or social primary goods]—liberty and opportunity, income and wealth, and the social bases of self-respect—are to be distributed equally unless an unequal distribution of any, or all, of these values is to everyone's advantage.[7]

Injustice, then, according to Rawls, becomes "inequalities that are not for the benefit of all."[8]

Rawls's theory and the principles he derives from it are based on a modified form of *social contract theory*. What is social contract theory? It is a theory that attempts to explain why there is order in society; it tells us that law-abiding individuals within a society have agreed, in an unspoken, informal way, to surrender some of their freedoms and submit to the authority of the government in exchange for the protection of their rights. This unspoken agreement is referred to as a "contract."

Rawls's theory of distributive justice works from a basis of social contract theory, but it departs from it in certain ways. For example, Rawls does not use the image of a contract. In describing his ideal of distributive justice, he imagines an "original position" from which a hypothetical committee of individuals would decide upon the best way to organize society. These individuals would go about this process without knowing the details of their own positions in the society-to-be. This way, they would not be tempted to create principles that served their own interests. This hypothetical process yields what Rawls calls "justice as fairness." This is the ideal of distributive justice.

DISTRIBUTIVE JUSTICE TODAY

Today, debates about distributive justice frequently arise in the context of automobile insurance and workers' compensation programs. The debates concern whether and how to "distribute" the cost of injuries. Should all members of a group pay premiums or fees for the

---

6   *Ibid* at paras 111-126.

7   John Rawls, *A Theory of Justice*, revised ed (Cambridge, Mass: Harvard University Press, 1999) at 54.

8   *Ibid.*

BOX 1.4

Pierre Trudeau's "Just Society"

The phrase "just society" was coined by former Canadian Prime Minister Pierre Elliott Trudeau (1919–2000) during his bid to win the 1968 Liberal Party leadership campaign. It has become part of Canada's political terminology.

Trudeau meant the phrase to apply not to any specific policy, but to his entire platform. In the years that followed, he applied it to all his policies: official bilingualism; decriminalizing sexual matters involving consenting adults; and his crowning achievement, the patriation of the Canadian Constitution and the enactment of the *Canadian Charter of Rights and Freedoms*. Equality was a central theme of the just society.

---

sake of the smaller number of members who will suffer injuries? If all members of the group contribute to the fund, then the few unlucky enough to suffer injuries will not have to bear the full weight of medical costs themselves. Outside of this type of context, distributive justice plays only a small role in Canadian private law.

Distributive justice is more concerned with public law matters than with private law. In Chapter 8, when we discuss the Canadian Constitution and constitutional principles of equality, we will see how Rawls's ideas provide a foundation for Canadian values and beliefs. During election periods, distributive justice ideas come to the fore. For instance, a liberal candidate might propose to raise taxes to pay for new programs to assist a minority community. In other words, the cost of the new program, which would benefit only a portion of the population, would be distributed among all taxpayers. This is a distributive justice matter.

Law and Religion

In Chapter 2, we will look at systems of law from around the world. These will include legal systems that are based on religious law, such as Islamic sharia law. In most of the world, there is now a separation between church and state. But that is a relatively recent phenomenon. In the West, the Christian religion has certainly influenced the law.

How has Christianity influenced the law? Take the example of one of the most important common law court decisions ever handed down. In it, Lord Atkin formulated his "neighbour principle." This principle deals with every person's obligation to take care when engaging in an activity—any activity—that might affect other people. In describing this principle, Atkin draws directly from the Biblical parable of the Good Samaritan:

> The rule that you are to love your neighbour becomes in law, you must not injure your neighbour; and the lawyer's question, Who is my neighbour? receives a restricted reply. You must take reasonable care to avoid acts or omissions which you can reasonably foresee would be likely to injure your neighbour. Who, then, in law is my neighbour? The answer seems to be—persons who are so closely and directly affected by my act that I ought reasonably to have them in contemplation as being so affected when I am directing my mind to the acts or omissions which are called in question.[9]

---

9 *M'Alister (or Donoghue) v Stevenson*, [1932] AC 562 at 580 (HL).

Atkin's decision and the principle it expresses continue to shape the law of torts in Canada today. Whenever the Canadian courts are asked to recognize new duties of care, they almost invariably refer to Lord Atkin's "neighbour principle" as a starting point for their analysis.

Our Constitution also reflects the influence of religion. The preamble to the *Canadian Charter of Rights and Freedoms* reads as follows: "Whereas Canada is founded upon principles that recognize the supremacy of God and the rule of law." This reference to God is slightly paradoxical, in the Canadian context; the Charter's guarantee of religious freedom (section 2) in our multicultural society has made references to specific religious influences—such as Atkin's reference to the parable of the Good Samaritan—less acceptable in recent years.

Theories of Law: "Ought" and "Is"

Jurisprudence—the philosophy or science of law—and the theories that compose it are our concern in this section. Theoretical approaches to the law are numerous and varied, and there is some overlap with justice theories. A common method of classification of theories of law is to divide them into two main camps: *analytical* (concerned with what the law is) and *normative* (concerned with what the law ought to be). The two are not mutually exclusive. There are hybrid theories, such as feminist legal theory, and other theories, such as legal realism, that seem to challenge or subvert the distinction between analytical and normative.

Analytical jurisprudence generally concerns critical, explanatory, and value-free assessments of the law. It may involve, for example, examining the internal logic of a system of rules. Sometimes the investigations are more empirical in nature. The common thread between analytical theories of law is that they do not involve value judgments. They are concerned with what law *is*, not what it *ought to be*.

Normative jurisprudence, on the other hand, generally concerns the rightness or wrongness of the law based on various conceptions of justice, fairness, and morality. It involves making value judgments; it is evaluative, not explanatory. Because there are no objective, universally accepted standards of right and wrong, normative legal analysis depends less on "logic" and empiricism than analytical jurisprudence does. (*Ought* is always a more debatable matter than *is*.) Some normative analysis focuses on the consequences of a particular law—in other words, the instrumentalist perspective, which, as we discussed above, views law as a means to an end. Other normative analysis is deontological in character; in other words, it is concerned less with the consequences of the legal response than with duty and responsibility without regard to extrinsic effects.

The following is a brief overview of three well-established fields of jurisprudence: natural law theory, legal positivism, and legal realism.

Natural Law Theory

The idea of a higher power or source that guides our behaviour or offers us an ideal standard is likely as old as human civilization itself. A person who believes this to be the case—who believes such external standards exist—believes that man-made or "positive" law is subject or subordinate to this higher or **natural law**.

What is the basis for this natural law? What is this "higher power"? Is it virtue, divine law, reason, human nature, morality, or some invisible wellspring? And how do we come to know it? How do we determine what the standards are to guide us? Do we base our standards on the beneficial results they promote? Or do we base our standards on unchangeable notions of what is right independent of the consequences they produce? Or is it sometimes a combination of these? The answers to these questions vary according to the specific theory being expounded.

Early Theories of Natural Law

The Greek philosopher Plato's ideas about justice and just laws are among the most ancient expressions of natural law. One of the starting points of Platonic thought is that there are eternal, immutable ideas of good—what he called the world of the Forms. These ideals, according to Plato, are more "real," in a sense, than the material world of change and sensation. In *The Republic*, Plato envisages a utopia governed by philosopher rulers whom the ordinary citizens trust to know these Forms and to rule by their light. Plato's student Aristotle, whom some consider the father of natural law theory, saw natural law as being based on virtue and the "golden mean" (that is, the idea that everything should be done in moderation). He developed these ideas in his *Nicomachean Ethics*.

In the Middle Ages, the theologian Thomas Aquinas (1225–1274) reworked Aristotle's ideas about natural law into a Christian context. Natural law was associated with God's will or divine law, and this was identified, in turn, with reason. According to Aquinas, when we correctly use our abilities to reason, we are participating in or identifying with God's reasoning.

Hugo Grotius (1583–1645) was a Dutch jurist who contributed to the natural law debate primarily by secularizing it. He believed that natural law would still exist even if God didn't. He grounded natural law in human nature itself, arguing that the natural law was discoverable through the use of "right reason," which is a human faculty rather than a divine one.

Connected to this secularizing shift was the development of social contract theory, which we discussed briefly above. This is the theory that human existence in a pre-civilization state of nature—a state in which people live without government, completely free—is not ideal but "nasty, brutish, and short," as Thomas Hobbes (1588–1679) wrote in *Leviathan*. To secure our safety and happiness, we surrendered (at some hypothetical point in our pre-history) our absolute freedom and agreed to be governed by rulers. Hobbes believed that these rulers' authority over their subjects was absolute, not subject to any natural law. English philosopher John Locke (1632–1704), on the other hand, believed that this contract was based on natural law, which he identified with human or natural reason. French philosopher and writer Jean-Jacques Rousseau (1712–1778) had similar ideas (see Box 1.5).

BOX 1.5

Natural Law and the US Declaration of Independence

The works of Locke and Rousseau, among others, provided a philosophical basis for the American Revolution in the late 1700s. With this event, 13 colonies fought a war to break free from British rule. According to Locke, natural law teaches us that we are all equal and have certain natural rights to life, health, liberty, and possessions. Locke also maintained that no government has the authority to deny its people these rights. If it does deny them these rights, it is placing its subjects in a state of nature, and war is justified.

Rousseau's most famous work is *The Social Contract* (1762). It begins as follows: "Man was born free, yet everywhere he is in chains. One man thinks himself the master of others, but remains more of a slave than they."

The second sentence of the Declaration reads as follows: "We hold these truths to be self-evident, that all men are created equal, that they are endowed by their Creator with certain unalienable Rights, that among these are Life, Liberty and the pursuit of Happiness."

These words constitute the philosophical justification for the American Revolution.

Modern Theories of Natural Law

An important modern exponent of natural law was the Harvard law professor Lon Fuller (1902–1978). In *The Morality of Law* (1964), Fuller wrote about the connection between morality and law. In Chapter 2 of this work, he begins with an allegory involving a fictional ruler called Rex, and he proceeds to describe "eight ways to fail to make law." These ways to fail are as follows:

1. *Deciding issues on an ad hoc basis, without laws.* This is the most obvious kind of failure: simply failing to make laws at all, necessitating decision making that is unpredictable. Laws must be made, despite the apparent difficulty in crafting them.

2. *Failing to publicize laws or make them available to the affected party.* The unfairness here is obvious. How can laws be effective if they are unknown?

3. *The abuse of retroactive legislation.* As a general rule, laws must be prospective. Retroactive legislation is legislation that applies to past behaviour. Without advance notice that such legislation will be passed, it cannot be a guide to conduct (unless you have the power of foresight), and if the power to make it is inappropriately used, it will undercut the integrity of prospective rules. Why follow an existing rule today if your now "legal" behaviour could be "punished" by a contrary law passed tomorrow, with retroactive effect?

4. *Failing to make rules understandable.* Rules that are too complex serve little purpose and suffer from the same failing as laws that are not publicized.

5. *The enactment of contradictory rules.* The only outcome here, for the person trying to obey the law, is failure. No matter which rule a person follows, she will be breaking another rule.

6. *Enacting rules with which the parties affected lack power to comply.* Rules that cannot be complied with cannot be a guide to action.

7. *Making frequent changes to law.* This challenges the stability of the legal system. If the law changes frequently, it becomes difficult if not impossible to plan ahead effectively.

8. *Announcing rules and then failing to enforce them.* If people come to believe that laws will not be enforced, they will not respect these laws and will treat them as window dressing. Fear of negative consequences motivates many to follow the rules.[10]

Fuller maintains that we need to avoid these pitfalls in order to achieve a legal system that is just and consistent. Unlike earlier natural law thinkers, Fuller does not believe that we discover natural law through external absolutes based on religion or reason. He believes that we find "natural" moral standards through analyzing social behaviour and human nature. However, he doesn't elaborate on what those moral standards are.

The work of Margaret Mead (1901–1978), an American cultural anthropologist, can be seen as filling in the gaps left by Fuller. Her research suggested interesting possibilities concerning natural moral standards—a natural law grounded in human nature itself, examined across cultures. Her study of different human populations revealed common standards of behaviour and common rules relating to such things as justified and unjustified killing, the prohibition of incest, and—in many cases—the right to own private property.[11]

---

10   Lon L Fuller, *The Morality of Law*, revised ed (New Haven, Conn: Yale University Press, 1965) ch 2.

11   Margaret Mead, "Some Anthropological Considerations Concerning Natural Law (1961)" in Michael DA Freeman, ed, *Lloyd's Introduction to Jurisprudence*, 8th ed (London: Sweet & Maxwell, 2008) at 225-27.

Ronald Dworkin (1931–2013), a student of Fuller, does not count himself as a natural law theorist, but he does believe in agreed-upon communal principles such as justice and fairness.[12] He believes these principles must inform the law and be used to resolve gaps and inconsistencies in it. The law, according to Dworkin, is a "seamless web" connected by these principles, dictating a correct answer to any legal problem.

Systems founded on natural law supply us with ideals. But they also raise many questions:

- What is the basis of natural law—virtue, religion, reason, or human nature?
- How do we determine what its rules are?
- Whom do we authorize to determine these rules?
- How do we resolve contradictions between natural law and positive (that is, man-made) law?

Legal Positivism

Natural law's main opposition as a legal theory is **legal positivism**. On the scale of *ought* and *is* (that is, normative versus analytic jurisprudence), legal positivism tends more toward the analytic. It evaluates laws and legal systems without, for the most part, placing value judgments on them. As legal theories go, it is a relatively recent development.

Backgrounds of Legal Positivism

One of the precursors to legal positivism was Thomas Hobbes. We discussed him above, in our discussion of social contract theory. There, we saw that, unlike other social contract theorists such as Locke and Rousseau, Hobbes was no believer in natural law. Instead, he believed in the absolute authority of the ruler to whom the people have given over power by way of the social contract. This belief in absolute authority is inconsistent with the idea that there are natural laws to which all members of the society, including the king, are subject. Hobbes, who was above all a pragmatist, also believed that people are free to do whatever the ruler's laws do not expressly forbid. Hobbes's pragmatic thinking in these matters, though it doesn't in itself qualify as legal positivism, would become a cornerstone for legal positivists.

David Hume (1711–1776) took the empirical method—in other words, the experimental method—further than Locke did, demystifying many of his society's most deeply held beliefs, including the religious ones. He also criticized social contract theory, natural law ideas, and certain established principles of justice on the grounds of their "artificiality" and lack of provability. He advocated for the use of the experimental method in questions of morality and justice. His work laid some ground rules for the analytic method in this area.

Legal Positivism in the Modern Era

Legal positivism's first real proponent was John Austin (1790–1859), a professor of jurisprudence at the University of London (now University College). He was a utilitarian, believing the goal of legislation to be "the greatest happiness of the greatest number." But he was better known for his analytic method and his use of precise terminology to define

---

12 His most famous works are Ronald M Dworkin, *Taking Rights Seriously* (Cambridge, Mass: Harvard University Press, 1977) and *Law's Empire* (Cambridge, Mass: Harvard University Press, 1986).

positivist thinking. His greatest work is the *Province of Jurisprudence Determined*.[13] The core positivist beliefs, according to Austin, are as follows:

1. All commands of the sovereign are valid and enforceable.
2. "Commands" means **positive law**—that is, man-made rules.
3. The "sovereign" refers to the person or agency who receives habitual obedience in a given society.
4. Laws made in accordance with the society's existing formalized and recognized process are valid, regardless of so-called natural law, morality, or any external standard.

More recently, H.L.A. Hart (1907–1992), a professor of jurisprudence at Oxford University, and his student Joseph Raz (1939–), also a professor at Oxford, have continued the positivist tradition. They have made the point that a person's holding positivist beliefs does not prevent her either from having moral standards or from advocating for their legal recognition. However, law and morality are separate, and the validity of the former is not tied to the latter.

Hart also writes about the frailty of language with respect to the law. There will be gaps and inconsistencies in the laws we make, however hard we try to avoid them. Gaps can be filled by judicial discretion, but at some point, Hart argues, the law simply breaks down. (Dworkin's response to this idea, in keeping with his natural law premises, is that justice and fairness fill these gaps.)

It is fair to say that the Anglo-Canadian legal tradition has a positivist basis. The principle of parliamentary sovereignty (which we discuss in more detail in Chapter 5) means that laws made in accordance with the recognized process are valid without reference to external standards. The Charter provides for self-imposed standards based on a kind of natural law, but legislators may disregard them in making law.

In times of political stability, when governments follow commonly accepted standards and the existing order is acceptable to the majority of people in the society, legal positivism is effective as an underlying theory. It is clear and relatively simple. It endorses the validity of what is. But during times of war or oppressive regimes, people begin to question the validity or fairness of existing laws and to measure them against external standards. For instance, how do we respond to positive laws that sanction the systematic killing of large numbers of people, or to laws that categorize people in certain ethnic groups as second-class? According to legal positivism, a bad law properly constituted under a cruel regime is a valid law. To many people, this might seem a shortcoming in the theory.

Legal Realism

Legal realism is a field of jurisprudence that arose in the 20th century. It was largely a response to the emphasis on logic that dominated British positivist theory in the 1800s. The first writers of legal realist theory were American (see Box 1.6). But Scandinavian countries, too, saw a strong theoretical movement in this direction. The adherents in both countries shared the positivist view that law is a human invention. But they also advocated a more intensely empirical study of the process by which laws are made and applied, and they argued that law is subject to many of the flaws and weaknesses of other human activities.

Another tenet of legal realism is that law does not operate in a vacuum; it is one of many parts in the whole social machine. It follows from this premise that an interdisciplinary

---

13 John Austin, *The Province of Jurisprudence* (London: John Murray, 1832).

Legal Realism and Oliver Wendell Holmes (1841–1935)

Oliver Wendell Holmes was born in Boston, Massachusetts and fought in the American Civil War on the Union side. He studied law at Harvard and practised law for 15 years before becoming, first, a legal editor, then a professor at Harvard Law School, and, finally, a judge of the Supreme Judicial Court of Massachusetts. He was appointed to the United States Supreme Court in 1902 and retired from the Court in 1932, aged 90, the oldest judge ever to serve on the Court. He left a legacy of ideas that are still relevant today.

Holmes was an early leading light in a new way of thinking about law. He is noted for many famous pithy sayings, including the following: "The life of the law has not been logic; it has been experience." * With this statement, Holmes was not denying that logic plays an important role in the law; he was merely affirming his belief that practical experience is a more important factor in the law than pure reason is. Opposed to the doctrine of natural law, he took a pragmatic approach to the study of law and felt it was largely about predicting what courts would decide. He is considered by some to be the father of legal realism in America.

* Oliver Wendell Holmes, *The Common Law* (Boston: Little, Brown and Company, 1881) at 1.

approach to the study of law offers advantages. Legal realism also holds that law should be seen as an instrument to further desired social objectives.

Many legal realists focus on the judicial process—a single part of the overall legal system—and, specifically, on how judges make their decisions. In theory, the primary role of judges is to make decisions by applying rules to specific "fact situations" (in other words, the cases appearing before them). Many of us believe, or would like to think, that certainty and objectivity surround this process. In go the facts and out comes the unerring, inevitable decision. But most experienced litigators, who are veterans of legal proceedings, believe the process works otherwise. If litigators often advise their clients to settle, it is to avoid the uncertainty of going to court.

How do we predict the legal decisions of judges? Many factors contribute to their decisions, including the following:

- how credible they find the witnesses,
- how much weight they give to documentary and other "real" evidence,
- how they go about synthesizing complex and conflicting legal principles,
- how they go about applying general principles to specific fact situations, and
- how far they are able to recognize and deal with uncertainties in the rules themselves and in the facts to which these rules are applied.

Oliver Wendell Holmes suggested that non-legal disciplines, such as history and economics, can help us understand judges' decision making. Also relevant are the intellectual ability, personality, morality, biases, and proclivities of the judge in question. Individual judges are likely to be inconsistent themselves from time to time, affected by their changing and personal circumstances. For instance, what tensions or conflicts is the judge who is hearing the case experiencing outside the courtroom, in her personal life? How rested and prepared is she for the case? One American jurist has remarked that a judicial decision "might be determined by what the judge had for breakfast." On days that a judge has multiple hearings, is your particular case at the beginning, at the middle, or at the end of her day—when she is starting to think about her daughter's hockey game, which she may miss if your application goes on much longer?

Study of legal realism has waned since the 1980s. It was a theory that pointed out some weaknesses in legal systems, but it did not come up with solutions. Other kinds of legal theories have arisen during this period, but most bear the influence of legal realism's empiricism, pragmatism, and openness to other disciplines.

Other Legal Theories

We have described three important theories of law, but there are many others, too many to describe in detail here. However, a brief mention of some of them will give you an idea of the scope of jurisprudential study.

Utilitarianism is a theory we mentioned in connection with John Austin and legal positivism. It originated with Jeremy Bentham (1748–1832), and it measures the utility or worth of actions in terms of the overall happiness they generate. It is instrumentalist (or consequentialist)—taking the law as a means to an end—and it underlies any current theory of law that considers the law to be a tool for social change.

Among such utilitarian theories is the *law and economics* movement (also referred to as the economic analysis of law), which measures a law's worth in terms of its capacity to increase social wealth. This theory substitutes wealth for the "happiness" of the utilitarian standard, happiness being difficult to measure. A prominent exponent of this legal theory is the American jurist Richard Posner (1939–). This theory of law has not had the same influence in Canada that it has had in the United States.

Another theory of law is the so-called *pure theory of law*, which owes its name to a book of the same name by the Czech legal scholar Hans Kelsen (1881–1973).[14] It is an outgrowth of legal positivism but acknowledges its "normative" aspects more openly than traditional positivism does. One interesting aspect of this theory is that it posits the existence of a basic norm called a "Grundnorm," from which all others can be derived. This basic norm is to be chosen based on a principle of efficiency. A principle is considered "efficient" if people in general can be shown to follow it independently of any legal rules requiring them to do so. However, the theory does not tell us what this basic norm is.

The **law and society** and **sociology of law** disciplines are related in that they look at law from a broad social, interdisciplinary perspective. The difference between these two theories is that the first identifies most closely with legal studies, and the second with sociology. One important issue debated in both is whether laws come about through consensus or through conflict within a society.

Marxist theories of law are based on the writings of Karl Marx (1818–1883), Friedrich Engels (1820–1895), and other advocates of communist policies. Such policies address the distribution of wealth and class structure within a society. These kinds of legal theories are compatible with distributive justice thinking, which, as we have seen, is also concerned with the distribution of wealth (among other benefits) in a society.

Feminist theories of law cover a wide range of issues, and can be seen as an outgrowth of the women's movement in the 1960s and 1970s, and as having connections with critical legal studies (described next). While works on women's rights are not new—for example, the seminal work *A Vindication of the Rights of Women* (1792) by Mary Wollstonecraft (1759–1797)—feminist jurisprudence arguably did not establish itself until the 1970s. The modern literature in this field is far-reaching and diverse, and goes well beyond issues concerning reproductive rights, violence against women, equal pay for equal work, and sex discrimination more generally. Feminist legal theories also examine such areas as how gender

---

14   Hans Kelsen, *Pure Theory of Law*, translated by Max Knight (Berkeley: University of California Press, 1960).

roles and women's subordination are perpetuated and concealed by the law's assumptions, language, and structure; how patriarchal interests are supported by the law; and what legal reforms are necessary to improve the position of women in society.

As a theory, **critical legal studies** (also known as "CLS" or "Crit") is an outgrowth of American legal realism. Forged as an independent theory in the late 1970s, it is largely concerned with exposing law as an instrument of the rich and powerful. Its adherents have suggested many legal reforms. Emerging from CLS is **critical race theory** (also known by its acronym, CRT), a kindred theory of feminist jurisprudence. The difference between feminist legal theory and critical race theory is that the latter focuses on race-based inequities in place of gender-related issues.

There are various other areas and sub-areas of legal study, as well as non-legal movements that touch on the law—for example, postmodernism, post-structuralism, deconstruction theory, and discourse analysis. All of these non-legal movements deal in some way with whether objective truth is ascertainable and with the logic of language systems and their hidden assumptions. Common to many current theories is a belief in the value of multi- and interdisciplinary study, and in the artificiality of trying to isolate any process, such as law, given that it is just one part of a complex social system.

Rule of Law

The term **rule of law** concerns fairness in the administration of the law. Its central tenets are that

1. everyone in a society, regardless of their social or political position, should be treated equally before the law; and
2. power under the law should not be used arbitrarily.

As we shall see, the rule of law is one of the cornerstones of the Canadian legal system, and is expressly referred to in the *Canadian Charter of Rights and Freedoms*.

Origins

Principles related to the rule of law appear in the legal culture of the Greeks and Romans. Cicero, a famous orator who lived in an era of Roman democracy, is quoted as saying the following: "[We] are servants of the law, that we all may be free."

The concept of the rule of law was generally not recognized in the next phase of world history, during the Dark Ages. It resurfaced in the Middle Ages. King John of England (1167–1216), after enjoying supreme power for much of his reign, was suddenly faced with a revolt by his barons. He capitulated by signing one of the most famous legal documents in the democratic world, the *Magna Carta* (1215). (See Box 1.7.) In this document, he agreed to give up some of his power and to protect his barons' liberties. The seeds of the rule of law were planted with the *Magna Carta*. Some of its provisions are still in force today in England.

Basic Principles

In the modern era, rule-of-law doctrine was given prominence through the work of A.V. Dicey, who is widely recognized as one of the fathers of modern English constitutional law. He popularized the phrase "rule of law" in his most influential work, *An Introduction to the*

Study of the Law of the Constitution (London, 1885). We may summarize Dicey's three core rule-of-law principles as follows:

1. Law must have supremacy over the influence of arbitrary power. It follows from this that no one can be punished except for breach of an established law as determined through an established process before the courts.

2. No one is above the law whatever his place in society or, to put it another way, the law applies equally to everyone. And, again, it is recognized judicial process that will make the rulings to ensure this occurs.

3. Personal rights and liberties must be protected by giving every person the ability to apply to the courts for a remedy should any of those rights and liberties be denied.

Dicey's first principle recognizes that the arbitrary application of state power will lead to discontent. Rules must be in place and then enforced according to a set process. Otherwise, punishment for their infringement will not be seen as fair. Adherence to the second principle is a key feature of true democracies; it distinguishes them from autocracies, where rulers have absolute power, and from societies where the law applies to people differently depending on their status. Equal application of the law promotes respect for the legal system. Dicey's third principle highlights the idea that the courts are instrumental in protecting our rights and liberties. How effective that protection is depends directly on how free our courts are

BOX 1.7

The Magna Carta: The Great Charter of English Liberties

In the early feudal era, when English kings were first establishing a strong, centralized kingdom in England, their powerful nobles resisted giving them total power. When King John raised taxes to help finance his wars in France, the nobles rebelled and forced him to sign the *Magna Carta*, which placed limits on royal powers. One notable limit on royal power was described in chapter 39 of this document:

> No free man shall be taken or imprisoned or disseised or outlawed or exiled or in any way ruined, nor will we go or send against him, except by the lawful judgement of his peers or by the law of the land.*

Arthur Hogue explains how the *Magna Carta* introduced the concept of the rule of law:

> In effect, each confirmation of the Charter became a solemn assurance to the realm that the king would act with a regard for the welfare of all subjects. It was an assurance, moreover, that the king would act according to clearly established procedure; in short, the king, like all of his subjects, was under the law.[†]

This idea—namely, that the same law applies equally to everyone and that a person's legal rights cannot be taken away

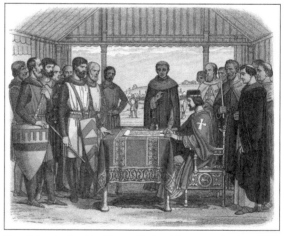

King John signing the *Magna Carta*, at Runnymede, June 1215.

from them except by the law of the land—is one of the great legal legacies that Canadians have inherited from English law.

* James C Holt, *Magna Carta* (Cambridge: Cambridge University Press, 1965) at 327.

† Arthur R Hogue, *Origins of the Common Law* (Bloomington, Ind: Indiana University Press, 1966) at 50-51.

from political interference (see Box 1.8). (The separation of powers between the legislative, executive, and judicial branches of government is discussed in Part II of this book.)

It has been frequently observed that Dicey's conception of the rule of law relates more to "procedural" fairness than to "substantive" fairness. In other words, it deals with when and how laws are applied rather than with the fairness of the laws themselves. Dicey does not propose any general guidelines for determining whether laws are fair.

Most modern definitions of the rule of law follow Dicey's approach; they leave substantive fairness issues to be dealt with in official bills of rights and human rights documents at both the national and international levels. This disregard for substantive fairness issues has interesting implications. For example, an established law permitting torture would not offend the idea of the rule of law so long as that law were clearly and equally applied through a recognized court process. But it might well violate whatever human rights document that society subscribes to.

No agreed-upon set of principles underlies the concept of the rule of law. There are principles other than Dicey's. For example, Joseph Raz has listed the following eight:

1. All laws should be prospective, open, and clear.
2. Laws should be relatively stable.
3. The making of particular laws (particular legal orders) should be guided by open, stable, clear, and general rules.
4. The independence of the judiciary must be guaranteed.
5. The principles of natural justice must be observed.
6. The courts should have review powers over the implementation of the other principles.
7. The courts should be easily accessible.
8. Crime-prevention agencies should not be allowed to pervert the law at their discretion.[15]

Raz's first three principles relate to the laws themselves. The clearer and more certain our laws are, the better they will guide us, and the less scope there will be for arbitrary power. The remaining five principles relate to fairness in the enforcement process, primarily through the court system but also through the police and other crime-prevention arms of government. You may notice that many of these rule-of-law principles are similar if not identical to Lon Fuller's "Eight Ways to Fail to Make Law," discussed above in connection with natural law.

Other legal scholars have suggested other requirements for the rule of law:

- The independence of the legal profession ("the bar") must be secure.
- Lawyer–client confidentiality must be guaranteed.
- Legal services must be affordable for the average person.

The principles above relate to the public's access to legal services generally and to the quality and integrity of those services. The legal system is complex, and most lay persons are not able to navigate their way successfully through its maze; most of us recognize the need for legally trained professionals to help us. And in Western societies, we recognize the need for an independent bench to uphold and apply the law. The need for an independent bar seems to be less obvious. In recent years, some countries have enacted laws changing

---

15   Joseph Raz, "The Rule of Law and Its Virtue" (1977) 93 Law Q Rev 195 at 198-202.

the regulatory structure of the legal profession. The legal systems in these countries have gone from being largely self-regulatory (in other words, lawyers regulating themselves through law societies) to being subject to government control. What usually happens is that government representatives are appointed to a newly created body charged with regulating the legal profession.

The arguments for these changes resemble arguments for government regulation of police forces and other professional bodies. People suspect that professional organizations that discipline their own members are inclined to be lenient. Members of the "club" will receive special treatment. The main arguments in support of self-regulation are that the professions undertake this responsibility seriously; there is no evidence that it is abused.

With respect to the legal profession, there is a need for it to be free from political control so that cases can be effectively argued before the courts. This is especially true of cases where rights and liberties are at issue. And there are options other than government control. So long as the self-regulatory process is open, measures can be taken to ensure that it

BOX 1.8

Roncarelli v Duplessis

The Supreme Court of Canada's decision in *Roncarelli v Duplessis* ([1959] SCR 121 [*Roncarelli*]) is one of Canada's defining decisions on abuse of power. It illustrates all three of Dicey's rule-of-law principles. It highlights how the arbitrary use of discretionary power violates the rule of law.

Roncarelli was a Jehovah's Witness and a successful restaurateur in Montreal. During this period, in the mid-20th century, Quebec was trying to control the distribution of religious literature. A number of Jehovah's Witnesses were arrested for contravening local bylaws that prohibited peddling without a licence. Roncarelli provided bail for many of those arrested. To prevent his further involvement, Maurice Duplessis, who was then the premier and attorney general of Quebec, ordered the province's liquor commissioner to permanently revoke Roncarelli's liquor licence, which had been issued under the *Liquor Act*. Roncarelli sued for damages.

A majority of the Supreme Court of Canada (SCC) found in favour of Roncarelli and ordered Duplessis to pay damages. Justice Rand's judgment, one of two majority judgments, is a classic from our country's highest court. Justice Rand reasoned that legislative discretion given to government administrators must be exercised in accordance with the general policies underlying the legislation itself. Extraneous factors such as different religious beliefs or opposing political views, which are wholly unconnected to the purpose of the legislation (here, the regulation of the sale of alcohol in the public interest), must not influence the use of the discretion. Justice Rand stated the following (at 140):

> In public regulation of this sort there is no such thing as absolute and untrammelled "discretion," that is, that action can be taken on any ground or for any

reason that can be suggested to the mind of the administrator. ... "Discretion" necessarily implies good faith in discharging public duty; there is always a perspective within which a statute is intended to operate; and any clear departure from its lines or objects is just as objectionable as fraud or corruption. Could an applicant be refused a permit because he had been born in another province, or because of the colour of his hair? The ordinary language of the legislature cannot be so distorted.

Justice Rand also said the following (at 141):

> To deny or revoke a permit because a citizen exercises an unchallengeable right totally irrelevant to the sale of liquor in a restaurant is equally beyond the scope of the discretion conferred. ... [W]hat could be more malicious than to punish this licensee for having done what he had an absolute right to do in a matter utterly irrelevant to the *Liquor Act*? Malice in the proper sense is simply acting for a reason and purpose knowingly foreign to the administration, to which was added here the element of intentional punishment by what was virtually vocation outlawry.

Justice Rand intimated that arbitrary power might be exercisable only if there were express statutory language authorizing such an action. He states the following (at 140):

> [N]o legislative Act can, *without express language*, be taken to contemplate an unlimited arbitrary power exercisable for any purpose, however capricious or irrelevant, regardless of the nature or purpose of the statute. [Emphasis added.]

is effective. For example, one could appoint an ombudsman who would have the power to embarrass through public exposure any law society that was lax in controlling its members.

Why is lawyer–client privilege needed to maintain the rule of law? The rationale here is that without this privilege of confidentiality, the client and the lawyer do not have the security they need to properly defend charges, to advance claims, and to seek and give advice.

Likewise, if legal services are not affordable, the existence of laws that assist or protect us will be of little use. One answer to this latter need is to promote and increase the use of para-professionals, such as paralegals and notaries public, to help reduce the overall cost of legal services.

Rule of Law in the International Context

Rule of law is not just an English or Western idea any more. It has a global influence. The United Nations, established in 1945 and now with 193 member states, has made the rule of law a standing agenda item for its General Assembly since 1992. The Security Council has focused on this issue on a number of occasions, emphasizing the need to adhere to rule-of-law principles in times of conflict.[16]

The United Nations has defined the rule of law as follows:

> For the United Nations, the rule of law refers to a principle of governance in which all persons, institutions and entities, public and private, including the State itself, are accountable to laws that are publicly promulgated, equally enforced and independently adjudicated, and which are consistent with international human rights norms and standards. It requires, as well, measures to ensure adherence to the principles of supremacy of law, equality before the law, accountability to the law, fairness in the application of the law, separation of powers, participation in decision making, legal certainty, avoidance of arbitrariness and procedural and legal transparency.[17]

Canada follows the rule of law, and all member states of the UN profess to do so. But other countries' interpretation of and adherence to its principles vary dramatically.

A number of organizations collect and summarize data that offer a snapshot of the rule of law around the world on an annual basis. Among them are the World Bank, which measures adherence to the rule of law in over 200 countries as one of its six governance indicators, and the World Justice Project, whose Rule of Law Index provides detailed data on 97 countries.[18]

Divisions of Law

The law includes many different subject areas. It is helpful, as a learning exercise, to see the law subdivided into discrete boxes (see Figure 1.1), each representing a different subject area. But it should be kept in mind that many of these subject areas overlap. To understand how the divisions of law interrelate, we might begin by considering Canadian constitutional

---

16 See United Nations, United Nations and the Rule of Law, <http://www.un.org/en/ruleoflaw/>.

17 *Report of the Secretary-General on the Rule of Law and Transitional Justice in Conflict and Post-Conflict Societies* (S/2004/616).

18 To view data maps and tables illustrating countries' rankings according to various factors, visit <http://info.worldbank.org/governance/wgi/index.aspx> and <http://worldjusticeproject.org/rule-law-index-map>.

law. The pattern we find there of separate and yet overlapping divisions exemplifies the law in general.

Canada's Constitution, as we will discuss at greater length in Chapter 5, divides the power to make law between the federal Parliament and the provincial legislatures. It does so by assigning specifically named areas of power to one jurisdiction or the other. Early in the interpretive history of our Constitution, it was remarked that these areas were "water-tight compartments."[19] After a few decades of federalism in practice, however, it became clear that these compartments were not as watertight as first thought; in a number of areas, the federal and provincial lawmakers were found to have shared jurisdiction.[20] In the law generally, there are many divisions, each with its own designation. However, many of them overlap, as in the constitutional context. As Dworkin has said, the law is a "seamless web."

Consider Figure 1.1. At the top is law in general—the whole concept. This concept is subdivided into positive law (that is, man-made law) and natural law (that is, transcendent or overarching law derived from sources such as religion or human reason). Figure 1.1 further subdivides positive law according to whether the laws deal with core rights and obligations (**substantive law**) or with the processes for determining and enforcing those rights and obligations (**procedural law**). Note how these two broad categories both feed into **domestic law**—in other words, the law of a particular state.

Public international law (or international law) deals primarily with international treaties, rules, and customs that govern inter-state relationships (we examine this area in Chapter 12). However, it also deals with other relationships, such as those between states and non-nationals. For example, when a state is trying to exercise control over foreign nationals for crimes against the state, and these non-nationals are outside the state's territorial jurisdiction, it becomes a matter for international law. In Figure 1.1, international law sits parallel to domestic law. This placement is meant to reflect the reality that the rules of international law do not in general have binding force on a state, unless the state accepts and implements those rules through its own domestic law. Whether international bodies such as the United Nations have the right to enforce international rules against an individual nation's will is a complex question, and one that is hotly debated.

Domestic law is divided into public law, military law, and private law. **Public law** deals with the legal relationship between a state and individual members of the state. It can be divided into a number of different areas, some of which are covered elsewhere in this book: constitutional law (Chapters 5–8) and criminal law (Chapter 13). **Private law**, which concerns the relationships between persons, can be subdivided into a great many areas. Some of the more common ones are set out in Figure 1.1, and a few of these will be examined in Part III of this text: private law (Chapters 9 and 10), and business and consumer law (Chapter 11). At the bottom of the figure, in the middle, is an area encompassing a few hybrid areas of law—in other words, areas that involve both public law (state-to-person) and private law (person-to-person) components. These hybrid areas include insolvency, environmental, natural resources, and entertainment law.

Military law is a special area, a constitutionally separate and largely self-contained system of law regulating the Canadian Forces. It governs the armed forces during times of conflict and in peace time, at home and abroad. It has domestic and international law aspects, and public law and private law aspects.

---

19 Lord Atkin in *Attorney-General of Canada v Attorney-General of Ontario (Labour Conventions)*, [1937] AC 326 at 354 (HL).

20 For example, the Supreme Court of Canada recently had to decide whether Parliament or the provincial legislatures had jurisdiction over "fertility" issues. The Court decided it was a shared jurisdiction: see *Reference re Assisted Human Reproduction Act*, 2010 SCC 61, [2010] 3 SCR 457 and the discussion of this case in Chapter 5.

FIGURE 1.1 Divisions of law

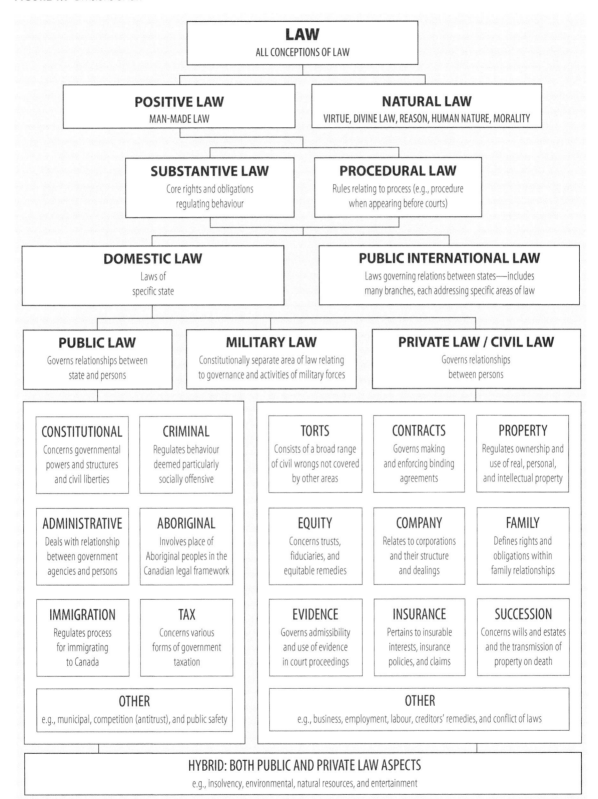

Legal Terminology

Law is expressed through language. Over the centuries, the language of the law has developed a separate life of its own. In fact, most students of law feel like they are learning a whole new language when they begin reading cases and legislation. It's not just that some of the words—particularly the Latin ones—are unfamiliar; it's also the way the words are used and how legal arguments are structured.

Legal terminology, like language in general, involves varying degrees of uncertainty. In reference to this, H.L.A. Hart has referred to the "penumbra" (that is, a surrounding shadow) of uncertainty around legal rules.

What is the source of this uncertainty? Consider the following example. Earlier in this chapter, in our discussion of the structure of rules, we referred to the negligence rule in the context of motor vehicle accidents. There we noted that the standard of care used to determine negligence was based on the "reasonable motorist." But who is the reasonable motorist? What does this phrase mean, exactly? How well does the reasonable motorist drive? Does it matter if it's dark and raining or if she's rushing to the hospital because her child is sick at the time of the accident? These are the kinds of uncertainties that the language of the law is often unable to avoid. What fills these shadows or grey areas of uncertainty around the legal rules? According to Hart, it is discretion. For Dworkin, who is friendlier to the doctrine of natural law, it is morality and justice; these, he claims, lead us to the correct answer.

Apart from the uncertainty it involves, legal language is very specialized. Its language is so unfamiliar that it may sometimes seem to you that the legal profession has conspired to make the law more difficult than it is. There may be some historical truth to this. S.M. Waddams has said the following in this regard: "George Bernard Shaw wrote that all professions are conspiracies against the laity, and no doubt the legal profession has earned its reputation for obscurantism."[21] Recently, there has been a reaction against such specialized, deliberately obscure professional language. This has been a positive development for students and legal practitioners alike. Archaic expressions such as "hereinafter," "aforesaid," "notwithstanding the generality of the foregoing," and "the said party of the first part" are no longer considered to be impressive.

A plain-language movement in business and law started in the 1970s. This change is often attributed to banks' wishing to simplify their contracts for consumers, so as to prevent unnecessary litigation. The benefits of this measure were soon clear to all, and the plain-language movement has continued to the present day. Nowadays, legislative draftsmen in most jurisdictions are directed to use plain language in writing or rewriting legislation. They are given lists of "difficult" words and told to replace them with clear ones. Newly appointed judges in many jurisdictions are now required to go to "judge school" for a few weeks to learn how to write clear, structured judgments.

Despite these developments, legal language remains a challenge to new law students. To help you navigate the language of the law, there are resources that you can use alongside your other course materials. These include dictionaries and collections of legal words and phrases. (See dictionary resources listed under Further Reading at the end of this chapter.) Also, be sure to use the glossaries in this and other law books. Finally, pay close attention to context when reading legal materials; there are many expressions, such as "common law" and "civil law," that have multiple meanings within the law (see Chapter 2). The context in which they are used should tell you the intended meaning.

---

21   In SM Waddams, *Introduction to the Study of Law*, 7th ed (Toronto: Carswell, 2010) at 35.

CHAPTER SUMMARY

Law is not easily or simply defined. We have seen that, at a basic level, it relates to the regulation of human activity by way of rules. The broad categories of rules and their forms are relatively standard, but the content of rules varies greatly. In many societies, especially liberal democracies of the West, the law is distinguished from other types of rules, such as those based on morality, justice, or religion.

There are numerous theories concerning the law and its development. Some of these theories are analytic (or positivist) in nature, describing what the law *is*. Others are normative in nature, describing what the law *ought to be*. Some

theories have both analytic and normative elements. Many countries, including Canada, have a positivist and analytic bias.

Law has many divisions and subdivisions, particularly within the domestic law category, and also many areas of overlap between these divisions. As you continue your legal studies, you will become more familiar with these specific areas, as well as with the legal terminology used to describe them. With that familiarity will come a greater comfort with the whole area of the law.

KEY TERMS

corrective justice theory of justice according to which (1) a person has a moral responsibility for harm caused to another, and (2) the latter's loss must be rectified or corrected *(p. 8)*

critical legal studies theory of law largely concerned with exposing law as an instrument of the rich and powerful *(p. 20)*

critical race theory theory of law that focuses on race-based inequities; an offshoot of critical legal studies *(p. 21)*

deontological theories that focus on the inherent rightness or wrongness of behaviour, without regard to the behaviour's consequences or outcomes *(p. 7)*

distributive justice theory of justice concerned with appropriate distributions of entitlements, such as wealth and power, in a society *(p. 12)*

domestic law the law of a particular state or society *(p. 26)*

ethics standards of right and wrong often applied to specific groups—for example, professions *(p. 7)*

feminist theories of law theories of law that generally concern the legal, social, and economic rights and opportunities of women *(p. 20)*

instrumentalist theories that focus on something—for example, justice or the law—as a means to an end *(p. 7)*

jurisprudence also known as "philosophy of law" or "science of law"; concerns theories that are used to describe, explain, or criticize the law *(p. 14)*

law and society a kind of legal study that looks at law from a broadly social, interdisciplinary perspective *(p. 20)*

legal positivism theory that the only valid source of law is the principles, rules, and regulations expressly enacted by the institutions or persons within a society that are generally recognized as having the power to enact them *(p. 17)*

legal realism a theory, developed in the US and Scandinavian countries, that encouraged a more thoroughly empirical study of the process by which laws are made and applied *(p. 18)*

Marxist theories of law legal theories, based on the writing of the communist philosopher Karl Marx, that are concerned with the distribution of wealth in a society; related to distributive justice theories *(p. 20)*

military law a constitutionally separate and relatively self-contained system of law regulating the Canadian Forces *(p. 26)*

morality standards of right and wrong, often associated with personal character *(p. 6)*

natural law theory that there is a source of law that is higher than man-made law, with which man-made law must try to comply *(p. 14)*

positive law man-made law, as opposed to a higher law (natural law) that transcends persons or institutions *(p. 18)*

private law law that concerns the relationships between persons *(p. 26)*

procedural law law relating to the process by which core rights and obligations are determined and enforced *(p. 26)*

public international law (or international law) the law relating to international treaties and customs, to inter-state relationships, and to the relationship between states and non-nationals *(p. 26)*

public law law dealing with the legal relationship be-tween a state and individual members of the state *(p. 26)*

retributive justice theory of justice based on *lex talionis*, or the law of retaliation *(p. 10)*

rule of law a key legal concept whose central tenets are that everyone is equal before the law and that power under the law should not be used arbitrarily *(p. 21)*

sociology of law a kind of sociological study that looks at law from a broadly social, interdisciplinary perspective *(p. 20)*

substantive laws laws that deal with core rights and obligations *(p. 26)*

FURTHER READING

BOOKS

Black's Law Dictionary, 9th ed (West Group, 2009) and the abridged version *Black's Law Dictionary, Abridged*, 9th ed (West Group, 2009).

Culver, Keith C, ed. *Readings in the Philosophy of Law*, 2d ed (Peterborough, Ont: Broadview Press, 2008).

The Dictionary of Canadian Law, 3d ed (Toronto: Carswell, 2004) and the abridged version, the *Pocket Dictionary of Canadian Law*, 4th ed (Toronto: Carswell, 2006).

Freeman, Michael DA. *Lloyd's Introduction to Jurisprudence*, 8th ed (London: Sweet & Maxwell, 2008).

Fuller, Lon L. "The Case of the Speluncean Explorers" (1949) 62 Harv L Rev 616.

Fuller, Lon L. *The Morality of Law*, revised ed (New Haven, Conn: Yale University Press, 1965).

Harris, Phil. *An Introduction to Law*, 7th ed (Cambridge: Cambridge University Press, 2007) ch 1.

Hart, HLA. *The Concept of Law*, 2d ed (Oxford: Oxford University Press, 1994)

Waddams, SM. *Introduction to the Study of Law*, 7th ed (Toronto: Carswell, 2010) ch 1, ch 3.

WEBSITES

Canadian Online Legal Dictionary by Irwin Law [online only]: <http://www.irwinlaw.com/cold>.

United Nations and the Rule of Law: <http://www.un.org/en/ruleoflaw/index.shtml>.

REVIEW QUESTIONS

1. Describe the basic structure(s) of legal rules.

2. What is one way to differentiate morality from ethics?

3. Briefly describe the relationship between the law and religion.

4. Is a lie ever justified in your opinion? Include in your answer the correct use of the words "deontological" and "instrumentalist."

5. Compare corrective justice with retributive justice, including the areas of law to which they most clearly apply.

6. How was natural law used to provide a philosophical justification for the American Revolution?

7. Describe legal realism in your own words.

8. How did the *Magna Carta* move English government closer to a government based on the rule of law?

9. How did government action in the *Roncarelli v Duplessis* case offend the rule of law?

10. What is the relationship between domestic law and international law?

EXERCISES

1. Choose a definition of law that, in your opinion, has both strengths and weaknesses. Describe the strengths and weaknesses and then rewrite the definition to remove the weaknesses.

2. Using the Internet, locate and read two speeches or articles by or about Pierre Elliott Trudeau and his "just society." Next, describe in your own words what you think a just society is.

3. In your view, does the law of retaliation reflect an innate need or a learned response? Provide reasons to support your view.

4. What is the basic difference between analytic and normative theories of law? If you had to write a paper on one or the other, which would you choose and why?

5. Using the United Nations rule-of-law website, locate, read, and summarize two UN documents dealing with the rule of law.

2 Legal Systems Around the World

After reading this chapter, you will understand:

- The common law's origins and defining characteristics
- The civil law's origins and defining characteristics
- The role that religion plays in legal systems
- What customary law is and its role in modern legal systems

- The prevalence of hybrid or mixed legal systems in the world today
- How the various legal systems are distributed worldwide

> As a new era in world history begins to unfold, and globalisation continues to play its part in the early years of the twenty-first century, there seems no better time … to utilise the techniques of comparative law.
>
> Peter de Cruz, *Comparative Law in a Changing World*, 3d ed (Abingdon, UK: Routledge-Cavendish, 2008) at 522

Introduction

The legal systems that exist in the world today reflect the diverse and sometimes complex histories of the world's peoples. As a student of law, you are likely to be involved with only one system of law. In Canada, that will likely be the system of **common law**. Still, Canadian law students have a number of good reasons to learn about other legal systems:

1. *Multiculturalism*. Canada is a multicultural society made up of people from all around the world. To understand something about the traditions of our fellow Canadians can only be a benefit.
2. *Bijuralism*. Canada is a *bijural nation*. This means that it has two legal systems— common law in most jurisdictions but **civil law** in Quebec, where roughly one quarter of our population lives. Legal matters often cross provincial boundaries.
3. *Trade*. International trade is necessary for a healthy economy. Knowing how our trading partners view legal rights and obligations will improve our business relations.
4. *Globalization*. The world is becoming a smaller place because of technology. The interconnectedness of all peoples is more apparent now than ever, making it increasingly important for us to understand our "neighbours" in other parts of the world.

Comparative law is the study of different legal systems. It is a relatively new field of legal study, and there is some debate about how best to go about classifying different systems of law. Here, we have opted for five categories:

1. common law,
2. civil law,

3. Muslim law (religion as law),
4. customary law, and
5. mixed or hybrid systems.

The first category we will discuss is the system used in most of Canada: the common law system.

Common Law

The common law system arose from circumstances unique to England. The system's defining feature is that judges follow precedent. The precedents that are the basis of the system originated with judges who sat in royal courts of justice. These courts were established by early English kings following the Norman invasion of England in 1066 CE.

Law in Pre-Norman England: Romans and Anglo-Saxons

The Roman era in England lasted from 43 CE, when the Romans conquered the island, until the fifth century CE, when they abandoned it. During this 400-year period, the Romans introduced their legal system to Britain. However, this system did not take root in England as it had in continental Europe, and little remained of it after the Roman departure.[1]

Other invaders succeeded the Romans in England. Germanic tribes—the Angles, Saxons, Jutes, and Danes—established the Anglo-Saxon era in Britain, which lasted from the fifth century until the Norman invasion of 1066. These tribes established separate kingdoms across southern England. Each had its own system of German laws based on tribal customs and principles of communal justice. Initially, their codes of justice were not written; they were transmitted orally. In time, some Anglo-Saxon kings had their tribes' legal codes compiled in written form. But each tribe's legal code applied only to its specific territory, and there was no centralized nationwide justice system. This changed with the invasion of the Norman king William the Conqueror, in 1066.

Origins of Common Law

William the Conqueror (1028–1087), unlike the Anglo-Saxon invaders before him, proceeded to establish a centralized royal kingdom in most of southern Britain. One way he accomplished this was through a political structure called **feudalism**. Under this system, William claimed ownership of all land on the island. He then distributed large areas of it to favoured nobles in return for their promises of loyalty and military support. And the nobles, in turn, granted portions of land to their subjects, known as vassals, in return for their oaths of allegiance. This new socio-political arrangement, with its hierarchical system of obligation and allegiance, helped unify the island under a single monarch. This centralization contributed greatly to the formation of the common law system.

Another way that William gained control over his English domain was to set up a centralized government administration. He and the kings that succeeded him established something called the *curia regis*. This was a group of nobles who advised the king on governing the country. They helped him in the following areas, in particular:

---

1 George W Keeton, *The Norman Conquest and the Common Law* (London: Ernest Benn, 1966).

- overseeing departments of state—for example, the **Chancery** for legal matters and the Exchequer for the king's finances;
- securing royal control throughout the island by issuing royal documents, such as charters, to establish new towns and villages; and
- creating administrative officers, such as sheriffs, who were responsible, within their respective regions of the country, for maintaining the king's powers and privileges.

Another centralizing measure that William introduced was to expand the island's legal system through royal courts of justice. These courts were particularly crucial to the emergence of the common law.[2]

Development of a Royal Court System

The Anglo-Norman kings, unlike their Anglo-Saxon predecessors, determined that justice was a royal obligation and that, as kings of Britain, they were responsible for the **king's peace**. This meant that an English king had the right and the duty to preserve public order and to punish anyone who disturbed the well-being of English subjects. A system of criminal law was initiated in the name of the king. In each county, the king appointed justices of the peace to keep order, and he established the grand jury to seek out suspected wrongdoers and bring them to his judges' attention. Through these measures, which were implemented across most of Britain, English law began to derive its authority directly from the king.[3]

The royal courts of justice evolved over time. English monarchs such as Henry I (1100–1135) and Henry II (1154–1189) appointed royal judges from the *curia regis* and sent them out on a circuit of the outlying counties, away from the London capital, to preside over the courts. The courts presided over by these travelling judges were known as *assizes*. Representing the monarch, these royal judges dealt with local offenders who had contravened the king's peace, and they helped to settle local disputes.

English monarchs set up three separate royal courts of justice—the Court of Common Pleas, the Court of King's (or Queen's) Bench, and the Exchequer Court—to decide legal disputes. The Court of Common Pleas decided civil and landholding disputes. The **Court of King's (or Queen's) Bench** decided criminal matters. The Exchequer Court decided revenue matters involving the king. The English people favoured these three royal courts. They appreciated the learned nature of the royal judges and other features of the courts, including the following:

- their power to summon witnesses;
- their use of juries rather than older modes of trial, such as ordeal or combat;
- their use of written records; and
- their power to enforce their judgments.[4]

The Writ System

The royal courts were popular, but they did involve one problematic feature: the writ system of civil procedure. A person who launched a civil or non-criminal action in these royal

---

2   Raoul C Van Caenegem, *The Birth of the English Common Law* (Cambridge: Cambridge University Press, 1988).

3   William R Cornish, *The Jury* (Harmondsworth, UK: Penguin, 1968).

4   Arthur R Hogue, *Origins of the Common Law* (Bloomington, Ind: Indiana University Press, 1966).

courts—a person known as the **plaintiff**—first had to purchase from the king a specific document called a **writ**. A writ was a written order to a defendant. It came not from the plaintiff but from the king. It was affixed with a royal seal, notifying a defendant that the plaintiff had a particular complaint or "cause of action" against him or her, such as breach of contract, trespass, or assault. It also stated that if the defendant wished to challenge a plaintiff's court action, he or she must precisely follow the procedures prescribed by the writ.

The problem with this system arose in the following way. The king could not issue all writs personally; they were too numerous. So the practice arose of having the chancellor, who headed the king's Chancery, issue them instead. Over the course of several centuries, many different writs developed for specific disputes, and each writ had its own formal procedures. The plaintiff's choice of writ became crucial. If plaintiffs chose the wrong writ for their cause of action, later amendment was impossible. At the same time, if no writ was appropriate for the plaintiff's cause of action, then no remedy was available from these royal courts. To overcome these formal, rigid, and increasingly technical pleading rules, litigants began to appeal to the king, who was seen as the fountainhead of justice, to intervene on their behalf.[5] Their appeals were heard by the chancellor, who was the king's representative.

Chancery Separates from Common Law

Over time, chancellors established a royal court that was separate from the three other royal courts of justice. It was called the **Court of Chancery**, and its purpose was to grant relief on grounds of equitable justice and to adjudicate petitions from plaintiffs appealing outside the writ system. Once established, this Court of Chancery developed a parallel system of civil procedure. The other royal courts of justice used the common law. The Court of Chancery created its own separate body of maxims or rules, called **equity**, to deal with plaintiffs' appeals.

For example, the common law courts interpreted contracts, and particularly contracts involving land, very strictly. If a person who had mortgaged his land (the mortgagor) missed a payment, the mortgagee (or lender) was permitted to exercise his contractual right to take the land in satisfaction. In many cases this would be unfair, especially if the mortgagor had paid off most of the debt. (The relevant maxim here is, "Equity abhors a forfeiture.") In such a case, the Court of Chancery could step in and give the mortgagor some extra time (a redemption period) to pay back the lender.

Another special feature of the Court of Chancery was that it could hear disputes informally and quickly, without a jury, and could provide a plaintiff with remedies—for example, specific performance, or rectification of a contract, or an injunction—other than monetary damages. These remedies were not available in the three other royal courts.

Judicature Acts

The existence of two completely separate court systems—the royal courts (using common law rules) on one hand, and the Court of Chancery (using equitable rules) on the other—created certain difficulties. These were not resolved until 1873, when the English Parliament passed a series of statutes, the *Judicature Acts*, unifying the courts under one court system. This system was made up of the High Court of Justice (with five specialist divisions) and the Court of Appeal. The system allowed for a further right of appeal to the House of Lords. Both common law and equitable rules could now be administered under one court system. This measure simplified court procedure considerably.

---

5 John H Baker, *An Introduction to English Legal History*, 4th ed (London: Butterworths, 2002).

In Canada, each province has its own unified high (or superior) court system with a trial level and an appeal level. These courts—except in Quebec, which employs the civil law system—apply both common law and equitable rules. Generally, the maxim "equity follows the law" governs the relationship between the two sets of rules. This means that the role of equity is to add to or fill in the gaps left by the common law, based on principles of fairness, but not to change the common law. However, in limited situations where there is a conflict between the two sets of rules, most provincial "judicature" statutes provide, as do the English *Judicature Acts*, that equity prevails.

Chief Features of Common Law

The distinguishing features of the common law system are the reliance on precedent, the principle of *stare decisis*, and the use of an adversarial process in court.

Use of Precedents

English common law was a product of centuries of evolution. This process began with the development of the royal courts during the medieval period, as described above. The itinerant royal judges, on returning to London from their county assizes, would meet and dine with their fellow judges at the **Inns of Court**. This collegial process promoted respect for and attention to one another's judgments. Court reporting began in 1283, with the Year Books. Two centuries later, the invention of the printing press made it even easier for English judges to critically examine one another's judgments. From there, it was a short distance to the practice of following **precedents**. In other words, a judge would apply an earlier judicial decision to the case before him if the facts and the law were similar.[6]

This practice became institutionalized when royal judges formally accepted the principle known as ***stare decisis***. According to this principle, cases that are alike should be treated alike. What this meant for English law, practically speaking, was that royal judges on the county circuit would decide cases by following precedents rather than by following local customs. As a result of this practice, there arose one cohesive system of judicial rules and practices common to England. This became known as the common law.

PRECEDENT AND STARE DECISIS IN A COURT HIERARCHY

Over time, changes in the English court system affected the operation of *stare decisis*. In the 16th century, the English court structure was eventually reorganized into a hierarchy, with trial courts at the bottom and superior appellate courts at the top. After this, a user of the system was required to enter first through a trial court, where one judge would decide on the matter. Those wanting to dispute the trial judge's decision were then required to "appeal" the judgment upward, to a higher appellate court at Westminster. At this upper level, a panel of appellate judges (usually three) would hear the trial judgment and decide whether it was correct in law.

The reorganization of the courts affected the principle of *stare decisis*; it was expanded to include the rule that a decision made by a higher appellate court is **binding**. In other words, the higher court's decision must be followed by a lower court in the same judicial hierarchy if the facts and the ***ratio decidendi*** ("reason for the decision") or principle of law in both cases are substantially similar.

---

6   Alan Harding, *The Law Courts of Medieval England* (London: Allen and Unwin, 1973).

The principle of *stare decisis* is very rational, but it has limitations. In 1966, the House of Lords issued the "Practice Statement." This was a formal recognition that "too rigid adherence to precedent may lead to injustice in a particular case and also unduly restrict the proper development of the law."[7] It gave the House of Lords the power to *overrule itself* and to depart from precedent to achieve justice. Since then, most courts in other common law jurisdictions have recognized a similar power to overrule themselves in appropriate circumstances. However, there has to be a good reason for a court to exercise this power. This development has had no effect on lower courts, which continue to be bound by higher court decisions in the same jurisdiction.

Even in the lower courts, the doctrine of precedent is not as absolute as it first appears. For example, lawyers and judges wishing *not* to follow an apparently binding precedent from a higher appellate court have certain arguments open to them. They might argue, for example, that there are material factual differences between the preceding case and the one under consideration. Such a precedent is said to be **distinguishable**. Other arguments can be made against an apparently binding precedent. You might argue, for example, that a precedent

- has been overruled by an even higher court,
- is no longer applicable because of changed social circumstances,
- was poorly reasoned and has lost its reputation as good law, or
- has been re-interpreted differently by other judges.

Any one of these arguments, if made successfully, could render a precedent non-binding. One English judge wrote the following in this regard: "The common law evolves not merely by breeding new principles but also, when they are fully grown, by burying their ancestors."[8]

Circumstances may arise where there is no binding precedent. In this case, a judge or lawyer may want to use a precedent from another jurisdiction that is directly on point. Such a precedent, taken from another province or from another common law country, is said to be **persuasive**. Today in Canada, a lawyer trying to "persuade" a judge to examine such a precedent would have to convince her that there was no relevant precedent from the judge's own province or from the Supreme Court of Canada (SCC).

Figure 2.1 shows the flow of precedent downward in the Canadian court system, with the SCC at the top. Each province is considered a separate jurisdiction; decisions from other provinces are therefore not binding but can be persuasive. How persuasive a decision is depends on a number of factors, including the level of the court, the particular judge writing the decision, the quality of the reasoning, and the date of the decision. The same standard applies to decisions from other countries.

In Chapter 7 we will look at Canada's court system in more detail, including the federal court system's place in it, as well as how lower courts and administrative tribunals form part of the hierarchy.

---

7 See *Practice Statement*, [1966] 3 All ER 77 (HL). Prior to 1966, the House of Lords had considered itself bound by its own decisions under the principle of *stare decisis*: see *London Tramways Co v London City Council*, [1898] AC 375 (HL). See also Gordon Bale, "Casting Off the Mooring Ropes of Precedent" (1980) 58 Can Bar Rev 255.

8 Lord Diplock in *Hong Kong Fir Shipping Co Ltd v Kawasaki Kisen Kaisha Ltd*, [1962] 1 All ER 474 at 488 (CA).

FIGURE 2.1 Flow of precedent in Canada

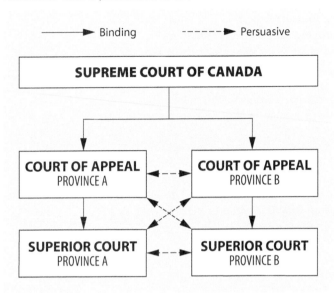

DEVELOPING NEW PRECEDENTS

If there is neither a binding precedent applicable to a case nor a persuasive precedent from another jurisdiction, litigants may call on the court to develop a new precedent (see Box 2.1). Under what circumstances would there be no binding precedent? The case might involve, for example, a novel issue, or it might be an old issue in an altered social context.

If a court feels that establishing a new precedent might be too contentious or radical a step, it can leave the matter for elected representatives to address through legislation. If the court is feeling bold or believes that a new precedent would represent a reasonable, incremental change to the common law, it may articulate the new precedent itself.

There are three important factors that a court may take into consideration when establishing a new precedent:

1. the existence of *similar* cases,
2. the approach taken in other jurisdictions, and
3. policy considerations.

In considering similar cases, the court might see a common thread that connects them all; these cases may reveal a common direction in which the law is moving. Under these circumstances, the new precedent established by the court's decision will simply be a logical extension of the decisions made in these similar cases.

A second factor that courts might consider is the approach that other courts, in other jurisdictions, have taken to the issue at hand. Such comparative analysis has become increasingly important in the last few decades, owing to globalization. More and more often, our courts ask the following question: How have courts elsewhere—in other provinces, other countries, even (on occasion) countries with other legal systems—treated a particular issue? If other jurisdictions have taken a consistent or reasoned approach to a particular problem, our courts might take a similar approach.[9]

Policy is the third factor the courts might consider when deciding whether or not to recognize a new precedent. A court might consider the possibility, for example, that a new rule would benefit society by providing a useful deterrent to some problematic behaviour. On the other hand, the court would shy away from creating a new precedent if it foresaw that the new rule might lead to negative economic consequences or to a flood of cases clogging up the courts (a policy argument known as the "floodgates" argument).

Adversarial System

In the common law system, the government appoints judges from among members of the legal profession—lawyers who have practised for a certain number of years. These judges

---

9   For example, in the *Whiten* (2002) case, referred to in Chapter 1, the SCC looked at how other common law countries (England, Australia, New Zealand, Ireland, and the United States) had dealt with the question of punitive damages before developing a rule for our country.

BOX 2.1

Applying Law Versus Making Law

Where an established rule (or precedent) seems relevant to a judge's decision in a case, he will *apply* that rule to the facts of the case. In a typical motor vehicle accident case involving liability, for example, the judge's decision will hinge on whether the defendant exercised "reasonable care" in all the circumstances (the standard of care element in a negligence action). Did the defendant breach any of the rules of the road by speeding or by not stopping at a stop sign or by not yielding at a courtesy corner? Was he impaired? Was he distracted by his cellphone? The judge will apply the reasonable care rule to the specific circumstances of the case and reach a conclusion.

The situation is different in cases where the judge or court is asked to articulate a new precedent and opts to do so. The *Donoghue v Stevenson* case (referred to in Chapter 1) was famous for a couple of reasons. First, Lord Atkin proposed something no one had proposed before—that people have a general legal obligation to take care where other people are concerned (the neighbour principle). Second, Lord Atkin applied the "neighbour principle" in a particular context, holding that manufacturers have a specific obligation or duty to ensure that their products are reasonably safe for consumers even though the manufacturer has no contractual relationship with the consumer. By establishing this new precedent, did the court *make* law?

What precisely is the role of judges and courts in the common law world? Historically, common law judges were tasked with "finding the law." In other words, they were supposed to determine what the existing law was according to common customs and then apply it to the facts before them. They were not charged with "making law," which was seen as too activist and not within their bailiwick. If a new law were required, Parliament or the Crown (during the period when the king or queen could make laws) was supposed to step in. But in cases where a matter was pressing, waiting for a legislative response was not always satisfactory. Under these circumstances, judges have sometimes taken the bold step of establishing a new precedent.

Still, some judges and commentators have argued that courts always *find* rather than *make* new precedents (or rules). This argument goes as follows. When judges recognize a new precedent, they do so in a rational manner, by searching for common threads in existing laws, by furthering established policies, and by effecting incremental change. A process of legal reasoning dictates the result. People who make this argument are reluctant to acknowledge the courts' power to make law. Their reluctance stems from the historical ideal of how the law was supposed to work. Judges were supposed to apply existing law, not create new laws. A greater creative authority on the part of judges could lead to uncontrolled change and instability.

Whether we characterize the creation of a new precedent as making law or finding it, the crucial element in the process seems to be the quality of the analytical reasoning that generates it.

---

preside over an **adversarial system** of justice. The adversarial system is based on the idea that truth will best be determined when lawyers oppose each other in the courtroom and present their respective cases without interference from the trial judge. Judges can ask questions to seek clarification and can do their own independent research, but the adversarial approach ensures that the *primary* responsibility for the presentation of cases lies with the opposing litigants and their counsel. At the end of the case, judges render their decisions based on the factual and legal material before them.

Other Sources of Law

Besides judge-made rules, other written laws have at various times been recognized as binding in England. Before 1689, the monarch was able to legislate by decree. This ended with the Glorious Revolution of 1688, when Parliament completely took over the Crown's power to legislate. The English **Bill of Rights (1689)** formally declared that the "pretended" power of the Crown to legislate without the consent of Parliament was illegal.

Since that time, jurisdictions that follow the common law tradition have recognized two primary sources of law:

1. legislation, and
2. case law (the decisions of the courts).

The doctrine of parliamentary sovereignty dictates that where there is a conflict between case law and legislation, the latter prevails. In Chapter 5, we examine this doctrine in more detail.

Common Law: A Summary

The distinguishing features of the common law, which developed over many centuries of English legal history, are as follows:

- It arose from the English kings' efforts, after the Norman invasion of 1066, to centralize their authority over the island through the use of royal courts of justice with experienced judges who travelled to and held court in the outlying counties. To begin with, these judges applied local customs in deciding their cases.
- Over time, judges of the royal courts of justice began the practice of following one another's precedents to decide cases. They did this when the facts and circumstances of a later case were the same as those of an earlier case.
- Once the courts were organized in a hierarchy, in the 16th century, the following of precedents became institutionalized in the legal principle of *stare decisis*.
- The court process is based on an adversarial approach, with lawyers opposing each other in the courtroom and presenting their respective cases without interference from the trial judge.
- The legal rules in common law jurisdictions are not set out in one central document or code.
- Judge-made rules are one of two main sources of law. The other is legislation.

Evolving over many centuries, with its own particular legal doctrines, courts, practices, and institutions, the common law system was unique to England and was too strong—too complex and well established—to be overcome by the civil law system used on the European continent. It was this common law legal system, carried to the New World by English settlers, that was received in Canada as well as in other countries that began as English colonies, including the United States, Australia, New Zealand, Jamaica, and Belize.

Civil Law

The civil law system evolved in continental Europe. Under this system, the civil code is the primary source of private law and is more important than judicial decisions. A **civil code**, according to *Black's Law Dictionary*, is a "comprehensive and systematic legislative pronouncement of the whole private, non-commercial law in a legal system of the continental civil law tradition."[10]

The civil law system's methods and techniques of analyzing legal issues are different from those of the common law system. When dealing with private law matters, judges must consult the civil code and decide the cases in accordance with the code's general principles

---

10   *Black's Law Dictionary*, 9th ed, *sub verbo* "civil code."

and laws. Judicial precedents are used in the civil law system, but they do not have the same binding nature as they do in the common law system, under the principle of *stare decisis*.

Origins of Civil Law

The most ancient legal code that has survived in its entirety is the *Code of Hammurabi* (see Figure 2.2), referred to briefly in Chapter 1. Other codes preceded it, such as the *Code of Ur-Nammu*, which dates from around 2050 BCE. But these earlier codes are not complete. The *Code of Hammurabi* was written around 1750 BCE, during the reign of the Babylonian king, Hammurabi, in the Akkadian language. Archaeologists unearthed the most famous copy of it in 1901, in Susa (now the modern Iranian town of Shush).

The following are some of the 282 laws from the Code:

> 5. If a judge try a case, reach a decision, and present his judgment in writing; if later error shall appear in his decision, and it be through his own fault, then he shall pay twelve times the fine set by him in the case, and he shall be publicly removed from the judge's bench, and never again shall he sit there to render judgment. …
>
> 22. If anyone is committing a robbery and is caught, then he shall be put to death. …
>
> 59. If any man, without the knowledge of the owner of a garden, fell a tree in a garden he shall pay half a mina in money. …
>
> 132. If the "finger is pointed" at a man's wife about another man, but she is not caught sleeping with the other man, she shall jump into the river for her husband. …
>
> 196. If a man put out the eye of another man, his eye shall be put out. …
>
> 229. If a builder build a house for someone, and does not construct it properly, and the house which he built fall in and kill its owner, then that builder shall be put to death. …
>
> 252. If [a man] kill [another] man's slave, he shall pay one-third of a mina. …
>
> 282. If a slave say to his master: "You are not my master," if they convict him his master shall cut off his ear. …[11]

FIGURE 2.2 Code of Hammurabi
In a relief on the upper part of this stela, which is 2.25 metres tall, Hammurabi (standing, left) is shown receiving the royal insignia from the god Shamash (seated, at right). The laws are carved into the stone below.

The laws in the *Code of Hammurabi* bear little resemblance to those in modern civil law jurisdictions. But any modern civil code, like the ancient Babylonian one, is essentially an authoritative statement of rules regulating conduct in a particular society.

Roman Era

Romans began keeping records of their laws as early as 450 BCE, with their *Law of the Twelve Tables*. This was not a comprehensive statement of all Roman law; it provided definitions of various private rights and procedures.

Rome's first conquests and settlements beyond the Italian peninsula began in the third century BCE. In the centuries that followed, during the time of the late Republic and early

---

11 The complete text is available through the Avalon Project at Yale Law School: go to <http://avalon .law.yale.edu>.

Empire, the Romans expanded into Europe and brought their legal system with them. A common body of laws, developed by Roman legal scholars over many centuries, was imposed on this increasingly vast territory.

In 534 CE, almost 1,000 years after the *Law of the Twelve Tables*, the emperor Justinian produced a comprehensive codification of Roman law in his monumental work **Corpus Juris Civilis**.[12] Also referred to as the *Justinian Code*, it is a compilation of the strongest features and principles of Roman law then in existence.

Justinian's work was an authoritative restatement of Roman legal scholarship and law concerning Roman citizens' private rights and obligations. It addressed, for example, the rights and obligations among family members, the rules about making contracts, and citizens' rights to acquire and dispose of property. The Code included four main parts:

1. the Codex, containing a collection of imperial edicts on private law matters;
2. the Digest, containing Roman jurists' commentary on these laws;
3. the Institutes, providing a textbook portion for Roman law students; and
4. the Novels, detailing new laws applicable to this area.

It was intended as a source of private law for all Roman citizens and as a reference work for Roman legal scholars and for Roman judges deciding cases.

Dark Ages

The Roman legal system did not entirely disappear in Europe, as it did in England, with the fall of the Roman Empire in the fifth century CE. The Germanic tribes that succeeded the Romans and settled the southern parts of Europe based many of their tribal customs and traditions on Roman laws.

This was not the case with the Germanic tribes in northern Europe. During the Dark Ages after Rome's collapse, these northern tribes—the Franks, Burgundians, and Visigoths, for example—established diverse regional kingdoms, each with its own customs and its own system of communal justice. Some of the Frankish (or French) kings summoned certain members of their council of noble advisers (the *curia regis*) to form a judicial assembly known as a *parlement*. A *parlement* compiled written accounts of local tribal customs, called *coutumes*. During the medieval period, many different French *parlements* developed many different *coutumes*, with the *coutume de Paris* being one of the most important.[13]

French law in the medieval era was not transformed, as English law was, by the centralizing ambitions of a foreign invader. No French king did what William the Conqueror had done in England, creating royal courts that applied a uniform law across the country. French law was changed by a different event: the Renaissance.

The Law in Post-Renaissance Europe

The Dark Ages in Europe gave way to the Renaissance in the late 12th and 13th centuries. During this period, there was a great revival of classical learning; people turned their attention to Greek and Roman art, medicine, literature, philosophy, and theology. A renewed interest in Roman law was part of this revival. Renaissance scholars at Italy's influential University of Bologna developed a special interest in the Roman law and in its formal codifications, such as the *Justinian Code*. Academics from across Europe who attended this

---

12   Alan Watson, *The Law of the Ancient Romans* (Dallas: Southern Methodist University Press, 1970).

13   René David & Henry P de Vries, *The French Legal System* (New York: Oceana, 1958).

university rediscovered the universal appeal of classical Roman law. They discussed how improved laws, based on the Roman model, could help European society.

Renaissance legal scholars realized that if classical Roman law were to be reapplied across modern Europe, it would need to be updated. Some sought to adapt classical Roman law to the new circumstances in modern Europe. Others felt the need of an entirely new legal system that would address contemporary European concerns related to human rights, justice, morality, order, and security. There was a long-standing debate between those who revered the old Roman law and those who believed that new systems were needed. This debate continued for several centuries. Over time, many European states established their own civil codes of law.[14]

Where Canada is concerned, France's *Code Civil*, established in 1804 by Napoleon (it is commonly called the *Napoleonic Code*), was the most influential. This influence is evident in Quebec's first code (enacted in 1866) and its current code, the **Civil Code of Quebec**, which replaced the first one in 1994. The *Napoleonic Code*, like Justinian's *Corpus Juris Civilis*, was designed to be an authoritative and universal statement of civil law covering private law areas. It also combined the following: (1) the laws and customs based on Roman influences that had remained the basis of law in southern France; and (2) the diverse Germanic-based laws and customs of northern France's *coutumes*. Other European countries followed the French lead and established their own civil codes. England was the main exception.[15]

As the foregoing account makes clear, the civil law system had a long and particular historical evolution on the European continent. It was shaped by Roman law more than English common law was. It also differed from English common law insofar as it was influenced more by university scholars than by judges.

Civil Law and Common Law: A Comparison

Both the civil law system and the common law system strive for certainty, stability, and predictability. The civil law achieves these things through a comprehensive civil code, with laws set out for all to see, understand, and follow. The common law achieves them chiefly by the legal principle of *stare decisis*, with judges following precedents based on the idea that similar cases should be treated in similar ways. Clearly, one of the key differences between the two systems is the different role each assigns to previous judicial decisions.

Despite this fundamental difference between these two major legal systems, in practice they have much in common. Judges in both systems consult prior decisions and legal scholarship when trying to resolve the issues before them. And in both systems, statutes are a source of law. The biggest challenge for newcomers to a common law jurisdiction is researching and analyzing the stand-alone judge-made rules that apply to their particular case. For newcomers to a civil law jurisdiction, the biggest adjustment tends to come in a litigation context, where judges play a more active role in an **inquisitorial system**. Table 2.1 summarizes the key differences between the civil law and common law systems.

As we have seen, some legal expressions have different meanings in different contexts. It addition to referring to legal *systems*, the phrases "common law" and "civil law" can have other meanings, too. The phrase *civil law* is sometimes used as a synonym for *private law*—

14   John H Merryman & Rogelio Pérez-Perdomo, *The Civil Law Tradition: An Introduction to the Legal Systems of Europe and Latin America*, 3d ed (Stanford, Cal: Stanford University Press, 2007); and Graham Stephenson & Peter Shears, *James' Introduction to English Law*, 13th ed (Oxford: Oxford University Press, 2005).

15   Alan Katz, "France" in Alan Katz, ed, *Legal Traditions and Systems: An International Handbook* (New York: Greenwood, 1986) ch 6.

in other words, laws governing the relationship between persons (as opposed to *public law*, which deals with the legal relationship between a state and its individual members). Apart from its reference to the legal system that originated in England, the phrase *common law* can also refer to decisions by courts exercising their "common law" jurisdiction (used in contradistinction to decisions by courts exercising their "equitable" jurisdiction), and to case law generally (used in contradistinction to legislation, or enacted laws).

In the practice of law in Canada, it is important to understand the civil law system because it applies to a significant portion of the Canadian population. To resolve social or business issues in our bijural nation, both legal systems are sometimes needed. Another good reason to learn about the civil law system is that it is the most common system worldwide. It is used in most of South and Central America, including Mexico, and in Continental Europe, including Russia. Many Asian countries, too—China and Japan, for example—use the civil law system, sometimes in combination with *customary law*, which we will discuss later in this chapter.

The legal systems in socialist countries that use the civil law system, such as Russia and China, have some features that distinguish them from most other civil law systems. For example, the role that doctrine (that is, academic commentary) plays in socialist countries varies with the government; authoritarian regimes tend not to permit academic criticism that is political or value-based. In such cases, academic commentary on existing laws will be confined to explanation and analysis.

TABLE 2.1   Comparison of Civil Law and Common Law

CHARACTERISTICS	CIVIL LAW SYSTEM	COMMON LAW SYSTEM
Judicial Decisions	*Not Authoritative* • not a primary or authoritative source of law; only legislation (civil code and other statutes) is binding • regard for precedent is informal (however, previous cases may be persuasive, along with academic commentary, as noted below)	*Authoritative* • a primary and authoritative source of law, along with legislation • judges are bound by precedent following the principle of *stare decisis*
Role of Judges in Dispute Resolution Process	*Inquisitorial System* • judges are appointed from a special school for judges in many civil law jurisdictions—prior experience as a lawyer not required • judges conscious of being part of civil service—i.e., representatives of government • courtroom process is based on the idea that judges should actively assist lawyers in presenting their case—truth is best determined this way • judges are free to call and question witnesses, and order investigations into other evidentiary matters	*Adversarial System* • judges are appointed from the legal profession, after years of practice as lawyer or law professor • judges are conscious of being independent of the government that appoints them • courtroom process is based on the idea that truth will best be determined by lawyers presenting their respective cases, unhindered by interference from the trial judge
Academic Commentary	*Important Interpretive Role* • academic commentary is one of the foundations of the civil law system and is called "doctrine" • scholarly texts and articles about the civil code play a significant role overall in helping judges decide cases	*Persuasive* • academic commentary is a type of "secondary source" and assists in the finding or interpretation of primary sources (judicial decisions and legislation) • texts and articles about the law have varying degrees of persuasiveness in cases in which they are cited, depending on the type of case and the author of the commentary
Juries	Generally not used	Can be used

Religion as Law

Historically, many countries have had a close connection between church and state. In classical Greece, for example, state power, law, and religion were closely intertwined, and the same was true in ancient Israel. Hindu law played a significant role in ancient India, and it continues to do so in India today.[16]

Most nations today separate church and state—in other words, religion and law. In the West, the idea that the two should be separated can be traced to John Locke and his social contract theory. One of the tenets of this theory was that the government should not interfere in matters of individual conscience, including religion. The specific phrase "separation of church and state" is often credited to US President Thomas Jefferson (1743–1826), one of the framers of the US Constitution. While the Constitution does not formally refer to the separation of church and state, the First Amendment guarantees religious freedom. Section 2 of Canada's Charter does the same thing (despite the preamble's reference to the "supremacy of God"). Judicial decisions in England, the United States, and Canada have also explicitly recognized this separation—between politics and law on the one hand, and religion on the other.

Some states guarantee religious freedom but do not recognize law and religion as being completely separate. In Israel, for instance, freedom of religion is protected under the country's Basic Law, and Judaism, the predominant religion, is not formally designated as the state religion. At the same time, religious law (Halacha) and state law converge in a number of areas, including marriage and divorce. Israel seems to fall somewhere between countries that declare a separation of church and state, and countries that acknowledge a significant connection between the state, its laws, and religion.

Finally, as we saw in Chapter 1, viewing religion and the law as belonging to different spheres does not mean that religion plays a limited role in the law. When a significant portion of the population holds similar religious views, they inevitably *influence* matters of state, including its laws. Lord Denning, a very religious man and perhaps the most famous English judge in the last 100 years, had this to say about the interplay between religion and the law:

> Although religion, law and morals can be separated, they are nevertheless still very much dependent on one another. Without religion, there can be no morality, there can be no law. … I will try to indicate how they [important legal principles] are challenged by a changing world which knows no religion, or which at best treats religion as something which is of no moment in practical affairs.[17]

Muslim Legal Systems

Legal systems based on Muslim law are the leading examples of religion-based legal systems. In discussing only Muslim law here, we concur, with some reservation,[18] with the JuriGlobe research group's view that other legal systems that were once religion-based have

---

16   Michael Gagarin & David Cohen, eds, *The Cambridge Companion to Ancient Greek Law* (Cambridge: Cambridge University Press, 2005) ch 3.

17   Lord Denning, *The Influence of Religion on Law* (Calgary: Canadian Institute for Law, Theology & Public, 1997) [reprint of an address given to the UK Lawyers' Christian Fellowship in 1952].

18   Our reservations stem from two concerns: (1) no Muslim nation is governed exclusively by Muslim law, and (2) other nations have legal systems with a significant religious law component (for instance, Israel and Jewish law, or Halacha; Bhutan, a mountain nation in the Himalayas, and Buddhist law; and India and Hindu law).

"since lost their character and distinct status due to the fact that a number of their components have more or less been absorbed into customary or other legal systems."[19]

Islam is the newest of the major world religions, with adherents today comprising between 20 and 25 percent of the world's population, according to most estimates. Muslims believe that Islam was revealed to the prophet Muhammad (570–632 CE) when he was 40 years old. Born in Mecca, Arabia, Muhammad began preaching publicly three years after his first revelation and soon gained many followers. By the time of his death, most of the inhabitants of the Arabian Peninsula had become adherents of a new faith—Islam.

After Muhammad's death, there were disagreements over succession, and these disagreements produced the differing sects and sub-sects that exist among Muslims today. The main sects are the following:

1. Sunni Islam, which is the largest Islamic denomination and covers most of the Islamic world;
2. Shia or Shiite Islam, which is centred mainly in Iran and parts of Iraq, but which also includes the Ismaili branch of Islam, with followers in over 25 countries.

In countries that use Muslim law, it is seen not as a branch of state regulation but as part of the Islamic religion. The rules of behaviour prescribed by Islam are known as sharia (the "way to follow"). To individuals from countries whose political traditions are based on the separation of church and state, the rules prescribed by sharia appear to blend legal rules with seemingly non-legal requirements. For example:

- Five times daily, Muslims are required to pray while facing Mecca.
- Affluent Muslims are required to pay an annual poor tax to indigent Muslims as part of a purification process and as an obligation to their community.
- Among sharia's complex laws concerning inheritance is a rule that if a man and a woman (a brother and sister, for example) both stand to inherit money or other property, the female's share generally will be half that of the male's share.
- Fasting between dawn and sunset is required daily during the month of Ramadan.

Disputes are heard in courts with judges (or *qadis*) and lawyers trained in sharia law.

There are three main sources of sharia. The first source, the Quran, is a collection of Muhammad's revelations, while the second, the *Sunna*, is a collection of traditions (*hadīth*) based on the acts and sayings of Muhammad. These two sources are considered fundamental or primary, but they do not cover all situations; there are legislative gaps. Legal scholars are authorized, based on specific verses in the Quran, to fill in these gaps through interpreting the Quran and the *Sunna*. If these scholars agree about an interpretation of this kind, it becomes a binding secondary authority and part of the *ijmā* (or consensus)—the third main source of sharia law.

A fourth source of sharia law, less central than the three listed above, is the *qiyās*, or analogical deduction. It is also a secondary source. This source is based on analogies to situations covered by the Quran. Like consensus (*ijmā*), it was developed to deal with circumstances not covered by the primary sources. Analogical deduction is accepted by Sunnis but not by Shiites, who replace it with *aql* or reason, which is based on intellect or logic. The difference between *qiyās* and *aql* is a matter of debate among sharia scholars.

---

19 See <http://www.juriglobe.ca/eng/sys-juri/intro.php>.

BOX 2.2

Sharia in Canada

Canada recognizes a separation between law and religion, but it also guarantees religious freedom under the Charter. It attempts to accommodate faiths—Judaism, Islam, Hinduism, or Buddhism, for example—that involve special practices, so long as these practices do not violate the law of the land. And it attempts to accommodate the religion-based laws of certain communities, provided that these laws do not offend the Charter.

In Ontario in 1991, the province amended its *Arbitration Act* to allow for "faith-based arbitration" in family law matters. Tribunals were set up so that adherents of Judaism and Catholicism could resolve their family law disputes according to their religious beliefs: Jews according to Halacha, Catholics according to their version of the Christian faith. Use of the new system was optional for Jewish and Catholic participants. But once they had agreed to use it, its decisions were binding.

In 2004, Muslims argued that they too ought to be entitled to faith-based arbitration in family law matters. In their case, the tribunals would be based on sharia law. The Ontario government reviewed the matter and concluded that the arbitration process could be expanded to include religious groups beyond Jews and Catholics, provided that Charter rights and freedoms were maintained.

Controversy ensued. Women's groups voiced their strong opposition to sharia-based decisions. Other organizations, too, argued that women are not accorded equal rights and protections under sharia. Religious groups newly entitled to faith-based arbitration responded to Muslim charges of inequity by agreeing to give up their own new-found rights under the *Arbitration Act* amendments.

Faced with this controversy, the Ontario government decided to repeal its faith-based arbitration procedures altogether.

In countries that use sharia law, there is a basic agreement about the nature of these sources. But the precise interpretation and application of sharia varies from country to country, and it varies among modernists, traditionalists, and fundamentalists.

As noted above, the legal systems in most Muslim states today blend Islamic law with other forms of law. Only three states today are Islamic law *monosystems*—in other words, countries that officially recognize Islam and whose legal systems are based almost entirely on Islamic law. The three states are Afghanistan, the Maldives (or Maldive Islands), and Saudi Arabia. In Afghanistan, the constitution (adopted in 2004) states that

1. Afghanistan is an Islamic republic with Islam as its "sacred religion" (articles 1 and 2), and
2. No law shall be contrary to the beliefs and practices of Islam (article 3).

Saudi Arabia's constitution, which was adopted in 1992, likewise declares the country to be an Islamic state and recognizes the primacy of sharia in legal matters. It includes the following provisions, for example:

1. Government in Saudi Arabia derives power from the Holy Quran and the Prophet's tradition (article 7).
2. The state protects Islam; it implements its Shariah; it orders people to do right and shun evil; it fulfills the duty regarding God's call (article 23).

It should be noted that even these so-called Muslim monosystems are not governed *exclusively* by sharia. Positive, man-made laws, based on legislation and custom, have been added to deal with administrative and other practical matters that lie outside the scope of Muslim law.

Customary Law

What is **customary law**? Lon Fuller defines it very broadly as follows: "Customary law is not the product of official enactment, but owes its force to the fact that it has found direct expression in the conduct of men toward one another."[20] In other words, customary law is made up of rules that have not been officially recognized or enacted but have become conventional or habitual within a society. For such rules to be considered customary *law*, the society's members must accept them as legally binding.

The term *customary law* is often applied to Aboriginal laws and to the laws of subgroups within a state—that is, laws that the subgroup considers binding but that differ from state-sanctioned positive laws.[21] Such laws are often based on oral tradition; there may only be a fragmentary written record of them. States will sometimes recognize them in some way, and customary law has in some cases influenced official systems. But customary law plays a much reduced role in the legal systems of the modern world. Only very rarely today does it operate as a major source of law at the state level.

The term *customary law* also refers to a type of international law—rules that are based on conventional, habitual practices in the relations between states. These rules may concern peaceful transactions between states or they may concern wartime conventions. What defines them as law in either case is that they are recognized as binding. We examine international law later in this text, in Chapter 12.

Customary law, whether at the local or at the international level, raises two basic questions. First, how widespread does a practice have to be before we regard it as customary? There is no precise test for determining when a tradition is sufficiently widespread to qualify as a tribal custom or a customary international law. Second, how do you define exactly what the custom is, in the absence of a formalized process for making, changing, or recording such practices? While there is definitional certainty in some local traditions, in many contexts this question needs to be addressed.

Other questions about customary law, related to these two basic ones, concern the following:

- the length of the tradition on which the rules are based (for example, one generation or five generations?),
- the regularity with which the rules are followed (which reflects the degree of consensus about the rules),
- dispute resolution mechanisms and enforcement methods, and
- how the customs are preserved (for example, by the memory of community elders, or by written records).

The following sections briefly describe the three ways that customary practices *within* states may come to have legal significance. They may be

1. recognized and applied by subgroups within a state,
2. incorporated into a mainstream system, or
3. adopted as the state system.

---

20 Lon Fuller, "Human Interaction and the Law" (1969) 14 Am J Juris 1 at 1.

21 Marianne Constable, *Just Silences: The Limits and Possibilities of Modern Law* (Princeton, NJ: Princeton University Press, 2005).

Aboriginal Rights Within the Canadian Legal System

Section 35(1) of the *Constitution Act, 1982* provides that the "existing aboriginal ... rights of the aboriginal peoples of Canada are hereby recognized and affirmed." Among the existing rights affirmed by this provision and as determined by the courts is the right of the Sault Ste Marie Métis to hunt without a licence. In the *Powley* case,* the Supreme Court of Canada (SCC) had to decide whether section 35(1) protected a father and son who were charged with hunting a moose without a licence and who claimed to be members of the Sault Ste Marie Métis community. Subsection (2) states that "'aboriginal peoples of Canada' includes the Indian, Inuit and Métis peoples of Canada."

Among other things, the Court had to determine was whether the accused were in fact members of this Métis community. The word *Métis* is not expressly defined in the Constitution. Generally speaking, Métis people are considered to be people who have a mixed First Nations and European heritage. The Court set out a non-exclusive list of criteria to help it determine whether the father and son were in fact Métis. The Court decided that, to qualify as Métis, a person must

1. "self-identify" as Métis,
2. be able to prove their "ancestral connection" with the Métis community, and
3. be "accepted by the modern community" (that is, the modern Métis community).

Concerning the third factor, the Court stated the following (at para 33): "The core of community acceptance is past and ongoing participation in a shared culture, in the *customs* and traditions that constitute a Métis community's identity and distinguish it from other groups" (emphasis added).

In the case of the accused father and son, the Court accepted that they qualified as Métis according to the criteria above. They were acquitted of the charge of unlawfully hunting without a licence. This case illustrates how the customs of Aboriginal groups can be recognized within the broader context of a state's legal system.

* *R v Powley*, 2003 SCC 43, [2003] 2 SCR 207.

Customary Law at the Sub-State Level

The world contains many instances of subgroups that adhere to their own legal systems within their multicultural societies. This can happen in various ways. In some cases, the subgroup exists outside the effective control of the state. Today, certain minority groups in Afghanistan fit into this category, as do some Amazonian tribes in Brazil.

In other cases, the state may not officially recognize the subgroup's legal system, but may tolerate it for political or other reasons. The state has the power to impose its own system but chooses not to. Some tribes in sub-Saharan African nations fall into this category. These tribes have not fully submitted to state control and have continued to maintain their own customary practices.

In other cases, a state may decide to officially recognize a subgroup's right to follow its own customary legal practices (see Box 2.3). Or the state may go further still and recognize an "enclave system" within the main state system—in other words, a legal system within a legal system. Some First Nations groups in British Columbia have negotiated such arrangements. For example, the Nisga'a Treaty, which was finalized in 2000, provides for self-government by the Nisga'a Nation within a defined region of British Columbia (see the discussion in Chapter 4).

Customary Law Incorporated into the Mainstream System

We distinguish between formally recognized positive law systems and customary law. But formal systems are ultimately derived from customary law. Ancient and modern codifications in the civil law tradition, from the *Code of Hammurabi* to Quebec's *Civil Code*, preserve and formalize common (that is, customary) rules and practices. The preamble to the latter code states the following: "The [Quebec] Civil Code comprises a body of rules which, in all matters within the letter, spirit or object of its provisions, lays down the *jus commune*, expressly or by implication."[22] The phrase *jus commune* refers to the society's customary law—the law commonly accepted by a society.

Customary practice was the basis of the common law system, too. In medieval England, the itinerant judges of the royal courts derived principles from the established practices they encountered on their travels through the English counties. And custom continues to play a role in the common law. In modern negligence actions, for example, when courts are trying to determine whether a defendant has behaved "unreasonably," they may look to local customs within the community. If the defendant was simply following accepted practice, her behaviour may be considered reasonable in the circumstances.[23]

Finally, in Canada, constitutional conventions (or customs) regulate the behaviour of government institutions and officials, such as the Senate and the governor general, and also the relations between the provinces and the federal government. We will consider constitutional conventions when we look at executive power in Chapter 6.

Customary Law at the State Level

Independent customary legal systems were numerous before the modern era. Examples include pre-colonial sub-Saharan Africa tribal law, early Germanic law, Celtic law, and Aboriginal law in Australia. Modern examples of purely customary systems are hard to find, however.

According to JuriGlobe, only three customary monosystems exist in the world today: the small nation of Andorra in the Pyrenees; and the two Channel Island UK dependencies, Guernsey and Jersey.

Other nations with customary systems have mixed them in varying combinations with common law, civil law, or Muslim law systems.

Hybrid or Mixed Systems

There are approximately 195 countries in the world today. Roughly half of these have monosystems based on one tradition, such as common law, civil law, or sharia law. The other half have hybrid systems—various mixes of common law, civil law, Muslim law, and customary law systems. We cannot describe all of these hybrid systems here, but we discuss the key ones below.

Common Law and Civil Law

Canada, the United Kingdom, and the United States are often said to have legal systems based on the common law tradition. But that is only partly true. All three of these countries contain regions—Quebec, Scotland, and Lousiana, respectively—in which civil law and common law systems are mixed (see Figures 2.3 and 2.4). The civil codes in these jurisdic-

---

22 *Civil Code of Quebec*, SQ 1991, c 64.

23 For example, see *Waldick v Malcolm*, [1991] 2 SCR 456, a slip-and-fall case. Here, the SCC was asked to determine whether there was a local custom of *not* salting or sanding icy walkways—a custom that might excuse the defendant for not doing so herself. The Court found that there was no such local custom, and the defendant was held liable in negligence.

tions apply to certain areas of the law and the common law system applies to others. A mix of two traditions is known as **bijuralism**.

In Chapter 3, we will look at how law was received into Canada, including Quebec. The *Civil Code of Quebec* covers much of the private law in that province.

The United Kingdom is a unique state because it comprises four other countries: England, Scotland, Wales, and Northern Ireland are countries within a country. England, Wales, and Northern Ireland have common law monosystems. Scotland, however, owing to its historical allegiances and connections with France, has a dual system based on civil law and common law. The US state of Louisiana, because it was formerly a French colony, has, like Quebec, a dual system.

This mix of systems has enriched the development of the law in these countries. For instance, the *Donoghue v Stevenson* case, referred to above as well as in Chapter 1, is in fact a civil law case, arising as it did in Scotland. Lord Atkin wrote the following:

> The case has to be determined in accordance with Scots law; but it has been a matter of agreement between the experienced counsel who argued this case … that for the purposes of determining this problem the laws of Scotland and of England are the same.[24]

The decision in this case, which concerns the tort of negligence, has become one of the most influential ever made in the common law world.

In Canada, the *Roncarelli* decision, also mentioned in Chapter 1, was a Quebec case decided under article 1053 of the *Civil Code of Quebec*, as it then was. It is still the leading case in Canada on abuse of power, and it has been cited repeatedly as a binding authority in the common law provinces as well as in Quebec.

Other Hybrid Systems

Some countries—former colonies of England—have maintained England's common law system after becoming independent but have added or revived other systems in the process. In India, for instance, the common law system applies generally throughout the country. On the local level, however, customary law, Hindu law, and Muslim law sometimes apply, depending on the region and the religion involved.

The legal systems in some countries mix civil law with customary law. This is true of China (not including Hong Kong and Macau), Taiwan, North and South Korea, and Japan. China and North Korea have socialist versions of civil law, and the degree to which local customary law plays a role is a matter of debate, at least in China. (The less tolerant the socialist system, the less influence a competing system will have.)

Many nations have a strong Muslim law base with other systems mixed in. Syria, Iraq, and Iran, for instance, mix Muslim law with civil law. Other countries primarily based on Muslim law have elements of three or four systems. The legal system in Indonesia, for example, incorporates Muslim law, civil law, and customary law. And there are four states—Bahrain, Qatar, Somalia, and Yemen—that have elements of all four legal systems (Muslim law, common law, civil law, and customary law). The majority of countries in Africa combine two or more legal systems.

Figures 2.5, 2.6, 2.7, and 2.8 detail four regions with the most complex mixes of legal systems: Africa, the Middle East, Southeast Asia, and Asia, respectively.

For a global overview of legal systems by continent, and for data on individual countries, visit JuriGlobe's website at <http://www.juriglobe.ca>.

---

24 *M'Alister (or Donoghue) v Stevenson*, [1932] AC 562 at 579 (HL).

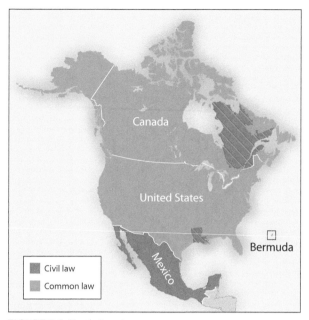

FIGURE 2.3 North America

Civil law
Common law

Civil law
Common law
Customary law

FIGURE 2.4 The United Kingdom

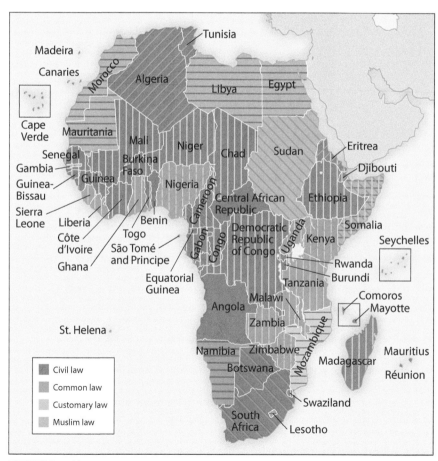

Civil law
Common law
Customary law
Muslim law

FIGURE 2.5 Africa

FIGURE 2.6 The Middle East

FIGURE 2.7 Southeast Asia

FIGURE 2.8 Asia

CHAPTER SUMMARY

There are four major legal system groups in the world today: common law, civil law, religious law, and customary law. Roughly half of the world's nations are monosystems, using predominantly one tradition. The other nations, including Canada, use a mix of traditions.

In Canada, the two most significant legal systems are the common law and the civil law. The common law developed in England over many centuries. It was brought to Canada by English settlers and became the legal system in all provinces and territories except for the province of Quebec. The key features of the common law system are the reliance on precedent and the principle of *stare decisis*. Another key feature of this system is the use of an adversarial process in the courtroom, with lawyers opposing each other and presenting their respective cases with (generally speaking) little interference from the trial judge.

The civil law system can be traced to ancient Rome and to societies even more ancient. Where Canada is concerned, the most important civil code is the *Napoleonic Code* of 1804; it strongly influenced the *Civil Code of Quebec*, which came into effect (as the *Civil Code of Lower Canada*) later in the 1800s. Codes of this kind, relatively unimportant in the common law system, play a central role in the civil law system and are more important than previous judicial decisions.

Another distinguishing feature of the civil law system is the inquisitorial nature of the decision-making process, with judges playing a much more active role than they do in the common law system.

Religion has influenced most political and legal structures, but legal traditions with a *significant* religious component today are found principally in nations with a substantial Muslim population. Sharia (or Muslim) law can be thought of as the "legal" part of Islam. It is based on a number of sources, including the Quran. There are few Muslim nations whose legal systems are based exclusively on sharia, however. Civil law usually plays a role in the legal systems of Muslim states.

We commonly associate customary law with local oral traditions and with international law. In the early stages of their development, however, all legal traditions were indebted to customary law. And yet few legal systems in the world today are based predominantly on customary law.

The need for an awareness of legal systems other than our own is greater now than it ever has been, as our world becomes ever more interconnected and we find ourselves doing business with people who live halfway around the globe.

KEY TERMS

adversarial system system, used in common law courts, whereby the primary responsibility for the presentation of cases lies with the opposing litigants and their counsel, not with the judge presiding over the case *(p. 41)*

bijuralism the operation of two legal systems in one jurisdiction, such as the common law and civil law systems in Canada *(p. 53)*

Bill of Rights (1689) English statute that formally ended the power of the Crown to legislate without the consent of Parliament *(p. 41)*

binding term used to describe a higher court decision that a lower court in the same jurisdiction must follow according to the principle of *stare decisis* *(p. 38)*

Chancery department of state established by English monarchs to assist with legal matters and to issue writs *(p. 36)*

civil code authoritative legislative encoding of a country's private law *(p. 42)*

Civil Code of Quebec (*Code Civil du Québec*) Quebec's current civil code, which came into effect on January 1, 1994, and which replaced the *Civil Code of Lower Canada* that had been in force since 1866 *(p. 45)*

civil law system of law based on codified rules; may also refer to private law *(p. 34)*

common law system of law based on the English legal tradition, which relies on precedent rather than on codified rules; may also refer to (1) decisions by courts exercising their "common law" jurisdiction as opposed to their "equitable" jurisdiction based on broad principles of fairness, or to (2) case law generally as opposed to legislation *(p. 34)*

Corpus Juris Civilis comprehensive codification of Roman civil law, compiled by the Emperor Justinian (483–565 CE) *(p. 44)*

Court of Chancery English court, existing separate from common law courts, established to provide equity *(p. 37)*

Court of King's (or Queen's) Bench English court that decided criminal matters *(p. 36)*

customary law system of law based on rules of conduct considered binding either at a local or an international level, with no formalized process in place for making, changing, or recording them *(p. 50)*

distinguishable term given to a precedent from a higher court that a lower court decides not to follow, usually on the grounds that the facts in the cases differ *(p. 39)*

equity discretionary legal decisions offered by judges in the Court of Chancery, based on fairness and providing relief from the rigid procedures that had evolved under common law courts *(p. 37)*

feudalism socio-political system in medieval Europe based on relationships of obligation and allegiance among king, nobles, and subjects, with land given to subordinates in return for loyalty and military support *(p. 35)*

Inns of Court professional associations for lawyers in England and Wales, with supervisory and disciplinary functions over their members and authority to call law students to the bar; the four Inns of Court today are Inner Temple, Middle Temple, Lincoln's Inn, and Gray's Inn *(p. 38)*

inquisitorial system a feature of civil law proceedings whereby trial judges actively assist lawyers in presenting their cases and are free to call and question witnesses and to order investigations into other evidentiary matters; contrasts with the adversarial system used in common law courts *(p. 45)*

king's peace the ideal peace and well-being of a nation that the English monarch was obliged to uphold and protect *(p. 36)*

persuasive describes a precedent that a court is persuaded to give some weight to but is not bound to follow, because the precedent is from another jurisdiction or is otherwise not binding *(p. 39)*

plaintiff individual, corporation, or other entity who initiates a non-criminal lawsuit *(p. 37)*

precedent court decision that, under the doctrine of *stare decisis*, is binding on lower courts in the same jurisdiction *(p. 38)*

ratio decidendi Latin phrase ("the reason for the decision") referring to the governing rule in a case or the way it was applied to the facts *(p. 38)*

stare decisis Latin phrase ("to stand by decided matters") referring to the common law principle that a precedent is binding on lower courts in the same jurisdiction *(p. 38)*

writ court document, obtained by a plaintiff, by which the defendant was informed that a particular type of action had been started against him or her *(p. 37)*

FURTHER READING

BOOKS

Baker, John H. *An Introduction to English Legal History*, 4th ed (London: Butterworths, 2002).

Cross, Rupert & James W Harris. *Precedent in English Law*, 4th ed (Oxford: Clarendon Press, 1991).

David, René & John EC Brierley. *Major Legal Systems in the World Today: An Introduction to the Comparative Study of Law*, 3d ed (London: Stevens & Sons, 1985).

Glenn, H Patrick. *Legal Traditions of the World*, 4th ed (Oxford: Oxford University Press, 2010).

Stephenson, Graham & Peter Shears. *James' Introduction to English Law*, 13th ed (Oxford: Oxford University Press, 2005).

WEBSITES

Avalon Project at Yale Law School: Documents in History, Law and Diplomacy: <http://avalon.law.yale.edu>.

JuriGlobe: <http://www.juriglobe.ca/eng/>.

The Osgoode Society for Canadian Legal History: <http://www.osgoodesociety.ca>.

REVIEW QUESTIONS

1. Why is it important to be aware of legal traditions other than our own? Give at least three reasons.

2. Explain how the common law developed in England.

3. Briefly describe the role of the English Court of Chancery.

4. What is the principle of *stare decisis*? Under what circumstances is a precedent found to be either (a) binding, (b) distinguishable, or (c) persuasive?

5. What are the benefits of the common law system's practice of following precedent?

6. Briefly describe how the civil law system in Europe was indebted to Roman law.

7. What is meant when we say that courts in civil law jurisdictions use an "inquisitorial system"?

8. Do any Islamic law monosystems exist in the world today? Explain.

9. Why is it difficult to find examples of customary law operating at the state level in the world today?

10. How is customary law inevitably part of the common law and civil law systems?

EXERCISES

1. When a common law judge recognizes a new precedent, is she *finding* new law or *making* new law? Explain why you think there is—or is not—a difference between these two processes within the common law system.

2. Consider one way in which the civil law is different from the common law, and describe a situation where you think that difference might affect the outcome of a case.

3. How is Canadian bijuralism an asset when it comes to Canadians doing business with other countries? In your answer, consider two of Canada's trading partners and their legal systems.

4. Do you believe there is a significant difference between a legal system that is *influenced by* religious beliefs and one that is *based on* religious beliefs? Support your answer with specific reasons and examples.

5. Choose an Aboriginal nation in Canada and research how it applies its own customary laws.

3 The Reception of Common Law and Civil Law into Canada

Hand-tinted postcard showing
Osgoode Hall, home of the oldest
law society in Canada, ca. 1912.

After reading this chapter, you will understand:

- General rules governing the reception of English law in England's colonies
- The different ways in which England acquired overseas colonies and how this affected the colonies' reception of English law

- The significance of the dates on which the different provinces and territories of Canada joined Confederation and the dates on which they are deemed to have received English (or French) law
- Some of the measures taken in Canada to harmonize common law with Quebec civil law

The Common law has been profoundly shaped by its history and this history is exclusively, at least until the eighteenth century, the history of the law of England.

R David & J Brierley, *Major Legal Systems in the World Today*, 3d ed
(London: Stevens, 1985) at 307

Canada, in sum, is bijural or bi-systemic by reason of the perpetuation in Quebec of French private law conceptual jurisprudence as expressed in the *droit civil* and Canada, in turn, is a bijural country by reason of this feature of Quebec law.

J Brierley, "Bijuralism in Canada," in *Contemporary Law: Canadian Reports
to the 1990 International Congress of Comparative Law, Montreal, 1990*
(Cowansville, Que: Yvon Blais, 1992) 22 at 24-25

Introduction

As we saw in Chapter 2, the common law and the civil law are two different legal systems. Canada received both systems from Europe in colonial times. The common law, which came from England, is the governing system in Canada in all provinces and territories except Quebec. In Quebec it applies, too, but only to its public law. The civil law, which Canada received from France, operates in Quebec alone and forms the basis of its private law. The coexistence of these two legal systems in Canada makes our country a **bijural nation**. Anne McLellan, a former minister of justice, has noticed that "Canadian bijuralism is an integral part of our legal heritage."[1]

This chapter outlines how British North America received both legal systems from Europe. It gives the dates on which the ten Canadian provinces and three territories were deemed to have received either English common law or (in the case of Quebec) French civil law. It also provides the dates on which the provinces and territories entered Confederation and thereby joined Canada. Lastly, the chapter considers some implications of Canadian bijuralism, and it reviews some of the ways that Canada's legal system has tried to accommodate both the common law and civil law working together in our country.

---

1   Quoted in M Brunet, *Out of the Shadows: The Civil Law Tradition in the Department of Justice
Canada, 1868-2000* (Ottawa: Queen's Printer, 2000) at ii.

Common Law Rules of Reception of English Law

In 1848, Chief Justice Brenton Halliburton of Nova Scotia wrote the following:

> To what extent the laws of the mother country prevail in the colonies settled by her descendants, is a question which has occasioned much discussion, without producing any rule approaching to precision for our guidance.[2]

A central concern for colonial judges like Chief Justice Halliburton was whether a particular English common law precedent or statute extended to a new colony in Canada and was in force here. Then, one of their most challenging problems was determining if some English law, which had evolved for centuries on that island, was compatible with all new world circumstances found in colonial Canada. As well, what would a colonial lawyer do if there were no English common law precedent to assist the client's case? Could a colonial judge in Canada be persuaded to consider contemporary law from the United States, a country that, like Canada, had also received English common law? (See Box 3.1.)

Faced with such questions, colonial Canadian judges looked to common law precedents from the mother country for guidance. They looked particularly to similar cases in other English colonies where there were similar reception uncertainties; and they looked to cases decided by respected English judges, such as Lord Mansfield. They also reviewed colonial law textbooks, as well as the work of William Blackstone, a prominent English scholar who wrote a widely read commentary on English law. General common law colonization rules concerning the reception of English law to Canada are explored in the following sections.[3] How the territory was acquired by England often determined what rule was followed. Other principles, too, governed reception.

Settlement

When England colonized a territory and sent English subjects there to settle it, that colony received English law then in force, including common law and statute law. These became the colony's first laws. This practice prevailed even though the territory was already inhabited; the first peoples' legal systems were simply disregarded (see Box 3.2). Colonial courts in Canada decided that the reception date—that is, the date on which the colony specifically received English laws—would be the same as the date on which a colony first established its own local legislature.

This first general reception rule was subject to some exceptions. Canadian judges were selective; for example, they did not always accept an English common law precedent that was unsuitable to local circumstances. They perceived that some conditions in a new colony in Canada differed significantly from those in England. For the same reason, not all English statutes were received in a colony. Colonial judges in Canada might not accept some English statutes as being in force here if these statutes were unsuitable and inapplicable to the conditions in this country. The position of colonial judges in this regard are discussed later in this chapter.

---

2 *Uniacke v Dickson*, [1848] 2 NSR 287 at 288-89 (Ch).

3 See also Peter W Hogg, *Constitutional Law of Canada*, 2013 student ed (Toronto: Carswell, 2013) ch 2; JE Cote, "The Reception of English Law" (1977) 15 Alta L Rev 29.

BOX 3.1

Sir John Beverley Robinson and American Law

Sir John Beverley Robinson (1791–1863; pictured at right) was one of the most important Canadian judges of the colonial legal era, the period in which English common law was first being introduced to Canada. In 1829, he was appointed by Britain and became the first Canadian-born chief justice of the Court of Queen's Bench in Upper Canada (later to become Ontario). He held this influential position until 1862. During this time, Upper Canada was being transformed from a pioneer frontier colony to a more modern society by the formation of new corporate institutions, such as banks, insurance companies, roads, navigation, and harbour companies. It was an era of rising urbanization and industrialization, with great advances in transportation, steam technology, the telegraph, and the railway. Writing the majority of judgments for the Court of Queen's Bench, Robinson consistently considered, used, and adapted English common law precedents to help develop the colony's legal system.

The influence of the United States, closer geographically to Canada than to England, meant that American law and cases competed with English law sometimes in a more influential way in this country. The argument for using American law did not persuade Robinson, however, who reminded lawyers that English common law was required by the colony's *Reception Act*. Under this Act, English common law (including legislation of general application) had officially been adopted in Upper Canada as of 1792.

In the case of *Hamilton v The Niagara Harbor and Dock Co*, an issue turned on whether this company was required, in accordance with English common law, to use its corporate seal to execute a contract. Lawyers in the case brought to Robinson's attention the fact that American law was moving away from the strict English common law in this regard. Robinson spoke out against the use of American law:

> [O]ur adherence to the principles of the English common law is a duty imposed upon us by written law, and is therefore more strongly obligatory than it may be acknowledged to be in the courts of the United States. Our statute says that we are to be governed by it "in all controversies relating to property and civil rights," and the English "rules of evidence" are expressly made binding upon us. Whatever liberties therefore may have been assumed in foreign countries in departing from principles which are binding upon English courts, we are not allowed to exercise any such discretion.*

* *Hamilton v The Niagara Harbor and Dock Co* (1841), 6 UCQB (OS) 381 at 399.

Imperial Statutes

As we have noted, colonial judges could decide whether some English domestic statutes were in force in Canada, and colonial legislatures could also amend them by legislation. This discretion did not apply to all English statutes, however. There were certain types, known as **imperial statutes**, that were made by England's imperial Parliament specifically for an overseas English colony. Such statutes were in force in the colonies owing to this special provenance, and they could not be amended or changed there.

Conquest or Cession

If England acquired an overseas colony by conquest (or by transfer or **cession** from another country, pursuant to a treaty), a second common law colonization rule held that laws already

BOX 3.2

Aboriginal Legal Systems

Canada's Aboriginal peoples had their own legal systems before contact with Europeans. [They] did not write their laws down ... but transmitted them orally from generation to generation. This tradition was one of the responsibilities of the elders in each nation's community. Sometimes the tribal laws were transmitted in the form of legends or stories to make them easier to remember and to inspire the listener with respect for the law.

The Iroquois Confederacy, located south of Lake Ontario, was one of the most powerful groups of Aboriginal peoples. Originally it consisted of five nations: the Mohawk, Seneca, Oneida, Onondaga, and Cayuga. The Confederacy was established by two great chiefs, Dekanawida and Hiawatha, around 1142 CE. According to their oral history, it took them 40 years to convince the tribes to form a union bound together by a formal constitution. This constitution was called the *Gayanashagowa*, Iroquois for "great binding law." It provided a system of checks and balances by giving every man and woman in the Confederacy a voice in tribal affairs. The powers of the war chiefs were held in check by those of the peace chiefs. All chiefs were appointed by the clan mothers, who also had the power to remove any chief who did not act in the interests of the people. At some point in the 18th century, the leaders of the Iroquois Confederacy agreed to write down their Great Binding Law. The framers of both the US constitution and the *Charter of the United Nations* referred to the Iroquois Great Binding Law in drawing up their own legal documents.

Source: Reproduced from George Alexandrowicz et al, *Dimensions of Law: Canadian and International Law in the 21st Century* (Toronto: Emond Montgomery, 2004) at 39-40.

existing in the colony continued in force until such time as they were specifically changed by the English government. Provided that no local legislature existed in the colony, English law could be imposed on the colony by the English monarch, exercising his or her prerogative power, or by England's imperial Parliament.

Adoption

A third way English law could be received into a British colony was by adoption. In this instance, a colony's legislature could pass a reception statute that adopted English law as of a certain date. From that time, English law would be received and in force in the colony.

Reception of English and French Law into Canada's Provinces and Territories

The following is an overview of how and when English or French law was received in each Canadian province and territory and the date on which each one joined Confederation. For the five provinces from Quebec east to Newfoundland, English and French laws were introduced by settlement or cession, the first two methods. For the five provinces from Ontario west and the territories, English laws were adopted by reception statutes, the third method. Table 3.1 on the following page provides a summary.

Newfoundland and Labrador

Newfoundland was England's first Canadian colony. British fishing fleets, along with others from Spain, France, and Portugal, sailed to the island as early as the 1500s to catch fish on the Grand Banks. In time, some members of the fishing crews began to spend the winter there, cutting wood and preparing for the fishing fleet's return the next spring. Generally speaking, fishing took priority over settlement in this early period.

TABLE 3.1 Reception Dates for Receiving English and French Law and Entering Confederation for Each Canadian Province and Territory

PROVINCE/TERRITORY	RECEPTION OF LAW	ENTERED CONFEDERATION
Newfoundland and Labrador	1832	March 31, 1949
Nova Scotia	1758	July 1, 1867
Prince Edward Island	1758 (or possibly 1773)	July 1, 1873
New Brunswick	1758 (or possibly 1660)	July 1, 1867
Quebec	French civil law restored in 1774	July 1, 1867
Ontario	1792	July 1, 1867
Manitoba	1870	July 15, 1870
Saskatchewan	1870	September 1, 1905
Alberta	1870	September 1, 1905
British Columbia	1858	July 20, 1871
Yukon	1870	June 13, 1898
Northwest Territories	1870	July 15, 1870
Nunavut	1870	April 1, 1999

In 1583, Sir Humphrey Gilbert claimed the island for England, and several British settlements were founded on the island's east coast. Settlers later came under the governance of the admiral of the English naval squadron that arrived each year to guard the fishing fleet. As a result of these developments, the island was considered a settled colony of England. Its first Legislative Assembly was held at St. John's in 1832, and this date became the reception date for English law in the colony.[4]

Although Newfoundland was England's first Canadian colony, it was actually the last to join **Confederation** and the last to be admitted to Canada, which occurred on March 31, 1949.

Nova Scotia

The reception of English law into Nova Scotia was complicated by the fact that this colony was originally part of French Acadia, that part of New France located in Canada's Atlantic region. French colonists first settled this area in the 1600s, and it was under French control until 1713. In that year, under the terms of the Treaty of Utrecht, France ceded Acadia to England.

Given that England acquired Nova Scotia by cession, following the second common law rule of reception noted earlier, French law ought to have continued there until England changed it. But things did not proceed according to this common law reception rule. In effect, once England established a colonial administration in Nova Scotia after the Treaty of Utrecht, and once Edward Cornwallis set up a seat of government and military base at Halifax in 1749, the colony was treated instead as having been acquired by settlement. The colony convened its first Legislative Assembly in 1758 and this was established as its reception date for English law.

---

4 C English, "From Fishing Schooner to Colony: The Legal Development of Newfoundland, 1791-1832" in LA Knafla & SWS Binnie, eds, *Law, Society, and the State: Essays in Modern Legal History* (Toronto: University of Toronto Press, 1995) 73; J Bannister, *The Rule of the Admirals: Law, Custom, and Naval Government in Newfoundland, 1699-1832* (Toronto: University of Toronto Press, 2003).

BOX 3.3

Difficulties Involving the Reception of English Law into Canada

Beamish Murdoch (1800–1876; pictured at right) was a Nova Scotia lawyer and author whose work, *Epitome of the Laws of Nova Scotia*, was an important early study of Nova Scotia law. Murdoch recognized that some circumstances in a young colony like Nova Scotia were different from those in England, and he suggested that colonial Canadian judges could use two criteria to determine whether English statutes should apply to local conditions. Murdoch suggested that English statutes, if they were to be binding on Canada, must be "applicable to our social condition" and "suitable to our local wants."*

The following case from Murdoch's lifetime shows Murdoch's criteria being applied:

> In the 1841 case of *Dillingham v Wilson*, a farmer apprenticed his son to a cabinet maker. The son complained to his father of some mistreatment and the father ended the apprenticeship. The plaintiff cabinet maker sued the defendant father under the terms of their apprenticeship agreement for failing to complete its terms. The issue was whether an old English apprenticeship statute, dating back to the 16th-century reign of Elizabeth I, applied to Upper Canada [Ontario]. Justice Sherwood held that it did

not, saying that the court considered the statute "a local act which was probably adapted to the state of society in England three hundred years ago, but is not now, and never was adapted to the population of a colony, and was never in force here."†

*   "'Nova Scotia's Blackstone' on the Origins of Nova Scotia Law. [Lecture by Beamish Murdoch, QC, 29 August 1863]" in Peter B Waite, Sandra Oxner, & Thomas Barnes, eds, *Law in a Colonial Society: The Nova Scotia Experience* (Toronto: Carswell, 1984) 187 at 190.

†   *Dillingham v Wilson* (1841), 6 UCQB (OS) 85 at 86-87.

In the next century, Nova Scotia was one of the original three colonies to join Confederation, doing so on July 1, 1867.

Prince Edward Island

The reception of English law in PEI was linked to its reception in Nova Scotia. The island was originally settled by France, and, under the 1713 Treaty of Utrecht, France kept it. However, in 1763, France ceded the island to England by the Treaty of Paris. Then, by the English Royal Proclamation of 1763, the island was annexed to Nova Scotia. Shortly afterwards, in 1769, the island became a separate colony, and its first elected Assembly was held there in 1773.

As with Nova Scotia, England apparently acquired the island by cession. However, the reception of English law in PEI was consistent with the island's being acquired by settlement. The probable date (legal scholars are not all in agreement about this) for its receiving English law may not be 1773 (the date of its own first elected Assembly) but 1758—the date of the first Legislative Assembly in Nova Scotia.[5]

---

5   See Hogg, *supra* note 3 at 2-15; JD Whyte & WR Lederman, "The Extension of Governmental Institutions and Legal Systems to British North America in the Colonial Period" in WR Lederman, ed, *Continuing Canadian Constitutional Dilemmas* (Toronto: Butterworths, 1981) 70.

Interestingly, though Charlottetown was the location of Canada's first meeting, in 1864, to discuss Confederation (see Chapter 4), the colony did not enter Confederation for another nine years; it was admitted to Canada on July 1, 1873.

New Brunswick

Like Nova Scotia and Prince Edward Island, New Brunswick was originally settled by French colonists and was also part of French Acadia. Like those colonies, it was ceded or transferred by France to England. Parts of it were ceded in 1713, by the Treaty of Utrecht, and the remainder by the Treaty of Paris, in 1763. In 1763, like Prince Edward Island, it was annexed to Nova Scotia, but subsequently (again like Prince Edward Island), it separated from Nova Scotia and became a separate colony. That was in 1784.

New Brunswick was also like the other two maritime colonies in that the reception of English law there was deemed to be by settlement and not by cession. However, the actual date for the reception of English law in the colony is unclear. Some legal scholars consider that New Brunswick's case is similar to Prince Edward Island's. In other words, though the province had its first Legislative Assembly in 1786, its being previously annexed to Nova Scotia makes Nova Scotia's reception date of 1758 applicable to New Brunswick. Other commentators on this matter, including the New Brunswick courts, have held 1660 as the reception date. According to Peter Hogg, this date was chosen because it was the year in which Charles II was restored to the English throne.[6]

New Brunswick was, like Nova Scotia, one of the three original colonies to join Confederation and was admitted to Canada on July 1, 1867.

Quebec

In contrast to the maritime colonies, Quebec's status as a colony was always clear. England acquired it from France by conquest and later by cession.

French colonists first settled Quebec in the early 1600s, and it thus became a French overseas colony, known as *la Nouvelle-France*. As such, the colony received French civil law for its legal system. However, the British general Wolfe defeated the French general Montcalm at the battle of the Plains of Abraham, also called the Battle of Quebec, near Quebec City, in 1759 (see Figure 3.1). Subsequently, in 1763, France ceded Quebec to England under the terms of the Treaty of Paris. What followed was the Royal Proclamation of 1763. Exercising his royal prerogative power, King George III of England declared that Quebec would have English law imposed there in place of French civil law.

This uneasy shift of affairs, with Quebec slated to receive English law, did not last long. The English government was influenced by its first civilian governors there, Murray and Carleton, who were both conciliatory to the French *Canadiens* and who were sensitive to the uncertain state of the legal system in Quebec in the wake of the Royal Proclamation. As a result, the English government passed the *Quebec Act, 1774*, a statute that restored French civil law there. Section 8 of the *Quebec Act* stated that "in all Matters of Controversy, relative to Property and Civil Rights, Resort shall be had to the Laws of Canada, as the Rule for the Decision of the same."[7] This provision restored pre-conquest French civil law to Quebec, although English criminal law was retained there, making 1774 the date for receiving (or restoring) civil law in the province.

---

6   See DG Bell, "A Note on the Reception of English Statutes in New Brunswick" (1979) 28 UNBLJ 195 at 196-200; Hogg, *supra* note 3 at 2-3.

7   *Quebec Act, 1774* (UK), 14 Geo III, c 83.

FIGURE 3.1 Anglo-American painter Benjamin West famously captured the death of General Wolfe on the Plains of Abraham. The French general, Montcalm, was also killed in the battle, which followed a three-month siege by the British and lasted only 15 minutes.

One related effect of this Act was also important. At that time, the territory of Quebec extended beyond its current western boundary (the Ottawa River) into what is now southern Ontario. After the American Revolution in 1776, many American settlers, still loyal to England, left their country and re-established themselves in present-day Ontario (at that time, part of Western Quebec). These United Empire Loyalists soon petitioned the English monarch to have the western part of Quebec, where they had relocated, separated from the older, eastern part. They were successful. In response to their demands, the English government passed the *Constitutional Act, 1791*.[8] This Act separated Quebec into two colonies, called Upper Canada (present-day Ontario) and Lower Canada (present-day Quebec) relative to their geographic location along the Great Lakes–St. Lawrence River watershed.

Quebec continued in this way until the *Union Act, 1840*, by which England once again reunited Lower Canada with Upper Canada into the new Province of Canada (see the discussion below). Under this Act, Quebec was then called Canada East and Ontario was then called Canada West. This united province lasted from 1841, when the *Union Act* took effect, until 1867, when the Province of Canada became one of the original colonies to enter Confederation. At this point, the province was once again divided into Quebec and Ontario. Quebec joined Confederation on July 1, 1867.

The Civil Code of Quebec

During the union period—that is, the period when Ontario and Quebec composed the Province of Canada—Quebec was undergoing a great economic transition; it was changing from an agrarian and rural society into a modern one, industrial, capitalist, and urban. The practical demands of this transformation—which involved, for example, the rapid

---

8 *Constitutional Act, 1791* (UK), 31 Geo III, c 31.

FIGURE 3.2 The Codification Commission at work, in their offices in Quebec City, about 1865. The three judges on the Commission were Charles Dewey Day (second from left), Augustin-Norbert Morin (second from right), and René-Édouard Caron (centre). Their secretaries are on the far left and right.

expansion of canals, roads, railways, banks, insurance companies, milling, and lumbering—in combination with an increased influx of British immigration, created the need for a less confusing legal system in the province, especially for commercial law. Uncertainty also arose over which legal system—the common law or the civil law—applied to diverse legal matters needing to be addressed.

The demands for more certainty forced politicians to act. George-Étienne Cartier, Quebec's attorney general, established a three-person Codification Commission in 1857 to revise existing laws in Quebec and consolidate them into a comprehensive civil code (see Figure 3.2). Its efforts resulted in the *Civil Code of Lower Canada*, or *Code civil du Bas Canada*, which took effect in 1866, the year before Confederation.

The Code was in force from 1866 until December 31, 1993. By the 1950s, it was increasingly felt that many of the Code's provisions were out of step with modern living conditions in Quebec. As a result, Quebec's Civil Code Revision Office, created in 1955, helped the government reform and modernize the Code. On January 1, 1994, a revised and newly comprehensive **Civil Code of Quebec (Code Civil du Québec)** became law. It was designed to reflect contemporary Quebec society's new social realities and modern attitudes to, among other things, marriage, children, human rights, and parental equality rights. The new Code comprises 10 books covering private law in Quebec. The topics, by book, are as follows:

1. persons;
2. the family;
3. succession;
4. property;
5. obligations;
6. prior claims and hypothecs;
7. evidence;
8. prescription;
9. publication of rights; and
10. private international law.

In Quebec, the 1866 Code and the 1994 Code have served as a bulwark against encroachments by the common law system practised in all other Canadian provinces. Gener-

The LSUC and the Osgoode Society for Canadian Legal History

The Law Society of Upper Canada (LSUC) regulates, licenses, and disciplines lawyers and licensed paralegals in Ontario. Created as a self-governing body by an act of the Legislative Assembly in 1797, the purpose of the LSUC was to ensure that individuals who practised law in the province were competent, adhered to professional ethics, and followed proper procedures. It was the first association of its kind in Canada and served as a model for the law societies that were subsequently founded in other provinces and territories. Following the creation of the province of Ontario, the LSUC retained its original name, which it holds to this day.

The LSUC did not have a permanent home until 1832, when it moved into Osgoode Hall, named for the first chief justice of Upper Canada, William Osgoode. The building (pictured on the opening page of this chapter) was constructed on six acres of land in what was originally a suburb of the Town of York but is today in the heart of downtown Toronto. It now houses the highest courts of the province of Ontario as well as offices, including those of the LSUC.

Founded by individuals including LSUC officials in 1979, the Osgoode Society is perhaps Canada's foremost organization for studying the history of Canadian law and promoting public interest in this history. The Society supports a number of academic activities and has a distinguished book-publishing program. Since 1981, it has published works on aspects of Canadian legal history, including famous trials, noted lawyers, critical issues affecting the legal profession, and histories of Canada's courts. A collection of oral histories—taped interviews with leading judges, lawyers, and others associated with Canada's legal profession—is available for scholarly research purposes.

ally speaking, these codes have helped preserve Quebec's separate civil law in predominantly common law North America.[9] It should be noted, however, that Quebec is not fully regulated by the civil law system. In general terms, the civil law system pertains to its private law and the common law system pertains to its public law (including criminal law). Quebec's bijuralism is what makes Canada a bijural nation.

Ontario

As we have seen, present-day Ontario originated when the *Constitutional Act, 1791* divided Quebec, and the western part became Upper Canada. However, the Act also provided, under section 33, that the laws of Quebec (that is, the civil law) were to continue in force in Upper and Lower Canada until such time as they were changed by the respective assemblies of each new colony.

Quebec retained its civil law unchanged, but Upper Canada did not. At the first Legislative Assembly for Upper Canada, in Newark (now Niagara-on-the-Lake) in 1792, the first statute passed was a reception act regarding English law. Section III of this Act provided that "in all matters of controversy relative to property and civil rights, resort shall be had to the Laws of England as the rule for the decision of the same." As a result of this Act, the legislature of Upper Canada adopted English law as of 1792. This is recognized as the date for the reception of English laws into the province of Ontario.

Upper Canada continued in this way until the *Union Act, 1840*, when, as noted earlier, the colony was re-united with Lower Canada (Quebec), and the Province of Canada was created. Ontario joined Confederation on July 1, 1867, separating from Quebec at the same time.

---

9   B Young, *George-Étienne Cartier: Montreal Bourgeois* (Montreal and Kingston, Ont: McGill-Queen's University Press, 1981); FP Eliadis, "The Legal System in Québec" in GL Gall, ed, *The Canadian Legal System*, 5th ed (Toronto: Thomson, 2004) 263.

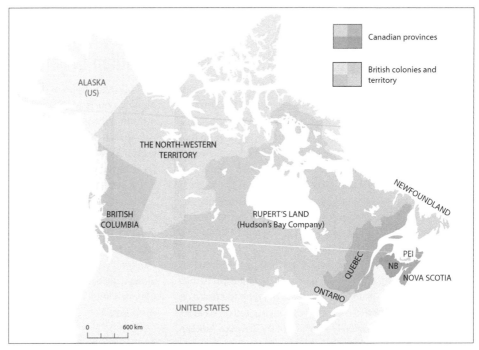

FIGURE 3.3 Dominion of Canada, 1867
Note the vast territory comprising Rupert's Land and the North-Western Territory.

Manitoba

At the time Ontario entered Confederation in 1867, the area on its western border, stretching west to the Rocky mountains, was divided between the Hudson's Bay Company's Rupert's Land and the North-Western Territory (see Figure 3.3).

For the newly formed Dominion of Canada, this western area was highly coveted; possession of it was crucial if Canada was to extend its borders "from sea to sea." Canada's first prime minister, John A. Macdonald, soon entered into negotiations with the Hudson's Bay Company to purchase their western landholdings with the help of the British government. Terms were reached in 1869, and the area was transferred to Canada in 1870. That same year, the federal Parliament created the province of Manitoba out of part of Rupert's Land, and created the Northwest Territories, as this area was renamed, out of the remainder of Rupert's Land and out of the former North-Western Territory. By statute, the reception date for English law into Manitoba was 1870. The actual date for Manitoba's joining Confederation, the fifth province to do so, was July 15, 1870.

Saskatchewan

This province, like Alberta and the three northern Canadian territories, was also created out of the vast Northwest Territories west and north of the province of Manitoba. Saskatchewan joined Confederation on September 1, 1905, and its reception date for English law was 1870. (See Figure 3.4.)

Alberta

Like Saskatchewan, this province too was created out of the Northwest Territories, and it joined Confederation at the same time as Saskatchewan, on September 1, 1905. The date of

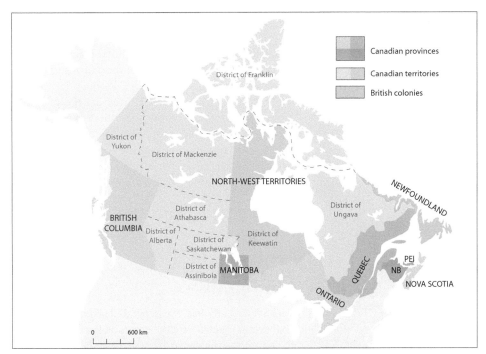

FIGURE 3.4 Map of Canada, 1895
The district boundaries of Saskatchewan, Manitoba, Alberta, and the Yukon are shown. Alberta and Saskatchewan had expanded to their northern boundaries by 1905 (into the area marked District of Athabasca), and Manitoba expanded northward in 1912.

reception for English law there was also the same as for Saskatchewan—that is, 1870. (See Figure 3.4.)

British Columbia

British Columbia was England's Pacific coast colony. Originally there were two of them: Vancouver Island, created in 1849; and British Columbia on the mainland, created in 1858. When England united these two separate colonies in 1866 and called the new territory British Columbia, the governor declared 1858 (later confirmed by its Legislative Council) as the reception date for English law. British Columbia joined Confederation on July 20, 1871, becoming Canada's sixth province (see Figure 3.5).

Yukon

The gold rush of 1898 was the primary reason for Yukon's being created as a separate territory. Mainly as a result of this event, Yukon was created out of the Northwest Territories and became a separate territory on June 13, 1898. The reception date for English law there, as in the three other western provinces created out of the Northwest Territories, was 1870.

Northwest Territories

The Northwest Territories, to the east of Yukon, has retained its original name, which dates from 1870. Its present area is of course smaller than it was originally; since 1870, as we have seen, the area has been divided into various other provinces and territories: Alberta, Saskatchewan, Yukon, and, most recently, the territory of Nunavut. The reception date for English law in the Northwest Territories was 1870, the year it originally entered Confederation.

THE EAST WELCOMES THE WEST.

PRESENTATION OF B. C. REPRESENTATIVES TO SIR JOHN A

FIGURE 3.5

This photoengraving, originally printed in the May 11, 1872 edition of the *Canadian Illustrated News*, shows the BC representatives presenting the terms of BC's entry into Confederation to Sir John A. Macdonald.

Nunavut

Nunavut is Canada's newest territory. It was officially created out of the eastern half of the Northwest Territories on April 1, 1999, though its boundaries had been established in 1993. The Inuit are the majority population in this territory, and the word *Nunavut* means "our land" in Inuktitut, the Inuit language. The date for the reception of English law there, as in the two other arctic territories, is 1870.

Canadian Bijuralism: English–French Connections

Because Canada has two separate legal systems—the civil law in Quebec and the common law elsewhere in the country—the government of Canada must ensure that federal laws are compatible with the civil law system in Quebec. Having a legal divide between the two systems would not be beneficial to our country.

The following are some areas and institutions in which measures have been taken to harmonize Canada's two legal systems:

- *The Supreme Court of Canada.* Canada's highest court is composed of nine judges. By law, under the *Supreme Court Act*, three of these nine judges must come from Quebec.[10] Thus, if a case involving Quebec's civil law comes before the Court, there are French civilian judges on the Court to help decide the appeal based on Quebec's civil law legal system. As well, the choice of who becomes chief justice of Canada has usually alternated between an anglophone and a francophone judge.
- *Legal Education.* Some law faculties—for example, the University of Ottawa and McGill University—offer both civil law and common law degrees. The University of Ottawa and the University of Moncton also offer a common law program in French, and McGill offers a civil law program in English.
- *The Canadian Bar Association.* This national organization, which represents Canada's legal community, has for some time sponsored events and seminars to promote a better understanding of Canada's two different legal systems among civilian and common law lawyers.
- *Federal Department of Justice.* This department was first created in 1868. A civil law section was established in 1952 and a new civil code section in 1993. The department's legislative bijuralism section is concerned, among other things, with developing proposals and programs that will harmonize federal common law legislation with the terms and concepts of Quebec's new civil code, in force as of January 1, 1994.

---

10   *Supreme Court Act*, RSC 1985, c S-26, s 6.

CHAPTER SUMMARY

The federal government in Canada and nine of the country's provinces and three territories use the common law, while one province, Quebec, uses the civil law. Both legal systems have deep roots in this country and have undergone unique developments since the period when Canada was a colony of both France and England. Quebec, originally a colony of France, received French civil law, while the rest of Canada's provinces and territories were originally English colonies or under England's jurisdiction and received English common law.

Common law rules of reception dictated how different regions of Canada received English law. These rules varied according to how the region came to be an English colony. If colonization came about through settlement, the mother country's laws—both common law and statutes—were deemed to be in force, subject to judicial discretion. If England acquired the territory by conquest (or cession), the region's pre-existing legal system continued until the English monarch or imperial Parliament formally imposed English law there, or until the colonial legislature passed a reception statute adopting the laws of England as of a certain date. Each province and territory has a unique history concerning their reception of English (or French) law.

Perhaps the most important aspect of reception, for the country as a whole, is that Canada retained civil law in Quebec. The efforts of Canada's legal community to harmonize both common law and civil law legal systems reflect the unique character of this country.

KEY TERMS

bijural nation a country, usually a federal state, having two different legal systems *(p. 60)*

cession the transfer of a colony from one country to another *(p. 62)*

Civil Code of Quebec (Code Civil du Québec) Quebec's current civil code, which came into effect on January 1, 1994, and which replaced the *Civil Code of Lower Canada* that had been in force since 1866 *(p. 68)*

Confederation the coming together of the three British North American colonies of Nova Scotia, New Brunswick, and the Province of Canada (Ontario and Quebec) to form the Dominion of Canada in 1867. The term later included all the provinces and territories that have joined Canada since that date *(p. 64)*

imperial statute law passed by the English Parliament applying specifically to an overseas English colony *(p. 62)*

FURTHER READING

BOOKS

Castel, J-G. *The Civil Law System of the Province of Quebec* (Toronto: Butterworths, 1962).

Girard, P & J Phillips, eds. *Essays in the History of Canadian Law*, vol 3, *Nova Scotia* (Toronto: Osgoode Society/ University of Toronto Press, 1990).

Guth, DeLloyd & W Wesley Pue, eds. *Canada's Legal Inheritances* (Winnipeg: Canadian Legal History Project, Faculty of Law, University of Manitoba, 2001).

Knafla, LA & J Swainger, eds. *Laws and Societies in the Canadian Prairie West, 1670-1940* (Vancouver: University of British Columbia Press, 2005).

Sworden, P. *Sir John Beverley Robinson: A Colonial Judge and the Development of Upper Canadian Law* (PhD Thesis, McMaster University, 1991) [unpublished].

Weaver, JC. *The Great Land Rush and the Making of the Modern World, 1650-1900* (Montreal and Kingston, Ont: McGill-Queen's University Press, 2003).

WEBSITES

Osgoode Society for Canadian Legal History: <http://www.osgoodesociety.ca>.

McCord Museum of Canadian History: <http://www.mccord-museum.qc.ca>.

REVIEW QUESTIONS

1. What is meant by the term "bijural nation"?

2. Why was the *Quebec Act, 1774* important for Quebec law?

3. How did the reception of English law in an overseas colony differ depending on whether England had acquired the colony by settlement or by conquest?

4. Describe three ways in which Canada has tried to harmonize the common law and civil law legal systems in this country.

5. Discuss one important reason why Sir John Beverley Robinson spoke out against the use of American law in Canada.

EXERCISES

1. What circumstances unique to Canada in our colonial past might have made applying an English case unsuitable here?

2. Consider ways in which having a separate civil law legal system is a benefit to the province of Quebec. Do you think that bijuralism is a good thing for the nation as a whole? Explain.

3. Do you think that an introductory course in both the civil law and the common law should be compulsory in all Canadian law schools? Why or why not?

4 From Confederation to the Charter

Prime Minister Pierre Trudeau and Queen Elizabeth II sign Canada's new Constitution in Ottawa, April 17, 1982, ushering in a new era for Canadian law.

LEARNING OUTCOMES

After reading this chapter, you will understand:

- Significant events leading to Canadian Confederation in 1867
- Why Confederation resulted in a federal government for Canada
- Some difficulties the *British North America Act* created for Canada
- The rise of Canadian nationalism, and Prime Minister Trudeau's efforts to patriate Canada's Constitution

- The activism of Aboriginal peoples and women preceding the Charter, and their influence in having several key provisions added to it
- How the *Canada Act 1982* satisfied Canadians' nationalistic wishes and their desire for an entrenched charter of rights and freedoms
- The nature and functions of Canada's Constitution

I n the hearts of the delegates who assembled in this room on September 1, 1864, was born the Dominion of Canada. Providence being their guide, they builded better than they knew.

> Inscription on plaque in Confederation chamber,
> Provincial Building, Charlottetown, Prince Edward Island

T he circumstances that led to the adoption of the Charter of Rights and Freedoms help to explain the form the document finally took.

> Ian Greene, *The Charter of Rights*
> (Toronto: Lorimer, 1989) at 37

Introduction

The idea of uniting some or all of Britain's six separate Canadian colonies—Newfoundland, Nova Scotia, Prince Edward Island, New Brunswick, the Province of Canada (Canada West and Canada East), and British Columbia—pre-dated 1867. In the early 1800s, politician and lawyer Richard Uniacke of Nova Scotia envisioned colonial union.[1] Lord Durham also wrote a notable report on intercolonial union in 1839; it contemplated the advantages of extending a "legislative union over all the British Provinces in North America."[2]

Unification gained further momentum when, in 1864, politicians from the Atlantic region met at Charlottetown, Prince Edward Island to discuss the possibility of a maritime union of Britain's Atlantic colonies. They were joined there by politicians from the Province of Canada, led by John A. Macdonald and George Étienne Cartier, who put forward an ambitious plan to unite more of Britain's Canadian colonies. Many of these politicians reconvened to

---

1   L Kernaghan, "Richard John Uniacke" in James H Marsh, ed, *The Canadian Encyclopedia*, 2d ed (Edmonton: Hurtig, 1988) vol 4 at 2211.

2   Gerald M Craig, ed, *Lord Durham's Report* (Toronto: McClelland & Stewart, 1963) at 160.

discuss this idea further at two subsequent conferences—one in Quebec City, later that same year, and another in London, England in 1866.

These conferences led to three of these colonies—Nova Scotia, New Brunswick, and the Province of Canada (Ontario and Quebec)—uniting into the new Dominion of Canada, in 1867. They did so under an imperial statute of the British Parliament called the *British North America Act* (BNA Act, now known as the *Constitution Act, 1867*). Note that the colonies were called "Provinces" in the preamble to the Act.

This chapter reviews significant events leading to Confederation, and explains why Canada's new national government became a federal one. It will also discuss how some ensuing problems and omissions in the BNA Act affected the later development of Canadian law. It examines Prime Minister Pierre Trudeau's political efforts, beginning in the 1960s, to patriate the BNA Act from Britain to Canada and to supplement it with a new *Charter of Rights and Freedoms*. In this context, we will show the important role undertaken by two groups—Aboriginal peoples and women—in having several key sections added to the Charter. Lastly, this chapter will consider how Canada's Constitution influences how laws are made in this country.

Prelude to Confederation

Canadian historians and political scientists have examined several key factors leading to Canadian Confederation in 1867 and ascertained important political, military, economic, and imperial forces behind this development.[3] Principal among these were the following:

1. political stalemate in the Province of Canada,
2. the influence of the United States,
3. expansion of railways across British North America,
4. hopes for a larger domestic market for manufactured goods, and
5. British support and approval for Confederation.

Political Stalemate in the Province of Canada

The *Union Act, 1840* reunited Upper Canada (Ontario) and Lower Canada (Quebec) as the Province of Canada. Section XII of this Act provided that Upper Canada and Lower Canada were to have an equal number of representatives in the new province's single elected Legislative Assembly. As well, sections XLVI and XLVII provided that, within the new Province of Canada, Canada West and Canada East, as Upper Canada and Lower Canada were now called, would each retain its own existing laws and courts of justice—the common law in Canada West and the civil law in Canada East. Problems with this new political arrangement arose from three main sources:

1. regional factions and rivalries,
2. disparities in population, and
3. the unsettled location of the Legislative Assembly.

---

3   See PB Waite, *The Life and Times of Confederation, 1864-1867* (Toronto: University of Toronto Press, 1962); R Cook, C Brown & C Berger, eds, *Confederation* (Toronto: University of Toronto Press, 1967); Patrick Malcolmson & Richard Myers, *The Canadian Regime: An Introduction to Parliamentary Government in Canada*, 3d ed (Peterborough, Ont: Broadview Press, 2005); and Roger Gibbins, *Conflict and Unity: An Introduction to Canadian Political Life*, 3d ed (Scarborough, Ont: Nelson, 1994).

In order to get bills passed into law in the Province of Canada, a bill had to receive support from both groups of representatives in the Legislative Assembly—those from Canada West and those from Canada East. This proved difficult to obtain. Union governments became, in effect, coalitions of English and French political factions. The two groups were divided on many issues by different language, geography, culture, and religion. Undermined by faction and instability, numerous government ministries were formed and fell during this union period (1841–1867). Such divisions between the French and English factions proved to be insurmountable.

Another problem was a growing disparity in population increase between Upper Canada and Lower Canada (these former terms remained in general use). This disparity posed problems for the principle of fair and equal representation within the Legislative Assembly. The western part of the new province (that is, Upper Canada) was receiving far more new immigrants than the eastern part (that is, Lower Canada). Responding to this disparity, politicians from the western part, in particular George Brown (1818–1880), argued forcefully for the principle of representation by population ("rep by pop"). He proposed a new form of government structure that would allow politicians in the western part, with its larger population base, to introduce and pass legislation according to its own particular needs without having to obtain French support.[4]

Over time, the location of the Legislative Assembly also became problematic. Kingston was the first capital of the Province of Canada. Thereafter the capital moved several times—to Montreal, then to Toronto, then to Quebec City, then back to Toronto in 1857. This meant continual upheaval for politicians and civil servants. They wanted a permanent capital city, particularly after it appeared that Confederation might be possible. Politicians finally asked Queen Victoria to choose a capital. Her choice was Ottawa, right on the border between Upper Canada and Lower Canada. It was there, in 1859, that Canada's new Parliament buildings began to be constructed.

As a result of these problems, political scientist Peter Russell noted that "the source of political energy that moved politicians to be constitutionally restless and creative, was the utter frustration of the leading Canadian politicians with the union system of government."[5] This frustration led union politicians, including George Brown, John A. Macdonald, George Étienne Cartier, Alexander Tilloch Galt, and Thomas D'Arcy McGee, to put aside their political differences in pursuit of a common goal. In 1864, they formed a "Great Coalition" to advocate a new, federal system of government for Canada whereby different regions of the country would control their own legislatures and their own legislation.

The Influence of the United States

Events in the United States also served as a catalyst to Canadian Confederation. One of these was their Civil War (1861–1865). In 1865, as the northern Union forces neared victory over the Confederate southern states, Canadian politicians began to worry about a large-scale demobilization of Union soldiers and a possible invasion northward. No such Union invasion occurred, though there was a cross-border raid from a particular military faction. Living in the northern United States were Irish–American Union veterans sympathetic to

---

4   George Brown, "Confederation Debates, Legislative Assembly Feb 8, 1865" in PB Waite, ed, *The Confederation Debates in the Province of Canada/1865* (Toronto: McClelland & Stewart, 1963) at 64.

5   Peter H Russell, *Constitutional Odyssey: Can Canadians Become a Sovereign People?* 2d ed (Toronto: University of Toronto Press, 1993) at 17.

the Irish independence movement then active in Ireland. Known as Fenians, they believed that by invading Canada, they could strike a blow against England in support of the Irish independence movement overseas. In 1866, a Fenian raid on the Niagara frontier across from New York state helped demonstrate to Canadian politicians that there was also a military need to unite the country; political union would better enable the colonies to defend themselves.[6]

Canadian politicians also worried about American westward expansion. This was occurring at a rapid pace after the Civil War. Underlying it was an American expansionist ideology called "manifest destiny"—the belief that the United States "was destined by the will of Heaven to become a country of political and territorial eminence."[7] Alarmed about this, Canadian politicians became even more concerned when the American government entered into talks to purchase Alaska from Russia, doing so in 1867, thereby threatening to outflank Canada on the west coast. Steps would have to be taken to counter America's aggressive westward push and to ensure that Canada would also be able to secure a Pacific coastline.

Railway Expansion Across British North America

The 1850s and 1860s were a boom time for railway building in North America. Canadian politicians realized that railways offered huge economic potential. In particular, they provided a solution to an annual Canadian problem: the closing of the St. Lawrence and Great Lakes waterway for nearly half the year due to winter ice. Railway construction was expensive, however, and huge amounts of overseas capital were needed. Both Macdonald and Cartier supported railways, and they believed that a union of Britain's separate colonies in North America would be better able to attract overseas investment capital for railway expansion.

Larger Domestic Market for Manufactured Goods

Politicians like Macdonald and Brown also saw Confederation as a means of securing new and larger domestic markets and encouraging more trade between Ontario, Quebec, and maritime Canada. They also hoped that a new national Canadian government might purchase Rupert's Land—that huge expanse of territory west of Lake Superior to the Rocky Mountains—from the Hudson's Bay Company and ultimately extend Canada to the Pacific Ocean, thus fulfilling a Canadian vision of westward expansion. A continental economy could result from such a union, with a larger internal market for domestic manufactured goods. At the same time, central Canadian banks, manufacturers, and railways could help develop the west and thereby encourage immigration there. This would yield a further benefit: the central government's stronger economic base would give it the ability to assume the colonial debt of future colonies that joined Confederation.[8]

British Support for Confederation

Perhaps the most influential factor in the movement toward Canadian Confederation was Britain's support for such a union. Britain favoured it for two main reasons:

---

6   Gibbins, *supra* note 3 at 15-16.

7   Norman A Graebner, "Introduction" in Norman A Graebner, ed, *Manifest Destiny* (Indianapolis, Ind: Bobbs-Merrill, 1968) at xv.

8   Roger Riendeau, *A Brief History of Canada* (Toronto: Fitzhenry & Whiteside, 2000) at 124-36.

1. In the 1840s, Britain was moving toward free trade and away from its former colonial mercantilism system. This meant that it would no longer favour and give protection to colonial Canadian imports. Accordingly, a larger economic union within Canada could help the colonies adjust to an uncertain British market for their goods.

2. Britain was also concerned about the high costs of administering its colonial presence in North America, especially the expense of maintaining British troops in Canada. By supporting British North American union, and by having Canadians accept more responsibility for their own defence, Britain could begin to withdraw its troops there and reduce its costs. Finally, Britain shared Canadian politicians' concern about American westward expansion. Supporting British North American union could also help ensure a Canadian presence on the Pacific coast—a benefit to the mother country.

As the review above indicates, there were many underlying forces leading to Confederation. Thus when pro-Confederation politicians from the Province of Canada, including Macdonald, Cartier, Brown, Galt, and McGee, arrived to present their idea of a larger British North American union to Atlantic politicians meeting at Charlottetown in 1864 (see Figure 4.1), the timing was auspicious. As noted, delegates at this conference were sufficiently interested in their presentation that they were willing to continue discussing this plan later that year, in Quebec City. It was there that these delegates finalized the terms of union, in 72 Resolutions.

Their last stop was London. Here, they made final revisions to their union plan. The statute that gave effect to these Quebec Resolutions was the *British North America Act*, referred to above. It was passed by the British Parliament on March 29, 1867 and proclaimed law on July 1, 1867. The newly completed Parliament buildings in Ottawa were set to host Canada's first national government.

FIGURE 4.1 Delegates to the Charlottetown Conference, 1864
The delegates discussed the idea for a union of Britain's separate North American colonies into a new Canadian federal state, achieved in 1867.

Confederation and the Formation of a Federal Government

The government structure eventually adopted by the framers of the BNA Act was **federalism**. This was something new to British constitutional history and was different from Britain's own unitary system of government. Federalism was an American, not an English, political idea, reflected in the Act's division of powers between the new Canadian federal government in Ottawa and the provinces.

Why did Canadian politicians end up adopting a federal system of government? It was not the first choice of Macdonald, our country's first prime minister. Macdonald desired a **unitary** (or legislative) **government** like Britain's, whereby all sovereign authority would be centred in one governing body for all of Canada. But he realized this would not be possible. He acknowledged this fact in his Legislative Assembly speech in support of Confederation, in 1865:

> The third and only means of solution for our difficulties was the junction of the provinces either in a Federal or a Legislative union. Now, as regards the comparative advantages of a Legislative and a Federal union, I have never hesitated to state my own opinions. I have again and again stated in the House, that, if practicable, I thought a Legislative union would be preferable. … I have always contended that if we could agree to have one government and one parliament, legislating for the whole of these peoples, it would be the best, the cheapest, the most vigorous, and the strongest system of government we could adopt. …
>
> But, on looking at the subject in the Conference, and discussing the matter as we did, most unreservedly, and with a desire to arrive at a satisfactory conclusion, we found that such a system was impracticable. In the first place, it would not meet the assent of the people of Lower Canada, because they felt that in their peculiar position—being in a minority, with a different language, nationality and religion from the majority,—in case of a junction with the other provinces, their institutions and their laws might be assailed, and their ancestral associations, on which they prided themselves, attacked and prejudiced; it was found that any proposition which involved the absorption of the individuality of Lower Canada— if I may use the expression—would not be received with favor by her people. We found too, that though their people speak the same language and enjoy the same system of law as the people of Upper Canada, a system founded on the common law of England, there was as great a disinclination on the part of the various Maritime Provinces to lose their individuality, as separate political organizations, as we observed in the case of Lower Canada herself. …
>
> Therefore, we were forced to the conclusion that we must either abandon the idea of Union altogether, or devise a system of union in which the separate provincial organizations would be in some degree preserved. So that those who were, like myself, in favor of a Legislative union, were obliged to modify their views and accept the project of a Federal union as the only scheme practicable, even for the Maritime Provinces.[9]

---

9   John A Macdonald, "Confederation Debates, Legislative Assembly, Feb 6, 1865" in PB Waite, *supra* note 4 at 40-41.

Macdonald recognized that a legislative union was unacceptable in two quarters: the maritime provinces and Quebec.

The inhabitants of the maritime provinces, though enticed by the prospect of a railway connection to central Canada that would reduce their geographic and economic isolation, feared that a legislative union would undermine their distinctive political culture. People in the maritime provinces had great affection for their separate local legislatures and, as Macdonald noted, were not inclined to lose them. A federal political union would better safeguard their local interests. The same was true for Quebec, which had, in addition, deep-seated cultural and language concerns. Quebec politicians saw the need for a French-controlled provincial government to legislate over areas such as language, schools, their civil law, religion, and political institutions. All of these elements were felt necessary for *la survivance* of their distinct culture in an otherwise English North America.

The role played by the Maritimes and Quebec in the ultimate adoption of Canadian federalism is summed up succinctly by historian G.F.G. Stanley:

> The decision to adopt a federal form of government rather than a legislative union was not the result of any philosophical theories of government, but of practical necessities. No other form of union was possible, regardless of the voiced preference for a unitary system on the part of some of the Canadian delegates. The French-Canadian province and the Maritimes possessed too strong a sense of their own identity willingly to surrender it for the sake of being ruled by an alien or a central Canadian majority. This determination to retain the maximum power over their own local affairs while yielding broad general powers to a central government was the basic fact of the negotiations, both at Charlottetown and at Quebec.[10]

Political instability in the Province of Canada was, as noted above, a leading underlying factor in the push for federal union. But the political system that created this instability was also, ironically, a key to Canadian federalism's future success. From 1841 to 1867, the Province of Canada already had an unacknowledged federal form of government. Its civil service and government departments were already *dual*; they operated in both English and French. It was governed under dual French–English premierships—for example, Baldwin and LaFontaine, Brown and Dorion, and Macdonald and Cartier. For legislation to pass, a double majority of votes was needed—in other words, a majority from representatives of both parts of the province. Though problematic, this political arrangement respected the regional and linguistic rights of the Province of Canada's two entities. As well, the later use of French and English in the province's Legislative Assembly showed that a bilingual Parliament could work in Canada.

John A. Macdonald and the New Federal Government

As noted, the framers of the BNA Act were aware of American federalism and borrowed some ideas from it. At the same time, however, Macdonald was wary of some negative aspects of American federalism. For one thing, he felt that the American Constitution gave too much power to individual states, at the expense of their federal government in Washington. Macdonald noted this also in his 1865 Legislative Assembly speech in support of Confederation:

---

10   George FG Stanley, *A Short History of the Canadian Constitution* (Toronto: Ryerson, 1969) at 78.

> We can now take advantage of the experience of the last seventy-eight years, during which that Constitution has existed, and I am strongly of the belief that we have, in a great measure, avoided in this system which we propose for the adoption of the people of Canada, the defects which time and events have shown to exist in the American Constitution … . They commenced, in fact, at the wrong end. They declared by their Constitution that each state was a sovereignty in itself, and that all the powers incident to a sovereignty belonged to each state, except those powers which, by the Constitution, were conferred upon the General Government and Congress. Here we have adopted a different system. We have strengthened the General Government. We have given the General Legislature all the great subjects of legislation. We have conferred on them, not only specifically and in detail, all the powers which are incident to sovereignty, but we have expressly declared that all subjects of general interest not distinctly and exclusively conferred upon the local governments and local legislatures, shall be conferred upon the General Government and Legislature. We have thus avoided that great source of weakness which has been the cause of the disruption of the United States.[11]

Such a perceived weakness in the American system helped convince Macdonald that Canada's new federal government had to be stronger than the provinces. This was reflected in the division of powers between the provinces and the federal government. Macdonald's vision was that "all the great questions which affect the general interests of the Confederacy as a whole, are confided to the Federal Parliament, while the local interests and local laws of each section are preserved intact, and entrusted to the care of the local bodies."[12]

Section 91 of the BNA Act lists a number of matters of national importance under the Parliament of Canada's areas of control, which included the following:

- The Regulation of Trade and Commerce [section 91(2)];
- The Raising of Money by any Mode or System of Taxation [section 91(3)];
- Militia, Military and Naval Service, and Defence [section 91(7)];
- Currency and Coinage [section 91(14)];
- Indians, and Lands reserved for the Indians [section 91(24)]; and
- Criminal Law [section 91(27)].

Section 91 also stated that the Parliament of Canada had residual power "to make Laws for the Peace, Order, and good Government of Canada, in relation to all Matters not coming within the Classes of Subjects by this Act assigned exclusively to the Legislatures of the Provinces."

Other sections of the BNA Act assigned further powers to the federal Parliament's control. For example, section 24 gave it the exclusive power to appoint senators; and section 58, the power to appoint the provinces' lieutenant governors. Section 92(10) gave the Parliament of Canada the power to declare some provincial works "to be for the general Advantage of Canada" and thus to come under federal control. Section 96 authorized the federal government to appoint judges to the highest courts in each province. Finally, section 101 provided for the Parliament of Canada to establish a "General Court of Appeal for Canada."

---

11 John A Macdonald, "Confederation Debates, Legislative Assembly, Feb 6, 1865" in PB Waite, *supra* note 4 at 44.

12 *Ibid* at 45.

Ensuing Problems with the BNA Act

The BNA Act was a crucial development in Canada's political history. But it later proved problematic in various ways. First, it was an imperial statute of the English Parliament, not of the Canadian Parliament, and it lacked a formula enabling Canadians to amend it themselves. "In constitutional and legal terms this was a major blunder," law professor E. McWhinney noted, "and undoubtedly stemmed from the ignorance of British constitutional lawyers with the problems of written constitutions and the practical necessity of having amendment formulae built in."[13]

The BNA Act's omission of a domestic amending formula was not a problem in 1867. However, it later emerged as a problem in the 1960s and 1970s, when Canadian nationalism became more pronounced. Many Canadians were getting frustrated at being unable to amend our Constitution by themselves, without Britain's approval.

A second problem with the BNA Act over time was that it did not contain an **entrenched** Charter or bill of rights for Canadian citizens. In this respect, it differed markedly from the American Constitution, whose first ten amendments are known as the Bill of Rights. The preamble to the BNA Act stated that Canada's Constitution was to be "similar in Principle to that of the United Kingdom." However, the United Kingdom's Constitution did not have anything similar to the American Constitution's Bill of Rights.

Britain's Constitution itself came from various sources. Its measures for protecting the civil liberties of English subjects were found, for example, in the 1689 Bill of Rights and written documents such as the *Magna Carta*; they were also based on common law court decisions, customs, political practices, public support for democracy, and legal principles like *habeas corpus*. The aim of making Canada's Constitution "similar in principle" to England's meant that Canada inherited Britain's varied civil liberties and legal inheritance, which contrasted with the American approach of protecting its citizens' civil rights in one central, entrenched document.

A third problem with the BNA Act, as later events were to reveal, was that it was formulated without consulting the first peoples to inhabit the land now called Canada: Canada's indigenous population. On the 100th anniversary of Confederation, Chief Dan George of the Tsleil-Waututh Nation, a Coast Salish band in North Vancouver, delivered his "Lament for Confederation" in Vancouver's Empire Stadium, offering a poignant reflection on the meaning of this centenary from an Aboriginal perspective (see Box 4.1).

Lastly, though Macdonald thought it "wise and expedient" to empower the Parliament of Canada, under section 101 of the BNA Act, to establish a General Court of Appeal for Canada, this section did not directly state whether this court would be the final Supreme Court of Appeal for Canada. Nor did the BNA Act indicate who would resolve future disputes likely to arise over the division of powers between the new federal government and the provinces.

Problems Interpreting Federalism: The Supreme Court of Canada

Using section 101 of the BNA Act, the federal government (under the Liberal administration of Prime Minister Alexander Mackenzie) passed the *Supreme Court Act* in 1875. This Act established the Supreme Court of Canada (SCC) as this country's "General Court of

---

13   Edward McWhinney, *Canada and the Constitution, 1979-1982* (Toronto: University of Toronto Press, 1982) at 65.

Appeal for Canada." However, a problem that later emerged with this court, as indicated above, was that it was not then the *final* appellate court for Canada. Litigants could still appeal a decision from the SCC to the **Judicial Committee of the Privy Council** in London, England. The Privy Council, established in 1833, was then the highest appeal authority for the British Empire. Litigants could even bypass the SCC altogether, taking their appeal from a lower provincial court of appeal directly to the Privy Council.

In a related matter, Peter Russell also noted that the fathers of Confederation were "remarkably insensitive" about the SCC's power to decide the constitutional validity of federal

BOX 4.1

Chief Dan George, "Lament for Confederation," July 1, 1967

How long have I known you, Oh Canada? A hundred years? Yes, a hundred years. And many, many years more. And today, when you celebrate your hundred years, Oh Canada, I am sad for all the Indian people throughout the land.

For I have known you when your forests were mine; when they gave me my meat and my clothing. I have known you in your streams and rivers where your fish splashed and danced in the sun, where the waters said, "Come, come and eat of my abundance." I have known you in the freedom of the winds. And my spirit, like the winds, once roamed your good lands.

But in the long hundred years since the white man came, I have seen my freedom disappear like the salmon going mysteriously out to sea. The white man's strange customs, which I could not understand, pressed down upon me until I could no longer breathe. When I fought to protect my land and my home, I was called a savage. When I neither understood nor welcomed his way of life, I was called lazy. When I tried to rule my people, I was stripped of my authority.

My nation was ignored in your history textbooks—they were little more important in the history of Canada than the buffalo that ranged the plains. I was ridiculed in your plays and motion pictures, and when I drank your fire-water, I got drunk—very, very drunk. And I forgot.

Oh Canada, how can I celebrate with you this Centenary, this hundred years? Shall I thank you for the reserves that are left to me of my beautiful forests? For the canned fish of my rivers? For the loss of my pride and authority, even among my own people? For the lack of my will to fight back? No! I must forget what's past and gone.

Oh God in Heaven! Give me back the courage of the olden chiefs. Let me wrestle with my surroundings. Let me again, as in the days of old, dominate my environment. Let me humbly accept this new culture and through it rise up and go on.

Oh God! Like the thunderbird of old I shall rise again out of the sea; I shall grab the instruments of the white man's success—his education, his skills—and with these new tools I shall build my race into the proudest segment of your society.

Before I follow the great chiefs that have gone before us, Oh Canada, I shall see these things come to pass. I shall see our young braves and our chiefs sitting in the house of law and government, ruling and being ruled by the knowledge and freedom of our great land.

So shall we shatter the barriers of our isolation. So shall the next hundred years be the greatest in the proud history of our tribes and nations.

Source: Reproduced from The Aboriginal Multi-Media Society (<http://www.ammsa.com>).

and provincial laws.[14] Another constitutional legal scholar, F.R. Scott, likewise found it surprising that the framers of the BNA Act did not expressly consider what is now known as **judicial review** of federal and provincial legislation passed under the Act. In this regard, said Scott, the framers "showed surprisingly little knowledge of its meaning or implications."[15]

This was a critical omission, noted G.F.G. Stanley, because: "The very essence of a federal constitution, the division of the powers of government, implies the existence of a tribunal free to determine the validity of legislation passed by the legislatures of the component parts of the federation."[16] Who would decide which legislative powers were validly federal and which were provincial if litigation over this matter were to occur?

Section 91 of the BNA Act listed federal powers. Section 92 of the Act listed provincial ones; it gave the provinces power over matters of local importance such as:

- Hospitals [section 92(7)],
- Municipal Institutions [section 92(8)],
- Property and Civil Rights [section 92(13)], and
- The Administration of Justice in the Province [section 92(14)].

The SCC was not Canada's final court of appeal until 1949, when appeals to the Judicial Committee of the Privy Council finally ended. Until then, this English body was both the final appeal court for Canadian legal matters *and* the final authority for judicial review when it came to settling inevitable disputes that arose after 1867 regarding the division of powers between the federal and provincial governments. Before 1949, in other words, the SCC was a subordinate court to the Privy Council. Though Canadian judges did not shy away from judicial review, notably in the case of *The Queen v Chandler* (see Box 4.2), the ultimate authority to determine this lay in London. As a result, initial decisions regarding federalism and the division of powers in Canada under the BNA Act—decisions that shaped the early evolution of Canadian federalism—came from the Privy Council, not from the SCC. It also meant that the SCC had a difficult beginning developing a distinctive Canadian jurisprudence for this country.

Patriation of the Constitution: Hope for a Charter of Rights

A growing concern among Canadians in the decades after the Second World War was protecting human rights. Many Canadians, concerned with wartime atrocities that came to light after the war, worried about the inadequacy of Canada's human rights legislation. They feared that the human rights of individuals, particularly visible minorities coming to Canada

---

14   Peter H Russell, "Introduction" in Peter H Russell et al, eds, *Federalism and the Charter: Leading Constitutional Decisions* (Ottawa: Carleton University Press, 1989) at 3.

15   FR Scott, "Foreword" in BL Strayer, *Judicial Review of Legislation in Canada* (Toronto: University of Toronto Press, 1968) at vii; see also BL Strayer, *The Canadian Constitution and the Courts: The Function and Scope of Judicial Review*, 3d ed (Toronto: Butterworths, 1988); and John T Saywell, *The Lawmakers: Judicial Power and the Shaping of Canadian Federalism* (Toronto: University of Toronto Press, 2002). Note that the term "judicial review" has a different meaning in the context of administrative law. See Chapter 12.

16   Stanley, *supra* note 10 at 111.

The Queen v Chandler (1869), 12 NBR 556 (NBSC)

This case is widely regarded as the first Canadian case dealing with judicial review of the Constitution.

In its division of powers between the new federal Parliament and provincial governments, the BNA Act gave the federal Parliament, under section 91(21), exclusive jurisdiction over "Bankruptcy and Insolvency." In 1868, shortly after the Act came into effect, the New Brunswick provincial legislature passed an amendment to its *Insolvment of Confined Debtors Act*. This amendment allowed a debtor confined in jail to apply to a county court judge for a discharge. Taking advantage of this amendment, a man named Hazelton, in jail in St. John for debt, applied to a county court judge (Chandler) to be discharged from his debts.

The issue was whether the New Brunswick government had power to make a provincial statute concerning insolvency—a legislative area over which the BNA Act had recently given the federal Parliament exclusive jurisdiction.

Chief Justice Ritchie of New Brunswick held that New Brunswick's 1868 amendment to the *Insolvment of Confined Debtors Act*, because it dealt with insolvency, was in "undoubted conflict" with section 91(21) of the BNA Act. His view was that the New Brunswick provincial legislature had "exceeded its powers" with this statute, and he issued an order prohibiting judge Chandler from proceeding under it.

Source: G Bale, *Chief Justice William Johnstone Ritchie: Responsible Government and Judicial Review* (Ottawa: Carleton University Press, 1991).

in increasing numbers after the war, were inadequately protected against racial, religious, and ethnic discrimination in such areas as housing and employment.

A growing number of civil liberty activists articulated an argument for, and hoped to entrench, a formal bill of rights in Canada's Constitution. They also wanted Canadian courts to have a more active role in protecting civil liberties. They were heartened by vanguard cases such as *Roncarelli v Duplessis* (see Chapter 1), which developed the theory of an "implied bill of rights" to help protect individuals against misuse of government power (see Chapter 8). However, many realized that, in the end, a concerted federal effort would be needed to achieve their goal. Here they found an ally in Prime Minister Trudeau.[17]

Pierre Trudeau and the Quest for a Domestic Amending Formula and Charter of Rights and Freedoms

As noted in his *Memoirs*, one main reason that Pierre Trudeau entered federal politics concerned the issue of "national unity and the place of Quebec within Canada."[18] During Trudeau's first period as prime minister (1968–1979), Canadian nationalism was on the rise. The 1960s saw the nation adopt a new maple-leaf flag, introduce the Canada Pension Plan, experience a glorious centennial in 1967, and welcome the world at Expo '67. This growing feeling of national pride helped weaken long-standing colonial ties to Britain. A corollary to this national pride was a desire to **patriate** Canada's Constitution from England so that amendments to it could be made by Canadians alone, without needing British approval.

Trudeau supported the idea of patriation and the idea of securing, through further constitutional reform, a domestic amending formula for Canada's Constitution, though he

---

17   B Dickson, "The Canadian Charter of Rights and Freedoms: Context and Evolution" in GA Beaudoin & E Mendes, eds, *Canadian Charter of Rights and Freedoms* 4th ed (Markham, Ont: LexisNexis, 2005) at 3.

18   Pierre Elliott Trudeau, *Memoirs* (Toronto: McClelland & Stewart, 1993) at 228.

knew that previous prime ministers who had tried to do this had been unsuccessful. However, he had an added incentive in his pursuit of these goals. Quebec nationalism was rising alongside Canadian nationalism in the 1960s and '70s, and was part of Quebec's "Quiet Revolution." In 1976, Quebec elected its first Parti Québécois government under René Lévesque. In 1980, the party held a referendum on sovereignty association regarding Quebec's future relationship with the rest of Canada. Trudeau, returning as prime minister in 1980 after losing the 1979 election, was determined to oppose Quebec separatists.

Including a charter to his patriation plan and opposition to separatism was important to Trudeau for several reasons. Such an accomplishment would be a cornerstone of the "just society" he was trying to achieve in Canada. (See also Box 1.4 in Chapter 1.) Later, looking back on this period, Trudeau wrote that the Charter expressed his long-held view that "the subject of law must be the individual human being … [who] has certain basic rights that cannot be taken away by any government."[19] Trudeau also recognized that the Charter would help promote Canadian identity and—since a majority of Canadians favoured the idea of having a charter of rights—that it would increase public support for his efforts in the patriation process. Strong public support could help him counter provincial opposition to his patriation process, help counter Quebec separatism, and be an instrument of national unity.[20]

When the federalist "no" side defeated the separatist "yes" side in Quebec's 1980 referendum on sovereignty association, Trudeau continued his commitment for a "renewed federalism" and continued to shepherd his patriation plan through to completion. He met with Canada's premiers, but found that they continued to add—as the price of their support—their own provincial demands to his undertaking. In response, a seemingly frustrated Trudeau decided to see if he could, as prime minister, patriate the Constitution unilaterally, amending the BNA Act without provincial consent. Though Ontario and New Brunswick supported him, he met strong opposition from the other eight provinces. They argued that such an important change to Canada's constitutional framework also required provincial approval. The question whether Trudeau could act unilaterally in this regard was put to the SCC. The SCC held that Trudeau's unilateral action to seek a proposed amendment to the BNA Act was legal, but that, under the circumstances, a substantial measure of provincial consent was necessary by constitutional convention for Trudeau to proceed further. (See Chapter 6 for a discussion of constitutional conventions.)

Faced with this judgment, in 1981 Trudeau once again met with provincial premiers to try to obtain their consent. At this stage, however, the patriation process was opened up for public input, and two interest groups in particular—Aboriginal peoples and women—came forward and pressed their proposals for reforms to members of Parliament. Both groups had been following the patriation process closely, and did not want to be excluded from it.

Aboriginal Peoples and the Patriation Process

Canada's Aboriginal peoples—First Nations (or Indians, as the government called them), Inuit, and Métis—were keenly aware of Trudeau's patriation plan for their own constitutional status and treaty rights. Having had their interests and treaty rights left out of the original BNA Act, they were determined not to be disregarded a second time.

---

19   *Ibid* at 322.

20   Malcolmson, *supra* note 3 at 37; Ian Greene, *The Charter of Rights* (Toronto: Lorimer, 1980); Stephen Clarkson & Christina McCall, *Trudeau and Our Times*, vol 1, *The Magnificent Obsession* (Toronto: McClelland & Stewart, 1990); Michael Mandel, *The Charter of Rights & the Legalization of Politics in Canada*, revised ed (Toronto: Thompson, 1994).

By the mid-20th century, Aboriginal peoples had experienced many decades of economic, social, and cultural hardship.[21] As the Royal Commission on Aboriginal Peoples summarized:

> The assimilation process enforced by the federal government severely disrupted family relationships in [Aboriginal] communities. Residential schools caused the greatest damage; the [widespread physical, emotional, sexual, and spiritual/cultural] abuse left the children with serious emotional scars. Those who escaped the worst abuse still suffered loss of both language and family relationships. Some were unable to develop healthy relationships with their own children.
>
> As the residential system wound down in the 1960s, a new form of family dislocation occurred: the child welfare system. Cross-cultural adoptions and foster placements were so common that many communities lost almost an entire generation of children. …
>
> Loss of land through the colonization process and economic collapse in Aboriginal communities led to extreme poverty and economic reliance on the Canadian government. At the conclusion of the era of colonization—an era that arguably continues to this day—Aboriginal people endured "ill health, run-down and overcrowded housing, polluted water, inadequate schools, poverty and family breakdown/violence at rates found more often in developing countries than in Canada."[22]

Aboriginal people wanted to improve their situation, a sentiment expressed by Chief Dan George in his "Lament for Confederation." They recognized the importance of organizing themselves politically and developing an infrastructure for activism. But it was not easy to accomplish this. They faced a number of difficulties:

- poor communication between Aboriginal groups across Canada, owing to isolation, vast geographical distances, and language differences;
- lack of funds for travel expenses for the delegates to attend meetings;
- hostility from the federal Department of Indian Affairs; and
- their unfamiliarity and lack of experience with such mobilization efforts.[23]

Yet Aboriginal organizations had slowly begun to form, first at the provincial and later, in the 1960s, at the national level. They began to inform Canadians about the difficulties Aboriginals experienced in trying to preserve their distinctive culture, about the hardships of life on reserves, and about the many problems they experienced in the areas of health, education, and unemployment. They pressured the Canadian government to change its

---

21   Darion Boyington, in John Roberts, Darion Boyington & Shahé S Kazarian, *Diversity and First Nations Issues in Canada*, 2d ed (Toronto: Emond Montgomery, 2012) ch 10.

22   Royal Commission on Aboriginal Peoples, *People to People, Nation to Nation: Highlights from the Report of the Royal Commission on Aboriginal Peoples* (Ottawa: Supply and Services Canada, 1996) <http://www.aadnc-aandc.gc.ca/eng/1100100014597/1100100014637>.

23   See Harold Cardinal, *The Unjust Society: The Tragedy of Canada's Indians* (Edmonton: Hurtig, 1969); DE Sanders, "The Indian Lobby" in Keith Banting & Richard Simeon, eds, *And No One Cheered: Federalism, Democracy and the Constitution Act* (Toronto: Methuen, 1983) 301; D Sanders, "Aboriginal Rights in Canada: An Overview" in Olive Patricia Dickason, ed, *The Native Imprint: The Contribution of First Peoples to Canada's Character*, vol 2, *From 1915* (Athabasca: Athabasca University Educational Enterprises, 1996) 518.

policies toward Aboriginal peoples, and their efforts began to meet with some success. For example, the government lifted its ban on the potlatch ceremony, gave all status Indians the right to vote in federal elections, and phased out residential schools. Two events in particular proved critical in bringing Aboriginal demands into the public's awareness during Trudeau's constitutional patriation process: the federal government's 1969 white paper on Aboriginals, and the SCC's recognition in 1973 of Aboriginal title to land in a case involving the Nisga'a in British Columbia (see Box 4.3).

Having achieved considerable unity and political organization, Aboriginal groups became alarmed when it appeared that Trudeau and many of the provincial premiers negotiating patriating the Constitution were once again ignoring them. In 1981, organizations representing the First Nations, Métis, and Inuit people of Canada—the National Indian Brotherhood, the Native Council of Canada, and Inuit *Tapirisat* of Canada—put pressure on these politicians to allow them to participate in the constitutional amending process. They had long-standing concerns about such issues as land claims, self-government, maintaining their special legal status,[24] and obtaining constitutional recognition from the Crown of their Aboriginal and treaty rights. They argued that Aboriginal peoples were key stakeholders in Trudeau's constitutional reform process.

Aboriginal organizations and their leaders soon realized that they needed to become even more active politically. They began speaking to Canadians with a unified voice, making skillful use of the media, and mobilizing across Canada to put pressure on the government to give more consideration to their interests. They even sent representatives to England to express their concerns before the British Parliament, using their historic treaty relationship with the English Crown. A key document in this relationship is the Royal Proclamation, issued by Britain in 1763; as we shall see, its importance was highlighted in a Charter provision.[25] In the end, the government acceded to the pressure from Aboriginal peoples to have their rights entrenched in and guaranteed by the new Constitution. The long-term impact of the resulting provisions remains to be seen.

Women, the Charter, and Equality Rights

Women were another group aware of the importance of Trudeau's patriation plan for a new Constitution, and similarly anxious not to be excluded from it. In Canada as elsewhere, women had traditionally been denied many political rights granted to men. They obtained the right to vote long after men: not until 1918 could they vote in federal elections, and not until 1951 could they vote in all provinces and territories. In 1917, the first woman was elected to provincial office, in Alberta, and in 1921 the first woman was elected to the federal Parliament. However, as late as 1929, women were still not considered "persons" eligible to become Canadian senators (see Box 4.4).

Since the end of the 19th century, volunteer women's groups, clubs, and organizations have been advocating for equal rights. In the 1960s and 1970s, the agenda of the women's

---

24   "[T]he doctrine of aboriginal rights exists ... because of one simple fact: when Europeans arrived in North America, aboriginal peoples were already here, living in communities on the land, and participating in distinctive cultures, as they had done for centuries. It is this fact ... above all others, which separates aboriginal peoples from all other minority groups in Canadian society and which mandates their special legal ... status." *R v Van der Peet,* [1996] 2 SCR 507.

25   The Royal Proclamation was issued by King George III to delineate British and Indian land in North America. It was the first public recognition of Aboriginal rights to lands and title. The Proclamation also stated that Indian lands could be purchased only by the Crown. It is the cornerstone of Aboriginal land claims today.

BOX 4.3

The White Paper and Land Claims: Increasing Awareness of Aboriginal Issues

In 1969, Prime Minister Trudeau and his minister of Indian affairs, Jean Chrétien, unveiled a "white paper," which set out the government's new policy for Aboriginal peoples. This white paper was issued in response to a government-commissioned report, which concluded Aboriginal peoples were Canada's most marginalized and disadvantaged population.* The government proposed measures including repealing the controversial *Indian Act* (the federal legislation that has regulated registered Indians and reserves since 1876, and that was part of the larger government agenda to absorb Aboriginal people into mainstream Canadian culture), dissolving the Department of Indian Affairs, eliminating Indian status, converting reserves to private property that could be sold by bands or their members, transferring responsibility for Aboriginal affairs to the provinces, and appointing a commissioner to address outstanding land claims, thereby terminating existing treaties over time.

The Aboriginal response to the white paper was one of fierce opposition. For one thing, the policy did not take into account the many concerns Aboriginal peoples had raised in their consultations with the government prior to the paper's release. As well, although the *Indian Act* severely compromised Aboriginal independence, it also secured important rights—namely, reserve lands, and a special status within the country. If the *Indian Act* were simply abolished, Aboriginal people imagined that whatever legislation replaced it would likely be worse. As well, the government's plan to transfer its responsibility for Aboriginal affairs to the provinces was

viewed as an effort to evade historic obligations. So angry was the Aboriginal reaction that the government withdrew the white paper shortly after it was issued.

Around the same time, a landmark Supreme Court case involving land claims in British Columbia further underscored another key issue. In its 1973 decision *Calder v Attorney General of British Columbia*,† the SCC affirmed the position of the Nisga'a people of BC that Aboriginal title to land, based on traditional occupancy, survived later European settlement and the Crown's assumption of sovereignty. In recognizing Aboriginal title, the Court weakened the federal and provincial governments' reluctance to negotiate land claims in parts of Canada not covered by existing treaties. In 1975, in Quebec, the Cree and Inuit were successful in securing the James Bay and Northern Quebec Agreement, which compensated Aboriginal peoples in that region for Quebec's building of power operations on their land. In 1977, Justice Thomas Berger, who had been appointed to head a royal commission tasked with studying and making recommendations on the effects of a proposed gas pipeline through the Mackenzie Valley, issued a report opposing any construction until Aboriginal land claims in the areas in question had been settled.

* H Hawthorne, "A Survey of the Contemporary Indians of Canada: Economic, Political, Educational Needs and Policies," October 1966 and 1967.

† [1973] SCR 313.

movement broadened. These decades saw the rise of women's liberation and a greater number of women entering the workforce and pursuing post-secondary education. Many in the women's movement began to lobby governments over concerns such as pay equity; access to good, affordable daycare; violence against women; sexual harassment; reproductive rights; family law reform; pension reform; and education. One of the women's movement's greatest victories during this pre-Charter period came in 1967, when the federal government appointed the Royal Commission on the Status of Women to examine women's concerns in a wide range of equality-related matters, including employment outside the home, child care, affirmative action, and discrimination.[26]

26 See C Hosek, "Women and Constitutional Process" in Banting & Simeon, *supra* note 23, 280; P Leclerc, "Women's Issues" in Patrick James & Mark Kasoff, eds, *Canadian Studies in the New Millennium* (Toronto: University of Toronto Press, 2008) 185; Lise Gotell, *The Canadian Women's Movement, Equality Rights, and the Charter* (Ottawa: Canadian Research Institute for the Advancement of Women, 1990).

Despite this success, women continued to have some major concerns about equality rights in Canada. Some of their dissatisfaction centred on former prime minister John Diefenbaker's 1960 Bill of Rights and its provision in section 1(b) regarding "the right of the individual to equality before the law and the protection of the law." Women were concerned that this section was not worded strongly enough to protect equality rights. Experience had shown that, in cases involving women's equality rights, courts tended to interpret this provision narrowly, to the disadvantage of women.

One of these cases was the 1974 *Lavell* case. It involved two Aboriginal women who married non-Aboriginal men, and it raised the question whether these women's Indian status ought to be affected by their marriage.[27] If a male status Indian married a non-Aboriginal, he would not lose his Indian status. However, section 12(1)(b) of the *Indian Act* denied Indian status to an Aboriginal woman who married a non-Aboriginal man. There was obvious inequality here. The issue was whether this section of the *Indian Act*, by discriminating on the basis of sex, violated the equality-before-the-law section 1(b) of the 1960 Bill of Rights. The SCC held that it did not.

In the wake of this and other SCC decisions, and with Trudeau's possible new Charter on the horizon, women from across Canada attended a conference in 1981 to discuss their concerns. Patrice Leclerc summarized these as follows:

> The consensus of the conference was that gender equality rights had to be in the Charter. Specific points were made, especially by the cadre of feminist lawyers: the use of the word "persons," which was familiar in Canadian law after the *Persons* case, should be used throughout. All points in the Charter were to apply equally to male and female persons. It was agreed that equality under the law must be stated as broadly as possible and that as many protections for this as necessary must be written in to cover eventualities. There was an enhanced emphasis on collective rights, on the rights of women as a group.[28]

As we shall see below, one measure taken by women's groups "to cover eventualities" was to have the framers of the Charter add another specific guarantee of equality rights. This, however, required further vigorous lobbying.

The Final Stage of the Patriation Process

Prime Minister Trudeau's patriation efforts culminated in the *Canada Act 1982*, enacted by the UK Parliament on March 29, 1982. Schedule B of the Act included the *Constitution Act, 1982*. The *Canada Act 1982* came into force on March 29, and the *Constitution Act, 1982* some two weeks later. The reason for the delay in the case of the latter statute was that section 58 of the *Constitution Act, 1982* specified that the Act "shall come into force on a day to be fixed by proclamation issued by the Queen or the Governor General under the Great Seal of Canada." In a public ceremony in Ottawa on April 17, 1982, Queen Elizabeth herself signed the proclamation, bringing it into force (see the opening photo of this chapter). It was the culmination of much hard work by many Canadians.

---

27   *Attorney General of Canada v Lavell and Bedard*, [1974] SCR 1349. See also *Bliss v AG Canada*, [1979] 1 SCR 183.

28   P LeClerc, *supra* note 26 at 203. See also Sherene Razack, *Canadian Feminism and the Law: The Women's Legal Education and Action Fund and the Pursuit of Equality* (Toronto: Second Story, 1991) at 34.

The Judicial Committee and the "Persons" Case

Emily Murphy of Edmonton, appointed in 1916 as the first female judge in the British Empire, initiated a drive to become a Canadian senator. But the federal government believed, based on section 24 of the BNA Act, that she was not a "qualified person" to become a senator. Murphy came up with a strategy. She petitioned the federal government to direct a reference—that is, a formal request for a tribunal's opinion about a certain matter—to the Supreme Court of Canada concerning section 24 and the question whether the phrase "qualified persons" could be interpreted to include female persons. She invited four other women to sign the petition with her.

Prime Minister King accepted their petition. His government then referred the matter to the SCC, which ruled against the "famous five," as these women became known. However, King's government agreed to support their appeal to the UK's Judicial Committee of the Privy Council, where Lord Sankey declared that women were "persons" and were eligible to be appointed to the Canadian Senate.

Sources: *Edwards v AG of Canada*, [1930] AC 124 (JCPC); RJ Sharpe & PI McMahon, *The Person's Case: The Origins and Legacy of the Fight for Legal Personhood* (Toronto: University of Toronto Press, 2007).

The *Canada Act 1982* and its Schedule B, the *Constitution Act, 1982*, provided solutions to many of the ensuing difficulties the BNA Act had created for Canada. For example, section 2 of the *Canada Act 1982* states the following: "No Act of the Parliament of the United Kingdom passed after the *Constitution Act, 1982* comes into force shall extend to Canada as part of its law." This provision, ending the authority of the English Parliament to legislate for Canada, satisfied this country's growing nationalist impulse. So did Part V of the *Constitution Act, 1982*, which sets out the general procedure by which Canadians could amend their own Constitution, without Britain's involvement. In another nod to Canadian nationalism, the *British North America Act* was renamed the *Constitution Act, 1867*. Part I of the *Constitution Act, 1982* also contains the *Canadian Charter of Rights and Freedoms*—which was something else many Canadians keenly wanted. And section 24 of the Charter gives the courts a wide-ranging power to remedy Charter infringements. Section 24(1) states that "Anyone whose rights or freedoms, as guaranteed by this Charter, have been infringed or denied may apply to a court of competent jurisdiction to obtain such remedy as the court considers appropriate and just in the circumstances." (See Box 8.4 for a more detailed discussion of section 24.) Chapter 5 summarizes all of Canada's constitutional statutes.

Aboriginal and Treaty Rights in the New Constitution

The aggressive lobbying of Canada's Aboriginal peoples brought the inclusion of section 25 in Part I of the Charter and of section 35 in Part II of the *Constitution Act, 1982*. The Charter provision reads as follows:

> 25. The guarantee in this Charter of certain rights and freedoms shall not be construed so as to abrogate or derogate from any aboriginal, treaty or other rights or freedoms that pertain to the aboriginal peoples of Canada including
>> (a) any rights or freedoms that have been recognized by the Royal Proclamation of October 7, 1763; and
>> (b) any rights or freedoms that now exist by way of land claims agreements or may be so acquired.

Part II of the *Constitution Act, 1982* is entitled "Rights of the Aboriginal Peoples of Canada." Section 35 reads as follows:

> 35(1) The existing aboriginal and treaty rights of the aboriginal peoples of Canada are hereby recognized and affirmed.
>
> (2) In this Act, "aboriginal peoples of Canada" includes the Indian, Inuit and Métis peoples of Canada.
>
> (3) For greater certainty, in subsection (1) "treaty rights" includes rights that now exist by way of land claims agreements or may be so acquired.
>
> (4) Notwithstanding any other provision of this Act, the aboriginal and treaty rights referred to in subsection (1) are guaranteed equally to male and female persons.

Section 35, in other words, recognizes existing Aboriginal and treaty rights, defines Aboriginal peoples of Canada, specifies that treaty rights include rights by way of land claims agreements, and guarantees Aboriginal and treaty rights equally to both sexes within the Aboriginal population. Finally, section 35.1 of Part II commits the government of Canada to include representatives of the nation's Aboriginal peoples in any constitutional conference where any amendments that may affect Aboriginal people are to be discussed. The inclusion of these provisions in the two parts means that Aboriginal and treaty rights cannot be unilaterally taken away by the federal government.

However, something these provisions did *not* do was define what, precisely, existing Aboriginal rights *are*, so it has fallen to the court system to determine this over time as questions and conflicts arise. In many cases, there has been disagreement between the government and Aboriginal peoples as to what is and what is not an Aboriginal right. The key Supreme Court decision defining aboriginal rights and setting out the legal test to determine an "existing aboriginal right" under section 35(1) of the *Constitution Act, 1982* was the case of *R v Van der Peet*.[29] In that case, the Court stated that "in order to be an aboriginal right an activity must be an element of a practice, custom or tradition integral to the distinctive culture of the aboriginal group asserting the right."[30] The central principle was that, to be recognized today, an Aboriginal right must be grounded in a pre-contact activity. Peter Hogg summarizes the elements of the test set out by the Court:

> In order for a practice to be "integral," the practice must be "of central significance" to the aboriginal society: it must be a "defining" characteristic of the society, "one of the things that made the culture of the society distinctive." The practice must have developed before "contact," that is, "before the arrival of Europeans in North America."[31]

The Constitution's definition of Aboriginal rights has been criticized by some for preventing the adaptation of these rights to today's needs and circumstances; in effect, rights in the post-contact era are largely "frozen" according to pre-contact practices.

Since *Van der Peet*, Aboriginal rights recognized by Canadian courts have included such rights as the right to hunt, fish, and trap for food and ceremonial purposes on ancestral lands[32] (see also Box 2.3 in Chapter 2). Professor Brian Slatterly, whose work has focused on

---

29 *Supra* note 24.

30 Quoted in Peter W Hogg, *Constitutional Law of Canada*, 2013 student ed (Toronto: Carswell, 2013) at 28-22 to 28-23.

31 *Ibid* at 28-23.

32 See Olthuis, Kleer, Townshend & Shin Imai, *Aboriginal Law Handbook*, 3d ed (Toronto: Carswell 2008) at 45-48.

Aboriginal rights and constitutional theory, distinguishes between generic and specific Aboriginal rights:[33]

- *Generic rights* are those held by all Aboriginal peoples in Canada. They include rights to land; rights to subsistence resources and activities; the right to self-determination and self-government; the right to enter into treaties; and the right to practise one's own culture and customs, including language and religion.
- *Specific rights* are those held by an individual Aboriginal group, either recognized in treaties or defined through a court case. For example, the Supreme Court in *R v Sparrow* found that Vancouver's Musqueam Band had an existing Aboriginal right to fish, though the right may not apply to other First Nations. In *R v Powley*, the Court found an existing Aboriginal right to hunt for the Métis of Sault Ste Marie, though other Métis groups may not enjoy this right.

Regarding the right of Aboriginal people to self-government, this is a right that Aboriginal peoples across Canada have long demanded. In 1887, for example, just 20 years after Confederation, the Nisga'a and Tsimshian chiefs pressed the government for a treaty and self-government in Victoria;[34] over a century later, in 2000, the Nisga'a Treaty was finally signed between the federal government and the Nisga'a. The Treaty authorizes the Nisga'a to operate their own government and make certain laws, and provides them with the authority to manage lands and resources.

At the time of writing, Canada has signed 20 comprehensive self-government agreements involving 34 Aboriginal communities across Canada, both independent of and in conjunction with land claim settlements.[35] Aboriginal Affairs and Northern Development Canada highlights some examples of the positive effects that modern treaties and self-government agreements have on Aboriginal communities as follows:

- In northern Quebec, the James Bay and Northern Quebec Agreement and the Northeastern Quebec agreement have led to the creation of a number of Inuit, Cree and Naskapi owned companies and joint ventures with the private sector in areas such as airlines, construction, clothing, communications/software, mining, shipping, tourism, arts/craftsmanship, fisheries, and biosciences.
- In British Columbia, the Sechelt First Nation has developed its traditional economy based on fishing, and more recently, increased economic activity in areas such as logging, gravel extraction, salmon farming and tourism. Large portions of Sechelt lands have also been developed and leased to non-member residents.
- In the Northwest Territories, the Tlicho have created several companies to engage in regionally specific economic development activities (e.g. remediation contracts) and through the negotiation of benefits agreements for their citizens and communities.[36]

---

33 Brian Slattery, "A Taxonomy of Aboriginal Rights" in Hamar Foster, Heather Raven & Jeremy Webber, eds, *Let Right Be Done: Aboriginal Title, the Calder Case, and the Future of Indigenous Rights* (Vancouver: UBC Press, 2007).

34 "Self-Government," online: BC Treaty Commission <http://www.bctreaty.net/files/issues_selfgovern.php>.

35 "Fact Sheet: Aboriginal Self-Government," online: Aboriginal Affairs and Northern Development Canada <http://www.aadnc-aandc.gc.ca/eng/1100100016293/1100100016294>.

36 "Fact Sheet: Economic Benefits of Modern Treaties and Self-Government Agreements," online: Aboriginal Affairs and Northern Development Canada <http://www.aadnc-aandc.gc.ca/eng/1346794349784/1346794380933>.

Government assessments of the well-being of self-governing communities have confirmed positive economic results.[37]

Despite many positive developments, the process of determining—and revising laws and policies to recognize—Aboriginal rights is ongoing, and, with a surge in activism in recent years, will likely continue for many years to come.

Women's Rights in Canada's New Constitution

As we have seen, women worked hard to have the new Charter include an equality section more strongly worded than the one in the 1960 Bill of Rights. The result of their efforts was section 15, which states the following:

> 15(1) Every individual is equal before and under the law and has the right to the equal protection and equal benefit of the law without discrimination and, in particular, without discrimination based on race, national or ethnic origin, colour, religion, sex, age or mental or physical disability.
>
> (2) Subsection (1) does not preclude any law, program or activity that has as its object the amelioration of conditions of disadvantaged individuals or groups including those that are disadvantaged because of race, national or ethnic origin, colour, religion, sex, age, or mental or physical disability.

Women also wanted the Charter to include as many protections as possible for gender equality. Section 28 constitutes such extra protection. It states the following: "Notwithstanding anything in this Charter, the rights and freedoms referred to in it are guaranteed equally to male and female persons."

The Nature and Functions of Canada's Constitution

Canada's Constitution is a collection of statutes and unwritten practices and traditions. It is the supreme law of Canada, outlining our system of government and guaranteeing our rights and freedoms under the *Canadian Charter of Rights and Freedoms*. Section 52(2) of the *Constitution Act, 1982* states that the Constitution of Canada includes

> (a) the *Canada Act 1982*, including this Act;
> (b) the Acts and orders referred to in the schedule; and
> (c) any amendment to any Act or order referred to in paragraph (a) or (b).

All of the acts and unwritten practices forming our present Constitution are interpreted through **constitutional law**—that area of law that deals with, among other things, the legislative jurisdiction of governments in Canada. We have seen, for example, that section 91 of the BNA Act (now the *Constitution Act, 1867*) gave the Parliament of Canada jurisdiction—the power to make laws—over areas of national importance, including Aboriginal

---

37   *Ibid*. Self-governing communities show consistently lower rates of unemployment, with recent figures showing a 13.4 percent increase in employment and a 12 percent growth in labour force participation.

peoples and the lands reserved for them, while section 92 of this Act gave the provinces jurisdiction over matters that were more local in scope, such as municipal institutions.

Peter Hogg defines constitutional law as follows:

> Constitutional law is the law prescribing the exercise of power by the organs of a State. It explains which organs can exercise legislative power (making new laws), executive power (implementing the laws) and judicial power (adjudicating disputes), and what the limitations on those powers are. In a federal state, the allocation of governmental powers (legislative, executive and judicial) among central and regional (state or provincial) authorities is a basic concern. The rules of federalism are especially significant in Canada because they protect the cultural, linguistic and regional diversity of the nation. Civil liberties are also part of constitutional law, because civil liberties may be created by the rules that limit the exercise of governmental power over individuals. A constitution has been described as "a mirror reflecting the national soul": it must recognize and protect the values of a nation.[38]

The chapters that follow in Part II of this text elaborate on this definition. They specifically discuss the processes by which legislative power makes new laws, executive power implements the laws, and judicial power decides disputes between them. They also discuss civil liberties, including those guaranteed by the Charter, and how they place important limits on the government's power in Canada.

---

38   Hogg, *supra* note 30 at 1-1.

CHAPTER SUMMARY

The *British North America Act* and the *Constitution Act, 1982*, which contains the *Canadian Charter of Rights and Freedoms*, were both the culmination of a long, difficult reform process. There were strong political, military, economic, and imperial reasons for the creation of the BNA Act and for the federal system of government the Act brought to this country. But the BNA Act left certain things unresolved. It lacked, for example, a domestic amending formula and a bill of rights. Its framers disregarded the interests and rights of Aboriginal peoples. It did not adequately address the role of the SCC as a final court of appeal, and it did not clearly define the power of the courts to review the constitutionality of legislation in disputes regarding the division of powers between the new federal government and the provinces.

As Canadian society became more multicultural and diverse, particularly after the Second World War, various political movements sought to reform the BNA Act. As Canadian nationalism became more pronounced in the 1960s, there arose an initiative, led by Prime Minister Pierre Trudeau, to patriate the Constitution from Britain so that Canadians could amend the Constitution by themselves. A corollary movement with this initiative was to add a charter of rights to Canada's new Constitution. Support for this idea was strong. Aboriginal people pushed to ensure that their special status and treaty rights were protected by the new Constitution, and women lobbied to have the proposed new Charter contain strongly worded equality rights.

KEY TERMS

constitutional law law dealing with the distribution of governmental powers under Canada's Constitution *(p. 96)*

entrenched in the Canadian context, law that is enshrined in the Constitution and cannot be changed unilaterally by the federal government or by any province, and cannot be changed except according to formal amending procedures set out in the Constitution *(p. 84)*

federalism in Canada, the division of state powers between the federal Parliament in Ottawa and the legislatures of the provinces and territories *(p. 81)*

Judicial Committee of the Privy Council the highest appeal authority for colonies in the British Empire; exercised final appeal for Canada until 1949 *(p. 85)*

judicial review process by which a court reviews the exercise of government power to ensure that it is constitutionally valid *(p. 86)*

patriate remove a nation's legislation or constitution from the control of the mother country and bring it under the control of the nation itself *(p. 87)*

unitary government a form of government whereby one supreme authority governs the whole country *(p. 81)*

FURTHER READING

BOOKS

Berger, Thomas R. *A Long and Terrible Shadow: White Values, Native Rights in the Americas, 1492-1992* (Vancouver/ Toronto: Douglas & McIntyre, 1991).

Coyne, Deborah & Michael Valpy. *To Match a Dream: A Practical Guide to Canada's Constitution* (Toronto: McClelland & Stewart, 1998).

Davenport, Paul & Richard H Leach, eds. *Reshaping Confederation: The 1982 Reform of the Canadian Constitution* (Durham, NC: Duke University Press, 1984).

James, Patrick & Mark Kasoff, eds. *Canadian Studies in the New Millennium* (Toronto: University of Toronto Press, 2008).

Reesor, Bayard. *The Canadian Constitution in Historical Perspective* (Scarborough, Ont: Prentice Hall, 1992).

Saywell, John T. *The Lawmakers: Judicial Power and the Shaping of Canadian Federalism* (Toronto: University of Toronto Press, 2002).

Sharpe, Robert J, Katherine E Swinton & Kent Roach. *The Charter of Rights and Freedoms*, 2d ed (Toronto: Irwin Law, 2002).

Strayer, Barry L. *Canada's Constitutional Revolution* (Edmonton: University of Alberta Press, 2013).

Waite, PB. *The Life and Times of Confederation, 1864-1867* (Toronto: University of Toronto Press, 1962).

WEBSITE

Indigenous Bar Association: <http://www.indigenousbar.ca>.

REVIEW QUESTIONS

1. List five key factors that led to Confederation.
2. What two events were occurring in the United States in the 1860s that served as a catalyst to Confederation?
3. What were two main reasons why Britain supported Confederation?
4. Why did Canadian politicians end up adopting a federal system of government in the BNA Act?
5. List six areas of law assigned to the federal government under section 91 of the BNA Act.
6. List four problems with the BNA Act that later proved to be problematic in Canada.
7. What difficulties did Aboriginal people encounter in organizing themselves politically and developing an infrastructure for activism?
8. Why was section 28 of the Charter important for protecting women's equality rights?

EXERCISES

1. Why do you think the BNA Act did not originally have a charter of rights in it?
2. Find and read a recent court case that addresses Aboriginal rights. Identify the issue, explain the arguments of each side, and state the court's decision. What implications could this decision have for other Aboriginal groups in Canada and for the public?
3. Look at the website for the Women's Legal Education and Action Fund (LEAF) and review materials on this public interest group. Why do you think LEAF has been so effective in supporting women's legal rights in Canada?

PART II
Law and the Canadian Constitution

5 The Legislature: The First Branch of Government

The Centre (pictured), East, and West blocks of the Parliament buildings, in Ottawa, were begun in 1859. The original Centre Block was destroyed by fire in 1916 and reopened in 1922. The new design and elements reflected the sense of Canadian identity that emerged from the First World War. The Centennial Flame symbolizes Canada's unity from sea to sea.

LEARNING OUTCOMES

After reading this chapter, you will understand:

- The nature of legislative assemblies
- The different types of statutory law in Canada
- How the power to make statutes is divided between the federal and regional governments
- The process by which statutes are enacted
- How statutes are structured and interpreted

- The nature of subordinate legislation and quasi-legislative materials
- The concept of parliamentary sovereignty and the relationship between the legislative branch of government and the executive and judicial branches
- How statutes are cited

> Canada is a federal state or a federation, that is, a country in which power to legislate, or make law, is divided between a national government and provincial or state governments. In Canada this distribution of authority is set out in a written document, the *British North America Act* of 1867, and neither of the governments can invade the sphere of power reserved to the other without consent.
>
> JC Ricker & JT Saywell, *How Are We Governed?*
> (Toronto: Clarke, Irwin, 1961) at 94

Introduction

As we noted in the previous chapter, constitutional law is primarily concerned with a nation's legislative, executive, and judicial powers. In a federal state such as Canada, it is also concerned with how these powers are divided between the national authority and the regional (provincial and territorial) authorities. These three powers—legislative, executive, and judicial—are sometimes referred to as the three branches or pillars of government. The **separation-of-powers doctrine** deals with the relationship between them. We can summarize this relationship as follows: the legislature makes the law; the executive implements the law; and the judiciary applies and interprets the law.

A **legislature** is a representative assembly charged under a constitution with making laws for a particular region or state. Legislatures go by various names, such as "parliament," "congress," or "legislative assembly." The members are usually elected but they can be appointed in other ways, depending on the political system. Legislatures have a settled number of members or seats. This number may be changed periodically in response to population changes and other factors.

Most legislatures are either **unicameral** or **bicameral**. A unicameral legislature has only one body. A bicameral legislature has two, with lower houses (with names like "House of Commons" and "House of Representatives") and upper houses (for example, "Senate" or "House of Lords"). Canada's Parliament, like the UK Parliament and the US Congress, has a bicameral structure. A bicameral legislature may be partly elected and partly appointed, as are the UK and Canadian Parliaments, with their elected House of Commons and their appointed House of Lords and Senate. Alternatively, both houses of a bicameral legislature can be elected. This is the case with the US Congress. Members of both the House of Representatives and the Senate are elected.

In unitary states such as the UK, governing power is not divided between central and regional authorities; there is one supreme legislative body. In federal states such as Canada, the US, and Australia, legislative jurisdiction is divided between central and regional authorities. Depending on how many regions the nation contains, its legislative power can be vested in a large number of separate legislative bodies.

Legislation refers to written laws made by legislative assemblies. The main form of legislation is statutory law. The legislature or law-making assembly enacts statutes according to a formal process. In addition to statutes, there is subordinate legislation, consisting mainly of regulations and municipal bylaws. Subordinate legislation is created under the authority of a statute, and it is made by a body to which the principal law-making body has delegated power to make such law.

Closely related to legislation are quasi-legislative materials consisting of policy statements, court practice directives, and certain kinds of agreements. Unlike legislation, the rules set out in these quasi-legislative materials are not technically binding. They are important, however; they fill in legislative gaps, and they regulate interactions among people and interactions between people and government institutions.

This chapter examines Canada's legislative branch of government and how it makes law. We consider the legislative bodies involved and the process by which statutes are enacted. We also look at the structure of statutes and at the principles of statutory interpretation. After a brief examination of subordinate legislation and quasi-legislative materials, the chapter concludes by considering the limits of legislative power and how the doctrine of parliamentary sovereignty applies to Canada. In an appendix to the chapter, we consider the rules for citing statutes.

Statutes

Statutes are the primary form of legislation. In Canada, which is a federal state, the power to make statutes is divided between the federal Parliament and the provincial legislatures. Most Canadian statutes are therefore either federal or provincial statutes.

However, our most important *constitutional* statutes are British. As described in Chapters 3 and 4, Canada before 1867 was a collection of British colonies. Therefore, our transition to nationhood required the cooperation of the UK Parliament. The principal constitutional statutes, including the *Constitution Act, 1867* itself (formerly called the *British North America Act*, or BNA Act), were written by and passed at the request of Canadians. But they were British statutes; the UK Parliament had to pass them. It was not until 1982 and the patriation of our Constitution that there existed a Canadian legislative formula or power for making legislation binding on both the federal and provincial governments.

There are four types of statutes, distinguished according to type or jurisdiction:

1. constitutionally entrenched statutes, which are mainly British;
2. federal statutes;
3. provincial statutes; and
4. territorial statutes.

We will discuss the four types of statutes in the following sections.

Constitutionally Entrenched Statutes

Canadian constitutional statutes are statutes that concern this country's governmental powers as well as important civil liberties matters. They include federal and provincial statutes, and statutes from the UK. Many federal and provincial statutes relating to government powers and civil liberties are not entrenched; they can be changed via the usual legislative process.

Our **constitutionally entrenched** statutes are ones that cannot be changed by ordinary federal or provincial legislation. Generally speaking, a statute is only *entrenched* if it requires a special process to change it. Specifically, a statute is constitutionally entrenched if it falls within the scope of the Constitution of Canada as set out in section 52 of the *Constitution Act, 1982.*

Section 52 of this Act is the "supremacy clause"; it states that the Constitution of Canada is our supreme law, overriding any laws that contradict it. It is an important provision because it clearly defines the Constitution of Canada, entrenches all laws that are part of the Constitution of Canada, and establishes that a special process is required to change them. The relevant subsections of section 52 are as follows:

> 52(2) The Constitution of Canada includes
> > (a) the *Canada Act 1982*, including this Act [that is, the *Constitution Act, 1982*];
> > (b) the Acts and orders referred to in the schedule; and
> > (c) any amendment to any Act or order referred to in paragraph (a) or (b).
> (3) Amendments to the Constitution of Canada shall be made only in accordance with the authority contained in the Constitution of Canada.

This provision tells us that the Constitution of Canada includes not only the *Canada Act 1982*, the *Constitution Act, 1982*, and the *Canadian Charter of Rights and Freedoms*, but also the 30 statutes and orders listed in the Schedule to the *Constitution Act, 1982* (see Appendix B). Listed in this schedule are the *Constitution Act, 1867* (formerly the BNA Act), the *Parliament of Canada Act, 1875*, the *Statute of Westminster, 1931*, a number of statutes and orders creating and/or admitting new provinces and territories into Canada, and various amending statutes.

The above are the main contents of the Constitution of Canada. Technically speaking, however, section 52's list of Acts and orders is not exhaustive. The Supreme Court of Canada (SCC) has held that other laws may be included in the Constitution of Canada. (See, later in this chapter, the section entitled "Statutory Interpretation," and the discussion of "Means/Includes.")

Any statute, law, or order is entrenched, then, if it is part of the Constitution of Canada, as defined by section 52 of the *Constitution Act, 1982*. Section 52(3) requires that these statutes, laws, or orders can only be changed through the use of the special constitutional amendment procedure set out in Part V of the *Constitution Act, 1982*.

Key Constitutional Statutes

Canada's key constitutional statutes are the following:

- *Constitution Act, 1867*
- *Statute of Westminster, 1931*
- *Canada Act 1982*
- *Constitution Act, 1982*

We discuss them in the following sections.

CONSTITUTION ACT, 1867

Before the enactment of the *Constitution Act, 1867*, what is now Canada (or then British North America) was a collection of British colonies and territories. As we saw in the last

FIGURE 5.1 House of Commons
Canada's 308 ridings are represented in the lower house by members of Parliament. The primary colour used (green) is the same colour used in Britain's House of Commons for more than 300 years.

chapter, this statute brought together three of those colonies—New Brunswick, Nova Scotia, and the Province of Canada (which would become Ontario and Quebec)—and created the new country of Canada in 1867. The new country was in the form of a federation, with government power divided between a central authority and the former colonies, now called provinces.

The *Constitution Act, 1867* is divided into 11 parts. Parts II–VIII and XI are the key ones:

- Part II, entitled "Union," united the three colonies mentioned above to form the new country.
- Part III outlines federal executive power.
- Sections 58–68 in Part V, headed "Provincial Constitutions," outline provincial executive power.
- Legislative power is covered in Parts IV, V (sections 69–90), and VI. The cornerstone sections are sections 91–92 in Part VI, which divide the power or **jurisdiction** to make laws between the federal Parliament and the provincial legislatures. Sections 93–95 are also important, however; they deal with jurisdiction over such things as natural resources, education, and immigration.
- Part VII is entitled "Judicature" and deals with the federal power to appoint judges and create new courts. It complements a parallel jurisdiction over courts and judges given to the provinces in section 92 (see Chapter 7).
- Part VIII deals with taxation and money issues and supplements the coverage given these areas in sections 91–92.
- Part XI, entitled "Admission of Other Colonies," gave the government special powers to admit new colonies. It is owing to Part XI that Canada now consists not of three but of ten provinces and three territories (see Chapter 3).

An excerpted version of the *Constitution Act, 1867* is reproduced in Appendix A.

STATUTE OF WESTMINSTER, 1931

The *Statute of Westminster, 1931* can be thought of as Canada's second step toward full legislative independence from Britain. The first step was the *Colonial Laws Validity Act, 1865*. This earlier Act provided that British colonies—including those in British North America (and the soon-to-be-formed country of Canada)—could enact laws contrary to English laws "of general application" that had been received by the colonies upon formation. They could not, however, enact laws contrary to British imperial statutes that were intended to extend to the colony in question. Laws of general application were English laws that weren't specifically directed at the colonies but had been received from England to avoid a legal vacuum when the colonies were established. Until the *Colonial Laws Validity Act, 1865* was passed, there was some doubt about the power of the colonies to change these laws. This Act made it clear they could.

The *Statute of Westminster, 1931* repealed the *Colonial Laws Validity Act, 1865*. It took colonial independence one step further. Not only did it confirm Canada's legislative autonomy, it also recognized Canada's legislative equality with Britain. However, Britain did reserve the power to amend key constitutional statutes such as the *British North America Act* (now the *Constitution Act, 1867*).

This reservation of power was due less to paternalism on Britain's part than to the fact that the federal government and the provinces were unable at the time to agree on a constitutional amending formula. Because of this disagreement, the UK Parliament still needed to be involved in Canada's constitutional amendments. Britain was always accepting of Canada's requests for such amendments, invariably passing them.

CANADA ACT 1982

In 1982, the UK Parliament, at the request of the federal government, passed the *Canada Act 1982*, giving up all legislative power over Canada. This was Canada's third and final step toward legislative independence from Britain. Section 2 of the Act provides as follows:

> 2. No Act of the Parliament of the United Kingdom passed after the
> *Constitution Act, 1982* comes into force shall extend to Canada as part of its law.

Schedule B of the *Canada Act 1982* is the *Constitution Act, 1982*. The amending formula it sets out in Part V empowered Canadians, for the first time, to make changes to their own Constitution. The Canadian Constitution had finally been patriated. Canada had achieved full legislative autonomy.

CONSTITUTION ACT, 1982

The *Constitution Act, 1982* is divided into seven parts and is set out in Appendix B. Part I is the *Canadian Charter of Rights and Freedoms* (the Charter), which is arguably the most significant legacy of the patriation process. It guarantees certain rights and freedoms, and has become the main basis of Canadian civil liberties (see Chapter 8 of this text).

Part II of the Act addresses Aboriginal rights, while Part III concerns the joint federal and provincial commitment to equal opportunities for Canadians regardless of regional disparities in wealth as well as the federal commitment to equalization payments for the less wealthy provinces. Parts IV and IV.I, now both repealed, dealt with constitutional conferences.

Part V sets out the amendment procedure for the Constitution of Canada. Part VI contains amendments concerning provincial power over natural resources, forestry resources, and electrical energy.

Part VII of the Act is entitled "General" and covers miscellaneous matters such as minor amendments, English and French versions of the legislation, commencement dates for certain provisions, and citation protocols. Significantly, it also includes section 52(1), the **supremacy clause**, which provides the following:

> 52(1) The Constitution of Canada is the supreme law of Canada, and any law that is inconsistent with the provisions of the Constitution is, to the extent of the inconsistency, of no force or effect.

If a federal or provincial statute offends or is inconsistent with the Constitution, section 52(1) states that the law is "of no force or effect." This may seem clear, but precisely what remedial responses are available when dealing with unconstitutional legislation is not always so clear. The courts have interpreted their power to deal with unconstitutional legislation broadly, such that a range of responses are possible. These include:

1. *striking down* the legislation altogether and declaring it invalid (this is the most extreme response);
2. *severance* of a portion of the legislation (if only part of the statute contravenes the Constitution—for example, a particular section—the court can declare that just that part is invalid and sever it from the rest of the legislation);
3. *reading down* (with this remedy, the courts narrowly interpret the legislation to ensure conformity with the Constitution);
4. *reading in* (this remedy is a little more activist and involves adding language to the legislation to ensure conformity with the Constitution—for example, adding a new class of persons covered by the legislation, or adding a new and unlisted ground of discrimination);

FIGURE 5.2 Senate
The Speech from the Throne is given in the Senate chamber. Canada adopted this custom from Britain, where neither the unelected members of the upper house (Senate) nor the sovereign are permitted to enter the House of Commons.

5. a *constitutional exemption* (with this rarely used remedy, and so far never used by the SCC, the court does not declare the legislation invalid, but finds that it doesn't apply to a particular person or class of persons); and

6. the *temporary suspension* of an order declaring the legislation or part of it invalid (this gives Parliament or the legislature the opportunity to enact new, valid legislation within a set period of time—see Box 13.2 for an example).

It should be noted that this power to deal with unconstitutional legislation can also extend to common law rules. This could occur, for example, if the government or agent of the government (such as a police officer or Crown prosecutor) were involved in a dispute and were relying on a common law rule that offended the Charter. This power does not extend, however, to common law rules being applied in private sector disputes not involving the government.

Since the *Constitution Act, 1982*, there are two main questions to ask about new (and sometimes existing) legislation:

1. Does jurisdiction to pass the statute belong to Parliament or to the provinces?

2. Does the statute infringe the Charter?

How the first question is answered will usually depend on sections 91–92 of the *Constitution Act, 1867*. Less often, it will depend on sections 93–95 of the Act and on other entrenched division-of-powers provisions. If either Parliament or a provincial legislature tries to pass legislation in an area that, according to the Constitution, belongs to the other's jurisdiction, the courts have the power to hold that the legislation in question is ***ultra vires*** and of no force or effect. Challenging legislation on the basis of the enacting authority's lack of jurisdiction is known as a **division-of-powers** (or division-of-authority) argument.

The second question is whether the legislation offends the Charter. It will if it infringes any of the rights and freedoms guaranteed by the Charter. If it does offend in this way, the issue then becomes whether it can be saved by section 1 of the Charter, the limiting provision.

The limiting provision, which we will examine more closely in Chapter 8 (see Box 8.2, on the *Oakes* case), is very important and qualifies the legal protection granted by the Charter. Under this provision, all the rights set out in the Charter are subject "to such reasonable limits prescribed by law as can be demonstrably justified in a free and democratic society." Soon after the Charter came into effect, the Supreme Court of Canada held that a two-step analysis was required to determine whether a particular government measure that offends a person's rights is nonetheless "saved" because, under section 1, it represents a justifiable limit on those rights. Simply put, the government has to show

1. that the measure serves an important social objective, and

2. that the measure is balanced (or proportionate) and fair.

For example, section 2 of the Charter guarantees "freedom of opinion and expression." Laws against defamation, obscenity, and hate propaganda might be seen as offending this guarantee. And yet such laws generally survive constitutional challenge because our society recognizes that they impose "reasonable limits" on "freedom of opinion and expression." They deal with important matters, and in most cases they are balanced and obtrude minimally on one's rights. Such laws are, in other words, saved by section 1, the limiting provision.

Challenging a statute's constitutionality on the basis of a division-of-powers argument is sometimes referred to as *judicial review on federalism grounds*. Challenging on the basis of a Charter infringement argument is sometimes referred to as *judicial review on Charter grounds* or just a *Charter challenge*. In conclusion, then, the power of the courts to review

BOX 5.1

History of Attempted Amendments

Since 1982, there have been no amendments to the Constitution that have followed either the general procedure or the special procedure requiring unanimous consent. There have been two attempts, however. One was the Meech Lake Accord of 1987, which aimed to encourage Quebec to endorse the 1982 constitutional changes (Quebec had been the only province not to give its consent when Canada approached England with the patriation proposal in 1982). The Accord included recognition of Quebec as a "distinct society," and it gave all provinces the power to veto constitutional amendments. But consensus was never reached and the Meech Lake Accord was never ratified.

The second attempt to amend the Constitution was the Charlottetown Accord, negotiated in 1992 by the federal and provincial governments. Proposing changes to the division of legislative powers, it gave the provinces exclusive jurisdiction in a few contentious areas where jurisdiction is divided, such as natural resources and cultural policy. The Charlottetown proposal also included a social charter that promoted health care, welfare, education, and environmental protection; and that formally recognized, by way of the "Canada Clause," certain "Canadian" values such as equality, diversity, and Quebec's status as a "distinct society." The Charlottetown Accord also proposed making some institutional changes to the SCC, to Parliament, and to the consultation process between the federal, provincial, and territorial governments. The proposal was put to a national referendum, and the results were 54.3 percent against and 45.7 percent in favour. The Charlottetown Accord therefore died before the other stages of the Part V legal amendment process were attempted.

Interestingly, in 1993, shortly after the failed Charlottetown Accord, New Brunswick succeeded in amending the Charter through the addition of a new section— section 16.1—guaranteeing the equal status of the English and French linguistic communities in that province. Under section 43 of the *Constitution Act, 1982*, the limited nature of the amendment meant that only the New Brunswick legislature and Parliament needed to approve it.

It remains to be seen whether as a nation we will ever be able to put aside our regional political differences sufficiently to amend the Constitution in any significant way. To this point, we have failed to meet even the relatively modest standards of the general procedure for amendment—that is, two-thirds of the provinces and 50 percent of the general population.

---

legislation and find that it is of no force and effect will generally be based on one of these two types of challenges. While the power existed before 1982, based on division-of-powers arguments, the supremacy clause makes this power *explicit* and has expanded it to cover Charter infringements.

Amendment Process

The making or changing of constitutionally entrenched statutes requires a special process. Section 52(3) states that "[a]mendments to the Constitution of Canada shall be made only in accordance with the authority contained in the Constitution of Canada."

Part V of the *Constitution Act, 1982* sets out the amendment procedure. Generally, an amendment will require the agreement of Parliament and of two-thirds of the provinces, with the support of at least 50 percent of the general population. This is known as the *general procedure* for amendment. The particular requirements are set out in section 38 of the Act. Currently, given the number of Canadian provinces and the way the population is distributed across the country, an amendment following the general procedure would need the support of seven provinces, and one of them would have to be either Ontario or Quebec.

There are certain kinds of amendments that require the *unanimous* agreement of Parliament and the provinces (see section 41 of the *Constitution Act, 1982*). These amendments include

- changes to the office of the Queen,
- the use of the English or French language when dealing with federal institutions,
- the composition of the SCC, and
- any changes to the amendment procedure itself.

Part V of the Act provides for simpler amendment procedures if the proposed change affects only one or two provinces or the federal government alone (see sections 43–45 of the *Constitution Act, 1982*). For instance, provinces can change their boundaries without the consent or agreement of provinces that are not affected by the change. Only Parliament and the provinces directly affected by the boundary change need agree to it. Similarly, the provinces—with parliamentary approval—can also independently make amendments concerning the use of either official language within the province (except, as noted above, where this use pertains to federal institutions).

Federal Statutes

Federal statutes are enacted by the Parliament of Canada. As we noted above, our Parliament is *bicameral*, which means there are two houses involved in the making of statutes. The House of Commons, which is elected, currently has 308 seats. The Senate, which is appointed, currently has 105 seats. Constitutional convention dictates that the House of Commons, as an elected body, takes the lead in making new legislation.

New statutes can only be passed while Parliament is in session. Each new session commences with a formal state opening at which the governor general (or occasionally the British monarch) reads the Speech from the Throne. Each session is formally brought to a close when it is **prorogued**. Most sessions are one to two years in length, sometimes with lengthy adjournments during that time. Under section 4 of the Charter, an election must be called at least once every five years. This means that, after each election, the governing party has five years in which to advance its legislative agenda through Parliament.

Federal Power

The principal sections of the Constitution that give power to Parliament are section 91 (many subject areas), section 93A (old age pensions), and section 95 (agriculture and immigration, though these areas are shared with the provinces). Any new legislation proposed by Parliament must be authorized by a section in the Constitution.

Section 91 is the source of most federal power. It lists 30 specific subject areas over which Parliament has exclusive jurisdiction. It also gives the federal government a general power to make laws for the "Peace, Order and good Government of Canada," in areas over which the provinces are not assigned exclusive jurisdiction. This is known as **POGG power**.

POGG POWER

The POGG power clause in section 91 appears to give Parliament a general *residuary power*— that is, jurisdiction in any area that the Constitution does not explicitly assign to either level of government. In other words, section 91 gives Parliament the power to fill the legislative gaps. This reflects the fact that the framers of the Constitution aimed to build a strong federal authority. In this respect, Canada contrasts with other federations, such as the US and Australia, where the residuary power is given to the regional or state legislatures.

The courts recognize the residuary aspect of the federal government's POGG power. At the same time, they have also taken a broad, inclusive view of the areas under provincial jurisdiction, and interpretations of POGG power by the courts since Confederation have placed limitations on it. Practically speaking, there have not been many legislative gaps for the federal government to fill.

Besides the use of the POGG clause to cover jurisdictional gaps, the courts have used it to authorize the federal government to legislate in areas that have a national dimension or concern. The *national concern approach* can be thought of as a counterbalance to the provinces' general authority, under section 92, over matters of a "merely local or Private nature."

What kinds of matters have a "national dimension or concern" and thereby fall, according to the POGG principle, under federal jurisdiction? Such matters must have wide-ranging importance; they must affect most or all parts of Canada. Further, a matter of this kind must be distinct, in the sense of having a "singleness, distinctiveness and indivisibility that clearly distinguishes it from matters of provincial concern."[1] Some areas of regulation that have been classed as matters of national concern include marine pollution, aeronautics, and nuclear power.

The third and final use of the POGG clause is to deal with emergencies. The federal government's *emergency power* has been used to justify legislation in times of war or insurrection and to control inflation. All legislative measures introduced on this basis must be temporary in nature, ending when the emergency ends.

SPECIFIC AREAS OF FEDERAL JURISDICTION

The list of subject areas in section 91 is extensive. According to this provision's introductory words, Parliament's authority "extends to all Matters coming within the Classes of Subjects" listed. Given that each area listed is a "class of subjects" and that federal jurisdiction is over "all matters" within those classes, the federal power to legislate appears to be quite far-reaching.

(For a full listing of the areas that fall under federal jurisdiction according to section 91 of the *Constitution Act, 1867*, see Table 5.1.)

To help determine whether a statute should be authorized, the courts try to determine what the "matter" of the law is. The courts are looking for the statute's essence here. Various phrases have been used to refer to a law's essence—for example, its "true meaning," its "true nature and character," and, most often, its "pith and substance."

Determining the statute's "pith and substance" requires looking at its dominant purpose and effect. If the courts find that the "dominant purpose and effect" address an appropriate area—that is, an area that falls within the jurisdiction of the legislature that made the statute—the statute will pass the division-of-powers test and will be accepted as constitutional. On the other hand, the new legislation may not pass this test. For instance, if a provincial legislature enacts a statute whose dominant effect and purpose relate to criminal law, which is a federal area, the law will be declared unconstitutional (see Box 5.2).

OVERLAPPING JURISDICTION

Determining a law's "pith and substance" is sometimes complicated by the fact that a law has multiple purposes and effects. A law can relate to more than one jurisdictional area. If the areas overlapping in this way are either all federal areas or all provincial ones, there is no constitutional problem. However, if the law involves complete overlap between a federal subject area and a provincial one—that is, if it falls fully within the jurisdiction of each—the law is said to have a *double aspect*.

---

1   *R v Crown Zellerbach*, [1988] 1 SCR 401 at 432. See also *Johanneson v West St Paul*, [1952] 1 SCR 292; and *Ontario Hydro v Ontario*, [1993] 3 SCR 327.

TABLE 5.1   Federal Powers Under Section 91 by Category

CATEGORY	RELATED SUBSECTION(S) OF SECTION 91	NOTES
Taxation, money, and public assets	1A. The Public Debt and Property 3. The Raising of Money by any Mode or System of Taxation 4. The Borrowing of Money on the Public Credit 14. Currency and Coinage 15. Banking, Incorporation of Banks, and the Issue of Paper Money 16. Savings Banks 18. Bills of Exchange and Promissory Notes 19. Interest 20. Legal Tender 21. Bankruptcy and Insolvency	The framers of the *Constitution Act, 1867* saw this category as important. Putting it under Parliament's jurisdiction was a means of creating a strong and effective central government. These powers are supplemented by Part VIII.
Trade and employment	2. The Regulation of Trade and Commerce 2A. Unemployment Insurance 17. Weights and Measures	The trade and commerce power was interpreted narrowly soon after confederation by the Privy Council as only applying to interprovincial and international trade and commerce, not intraprovincial trade and commerce, which was held to be a matter within provincial jurisdiction under s 92(13).*
Intellectual property	22. Patents of Invention and Discovery 23. Copyrights	The law in this area, which involves an intangible form of property without specific geographical context or connection, requires consistent rules across wide-ranging boundaries. It is also affected by international relations and agreements.
First Nations	24. Indians, and Lands reserved for the Indians	The reason for including this area under s 91 was apparently to protect First Nations against European expansion and to have a consistent set of policies across Canada.†
Immigration and citizenship	25. Naturalization and Aliens	In Canada, as in most countries, immigration and citizenship is primarily a national priority. However, the federal government collaborates with the provinces in establishing goals and policies in this area.
Marriage and divorce	26. Marriage and Divorce	Family law is also regulated by the provinces, which have some shared jurisdiction with Parliament (e.g., spousal support and child custody) and some exclusive jurisdiction (division of family assets).

CATEGORY	RELATED SUBSECTION(S) OF SECTION 91	NOTES

Transportation and communication	13. Ferries between a Province and any British or Foreign Country or between Two Provinces
	
	29. Such Classes of Subjects as are expressly excepted in the Enumeration of the Classes of Subjects by this Act assigned exclusively to the Legislatures of the Provinces
	
	s 91(29) must be read together with s 92(10):
	
	  10. Local Works and Undertakings other than such as are of the following Classes:
	    (*a*) Lines of Steam or other Ships, Railways, Canals, Telegraphs, and other Works and Undertakings connecting the Province with any other or others of the Provinces, or extending beyond the Limits of the Province:
	    (*b*) Lines of Steam Ships between the Province and any British or Foreign Country:
	    (*c*) Such Works as, although wholly situate within the Province, are before or after their Execution declared by the Parliament of Canada to be for the general Advantage of Canada or for the Advantage of Two or more of the Provinces.
		These areas are of national importance.

Water matters: coasts, shipping and fishing	9. Beacons, Buoys, Lighthouses, and Sable Island 10. Navigation and Shipping 11. Quarantine and the Establishment and Maintenance of Marine Hospitals 12. Sea Coast and Inland Fisheries	With so much water and coastline, federal jurisdiction was needed for reasons of safety, security, and uniformity.
Criminal law	27. The Criminal Law, except the Constitution of Courts of Criminal Jurisdiction, but including the Procedure in Criminal Matters 28. The Establishment, Maintenance, and Management of Penitentiaries	Parliament's jurisdiction over criminal law has been used to enact a variety of criminal statutes, including the *Criminal Code* and *Youth Criminal Justice Act*. Not all federations have a national criminal law system. In the US, for instance, criminal law jurisdiction rests with the individual states.
National defence	7. Militia, Military and Naval Service, and Defence	The need for a national armed services is clear.
Miscellaneous	5. Postal Service 6. The Census and Statistics 8. The fixing of and providing for the Salaries and Allowances of Civil and other Officers of the Government of Canada	National regulation in these areas was thought to be in the country's best interests.

*   *Citizens' Insurance Co v Parsons* (1881), 7 App Cas 96 (PC).

†   Peter W Hogg, *Constitutional Law of Canada*, 2013 student ed (Toronto: Carswell, 2013) at 28-2.

BOX 5.2

Assisted Human Reproduction Act, SC 2004, c 2

In 1989, Parliament established the Royal Commission on New Reproductive Technologies ("the Baird Commission"). In its report, the Baird Commission recommended that legislation be enacted to regulate what it and many others considered to be unethical practices. In 2004, after extensive consultations with the provinces, the territories, and various interest groups, Parliament passed the *Assisted Human Reproduction Act*. It prohibited human cloning and required licensing for certain "controlled activities." These activities included (1) manipulating human reproductive material or *in vitro* embryos, (2) transgenic engineering, and (3) paying for expenses of donors and surrogate mothers.

In a reference—that is, a formal request for a tribunal's opinion about a certain matter —to the Quebec Court of Appeal, the attorney general of Quebec conceded the constitutional validity of some provisions in the Act, such as the prohibition against human cloning. But the attorney general also argued that many sections in the Act, especially the ones dealing with "controlled activities," were an attempt by the federal government to regulate matters—the practice of medicine, and research related to assisted reproduction—that properly fall within provincial jurisdiction. In response, the attorney general of Canada argued that the entire Act was authorized by Parliament's jurisdiction over criminal law, a power given it by section 91(27) of the *Constitution Act, 1867*. The Quebec Court of Appeal held that the impugned provisions in question—

the ones dealing with "controlled activities"—were invalid, and the attorney general of Canada appealed to the SCC.

The SCC analyzed the legislation to determine its matter, or "pith and substance." The Court held that the dominant purpose and effect of the statutory scheme was to prohibit practices that would undercut moral values, generate public health evils, and threaten the security of people involved in assisted reproduction. These were criminal law matters, even though they touched on provincial jurisdiction over medical research and practice.

However, despite the *overall* characterization of the statute as criminal law, the SCC also found that the Act contained certain provisions whose dominant purpose and effect concerned provincial areas of jurisdiction. These included provisions dealing with the manipulation of human reproductive material to create embryos, keeping and handling gametes and embryos, combining human and non-human genes, and certain privacy of information rules that were not criminal in nature.

These provisions, according to the SCC, represented an attempt to regulate the medical profession in the field of assisted reproduction and did not address a criminal concern. The field of assisted reproduction was judged to be an area of provincial rather than federal jurisdiction, coming under the provincial powers over property and civil rights (section 92(13)) and matters of a merely local or private nature (section 92(16)). Hence these provisions were struck down as unconstitutional.

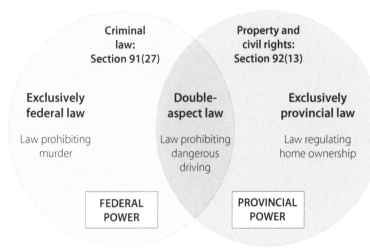

FIGURE 5.3 Double-aspect law

A **double-aspect law** can be enacted by either legislative body—either by Parliament or by a provincial legislature. For example, many laws dealing with traffic offences have a double aspect, covered both by the federal criminal law power (section 91(27)) and by the provincial power over property and civil rights (section 92(13)). (See Figure 5.3.) A law that falls fully within an area that belongs to one level of government, but that merely touches on an area belonging to the other, is not a true double-aspect law. For these kinds of laws, only the level of government with complete jurisdiction over the area can pass them.

As we have mentioned, either Parliament or the provinces can enact double-aspect laws. But what happens if both levels of government pass laws in a shared jurisdictional area and the laws conflict with one another? To deal with this situation, the courts have developed the **federal paramountcy doctrine**, according to which, in the event of conflict, the federal law prevails over the provincial one.[2]

How Parliament Makes Statutes

The responsibility for drafting proposed legislation falls to legislative counsel employed by Parliament and by the provincial and territorial legislatures. The legislative counsel is made up of lawyers specially trained in this area.

Statutes do not develop in a vacuum. They are influenced by the values and beliefs of the governing political party and of the society at large. A general consensus may emerge within the society that a new law is required or that an old one needs to be changed. More complicated statutes are often preceded by public hearings, commissions, studies, and other forms of reporting. Simpler statutes may be introduced (usually by Cabinet ministers) without much advance consultation.

Once a legislature has decided to pass a statute and the legislative counsel has prepared a draft, the legislative response begins. With Canada's bicameral federal Parliament, both the House of Commons and the Senate are involved in making statutes.

INTRODUCING A BILL

A proposed statute is first introduced as a **bill** either in the House of Commons (as a Commons bill), or in the Senate (as a Senate bill). Parliament employs parliamentary counsel to help members of Parliament (MPs) and senators draft bills and to answer questions in all areas of the legislative process. There are two types of bills: *public bills* and *private bills*.

A **public bill** can belong to one of two categories, the first being the most common:

1. *Government bills.* Most of these bills deal with matters of public policy. They are usually introduced by a minister in the House of Commons, after being reviewed and approved by the federal Cabinet. In a formal written notice, the minister responsible for the bill asks the clerk of the House for leave to introduce it, and the minister gives it a title at this point. Leave to introduce the bill is granted without debate, questions, or amendments. Government bills are occasionally introduced not in the House but in the Senate. If they originate in the House of Commons, they are numbered consecutively, from C-1 to C-200, in the order in which they are introduced. Senate bills are numbered from S-1 upward, also in their order of introduction.

2. *Private members' bills.* These bills, also dealing with matters of public policy, are introduced by individual MPs, who are usually members of the opposition. They are numbered C-201 to C-1000.

A **private bill** is one that is introduced and "sponsored" by a government, opposition, or Senate member and that deals with a private matter—for example, a matter relating to a particular individual, corporation, or charity. Private bills introduced in the Commons are numbered C-1001 upward. Those introduced in the Senate are numbered S-1 upward as they are introduced, and are numbered together with, not separate from, public bills.

---

2   For a detailed discussion of federal paramountcy, see Peter W Hogg, *Constitutional Law of Canada*, 2013 student ed (Toronto: Carswell, 2013) ch 16.

PASSAGE THROUGH PARLIAMENT

A bill's passage through Parliament, whether it is a public or a private bill, follows a set process. Parliamentary standing orders provide, among other things, the various procedural stages that all bills must pass through in order to become statutes. A federal bill requires six **readings**, three in the Commons and three in the Senate, followed by **royal assent**. Figure 5.5 illustrates this process.

On a motion by its initiator, the bill is read for the first time in the House. At this stage, the House passes the motion without debate and makes no amendments to the bill. A date is then set for second reading. The bill is given an alphanumeric order number and printed in French and English. It is then distributed to all members of Parliament.

On the date fixed for the second reading of the bill, members of the House debate the bill's general principle and main features. Amendments are still not permitted. If the bill is approved for second reading, it is referred to a House of Commons committee. If the matter is urgent and the bill has been approved with unanimous consent or involves a money bill,

FIGURE 5.4 Federal/provincial legislature

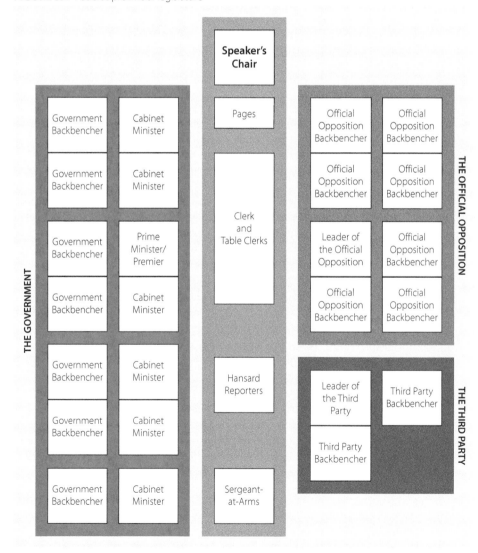

this committee may be a committee of the whole House. If not referred to a committee of the whole House, the bill will be referred to one of the House's standing, special, joint, or legislative committees. The committee examines the bill clause by clause, and can make amendments at this point. Ministers and public servants may be called for explanations, and public input is sometimes invited.

Once a legislative committee has examined the bill, the committee reports its findings back to the House, with or without amendments. The House can either concur with the committee's recommendations or suggest ("move") further amendments. A motion is then brought for the bill to be adopted and to proceed to the third reading.

The bill is read a third time. Debate is limited at this stage. A House vote is then held. If passed by the House of Commons, the bill goes to the Senate for approval.

The bill must now pass through a similar process in the Senate. Bills that are first introduced in the Senate (less common than those introduced in the House of Commons) follow the same steps as those introduced in the House, except that the starting points are reversed: the first three readings are in the Senate, followed by three more in the House of Commons.

Once the final reading has been given to the bill, a motion is made for it to be given royal assent. After receiving royal assent, the bill becomes a statute. The pomp and pageantry of the royal assent ceremony is described in Box 5.3.

If a bill does not receive all required readings and royal assent before the end of the legislative session in which it was introduced (in other words, before the session *prorogues*), it "dies on the order paper." However, it can be reintroduced in the next session if the opposition consents.

Assuming all six readings and royal assent occur before the end of the session, the newly enacted statute is assigned a chapter number and is published in the *Canada Gazette* Part III and, later, in annual statute volumes. The federal government also publishes electronic versions of its legislation. These were recently given official status alongside the print versions.

A bill becomes a statute once it receives royal assent, but it may not come into *effect* at this point. If a statute is silent on the question of when it comes into force, it is effective upon receiving royal assent. It may, however, specify some future date on which it comes into force or it may indicate that it will come into force on a day to be fixed by **proclamation**. Or (very rarely) it may provide for retroactive effect, specifying a date prior to royal assent on which it is deemed to have come into force. With complicated statutes, different portions may come into force at different times and in different ways—some portions on receiving royal assent, some on specified dates, and others upon proclamation.

FIGURE 5.5 Federal statutory enactment process

1. CANADIAN SOCIETY

Values, beliefs, politics, economics, wealth, capital, income, environmental issues, global events

2. PRE-PARLIAMENTARY RESPONSE

Consensus or conflict (public hearings, commissions, study papers, reports)

3. PARLIAMENTARY RESPONSE

HOUSE OF COMMONS OR SENATE	
1st Reading	• Bill is introduced on a motion • No debates or amendments
2nd Reading	• Bill is debated on its general principles and main features • Still no amendments are permitted
Committee Review	• Bill referred to committee after second reading • Committee examines proposed legislation, section by section, and can recommend amendments
3rd Reading	• Bill is read again with any recommended changes • Members vote

SENATE OR HOUSE OF COMMONS

For bills that begin in the House of Commons (C-bills, the majority of bills), the process above will be repeated in the Senate. For bills that begin in the Senate (S-bills), the process above will be repeated in the House of Commons. Federal bills, therefore, receive a total of six readings.

GOVERNOR GENERAL	
Royal Assent	• Bill is approved by governor general or representative • Formal ceremony

4. IMPLEMENTATION

- Proclamation (if statute requires)
- Regulations passed pursuant to statute (if required and statute authorizes)

BOX 5.3

Royal Assent

The ceremony of Royal Assent is one of the oldest of all parliamentary proceedings and brings all three elements of Parliament together (the Crown, the Senate and the House of Commons). Royal Assent is the stage that a bill must complete before officially becoming an Act of Parliament. A bill will not be given Royal Assent unless it has gone through all of the stages of the legislative process and been passed by both Houses in identical form [as shown in Figure 5.5].

Royal Assent may be granted in one of two ways: (1) through a written procedure, and (2) through the traditional ceremony, where Members of the House of Commons join with their Senate colleagues in the Senate Chamber.

The written procedure involves the Clerk of the Parliaments (the Clerk of the Senate), or his or her Deputy, meeting with the Governor General, or his or her Deputy, to present the bills with a letter indicating that they have been passed by both Houses and requesting that the bills be assented to.

An Act that has been given Royal Assent in written form is considered assented to on the day on which the two Houses of Parliament have been notified of the declaration. The *Royal Assent Act* preserves the traditional ceremony by requiring that it be used at least twice in each calendar year, including for the first bill in each session that authorizes government spending.

The traditional procedure for Royal Assent involves a formal ceremony that takes place in the Senate Chamber. When the House is sitting, it suspends its proceedings in order that its Members may proceed to the Senate Chamber, where the Governor General or his or her Deputy grants Royal Assent.

Once a bill has been granted Royal Assent, it becomes law and comes into force either on that date or at a date provided for within the Act or specified by an order of the Governor in Council.

Source: Reproduced from Parliament of Canada, "Compendium of Procedure: House of Commons Procedure Online," <http://www .parl.gc.ca/About/House/compendium/web-content/c_g_ legislativeprocess-e.htm#2i>.

Provincial Statutes

Provincial statutes are enacted by the provincial legislatures in each of the ten provinces. All provincial legislatures in Canada are elected bodies and are unicameral, with a single house involved in the legislative process.

With each provincial election, there is said to be a new "Parliament," even though the provincial bodies are called "assemblies" or "legislatures." Like federal statutes, provincial statutes can only be passed while the legislature is in session, with sessions lasting one to two years on average but permitted, under section 4 of the Charter, to continue for as many as five years, at which point an election must be called. The Charter also requires that provincial elections be called at least once every five years. Thus governing parties have as many as five years to advance their legislative agendas.

Provincial Power

The principal sections of the Constitution that distribute power to the provincial assemblies are

- section 92 (many subject areas),
- section 92A (natural resources, forestry, and electrical energy),
- section 93 (education), and
- section 95 (agriculture and immigration—though the provinces share jurisdiction in these areas with the federal level of government).

Provincial laws, like federal laws, must be authorized under the Constitution to be valid.

Section 92 is the source of most provincial power. Although the provinces have no general "residuary" power comparable to federal POGG power, there is a reasonable balance of power between the provincial and federal levels of government. This is because a few areas deemed to be under provincial jurisdiction—for example, property and civil rights, and matters of a merely local or private nature—have been broadly interpreted. For a full account of the subject areas listed in section 92, see Table 5.2.

How Provincial Legislatures Make Statutes

The process of making provincial statutes is generally the same in each province. It is very similar to the federal process. Much of what was said concerning the federal process applies here. Provincial bills can be public or private, but the vast majority are public and the vast majority of those are government bills.

One important difference between the federal and provincial processes is that provincial bills require only three readings. That is because there is only one chamber involved; there is no Senate. As with federal bills, there is a committee review stage between the second and third readings, and the final stage is royal assent. The provincial lieutenant governor—the Crown's representative at the provincial level—gives royal assent to provincial legislation.

As with a federal bill, if a provincial bill does not receive all required readings and royal assent before the legislative session prorogues, it "dies on the order paper." If this happens, a provincial bill (like a federal one) can, with the opposition's consent, be reintroduced in the next session.

Assuming the bill receives three readings and royal assent before the end of the session, it becomes a statute. It is assigned a chapter number and later published in print and electronic versions.

As to the timing of a provincial statute's coming into force, the rules that apply to federal statutes apply here, too. If silent about when it comes into force, the statute is effective upon royal assent. Alternatively, it may specify a date upon which it comes into force, or it may leave the date open, to be fixed by proclamation. Or a statute may come into force through a combination of these methods.

Territorial Statutes

Territorial statutes are enacted by the legislative assemblies in each of Canada's three territories: Yukon, the Northwest Territories, and Nunavut. All territorial assemblies in Canada are elected bodies and are unicameral, with just one house involved in the legislative process.

After each territorial election there is a new "assembly." As with federal and provincial statutes, territorial statutes can be passed only while the assembly is in session. As with Parliament and the provincial legislatures, these sessions may last up to five years, as prescribed by the Charter (sections 4 and 30).

The Yukon assembly is party-based, as the provinces and Parliament are, but the Northwest Territories and Nunavut have a consensus style of government. These are the only two jurisdictions in Canada with Aboriginal majorities, and the consensus style reflects the traditional decision-making custom of First Nations and Inuit peoples. In both territories, MLAs are elected as independent candidates, and there are no political parties. Unanimity is often achieved, though it is not required for decisions, such as the passage of motions or legislation. A majority vote often suffices.

TABLE 5.2   Provincial Powers Under Section 92 by Category

CATEGORY	RELATED SUBSECTION(S) OF SECTION 92	NOTES
Taxation, money, and public assets	2. Direct Taxation within the Province in order to the raising of a Revenue for Provincial Purposes 3. The borrowing of Money on the sole Credit of the Province 5. The Management and Sale of the Public Lands belonging to the Province and of the Timber and Wood thereon 9. Shop, Saloon, Tavern, Auctioneer, and other Licences in order to the raising of a Revenue for Provincial, Local, or Municipal Purposes	The power of the provinces in this area, though more limited than Parliament's, is still significant. It is supplemented by Part VIII of the *Constitution Act, 1867*. Forestry and natural resources are also covered by section 92A.
Property and civil rights	13. Property and Civil Rights in the Province	This category is a very important one for the provinces and has been interpreted to cover many specific areas, such as intraprovincial trade and commerce (business) (see also (11)), employment, regulation of the professions, contracts, torts, property, family law (see also (12)), civil liberties in the private sector, and many others.
Local matters	10. Local Works and Undertakings (subject to exceptions listed in the federal table) 16. Generally all Matters of a merely local or private Nature in the Province	The scope of property and civil rights has relegated these headings to the role of "backup" jurisdiction in many instances.
Health care	7. The Establishment, Maintenance, and Management of Hospitals, Asylums, Charities, and Eleemosynary Institutions in and for the Province, other than Marine Hospitals	Health care is mainly provincial and comes under a number of different heads of power, including property and civil rights (13), local matters (16), and the power over hospitals ("establishment, maintenance, and management") set out here (7). Parliament has jurisdiction over health matters under POGG power if they become serious enough to have national dimensions or to be classed as an emergency. Parliament also controls health care through substantial payments to the provinces. If a province wants to receive federal funding for health care it must comply with national standards set out in the *Canada Health Act*.
"Provincial" crime and punishment	6. The Establishment, Maintenance, and Management of Public and Reformatory Prisons in and for the Province 15. The Imposition of Punishment by Fine, Penalty, or Imprisonment for enforcing any Law of the Province made in relation to any Matter coming within any of the Classes of Subjects enumerated in this Section	"True" crime is a federal jurisdiction, but the provinces have the power to proscribe and punish lesser offences, such as traffic and regulatory offences.
Courts	14. The Administration of Justice in the Province, including the Constitution, Maintenance, and Organization of Provincial Courts, both of Civil and of Criminal Jurisdiction, and including Procedure in Civil Matters in those Courts	Each province has jurisdiction generally over its own courts but it is partly a shared jurisdiction (see Chapter 7).
Miscellaneous	4. The Establishment and Tenure of Provincial Offices and the Appointment and Payment of Provincial Officers 8. Municipal Institutions in the Province 11. The Incorporation of Companies with Provincial Objects 12. The Solemnization of Marriage in the Province	At the time of Confederation, regional regulation in these areas was considered most efficient.

Territorial Power

The territories do not have an equivalent to section 92 of the *Constitution Act, 1867* assigning them areas of legislative jurisdiction. Each territory is under the control of Parliament, and the source of each territory's power is a federal statute that grants provincial-like legislative power to each of them. These statutes are the *Yukon Act*, the *Northwest Territories Act*, and the *Nunavut Act*.[3] They are not constitutionally entrenched and can be legally changed by Parliament at any time, despite legislated and political promises not to do so without first consulting the territories.

The organizational arrangement between Parliament and the territories is one of **devolution**. This is the name for a legislative arrangement whereby a central authority grants power to regional authorities that are subordinate to it. The organization of the UK, with subordinate regional elected assemblies in Scotland, Wales, and Northern Ireland, is an example of devolution. Another example is the provinces' delegating authority to municipalities to make bylaws.

Devolution involves the delegation of legislative authority, which occurs any time a legislature gives power to another body to make legislation on the legislature's behalf. The most common form of delegation is a statute's enabling another body to make regulations. (For more on regulations, see below).

The legislative power that Parliament has granted the territories in their constituting statutes is similar to the power it has given the provinces. For example, section 18 of the *Yukon Act* states the following:

> **Legislative powers**
>
> 18(1) The Legislature may make laws in relation to the following classes of subjects in respect of Yukon:
>
> [(a)-(c), (g), (m), (n), (q), (r), (u)-(v) omitted]
>
> (d) the establishment and tenure of public offices in Yukon and the appointment, conditions of employment and payment of office-holders;
>
> (e) municipal and local institutions;
>
> (f) direct taxation and licensing in order to raise revenue for territorial, municipal or local purposes;
>
> (h) the incorporation of companies with territorial objects, other than railway, steamship, air transport, canal, telegraph or telephone companies, but including street railway companies;
>
> (i) the solemnization of marriage;
>
> (j) property and civil rights;
>
> (k) the administration of justice, including the constitution, maintenance and organization of territorial courts, both of civil and of criminal jurisdiction, and including procedure in civil matters in those courts;
>
> (l) the establishment, maintenance and management of prisons, jails or lock-ups;
>
> (o) education [clauses (i)-(ii) omitted]
>
> (p) immigration;
>
> (s) hospitals and charities;
>
> (t) agriculture;
>
> (x) generally, all matters of a merely local or private nature;
>
> (y) the imposition of fines, penalties, imprisonment or other punishments in respect of the contravention of the provisions of a law of the Legislature; and
>
> (z) any other matter that may be designated by order of the Governor in Council.

---

3 Respectively, SC 2002, c 7; RSC 1985, c N-27; and SC 1993, c 28.

TABLE 5.3   Provincial and Territorial Legislatures

PROVINCE/TERRITORY	NAME OF ASSEMBLY	MEMBER DESIGNATION*	SEATS
Alberta	Legislative Assembly of Alberta	MLA	83
British Columbia	Legislative Assembly of British Columbia	MLA	85
Manitoba	Legislative Assembly of Manitoba	MLA	57
New Brunswick	Legislative Assembly of New Brunswick	MLA	56
Newfoundland and Labrador	House of Assembly of Newfoundland and Labrador	MHA	48
Northwest Territories	Legislative Assembly of the Northwest Territories	MLA	18
Nova Scotia	Nova Scotia Legislature	MHA	52
Nunavut	Legislative Assembly of Nunavut	MLA	19
Ontario	Legislative Assembly of Ontario	MPP	107
Prince Edward Island	Legislative Assembly of Prince Edward Island	MLA	27
Quebec	National Assembly of Quebec	MNA	125
Saskatchewan	Legislative Assembly of Saskatchewan	MLA	58
Yukon	Yukon Legislative Assembly	MLA	18

*   MLA = Member of the Legislative Assembly; MHA = Member of the House of Assembly
     MPP = Member of the Provincial Parliament; MNA = Member of the National Assembly

Using the legislative powers granted them, the territorial assemblies have passed statutes equivalent to provincial statutes, such as taxation acts, motor vehicle acts, and human rights acts.

One constitutional question where the territories are concerned is whether Parliament actually has the power to delegate legislative jurisdiction to them in all the areas it has done. These are areas assigned to the provinces under the *Constitution Act, 1867* and not to Parliament. The specific source of Parliament's power to delegate authority to the territories is section 4 of the *Constitution Act, 1871*:

> 4. The Parliament of Canada may from time to time make provision for the administration, peace, order, and good government of any territory not for the time being included in any Province.[4]

The question is whether this statute—one of the statutes composing Canada's Constitution—gives Parliament the jurisdiction to delegate to the territories as it has done. So far, Parliament's power in this regard has not been challenged.

With their delegated power and their lack of constitutional entrenchment, the territories are legally analogous to municipalities. At the same time, the nature of their power, their geographical size, and their position on the national stage make them politically closer to provinces.

How Territorial Legislatures Make Statutes

Statute making in the territories is modelled on—and very close to—the provincial system. A public or private territorial bill becomes a statute after three readings, with a committee

---

4   (UK), 34 & 35 Vict, c 28.

review between the second and third readings, followed by assent. Assent comes from a federal appointee to each territory, called a "commissioner." When it comes to approving a bill, the commissioner's role in the territories is similar to that of the lieutenant governor in the provinces.

With respect to enactment, assent, and coming into force, territorial bills are like provincial or federal ones. The enactment process must be complete before the session prorogues or the bill "dies on the order paper." Assuming it passes in time, the bill is reborn as a statute, is assigned a chapter number, and is later published in print and electronic versions. Territorial statutes, like other statutes, come into force on assent. Alternatively, a statute may specify a date upon which it comes into force, or it may leave the date open, to be fixed by proclamation. Or a territorial statute may come into force through a combination of these methods.

Structure of Statutes

All Canadian statutes have structural components and features in common regardless of jurisdiction. The main elements of a statute are as follows:

- title,
- chapter number or citation,
- table of contents,
- preamble,
- parts,
- sections,
- sectional endnotes (legislative history),
- marginal notes or headnotes,
- schedules, and
- bilingual text.

For an illustration of the structure of statutes, see Figure 5.6.

Title

Many statutes have lengthy titles that include the purpose of and reason for the legislation. In this case, the statute will usually contain, either at its beginning or its end, a section that provides a short title for the statute, and the statute will state that it can be cited by its **short title**. For example, Canada's criminal law is contained in a statute whose long title is *An Act Respecting the Criminal Law*. However, section 1 of this statute states that it may be cited as the *Criminal Code*. If no short title is provided, the statute is cited by its long title. (Citation of statutes is described in Appendix 5.1.)

Chapter Number or Citation

The **chapter number** is usually set out just before or after the title. Sometimes the full citation is set out here, too. It identifies the statute's location in the relevant statute volume based on the legislative session or year in which it was passed or on the revision in which it was republished.

Table of Contents

A table of contents at the beginning of a statute used to be uncommon. Tables of contents are becoming more common, however, owing to the recent emphasis on plain language and clarity of expression in legislation. A table of contents allows the reader to quickly scan the contents of the entire statute and pinpoint the section he is looking for. In many jurisdictions now, all statutes, long or short, complex or simple, have tables of contents.

Preamble

A statute may have a **preamble**—an introductory sentence or two that succinctly states the statute's key purpose. For example, the preamble to the *Constitution Act, 1867* states that Canada is to have a "Constitution similar in Principle to that of the United Kingdom." The preamble to the *Canadian Charter of Rights and Freedoms* states the following: "Whereas Canada is founded upon principles that recognize the supremacy of God and the rule of law." The preamble is an official part of a statute and can help courts interpret it. (Statutory interpretation is examined in the next section.)

FIGURE 5.6 Structure of a statute

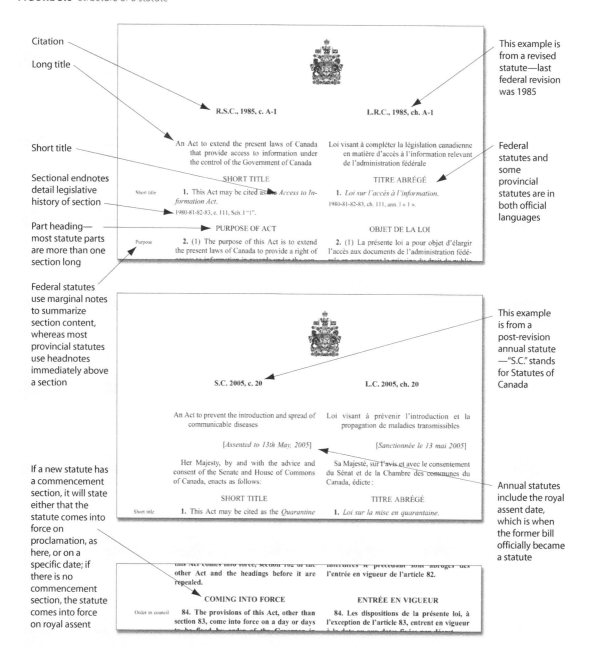

Parts

Lengthy statutes are usually divided into large divisions, called "parts," that are numbered consecutively. Each part contains the law pertaining to a specific subject area in the statute. For example, part XII of the *Criminal Code* pertains to offences relating to currency.

Sections

The basic "unit" of a statute is a **section**, also referred to as a "provision." The body of a statute is made up of consecutively numbered sections. Depending on its level of complexity, a section may be subdivided further into subsections, paragraphs, and subparagraphs (and, if necessary, clauses and subclauses).

The sections of a statute typically include *definition sections, enabling sections, consequential amendment sections,* and *commencement sections.* A **definition section**, usually found at the beginning of a statute or part of a statute, defines words intended to have a specific meaning in the statute. For example, section 2 of the *Criminal Code* lists definitions for terms such as "bank note," "day," "explosive substance," "motor vehicle," and "weapon." Apart from the definition section, the beginning of the statute may include other introductory sections that indicate the scope of the statute's application and how it is administered.

Some statutes require regulations to flesh out their legislative policy. For this to happen, the statute must authorize the passing of such regulations. The section in a statute that sets out this authority is called the **enabling section**. When researching statutes, always look for this possibility.

New statutes often affect existing legislation. A new statute may introduce a completely new set of laws in a particular area, and by doing so amend existing legislation "consequentially." Or the sole purpose of the statute may be to amend existing legislation. Usually the title of this latter type of statute has the word "amendment" in it, making its purpose clear—for example, *An Act to amend the Controlled Drugs and Substances Act (methamphetamine and ecstasy).*

To reconcile existing legislation with a new statute, the new statute will amend older statutes by way of a **consequential amendment section** or sections, usually located near the end of the statute. Often the changes are minor. For instance, if a new statute changes the name of a government department, all references to the old name in earlier statutes will have to be changed.

Some statutes have a **commencement (or coming into force) section**—a section that details when or how a statute comes into effect. As we have seen, the usual method of bringing statutes into force is to do so by proclamation at some unspecified time in the future. Other statutes, silent about when they come into force, do so upon receiving royal assent. But the coming into force of statutes is often delayed to allow governments time to make administrative adjustments to accommodate the new legislation. On occasion, too, statutes come into force retroactively. Such statutes will include a commencement (or coming into force) section.[5] This section will specify a date on which the statute or particular sections of it come into effect.

Sectional Endnotes (Legislative History)

Only consolidated or revised statutes include sectional endnotes. Placed at the end of each section of a revised statute, these endnotes give the reader details about the statute's legislative

---

5   Some jurisdictions, such as British Columbia, have recently started the practice of including a commencement section even when the statute or part comes into force on assent. Presumably this is for the sake of clarity and because most lay readers would be unfamiliar with the "silence rule."

history. When a statute is first passed, there will be no sectional endnotes because the statute has no history at this point. In the case of a consolidated or revised statute, the reader may need to find out when the statute was first passed—to determine, for example, when particular legal rights granted by the statute accrued for the first time.

This information tells the reader when the section first appeared or if it appeared in a previous revision or consolidation. The first number is the year, session, or revision in which it first or previously appeared. The chapter number is next. The final detail is the section number or other pinpoint information. Some jurisdictions no longer include legislative history information in revisions or consolidations in the form of endnotes. Instead, they publish separate tables with this information.

Marginal Notes or Headnotes

In the margin beside sections of a statute are brief words or **marginal notes**, which summarize the contents of each section. For example, beside a section on definitions will be found the marginal note "Definitions." The marginal notes are for guidance and ease of reference only. They do not qualify as part of the formal statute and cannot be used in interpretations of it. In some jurisdictions, the practice is to place the summaries *above* each section, in which case they are called **headnotes**.

Schedules

Some statutes have schedules. Schedules set out information in the form of lists or tables, for the reader's convenience. For example, sometimes a lengthy list of consequential amendments is set out in a schedule. If a statute has a schedule, one or more sections will refer you to it. The schedule itself will likewise indicate what the referring section(s) is.

Schedules are part of the statute and should be read carefully if they concern the issue that you are researching. They can contain very important information. The most famous example is the *Canadian Charter of Rights and Freedoms* (the Charter). As we have seen, the Charter is part of the *Constitution Act, 1982*, which is a schedule to another Act—the *Canada Act 1982*.

Bilingual Text

Federal and territorial statutes are bilingual. (Nunavut publishes its statutes in Inuktitut, too.) Among the provinces, Ontario, Quebec, Manitoba, and New Brunswick publish their statutes in both official languages. A few provinces—Saskatchewan, for example—publish certain statutes in both languages. The other provinces publish their statutes in English only.

For the rules concerning the citation of statutes, see Appendix 5.1.

Statutory Interpretation

Varying degrees of ambiguity inevitably exist in statutes, despite legislative counsels' best efforts to make them clear and consistent. Many statutes contain wordings and phrasings that are unclear. In these situations, the responsibility falls to the courts to resolve the ambiguity.

Courts faced with such ambiguity must engage in **statutory interpretation**. To help with this process, the courts have developed common law rules over hundreds of years, and these rules have been supplemented with various legislated rules regarding interpretation. Ultimately, what the courts are trying to establish in these cases is **legislative intent**.

In Canada today, there are three main contexts in which courts are called upon to interpret statutes:

1. cases where the search is for "jurisdictional meaning"—that is, whether the legislation is within the authority of the enacting legislature (for example, when there is a division-of-powers issue);
2. cases concerned with whether the statute offends one or more of the rights and freedoms guaranteed by the Charter; and
3. cases where the search is for "basic meaning"—that is, there is no concern about the legislation's validity.

The following is an overview of the rules and interpretive guides the courts can draw on when construing legislation.

General Rules of Statutory Interpretation

The courts have developed a number of general rules regarding statutory interpretation. The first three—the "mischief rule," the "literal rule" (or "plain meaning rule"), and the "golden rule"—are traditional common law rules that evolved over many centuries. The fourth one, the "modern principle," borrows parts of these earlier rules, adds to them, and creates a single all-encompassing principle. The SCC has cited this latter principle with approval, and it is *the* approach to follow today.

MISCHIEF RULE

Using this rule, which was derived from a 1584 English precedent called *Heydon's Case*, a judge looks at more than just the statute's words. She examines Parliament's objective or purpose in enacting a statute in relation to the "mischief" or deficiency that the statute was intended to remedy or correct, and interprets the statute in accordance with this view.[6]

LITERAL RULE

Using this rule, which is sometimes called the "plain meaning rule" or "ordinary meaning rule," a judge will not consider why the legislature passed a statute. The judge examines only the words and phrases of the statute itself—nothing more—and considers their ordinary sense or plain meaning. This rule entails a further consideration. When using it, a judge must interpret the legislation according to the meaning the words had at the time the statute was first enacted—that is, according to their original meaning and not to what their meaning may have become over time. These words and their ordinary plain—and original—meaning are followed, even if doing so leads to some injustice, difficulty, or absurdity. According to this rule, a judge must not assume that the legislature intended anything other than what is contained in the words of the statute itself.

GOLDEN RULE

This rule, based on the 1857 English case of *Grey v Pearson*, modifies the literal or plain meaning rule. The court in the *Grey* case stated that the ordinary sense or literal meaning of a statute's words are to be adhered to unless doing so "would lead to some absurdity, or some repugnance or inconsistency with the rest of the instrument, in which case the grammatical and ordinary sense of the words may be modified, so as to avoid the absurdity and inconsistency,

---

6 Edmund Kwaw, *The Guide to Legal Analysis, Legal Methodology, and Legal Writing* (Toronto: Emond Montgomery, 1992).

but no farther."[7] Using this rule, a judge will modify only the problematic words of a statute. For example, a court could read a statute's "and" as an "or" under circumstances where a conjunctive set of conditions (as established by the "and") would lead to an absurd result.

MODERN PRINCIPLE

In modern times, attempts have been made to unify the general rules. For example, Parliament enacted section 12 of the *Interpretation Act*, which provides as follows: "Every enactment is deemed remedial, and shall be given such fair, large and liberal construction and interpretation as best ensures the attainment of its objects."[8] The provinces and territories have similar provisions in their *Interpretation Acts*.

Elmer Driedger, summing up the modern principle (as he called it) in his seminal book on statutory interpretation, wrote the following:

> Today, there is only one principle or approach, namely, the words of an Act are to be read in their entire context and in their grammatical and ordinary sense harmoniously with the scheme of the Act, the object of the Act, and the intention of Parliament.[9]

Driedger's summary captures the spirit of the *Interpretation Act* provision and of the modern principle.

The SCC has cited the modern principle with approval in a number of its decisions. In 2011, in the *Celgene* case, the Court was called upon to interpret some provisions in the *Patent Act*. Abella J, writing for the Court, stated the following:

> The parties both relied on the approach used in *Canada Trustco Mortgage Co. v. Canada*, 2005 SCC 54, [2005] 2 S.C.R. 601, at para. 10, which confirmed that statutory interpretation involves a consideration of the ordinary meaning of the words used and the statutory context in which they are found:
>
> > It has been long established as a matter of statutory interpretation that *"the words of an Act are to be read in their entire context and in their grammatical and ordinary sense harmoniously with the scheme of the Act, the object of the Act, and the intention of Parliament* [emphasis added]": see *65302 British Columbia Ltd. v. Canada*, [1999] 3 S.C.R. 804, at para. 50. The interpretation of a statutory provision must be made according to a textual, contextual and purposive analysis to find a meaning that is harmonious with the Act as a whole. When the words of a provision are precise and unequivocal, the ordinary meaning of the words plays a dominant role in the interpretive process. On the other hand, where the words can support more than one reasonable meaning, the ordinary meaning of the words plays a lesser role. The relative effects of ordinary meaning, context and purpose on the interpretive process may vary, but in all cases the court must seek to read the provisions of an Act as a harmonious whole. [Emphasis added.]

---

7   *Ibid* at 126.

8   *Interpretation Act*, RSC 1985, c I-21, s 12.

9   Elmer A Driedger, *Construction of Statutes* (Toronto: Butterworths, 1974) at 67. Professor Driedger's text continues to be published, but with the 5th edition his name has been dropped. See Ruth Sullivan, *Sullivan on the Construction of Statutes*, 5th ed (Toronto: LexisNexis, 2008).

The words, if clear, will dominate; if not, they yield to an interpretation that best meets the overriding purpose of the statute.[10]

In all statutory interpretation cases, then, a "textual, contextual, and purposive analysis" is nowadays the approach to take. We might sum up this approach as follows:

- *textual analysis* focuses on the meaning of the words read by themselves;
- *contextual analysis* focuses on the meaning of the words in the context of the whole statute; and
- *purposive analysis* focuses on the meaning of the words in light of the underlying purpose or object of the Act.

Driedger's principle refers to all of these things. What the SCC appears to be adding to his principle is the dominance of the words themselves—provided they are clear—in the interpretive process.

In his classic 1938 article on statutory interpretation, John Willis, after describing the traditional common law rules concerning interpretation, wrote as follows:

Having inquired into the difference between the three familiar approaches and discussed the manner in which each is applied, we are now in a position to ask the final question which was posed at the beginning. ... [W]hich of these approaches does a court prefer and when? ... A court invokes whichever of the rules produces a result that satisfies its sense of justice in the case before it.[11]

Today, courts may and still do refer to the spirit of one or more of the three traditional common law rules—the "mischief rule," the "literal rule" (or "plain meaning rule")—and the "golden rule." However, given the position now taken by the SCC on statutory interpretation, the courts' guide in the final analysis must now be the modern principle.

Grammatical Rules

In addition to general rules of interpretation, the courts have developed some specific rules to help them construe grammatical patterns commonly found in statutes. These rules and patterns are as follows:

- *ejusdem generis*
- *noscitur a sociis*
- *expressio unius est exclusio alterius*
- and/or
- means/includes
- must/may.

EJUSDEM GENERIS

The *ejusdem generis* rule ("of the same kind or class") dictates that where two or more specific words (or a phrase) in a statute describe a class of objects that are followed by general words,

---

10   *Celgene Corp v Canada (Attorney General)*, 2011 SCC 1, [2011] 1 SCR 3 at para 21.

11   John Willis, "Statute Interpretation in a Nutshell" (1938) 16 Can Bar Rev 1.

the general words should be interpreted to be of the same type or class as the specific words preceding them. For example, if a statute states that "no dogs, cats, or other animals may wander in public places without being controlled by means of a leash," how should "other animals" be interpreted? According to the *ejusdem generis* rule, in this example "the specific words preceding the general phrase refer to the class of domestic animals, hence squirrels and rabbits would not fall within the provision."[12]

NOSCITUR A SOCIIS

The second grammatical rule is known as *noscitur a sociis* ("it is known by its associates"). Here, a general word in a statute can be interpreted as referring to things that are in the same class as other things specifically referred to in the same context. For example, if a statute states that "no vehicles, bicycles, skateboards, or scooters can enter this park," the general word "vehicles" could be interpreted as referring to a vehicle in the same class as bicycles, skateboards, or scooters—in other words, a recreational vehicle. This means that someone might be permitted to enter the park in a wheelchair—a non-recreational vehicle.

EXPRESSIO UNIUS EST EXCLUSIO ALTERIUS

The third grammatical rule is known as *expressio unius est exclusio alterius* ("to express one thing is to exclude another"). What this rule means is that if something was left out of a statute, it was meant to be left out. For example, as one commentator has said, "[a] bylaw that applies to owners of orange, blue, red, green, black, and yellow cars would not, it could be argued, apply to owners of brown cars."[13]

AND/OR

Many statutes list "elements" or "conditions" that relate to a definition or rule. Sometimes these lists are conjunctive, and sometimes they are disjunctive. With a conjunctive list, the last two items are connected by an "and." In this case, *all* elements or conditions must be present to satisfy the definition or rule. If the last two items are connected by an "or," it is a disjunctive list, and *only one* element or condition needs to be present to satisfy the definition or rule.

The definition of the Constitution of Canada, as described earlier, is an illustration of a conjunctive list. Section 52 of the *Constitution Act, 1982* states the following:

> 52(2) The Constitution of Canada includes
> (a) the *Canada Act 1982*, including this Act;
> (b) the Acts and orders referred to in the schedule; *and* [emphasis added]
> (c) any amendment to any Act or order referred to in paragraph (a) or (b).

This is a *conjunctive* list, and all the items listed are part of the definition.

The definition of culpable homicide in criminal law gives us an example of a *disjunctive* list. Homicide, of course, is when a person causes the death of another human being. Culpable homicide can be murder, manslaughter, or infanticide, and is defined in the *Criminal Code* as follows:

---

12   Kwaw, *supra* note 6 at 130.

13   Ted Tjaden, *Legal Research and Writing* (Toronto: Irwin Law, 2001) at 76.

222(5) A person commits culpable homicide when he causes the death of a human being,

    (a) by means of an unlawful act;

    (b) by criminal negligence;

    (c) by causing that human being, by threats or fear of violence or by deception, to do anything that causes his death; *or* [emphasis added]

    (d) by wilfully frightening that human being, in the case of a child or sick person.[14]

According to the "and/or rule" of statutory interpretation, the homicide is culpable if any one of the conditions listed above is present.

These examples are relatively straightforward. In more complex provisions, there can be lists within lists. For example, each paragraph could have a list of subparagraphs joined disjunctively or conjunctively. A reading of these provisions that takes careful note of the *and*'s and *or*'s will help determine the various relationships.

MEANS/INCLUDES

Statutes often refer to general concepts or tests. Then, to provide greater clarity, they go on to provide specific examples. When the word "means" precedes the examples, it indicates that the definition is complete and the list exhaustive. Conversely, the word "includes" or "including" before a list indicates an open definition and a non-exhaustive list.[15]

Again, section 52 of the *Constitution Act, 1982* provides an illustration:

52(2) The Constitution of Canada *includes* [emphasis added]

    (a) the *Canada Act 1982*, including this Act;

    (b) the Acts and orders referred to in the schedule; and

    (c) any amendment to any Act or order referred to in paragraph (a) or

(b). ...

The SCC has held that the word "includes" in section 52(2) permits an expansive interpretation; in other words, this list of the Constitution's contents is not an exhaustive one. In the *New Brunswick Broadcasting* case, accordingly, the SCC found that the unwritten doctrine of parliamentary privilege was included in the Constitution of Canada even though it was not listed in the definition.[16]

MUST/MAY

The word "must" is commonly used today to signify mandatory action or inaction; it implies a duty and the absence of discretion. The word "shall" was used to the same effect in older legislation and is still used in some jurisdictions. The word "may," on the other hand, signifies discretionary rather than mandatory action; it confers the power to do something, but does not make it a duty. The following section from BC's *Motor Vehicle Act* illustrates the use of both these words. Generally, drivers have a duty to stop at an intersection if there is a red light. However, bus drivers have a limited power to enter intersections on a red light.

---

14 *Criminal Code*, RSC 1985, c C-46, s 222(5).

15 Donald J Gifford, Kenneth H Gifford & Michael I Jeffery, *How to Understand Statutes and By-Laws* (Toronto: Carswell, 1996) at 66-68.

16 See *New Brunswick Broadcasting Co v Nova Scotia (Speaker of the House of Assembly)*, [1993] 1 SCR 319. See also Hogg, *supra* note 2 at 1-8.1.

Red light

> 129(1) Subject to subsection (2), when a red light alone is exhibited at an intersection by a traffic control signal, the driver of a vehicle approaching the intersection and facing the red light *must* cause it to stop … before entering the intersection. …
>
> (2) The driver of a bus approaching an intersection and facing a red light and a prescribed white rectangular indicator *may* cause the bus to proceed through the intersection.[17]

Internal Aids to Interpretation

Definition sections, usually located at the beginning of a statute or the part of the statute to which they relate, define specific words used in the legislation and should always be consulted. Words may have a special or unusual meaning within the statute.

The long or short titles of a statute, along with part headings, can be used to help determine the statute's purpose and scope. This can help, in turn, with the interpretation of the wording of a specific provision. The same applies to the preamble.

Marginal notes, head notes, and end notes can be helpful, but they are for ease of reference only and should not be used as the basis for interpretation. Section 14 of the federal *Interpretation Act* states the following: "Marginal notes and references to former enactments that appear after the end of a section or other division in an enactment form no part of the enactment, but are inserted for convenience of reference only."[18]

External Aids to Interpretation

DICTIONARIES

Judges sometimes consult legal dictionaries for assistance in defining a word. *Black's Law Dictionary*, a respected American reference text, is one example. Canadian legal dictionaries include Yogis's *Canadian Law Dictionary* and Dukelow's *Dictionary of Canadian Law*.

WORDS AND PHRASES REFERENCE SETS

There are legal reference works dealing specifically with words and legal phrases whose meanings have been considered by judges in previous cases. Carswell's *The Canadian Abridgment: Words & Phrases Judicially Defined in Canadian Courts and Tribunals* is one of the most comprehensive Canadian sets. Carswell also publishes *Sanagan's Encyclopedia of Words and Phrases, Legal Maxims*, which also focuses exclusively on interpretations from Canadian courts and tribunals.

INTERPRETATION ACTS

The federal, provincial, and territorial *Interpretation Acts* also define words that are intended to have a specific meaning whenever they are used in legislation.[19] However, the definitions provided by these general statutes are always subject to contrary definitions in particular statutes. When reading a statute, you must consult both the statute's definition section(s)

---

17 *Motor Vehicle Act*, RSBC 1996, c 318, s 129 (emphasis added).

18 *Interpretation Act*, RSC 1985, c I-21, s 14. See also the provincial and territorial equivalents.

19 For example, see *Interpretation Act*, *ibid*; *Interpretation Act*, RSA 2000, c I-8; *Interpretation Act*, RSBC 1996, c 238; *Interpretation Act*, RSNS 1989, c 235; *Legislation Act*, SO 2006, c 21, Schedule F (Part VI); *Interpretation Act*, RSY 2002, c 125.

and the relevant jurisdiction's *Interpretation Act* if you have doubts about the meaning of particular words.

HANSARD

Hansard, the common name for legislative debates, is the written record of parliamentary proceedings. Judges sometimes refer to it, especially for the purpose of determining Parliament's intent in passing a specific statute. However, judges have disagreed on whether *Hansard* can or cannot be used in all instances to help interpret a statute.[20]

Interpreting Bilingual Statutes

As noted earlier, federal and territorial statutes are published in both official languages, as are the statutes of Ontario, Quebec, Manitoba, and New Brunswick. A few provinces, such as Saskatchewan, publish select statutes in both languages, and the other provinces publish their statutes in English only. Where statutes are published in both languages, the English and French versions are usually arranged in columns side by side. Depending on the precise wording in a particular bilingual statute, there may be subtle differences in meaning between the two versions.

According to various constitutional provisions (including section 133 of the *Constitution Act, 1867*, section 23 of the *Manitoba Act, 1870*, and section 18 of the Charter), as well as the SCC's interpretation of these provisions, federal and territorial statutes—as well as the statutes of Quebec, Manitoba, and New Brunswick—must be enacted in both official languages, and both versions must be considered equally authoritative. One version is not paramount over the other; both have equal status when it comes to their application.

The "shared meaning rule" dictates the primary approach to interpreting bilingual statutes from these jurisdictions. Under this rule, both the French and English versions must be read together, and "the meaning that is shared by the French and English versions is presumed to be the meaning intended by the legislature."[21] In other words, the legislating body intended an English word and its French equivalent to mean the same thing in both the English and the French texts of the statute. Interpreting bilingual legislation is a matter of getting at this common meaning.

Subordinate Legislation

Subordinate or delegated legislation is legislation passed pursuant to a statute. This kind of legislation is made not by the principal law-making power but by a subordinate body to which the former has *delegated* authority to make laws. Above, we mentioned two limits on the primary legislator's power to delegate. They are as follows:

1. the power to legislate cannot be given away completely, and
2. the power delegated must be within the jurisdiction of the primary legislator.

Another general constitutional law principle relevant to this area is that of ***delegatus non potest delegare***. This means that the person or body to whom power is delegated cannot redelegate it.

The main types of subordinate legislation are regulations and municipal bylaws.

---

20   See Gifford, Gifford & Jeffery, *supra* note 15, ch 27.

21   Ruth Sullivan, *Statutory Interpretation*, 2d ed (Toronto: Irwin Law, 2007) at 85.

Regulations

Regulations are closely related to statutes. They can only be made under the authority of a particular statute and are always associated with that statute. As noted earlier, it is the statute's enabling section that delegates to another body—usually to the government Cabinet—the power to make regulations. Not all statutes have regulations. Those that do are usually longer, more complex statutes.

Regulations are passed differently from statutes. They are not passed by means of a series of readings, followed by royal assent. To become law, they are simply drafted and approved by the relevant body, filed with a government registrar or clerk (federally, with the clerk of the Privy Council), and then published in the relevant *Gazette* (federally, *Canada Gazette* Part II). Regulations are sometimes republished periodically in bound consolidations, like statutes. Almost all jurisdictions now publish ongoing loose-leaf and electronic versions of their regulations.

Regulations belong to one of two main categories:

1. "ordinary" regulations, and
2. rules of practice.

Ordinary regulations are simply referred to as "regulations." They are passed under statutes for the purpose of filling in the details of a statutory regime. Because regulations are much easier to make, amend, or repeal than statutes, they are a more appropriate place to include legislative details (for example, procedural rules or fees) that are changed frequently. For example, the federal *Access to Information Regulations* were passed under the *Access to Information Act*, RSC 1985, c A-1.

Rules of practice set out the procedure or practices to follow when pursuing particular types of claims, or when pursuing any kind of claim before particular courts or tribunals. Some federal examples of regulations that are rules of practice include the following: the *Bankruptcy and Insolvency General Rules*; the *Rules of the Supreme Court of Canada*; and the *Federal Court Immigration Rules*.

When dealing with regulations, you should be aware not only of the statute authorizing a particular regulation but of the *general regulations statute* for the jurisdiction in question. What is a general regulations statute? It is a special Act that sets out the precise rules for the making and publishing of regulations. Regulations can be challenged if they fail to follow the procedure set out in the relevant regulations statute (see, for example, the federal *Statutory Instruments Act*, RSC 1985, c S-22) or if they exceed the mandate outlined in the enabling section.

Municipal Bylaws

Municipal bylaws, like regulations, exist only in relation to a statute and are a form of delegated legislation. Under section 92 of the *Constitution Act, 1867*, the provinces have power over municipalities. The federal government has likewise given power to the territorial assemblies to regulate municipalities. Municipal bylaws are created pursuant to provincial or territorial statutes and can be thought of as a special type of provincial or territorial regulation. The authorizing legislation for these bylaws can be a general municipal statute or a special charter for an individual city.

Bylaws cover many topics. Some of the more familiar ones include property taxes, health and safety (for example, no-smoking areas), animals (for example, dog licensing and on-leash areas), structures and property maintenance (for example, clearance of snowy walkways), and business licensing.

Quasi-Legislative Materials

Quasi-legislative materials are non-legislated written rules. They play an important role in some areas of the law, but they are neither statutes nor a form of subordinate legislation. Strictly speaking, they are not legally binding. However, you must follow, observe, and consider these rules as you do legislated rules. If not, you risk having applications or documents rejected by the relevant authorities, delaying a legal process, or misunderstanding a related piece of legislation. Quasi-legislative materials relate to many different areas of the law. Examples of quasi-legislative materials include government policy statements, court directions, and certain kinds of agreements.

Policy Statements

Various government officials and regulatory bodies, and some non-governmental organizations, issue policy statements that you must follow in order to comply with various regulatory schemes or guidelines. These policy statements often explain how to interpret a particular piece of legislation setting out a regulatory scheme. In the area of corporate law, for instance, if you wish to incorporate a company, you need prior approval of the name. Corporate legislation often allows a corporate registrar to refuse to register a company under a name the registrar finds objectionable "for good and valid reason." Most registrars will have prepared a set of guidelines regarding names—the quasi-legislative material we are speaking of. These guidelines are not legislated. If you don't follow them, however, you won't get the company registered with the chosen name.

Another example concerns securities law. The securities industry in Canada is regulated through an extremely complex mix of statutes, regulations, and policies, as well as through the industry rules of self-regulatory organizations (SROs), such as the TSX Venture Exchange and the Investment Industry Regulatory Organization of Canada. Provincial securities commissions have issued a number of policies explaining how they intend to interpret relevant securities legislation. There are local policies (specific to one province) as well as national policies (agreed to by all Canadian securities regulators), among others. And there are SRO rules to consider as well. Without a working knowledge of these non-legislated policies and rules, no one can operate successfully in the securities field.

Court Directions

In the area of practice and procedure, many courts and administrative tribunals issue practice directives dealing with matters that are not covered in their legislated rules of practice. These directives might, for example, set conditions that must be in place for television coverage of proceedings, or they might specify the process for scheduling trials and hearings. The chief justice of the BC Court of Appeal has said the following about the set of Civil Practice Directives produced by that court:

> Practice Directives do not have the same force of law as the formal enactments in the *Court of Appeal Act* and *Rules*, but they express the view of the Court regarding matters of practice and procedure. Litigants and practitioners are expected to comply with them or show good reason for doing otherwise.[22]

---

22   Court of Appeal Practice Directives (Civil & Criminal Practice Directive, 19 September 2011), online: The Courts of British Columbia <http://www.courts.gov.bc.ca/court_of_appeal/Practice_and_Procedure/civil_practice_directives_/index.aspx>.

Agreements

Another area in which quasi-legislative materials have bearing is agreements. Certain kinds of agreements have ramifications beyond the particular parties involved, and approach the status of legislation. Agreements between provincial governments (for example, trade arrangements), between federal and provincial governments (for example, power sharing or shifting, and funding arrangements), or between countries (for example, treaties that have not been passed into law) have a quasi-legislative significance.[23]

Parliamentary Sovereignty

The doctrine of **parliamentary sovereignty** holds that Parliament has total power. It is a doctrine that became entrenched in 17th-century England, as parliamentary power superseded that of the Crown. Thus Parliament, rather than the monarch, became recognized as the country's supreme legislative authority (see Chapter 2). Parliamentary sovereignty implies at least three principles:

1. Parliament can make or unmake any law;
2. Parliament cannot bind itself against using its power in the future; and
3. a procedurally valid Act of Parliament cannot be questioned by the courts.[24]

In theory, these principles have been transplanted to Canada—part of the English political system we have inherited. In the Canadian context, however, the theory of parliamentary sovereignty is complicated by certain factors.

There are three features of the Canadian system that appear to qualify the notion of Parliament's "total power." First, we are a federation, with legislative power split between two levels of government, the federal and the regional. Second, we have an entrenched Charter (discussed in detail in Chapter 8) that limits the power of our legislators. Third, the power to amend the Constitution lies outside the sole jurisdiction either of Parliament or of the provinces.

Federalism and Parliamentary Power

Canada is a federal state, with split jurisdiction. This means that no legislative body in Canada has total power, as the UK Parliament does. However, it is accepted that we have modelled our system on the British one. This means that between the two levels of government, federal and provincial, there is no power vacuum; between the two levels of government, in other words, there exists law-making power over all subject areas. One or the other authority can enact any law. In the *Reference re Same-Sex Marriage*,[25] the SCC affirmed this principle, which Hogg summarizes as follows:

> The Supreme Court of Canada reaffirmed "the principle of exhaustiveness," which
> it described as "an essential characteristic of the federal distribution of powers." A
> "legislative void is precluded." It followed that "legislative competence over same-sex

---

23   If an international treaty (international agreement) is implemented through the passage of legislation, then the agreement at that point has the force of law.

24   Hogg, *supra* note 2 at 12-1ff.

25   2004 SCC 79, [2004] 3 SCR 698.

marriage must be vested in either Parliament or the Legislatures," and the most apt home for the matter was s 91(26).[26]

The conclusion we can draw from this is that, in our federal system, there are no limits on the *combined* power of the federal and provincial legislatures. Parliamentary sovereignty—of a kind—exists.

The Charter and Parliamentary Power

The next challenge to the notion of parliamentary sovereignty in Canada comes from the Charter. As an entrenched statute, it places limits on the powers of Parliament and the provincial and territorial legislatures to pass laws that offend the Charter's guaranteed rights and freedoms. These limits are qualified, however, by the Charter's "opting out" or "notwithstanding" clause (section 33), which is as follows:

> 33(1) Parliament or the legislature of a province may expressly declare in an
> Act of Parliament or of the legislature, as the case may be, that the Act or a
> provision thereof shall operate notwithstanding a provision included in section 2
> or sections 7 to 15 of this Charter.

Under this provision, our legislators can in theory pass laws that offend the Charter and that are not subject to it.

Constitutional Amendment and Parliamentary Power

Finally, we must address the fact that the power to amend the Canadian Constitution lies outside the unilateral jurisdiction of either Parliament or the provinces. This also seems a challenge to the doctrine of parliamentary sovereignty in this country. The answer to this is as follows. While it is true that, subject to a few limited exceptions, neither Parliament nor the provinces can amend the Constitution *unilaterally*, there is no "legislative void" in this regard. Provided the two levels of government cooperate according to the legislative process established in Part V of the *Constitution Act, 1982*, they can make any amendment to the Constitution. Though they have yet to exercise this power successfully, it is available to them.

When we consider legislative authority in Canada as a collective of federal and provincial power, we see that the principle of parliamentary sovereignty applies in this country as it does in Britain. The English system has, at least theoretically, been transplanted onto Canadian soil. Of the three branches of government—legislative, executive, and judicial—the legislative branch is supreme. The executive and judicial branches are ultimately subject to its control.

---

26   Hogg, *supra* note 2 at 12-5.

APPENDIX 5.1

Citation of Statutes

Canadian statutes, like cases and other legal sources, are cited according to specialized rules. There are many such rules, too many to discuss comprehensively here; below, we offer only the basic ones. See the *Canadian Guide to Uniform Legal Citation* (or "McGill Guide," for short) for more in-depth coverage.[27]

Proper citation of legal sources is expected in all legal writing, both practical and academic. Members of the legal community are not in complete agreement about what the rules for citation should be. In Canada, however, courts, law schools, law offices, and legal publications are increasingly adopting the rules set out in the McGill Guide. That is the guide we follow in this text. The citation for a statute generally consists of the following components: title, jurisdiction and year, chapter, and section.

Title

The title or name of the statute is cited first. As noted above, a statute often has a long title. If the title is long, and if the statute also has a short title, the statute is cited by its short title. The title is italicized.

Jurisdiction and Year

The next part of the citation refers to the statute's jurisdiction and year. Abbreviations are always used to indicate which jurisdiction enacted the statute and the year it was enacted or, for older statutes, the most recent revision in which it appeared. For example, a federal statute enacted in 2012 would be published in the *Statutes of Canada* 2012 volume, which is abbreviated "SC 2012." For older statutes appearing in the *Revised Statutes of Canada* 1985—the most recent federal revision—the abbreviation is "RSC 1985."

Statutes are published in hardbound volumes at the end of the year in which they are enacted. Federal statutes are also published every three months in a softcover volume of the *Canada Gazette* Part III. This ensures that a print version of all federal statutes is available soon after they are enacted. The hardbound volumes in which they

are published are called "annual" or "sessional" volumes. Today, statutes are also published electronically.

Periodically, print versions of a jurisdiction's entire catalogue of public statutes are republished in hardbound **revised statutes** volumes. A statute revision is a "snapshot" of all public statutes in a jurisdiction as of the revision date. All amendments or changes to the statutes are incorporated into the revised versions of the statutes. Repealed statutes are not included in the revision. Most jurisdictions also publish ongoing loose-leaf revisions and online consolidations.

Chapter

As soon as a bill becomes a statute, it is assigned a chapter number. From that point on, it is properly referred to by its statute citation rather than its bill number. (Sometimes we find the news media continuing to use the bill number in cases where the bill has achieved some notoriety.) "Chapter" is abbreviated as lowercase "c". Statutes in the annual or sessional statute volumes are ordered according to their chapter numbers (numeric).

When statutes are republished in a revision, they are assigned new chapter numbers (sometimes numeric and sometimes alphanumeric) to correspond with their position in the consolidation. For example, when the *Access to Information Act* was first enacted in the 1980–1983 federal legislative session, it was cited as *Access to Information Act*, SC 1980-81-82-83, c 111. When it was republished in the 1985 revision, it was given a new citation: *Access to Information Act*, RSC 1985, c A-1.

Section

You will often need to refer to a specific section(s) of a statute. If so, the abbreviations used are "s" for "section" and "ss" for "sections" (with no periods, according to the McGill Guide rules). Sections can be broken down into subdivisions (called subsections), paragraphs, and subparagraphs (and sometimes further still, into clauses and subclauses), depending on their complexity.

---

27   McGill Law Journal, *Canadian Guide to Uniform Legal Citation*, 7th ed (Toronto: Carswell, 2010). In the 7th edition, the editors made one of the most noticeable changes to legal citation conventions in a long time, omitting periods after abbreviation letters. This changes a practice that goes back centuries. For example, the Revised Statutes of Canada used to be "R.S.C." Now it is abbreviated "RSC". Similarly, the Supreme Court Reports used to be abbreviated "S.C.R." but is now abbreviated "SCR".

FIGURE 5.7 Components of a statutory citation

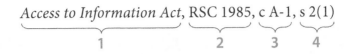

Access to Information Act, RSC 1985, c A-1, s 2(1)

1   2   3   4

1   **Title**
The title is italicized, followed by a comma (not italicized) and a space.

2   **Jurisdiction and Year**
The jurisdictional reference is abbreviated, then a space and the year, followed by a comma and another space. In this example of a federal revised statute, "R" is for revised, "S" is for statutes, and "C" is for Canada. If it were an annual statute it would be just "SC". Each province and territory has its own abbreviation—for example, "A" for Alberta, "BC" for British Columbia, and "M" for Manitoba. When citing provincial or territorial statutes, "RS" or "S" would precede the relevant jurisdictional abbreviation. The *Canadian Guide to Uniform Legal Citation* has a comprehensive listing of abbreviations used in legal citations of all types.

3   **Chapter**
Chapter is abbreviated to "c". Then comes a space and the numeric or alphanumeric designation ("A-1"), followed by a comma and another space if there is a section reference.

4   **Section**
Section is abbreviated to "s". Then comes a space and the number along with any subdivisions, which are placed in parentheses with no spaces in between. Regardless of the particular level or sublevel being referred to, when written as part of a full citation, it always begins with the abbreviation for section, "s". When spoken, the level is noted. For example, at the third level, you would say, "section 2, subsection 1, paragraph b."

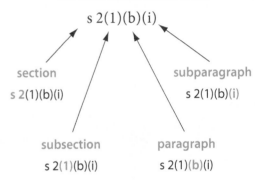

The Subdivisions of a Section

s 2(1)(b)(i)

section
s 2(1)(b)(i)

subparagraph
s 2(1)(b)(i)

subsection
s 2(1)(b)(i)

paragraph
s 2(1)(b)(i)

Citation of Regulations

Regulations are cited, much like statutes, according to their chapter or other number in a consolidation or according to the year in which they were made and to their chronological number for that year. Including the title is optional. Older federal regulations that appear in the 1978 consolidation (the most recent one) are abbreviated "CRC" for "Consolidated Regulations of Canada." If they are more recent, they are abbreviated "SOR" for "Statutory Orders and Regulations." Provincial regulations are usually abbreviated by province, and "regulation" is shortened to "Reg". Older Ontario regulations appearing in the 1990 revision are cited as "RRO" ("revised regulations of Ontario").

The following are some sample citations from federal and provincial regulations:

- *Coastal Fisheries Protection Regulations*, CRC, c 413, s 12;
- *Citizenship Regulations*, SOR/93-246;
- *Federal Court Immigration Rules*, r 10;
- *Clean and Renewable Resource Regulation*, BC Reg 291/2010, s 2; and
- *Critical Defects of Commercial Motor Vehicle Regulation*, O Reg 512/97, s 1.

The citations for rules of practice are simpler than those for ordinary regulations. The jurisdiction is set out first (unless it's clear from the title), followed by the title, which is not optional, and then the rule number. Rule is abbreviated "r". The regulation number is omitted.

CHAPTER SUMMARY

There are three branches of government: the legislative branch, the executive branch, and the judicial branch. The legislative branch is the most powerful of the three, with ultimate control over the other two.

Canada is a former colony of England and, prior to the patriation of the Constitution in 1982, was theoretically subject to control by the UK Parliament. A number of British statutes are a part of our Constitution. The most important of these are the *Constitution Act, 1867* (formerly the BNA Act) and the *Constitution Act, 1982*. The *Constitution Act, 1867*, passed at the request of Canadians, established the country of Canada. It includes many important provisions, including key sections (sections 91 and 92) that divide legislative authority over particular areas between the federal Parliament and the provincial legislatures. The *Constitution Act, 1982* is important because it contains the *Canadian Charter of Rights and Freedoms*, which places limits on legislative power, and because it contains an amending formula for our Constitution. Such a formula did not exist prior to 1982.

In Canada, the power to make legislation is divided more or less equally between Parliament and the provinces. Whenever either level of government enacts legislation in a certain area, it must find authority in the Constitution to support its doing so. Parliament has broad jurisdiction over money matters as well as over a number of other areas, including international trade and criminal law. The provinces have primary jurisdiction over private law and local matters, as well as over areas such as education and natural resources. Parliament has devolved province-like jurisdictional authority over the territories.

The process of making statutory law in this country follows a set process based on the English system. A bill is introduced into the legislative chamber, and after a number of readings, followed by assent, it becomes a statute.

Canadian statutes are structured similarly regardless of their enacting jurisdiction. Common elements include a title, a body of text divided up into parts and sections, and schedules that provide information best conveyed in the form of lists or tables. The courts have various rules and principles and interpretive aids to help them interpret ambiguous legislation.

Besides statutory law, there are subordinate legislation (which includes regulations and municipal bylaws) and certain non-legislated rules, such as policy statements and government agreements. Collectively, this varied legislation and quasi-legislative material provides an ever-growing mass of regulation that touches on almost every aspect of our lives.

KEY TERMS

bicameral legislature with two houses involved in the passage of legislation *(p. 104)*

bill the draft version of a proposed new statute *(p. 117)*

chapter number the number assigned to a statute when it is first passed or when it is republished in a statutory revision—refers to the chronological position of the statute within a particular legislative session, year, or revision *(p. 125)*

commencement (or coming into force) section section that details when or how a statute comes into effect *(p. 127)*

consequential amendment section section in a new statute that amends existing legislation to make it consistent with the new statute *(p. 127)*

constitutionally entrenched describes a statute that falls within the definition of the Constitution of Canada as set out in section 52 of the *Constitution Act, 1982* *(p. 106)*

definition section a statute section that defines words that have a specific meaning in the statute *(p. 127)*

delegates non potest delegare principle that a person or body to whom power is delegated cannot subdelegate that power (Latin: "one to whom power is delegated cannot himself further delegate that power") *(p. 135)*

devolution the legislative arrangement whereby a central authority grants power to regional authorities that are subordinate to the central authority *(p. 123)*

division of powers refers to the divided jurisdiction—between Parliament, on one hand, and the provinces, on the other hand—to make legislation in a federal state such as Canada *(p. 110)*

double-aspect law a law whose subject matter falls within a federal subject area *and* a provincial one *(p. 116)*

enabling section section that delegates authority to make regulations to another person or body *(p. 127)*

federal paramountcy doctrine doctrine according to which, in the event of conflict between a federal law and a provincial law in an area over which both levels of government have jurisdiction, the federal law governs and overrides the provincial one *(p. 117)*

headnotes notes immediately above a section briefly summarizing its contents, serving the same purpose as marginal notes *(p. 128)*

jurisdiction refers (in the context of legislative power under the Constitution) to the specific subject areas over which the federal Parliament and the provincial legislatures have been assigned authority *(p. 107)*

legislation written laws made by legislative assemblies *(p. 105)*

legislative intent a legislature's express or implied intent in passing a statute *(p. 128)*

legislature representative assembly charged under a constitution with making laws for a particular region or state *(p. 104)*

marginal notes notes in the margin beside a section briefly summarizing its contents *(p. 128)*

municipal bylaws form of subordinate legislation passed by municipalities *(p. 136)*

parliamentary sovereignty doctrine that Parliament has ultimate and complete power to pass any law *(p. 138)*

POGG power the general *residuary power* given to Parliament—in other words, the power to fill in the gaps left by the specifically enumerated areas of jurisdiction assigned to the two levels of government *(p. 112)*

preamble an introductory sentence or two at the beginning of a statute that succinctly states the statute's key philosophical aspect or purpose *(p. 126)*

private bill a bill dealing with a private matter that relates, for example, to a particular individual, corporation, or charity *(p. 117)*

proclamation a special government order bringing a statute into force *(p. 119)*

prorogued the formal closing of a legislative session *(p. 112)*

public bill a bill dealing with a matter of public policy *(p. 117)*

quasi-legislative materials non-legislated written rules that relate to and affect a legal process *(p. 137)*

reading a bill's formal presentation to the legislature before it becomes a statute *(p. 118)*

regulations form of subordinate legislation passed by a person or body (frequently the government Cabinet) to expand on or fill out a statute's legislative scheme *(p. 136)*

revised statutes republished, revised collection of all public statutes for a jurisdiction, providing a comprehensive statutory "snapshot" as of the revision date *(p. 140)*

royal assent formal approval of a bill by the Queen's representative *(p. 118)*

section the basic unit of a statute *(p. 127)*

separation-of-powers doctrine doctrine according to which separate powers are assigned to the legislative, executive, and judicial branches of government *(p. 104)*

short title abbreviated version of the full statute title *(p. 125)*

statutes the primary form of legislation *(p. 105)*

statutory interpretation process of interpreting legislation to resolve any ambiguities regarding its meaning or effect *(p. 128)*

subordinate (or delegated) legislation legislation passed pursuant to a statute, whereby the principal law-making power has *delegated* authority to another body to make laws *(p. 135)*

supremacy clause section 52(1) of the *Constitution Act, 1982*, which provides that the Constitution is the supreme law of Canada and empowers the courts to find that laws that are inconsistent with the Constitution are of no force or effect *(p. 109)*

ultra vires outside the jurisdiction of the enacting authority *(p. 110)*

unicameral legislature with one house involved in the passage of legislation *(p. 104)*

FURTHER READING

BOOKS

The Constitutional Law Group. *Canadian Constitutional Law*, 4th ed (Toronto: Emond Montgomery, 2010).

Funston, Bernard W & Eugene Meehan. *Canada's Constitutional Law*, 3d ed (Toronto: Carswell, 2003).

Gifford, Donald J, Kenneth H Gifford & Michael I Jeffery. *How to Understand Statutes and By-Laws* (Toronto: Carswell, 1996).

Hogg, Peter W. *Constitutional Law of Canada*, 2013 student ed (Toronto: Carswell, 2013).

Sullivan, Ruth. *Statutory Interpretation*, 2d ed (Toronto: Irwin Law, 2007).

Sullivan, Ruth. *Sullivan on the Construction of Statutes*, 5th ed (Toronto: LexisNexis, 2008) [original and earlier editions by Elmer Driedger].

WEBSITES

Gateway Site for Canadian Legal Databases

Canadian Legal Information Institute (CanLII): <http://www.canlii.org>.

Canadian Legislature and Legislation Databases

Federal

Parliament of Canada: <http://www.parl.gc.ca>.

Justice Laws Website: <http://laws.justice.gc.ca/eng/>.

Alberta

Legislative Assembly of Alberta: <http://www.assembly.ab.ca>.

Alberta Laws: <http://www.qp.alberta.ca/Laws_Online.cfm>.

British Columbia

Legislative Assembly of British Columbia: <http://www.leg.bc.ca>.

British Columbia Laws: <http://www.bclaws.ca>.

Manitoba

Legislative Assembly of Manitoba: <http://www.gov.mb.ca/legislature>.

Manitoba Laws: <http://web2.gov.mb.ca/laws>.

New Brunswick

Legislative Assembly of New Brunswick: <http://www.gnb.ca/legis>.

New Brunswick Laws: <http://www.gnb.ca/0062/acts/index-e.asp>.

Newfoundland and Labrador

House of Assembly of Newfoundland and Labrador: <http://www.assembly.nl.ca>.

Newfoundland and Labrador Laws: <http://www.assembly.nl.ca/legislation>.

Nova Scotia

Nova Scotia Legislature: <http://nslegislature.ca>.

Nova Scotia Laws: <http://www.gov.ns.ca/just/acts.asp>.

Ontario

Legislative Assembly of Ontario: <http://www.ontla.on.ca>.

Ontario Laws: <http://www.e-laws.gov.on.ca>.

Prince Edward Island

Legislative Assembly of Prince Edward Island: <http://www.assembly.pe.ca>.

Prince Edward Island Laws: <http://www.gov.pe.ca/law/statutes>.

Quebec

Assemblée Nationale Québec: <http://www.assnat.qc.ca>.

Québec Laws: <http://www.justice.gouv.qc.ca/english/sites/lois/quebec-a.htm>.

Saskatchewan

Legislative Assembly of Saskatchewan:
<http://www.legassembly.sk.ca>.

Saskatchewan Laws: <http://www.qp.gov.sk.ca>.

Northwest Territories

Legislative Assembly of the Northwest Territories:
<http://www.assembly.gov.nt.ca>.

Northwest Territories Laws: <http://www.justice.gov.nt.ca/
Legislation/SearchLeg&Reg.shtml>.

Nunavut

Legislative Assembly of Nunavut:
<http://www.assembly.nu.ca>.

Nunavut Laws: <http://www.nucj.ca/library/amended.htm>.

Yukon

Legislative Assembly of the Yukon:
<http://www.assembly.gov.nt.ca>.

Yukon Laws: <http://www.justice.gov.yk.ca/legislation/
index.html>.

REVIEW QUESTIONS

1. What are the three branches of government in Canada?

2. List the four types of statutes in Canada.

3. Describe the process for enacting a federal statute, from the introduction of a new bill to the statute's coming into force.

4. What does it mean to say that a statute is "constitutionally entrenched"? Name and briefly describe three entrenched statutes under the Canadian Constitution.

5. What is POGG power?

6. What is a double-aspect law? How is conflict between federal and provincial double-aspect laws resolved?

7. What is the source of territorial power to make statutes?

8. Describe the "modern principle" of statutory interpretation.

9. What are the two main types of regulations? Briefly explain each.

10. Name two types of "quasi-legislative materials" and explain why it is important to have a working knowledge of them.

11. Describe the doctrine of parliamentary sovereignty and its relation to the separation-of-powers doctrine as applied in Canada.

EXERCISES

1. Research the website for the legislative assembly in your province or territory. Find and read all available information about the assembly's location, its members, and the legislative process it follows.

2. Section 37 of the *Constitution Act, 1867* states that the House of Commons shall

   > consist of three hundred and eight members of whom one hundred and six shall be elected for Ontario, seventy-five for Quebec, eleven for Nova Scotia, ten for New Brunswick, fourteen for Manitoba, thirty-six for British Columbia, four for Prince Edward Island, twenty-eight for Alberta, fourteen for Saskatchewan, seven for Newfoundland, one for the Yukon Territory, one for the Northwest Territories and one for Nunavut.

   These are the current membership and distribution numbers (as of the May 2011 federal election). When section 37 was first enacted in 1867, the total membership was 181. Parliament amended section 37 to reflect present-day circumstances. Start by reading section 37, including the footnotes at <http://www.emp.ca/ilc>, and then locate any other relevant sections in the Constitution to determine the following: (a) the source of Parliament's power to amend the Constitution this way unilaterally; and (b) the statute which effected the change.

3. Go to the Supreme Court of Canada judgments website (<http://scc-csc.lexum.org>) and type "division of powers" (in quotation marks) in the Decisions search field. Scan through the judgments to find one of interest to you, and then read the case to determine how the SCC resolved the argument about which level of government had jurisdiction to enact the challenged legislation.

4. Locate the following statutes online and provide full citations according to the format outlined in the appendix to this chapter:

   - *Identification of Criminals Act* (federal)
   - *Gaming and Liquor Act* (Alberta)
   - *Sale of Goods Act* (Ontario)
   - *Official Tree Act* (Nova Scotia)
   - *Legal Profession Act* (Yukon)

5. Visit the federal Justice Laws website (<http://laws-lois.justice.gc.ca>). Click the Consolidated Acts link under the Laws sidebar heading. Search through the alphabetical listing of statutes and choose one of interest to you. Locate as many of the structural features of statutes covered in this chapter (for example, the title, preamble, part headings, and different types of sections) as you can. Next, try to find sections that illustrate some of the grammatical rules described earlier, such as the use of "must" or "may," or "includes" versus "means."

6. Consider the idea of parliamentary sovereignty in the context of Canadian Confederation, and discuss whether you believe that legislative power considered in its totality *should* be limited (and if so, how any limits could be imposed). If not, consider whether legislative power is, in practical terms, sufficiently limited or too limited. Provide specific examples and reasons for your opinion.

6 The Executive: The Second Branch of Government

Canada's longest-serving prime minister, William Lyon Mackenzie King (centre), at a meeting with his Cabinet ministers in the Privy Council Chamber in the East Block of Parliament, in 1930.

After reading this chapter, you will understand:

- The nature of executive power
- The nature of the Canadian system of responsible government
- The key constitutional, conventional, common law, and statutory sources defining executive government in Canada

- The concept of Crown immunity
- The basic limits of executive power

It is the executive branch which is at the centre of government in Canada today. In practice, the executive is the controlling mind of the legislative branch.

Bernard W Funston & Eugene Meehan, *Canada's Constitutional Law*, 3d ed
(Toronto: Carswell, 2003) at 63

Introduction

The second branch of government is the **executive**. It is responsible for administering and implementing our laws. In Canada, it is common to refer to the executive branch simply as "the government," although it is, technically, only one of the three branches of government. In the US, it is more common to refer to the executive as "the administration," particularly in reference to the federal executive branch.

The formal head of state and chief executive in Canada is the British monarch—that is, the **Crown**. At the time of Confederation, this was Queen Victoria. Since 1952, it has been Queen Elizabeth II. The Queen "reigns" in Canada through her representatives: the governor general at the federal level, and the lieutenant governors at the provincial level. Legally, according to the Constitution, the Queen and her representatives wield executive power in Canada.

As we will see, however, this legal power has passed, by convention, to the Queen's representatives in council—that is, the federal and provincial Cabinets, who hold the *real* executive power. Most people examining our Constitution for the first time find it confusing that executive power, as spelled out in the *Constitution Act, 1867*, is so divorced from political reality, and that the Constitution contains no mention of the prime minister of Canada or the provincial premiers.

In this chapter, we will look first at our system of executive government, which is based on the system of "responsible government" that evolved over many centuries in the United Kingdom (UK). Next, we examine the various sources of executive power: the Constitution, convention, royal prerogative, common law, and ordinary statute. Then we consider the main principles of Crown immunity. Lastly, we take a brief look at the limits of executive power.

Responsible Government

Our system of government evolved in the UK over hundreds of years and is known as **responsible (or parliamentary) government**. This system was formally recognized and named in Great Britain in 1835. In 1848, Nova Scotia became the first colony in the British Empire to adopt the system. In 1867, with Confederation, responsible government became the system for the new country of Canada.

Three main features distinguish the system of responsible government:

1. a dual executive;
2. elected office—that is, members of the political executive must have elected seats in the legislature; and
3. a reliance on convention.

Dual Executive

Peter Hogg describes the system of responsible government in the Canadian context as follows:

> In a system of responsible government, there is a "dual executive," consisting of a formal head of state and a political head of state. The *formal* head of state for Canada is the Queen, but she is represented in Canada by the Governor General of Canada and the Lieutenant Governors of the provinces. … The *political* head of state for Canada is the Prime Minister, who is the leader of the party that commands a majority in the elected House of Commons. In each province, the equivalent of the Prime Minister is the Premier, who is the leader of the party that commands a majority in the elected Legislative Assembly.[1]

The Canadian system of executive government is unusual, then, in having both a formal executive (that is, the Queen and her representatives) *and* a political executive. It is the latter that exercises real administrative power.

Elected Office

Another distinctive feature of the Canadian system is that the members of the political executive must have elected seats in the legislature. (In the US system, by contrast, the members of the president's Cabinet need not be elected). The members of the political executive are "responsible" to the legislature in the sense that they must enjoy the confidence of the majority of the assembly. And the elected members of the assembly must, in turn, have the support of the people or risk losing their seats in the next election.

When one political party has a majority in a legislature, the *political* head of state will always enjoy the confidence of the majority, so long as party members vote as a block. The principles of responsible government become very clear when there is a minority government. In this case, the lead party requires cooperation from other parties if it is to have majority support for its key legislative initiatives. If that support is lost, the "government" falls and an election must be called.

There are exceptions to the requirement that the members of the executive must hold elected office. For instance, a new party leader is temporarily permitted to be without a seat in the legislature. But such a situation may last only until an election is arranged. If the leader subsequently fails to get elected, she would have to forfeit her position as a member of the executive. At the federal level, it is usual for the government leader in the Senate, which

---

1   Peter W Hogg, *Constitutional Law of Canada*, 2013 student ed (Toronto: Carswell, 2013) at 9-2.

FIGURE 6.1 Under the Constitution, Queen Elizabeth II, as the reigning British monarch, is the formal head of the executive government in Canada.

is an unelected position, to be part of the Cabinet. Less often, another Senate member may be appointed to Cabinet, usually to fill a representational void in one of the regions of the country. In 2006, for example, Prime Minister Harper appointed Senator Michael Fortier from the Montreal region to his Cabinet. At the time, there were no elected Conservative members from that region in his minority government.

The classic model of government from which ours is derived requires a separation of powers between the legislative, executive, and judicial branches. However, our system of responsible government, with its (by and large) elected Cabinet, significantly modifies this classic model. In Canada, the executive exercises significant control over the legislature, particularly when it holds a majority there. At the same time, the executive only maintains its authority while it has the support of the majority of the elected assembly. In the US, by contrast, the administration, federally or at the state level, is not part of the legislative branch. If there is a political divide between the two branches—if, for example, the administration is Democratic and the legislative branch is predominantly Republican—the administration will simply have less say in the legislative agenda.

Convention

Perhaps the most surprising aspect of responsible government is that, as Peter Hogg has said, "the rules which govern it are almost entirely 'conventional,' that is to say, they are not to be found in the ordinary legal sources of statute or decided cases."[2] When we say that the rules are "conventional," we mean that they are based on tradition and past practice rather than on principles set out in formal documents. Again, the US model serves as a contrast to the Canadian system of responsible government; in the US, the national system of government is clearly spelled out in its written Constitution.

It is the view of some people that responsible government does in fact have "legal" constitutional status in Canada. The basis for this view is the preamble clause to the *Constitution Act, 1867*, which states that we have "a Constitution similar in Principle to that of the United Kingdom." Some people take this preamble clause to mean that the rules of responsible government (though they may have been merely conventional in the UK) have become constitutionally entrenched in Canada.

The question whether the rules of responsible government are conventional or legal within the Canadian system would become pressing if we were ever faced with a constitutional crisis in this country, set off by the conventional rules not being followed. We would face such a crisis, for example, if a government refused to resign after losing a vote of confidence in the legislature. If the courts—that is, the third branch of government—were called upon to adjudicate the matter, their hands would be tied if the rules were conventional rather than legal. If, on the other hand, the rules were legally binding, the machinery of the state, represented by the courts, could be called upon to enforce them.

As we will see in the next section, such a crisis could be averted if the governor general exercised his or her legal power under the Constitution.

---

2 *Ibid* at 9-5.

Executive Power

What are the sources of executive power in Canada? Our constitutional legislation is one source, especially the *Constitution Act, 1867*. But this legislation does not fully define the extent of executive power in the Canadian government. Convention (that is, agreed-upon customary practice), too, plays an essential role in this area. Also relevant are certain statutory (federal, provincial, and territorial) and common law rules. All of these sources of executive power are examined in this section.

Constitutional Basis

The *Constitution Act, 1867* contains many of the key constitutional provisions dealing with formal executive power in Canada. These provisions include the following: all of Part III (sections 9–16), relating to federal executive power; and part of Part V (sections 58–68), concerning provincial executive power.

Peter Hogg summarizes these provisions as follows:

> [Section] 9 provides that the "executive government" of Canada is vested in "the Queen"; s. 10 contemplates that the Queen's powers may be exercised by a "Governor General"; and s. 11 establishes a "Queen's Privy Council for Canada" whose function is "to aid and advise in the government of Canada" and whose members are to be appointed and removed by the Governor General. …
>
> In each province, there is a "Lieutenant Governor" and an "Executive Council" with powers similar to those of the Governor General and Privy Council [ss. 58-68]. The Lieutenant Governors are appointed by the Governor General in Council (s. 58).[3]

The *Constitution Act, 1867* does not make it expressly clear who is responsible for appointing the **governor general**, but by implication it is the reigning British monarch, and this is the practice that is followed.

Early in our history, there was a question about the nature of the power of the **lieutenant governor**, given that he was an appointee of the Governor General in Council (that is, the federal Cabinet, often shortened to **Governor in Council**). Did he, like the governor general, represent the Crown, or was he a delegate of the Governor in Council? The answer to this question was significant. If the lieutenant governor represented the Crown, he would be vested with all the executive powers and prerogatives of the Crown in relation to provincial matters. However, if he were merely a delegate of the federal Governor in Council, his power would be limited to whatever that committee expressly delegated to him. In the latter case, all executive power in Canada would be federally controlled. The Judicial Committee of the Privy Council (that is, the British appeal court, not to be confused with Queen's Privy Council for Canada) ruled in 1892 that lieutenant governors are representatives of the Crown, not delegates of the federal Cabinet.

The governor general and lieutenant governors also play a part in the legislative process. Under sections 17 and 55 of the *Constitution Act, 1867*, the governor general (it could also be the Queen) is required to sign federal bills as a final formal step before they become law. Similarly, the lieutenant governors are required to sign provincial bills into law (section 90). This last step of the legislative process, which we described in Chapter 5, is known

---

3 *Ibid* at 9-6.

FIGURE 6.2 Governor General David Johnston signs bills into law in Parliament as Prime Minister Stephen Harper looks on (2011).

as "royal assent"; it is another example of how the Canadian system of government has modified the separation-of-powers doctrine with respect to the executive and legislative branches.

The *Constitution Act, 1982* includes an important constitutional provision relating to executive power. Section 44 of the Act provides that Parliament "may exclusively make laws amending the Constitution of Canada in relation to the executive government of Canada." So far, this amendment power has not been used.

On the surface, then, it looks like formal executive power in Canada resides with the British monarch and her representatives, with few restrictions on their power. For instance, a literal reading of section 55 of the *Constitution Act, 1867* would suggest that the Queen has unlimited discretion to refuse to sign into law any legislation she doesn't like and thereby to bring the law-making process in Canada to a halt.

Conventional Practice

As mentioned above, responsible government in Canada is primarily based on **convention**—that is, agreed-upon customary practice—rather than on principles explicitly set out in the Constitution. Knowing the conventional practice in this area is important because it qualifies—that is, modifies—the rules explicitly set out in the Constitution. The key conventions are set out below.

As far as the "legality" of constitutional conventions is concerned, the Supreme Court of Canada (SCC) ruled in the *Patriation Reference*, in 1981, that these conventions are not legally binding.[4] This case dealt with whether the federal executive could, without the unanimous consent of all provinces, approach the UK Parliament to request an amendment to the *British North America Act* (now known as the *Constitution Act, 1867*) that would affect provincial powers. There was a convention that such consent was required. The SCC held

---

4 *Reference re a Resolution to amend the Constitution*, [1981] 1 SCR 753 [*Patriation Reference*].

that because conventions are not legally binding, the federal government could ignore past practice without offending the law. In other words, it is not the role of the courts to enforce constitutional conventions. Whether there would be political consequences if such conventions were breached was another matter.

Are there any situations where the governor general or lieutenant governor (or the Queen, for that matter) could—acting independently, without the advice of Cabinet ministers appointed by the prime minister—exercise the legal power vested in them under the Constitution without offending conventional practice? When might this option seem compelling? Think of situations in which the confidence conventions were being rejected or ignored—if, for example:

- a government refused to resign after losing the confidence of the majority of members in the legislature;
- a prime minister or premier refused to resign after losing an election; or
- a prime minister or premier wanted to call an election immediately after one had just taken place, with the aim of increasing his or her party's number of seats.

Faced with these situations, the governor general or lieutenant governor (or the Queen) could, in theory, exercise her legal powers in opposition to the "political" executive. In other words, if the "political" executive government were ignoring the conventional constraints on its power, the Queen's representatives—the governor general or the lieutenant governor—could use their legal power to override the government. They could force a government to resign, call an election, or refuse to call an election. Has this ever happened?

There have been instances in our history where governors general and lieutenant governors have independently exercised their legal powers of reservation and disallowance (essentially refusing to grant royal assent) to prevent bills from becoming statutes. Their power to do so is set out in sections 55–57 and section 90 of the *Constitution Act, 1867*. But they have not exercised this power in over 50 years. Most likely, a modern convention has developed according to which the Queen's representatives are never to use these powers. This means that if a government wants to push through a truly objectionable law, it can do so, but then must answer for it not to the Queen's representatives but to the electorate alone (and perhaps to the courts, if the new law offends the Charter).

The political reality concerning executive power differs significantly from the legal reality spelled out in the Constitution. Does it matter that our administration operates according to a set of rules that are not legally enforceable? Does it matter that those with legal power—namely, the governor general and the lieutenant governor—are expected not to use it except as directed by political leaders? Perhaps not, as long as everyone involved respects and accepts the system. So far, this has been the case in Canada. But there is no guarantee that it will always be the case. Arguably, in times of extreme political uncertainty, rules based on convention are less stable than those enshrined in law.

Key Conventions

The following are conventions relating to the federal executive in the Canadian political system:

- *Prime minister.* The political executive is headed by the leader of the political party that controls the majority of Parliament (either by way of an outright party majority or, in the case of a minority government, by way of a coalition with other parties)—namely, the **prime minister**.

- *Appointment of the governor general.* Section 10 of the *Constitution Act, 1867* describes the office of the governor general, who is appointed by the Queen. By convention, the Queen now appoints the person nominated by the prime minister.
- *Cabinet.* Section 11 provides that the governor general has the aid and advice of the **Queen's Privy Council for Canada**, referred to more informally as the Privy Council. By convention, the key members of the Privy Council are the Cabinet ministers appointed by the prime minister. The Cabinet is the part of the Privy Council which, under the direction of the prime minister, has members who currently sit as members of Parliament. There are other members of the Privy Council, including former ministers of government, whose status is nominal rather than practical; they have no real influence. It is extremely rare for the entire Privy Council to meet, and when it does it is usually for ceremonial purposes. As noted above, the Governor General in Council is generally taken to refer to the federal Cabinet and is often shortened to Governor in Council. When legislation refers to Governor General in Council or Governor in Council, it means the federal Cabinet.
- *Political and legislative agenda.* The prime minister takes the lead in setting the government's agenda as well as the composition, organization, and procedures of Cabinet. By convention, the prime minister appoints members of Cabinet from each province of Canada.
- *Ministerial responsibility.* Although the government stands or falls as one, individual ministers are responsible in the sense that each is the executive head of his portfolio and must take responsibility not only for his own actions but for those of his subordinates within the Ministry. Ministers are also required to answer to Cabinet and to Parliament for their activities within the Ministry.
- *Confidence convention.* Arguably, the most important convention of all is the **confidence convention**. If the government loses the support of the majority of the elected representatives in the House of Commons, the confidence convention requires the government to resign and, if a new government cannot be formed, it must call an election.

Most of these conventions apply, with certain modifications, to the provinces (see Figure 6.3). The political head provincially is the **premier**. The lieutenant governor is appointed by the governor general under the Constitution, but, by convention, the governor general follows the recommendation of the premier. The **Lieutenant Governor in Council** is the official name for the provincial Cabinet. The provincial Executive Councils, as they are referred to in Part V of the *Constitution Act, 1867*, are made up exclusively of current Cabinet ministers; there are no "outsiders" as there are with the federal Privy Council.

Similar conventions apply in the Yukon and the Northwest Territories. Although, as we saw in Chapter 5, the territories are federal "dependencies," their executive governments operate much as the provincial ones do. The federal government appoints a **commissioner** who acts as the formal head of the territorial executive government. The **Commissioner in Executive Council** is the official name for a territorial Cabinet. The system is different in Nunavut; it operates according to a system of consensus democracy, not responsible government, and it has no political parties.

Common Law and Royal Prerogative

As Chapter 2 explained, the power of the British Crown to legislate by decree or otherwise was limited by the *Magna Carta* and was finally taken over completely by Parliament when

FIGURE 6.3 Executive and legislative government in Canada

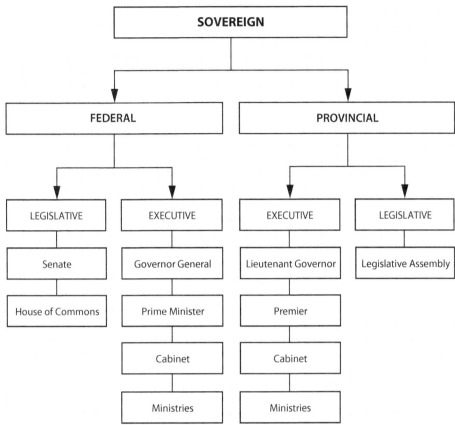

the English Bill of Rights (1689) was passed. Similarly, the Crown lost the right to adjudicate disputes, criminal and civil, early in its legal history. This was confirmed in the 1607 *Case of Prohibitions*, in which Chief Justice Edward Coke stated the following for the court: "[No] King after the Conquest assumed to himself to give any judgment in any cause whatsoever, which concerned the administration of justice within this realm, but these were solely determined in the Courts of Justice."[5]

However, the Crown had long exercised *executive* authority. The expression **royal prerogative** refers to one of the sources of the Crown's executive authority. Royal prerogative is exercised through various kinds of orders, which have different names depending on the context. One of them is the **royal proclamation**. This is a formal order concerning some executive action, such as declaring war, and it announces this action to subjects of the realm. For example, the Royal Proclamation of 1763, issued by King George III after the end of the Seven Years War, was meant to organize Great Britain's new North American empire and to stabilize relations with North American Aboriginals.

Another class of order, expressing the royal prerogative in a more limited way, consists of **letters patent**. These are usually orders that establish rights, titles, or offices of particular

5   See *Prohibitions del Roy*, [1607] EWHC KB J23, 12 Co Rep 63, 77 ER 1342 [*Case of Prohibitions*].

persons or corporations. In 1947, for example, King George VI officially constituted the office of the governor general in Canada by letters patent—although the office had already been constituted, by implication, under the terms of the *Constitution Act, 1867*.

The Crown's ability to *independently* exercise prerogative power survived much longer than its adjudicative and legislative powers. But this independent prerogative power, too, came to be curtailed as responsible government took hold in the 1700s. Since then, it has been exercised only on the advice of the prime minister and Cabinet (with a few exceptions, as in matters relating to the royal family itself).

The common law courts have defined the exact nature and extent of the Crown's prerogative. It is therefore a part of the common law and not a separate source of law. As Peter Hogg writes,

> The royal prerogative consists of the powers and privileges accorded by the common law to the Crown. Dicey described it as "the residue of discretionary or arbitrary authority, which at any given time is left in the hands of the Crown." The prerogative is a branch of the common law, because it is the decisions of the courts which have determined its existence and extent.[6]

In Canada, royal prerogative survives and is exercised by the federal and provincial Cabinets, or—to give these bodies their more formal titles—by the Governor General in Council (or Governor in Council) and the Lieutenant Governors in Council. As mentioned above, even though the lieutenant governors are appointed by the governor general, they are also representatives of the Crown. Because we are a federation, the Crown's executive authority is split between

1. the federal Crown (or Crown in right of Canada), which exercises prerogative in relation to matters under its legislative authority; and
2. the provincial Crown (or Crown in right of Alberta and other provinces), which exercises prerogative in relation to matters under its legislative authority.

For examples of prerogative power, see Box 6.1.

Prerogative Power Today

Many executive actions that were at one time authorized by prerogative power are now authorized by statute. For example, the power to confer honours such as the Queen's Counsel (QC) designation on lawyers (usually conferred by the provincial Crown) is now based on legislation. The *Queen's Counsel Act* in BC, for example, contains the following provision:

> 2(1) On the recommendation of the Attorney General, the Lieutenant Governor in Council, by letters patent under the Great Seal, may appoint, from among the members of the Bar of British Columbia, Provincial officers under the names of Her Majesty's Counsel learned in the law for the Province of British Columbia.[7]

This general trend toward statutory authority has reduced the actual scope of prerogative power. Even where a general prerogative power continues to exist, as in the case of the royal prerogative of mercy (confirmed in section 749 of the *Criminal Code*), statutes may

---

6 Hogg, *supra* note 1 at 1-18.

7 *Queen's Counsel Act*, RSBC 1996, c 393, s 2(1).

BOX 6.1

Examples of Prerogative Power

A well-known example of prerogative power is the federal Crown's power to grant mercy in criminal cases. The *Criminal Code* provides that nothing in the Code "in any manner limits or affects Her Majesty's royal prerogative of mercy." * Although its exact bounds are not entirely clear, the royal prerogative of mercy (RPM) is considered a far-reaching power that includes all forms of clemency, from free pardons (total expungement of a conviction together with its record) to conditional pardons (expungement, but with the record kept) to the remission or reduction of sentences. The RPM is traditionally associated with the commutation of a death sentence to prison time—an instance of RPM that no longer applies in Canada because we abolished the death penalty in 1976.

Some other areas where prerogative power is exercised, as Hogg has noted, include the following:

- conduct of foreign affairs, including making treaties;
- declarations of war;
- appointment of the prime minister and other ministers;
- issuance of passports; and
- creation of Indian reserves.[†]

The power to appoint provincial premiers and ministers is an example of the provincial Crown's prerogative power.

*   *Criminal Code*, RSC 1985, c C-46, s 749.

†   Peter W Hogg, *Constitutional Law of Canada*, 2013 student ed (Toronto: Carswell, 2013) at 1-20.

---

provide authority in the same area. For example, sections 748 and 748.1 of the *Criminal Code* deal with pardons and remissions of fines and forfeitures. Such legislative duplication reduces the need to resort to prerogative power.

The common law now defines in positive terms the extent of royal prerogative; in other words, it provides rules authorizing Crown conduct. It has also developed "negative" rules—that is, rules that impose limits both on others' conduct that affects the Crown and on Crown conduct that affects others. In particular, the courts have developed rules relating to Crown immunity (see below) and, on the other side of the coin, rules imposing limits on executive action (the subject of the final section of this chapter).

Finally, it should be noted that the common law relating to executive power is subject to change by the appropriate legislative authority. As noted above, some instances of royal prerogative have been changed, replaced, or confirmed by statutory rules.

Statute

The main source of executive power today is statutory law. Federal, provincial, and territorial statutes assign specific executive powers to their respective governments.

Most ministries or departments have their own statutes that define, among other things, the powers and duties of the responsible minister. For example, the *Department of Health Act* and the *Department of the Environment Act* grant the federal minister of health and the minister of the environment, respectively, specific executive authority. The pattern is the same at the provincial and territorial levels. For example, Ontario's *Ministry of Energy Act* grants specific administrative powers to the Ontario minister of energy; Saskatchewan's *Department of Social Services Act* gives such powers to the Saskatchewan minister of social services; and the Yukon *Education Act* empowers the Yukon minister of education. There are many statutes of this kind.

The various powers granted to ministers by these various federal, provincial, and territorial statutes include the authority

- to enter into contracts to facilitate ministry business,
- to hire and manage staff, and
- to pursue actions to enforce the liabilities of others.

Sometimes, when it comes to particular matters over which the responsible minister has general administrative control, the legislation will grant executive power to the entire Cabinet, or impose a Cabinet approval requirement. In BC, for example, the *Ministry of Environment Act* requires the minister of the environment to gain Cabinet approval before entering into agreements with other provincial governments or with the federal government.[8]

There are many statutes creating institutions under the control of the executive government. For example, there are statutes that authorize

- setting up and regulating the armed forces and the national security service (the Canadian Security Intelligence Service, or CSIS);
- setting up and regulating law enforcement agencies (such as the Royal Canadian Mounted Police, or RCMP, and the Canada Border Services Agency, or CBSA); and
- setting up administrative boards and tribunals to regulate almost every area of society, from energy to human rights to transportation.

Finally, where statutes come into force by proclamation, the Cabinet is almost always given the power to fix the date of their coming into force. This makes sense, given that Cabinet is well informed about new legislation and receives regular reports about it. The proclamation language for federal statutes is that the Act comes into force "by order of the Governor in Council."

The proclamation language for provincial and territorial statutes is less settled. It might say that the Act commences "by order of the Lieutenant Governor in Council," "by regulation of the Lieutenant Governor in Council," or "by proclamation." Yukon legislation states that legislation comes into force on dates fixed "by the Commissioner in Executive Council." In the Northwest Territories and Nunavut, the commissioner for the territory, not Cabinet, is assigned the administrative power to proclaim statutes in force.

In modern times, statutory law has become the main source of executive authority. In other words, most day-to-day executive power finds its basis in legislation that confers authority on Cabinets and individual ministers.

Crown Immunity

Crown immunity is sometimes seen as part of the law of royal prerogative. It includes the Crown's immunity from liability as well as any privileges and presumptions that operate in favour of the Crown. It is a complicated area, and a detailed examination of all the issues involved in it is beyond the scope of this text (for example, we do not discuss Crown immunity from criminal liability and its limits). However, a basic awareness of the area is important.

---

8 *Ministry of Environment Act*, RSBC 1996, c 299, s 6.

To Whom It Applies

Crown immunity in Canada today, when it does apply, applies to the federal Crown and to the provincial Crown (that is, the federal and provincial Cabinets) and also to agents of the Crown. Not all government bodies or organizations are "agents" of the Crown. There are three factors determining which of them meet this qualification:

1. the legislation that constitutes (and defines) them,
2. the degree of authority granted to the organization by Cabinet, and
3. the degree of Cabinet's control over the organization.

Generally speaking, the more closely the organization is associated with and controlled by Cabinet, the more likely it is to qualify as a Crown agency and to be afforded the same protections as the Crown. But there are many government agencies that operate at arm's length from the executive, are not considered agents of the Crown, and are not accorded the same privileges.[9]

There are three main forms of Crown immunity:

1. Crown privilege,
2. the presumption against legislation applying to the Crown, and
3. Crown immunity in civil cases.

Crown Privilege

Crown privilege, also known as "public interest immunity," is an evidentiary rule that originates in common law. It permits the Crown to claim that evidence relevant to the case at hand—evidence that ordinarily would have to be disclosed—is privileged on the ground that its disclosure would adversely affect some matter of public interest. Such privileged areas might include, for example, matters of national security or defence, and certain Cabinet communications.

Federally, the *Canada Evidence Act* now codifies the rules relating to public interest immunity, so Crown privilege no longer needs to be claimed at common law.[10] At the provincial level, Crown privilege exists but it is qualified according to the common law, statutory rules, and combinations of the two. Both under the common law and statutory rules, Crown privilege is restricted and involves a balancing of interests—on the one hand, the interest of resolving disputes fairly through full disclosure; and, on the other hand, the interest of protecting the state from undue harm by disclosure.

---

9 It should also be noted that Crown corporations are not necessarily Crown *agents*. At the federal level, for example, Atomic Energy of Canada Limited (AECL), Canada Post Corporation, the Canadian Broadcasting Corporation (CBC), and the Royal Canadian Mint—along with over 20 other Crown corporations—*are* Crown agents. But the Bank of Canada, the Canada Pension Plan Investment Board, and VIA Rail, among others, are not. Each year, the Treasury Board's *Annual Report to Parliament: Crown Corporations and Other Corporate Interests of Canada* details the operations of the various federal corporations and organizations, and it includes their Crown agency status. Similarly, at the provincial and territorial levels, government corporations and institutions may or may not have Crown agency status.

10 RSC 1985, c C-5, ss 37-39.

Presumption Against Legislation Applying to the Crown

At common law, there is a presumption against legislation applying to the Crown. This presumption exists unless the legislation itself expresses or clearly implies that it does in fact apply to the Crown. This common law presumption has been confirmed by section 17 of the federal *Interpretation Act*, which states the following: "No enactment is binding on Her Majesty or affects Her Majesty or Her Majesty's rights or prerogatives in any manner, except as mentioned or referred to in the enactment."[11] Most provinces contain statutes with equivalent provisions. The two exceptions are British Columbia and Prince Edward Island, which have removed the presumption, thus putting the government in these provinces on an equal footing with other people.[12] In other words, legislation in British Columbia and Prince Edward Island is presumed to apply to the government unless the legislation states otherwise.

Crown Immunity in Civil Cases

The Crown has always been able to enter into contracts itself and to appoint agents to do so on its behalf. The general rules of contract apply to the Crown; when it enters into a contract, it is subject to the same rights and liabilities as an ordinary person.

However, at common law, while the Crown could sue others in tort, in the past it was immune from tortious liability to others. Federal and provincial legislation has now removed this common law immunity. The federal and provincial governments—in other words, the federal Crown and the Crown "in right of all the provinces"—can now be sued in tort. However, the relevant legislation needs to be examined carefully because there are still some limitations on the Crown's liability, particularly in the area of remedies. Often, for instance, it is not possible to get injunctive relief against the Crown—that is, an order requiring the Crown to perform or refrain from performing a certain act (other than an order to pay a judgment for money).

Limits of Executive Influence

As noted in the discussion of responsible government, the separation-of-powers doctrine is modified under the Anglo-Canadian system. The modification consists in the fact that, in our system, the executive branch is made up of elected members of the legislature who exert control over the majority of members. The executive in our system therefore controls the legislature with its majority.

It is important to remember that the reverse is also true; if the executive loses majority control, the legislature controls the executive. Majority control can be lost if a minority government loses the support of its coalition partners, or if a party with a majority loses control of its own members. In these situations, the legislature exercises its ultimate authority by forcing the government to resign.

Assuming, however, that the executive branch has clear control of the legislature, there are still limits to its power. In this section, we look at the two main kinds of limits.

---

11   RSC 1985, c I-21, s 17.

12   See *Interpretation Act*, RSBC 1996, c 238, s 14, and *Interpretation Act*, RSPEI 1988, c I-8, s 14.

Separation-of-Powers Limits

The separation of the legislative and executive branches of government is, as we have seen, not absolute in Canada; it is qualified. Nonetheless, there are boundaries that cannot be crossed. For instance, legislators—that is, elected representatives—cannot act as administrators unless they have been given the authority to do so. And members of the executive cannot overstep the bounds of their appointed executive authority. A minister, for example, who, under a statute, has been assigned executive authority in relation to a particular matter must not exceed the stated bounds of that authority.

The separation of powers between the legislative and executive branches may be murky at times in the Canadian system. But the separation between the executive and judicial branches is clear. It becomes especially clear when a government official attempts to directly influence the outcome of a case before the courts. Politicians who do this risk ending their careers. Perhaps the most famous example of such political interference is the so-called Judges Affair (see Box 6.2).

According to Peter Russell, the **principle of non-interference** is a principle based on convention; therefore, it is a principle of political rather of than legal consequence.[13] However, the fact that a minister who attempts to influence a judge might be cited for contempt of court suggests that the legal consequences for violating the principle of non-interference are real. This principle is an aspect of judicial independence; it concerns the administrative independence of the courts. And the SCC has held that judicial independence has become legally entrenched by way of the preamble clause to the *Constitution Act, 1867*, which states that we have "a Constitution similar in Principle to that of the United Kingdom." Judicial independence and its constitutional protection are described in more detail in Chapter 7.

Although the existence of the principle of non-interference is clear, its exact *scope*—and that of judicial independence generally—is not. Certain forms of interference clearly offend the principle. For example, politicians must not communicate with judges concerning matters before them. But other forms of interference are not so clear. For instance, it was at one time considered unacceptable for a politician to criticize court judgments publicly. As seen in Box 6.2, André Ouellet was cited for contempt after publicly criticizing Justice Mackay's decision. Since then, however, there have been no similar contempt citations despite several instances of politicians' criticizing judgments and the judicial process.

The Canadian judicial system's increased tolerance for public criticism by politicians has several possible causes. Legal scholars have cited the following:

- the rise of the "rights culture,"
- the value placed on freedom of expression,
- the increasing involvement of the courts in social policy by way of Charter decisions (and the invitation to criticism that comes with such involvement),
- the "rise of neo-conservative (and often populist) ideology" and the "decline of deference" within society toward traditional institutions.[14]

---

13 Peter Russell, *The Judiciary in Canada: The Third Branch of Government* (Toronto: McGraw-Hill Ryerson, 1987) at 78.

14 See Lori Hausegger, Matthew Hennigar & Troy Riddell, *Canadian Courts: Law, Politics, and Process* (Toronto: Oxford University Press, 2009) at 204; and Neil Nevitte, *The Decline of Deference: Canadian Value Change in Cross National Perspective* (Peterborough, Ont: Broadview Press, 1996).

BOX 6.2

The Judges Affair of 1976

In December 1975, a federal Cabinet minister in the Trudeau government, André Ouellet, was cited by Justice Kenneth Mackay of the Quebec Superior Court for contempt when Ouellet criticized Justice Mackay for acquitting three companies that had been charged with price fixing. In the months that followed the citation, other instances of interference with the judicial process came to light, and material in support was placed before the House of Commons in March 1976. Three occurrences were noted:

- In 1969, Marc Lalonde, who was at the time an official with the Prime Minister's Office, called on Justice Mackay at his home concerning the trial of three persons from Trinidad who had been charged with property damage at a university. Lalonde had received information from the High Commission for Canada in Trinidad and was concerned that a conviction could lead to riots in Trinidad.

- 1n 1971, Jean Chrétien, then minister of Indian Affairs and Northern Development, telephoned Justice Aronovitch about a bankruptcy case in his constituency on behalf of some unemployed persons who were affected by the proceedings.

- Bud Drury, minister of public works, telephoned Justice Hugessen of the Quebec Superior Court, who was hearing the Ouellet contempt proceedings, to ask if an apology

from Ouellet would end the proceedings. Justice Hugessen refused to make any commitments on that point, and in the end Ouellet's contempt citation was upheld.

No firings or resignations actually resulted from these three disclosures. Bud Drury did offer his resignation but Trudeau refused it. Ouellet resigned but gave reasons other than the contempt citation.

In March 1976, however, Prime Minister Trudeau issued the following statement in the House of Commons:

> In future no member of the Cabinet may communicate with members of the judiciary concerning any matter which they have before them in the judicial capacities, except through the minister of justice, his duly authorized officials, or counsel acting for him.

This whole affair came to be known as the Judges Affair. After Trudeau issued this statement, other statements, similar in spirit, were issued in provincial assemblies. In the time since this affair, a number of ministers have been forced to resign where there was evidence of their communicating directly with judges concerning cases before them.

Source: Peter Russell, *The Judiciary in Canada: The Third Branch of Government* (Toronto: McGraw-Hill Ryerson, 1987) at 78-81.

As a final point, it should be noted that the federal and provincial governments recognize the non-interference principle as applying not only to courts but also to administrative tribunals that are exercising quasi-judicial functions. A recent guide for ministers contained the following directive concerning tribunals of this sort:

> Parliament's intention to lessen or remove political influence in decision making in such areas underlies the principle that Ministers should not intervene with administrative or "quasi-judicial" tribunals on any matter that requires a decision *in their quasi-judicial capacity*.[15]

Civil Liberties Limits

The area of civil liberties is the subject of Chapter 8, but we mention it here briefly concerning its relationship to executive power and the limits on that power.

---

15   *Accountable Government: A Guide for Ministers and Ministers of State 2011* (Ottawa: Privy Council Office, 2011) Annex H at 67.

At common law, the starting point is that basic freedoms, such as freedom of expression and freedom of movement, exist until they are taken away by law. The doctrine of parliamentary sovereignty allows the legislative branch to restrict or eliminate these freedoms. But the executive branch in itself has no power, except under legislative authority, to restrict these freedoms.

With the increasing regulation of society, more administrative power has been given to governments. The common law has responded by developing rules that protect civil liberties where they haven't been clearly taken away by law. Two examples will serve to illustrate this, the first related to police power and the second to administrative agencies.

Police forces are agents of the executive branch and have various powers to arrest individuals. At common law (and now by ordinary legislation and the Charter), the police are required to give individuals reasons for their being arrested. This requirement helps to protect the individual against the arbitrary use of power.

In the area of administrative agencies, the common law has responded similarly. The *Roncarelli* case, which we discussed in Chapter 1, showed how the courts would not permit discretionary executive power to be used arbitrarily. They determined that the discretion to grant or refuse to grant a liquor licence could only be based on the legislative policies set out in the relevant statute, and not on extraneous factors. And, more generally, the courts have held that any administrative action affecting a person's interests is reviewable if it doesn't satisfy certain rules of fairness and if it doesn't permit that person the "right to know the case to be met and the right to respond."[16]

In addition to common law rules, there is legislation—most notably, the *Canadian Bill of Rights* and the constitutionally entrenched Charter—to curtail executive action and protect civil liberties. These statutes and others are examined in Chapter 8.

---

16 See Sara Blake, *Administrative Law in Canada*, 4th ed (Toronto: LexisNexis Canada, 2006) ch 2.5 and *Nicholson v Haldimand-Norfolk Regional Police Commissioners*, [1979] 1 SCR 311.

CHAPTER SUMMARY

The formal head of state in Canada is the British monarch, Queen Elizabeth II. Her official representative at the federal level is the governor general and, at the provincial level, the lieutenant governors. By convention, her representatives in council, the Governor in Council (the federal Cabinet) and the Lieutenant Governors in Council (the provincial Cabinets), exercise the executive power that is formally vested in her under the Constitution.

The executive branch of government is charged with implementing and enforcing the law. Under the classic separation-of-powers doctrine, the executive branch would operate independently of the legislative branch, as it does in the United States. But under the Anglo-Canadian system of responsible government, the executive branch is composed of elected members of the legislature. Federally, the political party that controls the majority of the House of Commons chooses its leader. This leader becomes the prime minister of Canada and in turn chooses his or her Cabinet, primarily from the House of Commons. Provincially, the political party that controls the majority of the Legislative Assembly chooses its leader, who becomes the premier of the province and who similarly chooses a Cabinet. Executive governments that lose the support of the majority of the relevant legislature must resign. In that sense, the prime minister or premier and his or her Cabinets are accountable or "responsible" to the elected assembly.

Executive power comes from a variety of sources: constitutional rules, convention, common law and royal prerogative, and statutory law. Most of the constitutional rules are located in the *Constitution Act, 1867*, and most of them are followed in form only. The *real* basis of executive power is political and democratic convention—that is, agreed-upon customary tradition. It is the federal Cabinet ("the Crown in right of Canada") and the provincial Cabinets ("the Crown in

right of the provinces") who hold that power as "advisors" to Her Majesty's representatives. The federal Cabinet administers federal law and the provincial Cabinets administer provincial law.

Royal prerogative, rooted in the common law, is also a source of some executive power. Examples of royal prerogative are the power to conduct foreign affairs and the power to issue passports. Most of the surviving instances of royal prerogative relate to matters within the jurisdiction of the federal Crown. The main source of executive power is statutory law. Federal and provincial statutes define many of the day-to-day powers and duties of executive government.

Because of the Crown's special status and because of the power and responsibility it must continuously exercise, the common law has developed a number of "immunities" to protect the Crown and its agents (that is, the executive government). These immunities have traditionally included the following: a Crown privilege to hold back evidence that would harm the public interest; a presumption in the Crown's favour that legislation does not apply to it unless the legislation contains a clear indication otherwise; and, most importantly, immunity from liability in tort. This last immunity has been significantly modified by statute. Today, in fact, the federal government and all the provincial governments have given up this protection to varying degrees.

Finally, the Crown's practical need to maintain its status and power—things that it needs in order to govern effectively—justifies the principle of Crown immunity (to the extent that it still exists). And it is the potential for abuse *by* the Crown that justifies the various limits that have been placed on its power. Two of the most important of these limits today are the requirements that executive governments not interfere with judicial proceedings and that they adhere to various standards prescribed by law relating to civil liberties.

KEY TERMS

commissioner federally appointed official who is the formal head of the territorial executive government *(p. 154)*

Commissioner in Executive Council official name for a territorial Cabinet *(p. 154)*

confidence convention convention requiring the government to resign if it loses the support of the majority of the elected representatives in the House of Commons and, if a new government cannot be formed, to call an election *(p. 154)*

convention established and traditional "rules" on which our system of responsible government is based and which qualify many of the rules of government set out in constitutional legislation such as the *Constitution Act, 1867*, but which are not, technically, legally binding *(p. 152)*

Crown the sovereign (currently the Queen), whose authority in Canada has been formally delegated to the governor general (federally) and to the lieutenant governor (provincially), but is actually exercised by the executive branch of government *(p. 148)*

Crown immunity covering term for the various protections afforded the Crown, including Crown privilege, the presumptions of legislation not applying to the Crown, and (formerly) immunity from tortious liability *(p. 158)*

Crown privilege aspect of Crown immunity that permits the Crown to claim that evidence is privileged on the ground that its disclosure would adversely affect some matter of public interest *(p. 159)*

executive the branch of government that is responsible for administering or implementing the laws in Canada and whose authority, in this country, is divided between the federal, provincial, and territorial governments based on the division of legislative authority under the Constitution *(p. 148)*

governor general Queen's representative in Canada, formally authorized to exercise her powers as head of the executive government in Canada, but who, by convention, exercises these powers only on the advice of the prime minister and federal Cabinet *(p. 151)*

Governor in Council official name for the federal Cabinet *(p. 151)*

letters patent orders, based on royal prerogative, that establish rights, titles, or offices of particular persons or corporations *(p. 155)*

lieutenant governor formal head of the provincial executive government who, by convention, exercises executive power on the advice of the provincial premier and Cabinet *(p. 151)*

Lieutenant Governor in Council official name for a provincial Cabinet *(p. 154)*

premier the political head of a provincial or territorial government who leads the party with control of the majority in the Legislative Assembly (in Nunavut, there are no political parties but the premier must command the support of the majority in the Assembly) *(p. 154)*

prime minister the political head of state in Canada who leads the party with control of the majority of in the House of Commons *(p. 153)*

principle of non-interference the convention prohibiting direct interference by politicians with court proceedings *(p. 161)*

Queen's Privy Council for Canada formal advisory council of the governor general, the active portion of which consists of the federal Cabinet *(p. 154)*

responsible (or parliamentary) government system of government in which the members of the executive branch are drawn from the elected members of the legislative branch and in which their power continues only so long as they enjoy the support of the majority in the legislature *(p. 148)*

royal prerogative powers and privileges given by the common law to the Crown; a source of limited executive power *(p. 155)*

royal proclamation public announcement of a formal order concerning some executive action based on royal prerogative, such as a declaration of war *(p. 155)*

FURTHER READING

BOOKS

Aucoin, Peter, Jennifer Smith & Geoff Dinsdale. *Responsible Government: Clarifying Essentials, Dispelling Myths and Exploring Change* (Ottawa: Canadian Centre for Management Development, 2004). <http://publications.gc.ca/collections/Collection/SC94-107-2004E.pdf>.

Bernier, Luc, Keith Brownsey & Michael Howlett, eds. *Executive Styles in Canada: Cabinet Structures and Leadership Practices in Canadian Government* (Toronto: University of Toronto Press, 2005).

Government of Canada. *Accountable Government: A Guide for Ministers and Ministers of State 2011* (Ottawa: Privy Council Office, 2011). <http://pm.gc.ca/grfx/docs/guidemin_e.pdf>.

Heard, Andrew. *Canadian Constitutional Conventions: The Marriage of Law and Politics*, 2d ed (Don Mills, Ont: Oxford University Press, 2014).

Hogg, Peter W. *Constitutional Law of Canada*, 2013 student ed (Toronto: Carswell, 2013), ch 9.

MacKinnon, Frank. *The Crown in Canada* (Calgary: McClelland & Stewart West, 1976).

Saywell, John T. *The Office of Lieutenant-Governor* (Toronto: Copp Clark Pitman, 1986).

Seidle, FL & Louis Massicotte, eds. *Taking Stock of 150 Years of Responsible Government in Canada* (Ottawa: Canadian Study of Parliament Group, 1999). <http://www.studyparliament.ca/English/pdf/ongoing/1999_b_E.pdf>.

WEBSITES

Gateway Site for Canadian Legal Databases

Canadian Legal Information Institute (CanLII): <http://www.canlii.org>.

Canadian Government Databases

Federal Government: <http://www.canada.gc.ca>.

Alberta Government: <http://alberta.ca>.

British Columbia Government: <http://www2.gov.bc.ca>.

Manitoba Government: <http://www.gov.mb.ca>.

New Brunswick Government: <http://www2.gnb.ca>.

Newfoundland and Labrador Government: <http://www.gov.nl.ca>.

Nova Scotia Government: <http://www.gov.ns.ca>.

Ontario Government: <http://www.ontario.ca>.

Prince Edward Island Government: <http://www.gov.pe.ca>.

Quebec Government: <http://www.gouv.qc.ca>.

Saskatchewan Government: <http://www.gov.sk.ca>.

Northwest Territories Government: <http://www.gov.nt.ca>.

Nunavut Government: <http://www.gov.nu.ca>.

Yukon Government: <http://www.gov.yk.ca>.

REVIEW QUESTIONS

1. What is the role of the executive branch of government?

2. Who is the formal head of state in Canada?

3. Briefly describe how the system of responsible government modifies the separation-of-powers doctrine.

4. Why is it important to read the provisions of the *Constitution Act, 1867* in light of convention? Describe at least three specific situations to support your answer.

5. Name three instances where the federal Crown could invoke royal prerogative as the basis of executive action.

6. What is the source of power for most executive authority in Canada today?

7. How is executive authority divided between the federal and provincial governments?

8. Name and describe three examples of Crown immunity.

9. What is a Crown agent?

10. What are the principle limits on executive power?

EXERCISES

1. In your opinion, is having a *dual* executive, with a formal and a political head of state, a good system or a bad system? Support your answer with specific reasons. If you think the system should be changed, indicate how.

2. For your province or territory, find the statute that assigns specific executive authority to the provincial or territorial minister of health. Use the websites listed under Further Reading.

3. Although executive (and legislative) power is divided in Canada, there are certain areas—for example, education, the environment, and tourism—in which the federal and provincial/territorial governments cooperate in implementing laws, either because of jurisdictional overlap or because of the availability of federal funding. Choose one of the areas in which such cooperation occurs and research *how* the federal government and your regional government have together implemented the program that has resulted. Consider, for example, the funding and administrative structures that have been used.

4. Prepare an argument setting out why you think the protection afforded the Crown under existing Crown immunity rules is adequate or inadequate. Provide at least three reasons to support your argument.

5. While it is clear that politicians cannot interfere directly with the judicial process, it is less clear whether they can criticize judges and judgments after proceedings have been concluded. Do you believe that politicians should be able to call into question the judicial process in this way? Should it depend on what type of case is involved? In your answer, refer to the separation-of-powers doctrine and provide specific reasons and examples (hypothetical or real) for your position.

7 The Judiciary: The Third Branch of Government

The Supreme Court Building in Ottawa, designed by Ernest Cormier, is a national landmark and a symbol of the Canadian justice system. Begun in 1938, it is constructed from granite and includes a chateau-style copper roof.

After reading this chapter, you will understand:

- The role of the judiciary in Canada
- The constitutional basis of the Canadian court system
- How the Canadian court system is organized and how the different types and levels of courts function, from the Supreme Court of Canada to the military courts
- How the doctrine of precedent operates within the Canadian court system

- How judges are appointed to the various types of courts
- How the open court principle and the principle of judicial independence inform the Canadian judicial system
- How judgments are structured and reported
- How to brief cases and how to cite them

Adjudication, the resolution of disputes through a decision of a court of law, achieves an authoritative settling of issues between the parties, a definitive determination of their legal rights and obligations, and, ideally, a result that accords with justice.

Patrick Fitzgerald, Barry Wright & Vincent Kazmierski,
Looking at Law: Canada's Legal System, 6th ed
(Markham, Ont: LexisNexis, 2010) at 107

Courts are the operating rooms of the legal system: theatres where preparation and expertise are brought to bear in critical moments of questioning and arguing, where decisions sometimes have to be made on the fly, where blood sometimes flows—at least metaphorically.

Jessie J Horner,
Canadian Law and the Canadian Legal System
(Toronto: Pearson, 2007) at 238

Introduction

The third branch of government is the judiciary. Judges exercise their power by rendering decisions in our country's courts. A **court** is a state-sanctioned forum where disputes between opposing litigants are formally adjudicated. As we will see, the Canadian court system is complex. This is largely because, under the Constitution, the authority over the courts themselves and over the appointment of judges is divided between Parliament and the provinces.

Most courts in Canada are so-called *inferior* courts. ("Inferior" here is not a pejorative term. It refers not to the quality or value of these courts, but to their *level* in the overall hierarchy of the court system.) All such courts are courts of first instance—that is, trial courts—that hear matters for the first time and have a single judge. The provincial inferior courts are the main point of entry for most people when they interact with the justice system. They deal with less serious criminal matters and matters related to traffic, family, and small claims. Inferior courts do not hear appeals.

Other courts in Canada are *superior* courts. Some superior courts are courts of first instance—that is, trial courts. These courts have a general (or inherent) jurisdiction to deal with most legal cases but are most often used for important matters such as civil disputes involving large sums of money or serious criminal cases—murder, for example. Other superior courts are appellate courts. These courts hear appeals from courts of first instance and have more than one judge (and sometimes as many as nine).

It is important for anyone involved with the court system to understand each court's jurisdictional limitations and its place in the overall hierarchy. Such understanding will guide litigants, for example, to the right forum and help them determine routes of appeal.

This chapter begins with a general overview of the Canadian court system. We consider the role of the judiciary and the constitutional basis for the different types of courts in Canada. Then we look more closely at the organization and function of the various courts—the Supreme Court of Canada, the provincial court systems, the territorial court systems, the federal court systems, and the military courts. We explain the flow of precedent within the Canadian court system. Then we consider how judges are appointed and discuss the two overarching principles of the Canadian judicial system: the open court principle and the principle of judicial independence.

In the last part of the chapter, we discuss cases, case reports, and the judicial reasoning process. Appendixes 7.1 and 7.2 at the end of this chapter outline the conventions of briefing cases and of legal citation.

Role of the Judiciary

A court's **judgment** or decision is the final outcome of the dispute heard before it. In cases where the court provides reasons for its decision, the record of those reasons becomes part of our law and—depending on the court's position in the hierarchy—may bind later courts under the doctrine of precedent (see Chapter 2, as well as the discussion of precedent and *stare decisis* later in this chapter). Canadian courts make decisions that affect all aspects of our public and private lives.

In the common law provinces (in other words, all provinces except Quebec) and in the territories, judge-made rules play an important if diminishing role in the whole body of the law. Statutes, which are made by legislatures, play an increasing role, as the state regulation of society expands. Despite this trend, the judiciary's role is as significant as ever in Canada.

As we saw in Chapter 5, judges add to legislated rules by interpreting statutes. Specifically, they establish the basic meanings of statutory provisions; they determine the jurisdictional validity of statutes; and they decide whether a particular statute offends the Charter. Once judges have interpreted a statute, the statute will, from that point on, have to be read in light of that interpretation.

On occasion, judges perform a fourth interpretive exercise with respect to statutes; they may be asked to decide if a statute has superseded a common law rule. According to the principle of parliamentary sovereignty, statutes, which are made by legislators, take precedence over judge-made common law rules. In the case of a new statute or changes to an existing one, it is not always clear whether the new legislation has superseded a common law rule. Where uncertainty exists, judges may be called upon to rule in this regard.

Canadian Courts: Constitutional Basis

The *Constitution Act, 1867* sets out the power over courts and judicial appointments. The key provisions are the following:

92. In each Province the Legislature may exclusively make Laws in relation to Matters coming within the Classes of Subject next hereinafter enumerated; that is to say, …

    4. The Establishment and Tenure of Provincial Offices and the Appointment and Payment of Provincial Officers. …

    14. The Administration of Justice in the Province, including *the Constitution, Maintenance, and Organization of Provincial Courts, both of Civil and of Criminal Jurisdiction* [emphasis added], and including Procedure in Civil Matters in those Courts. …

96. The *Governor General shall appoint the Judges of the Superior, District, and County Courts in each Province* [emphasis added], except those of the Courts of Probate in Nova Scotia and New Brunswick. …

99(1) Subject to subsection (2) of this section, the judges of the superior courts shall hold office during good behaviour, but shall be removable by the Governor General on address of the Senate and House of Commons.

(2) A judge of a superior court … shall cease to hold office upon attaining the age of seventy-five years. …

101. *The Parliament of Canada may*, notwithstanding anything in this Act, from Time to Time *provide for the Constitution, Maintenance, and Organization of a General Court of Appeal for Canada, and for the Establishment of any additional Courts for the better Administration of the Laws of Canada* [emphasis added].

Since Confederation, Parliament and the provinces have used their constitutional powers to create three types of court:

1. inferior courts,
2. superior courts, and
3. the Supreme Court of Canada (SCC).

They have also used their powers to create a fourth related institution, the administrative tribunal (discussed in Chapter 12).

Inferior Courts

The inferior courts fall into two categories: provincial/territorial and federal.

Provincial and Territorial

The main **inferior courts** are the provincial and territorial ones. Their jurisdiction typically is over the following:

- criminal matters (not the most serious crimes, such as murder and treason, which go before the provincial superior courts),
- family and youth matters, and
- small claims disputes.

The provincial inferior courts, as noted above, are constituted under section 92(14) of the *Constitution Act, 1867*, with provincially appointed judges under section 92(4). Parallel provisions exist in the various federal statutes devolving legislative powers to the territories— that is, provisions that set out the power to establish inferior courts and appoint territorial

Terminology: Provincial and Territorial Courts

The nomenclature applied to the provincial courts, inferior and superior, is inconsistent. This inconsistency adds to the complexity of the Canadian court system. For example, provincial superior courts are known variously as Superior Courts, Superior Courts of Justice, Supreme Courts, or Courts of Queen's Bench.

The provincial inferior courts are often simply referred to as the *provincial courts*. However, the phrase *provincial courts* sometimes refers to the provincial *superior* courts, and at other times to all provincially constituted courts, superior and inferior. The context should make the intended meaning clear. There is a similar ambiguity with territorial inferior courts. They are often referred to as the *territorial courts*. But this name may also refer to the territorial superior courts or to all of the territorial courts, both superior and inferior. Again, the context should make the reference clear.

judges.[1] These inferior courts, provincial and territorial, are the workhorses of the court system, and they are where most Canadians are likely to experience their "day in court."

Federal

Apart from the provincial inferior courts, there is also a very specialized set of *federal* inferior courts—namely, the military courts martial. These include the General Court Martial and the Standing Court Martial, and they have jurisdiction over armed forces personnel who commit "service" offences.

Superior Courts

Like the inferior courts, the superior courts fall into two categories: provincial/territorial and federal.

Provincial and Territorial

The **provincial superior courts**, as noted above, are constituted under section 92(14) of the *Constitution Act, 1867*, with their judges appointed *federally* under section 96 of the Act. Because of this they are sometimes referred to as **section 96 courts**. Why are the judges in these provincial courts appointed federally? Though these are provincial courts, they can, under section 92(14), hear not only matters falling under provincial legislative power (for example, motor vehicle accident cases) but also some matters falling under federal legislative power (for example, bankruptcy cases). (See Chapter 5 for a discussion of how legislative power is divided under Canada's Constitution.) The fact that the judges in these provincial superior courts are federally appointed ensures balance. Balance is needed because of the power these provincial courts have to adjudicate certain federal matters.

It should also be noted that it would be unconstitutional for the provinces to assign to provincial inferior courts (with provincially appointed judges) matters that historically—at

---

1   See the *Yukon Act*, SC 2002, c 7 and the *Northwest Territories Act*, RSC 1985, c N-27. Nunavut is an exception, however. It has a unified superior and territorial court called the Nunavut Court of Justice, which has the combined jurisdiction of an inferior and a superior court. It is the only jurisdiction with such an arrangement.

the time of Confederation—were adjudicated by superior courts. Such matters must be heard by section 96 courts, with their federally appointed judges.[2]

The provincial superior courts—that is, section 96 courts—have two levels: a trial level and an appeal level. The provincial courts of appeal are the highest level of court in the provinces.

The **territorial superior courts** are very similar, in terms of their function, to the provincial superior courts, and they likewise have federally appointed judges. They differ, however, in that they are constituted under federal legislation. The source of Parliament's jurisdiction over the territorial courts, superior and inferior, is section 4 of the *Constitution Act, 1871* (see Chapter 5).

Federal

The **federal superior courts** (sometimes just called **federal courts**) are:

- the Federal Court,
- the Federal Court of Appeal,
- the Tax Court of Canada, and
- the Court Martial Appeal Court.

These courts are constituted under federal legislation, with federally appointed judges. Parliament's authority over these courts flows from the second leg of section 101 of the *Constitution Act, 1867*, which gives Parliament the power to create "additional Courts for the better Administration of the Laws of Canada." The phrase "Laws of Canada" in section 101 has been interpreted as limiting the jurisdiction of these courts to disputes involving federal (as opposed to provincial) laws.

The Federal Court and the Federal Court of Appeal have jurisdiction throughout Canada. The authority of these courts overlaps with that of the provincial superior courts, and this has given rise to a number of jurisdictional disputes. The Tax Court of Canada has jurisdiction throughout Canada, but only in the area of tax law. The jurisdiction of the Court Martial Appeal Court is limited to appeals from the courts martial.

The Supreme Court of Canada

The **Supreme Court of Canada** (SCC) is also a federal superior court. But it has a special status and occupies its own category. Parliament's authority over this court flows from the first leg of section 101, which gives Parliament the power to create a "General Court of Appeal for Canada." The SCC has been Canada's "general court of appeal" since 1875 and its final court of appeal since 1949.

Canadian Courts: Organization and Function

Figure 7.1 shows how the three types or categories of courts in Canada are organized. Administrative tribunals sit just below the fourth level. (For more on administrative tribunals, see Chapter 12.)

---

2 See *Toronto v York*, [1938] AC 415 (JCPC).

FIGURE 7.1 Overview of the Canadian court system

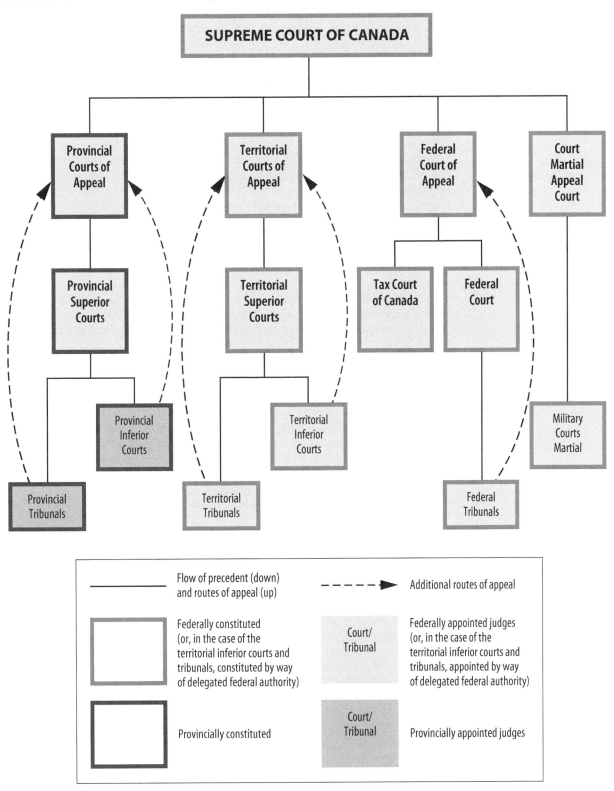

The Supreme Court of Canada

Courts of law existed in the separate British North American colonies before Confederation in 1867. At that time, the English Judicial Committee of the Privy Council was still the final appeal authority for Canada. With Confederation (as we saw in Chapter 4), Canadian statesmen recognized that a general court of appeal would be desirable for the country. Such a court was needed to interpret statutes and to decide future constitutional disputes likely to arise over the division of powers between the new federal government in Ottawa and the provinces.[3]

As a result, section 101 was included in the *Constitution Act, 1867*, giving Parliament the power to "provide for the Constitution, Maintenance, and Organization of a General Court of Appeal for Canada." Using this authority, the federal government passed the *Supreme Court Act* in 1875 and created the SCC. As a general Court of Appeal sitting at the top of Canada's judicial system, the SCC has jurisdiction to hear appeals from the following:

- all of the provincial and territorial Courts of Appeal,
- the Federal Court of Appeal, and
- the Court Martial Appeal Court of Canada.

Until the 1970s, the SCC often heard private law appeals regarding tort, contract, real property, and commercial law disputes.[4] Since the 1980s, its mainstay has been public law appeals involving criminal matters, statutory interpretation questions, and Charter and other constitutional law issues.[5] The SCC also hears appeals from Quebec concerning that province's civil law, as well as appeals from the other provinces concerning the common law.

Historically, Quebec jurists have feared that the common law majority on the SCC would graft common law precepts and techniques onto Quebec's civil law system. This has affected the geographic representation of the Court.[6] Originally, two of the Court's six judges came from Quebec. The total number of judges was increased to seven in 1927, and in 1949 that number reached nine, where it remains. The *Supreme Court Act* requires that three of these judges be appointed from Quebec.[7] By convention, three are from Ontario, two from the west, and one from the Atlantic provinces.[8] One judge is given the title of chief justice of Canada, and the other eight are called **puisne** ("inferior in rank") judges.

Table 7.1 summarizes the key organizational and jurisdictional aspects of the SCC.

---

3   See James G Snell & Frederick Vaughan, *The Supreme Court of Canada: History of the Institution* (Toronto: University of Toronto Press, 1985). Also available online: <http://www.thecourt.ca/resources/snell-and-vaughan>.

4   See Peter McCormick, *Supreme At Last: The Evolution of the Supreme Court of Canada* (Toronto: Lorimer, 2000); Ronald I Cheffins, "The Supreme Court of Canada: The Quiet Court in an Unquiet Country" (1965-66) 4 Osgoode Hall LJ 259; and Peter H Russell, "The Political Role of the Supreme Court of Canada in Its First Century" (1975) 53 Can Bar Rev 576.

5   See Patrick J Monahan, *Politics and the Constitution: The Charter, Federalism and the Supreme Court of Canada* (Toronto: Carswell, 1987); Peter H Russell, "Introduction: History and Development of the Court in National Society and the Canadian Supreme Court" (1980) 3 Can-USLJ 4.

6   Peter H Russell, *The Supreme Court of Canada as a Bilingual and Bicultural Institution: Documents of the Royal Commission on Bilingualism and Biculturalism* (Ottawa: Queen's Printer, 1969) at 215.

7   *Supreme Court Act*, RSC 1985, c S-26, s 6.

8   Peter W Hogg, *Constitutional Law of Canada*, 2013 student ed (Toronto: Carswell, 2013) at 8-25.

How Cases Come Before the SCC

Cases come before the SCC in one of three ways: (1) leave to appeal, (2) appeal as of right, or (3) on a reference.

LEAVE TO APPEAL

This occurs when a court grants a party leave to appeal his case to the SCC. It is the most common way for non-criminal cases to come before the SCC. In some instances, a provincial Court of Appeal or the Federal Court of Appeal can grant such leave. However, most parties who want to appeal their cases to the SCC must get permission or leave to appeal from the Court itself.

Applicants must file written submissions with the Court. In most cases, these submissions are considered by one of three panels (each composed of three SCC judges) that have been selected by the chief justice of Canada. The panel will either grant leave or it will not, and it does not provide reasons either way.

Section 40(1) of the *Supreme Court Act* sets out the main criteria the Court considers when deciding whether to grant a party leave to appeal. Under this section, the SCC may grant leave if it is of the opinion that the case involves

- a matter of public importance,
- a significant legal question, or
- any other matter the Court believes warrants its attention.

Cases involving constitutional issues (including civil liberties) or Aboriginal rights, or important matters dealing with criminal law, administrative law, or private law, stand the greatest chance of success on a leave application. Cases that are purely factual or that involve matters that are specific to a particular province or territory are less likely to succeed.

APPEAL AS OF RIGHT

With certain kinds of criminal cases, there is a right of appeal to the SCC without the need for prior leave. Section 691 of the *Criminal Code* identifies these cases. Circumstances under which an *appeal as of right* exists for an accused person include the following:

1. He is convicted of an indictable offence at trial and the conviction is upheld by the Court of Appeal, but one of the appeal court judges dissents on a question of law.
2. She is acquitted of an indictable offence, but the Court of Appeal sets aside the acquittal and substitutes a guilty verdict.

If there is no prescribed right of appeal under section 691, an accused can still apply for leave to appeal, just as parties in *non-criminal* cases can. (See the discussion of leave to appeal, above.)

ON A REFERENCE

Section 53 of the *Supreme Court Act* provides a third way for a matter to come before the SCC. Unlike the two preceding ways, this one is not dependent on an existing legal action in a lower court. Under this section, the Governor in Council (the federal Cabinet) may

TABLE 7.1   SCC: Key Facts and Features

Name	Supreme Court of Canada (1875–)
Constitutional Authority	Section 101, *Constitution Act, 1867*
Act	*Supreme Court Act*, RSC 1985, c S-26
Rules	*Rules of the Supreme Court of Canada*
Judges	• 1 chief justice of Canada • 8 puisne judges • Quorum: 5-9 judges
Key Jurisdictional Features	• Hears appeals in criminal and non-criminal cases (if the case concerns a matter of public importance or significant legal question) • Leave to appeal is required • Hears appeals in criminal cases involving indictable offences where the court of appeal upholds a conviction but with a dissenting opinion • Hears appeals in criminal cases where the court of appeal substitutes a guilty verdict for an acquittal • Hears references

The Supreme Court: From 1875 to the Present

For a long time, the SCC was not well understood by Canadians. Few grasped its role in the nation. The Court was created in 1875 but, as we have noted elsewhere, it was not Canada's final court until 1949, when all appeals to the Judicial Committee of the Privy Council ended. Until then, it was "a captive court" (as former Chief Justice Laskin noted), with little opportunity to develop any jurisprudence "distinctively its own."* Indeed, for the Court's first sitting on January 17, 1876, it had literally no work to do.

The situation is different now. Today, the SCC is an active player in the political and legal life of this country. Its decisions have a major impact on the lives of all Canadians, who see and read about the Court frequently on television and in newspaper accounts. Its docket is now increasingly concerned with criminal cases, civil liberty matters, statutory interpretation, and constitutional law cases. The Court's pivotal role for Canadian law has expanded even more since the introduction of the *Canadian Charter of Rights and Freedoms*.

* Bora Laskin, "The Supreme Court of Canada: A Final Court of and for Canadians" (1951) 29 Can Bar Rev 1038 at 1075; see also Bora Laskin, "The Supreme Court of Canada, the First One Hundred Years: A Capsule Institutional History" (1975) 53 Can Bar Rev 459.

refer important questions of law or fact to the SCC for an advisory opinion. Typically, these questions would concern the constitutionality of a proposed statute or of a course of action the government is considering.

These questions don't only originate with the federal Cabinet. A provincial Cabinet might direct a **reference** question to its own provincial Court of Appeal. That court's decision regarding the reference question can be appealed as of right (by the provincial Cabinet) to the SCC.[9]

Hearings

Before an appeal is heard, the parties must file with the Supreme Court registrar all of the documents, in both paper and electronic versions, that the Supreme Court judges need in order to prepare for the appeal. These documents include the following:

- the trial transcripts;
- the **facta** of all parties, which contain the written legal arguments to be presented on the appeal; and
- a book of authorities containing copies of all precedent cases, statutes, and secondary sources, such as excerpts from books and articles.

The Supreme Court registrar then schedules a date for the hearing of the appeal. At the hearing, the parties may appear before a panel consisting of five, seven, or all nine Supreme Court judges. The chief justice determines the size of the panel, with five judges constituting a quorum—that is, a minimum number of members. The modern practice is generally for all nine judges to hear the appeal.[10]

The Supreme Court judges hear the appeal from a semicircular bench (see Figure 7.2). The chief justice sits in the middle, flanked by the puisne judges who range outward from

---

9 *Ibid* at 8-15ff.

10 See McCormick, *supra* note 4; and Bora Laskin, "The Supreme Court of Canada: A Final Court of and for Canadians" (1951) 29 Can Bar Rev 1038 at 1075.

the chief justice in order of seniority. Judges are normally gowned in black silk robes, but they wear red ones for ceremonial occasions (see Figure 7.3). The courtroom is open to the public. Oral argument is permitted at the appeal hearing, but with strict time limits imposed. Hearings are conducted in either English or French. The judges can (and often do) ask the lawyers questions, and they can also hear from intervenors—persons or groups who are not parties to the lawsuit but who can participate in the hearing with the Court's permission.

FIGURE 7.2 The nine judges' benches in the main courtroom of the Supreme Court of Canada.

Judgments

After the appeal hearing concludes, the judges move directly to a conference room for initial discussion of the case. Though the judges can return from this discussion and give the Court's judgment directly from the bench, the usual practice is to **reserve** their decision. This means that they reserve for themselves a period of time in which to reflect further on the case, to do more research, possibly to review how other common law courts in other countries might have decided a similar matter, and to allow themselves more time to write the reasons for their decision.[11]

In the conference room immediately after the hearing, during the judges' initial discussion of the case (which is presided over by the chief justice), the most junior member appointed to the Court first gives his or her opinion. The other judges follow, in reverse order of seniority.[12] The main aim of this formalized, private preliminary conference is not just to canvass initial views but also to determine in a collegial way who will write the court's judgment.

Writing a judgment is labour-intensive and time-consuming. Judges often confer with their clerks and develop a draft judgment, which may require further research at the Court's own library. The draft is then circulated among the other panel judges for comments until a consensus is (ideally) reached and a final judgment is completed. The Court's judgment on an appeal is decided by a **majority**, and need not be unanimous. Unanimity is preferred, however, because it signals most forcefully the Court's position regarding the appeal, and this kind of clarity is helpful to the legal profession. A judge may also concur (or agree) with the Court's decision and be part of the majority, but write different reasons. Another judge may **dissent**, or disagree with the majority, and write the reasons for her dissent. Dissenting judgments may later become influential if shown to be better reasoned than the majority decision.

---

11   Michael J Herman, "Law Clerking at the Supreme Court of Canada" (1975) 13 Osgoode Hall LJ 279; Jack Batten, "The Supreme Court of Canada" in *Judges* (Toronto: Macmillan, 1986); Ian Greene et al, *Final Appeal: Decision-Making in Canadian Courts of Appeal* (Toronto: Lorimer, 1998).

12   Antonio Lamer, "A Brief History of the Court" in *The Supreme Court of Canada and Its Justices, 1875-2000: A Commemorative Book* (Toronto: Dundurn Group, 2000) at 23-25.

FIGURE 7.3 Justice Bertha Wilson, who in 1982 became the first woman appointed to the Supreme Court, wearing the red ceremonial robe.

Once made, the decision is deposited with the Supreme Court registrar, who releases it in both English and French. It can then be accessed on the Court's website or read in the Supreme Court Reports.

Provincial Court Systems

A plaintiff in a civil or non-criminal matter, or an accused in a criminal matter, enters a specific level of the Canadian court system in accordance with pre-established criteria—for example, the monetary amount involved in the plaintiff's civil action or the nature of the accused's criminal charge. Serious criminal charges, such as murder or treason, are tried in a provincial superior trial court, while civil claims lower than a specified amount ($25,000 in most provinces) involve trials in small claims court at the lowest level of the judicial hierarchy.

Most provinces structure their court systems as described earlier in this chapter (see Figure 7.1). In all provinces, there are two levels of superior court—a trial level superior court and, above it, a provincial Court of Appeal. The chief justice of the latter is usually the chief justice of the province. Beneath the trial level superior courts are the inferior courts. Cousins to the inferior courts, but beneath them in the overall system of justice, are the many provincial administrative tribunals.

Not all cases can move up the judicial hierarchy from lower level trial courts to the SCC. Parties must have solid grounds in law to appeal decisions made by a trial judge. Trial cases first must reach the provincial superior Court of Appeal—in other words, the top court in each province—and this court decides whether an appeal is warranted. A case can only proceed from the provincial superior Court of Appeal to the SCC if certain appeal criteria are met, as described above in our discussion of the SCC.

Provincial Superior Courts

The provincial superior courts are historically related to the English royal courts of justice (see Chapter 2) and have inherent jurisdiction over *all* civil and criminal law disputes in their respective provinces. This absolute jurisdiction is granted by the common law and is only limited where some aspect of it has been exclusively assigned, by clear and constitutionally valid legislation, to another court or tribunal (such as a provincial inferior court).

The provincial superior court's jurisdiction very often overlaps with that of the inferior court. In most provinces, for instance, a small claims court has been created to adjudicate civil claims below $25,000. However, the provincial superior court, with its inherent jurisdiction over all civil and criminal disputes in the province, is still authorized to hear such claims.

Why would a plaintiff choose to go to a higher court for resolution of a dispute involving a small amount of money? After all, costs are less and procedures simpler in small claims court. The rationale for going to the provincial superior court, under these circumstances, might be that the higher court's decision will have greater precedential value. For example, the plaintiff might be an insurance company suing to recover moneys it paid out on the basis of a misinterpretation of contract language. If the insurance company is successful, the superior court's decision could subsequently serve as a precedent for similar cases. Each claim might be small, but the cumulative effect could be large, and the insurance company stands to benefit a great deal from the higher court's authoritative decision.

The higher provincial courts are not required to hear all claims brought before them. In certain circumstances, the superior court can transfer such cases to the lower court on its own initiative. For example, if the court's docket were backlogged, or the matter were insignificant and only of concern to the particular parties, the court could refer the case down.

The superior courts also have an inherent jurisdiction, as modified by legislation, to review the decisions of the inferior courts and administrative tribunals, as well as the right to hear appeals from these courts and tribunals if permitted by the superior courts' constituting statutes. (See Chapter 12.) The provincial superior courts' wide-ranging adjudicative power means they have the largest share of overall judicial power in Canada.

Table 7.2 summarizes the key organizational and jurisdictional aspects of the provincial superior courts.

FAMILY LAW IN THE PROVINCIAL COURT SYSTEMS

We should also note that a number of provinces have modified their court systems in the area of family law. Traditionally, family law disputes are heard in either the provincial inferior or superior courts—or in both, depending on the issues. (As we noted in Chapter 5, constitutional jurisdiction over family law is split between Parliament and the provinces.) Family breakups are emotionally and financially trying enough without the added stress of having to deal with complicated jurisdictional divisions within the court system. To help with this, initiatives in seven provinces—Manitoba, New Brunswick, Newfoundland and Labrador, Nova Scotia, Ontario, Prince Edward Island and Saskatchewan—have resulted in **unified family courts (UFCs)**.

UFCs are special divisions of the trial level of the superior court, and they have complete jurisdiction over family law matters. Judges with special training or expertise oversee these disputes, and the parties are encouraged to use non-adversarial approaches to resolve their claims. The objective is to make the process less onerous. Should the court be called upon to finally adjudicate any issues, there is, at least, only one court involved. The UFCs only operate in select cities and venues within the province, so parties not able or willing to go to these locations must follow the traditional route.

Provincial Inferior Courts

Most provinces have one provincial inferior court with multiple divisions. The following divisions are typical:

- criminal,
- youth (young offender matters),
- traffic,
- family, and
- small claims (civil claims usually up to $25,000).

These divisions vary among the provinces. For instance, Nova Scotia has multiple provincial courts with separate constituting legislation for each, and Manitoba's small claims disputes are handled by a division of its superior court, the Manitoba Court of Queen's Bench.

TABLE 7.2   Provincial Superior Courts: Key Facts and Features

Constitutional Authority	Sections 92(14) and 96, *Constitution Act, 1867*
Key Jurisdictional Features at the Appeal Level	• Is the general court of appeal for the province in both civil and criminal matters • Hears appeals from the provincial superior trial level • Hears some appeals from provincial court decisions • Hears some appeals from provincial administrative tribunal decisions
Key Jurisdictional Features at the Trial Level	• Has inherent jurisdiction in all cases arising in the province • Hears some appeals from provincial court decisions (e.g., from small claims court) • Hears some appeals from provincial administrative tribunal decisions • Hears applications for judicial review of some provincial administrative tribunal decisions

Regardless of the precise organizational setup, it is important to understand that the provincial inferior courts are the main point of entry for most people when they interact with the justice system. These courts handle the vast majority of criminal and civil cases in Canada.

Provincial inferior courts are creatures of statute and have no inherent jurisdiction as the provincial superior courts do. In other words, inferior courts can only exercise powers given to them by legislation. (The source of the inherent jurisdiction of the superior courts, as we mentioned above, is the common law.)

Each division within a provincial inferior court—or, in Nova Scotia, each separate specialized provincial court—must look to its constituting provincial statute to determine the criminal, quasi-criminal, or civil matters over which it has jurisdiction. In the case of jurisdiction over criminal matters, the *Criminal Code* must also be considered; it requires that certain serious offences, such as murder and treason, be tried by a superior court. The provincial inferior courts also have rules of practice governing procedure in all areas over which they have jurisdiction. In civil matters particularly, their court procedures are generally set up to be simpler, faster, and less expensive than those of the superior courts.

As mentioned above, the superior courts have an inherent power to review the provincial inferior courts' decisions. This power is generally confined to reviewing the procedural "fairness" of the lower court's decision, and this power can be modified by statute. Also, the legislation constituting most provincial inferior courts provides for a general right of appeal to the superior court, which allows the superior court to assess the "merits" of the lower court's decisions, a much broader power than judicial review.

At its most basic level, judicial review involves an examination of the fairness of the *process* by which a decision was reached. For example, did the applicant have a right to be heard and be represented by legal counsel? If the applicant was denied these rights, the decision being reviewed might be overturned. On the other hand, a right of appeal, if granted by legislation, will usually allow the superior court to look beyond process and examine the soundness of the reasoning of the inferior court or tribunal. For example, were the proper principles of law considered and were they applied correctly? If not, the decision might be overturned. (For a discussion of judicial review and rights of appeal as they apply to administrative decisions, see Chapter 12. The basic principles discussed there also apply to inferior courts.)

Territorial Court Systems

Most of what we have said about the provincial court systems applies to the territorial court systems. Perhaps the most significant difference between the two systems is their constitutional basis. As we have seen, the territorial systems are not rooted in a constitutionally entrenched statute, as the provincial ones are, but in federal statutes that can be changed unilaterally by Parliament.[13]

We may assume, however, that this lack of constitutional protection for the territorial court systems is mostly a matter of legal theory. The political and practical difficulties involved in unilaterally changing them would be significant. In terms of functionality and jurisdiction, the territorial court systems are very similar to the provincial ones.

---

13   *Yukon Act*, SC 2002, c 7; *Northwest Territories Act*, RSC 1985, c N-27; and *Nunavut Act*, SC 1993, c 28. Again, the power of Parliament to legislate for the territories is based on s 4 of the *Constitution Act, 1871*.

Territorial Superior Courts

Yukon and the Northwest Territories structure their superior courts as set out in Figure 7.1. There are two superior court levels, with jurisdiction similar to that of the provincial superior courts.

In the Yukon, the Court of Appeal of the Yukon Territory is the top court and hears appeals from the Supreme Court of Yukon and the Territorial Court. The Court of Appeal is made up of justices from British Columbia, Yukon, the Northwest Territories, and Nunavut. This court's small case load is the reason for its not having a full complement of resident justices. It only sits for one week each year in Whitehorse; at other times, it sits in Vancouver, from which the court "borrows" some of its judges.

Similarly, the Court of Appeal for the Northwest Territories hears appeals from the Supreme Court of the Northwest Territories and the Territorial Court. It sits regularly in Yellowknife (occasionally it sits in other territorial locations and in Alberta) and is made up of justices from Alberta, Saskatchewan, and the Northwest Territories.

Nunavut is unique. It has a unified court, the Nunavut Court of Justice, which combines the jurisdiction of an inferior court with the jurisdiction of the trial level of a superior court. It is like a unified family court (UFC) except that it covers not just family law but all jurisdictional areas. There is a single court for Nunavut because its population is very small—30,000 to 40,000 people, spread over a region roughly the size of Western Europe. There is a separate Court of Appeal, however. The Court of Appeal of Nunavut sits mainly in the territorial capital, Iqaluit, and is composed of justices from Alberta, Yukon, the Northwest Territories, and Nunavut.

Territorial Inferior Courts

Yukon and the Northwest Territories each have a territorial inferior court (in each territory, simply called the Territorial Court) that is organized along the lines of the provincial inferior courts. The territorial courts are creatures of the territorial assemblies, which exercise provincial-like statutory power under the federal statutes that devolve power to them. Nunavut is an exception to this, as mentioned above.

Federal Court System

As we have seen, the federal court system includes the SCC and four other superior courts (the Federal Court, the Federal Court of Appeal, the Tax Court of Canada, and the Court Martial Appeal Court). Additionally, it includes the two military courts martial (the General Court Martial and the Standing Court Martial), which qualify as federal inferior courts. The SCC, discussed above, has been the focus of our discussion because of its relative importance.

Federal Court and Federal Court of Appeal

In 1971, Parliament created the Federal Court of Canada under the *Federal Court Act*. This court replaced the Exchequer Court of Canada. The jurisdiction of the Federal Court of Canada was increased to include not only the matters formerly under the Exchequer Court's jurisdiction—revenue matters, disputes involving the federal government, and other types of claims concerned with copyright, trademarks, and patents—but also (among other things) the review of federal boards and tribunals. The Federal Court of Canada had two divisions: the trial division, and the appeal division.

In 2003, the new *Courts Administration Service Act* came into force, amending a number of federal statutes involving the administration of justice, including the *Federal Court Act*. The *Courts Administration Service Act* reconstituted the Federal Court of Canada, converting its two divisions (the trial division and the appeal division) into two separate courts: (1) the Federal Court, and (2) the Federal Court of Canada. The *Federal Court Act* was renamed the *Federal Courts Act*. One of the main purposes of the new *Courts Administration Service Act* was to "facilitate coordination and cooperation among the Federal Court of Appeal, the Federal Court, the Court Martial Appeal Court and the Tax Court of Canada for the purpose of ensuring the effective and efficient provision of administrative services to those courts."[14]

The Federal Court and Federal Court of Appeal are both itinerant courts, with hearing locations in major cities across Canada. Judges from both courts travel to hear disputes according to a set schedule. The key features of the two courts are summarized in Table 7.3.

Tax Court of Canada

The Tax Court of Canada used to be characterized as an inferior court or administrative tribunal but is now considered a superior court. It was created in 1983 pursuant to the *Tax Court of Canada Act*. It has a chief justice and an associate chief justice and numerous puisne judges. Like the Federal Court and Federal Court of Appeal, the Tax Court of Canada is an itinerant court with hearing locations in cities across Canada and regular sittings in those locations.

The court has jurisdiction to hear appeals from individuals and corporations concerning matters arising out of a number of federal statutes, including the *Income Tax Act*, the *Employment Insurance Act*, the *Excise Tax Act* (GST), the *Canada Pension Plan*, and the *Old Age Security Act*. It is an independent court and not an instrument of the Canada Revenue Agency or other government departments.

Military Court System

Military law is a specialized area and something of which most Canadians who are not in the military have only a vague understanding. Section 91(7) of the *Constitution Act, 1867* gives Parliament jurisdiction over "Militia, Military and Naval Service, and Defence." The *National Defence Act* passed pursuant to this authority is the governing statute for the armed forces. The Office of the Judge Advocate General (JAG) is responsible for the prosecution and defence functions of the military justice system, which is parallel to but separate from the regular justice system.

As mentioned above, the courts martial (the General Court Martial and Standing Court Martial) are a very specialized set of *federal* inferior courts with jurisdiction over armed forces personnel who commit "service" offences. These courts are constituted under the *National Defence Act* and are analogous to the provincial and territorial inferior courts that have jurisdiction over criminal cases. However, unlike the provincial and territorial inferior courts, they also have jurisdiction over serious offences and are vested with the same powers as superior courts. Parliament's constitutional jurisdiction over these courts is either based on section 91(7) or section 101 of the *Constitution Act, 1867*.

The Court Martial Appeal Court hears appeals from the courts martial. It is a superior court and is also constituted under the *National Defence Act*. Parliament's jurisdiction over this court is clearly based on section 101.

---

14 *Courts Administration Service Act*, SC 2002, c 8, s 2.

TABLE 7.3   Federal Court and Federal Court of Appeal: Key Facts and Features

	FEDERAL COURT	FEDERAL COURT OF APPEAL
Name	• Federal Court (1971–)	• Federal Court of Appeal (1971–)
Constitutional Authority	• Section 101, *Constitution Act, 1867*	• Section 101, *Constitution Act, 1867*
Act	• *Federal Courts Act*, RSC 1985, c F-7	• *Federal Courts Act*, RSC 1985, c F-7
Rules	• *Federal Courts Rules* • *Federal Courts Immigration and Refugee Protection Rules*	• *Federal Courts Rules* • *Federal Courts Immigration and Refugee Protection Rules*
Judges	• 1 chief justice of the Federal Court • Numerous itinerant judges and deputy judges • Quorum: 1 judge	• 1 chief justice of the Federal Court of Appeal • 12 puisne judges • Quorum: usually 3–5 judges
Key Jurisdictional Features	• Has *exclusive jurisdiction* in the following areas: (1) reviewing decisions of most federal boards and tribunals, with the exception of those assigned to the Federal Court of Appeal; (2) hearing copyright, trademark, patent, and industrial design matters; hearing citizenship appeals; hearing certain armed forces matters • Has *concurrent jurisdiction* with provincial superior courts in certain disputes (e.g., those involving bills of exchange and promissory notes, aeronautics, and interprovincial works and undertakings) • Has *residuary jurisdiction* to hear matters over which no other court has jurisdiction	• Hears appeals from the Federal Court • Hears appeals from the Tax Court of Canada • Has exclusive jurisdiction to review decisions of certain federal boards and tribunals as specified in the *Federal Courts Act* (e.g., the Canadian Radio-television and Telecommunications Commission, the National Energy Board, and the Copyright Board)

Precedent and Stare Decisis in the Canadian Court System

In order to research the law effectively and to assess the binding or persuasive value of earlier decisions properly, you need some familiarity with the hierarchical structure of the courts and their jurisdiction. In Chapter 2, we described the doctrine of ***stare decisis***. According to this doctrine, the decision in an earlier court case (in other words, a **precedent**) binds lower level courts *in the same jurisdiction*. It does so in cases where the facts and applicable legal principle (sometimes referred to as ***ratio decidendi***, or simply ***ratio***) in the later case are materially similar to those in the earlier one.

What is meant by *jurisdiction* in this context? And more specifically, what does it mean in the context of the Canadian court system? Each of the four pathways (or court systems) leading up to the SCC, as shown in Figure 7.1, is considered a separate jurisdiction or jurisdictional grouping. The federal court system is considered a separate jurisdiction, as is the system of courts martial (the military courts). The provincial and territorial court systems are jurisdictional groupings—each province and territory is its own jurisdiction within the general provincial and territorial court pathways. For example, a decision by a court in one province would not bind a court in another province. Precedent only flows downward and only within the jurisdiction in which the decision was made. Decisions of the SCC, however, as Canada's highest court and "general court of appeal," are binding on all courts across Canada.

Cases from the same level of court within the same jurisdiction aren't, strictly speaking, binding on each other (for example, an earlier decision from the Manitoba Court of Appeal isn't technically binding on a later decision by that same court), but the principle of comity—that is, respect for the decisions of fellow judges at the same level—requires they be followed, unless there is a good reason not to follow them. A judge might choose not to follow an earlier decision if it involved, for example, a missed precedent or a missed statutory provision.

Legal researchers start by looking for **binding** authority from the decisions of higher courts. For example, if researching a matter within the jurisdiction of the provincial superior or inferior court system, they would start by looking for SCC decisions. Then they would look for Court of Appeal decisions from the relevant province, then for decisions of the provincial superior court (trial level). Finally, they would look for decisions from provincial inferior courts and, possibly, from administrative tribunal decisions.

If no binding authority is found—and sometimes even if it is—researchers may find it helpful to search for **persuasive** authority from other jurisdictions. A person researching a matter within the provincial court systems would look at decisions from other provinces or territories, from the federal courts (if there is joint authority over the matter in question), and possibly also from other countries with common law traditions, such as England, Australia, and the United States (generally, in that order of preference). The higher the level of court from the other jurisdiction, the more persuasive the decision. Intangibles, such as the reputation of the particular judge who rendered the decision, may also influence the weight given to a particular decision.

As a general rule, the more recent the authority, the better. It should also be noted that decisions that initially appear to be binding or persuasive may seem less so (in other words, they may be *distinguishable*) upon careful examination. A precedent may be distinguishable for a variety of reasons (see Chapter 2).

Judicial Appointments

There is essentially one appointment process for superior court judges—that is, provincial and territorial superior court judges, Federal Court and Federal Court of Appeal judges, and judges of the SCC. All are federally appointed. When it comes to provincially and territorially appointed judges (that is, judges in the inferior courts), the provinces and territories each have separate but parallel appointment processes.

Superior Court Judges

In the following sections we will look at the appointment authority, appointment process, and the qualifications of superior court judges.

Appointment Authority

The appointment power set out in section 96 of the *Constitution Act, 1867* states that the governor general shall appoint the provincial superior court judges. By constitutional convention, this means that the Governor in Council (that is, the federal Cabinet) makes the appointments.

Section 96 says nothing, however, about the Cabinet's appointing *federal* superior court judges. In their case, the federal Cabinet's appointment power comes from section 101. This provision, as we have seen, states that Parliament may from time to time "provide for the Constitution, Maintenance, and Organization of a General Court of Appeal for Canada, and for the Establishment of any additional Courts for the better Administration of the Laws of Canada." This provision has been interpreted as giving the federal Cabinet the executive power to appoint federal superior court judges, including SCC judges. The *Federal Courts Act* and the *Supreme Court Act* have since expressly given the federal Cabinet this power.

The appointment of territorial superior court judges follows the same process as that of provincial superior court judges. The only difference is the constitutional basis of this power. Parliament, exercising its authority over the territories under section 4 of the *Constitution Act, 1871*, has delegated the appointment power to the federal Cabinet in the various federal territorial statutes.

Appointment Process

There are many judicial appointments, and the federal Cabinet cannot be closely involved with all of them. To deal with the volume, a special federal office called the Office of the Commissioner for Federal Judicial Affairs Canada (FJA) was created under the *Judges Act*. Since 1988, the FJA has played a major role in vetting proposed appointments. To assist it in this process, the FJA has overseen the creation of judicial advisory committees in the ten provinces and three territories. Most provinces have one such committee, but Ontario and Quebec, because of their size, have multiple committees (three and two, respectively).

Potential judges now have to apply for the position and go through background checks by the advisory committee. The advisory committee puts forward a list of names, which is then reviewed by the federal minister of justice and the FJA. From this list and following this review, recommendations are made to Cabinet. One of the main purposes in setting up the appointment process this way was to eliminate patronage (that is, appointments based on political connections rather than merit). The advisory committees have members from all corners of the legal profession, so no one person on the committee can dominate the selection process. This diversity inhibits patronage. Patronage may still exist in some degree, but these measures have helped reduce it.

The FJA process is now used for all federally appointed superior court judges. There is an extra step with SCC appointments, which receive more attention because of the high profile and influential nature of the Court. Starting in 2006, Prime Minister Harper introduced the step of having a public hearing before an ad hoc all-party committee of the House of Commons. The federal Cabinet still makes the final decision about SCC appointments, however, and the prime minister, as head of the Cabinet, plays a major role. By convention, the prime minister also decides who will be chief justice of the SCC.

Qualifications

To qualify for appointment as a provincial superior court judge, a candidate must

1. be a barrister or advocate of at least ten years standing at the bar of any province, or
2. have had a total of at least ten years in which she (a) was a barrister or advocate at the bar of any province and then (b) served full-time as a member of a body that performed duties of a judicial nature.[15]

Qualifications for the Federal Court and Federal Court of Appeal are identical, except that a candidate must also be or have been "a judge of a superior, county or district court in Canada."[16]

---

15 *Judges Act*, RSC 1985, c J-1, s 3.

16 *Federal Courts Act*, RSC 1985, c F-7, s 5.3.

The required qualifications for the SCC judges are the following:

1. prior appointment as a judge of a superior court of a province, or
2. being a barrister of at least 10 years standing at the bar of a province.[17]

Inferior Court Judges

In the following sections we will look at the appointment authority, appointment process, and the qualifications for provincial/territorial and federal court judges.

Provincial

APPOINTMENT AUTHORITY AND PROCESS

The constitutional jurisdiction for the appointment of judges to the provincial inferior courts flows from sections 92(4) and (14) of the *Constitution Act, 1867*. Jurisdiction over these appointments belongs to the provincial legislatures. Each provincial legislature has in turn delegated this power, by way of its provincial courts legislation, to the Lieutenant Governor in Council (that is, the provincial Cabinet). The provincial executive branch, therefore, is responsible for appointing judges to this level of court.

The appointment process varies slightly from province to province, but all provinces now have judicial councils created under their respective provincial courts legislation. These provincial councils recruit, screen, and recommend potential candidates for judgeships. Their purpose is to accomplish at the provincial level what the FJA accomplishes at the federal level—that is, to promote quality in judicial appointments and eliminate patronage. The provincial Cabinet still makes the final decision on appointments.

QUALIFICATIONS

The basic qualification for judicial appointment to a provincial inferior court is five years' practice as a lawyer in good standing with the provincial bar, or other legal or judicial experience considered satisfactory to the council. The experience requirement, in other words, is half what it is for superior court judges. Close to 50 percent of all Canadian judges are appointed to provincial inferior courts.

Territorial

The appointment process for the territorial inferior courts operates in much the same way as for the provincial ones. Section 4 of the *Constitution Act, 1871*, along with the federal territorial statutes delegating authority to each territorial assembly, provides the constitutional basis for the appointment of territorial judges. The territorial assemblies have, in turn, passed legislation creating their own territorial courts as well as their own territorial judicial councils—equivalent to the provincial councils—to assist with the appointment process. In the Yukon, for example, the statute that accomplishes this is the *Territorial Court Act*.

---

17 *Supreme Court Act*, RSC 1985, c S-26, s 5.

Federal

The *National Defence Act* sets out the process for appointing judges to the federal courts martial, which are the only federal inferior courts. It gives the power of appointment to the federal Cabinet. However, the FJA process does not apply to these judges. The basic qualification level is ten years' practice as a lawyer at a provincial bar.

Public Proceedings

The **open court principle** is generally taken for granted today in Canada. In the context of criminal charges, it is guaranteed under the Charter, subject to reasonable limits.[18] In Jeremy Bentham's words, publicity is the "security of securities." We expect to be able to observe our justice system at work and to ensure that it is fair.

Courts have not always been open in this way. In England in the 1600s, the Star Chamber abuses highlighted the importance of having open courts. The Star Chamber was a special court set up alongside the well-established common law and equity courts (see Chapter 2). Its jurisdiction was to hear cases considered too important to be handled by the ordinary courts. Its proceedings were secret, and in its final days it became a political instrument used by the Stuart monarchy to punish those who opposed them. After a number of cases of unfair treatment involving prominent political and religious activists, it was abolished by an act of Parliament, the *Habeas Corpus Act* of 1640, just before the English Civil War.

The open court principle has been called "the best security for the pure, impartial, and efficient administration of justice, the best means of winning for it public confidence and respect."[19] What this means is that public proceedings are a check against the injustices that can flourish in private or secret proceedings. Where power is not scrutinized, civil liberties tend to suffer. The English historian Henry Hallam has cited public proceedings—the "open administration of justice"—as among the most important safeguards of civil liberty:

> Civil liberty in this kingdom has two direct guarantees; the open administration of justice according to known laws truly interpreted, and fair constructions of evidence; and the right of Parliament, without let or interruption, to inquire into, and obtain redress of, public grievances. Of these, the first is by far most indispensable; nor can the subjects of any State be reckoned to enjoy a real freedom, where this condition is not found both in its judicial institutions and in their constant exercises.[20]

Judicial Independence

According to the principle of **judicial independence**, judges should be free to make decisions based on the law without threat of negative consequences should their decisions be unpopular. Also, the public needs to see such independence in order to have confidence in

---

18 See ss 1 and 11(d) of the Charter. Some of the limits that have been recognized include cases involving vulnerable victims (for example, children and individuals who have been sexually abused) and national security issues. In these cases the court may protect a person's identity from being disclosed or may even close the court to the public altogether.

19 *Scott v Scott*, [1913] AC 417 at 463 (HL).

20 As quoted in *Scott v Scott*, *ibid* at 477.

the justice system. The idea that the judicial arm of government should be independent of the other branches is related to the rule-of-law doctrine described in Chapter 1 and to the separation-of-powers doctrine that provides a framework for constitutional law.

In Canada, there are recognized to be three main aspects of judicial independence:

1. security of tenure,
2. financial security, and
3. administrative independence.[21]

Security of tenure ensures that judges can render decisions without fear of losing their jobs if their decisions are not well received. Financial security ensures that any temptation to accept bribes will be minimized. And administrative independence ensures that the running of the courts is by the judges themselves and not by outside parties who may subject the judges to external biases.

Constitutional protection for the independence of the judiciary comes from a number of sources, most notably the following:

- The preamble clause to the *Constitution Act, 1867*. The preamble clause provides implied protection by stating that we in Canada have "a Constitution similar in Principle to that of the United Kingdom."[22] Protection is *implied* because, although it exists under the Constitution of the UK, protection is not expressly referred to in the preamble clause.

- Section 99 of the *Constitution Act, 1867*. This section provides that superior court judges "hold office during good behaviour" and that they are "removable by the Governor General on address of the Senate and House of Commons." (Security of tenure consists in the fact they cannot be removed otherwise.)

- *Section 11(d) of the Charter*. This section provides that any person charged with an offence has the right to a "public hearing by an independent and impartial tribunal."[23] The terms "independent" and "impartial" indicate a general standard for the judiciary in Canada.

Judicial independence finds protection as well in various federal, provincial, and territorial statutes.[24] Their provisions recognize judicial independence through salary guarantees and institutional structures. Also, the "good behaviour" tenure provision in section 99 of the *Constitution Act, 1867*, a provision directed at provincial superior court judges, is echoed in provisions directed at federal superior court judges and at provincial and territorial inferior court judges.

---

21   Lori Hausegger, Matthew Hennigar & Troy Riddell, *Canadian Courts: Law, Politics, and Process* (Toronto: Oxford University Press, 2009) ch 6.

22   In *Reference re Remuneration of Judges of the Provincial Court (PEI)*, [1997] 3 SCR 3, the Supreme Court of Canada stated that judicial independence is an unwritten norm, constitutionally entrenched by virtue of the preamble clause to the *Constitution Act, 1867*. Further, this "norm" is not restricted to superior courts but applies to all courts, including inferior courts.

23   Although this Charter guarantee of an independent tribunal only applies to courts and tribunals exercising "criminal" jurisdiction, it is clear that judicial independence applies to all courts regardless of the nature of the claim. The protection provided by the preamble clause is not qualified, as the Charter guarantee is.

24   Federally, for example, see the *Judges Act*, RSC 1985, c J-1; the *Federal Courts Act*, RSC 1985, c F-7; and the *Supreme Court Act*, RSC 1985, c S-26.

The National Judicial Institute

Who educates and trains the judges? How confident are you that a judge will really know the law and the context within which a dispute has arisen?

Judges in Canada are appointed from the practising bar and, sometimes, from the academic world. This means that the usual preparation for a career as a judge is a law practice or an academic position. These experiences don't necessarily give someone a wide experience of the law. A new judge often faces areas of the law that are relatively unfamiliar to her. For example, a lawyer whose practice has been confined to personal injury disputes may, once she becomes a judge, have to deal with family disputes or criminal law cases.

New judges face two significant challenges. First, they must learn about areas of the law in which they have no previous experience. A second challenge has to do with achieving objectivity. Most lawyers are professional advocates. Lawyers who have spent long careers practising advocacy must, once they become judges, move beyond the professional mindset of many years and make themselves sensitive to the circumstances of both parties in a case.

This second requirement is especially challenging. How does a judge fully understand, for example, the social and economic obstacles facing a single mother charged with welfare fraud? How does a judge make sense of the cultural aspects of a case involving a First Nations person charged with hunting out of season? How do judges make themselves sensitive to the social, cultural, and power elements of a case? Where do they obtain the necessary sensitivity training?

In 1988, the National Judicial Institute (NJI) was formed. It is an independent, non-profit organization that serves the Canadian judiciary by planning, coordinating, and delivering judicial education concerning the law, the craft of judging, and the social context in which legal disputes arise.

The NJI's mandate is to "engender a high level of social awareness, ethical sensitivity, and pride of excellence within an independent judiciary." For example, new judges are encouraged to attend a four-and-a-half-day seminar that focuses on the craft of judging and the role of judges in the social context. The program includes such topics as:

- judicial independence,
- judicial ethics,
- equality issues in the courtroom,
- Aboriginal law,
- persons with disabilities and the judicial system, and
- introduction to judicial dispute resolution.

The seminars are conducted by experienced judges, legal academics, and other experts.

Canada is widely regarded as having one of the finest judiciaries in the world. The NJI's seminars and workshops, together with training and educational programs from other organizations, play a large part in ensuring that Canada's judiciary lives up to its reputation.

Source: Reproduced from George Alexandrowicz et al, *Dimensions of Law: Canadian and International Law in the 21st Century* (Toronto: Emond Montgomery, 2004) at 54.

"Good behaviour" tenure means that judges can only be removed from office if their behaviour falls below a certain standard, into what could be termed "bad behaviour." There is no generally accepted common law or statutory definition of bad behaviour or misconduct. Section 65 of the federal *Judges Act* sets up the Canadian Judicial Council, which can investigate a superior court judge if he becomes "incapacitated or disabled from the due execution of his office" owing to age or infirmity, misconduct, incompetence, or to "having been placed, by his or her conduct or otherwise, in a position incompatible with the due execution of that office."[25] This provision goes some way toward defining "bad behaviour." After an investigation, the Council can recommend that a judge be removed for misconduct. The provinces and territories have constituted similar judicial councils with similar powers in relation to provincially and territorially appointed judges.

---

25 *Judges Act*, RSC 1985, c J-1, s 65.

Since Confederation, four attempts have been made to remove superior court judges, but none of these attempts have been successful. No superior court judge has ever been removed from office following the required joint address process set out in section 99 of the *Constitution Act, 1867*. Because this process has never been followed through to completion and because the statutory language is broad, there is some doubt as to what exactly is involved. At the very least, it would appear to require a resolution of the members of the House of Commons and Senate sitting together directing the governor general to remove the judge. A handful of lower court judges have been removed, however, through less stringent processes.[26]

Judicial independence finds further support in the common law doctrine of judicial immunity (now also legislated in many jurisdictions). This immunity protects judges in courts at all levels from civil liability in lawsuits instigated by dissatisfied litigants or accused persons.

Judicial independence, in its many facets, plays a key role in supporting the freedoms we enjoy in Canadian society.

Decisions of the Courts: Case Law

The term *case law* refers to decisions of the courts. There are hundreds of thousands of Canadian cases, and they are incredibly diverse. They range from complex constitutional law appeal cases with multiple judgments hundreds of pages long, to simple one-paragraph oral decisions; from clearly written, well-reasoned, and well-researched judgments that have become leading precedents, to poorly written and reasoned decisions that are soon forgotten.

It is not possible for anyone, legal professional or lay person, to master all the case law in Canada. There is too much of it, and it is always growing and changing. But you can learn to understand cases and appreciate the legal significance of their judgments. Case law is diverse, but the structure of most cases is very similar. Once you have learned that structure, you will be able to read and understand any case. Reading and briefing cases is an effective way of learning that structure. (See Appendix 7.1.)

Format of Case Reports

Cases published in print law reports contain several standard structural components in addition to the actual reasons for judgment written by the court. The law report publisher prepares this additional information and sets it out, together with the court's reasons for judgment, in a particular format. Online versions generally follow the same format. For an illustration of the format of a case report, see Figure 7.4.

Names of Parties

Cases normally begin with the names of the parties on opposite sides of the legal dispute. In non-criminal disputes, the individual, corporation, or other entity who initiates the lawsuit is called the **plaintiff**. The plaintiff's name is listed first. The abbreviation "*v*" (meaning "versus," with no period according to the current McGill Guide rules) separates the plaintiff's name from that of the individual, corporation, or other entity being sued, who is called the **defendant**. In criminal cases, there is no plaintiff. The government initiates cases in the name of the Queen. For this reason, almost all Canadian criminal cases begin with "*R*". This

---

26   Hausegger, Hennigar & Riddell, *supra* note 21 at 186-89.

BOX 7.4

Terminology: "Judgment," "Decision," and "Case"

The words judgment, **decision**, and **case** are sometimes used interchangeably to refer to the *entire set of reasons* the court provides to justify the outcome of a dispute. In a court file, this set of reasons is usually the last document in the paper or electronic folder. Unfortunately, all three words have alternate meanings, and so it is important to pay close attention to the context in which they appear.

"Judgment," for example, can simply refer to the disposition or outcome of the case, as in "judgment for the plaintiff." Likewise, "decision" can refer to the disposition or outcome of the case. It can also refer to a specific part of the reasons, that is, the *holding* (in other words, the court's answer to an issue).

The word "case" is prone to similar ambiguities. To the parties and the court, it can mean the entire proceedings before the court. To the lawyer, paralegals, and others who worked on the file, it can mean the whole process, starting with the client interview and proceeding through to trial, then to the appeal (if there is one), and then to the final judgment of the court.

---

is an abbreviation for *regina* (or *rex*), which is the Latin word for queen (or king). It is followed by "*v*" and the name of the defendant or accused.

On an appeal, the individual, corporation, or other entity who lost at trial and who initiates an appeal to a higher court is called the **appellant**. The other party is called the **respondent**. In such instances, the name of the appellant is generally placed first, followed by "*v*" and then the name of the respondent.

Other terms found in case names are "*Re*" and "*Ex parte*." The first means "in the matter of" and it precedes a named party. It is used in cases where someone is applying to the court for an interpretation of someone's rights. Cases in this category include bankruptcy, adoption and certain estate matters. "*Ex parte*," meaning "on the application of one party," is used when only one side is before the court. This might occur, for example, where, prior to trial, one party is applying to the court for an order to prevent the other party from dissipating certain assets. (Generally, these kinds of applications involve some kind of urgency.)

Date of Decision

After the names of the parties, the law report lists the date of the court's decision. Be alert to the date. A very old case may not be a reliable precedent.

Court and Judges

After the date of the court's decision, the law report notes the court that decided the case, along with the judge or judges involved. It could list either a single judge, if the case involves a trial; or a panel of judges, if the case is heard on appeal.

Headnote

A **headnote** is a concise summary of the entire case. The headnote is prepared by the editor of the law report, not by the judge or judges who wrote the decision. It is placed before the reasons for judgment, enabling the reader to quickly obtain an overview of the facts, issues, and reasons for the court's decision. It also lists the cases, legislation, and other secondary sources that the court examined in making its judgment. These features of the headnote make it an invaluable source for further research in the area. Note, however, that it is only there to assist the researcher and is not part of the judgment—it is not something you would rely on in court when making a legal argument, for instance.

FIGURE 7.4 Sample case report

The *Doern* case was seen as a case of interest to the legal community and was published in a number of report series. This excerpt is from the *British Columbia Law Reports*. At the beginning, the publisher has added a catchwords summary followed by a headnote.

Doern v. Phillips Estate   Kirkpatrick J. 349

[Indexed as: Doern v. Phillips Estate]

DOUGLAS ALLEN DOERN

v.

Estate of RONALD MICHAEL PHILLIPS, DECEASED,
his representative ad litem, PUBLIC TRUSTEE, said
PUBLIC TRUSTEE, VANCOUVER POLICE DEPARTMENT,
CITY OF VANCOUVER, FRED MANSVELD and R.. IN
RIGHT OF PROVINCE OF BRITISH COLUMBIA;

FRED MANSVELD, VANCOUVER CITY POLICE
DEPARTMENT, CITY OF VANCOUVER, R. IN RIGHT
OF PROVINCE OF BRITISH COLUMBIA, Estate of
RONALD MICHAEL PHILLIPS, DECEASED, his
representative ad litem, PUBLIC TRUSTEE and
said PUBLIC TRUSTEE (Third Parties)

Supreme Court
Kirkpatrick J.

Heard – September 14-16, 21, 26-30, October 3-7, 13-14
and 24-26, 1994
Judgment – December 13, 1994

Catchwords summary

Police — Duties and liability — Negligence — During police chase fleeing driver striking and severely injuring plaintiff driver — Injured driver suing police department and one officer — Court considering standard of care of police under s. 118 of Motor Vehicle Act and protection of officers from liability under s. 21 of Police Act — Police department 25 per cent liable for negligence involving pursuit guidelines — Officer not following guidelines but not liable as not grossly negligent — Fleeing driver 75 per cent liable.

Negligence — Remoteness of damage — Causation — During police chase fleeing driver striking and severely injuring plaintiff driver — Police negligence being one proximate cause of accident — Police 25 per cent liable to injured driver — Fleeing driver 75 per cent liable.

Administrative law — Judicial review of decisions — Characterization of function of tribunal — During police chase fleeing driver striking and severely injuring plaintiff driver — Police implementation of pursuit guidelines being operational matter and open to judicial review — Police negligent in implementation of guidelines.

Headnote

The Vancouver police manual prescribed the policy for police pursuits by car. The underlying principle was the capture of a fleeing suspect without unnecessarily endangering the police or other persons. Pursuits were normally limited to the primary unit which started the pursuit and one secondary unit. Other units were not to join the pursuit unless assigned. "Paralleling" a pursuit on a nearby street was forbidden. The duties of the chief dispatcher and field supervisor were to assume command, control police actions and ensure that police procedure was followed. The chief dispatcher was to obtain, assess and disseminate information. The pursuing units were to inform him of all relevant facts. If the police "lost" the fleeing car, the primary unit was immediately to inform the chief dispatcher and all police units were to resume their normal duties. Discontinuing a pursuit was to be considered when a

FIGURE 7.4 Sample case report *continued*

Doern v. Phillips Estate   Kirkpatrick J. 351

command and the dispatcher failed to elicit vital information. The accumulation of occurrences of clear danger in the pursuit, which went unreported to those in command, would have mandated ending the pursuit. In failing to terminate in the face of clear danger, the police failed to meet the required standard of care.

Section 21(3) of the *Police Act* holds an officer liable for acts of gross negligence. "Gross negligence" is a very marked departure from the standards by which responsible people habitually govern themselves. The definition is not rigid, but reflects the degree to which the conduct falls below the appropriate standard of care. Police officers engaged in a pursuit have a reasonably high standard of care because of the inherent danger of such pursuits. Such higher standard of care raises the standard for gross negligence. The officer in the third unit had the hardest role in the pursuit because he had no partner to communicate with the dispatcher. In the circumstances, the line between negligence and gross negligence was very fine indeed. However, the officer's conduct was not grossly negligent.

The test for causation-in-fact is the "but-for" test. A defendant has caused a plaintiff's loss if the plaintiff would not have suffered the loss but for the defendant's act. Where a defendant creates or materially contributes to a significant risk of injury, and injury occurs that is squarely within the risk, the defendant is liable for the injury even though there are other later factors also causing or materially contributing to that injury. "But for" the pursuit the police initiated and negligently conducted, the injured driver's injuries would not have occurred. The police thus caused his loss. Further, the police materially increased his risk of injury by conducting the pursuit as they did, and by so doing materially contributed to the cause of his injury. The fact that the fleeing suspect actually collided with the injured driver's car was immaterial. Such an event was within the risk created by the police. As such, their negligence was also a proximate cause of the accident.

The implementation of government policy decisions is an operational matter and thus open to judicial review. The police implementation of their pursuit guidelines was negligent. That implementation was an operational matter. Thus whether the guidelines themselves were policy or operational decisions was immaterial. The police were not exempt from the duty which they would otherwise owe to users of the road.

Section 1 of the *Negligence Act* provides that where it is not possible to establish different degrees of fault, liability shall be apportioned equally. Here, it was not impossible to establish different degrees of fault. While the police were negligent and a proximate cause of the accident, one could not ignore the fleeing driver's negligence. Having regard to his reckless actions and his apparent response to the accelerations of the police, he should be found 75 per cent liable and the police 25 per cent liable.

Cases considered

Almeida v. Town of North Providence, 468 A. 2d 915 (R.I. Sup. Ct., 1983) — referred to.
Anns v. Merton London Borough Council, [1978] A.C. 728, (sub nom. *Anns v. London Borough Council of Merton*) [1977] 2 All E.R. 492 (H.L.) – considered.

At the end of the headnote, the *Cases considered* section lists all cases considered in the decision.

FIGURE 7.4 Sample case report *continued*

BRITISH COLUMBIA LAW REPORTS 2 B.C.L.R. (3d)

Barratt v. North Vancouver (District), [1980] 2 S.C.R. 418, 27 B.C.L.R. 182, 8 M.V.R. 294, 13 M.P.L.R. 116, 14 C.C.L.T. 169, 114 D.L.R. (3d) 577, 33 N.R. 293 — considered.

Brown v. British Columbia (Minister of Transportation & Highways), [1994] 1 S.C.R. 420, [1994] 4 W.W.R. 194, 89 B.C.L.R. (2d) 1, 19 C.C.L.T. (2d) 268, 164 N.R. 161, 42 B.C.A.C. 1, 112 D.L.R. (4th) 1, 20 Admin. L.R. (2d) 1, 2 M.V.R. (3d) 43 — applied.

Jones v. Denomme (February 28, 1994), Doc. 5411/90 (Ont. Gen. Div.) — considered.

Just v. British Columbia (1989), [1989] 2 S.C.R. 1228, [1990] 1 W.W.R. 385, 41 B.C.L.R. (2d) 350, 1 C.C.L.T. (2d) 1, 18 M.V.R. (2d) 1, 103 N.R. 1, 64 D.L.R. (4th) 689, 41 Admin. L.R. 161 — applied.

McCulloch v. Murray, [1942] S.C.R. 141, [1942] 2 D.L.R. 179 — applied.

McGhee v. National Coal Board, [1973] 1 W.L.R. 1, [1972] 3 All E.R. 1008 (H.L.) — considered.

Moore v. Fanning (1987), 49 M.V.R. 161, 60 O.R. (2d) 225, 41 C.C.L.T. 67 (H.C.) — considered.

Ogilvie v. Donkin, [1949] 1 W.W.R. 439 (B.C. C.A.) — applied.

O'Reilly v. C., [1978] 3 W.W.R. 145, affirmed [1979] 3 W.W.R. 124, 8 C.C.L.T. 188, 99 D.L.R. (3d) 45 (Man. C.A.) — considered.

Pepper v. Hoover (1976), 71 D.L.R. (3d) 129 (Alta. T.D.) — considered.

Powell v. Guttman, [1978] 5 W.W.R. 228, 6 C.C.L.T. 183, 89 D.L.R. (2d) 180, 2 L. Med. Q. 279 at 291 (Man. C.A.) — applied.

Priestman v. Colangelo, [1959] S.C.R. 615, 30 C.R. 209, 124 C.C.C. 1, 19 D.L.R. (2d) 1 — applied.

R. v. Rahey, [1987] 1 S.C.R. 588, 75 N.R. 81, 78 N.S.R. (2d) 183, 193 A.P.R. 183, 57 C.R. (3d) 289, 33 C.C.C. (3d) 289, 39 D.L.R. (4th) 481, 33 C.R.R. 275 — applied.

Smith v. British Columbia (Attorney General) (1988), 30 B.C.L.R. (2d) 356 (C.A.) — considered.

Snell v. Farrell, [1990] 2 S.C.R. 311, 110 N.R. 200, 4 C.C.L.T. (2d) 229, 72 D.L.R. (4th) 289, 107 N.B.R. (2d) 94, 267 A.P.R. 94 — considered.

Thornton v. Shore, 666 P. 2d 655, 233 Kan. 737 (Sup. Ct., 1983) — referred to.

Vallery v. Po (1971), 23 D.L.R. (3d) 92 (B.C. S.C.) — applied.

Walker v. Coates, [1968] S.C.R. 599, 64 W.W.R. 449, 68 D.L.R. (2d) 436 — considered.

Watt v. Hertfordshire County Council, [1954] 1 W.L.R. 835, [1954] 2 All E.R. 368 (C.A.) — applied.

Whitehouse v. Jordan, [1981] 1 W.L.R. 246, [1981] 1 All E.R. 267 (H.L.) — applied.

Statutes considered

Good Samaritan Act, R.S.B.C. 1979, c. 155
    s. 1 — considered.
Motor Vehicle Act, R.S.B.C. 1979, c. 288
    s. 76 — considered.
    s. 79 — considered.
    s. 118 — considered.
Municipal Act, R.S.B.C. 1979, c. 290
    s. 755.1(3) — considered.

Most editors also include a *Statutes considered* section.

FIGURE 7.4 Sample case report *concluded*

The final piece of "value added" information is the *Words and phrases considered* section.

Next, counsel are listed.

The judgment, taken word for word from the registry file, is then set out.

Doern v. Phillips Estate   Kirkpatrick J. 353

Negligence Act, R.S.B.C. 1979, c. 298
s. 1 — considered.
Offence Act, R.S.B.C. 1979, c. 305
s. 14(5) — considered.
s. 22 — considered.
Police Act, S.B.C. 1988, c. 53
s. 21 — considered.
s. 28 — referred to.

Words and phrases considered
gross negligence

ACTION by plaintiff driver for damages incurred when struck by fleeing driver being pursued by police.

Soren Hammerberg and *James T. McBride*, for plaintiff.

Paul D.K. Fraser, Q.C., and *Patrice M.E. Abrioux*, for defendants and third parties, Estate of Ronald Michael Phillips, Deceased, his representative ad litem, Public Trustee, and said Public Trustee.

Richard B. Lindsay and *Michael A. Girard*, for defendants and third parties, Fred Mansveld, Vancouver City Police Department and City of Vancouver.

Colleen Smith, for the Crown.

(Doc. Vancouver B895010)

1 December 13, 1994. KIRKPATRICK J.: — At 3:45 a.m. on October 19, 1989, Douglas Allen Doern drove his 1982 Volkswagen Cabriolet convertible north on Boundary Road through a green light at Kingsway. At the same instant, Ronald Michael Phillips was driving his 1976 Lincoln west on Kingsway at a high speed. Mr. Phillips was being pursued by Constable Mansveld of the Vancouver City Police Department. Mr. Phillips' car sped through the red light at Boundary and collided with Mr. Doern's car. The force of the impact propelled Mr. Doern's car approximately 250 feet west on Kingsway. The Phillips' car veered into a power pole, spun into a cement planter, and exploded into flames. Mr. Phillips died instantly. Mr. Doern suffered injuries that, it is alleged, include a fracture to the thoracic vertebrae; basal skull fracture; blood clot to the frontal portion of the brain; renal contusions; injury to the neck, jaw, shoulder and pelvis; lacerations; and cognitive and intellectual dysfunction.

2 On the first day of trial, counsel advised that liability alone was in issue. Counsel also asked that the claim against the defendant and third party, Her Majesty the Queen in Right of the Province of British Columbia, be dismissed, by consent. On the last day of trial, counsel asked that, by consent, the claim against the Vancouver Police Department be dismissed

Source: *Doern v Phillips (Estate of)* (1994), 2 BCLR (3d) 349 (SC), aff'd (1997), 43 BCLR (3d) 53 (CA).
From Carswell's *British Columbia Law Reports*.

Nature of the Proceedings and Counsel

Before reporting the actual decision, the law report generally states the purpose or nature of the proceeding—for example, "an appeal from a decision of Justice Smith"—and provides the names of the lawyers (counsel) representing each side of the dispute.

Reasons for Judgment

This part of the law report contains the actual decision by the court. A student of case law will soon discover that individual judges have their own unique writing style. Generally, most judges adhere to the following format and order of presentation:

1. the nature of the proceedings,
2. the relevant facts of the case,
3. the legal issue(s) that must be resolved,
4. the argument of both lawyers at trial or on appeal,
5. the legal rule(s) pertaining to the issue(s),
6. the application of the rule(s), and
7. the court's conclusion(s).

The *ratio* of the case usually refers to the governing legal rule. It can also refer to the way in which a rule is applied to a given set of facts. Isolating the rule and the key facts to which it relates takes practice, and being able to determine the *ratio* of a case is the mark of a good legal researcher. Judicial statements about the law that may be of interest but that are not necessary to the decision in the case are called **obiter dicta** (sometimes shortened to **obiter**). This is Latin for "statements said in passing."

Disposition

After the reasons for judgment, and at the end of the case, the formal order of the court is given. It could be, for example, "motion dismissed" or "judgment for the plaintiff" or "appeal dismissed."

APPENDIX 7.1

Briefing Cases

One of the most effective techniques for learning how to analyze legal problems is to study how judges reach their decisions. A time-honoured method for doing this is to summarize—that is, brief—the cases you read. A **case brief** follows a defined pattern, with the constituent parts of the court's reasons for judgment summarized in a set order. Briefing a case helps you grasp it much more fully than just reading it does. The brief gives you a concise, easily remembered overview of the case.

There is no one way to do a case brief, and different names may be used for the components that comprise a brief. What is important is that you understand what you are summarizing and how it relates to the overall process of reaching a reasoned legal decision.

Case Brief Format

Summarizing a case with the headings and components described below will help you understand and remember it, and will help you become more proficient at legal analysis. A sample case and the brief that was created from it are included following this discussion.

Style of Cause

It is useful to begin with the name of the case.

Facts

The facts make up the context that has given rise to the legal question(s) or issue(s) in a particular case. Sometimes the facts are complex, sometimes simple, and often the judgment includes more facts than are necessary to understand the issues. Only include the facts that are necessary in this regard. (Some rare cases—cases where purely legal questions are referred to the court—have no facts.)

Proceedings

This is where you describe the claim (who is suing whom for what) and, if the case is on appeal, the result in the lower court(s) and the grounds for appeal and cross-appeal (if there is one). This section is sometimes refer-red to as the "procedural history." Note also that another way to format a case brief is to put the proceedings or procedural history information at the end of the facts section, combining these two sections.

Issue(s)

There may be one or more issues that arise from a given set of facts. Issues fall into two broad categories or types:

1. issues concerned with defining what the rules are, and
2. issues concerned with how the rules should be applied to the facts.

Most issues that arise in everyday cases are of the second type. The first type arises where the law is unclear or complex and the court needs to or is asked to sort it out. Both types may be found in the same judgment.

Holding(s)

For every issue there must be a holding. A holding is the court's answer to an issue. If the issue is of the first type, the holding will be a statement of the rule. If it is of the second type, the holding will concern how the rule is applied to the facts. If there is just one main rule relevant to the disposition of the case, this heading is sometimes named *Ratio Decidendi* or *Ratio* for short (as described earlier in the chapter).

Reasoning/Reasons

The reasoning is the court's explanation and justification for its holding(s). The court may refer to policy reasons for adopting or not adopting a particular rule—for example, a concern that it will flood the courts with litigation (the "floodgates" argument) or that it will cost the government or industry too much money ("indeterminate liability"). At other times, the court may apply or not apply an established rule based on a simple assessment of the facts, or because it feels bound by precedent. Note that some other case brief formats combine the holdings and reasons under one heading.

Disposition/Judgment

The disposition is the result of the case (for example, judgment for the plaintiff, appeal granted, new trial ordered) and is usually found at the end of a court's decision. As noted earlier, the word "judgment" sometimes refers to the disposition of the case as well; it can also refer to the entire set of reasons. Context should make it clear.

With some cases it is easy to find these elements because the judgment has headings similar or identical to those we have used in this discussion. The use of headings is more common in recent judgments—newly appointed judges now receive training in judgment writing, among other things. In older judgments, headings were rarely used. Another challenge for the researcher who is trying to isolate the various parts of a judgment is ambiguous writing. Ambiguity is the result of hastily written reasons and sometimes, one suspects, of the judge's fear of committing to a clear position.

The ease with which the researcher or student will be able to break down a judgment depends on his or her level of experience and training. It is difficult for most people at first, but gets easier with practice.

MULTIPLE JUDGMENTS

To this point, we have been assuming a single judgment in the case. This will always be the case for trial judgments, because they involve a single judge. On appeals, however, there will be more than one judge. Provincial and territorial courts of appeal can have as many as five judges hearing the appeal. In the SCC, it can be up to nine. If the judges are unanimous on an appeal, there will be a single judgment. But often they are not unanimous, and two or more of the judges write their own reasons or judgments. Although the court *as a whole* will have disposed of the case in one way, there are multiple judgments.

The difficulty with multiple judgments is figuring out which judgment represents the judgment of the court. What is the governing rule or *ratio* in the case? Sometimes it is easy to answer this question, sometimes not. In cases where there are two are three judgments, you must first note which judges are agreeing with which judgment. (The names of the concurring judges are usually in brackets next to the name of the judge writing the judgment.) The number of concurring judges plus one (that is, the writer) gives the weight of the judgment in relation to the total number of judges hearing the appeal.

The following examples, all with a quorum of nine, illustrate some of the possibilities.

First, consider this example:

Disposition A (majority)	Disposition B (dissent)
Judgment X (5)	Judgment Y (4)

This is a simple case where there are only two judgments and there is a clear majority—a five/four split (four judges agreed with one writer's judgment and three agreed with the other writer's judgment). In this case, judgment X is the judgment of the court and is binding.

Now consider the following example:

Disposition A (majority)	Disposition B (dissent)
Judgment X (4)	Judgment Z (3)
Judgment Y (2)	

Here, there is a majority for Disposition A, but there is division within this majority with respect to reasons. Judgment X has the support of only four of the six judges agreeing with Disposition A. This means that, in the court as a whole, five judges do not agree with Judgment X. In other words, Judgment X is not the majority judgment of the whole court, only of the "majority of the majority." In practice, in cases of this type, Judgment X is generally followed by later courts because its weight exceeds Judgment Z. Strictly speaking, however, it is not binding because it does not have the support of the majority of the court.

Now consider the following example:

Disposition A (majority)	Disposition B (dissent)
Judgment X (3)	Judgment Z (4)
Judgment Y (2)	

Again, we have a split majority, but this time the number in dissent actually exceeds Judgment X. While Disposition A has gained a majority, it is arguable that no binding rule or holding emerges from a case like this.

When briefing multiple-judgment cases, isolate the most important judgment—in the examples above, Judgment X—and do a case brief of it. In a note following the brief, summarize the differences between that judgment and the others. Were different rules applied? Or were the same rules applied but with a different conclusion or holding?

Sample Case and Case Brief

Case: Matthews v MacLaren (1969), 4 DLR (3d) 557 (Ont HC)

The *Matthews* case was based on a claim in negligence, an area of tort law that generates more litigation than any other type of claim (see Chapter 9, which includes an overview of the law of negligence). The argument in *Matthews* focused on the limited duty of a person to rescue another in distress. Two fatalities resulted from a boating mishap, and the estates of both victims, Matthews and Horsley, sued the boat owner. As explained in the case, the Matthews claim was actually one-half of the two combined claims. Only the portion of the judgment dealing with liability in the Matthews claim is set out.

REASONS FOR JUDGMENT

LACOURCIERE J.: – These two actions under the *Fatal Accidents Act*, R.S.O. 1960, c. 138, were tried together, and involve the claim of the widows and children respectively of the late Roland Edgar Matthews and the late John Albert Horsley, both of whom lost their lives in a tragedy on Lake Ontario on May 7, 1966. The defendant Kenneth MacLaren was at the material time the owner and operator of an Owens, Empress 30-foot six inch cabin cruiser known as the "Ogopogo" powered by two inboard 100 h.p. engines driving two propellers or twin screws. At the opening of trial, on consent, the action was discontinued against the defendant, Richard J. Jones, on terms. Any reference to the defendant hereafter will be to the defendant MacLaren only. A Halton County jury listened to the evidence during five days of the trial, and on January 24th defence counsel renewed a motion, which had been dismissed at the opening of trial, to strike out the jury notice; plaintiffs' counsel agreed and the jury was dismissed by me with regret.

On the day of the fatal accident, the late Roland Edgar Matthews and the late John Albert Horsley were gratuitous passengers, or invited guests, of the defendant on this boat, which left Port Credit Yacht Club at approximately 6:30 p.m. for the return voyage to Oakville. The weather at that time was starting to cool and a wind, blowing from the north-west crated a light chop on Lake Ontario. The "Ogopogo" with the defendant at the helm was proceeding at a speed of 10 to 12 knots; at that time Matthews, who had looked after the bowline on leaving Port Credit, was still sitting on the port side of the foredeck: another passenger, the defendant Richard J. Jones, was in the pilot's cockpit and the other four passengers, i.e., Horsley, one Donald Marck, and the two ladies -- Mrs. MacLaren and Mrs. Jones -- were in the cabin below. Jones observed Matthews get up and proceed towards the stern along the narrow catwalk on the port side of the boat, holding on to the rail, with his back to the water, and topple over backwards at the level of the windscreen. Jones immediately hollered "Roly's overboard" and the rescue operation began.

The defendant threw the boat controls in the neutral position and on leaning back could see Matthews, floating, with head and shoulders out of the water, some 40 to 50 ft. astern to starboard: he reversed the motors and backed towards Matthews, having pinned the control wheel with his stomach and looking over his shoulder using the throttle to manoeuvre and, according to Jones, swerving a bit, until the man in the water disappeared from his view behind the transom. The defendant then shut the engines down completely to drift towards Matthews: meanwhile, Jones had gone to the stern and thrown a life ring which landed some 10 ft. in front of Matthews, and as the boat got closer Donald Marck, also at the stern, was attempting to hook Matthews with a six-foot pikepole. Matthews was still floating -- arms outwards with his eyes open and staring, apparently unconscious. The motors had been shut down when the stern of the boat got to within four or five feet from Matthews, who could not be hooked when the boat was blown or drifted away a distance of 10 to 20 ft. The defendant MacLaren started the engines and reversed again towards Matthews.

A recounting of the facts begins here. Sometimes judges use headings for the various parts of their judgment. Lacourciere J used some headings, but not many.

Judges often start their reasons with a description of the action, and the appeal history, if there is one. Because this is a trial judgment, there is no appeal history.

Meanwhile, Jones had thrown a second lifejacket which had fallen on top of Matthews or under his nose.

By then some three or four minutes had elapsed since Matthews had fallen overboard and the situation was getting desperate. Horsley from the stern took off his shoes and trousers and yelling "my friend, my friend!" dived in while the boat was moving, and surfaced some 10 ft. away from Matthews. Mrs. Jones then noticed Matthews' body fall forward -- face and head in the water: she then courageously jumped in, one foot away, to hold his head up but Matthews had gone under the starboard quarter and could not be helped. Jones, seeing his wife in the water, ran up to the defendant and took over the controls without argument, swung the boat around and approached his wife "bow on", getting her on the starboard side. MacLaren and Marck grabbed her arms and pulled her out of the water. MacLaren reassumed the controls and shortly thereafter Horsley was picked up, but could not be resuscitated and was pronounced dead later at Port Credit.

The court is describing some of the evidence here. Be careful to distinguish between "evidence" and "fact." What is important are the factual conclusions of the judge (or jury), not the evidence of a particular witness.

Although the outside temperature had been warm and pleasant in the afternoon, with a temperature of approximately 65°, the water was extremely cold: the only person who survived the immersion, Jean Jones, described how she felt paralysed, as if in a vat of ice cubes. The witness Burtershaw, chief operator of the Waterworks Department of the Oakville Public Utilities, gave evidence that the recorded water temperature at the intake pipe some 2,400 ft. from shore was a constant 39° on that day, with surface temperature probably five degrees higher.

The pathologist, Dr. D.F. Brunsdon, who examined Horsley's body, ascribed the cause of death to cardiac failure resulting from either sudden shock on immersion or from prolonged immersion in cold water. In the latter case, unconsciousness would precede death. It was his opinion after conducting the autopsy that death was probably due to sudden shock as a result of immersion, in which case death would be immediate or extremely quick; the deceased had been perfectly healthy before and there was no evidence of heart or any other disease. The body of Matthews was never recovered and the cause of his death remains undetermined.

Because of the allegation made in both actions (among other items of negligence) that the defendant was operating his motor boat while his ability to do so was impaired by alcohol, I will summarize the events leading up to the tragic occurrence.

The defendant, then a 51-year old steel salesman, had earlier in the morning one pint of beer with a sandwich at the Oakville Club, later a hamburger and one beer at the Oakville Powerboard Club with Mr. and Mrs. Jones; the outing was improvised, and a case of 24 pints of beer put on board: the defendant and each passenger had one pint of beer on the trip to Port Credit. The arrival of the "Ogopogo" at the Port Credit Club, and the docking process there was described in great detail by various witnesses because of the incident of damage to the stanchion, a vertical member of the stainless steel pulpit, on the stern of the "Stormalong" which was slightly damaged when hit by the bow of the "Ogopogo". I am satisfied that this was a mere mishap caused by the temporary failure of one engine of the "Ogopogo", which can in no way reflect on the ability of the defendant who was at the helm.

The defendant, as captain of the first boat -- so he claimed -- to dock at the Port Credit Yacht Club that season, arrived in jovial and exuberant mood and ordered champagne for all present. The steward of the yacht club relates that approximately forty people in the club shared four large (32 oz.) bottles of champagne. The MacLaren party was in the club between 3:30 and 6:30. The defendant admits having consumed two glasses of champagne during that period, intermingling freely with the Port Credit members, many of whom were friends. There is no evidence that the defendant had any of the other drinks being ordered and served that afternoon. After the accident, a glass of amber coloured liquid, presumably containing whisky, was found in a glass-holder near the controls of the cockpit. The defendant disclaims any knowledge of its contents and says that it must have been pressed upon him by friends upon leaving the dock of the Port Credit Yacht Club and forgotten and untouched by him.

This heading tells us that the analysis of issues dealing with liability begins here. Headings make judgments easier to read.

Liability:

1. Re Matthews' Claim

Notwithstanding the allegations pleaded that the defendant failed to ensure the safety of his passengers and particularly of the deceased Matthews by having them wear life-preservers on board, I am satisfied that in the circumstances this does not constitute actionable negligence. The only negligence argued here relates to the defendant's condition and to his conduct following Matthews' fall into the water. The first question therefore is whether there existed a legal duty on the part of the defendant to come to the rescue of a passenger who fell overboard by reason of his own misfortune or carelessness, and without any negligence on the part of the defendant or any person for whom the defendant would be vicariously responsible. This question, strictly a determination of law for the Court and not a question of fact for the jury, was repeatedly answered in the negative in the 19th century decisions (based on the distinction between "misfeasance" and "non-feasance") illustrated in Ontario by the 1913 decision of the Ontario Court of Appeal in *Vanvalkenburg* v. *Northern Navigation Co.* (1913), 30 O.L.R. 142, 19 D.L.R. 649. In that case, a seaman employed on a steamboat had fallen overboard by his own carelessness, and drowned: Mulock, C.J.Ex., speaking for the Appellate Division said at p. 146 O.L.R., p. 652 D.L.R.:

Lacourciere J begins his discussion of the first issue here. Look for pointer words and phrases, such as "The question is..." to help isolate the issues in a case. Based on the detailed analysis that follows, it is clear that this is the most significant issue in the case.

> The question then arises whether the defendants were guilty of any actionable negligence in not using all reasonable means in order to rescue the drowning man. Undoubtedly such is one's moral duty, but what legal duty did the defendants owe to the deceased to rescue him if possible, from his position of danger, brought about, not by their, but his own, negligence?

And at p. 148 O.L.R., p. 653 D.L.R.:

> His voluntary act in thus putting himself in a position of danger, from the fatal consequences of which, unfortunately, there was no escape except through the defendants' intervention, could not create a legal obligation on the defendants' part to stop the ship or adopt other means to save the deceased.

This decision was followed by an amendment to the *Canada Shipping Act*, R.S.C. 1927, c. 186, enacting [1934, c. 44, s. 519] what is now s. 526 [R.S.C. 1952, c. 29]:

> 526(1) The master or person in charge of a vessel shall, so far as he can do so without serious danger to his own vessel, her crew and passengers, if any, render assistance to every person, even if that person be a subject of a foreign state at war with Her Majesty, who is found at sea and in danger of being lost, and if he fails to do so he is liable to a fine not exceeding one thousand dollars.

The section may not be applicable to or refer to the assistance to a passenger who falls overboard, but the shocking reluctance of the common law to recognize as a legal duty the moral obligation to assist a fellow human being in this predicament has been overcome in cases where a special relation exists, such as that of a carrier to a passenger in peril overboard, by thinly disguising the moral obligation as an "implied contract": See *Prosser on Torts,* 3rd ed., c.10, p. 336 under the heading "Duty to Aid One in Peril"; *Fleming on Torts,* 2nd ed., p. 166; *Salmond on Torts,* 14th ed., p. 57.

Two American decisions illustrate this trend: In *Harris* v. *Pennsylvania Railroad Co.* (1931), 50 F. 2d 866, where the evidence disclosed that a seaman on a flat had fallen overboard, it was held on appeal that the negligence of the crew in failing to assist the seaman should have been left to the jury on the evidence, the Court making the following comment at pp. 868-9:

> . . . it is implied in the contract that the ship shall use every reasonable means to save the life of a human being who has no other source of help. The universal custom of the sea demands as much wherever human life is in danger. The seaman's contract of employment requires it as a matter of right.

The decision, *The "Cappy", Hutchinson* v. *Dickie*, [1947] Am. Mar. Cas. 1467, 162 F. 2d 103, was quoted and relied upon by the defendant's counsel. The facts of the case are somewhat similar to those of the present case, in that during the daylight hours, after the consumption of intoxicating liquor, the owner of a 38-foot cabin cruiser who was at the wheel lost an invited guest who fell overboard in Lake Erie near Cleveland. The trial Judy found that the helmsman was incapable of co-ordination due to the excessive use of alcoholic stimulants coupled with physical impairment, and was negligent in failing to turn his cruiser about instead of back it astern. The Circuit Court of Appeal reversed the trial judgment and dismissed the case, on the basis that the decree had no substantial support in the evidence, and commenting at p. 1473:

> We think that if appellant erred at all in backing instead of turning the cruiser, the error was one of judgement and not of negligence. Further, we think an insurmountable objection to the judgement in appellee's favor is the entire lack of evidence that anything appellant did or left undone caused his efforts at rescue to fail. It does not appear that if appellant had turned the cruiser instead of backing it, Dickie would or should have been save.

The Court did not disagree, however, with the universally recognized duty of the owner to make a reasonable effort to rescue the man overboard.

In *Silva's Fishing Corporation (Pty.) Ltd.* v. *Maweza*, [1957] (2) So. Afr. L.R. 256 at p. 263, the following appears in a discussion whether there exists a legal or a moral duty to rescue:

> A duty to rescue is not special or subject to peculiarly restricted rules. It is simply a duty to act reasonably and such a duty may arise out of the circumstances of the case. It will be for the Court to decide in each case whether the circumstances are such as to give rise to a legal duty.

The learned author of *Fleming on Torts*, 3rd ed., discussed at p. 145 under the heading "Duty of Care", "Duties of Affirmative Action", the distinction above referred to, between misfeasance and nonfeasance, and compares it to the distinction, ". . . between active misconduct working positive injury to others and passive inaction, failing merely to take positive steps to benefit others or to protect them from some impending harm". It is still in the modern law of negligence that there is no general duty to come to the rescue of a person who finds himself in peril from a source completely unrelated to the defendant, even where little risk or effort would be involved in assisting: thus a person on a dock can with legal impunity ignore the call for help of a drowning person, even refusing to throw a life ring. The law leaves the remedy to a person's conscience.

There is, however, in the words of Fleming, *ibid*, at p. 148, ". . . strong support for a duty of affirmative care, including aid and rescue, incidental to certain special relations, like that of employer and employee, carrier and passenger, and occupier and his lawful visitors".

Extending the *quasi*-contractual duty of a carrier to his passenger in peril, it seems to me that the relation between the master of a pleasure boat and his invited guest should also require a legal duty to aid and rescue. Parliament reflecting the conscience of the community has seen fit to impose on the master a duty to render assistance to any stranger, including an enemy alien "found at sea and in danger of being lost" (s. 526, *Canada Shipping Act*); the common law

After a lengthy discussion of the law that included cases (precedents), a statute, and some texts (secondary authorities), the judge reaches his conclusion as to the applicable principle. He has extended the rule to include a new situation, and in so doing has created new law. This is one way that the common law develops, by incremental changes to existing rules.

can be no less solicitous for the safety of an invited guest and must impose upon the master the duty to attempt a rescue when this can be done without imperilling the safety of the vessel, her crew and passengers. The common law must keep pace with the demand and expectations of a civilized community, the sense of social obligation, and brand as tortuous negligence the failure to help a man overboard in accordance with the universal custom of the sea.

Lacourciere J applies another principle (apparently, this one is "established") to resolve the first issue.

In any event, if the defendant, as he did here, affirmatively undertakes the rescue operation, he is by law regarded as assuming a duty to act, and will thereafter be liable for his negligence: *Prosser on Torts* (1941), pp. 194-5, puts it this way:

> But further, if the defendant attempts to aid him, and takes control of the situation, he is regarded as entering voluntarily into a relation of responsibility, and hence as assuming a duty. Thereafter he will be liable for any failure to use reasonable care in dealing with him, until the emergency has ended, and particularly if he abandons him in a position of danger.

The analysis of the second issue starts here.

Having found a legal duty to rescue, or a voluntary assumption of duty, the next question is, is the standard of conduct applicable in the performance of such duty? Bearing in mind that the man in the street would not have any knowledge of a sea rescue operation, the test here is: what would the reasonable boat operator do in the circumstances, attributing to such person the reasonable skill and experience required of the master of a cabin cruiser who is responsible for the safety and rescue of his passengers?

Expert witnesses were called on behalf of the plaintiffs to assist the Court in setting out what such ordinary, prudent, reasonable boat operator would have done in the circumstances. The first was Captain Livingstone, Chairman of the Marine Department at George Brown Community College, Toronto, a qualified sea captain under a British certificate who recently acted as Education Vice-Commander of the Toronto Power Squadron, with considerable experience since 1925 on all ships including yachts of the "Ogopogo" type. The other expert was Captain John Kenneth Mumford, Communications Office of the Toronto Harbour Commission, British Master's Certificate 1957, and the author of a boating course covering all safety aspects of operating a power cruiser, and winner of every major navigation contest on Lake Ontario. These two highly qualified seamen agree that there are no statutory regulations or guidelines covering the rescue procedure in a "man overboard" situation, and that none is mentioned in the well-known Canadian booklet "Safety Afloat". This situation, according to them, is a common emergency calling for the common sense of every prudent seaman who should be prepared to react quickly and instinctively, so to speak automatically.

The following should be the procedure followed: having ascertained on which side the man fell, the master first turns his boat towards the same side to clear the propellers and leaves the engine in neutral unless the man overboard is astern and in no danger from them. A life ring is cast, and the master then turns around to approach the man against the wind, allowing him to come on the leeward side where passengers or crewmen can grasp him and haul him in at the lowest point of the boat. The maximum time involved would be one to two minutes or slightly more. Both experts emphasized many reasons why the procedure of reversing the engines and backing should never be adopted, unless in a confined area where the boat cannot be turned around: in addition to loss of control and manoeuvrability, there is the impossibility of keeping sight of the man astern when approaching, the danger of the propellers, and complete loss of control, at the mercy of wind and wave, on shutting down the engines. In the opinion of Captain Mumford, the bearing down stern first here adopted by the defendant was the sign of an incompetent operator: the average prudent owner of a 30-foot boat according to both experts should be competent in the rescue procedure described, and if not should not undertake to operate his boat. It is the procedure taught to students, and one in fact known by the defendant and practised by him on many previous occasions.

I can only conclude that the defendant's adoption of the wrong procedure in the circumstances was negligent, being a failure to exercise the reasonable care that the ordinary, prudent, reasonable operator would have shown in effecting the "man overboard" rescue. The defendant in his evidence admitted that he made what he described as an error of judgement and did not attempt to justify the rescue procedure adopted.

Detective Sergeant John Brooks of the Town of Port Credit Police, who had ample opportunity to observe the defendant at the yacht club, and at the Police Station after the accident, formed the opinion that MacLaren's ability to drive an automobile or operate a vessel was impaired by alcohol, and he would have recommended the laying of criminal charges to the Crown Attorney. The admitted consumption by the defendant and the necessary inferences from surrounding circumstances, plus the extraordinary conduct of the defendant during the rescue attempt, force me to the conclusion that the defendant was unable to exercise proper judgement in the emergency created because of his excessive consumption of alcohol.

The third issue. —— It is trite law that liability does not follow a finding of negligence, even where there exists a legally recognized duty, unless the defendant's conduct is the effective cause of the loss: *Cork* v. *Kirby MacLean, Ltd.*, [1952] 2 All E.R. 402 at p. 407, *per* Denning, L.J.:

> Subject to the question of remoteness, causation is, I think, a question of fact. If you can say that the damage would not have happened but for a particular fault, then that fault is in fact a cause of the damage; but if you can say that the damage would have happened just the same, fault or no fault, then the fault is not a cause of the damage.

In the present case the burden is on the plaintiff to prove by a preponderance of evidence that the defendant's negligence was the effective cause of Matthews' death. Obviously the defendant is not responsible for Matthews' fall overboard. There is no evidence in the present case that Matthews was ever alive after falling in the water: all witnesses agree that he was motionless and staring. Bearing in mind that Horsley, a young man than Matthews, in the opinion of the pathologist probably died of shock immediately or shortly after his immersion, it is reasonable to think that Matthews, 16 years older, did not survive longer, and after he hit the water there never was a sign of life or consciousness. It was impossible in the present case to discharge this burden by a pathologist's report; in the case of a missing body, witnesses' evidence of some struggle or sign of life on the part of the deceased during rescue operations would be required. I am reluctantly forced to the conclusion that, on the balance of probabilities, it

The plaintiffs have —— has not been shown that Matthews' life could have been saved. The defendant's negligence therefore was not the cause of Matthews' death and there can be no liability.

failed to prove one of the essential elements in a negligence action: causation. While they succeeded on the first two points, their failure on this one means they lose the whole case.

* * *

Case Brief

Matthews v MacLaren

Facts

The defendant (Δ) was the owner/operator of a cabin cruiser. On the day in question, he invited some guests for an outing on his boat. One of his guests, Matthews, fell overboard. The Δ reversed the motors and backed toward Matthews. Approximately four minutes elapsed as various rescue attempts were made. Matthews was apparently unconscious in the water, and he eventually disappeared under the boat and his body was never found. The Δ was impaired because of excessive consumption of alcohol. The "standard" rescue procedure in a "man overboard" situation is to approach the person overboard "bow on."

The Greek letter delta (Δ) is often used as an abbreviation for the defendant, and the Greek letter pi (Π) is used for the plaintiff.

In applying the guidelines to isolate the key facts, the parties, the cause of action, and the elements of the claim were noted. Only facts relating to these specifics were included.

Proceedings

The plaintiffs (Πs), the widow and children of Matthews, commenced this action under fatal accidents legislation claiming negligence on the part of the Δ.

Issues

1 a) Whether there exists a duty on the part of the master of a pleasure boat to rescue a gratuitous passenger who falls overboard through no negligence on the part of the former?

b) In any event, whether there existed a duty on the Δ to rescue Matthews having commenced the rescue operation?

2 a) Assuming the Δ owed a duty to rescue, what is the requisite standard of care?

b) Assuming the Δ owed a duty to rescue, did the Δ breach the requisite standard of care by using the wrong procedure and by being impaired?

Note the two types of issues. 1a and 2a are *rule formulation issues*. The questions were about the nature of the applicable rule. The law was not clear and required some analysis (although for 2a, not much). 1b and 2b were *rule application issues*.

Holdings

1 a) Extending the quasi-contractual duty of a carrier to his passenger in peril, the relation between the master of a pleasure boat and his invited guest requires a duty to aid and rescue.

b) Also, the Δ having commenced the rescue operation was by law regarded as having assumed a duty to act.

2 a) The test here is: what would the reasonable boat operator do in the circumstances, attributing to such person the reasonable skill and experience required of the master of a cabin cruiser who is responsible for the safety and rescue of his passengers?

b) The Δ failed to exercise the reasonable care of a reasonable boat operator in his rescue attempt by adopting the wrong procedure and by being impaired.

Reasoning

1 a) The court affirmed the rule that there is no general duty to rescue, but declined to follow the *Vanvalkenburg* case where the court held that the operators of a ship were not under a duty to rescue a seaman in their employ, who had fallen overboard through his own negligence. The court cited an amendment to the *Canada Shipping Act* enacted after the *Vanvalkenburg* case imposing a statutory duty on the master or person in charge of a vessel to rescue every person found at sea. The court also cited *Fleming on Torts* where it was stated that there was support for a duty to rescue incidental to certain special relations, like that of employer–employee, carrier–passenger, and occupier–visitor. In light of these authorities and the "expectations of a civilized community," the court extended the common law duty to rescue to include the relation of master of a pleasure boat and his invited guest.

b) The court simply applied the established rule that where a person attempts to rescue someone and takes control of the situation, he is regarded as entering voluntarily into a relation of responsibility, and hence assuming a duty.

2 a) The court adopted the standard of the reasonable boat operator stating that the man in the street would not have any knowledge of a sea rescue operation.

b) The court offered no arguments in support of its finding as a fact that the Δ had not exercised the care of an ordinary, prudent, reasonable boat operator.

Disposition/Judgment

The Πs' action was dismissed. Although the court found the Δ in breach of his duty to Matthews, the court found that the Δ's conduct had not in fact caused Matthew's death.

Causation was not set out as a separate issue because there was no analysis of the legal principle involved. The judge made a purely factual determination: the Δ did not cause the loss.

APPENDIX 7.2

Citation of Cases

As explained in Chapter 5, Canadian legal sources are cited according to rules different from citation rules for other kinds of academic writing. Proper citation of legal sources is expected in

- legal memoranda (written analyses of legal problems prepared to assist lawyers advise clients),
- written submissions, briefs, and books of authorities for argument at trial,
- appeal facta for argument on appeals, and
- various legal publications.

We follow the rules set out in the *Canadian Guide to Uniform Legal Citation*.[27] Rules for citing cases traditionally dealt with how to refer to them as they appeared in print report series. However, beginning in 2000, many courts in Canada and internationally began to adopt and require an additional citation for their decisions: a **neutral citation**. As of 2010, when the Ontario courts adopted neutral citations, all Canadian court systems use them.

Neutral Citations

A court that has adopted the neutral citation protocol numbers each of its judgments consecutively for the year in question. This requires coordination between all the court registries in the relevant jurisdiction. Another feature of the neutral citation method is that each paragraph within each judgment is numbered consecutively (prior to this, paragraphs were usually unnumbered). Once the decision is released by the court and reproduced online or in a print report series, the yearly decision number and paragraph numbers must remain unaltered. The purpose of this new approach is to make cases, and passages within them, easy to find, whether paper or electronic sources are being used. Now all references to passages are to the court-assigned paragraph numbers, which are consistently used in all publications.

Following is an example of a neutral citation:

Kerr v Baranow, 2011 SCC 10 at paras 12-15
1   2 3 4   5

The components in this neutral citation are as follows:

1   **Style of cause**
The **style of cause** is the name of the case or title of the proceeding, and it consists of the names of the parties to the dispute. It is italicized, with a "*v*" (no period) separating the parties, followed by a comma (not italicized).

2   **Year of the decision**

3   **Unique jurisdiction and court abbreviation**
In this example, the abbreviation is for the Supreme Court of Canada (SCC).

4   **Decision number**
The decision number, followed by a space if a pinpoint reference follows as it does here.

5   **Pinpoint**
Where a particular passage from the judgment is being quoted, individual or multiple paragraph numbers are preceded by "para" or "paras," respectively; or the symbol "¶" can be used in place of either.

Where available, the neutral citation must be used. In some instances, where the decision has not been reported in a print report series, it will be the only citation available. Such cases will often be available online, because most courts now publish their decisions online soon after they are handed down. In other instances, where the case has been reported in one or more report series, the neutral citation is set out first and then followed by the citation for the print report(s). The implementation of the neutral citation protocol does not render traditional citation rules redundant; if you wish the reader to be able to look up a reported case in a print report series, you must *also* include the traditional citation.

---

27   McGill Law Journal, *Canadian Guide to Uniform Legal Citation*, 7th ed (Toronto: Carswell, 2010) ["McGill Guide"]. See also footnote 27 in Chapter 5.

Print Report Citations

As of 2010, all Canadian court systems have adopted the neutral citation protocol. For the past four years, then, all reported citations have included a neutral citation as well as the information traditionally included. The following shows a citation of this type, which is now standard:

> *Kerr v Baranow*, 2011 SCC 10 at paras 12-15, 18, [2011] 1 SCR 269.

As you can see, the neutral citation is set out first, together with any pinpoint reference ("paras 12-15, 18"). Where the report series reports by year (rather than by volume), the year is set out in square brackets. In this particular instance, the year of the decision and the year of publication are the same. (Sometimes, the year of publication is later than the year of the decision). Set out the volume number after the year of the publication. Next is the law report abbreviation ("SCR"). Note that no periods separate the letters, in keeping with the McGill style. The last element in the citation is the page number—the first page of the case in the report series volume.

Following is an example of a print report citation *without* a neutral citation:

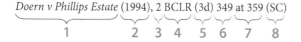

> *Doern v Phillips Estate* (1994), 2 BCLR (3d) 349 at 359 (SC)
> 1   2   3   4   5   6   7   8

The components shown in this example are as follows:

1   **Style of cause**
Appearing first in a case citation is the style of cause, which is italicized. As with neutral citations, the plaintiff's name precedes the defendant's, and the names are separated with a "*v*" (no period). Usually, last names are used, not titles or first names. When referring to a corporate entity, always include "Ltd" and "Limited," but omit "Inc," "Co," or "Corp," except where it is unclear from the name that the party is a company or where these abbreviations form an integral part of the name (for example, *Canadian Broadcasting Corp*).

In criminal cases, the Crown is usually "*R*"; however, if the Crown is the defendant/respondent, terms such as "The Queen" or "Regina" are used. In civil cases, the Crown is "Canada" or "Manitoba," for example (depending on whether it is the federal Crown or a provincial Crown which is the party to the lawsuit). Specific bodies representing the Crown are designated in parentheses: for example, "New Brunswick (Workplace Health, Safety

and Compensation Commission)." Where there are multiple parties, only the names of the first plaintiff and the first defendant are shown.

2   **Year of decision**
After the style of cause, the decision year is included in round brackets. This is done in cases where, as here, the report series reports by volume number and not by year. If the report series reports by year, include the year in the report series portion of the citation, in square brackets. Sometimes a case is published in the year after the case is decided, in which case you may need to include both a year in round brackets (indicating the year of decision) and a year in square brackets. (Note, however, that if there is a neutral citation preceding a report series citation, it will never be necessary to include the year in round brackets; the neutral citation makes it clear what the year of the decision is.)

3   **Volume of law report**
Set out the volume number, followed by a space. Law reports consist of numerous volumes that cover many years. If the report series being cited reports by volume number and not by year, the volume numbers can get quite high, sometimes in the hundreds. If the report series reports by year, there still may be a volume number following the year in square brackets, but the numbers only run for the year in question and will never be that high.

4   **Law report abbreviation**
Next is the law report abbreviation. Cases are always cited according to the abbreviated form of the law report in which they are found. Many law reports state in the front of each volume how they are to be cited—what abbreviations should be used.

5   **Law report series**
The law report series appears, where applicable, after the law report abbreviation. Periodically, a law report may change its format and binding, or make other editorial changes. When this occurs, the law report may begin a new series. This means that the numbering system begins over again. If a law report has multiple series, the series number, starting with the second one, is indicated in round brackets "(2d)" followed by a space. The abbreviations are: 2d, 3d, 4th, 5th, and so on. Superscript is not used, and there is no *n* in 2d or *r* 3d.

6   **Page**
After the law report abbreviation or (if there is one) series indication, the page number on which the case begins in the law report is set out. The reference is to the first page only, and does not include "p" for page.

7   Pinpoint

Indicate the relevant page number in the form "at *n*". There is no "p" or "pg" prior to the number.

8   Jurisdiction and court

The jurisdiction of the case—that is, the province or territory in which the case originated—and the court that rendered the decision are often placed in round brackets after the page reference. Some or all of this information may be omitted where it is redundant. In the above example, only "SC" is included to indicate the British Columbia Supreme Court, since the jurisdiction is clear from the name of the law report ("BCLR"). To take another example, the *Supreme Court Reports* contain only decisions of the SCC, so it is not necessary to include "(SCC)" at the end of the citation. Only include necessary information. (Note that where there is a neutral citation, it will never be necessary to include this information; it will already be part of the neutral citation.)

Legal Abbreviations

Most legal citations, whether of statutes, cases, or secondary material, use abbreviations. The publication in which you have located the relevant legal source will often indicate how it is to be abbreviated when cited. However, sometimes it is not clear how to abbreviate a particular source, either because the original source omits this information or because you are not looking at the original source. When this occurs, it is necessary to consult a secondary source that lists abbreviations. Two excellent resources are the following:

- The appendices to the McGill Guide, which include comprehensive listings of abbreviations required to correctly cite legal materials.
- The online Cardiff Index to Legal Abbreviations.[28]

---

28   <http://www.legalabbrevs.cardiff.ac.uk>.

CHAPTER SUMMARY

The third branch of government, the judiciary, plays an important role in resolving all manner of disputes. Some of these disputes involve private law claims, some involve public law issues, and some involve common law principles. Other disputes deal with statutory interpretation, and still others require answers to important questions concerning the constitutional validity of our laws.

Two overarching principles inform the Canadian judicial system: (1) the open court principle, which requires proceedings to take place in public unless there is a justifiable exception; and (2) the principle of judicial independence. These two principles, when adhered to, help safeguard the rule of law and promote public confidence in our justice system.

Understanding how cases get before the courts requires a basic knowledge of the constitutional basis and structure of our courts. There are three broad categories of courts: (1) inferior courts, (2) superior courts, and (3) the SCC. The jurisdiction to create courts is split between the federal and provincial legislative branches. The power to appoint judges is also a split jurisdiction, between the federal and provincial executive branches. The involvement of both levels of government creates a balance of power in the judicial branch.

The provincial and territorial inferior courts handle most of the cases in the system overall, dealing as they do with the less serious criminal and civil cases. The provincial superior courts have inherent jurisdiction to hear most disputes but are used primarily to resolve more serious claims. The federal courts have a more limited jurisdiction; they hear matters concerned with federal laws, such as intellectual property and taxation disputes. The SCC is the final court of appeal for Canada and generally only hears matters of national importance, whether criminal, civil, or constitutional in nature. Precedent flows downward, from the SCC to the various jurisdictionally separated court systems.

Understanding the structure and jurisdiction of the courts is only part of the puzzle, however. It is also important to understand how to read, cite, and analyze court judgments. Most judgments have similar components, such as a factual base, defined legal issues, holdings (or decisions), and reasons for those holdings. The governing rule is often referred to as the *ratio* of the case, and is one of the most important components to isolate when you are trying to understand a case. Reading and briefing cases is one of the most effective ways to learn how to analyze legal problems.

KEY TERMS

appellant individual, corporation, or other entity who lost at trial and who initiates an appeal to a higher court *(p. 193)*

binding term used to describe a higher court decision that a lower court in the same jurisdiction must follow according to the principle of *stare decisis* *(p. 186)*

case depending on context, refers to the reasons for judgment (where the court provides them), to the court process more generally, or to the entire dispute from beginning to end *(p. 193)*

case brief summary of a case, with the constituent parts of the court's reasons for judgment arranged in a set order *(p. 199)*

court state-sanctioned forum where disputes between opposing litigants are formally adjudicated *(p. 170)*

decision depending on context, refers to the outcome or disposition of a case, to the holding in the case, or (where the court provides them) to the entire set of reasons the court gives for its judgment *(p. 193)*

defendant individual, corporation, or other entity who defends a non-criminal lawsuit initiated by the plaintiff *(p. 192)*

dissent refers (in the context of a split decision on appeal) to the judgment of one or more justices in the minority *(p. 179)*

facta (sing. factum) written legal arguments to be presented on an appeal *(p. 178)*

federal superior courts (or federal courts) the Federal Court, the Federal Court of Appeal, the Tax Court of Canada, and the Court Martial Appeal Court *(p. 174)*

headnote concise summary of reasons for judgment, located near the beginning of a reported version of the case *(p. 193)*

inferior courts provincial and territorial courts whose jurisdiction is limited to the less serious criminal matters, family and youth matters, and small claims disputes; the federal courts martial, part of the military court system, are also inferior courts *(p. 172)*

judgment final outcome or disposition of the dispute heard before the court, or, when the court provides reasons for its judgment, the entire set of reasons *(p. 171)*

judicial independence principle that judges should be free to make decisions based on the law and free from outside interference *(p. 189)*

majority refers (in the context of a split decision on appeal) to the group of justices who form the majority and whose decision becomes the decision of the court *(p. 179)*

neutral citation unique citation protocol, recognized internationally and in all Canadian courts, according to which courts number each of their judgments consecutively for the year in question, as well as the paragraphs within judgments *(p. 209)*

***obiter dicta* or *obiter* (sing. *obiter dictum*)** statements made by the court in its reasons for judgment that may be of interest but that are inessential to the decision and therefore have no binding authority *(p. 198)*

open court principle principle that judicial proceedings should be administered in public *(p. 189)*

persuasive describes a precedent that a court is persuaded to give some weight to but is not bound to follow, because the precedent is from another jurisdiction or is otherwise not binding *(p. 186)*

plaintiff individual, corporation, or other entity who initiates a non-criminal lawsuit *(p. 192)*

precedent court decision that, under the doctrine of *stare decisis*, is binding on lower courts in the same jurisdiction *(p. 185)*

provincial superior courts provincially constituted courts with inherent jurisdiction to hear all matters (unless taken away by legislation) with two levels, a trial level and an appeal level—sometimes refers just to the trial level *(p. 173)*

puisne term applied to describe judges who rank below another judge or judges on the same court—for example, the judges below the chief justice on an appeal court *(p. 176)*

ratio* or *ratio decidendi Latin phrase ("the reason for the decision") referring to the governing rule in a case or the way it was applied to the facts *(p. 185)*

reference special case in which the executive branch of government refers a question of law to a court of appeal, usually a question concerning the constitutionality of a statute or course of action the government is considering *(p. 178)*

reserve postpone rendering its decision, after a hearing has concluded, so the court can carefully prepare the reasons for its judgment *(p. 179)*

respondent individual, corporation, or other entity who won at trial and who is responding to the appellant on an appeal to a higher court *(p. 193)*

section 96 courts provincial superior courts, so called because their judges are federally appointed under section 96 of the *Constitution Act, 1867 (p. 173)*

stare decisis Latin phrase ("to stand by decided matters") referring to the common law principle that a precedent is binding on lower courts in the same jurisdiction *(p. 185)*

style of cause the name of the case or title of the proceeding, consisting of the names of the parties to the dispute *(p. 209)*

Supreme Court of Canada Canada's highest court and final court of appeal *(p. 174)*

territorial superior courts federally constituted superior courts with jurisdiction in the territories *(p. 174)*

unified family courts special divisions of the trial level of a provincial superior court with complete jurisdiction over family law matters, including matters that would otherwise be heard in a provincial inferior court *(p. 181)*

FURTHER READING

BOOKS

Bushnell, Ian. *The Captive Court: A Study of the Supreme Court of Canada* (Montreal: McGill-Queen's University Press, 1992).

Hausegger, Lori, Matthew Hennigar & Troy Riddell. *Canadian Courts: Law, Politics, and Process* (Toronto: Oxford University Press, 2009).

Hogg, Peter W. *Constitutional Law of Canada*, 2013 student ed (Toronto: Carswell, 2013) ch 7 ("Courts"), ch 8 ("Supreme Court of Canada").

McGill Law Journal. *Canadian Guide to Uniform Legal Citation*, 7th ed (Toronto: Carswell, 2010).

Russell, Peter H. *The Judiciary in Canada: The Third Branch of Government* (Toronto: McGraw-Hill Ryerson, 1987).

WEBSITES

Gateway Site for Canadian Legal Databases

Canadian Legal Information Institute (CanLII): <http://www.canlii.org>.

Federal Courts

Supreme Court of Canada: <http://www.scc-csc.gc.ca>.

Federal Court of Appeal: <http://www.fca-caf.gc.ca>.

Federal Court: <http://www.fct-cf.gc.ca>.

Tax Court of Canada: <http://tcc-cci.gc.ca>.

Court Martial Appeal Court: <http://www.cmac-cacm.ca>.

Courts of the Provinces and Territories

Alberta Courts: <http://www.albertacourts.ab.ca>.

British Columbia Courts: <http://www.courts.gov.bc.ca>.

Manitoba Courts: <http://www.manitobacourts.mb.ca>.

New Brunswick Courts: <http://www.gnb.ca/cour>.

Newfoundland and Labrador Courts: <http://www.court.nl.ca>.

Nova Scotia Courts: <http://www.courts.ns.ca>.

Ontario Courts: <http://www.ontariocourts.on.ca>.

Prince Edward Island Courts: <http://www.gov.pe.ca/courts>.

Quebec Courts: <http://www.tribunaux.qc.ca>.

Saskatchewan Courts: <http://www.sasklawcourts.ca>.

Northwest Territories Courts: <http://www.nwtcourts.ca>.

Nunavut Courts: <http://www.nucj.ca>.

Yukon Courts: <http://www.yukoncourts.ca>.

Legal Abbreviations

Cardiff Index to Legal Abbreviations: <http://www.legalabbrevs.cardiff.ac.uk>.

REVIEW QUESTIONS

1. Explain how the role of the judiciary is still significant despite the prevalence today of legislated rules as a means of regulating society.

2. Explain why the provincial superior courts, which are constituted under section 92 of the *Constitution Act, 1867*, are sometimes referred to as "section 96 courts."

3. What are the main criteria the SCC considers when deciding whether or not to grant leave to a party to appeal to the Court?

4. How does the source of the jurisdiction of provincial and territorial *inferior* courts to hear cases differ from that of their superior court relatives?

5. Name three types of cases over which the Federal Court of Appeal has jurisdiction.

6. Describe the flow of precedent in the Canadian court system.

7. Describe the role of the Office of the Commissioner for Federal Judicial Affairs Canada (FJA) in the appointment process of superior court judges.

8. How does the National Judicial Institute (NJI) help prepare new judges for the transition from lawyer to adjudicator?

9. Explain the purpose of the open court principle and name two exceptions to it.

10. What are the three main facets of judicial independence?

11. What is the *ratio* (or *ratio decidendi*) of a case?

EXERCISES

1. Using Figure 7.1 as a reference point, research the website for the courts in your province or territory, and chart the four levels of the court system using the correct names for the courts at all levels.

2. Using the website for the courts in your province or territory, determine who are the three most recent appointees to the trial level of the superior court. Read their biographical information and prepare a short opinion concerning each, focused on the following question: Do you think political patronage or professional competence was the primary factor in his or her appointment?

3. Search the SCC website to locate the judgments database and the following case, which involves the open court principle. Following the citation rules described in Appendix 7.2, provide the full citation including both the neutral citation and the *Supreme Court Reports* citation:

   Canadian Broadcasting Corp v Canada (Attorney General) (2011)

4. The following case citations all contain mistakes. Circle the mistakes and redo the citations in the correct format, following the style prescribed by the McGill Guide:

   a. Westendorp v The Queen, [1983] 1 S.C.R. 43 (SCC

   b. *Downing v Graydon* [1978], 92 DLR (3rd) 355 at pp. 370-71 (Ont CA)

   c. *Fullowka v. Pinkerton's of Canada Ltd*, 2010 S.C.C. 5, (2010) 1 SCR 132

   d. *Blair v Western Mutual Benefit Association*, 1972 4 W.W.R. 284 (BC CA)

5. Read Appendix 7.1 on briefing cases, and then prepare a case brief of the following SCC case, which is available online (there are two judgments):

   Skoke-Graham v The Queen, [1985] 1 SCR 106

6. Locate the statute for your province or territory that constitutes the provincial/territorial court. Review the provisions in the statute dealing with judicial independence and then prepare a reasoned argument as to why, in your opinion, these provisions adequately or inadequately support judicial independence.

8 Civil Liberties

CANADIAN CHARTER OF RIGHTS AND FREEDOMS

The *Canadian Charter of Rights and Freedoms*, bearing the signature of Pierre Trudeau in the bottom right corner.

After reading this chapter, you will understand:

- The historical evolution of civil liberties and human rights in Canada
- How human rights are protected in the private sector by provincial and federal human rights legislation
- How rights and freedoms are protected in the public sector by the *Canadian Charter of Rights and Freedoms*

- The role played by the Supreme Court of Canada in interpreting the Charter
- The possibility of the Charter's evolving to include new grounds for discrimination and new rights and freedoms

Civil liberties encompass a broad range of values that support the freedom and dignity of the individual, and that are given recognition in various ways by Canadian law. The political civil liberties include the freedoms of speech, religion, assembly and association; the right to vote and be a candidate for elected office; and the freedom to enter and leave Canada and to move from one province to another. Legal civil liberties include the freedom from search, seizure, arrest, imprisonment, cruel and unusual punishment and unfair trial procedures. Egalitarian civil liberties include equality of access to accommodation, employment, education and other benefits, implying, at least, an absence of racial, sexual or other illegitimate criteria of discrimination. Particular to Canada are language rights, covering the right to use the English or the French language; and educational rights, covering the rights of denominational (or separate) schools.

Peter W Hogg, *Constitutional Law of Canada*,
2013 student ed (Toronto: Carswell, 2013) at 34-1

Introduction

In Canada, there is a distinction between the terms "civil rights" and "civil liberties." Section 92(13) of the *Constitution Act, 1867* gave provinces jurisdiction over "Property and Civil Rights in the Province." At the time the Act was drafted (then called the *British North America Act*), it was understood that the term "civil rights" referred to *private law rights* between individuals in areas such as contracts, torts, and property.[1]

The term "civil liberties" has a different meaning. As our chapter's opening quotation from Peter Hogg suggests, civil liberties encompass values related to the freedom and dignity of all individuals in the context of public sector areas such as politics and the justice system. These values, as Hogg notes, are reflected in principles such as freedom of speech, the right to a fair trial, and the right to equal access to accommodation, jobs, and education. This last principle, concerning equal access, relates to the idea that discrimination is very harmful to the dignity of an individual. Accordingly, legislation in this country—provincial,

---

1   Peter W Hogg, *Constitutional Law of Canada*, 2013 student ed (Toronto: Carswell, 2013) at 21-3, 21-4.

territorial, and federal human rights acts, and the *Canadian Charter of Rights and Freedoms*—prohibits discrimination in certain defined areas, both in the private and in the public sectors.

This chapter will trace the historical evolution of civil liberties in Canada, from their origins in England to their eventual inclusion in our regional and federal human rights acts and in our *Canadian Charter of Rights and Freedoms*. We will explain how these human rights acts differ from the Charter in their protection of rights and freedoms. We will also provide a concise overview of the Charter, and take into account the Supreme Court of Canada's key supporting role in interpreting the rights and freedoms that the Charter guarantees. Lastly, the chapter contemplates future areas to which the Charter's grounds for discrimination and rights and freedoms coverage might be extended.

The Evolution of Civil Liberties in Canada

How did civil liberties in Canada eventually gain legislative protection in provincial, territorial, and federal human rights acts and in the Charter? Many scholars and jurists have considered this question.[2] Four main factors in the development of this protection can be identified:

1. growing dissatisfaction in Canada, after the Second World War, with an "implied" bill of rights (according to this position, a bill of rights inferred to be in the preamble to the *Constitution Act, 1867*);
2. the influence of the civil rights movement in the United States;
3. dissatisfaction with the *Canadian Bill of Rights* (1960); and
4. the advent of the *Canadian Charter of Rights and Freedoms* in 1982.

Each of these factors is discussed below.

Canada's "Implied" Bill of Rights

The *Constitution Act, 1867* states in its preamble that Canada is to have "a Constitution similar in Principle to that of the United Kingdom." These words reflect the drafters' intention to imply that England's historical legacy of civil liberties—and the rules that were developed to safeguard them—were included in our Canadian Constitution. What were some examples of the **civil liberties** and safeguards that Canada derived from England?

Human rights in England had a long evolution under that country's common law. One of the earliest and most important documents in this regard was the *Magna Carta* (1215), which stated that certain actions could not be taken against a person except in accordance with the "law of the land." Over time, this principle came to be known as "due process of law." Other legal rights were subsequently recognized in England, including the following: the presumption of innocence (that is, the right to be presumed innocent of a crime until proven guilty in a court of law); the right to trial by jury; *habeas corpus* (that is, a prisoner's right to be brought before the court to determine whether the government has the right to continue detaining him); and the right to an open and fair trial.

---

2   See, for example, Ian Greene, *The Charter of Rights* (Toronto: Lorimer, 1989); R Sharpe, K Swinton & K Roach, *The Charter of Rights and Freedoms*, 2d ed (Toronto: Irwin Law, 2002); Gerald-A Beaudoin & Errol Mendes, eds, *Canadian Charter of Rights and Freedoms*, 4th ed (Markham, Ont: LexisNexis, 2005); Hogg, *supra* note 1.

In addition to these legal rights, there developed certain political civil rights that stemmed from England's having a democratic government. Among such values were the rights to freedom of speech, freedom of religion, freedom of the press, and peaceful assembly. There were also certain conventions and practices, related to England's parliamentary form of government, that helped safeguard civil liberties in that country. Some of these were:

- respect for the rule of law,
- the independence of the judiciary from interference by the executive and legislative branches of government, and
- the independence of the legal profession from government control.

What is significant about the English system, from a Canadian perspective, was that civil liberties in that country were not guaranteed by any single entrenched constitutional bill of rights. They were protected, instead, by a combination of the common law, Parliament, public opinion, a free press, and the country's popular support for democracy.

As noted, the preamble to the *Constitution Act, 1867* states that Canada is to have "a Constitution similar in Principle to that of the United Kingdom," which implies that these English civil liberty concepts have been inherited by Canada. In doing so, according to some Canadian court decisions, including some from the Supreme Court of Canada (SCC), the Act gives Canada an "implied bill of rights" that pre-dates the Charter and protects Canadians against misuse of government power.[3]

What concerned civil libertarian activists in Canada, particularly in the period after the Second World War, was a sense that such an implied bill of rights was not effective to protect the civil liberty rights of Canadians. In short, was an implied bill of rights adequate? This post-war period saw an international trend toward the global protection of human rights. The genocide and atrocities of the Second World War, once they came fully to light at the end of the war, led to the founding of the United Nations and to the proclamation, in 1948, of the UN's Universal Declaration of Human Rights. A growing number of Canadians, some important lawyers among them, believed that civil liberties in this country likewise needed to be codified and protected by constitutional legislation.[4]

Influence of the Civil Rights Movement in the United States

The 1950s and 1960s were important decades for civil rights in the United States. The civil rights movement had awoken in that country in the 1950s, when court action against the segregation of blacks and whites—most notably, the landmark 1954 US Supreme Court case of *Brown v Board of Education*—outlawed racial segregation in public schools. The 1950s also saw the mobilization of activist organizations such as the National Association for the Advancement of Colored Peoples (NAACP), which sought to advance the cause of civil rights for black Americans and to ensure that desegregation prescribed by the *Brown* case was followed at the state level. Inspired by Dr. Martin Luther King Jr., black Americans began to engage in protest marches, boycotts, and sit-ins, particularly in the American

---

3 See Sharpe, Swinton & Roach, *supra* note 2. See also *Reference Re Alberta Statutes*, [1938] 2 SCR 100; *Saumur v Quebec and Attorney General of Canada*, [1953] 2 SCR 299; *Roncarelli v Duplessis*, [1959] SCR 121; and Hogg, *supra* note 2 at 34-10.

4 See EM Adams, "'Guardians of Liberty': RMW Chitty and the Wartime Idea of Constitutional Rights" in Constance Backhouse & W Wesley Pue, eds, *The Promise and Perils of Law: Lawyers in Canadian History* (Toronto: Irwin Law, 2009) 173; FR Scott, *Civil Liberties and Canadian Federalism* (Toronto: University of Toronto Press, 1959).

South, with the common aim of ending segregation in public places such as transit systems, lunch counters, and voting districts.

Such actions in America, as well as civil rights movements abroad—for example, the movement to end apartheid in South Africa—further influenced civil rights activists in Canada to seek anti-discrimination legislation here.

Dissatisfaction with Canada's 1960 Bill of Rights

Among Canadians strongly influenced by these civil rights movements in the US and elsewhere was Prime Minister John Diefenbaker. In 1960, his government enacted the *Canadian Bill of Rights*. One of its notable provisions was section 1, which states:

FIGURE 8.1 When Martin Luther King (1929–1968) became the youngest man to receive the Nobel Peace Prize, in 1964, he contributed all of the prize money to the civil rights movement.

It is hereby recognized and declared that in Canada there have existed and shall continue to exist without discrimination by reason of race, national origin, colour, religion or sex, the following human rights and fundamental freedoms, namely,

(a) the right of the individual to life, liberty, security of the person and enjoyment of property, and the right not to be deprived thereof except by due process of law;
(b) the right of the individual to equality before the law and the protection of the law;
(c) freedom of religion;
(d) freedom of speech;
(e) freedom of assembly and association; and
(f) freedom of the press.[5]

Diefenbaker's initiative started a new approach to protecting civil liberties in this country—a movement away from the older, convention-based Anglo-Canadian implied-bill-of-rights idea, toward the American approach of having rights codified in one central document. Many Canadians welcomed this initiative.

However, Diefenbaker's 1960 Bill of Rights proved disappointing. Where the US Bill of Rights was entrenched in that country's Constitution, Diefenbaker's Bill of Rights was not. It was also an ordinary act of the federal Parliament and applied only to federal laws, not provincial ones. Furthermore, in several cases pertaining to equality before the law using the Bill of Rights, the SCC was reluctant to use section 1 in any forceful way to invalidate federal legislation that concerned equality under the law between men and women (see Chapter 4).

The SCC's cautious interpretation of the Bill of Rights and deference to legislative supremacy concerned many civil rights activists and, especially, many women.[6] They were highly motivated to support Prime Minister Trudeau's efforts in the 1970s and 1980s to patriate

5 *Canadian Bill of Rights*, SC 1960, c 44, reprinted in RSC 1985, App III.

6 See Anne F Bayefsky, "Defining Equality Rights" in Anne F Bayefsky & Mary Eberts, eds, *Equality Rights and the Canadian Charter of Rights and Freedoms* (Toronto: Carswell, 1985) at 1; Lise Gotell, *The Canadian Women's Movement, Equality Rights and the Charter* (Ottawa: Canadian Research Institute for the Advancement of Women, 1990).

Canada's Constitution from England and supplement it with a charter of rights and freedoms that *would* be entrenched. In particular, they wanted stronger wording to overcome perceived limitations in section 1 and a document that was more effective than Diefenbaker's Bill of Rights.[7] By the 1980s, conditions at last were ripe for such a development. Former Chief Justice Dickson succinctly summarized the legal and sociohistorical context in which Canada acquired the Charter:

> By the 1980s, many of the elements necessary for a *Charter of Rights* were present: a commitment to a unified set of norms governing the individual's relation with the state in a criminal law setting; experience with constitutionally mandated judicial review of legislative action in the realm of the division of powers; tentative steps by the judiciary to uphold rights in the implied *Bill of Rights* cases; a growing recognition at an international level that human rights should be constitutionally protected; and further steps on the part of the legislature and the courts to marry this international movement with the dictates of a parliamentary democracy through the adoption of a *Bill of Rights*. In this rich environment, one critical ingredient was lacking: constitutional legitimization of these fundamental rights.[8]

The Advent of Canada's New Charter of Rights and Freedoms

The "critical ingredient" referred to by Chief Justice Dickson eventually arrived. It came as a result of Prime Minister Trudeau's successful efforts to patriate Canada's Constitution and add a new charter of rights and freedoms. As described in Chapter 4, this was the final step in Canada's constitutional legitimization of fundamental rights. On April 17, 1982, Queen Elizabeth visited Ottawa and proclaimed the *Constitution Act, 1982* in force. The *Canadian Charter of Rights and Freedoms* was officially entrenched in Canada's Constitution.

Private Sector Protection of Human Rights

The Charter provided new and important protections for civil liberties in Canadian law. However, we should keep in mind, too, that the Charter was not the only example of legislation that arose after the Second World War to protect the rights and freedoms of Canadians. In this regard, the provinces had taken the lead.

Provincial and Territorial Legislation

Canada's provinces introduced **human rights** legislation in this country before the federal government did. Ontario passed a *Racial Discrimination Act* in 1944, and Saskatchewan enacted a *Bill of Rights* in 1947—the first legislation of their kind in Canada. Canada at that time was starting to undergo demographic changes, because of a growing influx of visible-minority immigrants arriving here from non-European countries.[9] Many of these new

---

7   Sandra Burt, "What's Fair? Changing Feminist Perceptions of Justice in English Canada" (1992) 12 Windsor YB Access Just 337; P Leclerc, "Women's Issues" in P James & M Kasoff, eds, *Canadian Studies in the New Millenium* (Toronto: University of Toronto Press, 2008) 185.

8   B Dickson, "The Canadian Charter of Rights and Freedoms: Context and Evolution" in Beaudoin & Mendes, *supra* note 2 at 10.

9   WS Tarnopolsky, *Discrimination and the Law in Canada* (Toronto: Richard De Boo, 1982).

Canadians encountered **discrimination**, especially in finding housing, getting service in restaurants and hotels and in other public areas, and finding employment.[10] This discrimination was meted out mainly in the private sector—that is, by landlords, employers, service providers, and companies. To help prevent it, provinces and territories began to enact human rights codes that prohibited discrimination in the private sector on certain defined grounds. The codes also applied to provincial and territorial governments when they engaged in private sector activities (for example, when acting as landlords or employers). Ontario became one of the first provinces in Canada to enact a human rights code, and it also established a human rights commission to hear complaints involving discrimination, to investigate and remedy them, and to take measures to help prevent discrimination from occurring. All provinces and territories now have similar legislation.

Federal Legislation: The Canadian Human Rights Act

The federal government passed its own *Canadian Human Rights Act* in 1977 and established the Canadian Human Rights Commission one year later, to administer it. The Act applies to private sector matters that, under section 91 of the *Constitution Act, 1867*, come under the federal government's jurisdiction (see Chapters 4 and 5). For example, section 91(15) of the *Constitution Act, 1867* gave jurisdiction over banking to the federal government. Accordingly, if a human rights complaint was made against a bank manager, the federal *Canadian Human Rights Act*, not one of the provincial human rights acts, would apply to the complaint.

This federal act, like human rights statutes in each of the provinces and territories, prohibits discrimination on certain grounds. The prohibited grounds of discrimination are set out in section 3:

> 3(1) For all purposes of this Act, the prohibited grounds of discrimination are race, national or ethnic origin, colour, religion, age, sex, sexual orientation, marital status, family status, disability, and conviction for which a pardon has been granted.
> (2) Where the ground of discrimination is pregnancy or child-birth, the discrimination shall be deemed to be on the ground of sex.[11]

The Act goes on the define certain specific practices described in sections 5 to 14.1 where discrimination on any of the grounds referred to in section 3 is forbidden. These practices occur most often in the private sector and include the provision of goods and services, real estate dealings (commercial or residential), employment, and harassment in any of these contexts. The federal government is also subject to this legislation if it engages in any of these activities, such as employment, and discriminates against someone on a prohibited ground while doing so (section 66). Concerning harassment (section 14), there have been an increasing number of cases recently, particularly in the employment context. While harassment can take many forms, section 14(2) makes it clear that "sexual harassment shall … be deemed to be harassment on a prohibited ground of discrimination."

10   See George Tanaka, "Wartime Toronto and Japanese Canadians" (1984) 6 Polyphony 240; Constance Backhouse, *Colour-Coded: A Legal History of Racism in Canada, 1900-1950* (Toronto: University of Toronto Press, 1999).

11   *Canadian Human Rights Act*, RSC 1985, c H-6.

Aboriginal People and the Canadian Human Rights Act

The original version of the *Canadian Human Rights Act* included section 67, which stated: "Nothing in this Act affects any provision of the *Indian Act* or any provision made under or pursuant to that Act." Effectively, this prevented anyone from filing a complaint with the Canadian Human Rights Commission (CHRC) about a decision that was made or an action that was taken by the federal government, a band council, or a related agency, such as a school board, pursuant to or under the *Indian Act*. While the *Human Rights Act* protected Canadians and Aboriginal persons living or working *off* reserves from discrimination by an employer or a service provider, First Nations persons living or working *on* a reserve were unable to file complaints with the CHRC. In other words, they did not have full access to human rights protection.*

In 2008, section 67 was repealed, and since then Aboriginal people have filed complaints against the federal government on issues such as federal funding for services on reserves, including policing, education, and child welfare. As of 2011, Aboriginal people could also file human rights complaints against First Nations governments and federally regulated Aboriginal organizations. Complaints have been filed on issues such as voting eligibility in band council elections and housing on reserves.

*   Aboriginal Affairs and Northern Development Canada, "Repeal of Section 67 of the *Canadian Human Rights Act*," online <http://www.aadnc-aandc.gc.ca>.

In today's workplace, dealing with sexual harassment has become particularly important. What happens, for example, if an employee displays an offensive symbol in the lunchroom? What if a boss approaches his or her employee and makes sexually suggestive jokes? One can see the value of section 14 in helping prevent this.

Exceptions

A number of exceptions are built into human rights acts. Under the *Canadian Human Rights Act*, there are certain defined exceptions in which a *discriminatory practice* cannot be applied to an employer's actions. A key one is where a **bona fide occupational requirement** for a job is involved. This means that a job requirement exists for a legitimate reason and that it cannot be removed without undue hardship for the employer. Section 15(1)(a) states:

> 15(1) It is not a discriminatory practice if
> (a) any refusal, exclusion, expulsion, suspension, limitation, specification or preference in relation to any employment is established by an employer to be based on a *bona fide* occupational requirement.

One example of this could be where an employer specified that all its employees must wear a hard hat on the company's construction site. If an employee on the job site is a Sikh, required by his religion to wear only a turban on his head, would the company be discriminating against him on religious grounds by requiring him to wear a hard hat, or is this a bona fide occupational requirement to ensure worker safety?

Other exceptions in which discrimination of a kind is permitted by the *Canadian Human Rights Act* are **affirmative action** programs, under section 16(1). These are special government or business initiatives to help certain identifiable groups who have experienced discrimination in the past—for example, women, Aboriginals, visible minorities, and persons with disabilities—achieve equality with others. Section 16(1) states:

16(1) It is not a discriminatory practice for a person to adopt or carry out a special program, plan or arrangement designed to prevent disadvantages that are likely to be suffered by, or to eliminate or reduce disadvantages that are suffered by, any group of individuals when those disadvantages would be based on or related to the prohibited grounds of discrimination, by improving opportunities respecting goods, services, facilities, accommodation or employment in relation to that group.

In the context of employment, what this provision means, practically speaking, is that an unsuccessful job applicant will have no grounds for a complaint of discrimination if the prospective employer can claim to have passed over the applicant (and chosen another candidate) on the basis of an affirmative action program—that is, "a special program, plan or arrangement designed to prevent disadvantages" toward groups of people who have suffered discrimination in the past.

Public Sector Protection of Civil Liberties: The Charter

As we have noted, the arrival of the *Canadian Charter of Rights and Freedoms* was a significant milestone in the history of civil liberties in this country. That said, it bears repeating that many of the rights, freedoms, and protections provided by the Charter—for example, freedom of speech, the presumption of innocence, and the right to a fair and public hearing before an independent and impartial tribunal—were already among the civil liberties that Canada inherited from England.

An Overview of the Charter

What the Charter did was entrench many of the rights, freedoms, and protections inherited from England and add new ones, making them part of our Constitution, so that they could only be changed following a formal constitutional amendment procedure. As well, section 52(1) of the *Constitution Act, 1982* states that "[t]he Constitution of Canada is the supreme law of Canada, and any law that is inconsistent with the provisions of the Constitution is, to the extent of the inconsistency, of no force or effect."

The Charter also differs from provincial and federal human rights acts in one other important way: it does not apply to matters in the private sector—that is, to disputes involving only individuals or corporations. Instead, it applies

1. to the actions of the federal, provincial, and territorial governments of Canada in making and administering laws; and
2. to relations that involve an individual or corporation (depending on the section) on one side and a government on the other side (for example, in a criminal trial).

The full text of the Charter is reproduced in Appendix B.

Section 1: Guarantee of Rights and Freedoms

Section 1 of the Charter guarantees the rights and freedoms it sets out, but also states that they are not absolute. They are subject to "reasonable limits." The wording is as follows:

> 1. The *Canadian Charter of Rights and Freedoms* guarantees the rights and freedoms set out in it subject only to such reasonable limits prescribed by law as can be demonstrably justified in a free and democratic society.

What does this limitation on our rights mean? Take section 2 of the Charter, which states, among other things, that we have freedom of opinion and expression in this country. What section 1 means is that this freedom is subject to limits. For example, this freedom does not allow you to threaten to kill someone; to make, distribute, or possess obscene materials; or to incite hatred against an identifiable group. Laws prohibiting such behaviour may be acceptable insofar as they impose "reasonable limits" on this Charter freedom. One of the most important early Charter cases for the SCC—the *R v Oakes* decision in 1986—concerned the test for determining whether a law can be justified under section 1 even if it infringes a Charter right (see Box 8.2). Normally, a law that is inconsistent with the Constitution runs the risk of being stuck down pursuant to the supremacy clause, section 52 of the *Constitution Act, 1982*. However, if the law is a reasonable limit on one's rights, it can be "saved" under section 1. The courts still apply the test from the *Oakes* case today when making this determination under section 1.

Section 2: Fundamental Freedoms

Section 2 of the Charter lists four fundamental freedoms provided to Canadians. It states the following:

> 2. Everyone has the following fundamental freedoms:
>   (a) freedom of conscience and religion;
>   (b) freedom of thought, belief, opinion and expression, including freedom
> of the press and other media of communication;
>   (c) freedom of peaceful assembly; and
>   (d) freedom of association.

These freedoms were established ones in English constitutional history and are essential to the functioning of our democracy in Canada. For example, our right to criticize government action or policy on television or in a newspaper, without fear of reprisal, or to peacefully protest against government actions, are fundamental to our parliamentary system of government and free and democratic society.

Sections 3–5: Democratic Rights

Sections 3–5 of the Charter further allow our democratic system of government to function by giving every citizen of Canada the right to vote, and by limiting the duration of legislatures and ensuring that there is an annual sitting of our legislative bodies. These sections are as follows:

> 3. Every citizen of Canada has the right to vote in an election of members of the House of Commons or of a legislative assembly and to be qualified for membership therein.
> 4(1) No House of Commons and no legislative assembly shall continue for longer than five years from the date fixed for the return of the writs of a general election of its members.

Section 1: The "Reasonable Limits" Clause and the *Oakes* Test

In 1982, David Oakes was found with a small quantity of narcotics and charged with unlawful possession of a narcotic for the purpose of trafficking, an offence under section 4(2) of the *Narcotic Control Act*. At the time, section 8 of the Act stated: "[I]f the court finds that the accused was in possession of the narcotic he shall be given an opportunity of establishing that he was not in possession for the purpose of trafficking." The constitutionality of this provision, which placed a reverse onus on the defendant by requiring him to prove he did *not* intend to traffic, was challenged by Oakes on the grounds that it infringed his right under section 11(d) of the Charter to be presumed innocent until proven guilty.

The case eventually made its way up to the SCC (*R v Oakes*, [1986] 1 SCR 103). The SCC noted that Canadian Charter jurisprudence accords a high degree of protection to the presumption of innocence and that section 11(d) had been infringed. The Court then had to determine whether, in light of this, the infringement was justified by section 1 of the Charter. In other words, was section 8 of the *Narcotic Control Act* and its reverse onus a "reasonable limit" on Mr. Oakes' right to be presumed innocent under section 11(d) of the Charter? Under section 1, it had to first be established that the limit was "prescribed by law." This was easy to show—the reverse-onus requirement was set out in section 8 of the *Narcotic Control Act*. Next, it had to be shown that the infringement was a "reasonable limit … demonstrably justified in a free and democratic society." The Court developed a general two-part test, now known as the *Oakes* test, to determine whether a law that infringes the Charter, is a "reasonable limit" on one's Charter rights. The onus is on the Crown to show on a balance of probabilities (or preponderance of probability) that the limit is a reasonable one by proving (1) that it relates to an important social objective, and (2) that it is a proportionate response to the problem. Specifically, the Crown must prove the following:

1. *Important social objective ("pressing and substantial" concern)*

   The government's objective in creating the law must be shown to be "of sufficient importance" to warrant overriding a Charter right. The standard for this part of the test is high, but is often met by the government in Charter cases. In the words of the SCC, for an objective to qualify as sufficiently important, it must relate "to concerns which are *pressing and substantial* in a free and democratic society."

2. *Proportionality*

   If the objective is found to be sufficiently important, the government must then show that the means used are a reasonable and fair way to achieve its legislative objective. To make this determination, a court considers three components or criteria, all of which must be satisfied in the circumstances:

   i. *Rational connection:* The measures that impair the Charter right must be designed to achieve the government's objective—in other words, the measures must be "rationally connected" to the objective. They must not be "arbitrary, unfair, or based on irrational considerations."

   ii. *Minimal impairment:* If a rational connection exists, the court will then examine the degree to which the measures impair the right or freedom. The right should be impaired "as little as possible," and if it is possible to impair a right to a lesser degree and still achieve the objective, the government must do so in drafting its legislation. Many arguments put forward by governments in defending legislation fail this part of the test.

   iii. *Proportionate effect:* The effects of the measures that limit the right or freedom

(Continued on the next page.)

BOX 8.2 *Continued*

must be proportionate to the objective identified in the first part of the test. In other words, this third part of the test weighs the benefit to society as a result of the law's being in place with the negative effects on those whose rights the law impairs. The greater the impairment of the right, the more important the objective must be.

Applying the test to section 8 of the *Narcotic Control Act*, the Court held that the social objective involved was "pressing and substantial" and that first part of the "reasonable limits" determination was satisfied. Controlling drug trafficking is a sufficiently important social objective to justify a violation of Charter rights. However, the provision failed to pass the proportionality test. Specifically, the first component of the test was not satisfied because the Court found that there was no rational connection between the reverse-onus requirement and the ob-

jective of controlling trafficking. Chief Justice Dickson stated:

> [I]t would be irrational to infer that a person had an intent to traffic on the basis of his or her possession of a very small quantity of narcotics. The presumption required under s. 8 of the *Narcotic Control Act* is overinclusive and could lead to results in certain cases which would defy both rationality and fairness. In light of the seriousness of the offence in question, which carries with it the possibility of imprisonment for life, I am further convinced that the first component of the proportionality test has not been satisfied by the Crown.

As a result of its analysis, the SCC found that section 8 of the *Narcotic Control Act*, which infringed the Charter, could not be saved under section 1 and was therefore of no force or effect.

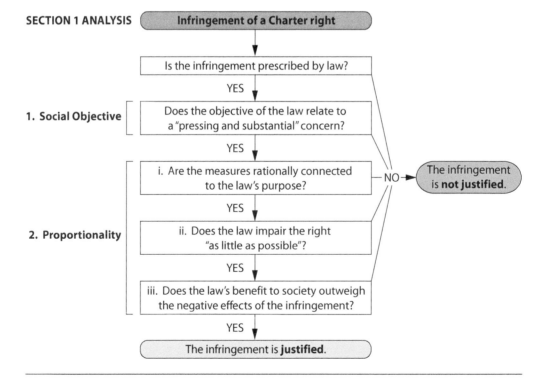

(2) In time of real or apprehended war, invasion or insurrection, a House of Commons may be continued by Parliament and a legislative assembly may be continued by the legislature beyond five years if such continuation is not opposed by the votes of more than one-third of the members of the House of Commons or the legislative assembly, as the case may be.

5. There shall be a sitting of Parliament and of each legislature at least once every twelve months.

Clearly, Canadian women would have had the right to vote long ago if our country had the Charter decades earlier. Recently, section 3 of the Charter has been used successfully to give prison inmates in Canada the right to vote.[12]

Section 6: Mobility Rights

Section 6 of the Charter makes it easier for Canadians living in one part of the country to move to another province, or to obtain a job in one province while living in another. For example, many people living in the maritime provinces of eastern Canada work in the oil sands of Alberta. They can do so by section 6, which is as follows:

6(1) Every citizen of Canada has the right to enter, remain in and leave Canada.

(2) Every citizen of Canada and every person who has the status of a permanent resident of Canada has the right

(a) to move to and take up residence in any province; and

(b) to pursue the gaining of a livelihood in any province.

(3) The rights specified in subsection (2) are subject to

(a) any laws or practices of general application in force in a province other than those that discriminate among persons primarily on the basis of province of present or previous residence; and

(b) any laws providing for reasonable residency requirements as a qualification for the receipt of publicly provided social services.

(4) Subsections (2) and (3) do not preclude any law, program or activity that has as its object the amelioration in a province of conditions of individuals in that province who are socially or economically disadvantaged if the rate of employment in that province is below the rate of employment in Canada.

The guarantee of mobility rights provided for by section 6 brings up an interesting issue related to doctors. Canadians living in rural and remote areas of many provinces face a doctor shortage. Would a provincial law ordering newly qualified doctors to begin their practice in a rural or remote part of the province infringe this section of the Charter, given that it would occur wholly within the province?

Sections 7–14: Legal Rights

Sections 7–14 of the Charter provide important legal rights for Canadians who may enter the criminal justice system, protecting people charged with an offence. They ensure that a person is treated fairly and that procedural safeguards and principles of fundamental justice are observed. Sections 7–10 read as follows:

---

12 *Sauvé v Canada (Chief Electoral Officer)*, 2002 SCC 68, [2002] 3 SCR 519.

7. Everyone has the right to life, liberty and security of the person and the right not to be deprived thereof except in accordance with the principles of fundamental justice.

8. Everyone has the right to be secure against unreasonable search or seizure.

9. Everyone has the right not to be arbitrarily detained or imprisoned.

10. Everyone has the right on arrest or detention

(a) to be informed promptly of the reasons therefor;

(b) to retain and instruct counsel without delay and to be informed of that right; and

(c) to have the validity of the detention determined by way of *habeas corpus* and to be released if the detention is not lawful.

Section 11 sets out the rights of individuals who are charged with an offence, while section 12 safeguards against cruel and unusual treatment or punishment. Section 13 protects witnesses against self-incrimination, providing that "[a] witness who testifies in any proceedings has the right not to have any incriminating evidence so given used to incriminate that witness in any other proceedings, except in a prosecution for perjury or for the giving of contradictory evidence." Finally, section 14 guarantees the right to an interpreter.

Section 15: Equality Rights

Section 15(1) of the Charter concerns equality rights, and it provides protection against discrimination that is based on certain defined grounds—namely, "race, national or ethnic origin, colour, religion, sex, age, or mental or physical disability." The SCC has also interpreted it as providing protection against discrimination based on sexual orientation (see Box 8.3).

As noted in Chapter 4, many women were concerned when the SCC, considering Diefenbaker's 1960 Bill of Rights, adopted a narrow interpretation of equality rights. To prevent this from happening again, they sought to make the language in the Charter's equality section stronger than it had been in the earlier Act. The Bill of Rights, for example, speaks of the "right of the individual to equality before the law and the protection of the law." The Charter's added wording protects every individual's equality "before *and under the law*" and grants every individual "the right to the equal protection *and equal benefit of the law*."

Women were not the only ones who had input into the wording of the Charter's equality-rights provision. During Charter negotiations, activists concerned about seniors and Canadians with mental and physical disabilities also put concerted pressure on the government to include "age" and "mental or physical disability" as prohibited grounds of discrimination.[13] Section 15(2) also expressly permits affirmative action programs, which, as we noted earlier, help disadvantaged groups overcome discrimination by giving them special consideration. Section 15 is as follows:

15(1) Every individual is equal before and under the law and has the right to the equal protection and equal benefit of the law without discrimination and, in particular, without discrimination based on race, national or ethnic origin, colour, religion, sex, age or mental or physical disability.

(2) Subsection (1) does not preclude any law, program or activity that has as its object the amelioration of conditions of disadvantaged individuals or groups including those that are disadvantaged because of race, national or ethnic origin, colour, religion, sex, age or mental or physical disability.

13 William Boyce et al, *A Seat at the Table: Persons with Disabilities and Policy Making* (Montreal and Kingston, Ont: McGill-Queen's University Press, 2001); Sharpe, Swinton & Roach, *supra* note 2.

BOX 8.3

Sexual Orientation: A New Prohibited Ground

Delwin Vriend worked for a Christian college in Alberta. When the college found out that Vriend was homosexual, it terminated his employment. Vriend complained about this to the Alberta Human Rights Commission. The Commission said that it could not intervene on Vriend's behalf because Alberta's *Individual's Rights Protection Act* (IRPA) did not have "sexual orientation" as a prohibited ground of discrimination.

The case was appealed to the SCC. The issue the Court had to decide was whether Alberta's IRPA violated the Charter by not including sexual orientation as a prohibited ground of discrimination. Justice Cory stated that sexual orientation was a "personal characteristic which has been found to be analogous to the grounds enumerated in s. 15" (*Vriend v Alberta*, [1998] 1 SCR 493 at para 107). However, rather than strike down the Alberta Act, the Court instead made it comply with the Charter. Sexual orientation was "read into" Alberta's IRPA—in other words, added by analogy to the Act's prohibited grounds of protection. Justice Iacobucci stated the following: "I conclude that reading sexual orientation into the impugned provisions of the IRPA is the most appropriate way of remedying this underinclusive legislation" (at para 179).

Delwin Vriend (right) and his partner, Andrew Gagnon, at the Supreme Court in 1997.

Sections 16–23: Official Languages of Canada and Minority Language Educational Rights

These sections of the Charter include a number of language provisions that are important for our country. Section 16(1) provides, for example, that "English and French are the official languages of Canada and have equality of status and equal rights and privileges as to their use in all institutions of the Parliament and government of Canada." They also provide that Canadians have the right to communicate with and to receive bilingual services in either English or French when dealing with any institution of the federal government. Section 23 also covers minority language educational rights for citizens of Canada.

Section 24: Enforcement

Section 24 reflects the desire of many in Canada, as noted above, to formally entrench civil liberties and rights in a central document that Canadians could use to protect and enforce their rights and freedoms. It provides that if a person believes her Charter rights have been infringed or denied, she can turn to our courts for assistance (see Box 8.4). The section states:

> 24(1) Anyone whose rights or freedoms, as guaranteed by this Charter, have been infringed or denied may apply to a court of competent jurisdiction to obtain such remedy as the court considers appropriate and just in the circumstances.
>
> (2) Where, in proceedings under subsection (1), a court concludes that evidence was obtained in a manner that infringed or denied any rights or freedoms guaranteed by this Charter, the evidence shall be excluded if it is established that, having regard to all the circumstances, the admission of it in the proceedings would bring the administration of justice into disrepute.

BOX 8.4

Section 24: The "Remedies" Section

In most cases, when a *law* is inconsistent with the Constitution, including when it infringes the Charter and cannot be saved under section 1 (see Box 8.2), the courts will use their power to provide some form of relief under section 52 of the *Constitution Act, 1982*. As described in Chapter 5, section 52, the supremacy clause, has been interpreted as allowing for a range of responses or remedies, including striking down the legislation or a part of it, or interpreting it narrowly to bring it in line with the Constitution.

Section 24 can be contrasted to courts' remedial powers under section 52 in several respects. Some of the more important distinctions are:

- section 24 is restricted to remedies for Charter infringements;
- the range of possible relief is broader, and is only limited by what is "appropriate and just in the circumstances";
- only "courts of competent jurisdiction" can hear applications under this section (this often means a superior court, because they have the broadest power to grant remedies); and
- a section 24 remedy is possible not only when a law infringes the Charter, but also when *administrative action* offends the Charter (such as when a police officer performs an illegal search and seizure).

Section 24 has two subsections, the first of which deals with general remedial relief, and the second with the exclusion of evidence.

Section 24(1): General Relief

A wide range of remedies is possible under section 24(1), and what is "appropriate and just" will vary with the specific circumstances of the case. "Defensive" remedies may be issued to prevent the continuation of an illegal state of affairs (for example, a court may dismiss a charge, quash a search warrant, or declare a law invalid, which is also a possible remedy under section 52). The courts may also provide "affirmative" remedies (for example, by ordering the return of property that has been seized or by awarding damages to a person whose Charter rights have

been infringed). In one case, the SCC ordered a provincial government to use its best efforts to build French-language schools to enforce minority-language education rights under section 23 (see *Doucet-Boudreau v Nova Scotia (Minister of Education)*, 2003 SCC 62, [2003] 3 SCR 3). Finally, the court may issue a declaration, in which it declares a particular state of affairs unconstitutional (for example, declaring that it is a contravention of the Charter for a province not to have a law providing for absentee voting). A declaration does not positively order the government to change its laws or act in a particular way, but in practice it may have this effect, because the government may need to make changes to avoid a continued breach of its Charter obligations.

Section 24(2): Exclusion of Evidence

When an application is made under section 24(1) and the court finds that evidence was obtained in contravention of the Charter, the court is required to exclude the evidence under section 24(2) if its admission "would bring the administration of justice into disrepute." At common law, the primary guide for the admissibility of evidence is its relevance; the admissibility of relevant evidence is not affected by the way in which it was obtained (that is, legally or illegally). Section 24(2) changes this rule to exclude illegally obtained evidence in some situations.

The leading case on section 24(2) is *R v Grant* (2009 SCC 32, [2009] 2 SCR 353). In 2003, Donnohue Grant attracted the attention of several officers while walking in an area known for its high crime rate. The officers questioned him, and while doing so required him to keep his hands in front of him and obstructed his movement so that he was prevented from leaving. In the course of the questioning, Mr. Grant admitted to having "a small bag of weed" and a firearm. The officers arrested and searched Mr. Grant, seizing the marijuana and a loaded revolver. They then advised him of his right to counsel and took him into custody. He was later charged with a number of firearms offences.

Mr. Grant was convicted at trial and his case ultimately went to the SCC. There were several issues before

BOX 8.4   *Continued*

the Court, including whether the evidence the police had obtained was admissible. The Court found that Mr. Grant had been psychologically detained when he was first questioned, and that his legal rights under sections 9 and 10 of the Charter had been infringed. In assessing whether admitting the evidence thus obtained would "bring the administration of justice into disrepute," the Court set out a three-part test that assesses and balances the following factors:

1. *The seriousness of the Charter-infringing state conduct.* The more serious the Charter violation, the more likely the administration of justice will be brought into disrepute. Deliberate or blatant breaches, for example, are more serious than breaches occurring where the police are acting in good faith.
2. *The impact on the Charter-protected interests of the accused.* The greater the intrusion on the Charter right, the more likely the evidence will be excluded. For example, serious intrusions into one's privacy or dignity, such as might occur from an illegal search, would have more impact than a "fleeting and tech-

nical" breach, such as where a slight delay occurs in informing a person of the reasons for his arrest.
3. *Society's interest in an adjudication on the merits.* This last factor focuses on whether the conduct calls into question the reliability of the evidence (for example, was the conduct of police likely to produce a false confession?), and the importance of the evidence to the Crown's case. The less reliable the evidence appears to be, the more likely its admission will bring the administration of justice into disrepute.

On the facts of this case, the Court concluded that the evidence could be admitted. First, the police conduct in breaching Mr. Grant's Charter rights was not "deliberate or egregious" and could not be characterized as serious. Second, there was no physical coercion or abuse and, therefore, while the impact on Mr. Grant's rights was more than minimal, it was not severe. Finally, the gun was important evidence and the method by which it was obtained in this case did not affect its reliability.

Sections 25–31: General

As discussed in Chapter 4, Canada's Aboriginal peoples worked hard to include a section of the Charter to protect their Aboriginal, treaty, or other rights and freedoms. Their efforts produced section 25 of the Charter, which is as follows:

> 25. The guarantee in this Charter of certain rights and freedoms shall not be construed so as to abrogate or derogate from any aboriginal, treaty or other rights or freedoms that pertain to the aboriginal peoples of Canada including
>> (a) any rights or freedoms that have been recognized by the Royal Proclamation of October 7, 1763; and
>> (b) any rights or freedoms that now exist by way of land claims agreements or may be so acquired.

Finally, we mentioned that women wanted as many protections for equality rights as possible put into the Charter. Thus, in addition to section 15, women were successful in also having section 28 added to the Charter. An added guarantee of sexual equality, it reads:

> 28. Notwithstanding anything in this Charter, the rights and freedoms referred to in it are guaranteed equally to male and female persons.

Sections 32 and 33: Application of the Charter

Section 32 states that the Charter applies to all matters of the federal, provincial, and territorial governments within their respective jurisdictions or spheres of authority. The wording is as follows:

> 32(1) This Charter applies
>
> (a) to the Parliament and government of Canada in respect of all matters within the authority of Parliament including all matters relating to the Yukon Territory and Northwest Territories; and
>
> (b) to the legislature and government of each province in respect of all matters within the authority of the legislature of each province.
>
> (2) Notwithstanding subsection (1), section 15 shall not have effect until three years after this section comes into force.

Accordingly, the Charter does not apply to the private sector—for example, to actions between you and your neighbour, your landlord, or your employer; or to how you are treated in a restaurant or a department store. The government is generally not involved in such situations, so the Charter usually will not apply to these kinds of relationships and activities. Such actions are, however, covered by federal, provincial, or territorial human rights acts. In those situations where the government is involved in private sector activities, though (for example, as a landlord or employer), the Charter will apply, *as well as* the relevant human rights legislation.

Lastly, section 33 of the Charter allows the federal Parliament or provincial legislatures to pass legislation that may operate even though it may infringe certain sections of the Charter. This section retains the idea of parliamentary sovereignty. Section 33 is as follows:

> 33(1) Parliament or the legislature of a province may expressly declare in an Act of Parliament or of the legislature, as the case may be, that the Act or a provision thereof shall operate notwithstanding a provision included in section 2 or sections 7 to 15 of this Charter.
>
> (2) An Act or a provision of an Act in respect of which a declaration made under this section is in effect shall have such operation as it would have but for the provision of this Charter referred to in the declaration.
>
> (3) A declaration made under subsection (1) shall cease to have effect five years after it comes into force or on such earlier date as may be specified in the declaration.
>
> (4) Parliament or the legislature of a province may re-enact a declaration made under subsection (1).
>
> (5) Subsection (3) applies in respect of a re-enactment made under subsection (4).

Section 33 is commonly referred to as the "notwithstanding" or "override" clause. Governments rarely exercise their power under this provision because of the political consequences of openly stating that the Charter is being ignored when enacting a particular law. So far, the most noteworthy example of a government using this power was when the Quebec government used it in the late 1980s to protect its language law—the *Charter of the French Language* (also referred to as Bill 101)—from Charter challenges. In the previous year, the SCC had found that some of the provisions in this legislation contravened the Charter.[14] Following this case, the language law was re-enacted and section 33 was invoked to shield it from further Charter challenges for five years. In 1993, the language law was amended so

---

14 See *Ford v Quebec (Attorney General)*, [1988] 2 SCR 712.

that it no longer contravened the Charter—the use of the "notwithstanding" clause was no longer necessary.

Note also that section 33 applies only to *specific sections* of the Charter (namely, to section 2 and sections 7 to 15). Voting rights under section 3 and Aboriginal rights under section 25, for example, cannot be overridden through the use of section 33.

The Courts and the Charter

Courts across Canada hear cases involving Charter issues, and those cases with very important Charter issues may find their way up to the SCC, which will set a precedent for the whole country to follow.

The SCC has the final role in upholding and supporting the Charter. Two main facets of this role involve (1) interpreting the Charter, and (2) determining the public interest of its decisions.

Interpretation of the Charter

The SCC plays a key role in interpreting general words and phrases used in the Charter, some of which are unclear. In section 2, for example, what does the phrase "freedom of religion" mean, exactly? What are the "principles of fundamental justice" referred to in section 7? Section 11(b) states that any person charged with an offence has the right "to be tried within a reasonable time." What is a "reasonable time"? Two months? Two years? Section 12 states that everyone has the right not to be subjected to "any cruel and unusual treatment or punishment." What does this mean? Former Chief Justice Dickson described the Court's supporting role in interpreting the Charter as follows:

> The words and expressions used in the Charter are broad and in many instances seem purposely vague. What is meant by "freedom of expression"? At what point does "expression" run into action? What is meant by the right to "security of the person"? What are the "principles of fundamental justice"? The admission of what sort of evidence would "bring the administration of justice into disrepute"? The answers to these questions are not to be found by consulting a dictionary. Nor will the traditional maxims of statutory interpretation shed much light on the issue. The determination of the meaning of such terms requires a philosophic, and possibly a political, theory as a context. It is only if you know *why* freedom of expression or security of the person or the principles of fundamental justice are suitable for protection in a *Charter of Rights and Freedoms* that you can know whether a given situation falls within or outside of these terms and whether admitting evidence obtained through a violation of such a right would bring the administration of justice into disrepute.[15]

Determination of the Public Interest

The Supreme Court is increasingly conscious of the fact that its decisions on Charter cases, and on constitutional and public law cases generally, have significant public consequences in Canada. With this in mind, the Court not only reviews statutes and cases but also consults

---

15   B Dickson, "The Role of the Supreme Court of Canada" (1984) 3 Advocates' Soc J 3 at 5.

academic books and articles applicable to its cases, and can also receive, at its discretion, the views of public interest groups on its cases through **intervenors**. Examples of public interest group intervenors who have appeared before the Court are the Canadian Civil Liberties Association and LEAF, the Women's Legal Education and Action Fund. Former Justice Bertha Wilson has acknowledged the role of such groups in helping the Court consider the broader implications of its decisions:

> The participation of third parties as intervenors in court cases is an issue on which views may legitimately differ. Some view it as incompatible with the adversarial nature of our litigation process and particularly inappropriate in criminal litigation where the defence should face off only against the prosecution. Some rule it out on purely pragmatic grounds: it adds time to the length of the proceedings, produces more paperwork and clutters up the issues with tangential and sometimes irrelevant evidence and argument. Personally, I found it invaluable in most cases. ... Enter the intervenor whose proper role, I believe, is to distance him or herself from the narrow facts of the case, to paint a broader picture and to assist the court by hypothesizing a wide range of contexts in which the section might be invoked, all with a view to discerning its purpose and delineating and defining its contours.[16]

The Extension of New Rights and Freedoms in the Future

Review once again the grounds for discrimination under section 15 of the Charter. Do you think other new grounds of discrimination might be added to section 15 as our future society evolves? Could a person's political belief, for example, eventually be included as another prohibited ground of discrimination? Might a person's weight become a future prohibited ground of discrimination?

We do know, from the SCC's ruling in *Vriend*, that this section may not be exhaustive and that any new prohibited ground of discrimination would have to be "analogous" (similar) to those specifically listed in section 15. For example, someone's sexual orientation was recognized in *Vriend* as analogous to the already listed ground of "sex." Determining what potential new grounds might be analogous to those already listed in section 15 will be challenging.[17]

Another aspect to also consider is whether any future new rights might be added to the Charter. For example, many Canadians are trying to get a better job. Most of those people, and especially students, recognize that having a good education is critical to finding better employment. Should there be a right to higher education added to the Charter? Consider another example. Poverty and homelessness constitute a serious socio-economic problem in this country. Many Canadians now rely on food banks. Given this fact, should a new right to adequate food and shelter be added to the Charter?

---

16 B Wilson, "Foreword" in Women's Legal Education and Action Fund, *Equality and the Charter: Ten Years of Feminist Advocacy Before the Supreme Court of Canada* (Toronto: Emond Montgomery, 1996) at ix; see also P Weiler, *In the Last Resort: A Critical Study of the Supreme Court of Canada* (Toronto: Carswell/Methuen, 1974).

17 W Black & L Smith, "The Equality Rights" in Beaudoin & Mendes, *supra* note 2 at 927.

CHAPTER SUMMARY

In Canada, we distinguish between the private sector protection of civil rights and the public sector protection of civil liberties. The former concerns civil rights in the "private" sphere—in other words, in relations between (for example) landlords and tenants, employers and employees, or customers and service providers. Various provincial and territorial human rights statutes and codes—and, at the federal level, the 1977 *Canadian Human Rights Act*—provide private sector protection against such discrimination by private persons and companies. Sections 91 and 92 of the *Constitution Act, 1867* set out the different jurisdictional areas and are used to determine whether a particular private sector civil rights matter falls under federal or provincial jurisdiction.

Public sector protection of civil liberties concerns two areas: (1) the governments of Canada—federal, provincial, and territorial—in their legislative activity; and (2) disputes that involve an individual on one side and the government on the other, as in the criminal justice system. In Canada today, these public sector protections are provided by the *Canadian Charter of Rights and Freedoms*. The Charter entrenches certain traditional rights and freedoms so that they cannot be changed except by following a formal constitutional amendment process set out in the Charter.

Both the Charter (protecting civil liberties in the public sector) and the various provincial, territorial, and federal human rights acts (protecting civil rights in the private sector) were the end results of a long and difficult political process of codifying civil rights and human rights in Canada. Canadians inherited many civil liberties rights from England. However, the United Kingdom had no one central civil rights code—no equivalent, in other words, to the US Bill of Rights. Our Constitution, based on the preamble to the *Constitution Act, 1867*, was to be "similar in principle to that of the United Kingdom," and for nearly a century Canadians made do, as did the British, with civil liberties protections based on the supremacy of Parliament, on an "implied bill of rights," respect for the rule of law, and public support for democracy.

By the middle of the 20th century, various factors—US influence, for example, and an international trend, after the atrocities and genocide of World War II, toward civil rights codes—left Canadians dissatisfied with the country's implied, derivative bill of rights. Many wanted a central, authoritative code like the one in place in the United States to protect their civil liberties. Diefenbaker's 1960 Bill of Rights was a first—but relatively unsuccessful—attempt at bringing about such a document. Trudeau's *Canadian Charter of Rights and Freedoms*, which entrenched certain rights and freedoms in the country's new Constitution, was more successful.

KEY TERMS

affirmative action policy, particularly in relation to education or employment, intended to assist groups who have suffered past discrimination *(p. 224)*

bona fide occupational requirement in the context of employment, a bona fide (Latin for "in good faith") requirement is one that exists for a legitimate reason—for example, safety—and that cannot be removed without undue hardship on the employer *(p. 224)*

civil liberties rights and freedoms protected by the Charter *(p. 219)*

discrimination prejudicial treatment of people on the ground of race, age, or sex; prohibited by human rights legislation *(p. 223)*

human rights rights that respect the dignity and worth of an individual *(p. 222)*

intervenor a party, other than the original parties to a court proceeding, who does not have a substantial and direct interest in the proceeding but has interests and perspectives helpful to the judicial determination and whose input is accepted by the court *(p. 236)*

FURTHER READING

BOOKS

Backhouse, C. *Petticoats and Prejudice: Women and Law in Nineteenth-Century Canada* (Toronto: Women's Press 1991).

Bryden, Philip, Steven Davis & J Russell, eds. *Protecting Rights and Freedoms: Essays on the Charter's Place in Canada's Political, Legal, and Intellectual Life* (Toronto: University of Toronto Press, 1994).

Corbett, SM. *Canadian Human Rights Law and Commentary* (Markham, Ont: LexisNexis, 2007).

Gibson, D. *The Law of the Charter: Equality Rights* (Toronto: Carswell, 1990).

Kaplan, W. *State and Salvation: The Jehovah's Witnesses and Their Fight for Civil Rights* (Toronto: University of Toronto Press, 1989).

Mosher, CJ. *Discrimination and Denial: Systemic Racism in Ontario's Legal and Criminal Justice Systems, 1892-1961* (Toronto: University of Toronto Press, 1998).

LEGISLATION

Canada

Canadian Bill of Rights, SC 1960, c 44, reprinted in RSC 1985, App III.

Canadian Human Rights Act, RSC 1985, c H-6.

Alberta

Alberta Human Rights Act, RSA 2000, c A-25.5.

British Columbia

Human Rights Code, RSBC 1996, c 210.

Manitoba

The Human Rights Code, CCSM c H175.

New Brunswick

Human Rights Act, RSNB 2011, c 171.

Newfoundland and Labrador

Human Rights Act, 2010, SNL 2010, c H-13.1.

Northwest Territories

Human Rights Act, SNWT 2002, c 18.

Nova Scotia

Human Rights Act, RSNS 1989, c 214.

Nunavut

Human Rights Act, SNu 2003, c 12.

Ontario

Human Rights Code, RSO 1990, c H.19.

Prince Edward Island

Human Rights Act, RSPEI 1988, c H-12.

Quebec

Charter of Human Rights and Freedoms, RSQ c C-12.

Saskatchewan

The Saskatchewan Human Rights Code, SS 1979, c S-24.1.

Yukon

Human Rights Act, RSY 2002, c 116.

REVIEW QUESTIONS

1. What is the distinction between "civil rights" and "civil liberties" in the Canadian context?

2. In Canada, what were four main factors in the development of legislative protection for civil liberties?

3. What is the basis of Canada's "implied bill of rights"?

4. Why did Diefenbaker's 1960 Bill of Rights prove disappointing?

5. Why do you think the US civil rights movement was so important for the development of Canadian human rights legislation?

6. What is a bona fide occupational requirement? What do you think would be a bona fide occupational requirement for a firefighter?

7. If an employee were fired from his job at Canadian Tire, would the Charter or a provincial/territorial human rights act apply?

8. If there were a human rights complaint brought against a bank manager, what human rights act would apply—federal or provincial/territorial? Give reasons.

EXERCISES

1. Weigh the pros and cons of affirmative action programs. Do you approve or disapprove of them? Explain.

2. Assume you are an employer concerned to prohibit harassment in your workplace. You are determined to be proactive in preventing occurrences of it. List three steps you might implement in this regard.

3. Using the Internet, find the human rights code for your province or territory. Compare and contrast your provincial or territorial code's prohibited grounds of discrimination with those in section 15 of the Charter.

4. Do you think that an SCC hearing that permits submissions from an intervenor is stronger than one that does not permit them? Discuss.

5. Discuss what you think might in time become a new prohibited ground of discrimination under section 15 of the Charter.

PART III
Private Law and Public Law

9 Private Law I: Torts, Contracts, and Related Areas

After reading this chapter, you will understand:

- The nature of private law and how it differs from public law
- The nature of tort law, and the main categories and subcategories of torts
- The main defences available to those who commit torts
- The remedies available to victims of torts
- The function of contracts in society, how they are formed, and the elements of a valid contract

- The main types of contracts, and the terms and terminology commonly found in contracts
- The excuses available for the non-performance of contracts
- The remedies in contract disputes
- The private law areas that are related to torts and contracts

Private law: a branch of law concerned with private persons, property, and relationships

Merriam-Webster's Dictionary of Law,
sub verbo "private law"

Introduction

In Chapter 1, we described the divisions of law in broad terms, dividing domestic law into three categories: public law, military law, and private law. In Part III of this text, comprising Chapters 9–13, we examine private law and public law in more detail. Private law, the focus of Chapters 9–11, governs the relationships between persons. Public *domestic* law governs the relationships between persons and the state (and includes the key area of criminal law), and public *international* law is primarily concerned with the relationship between states. Public law is covered in Chapters 12 and 13. Unless we are career criminals or tax evaders, or are involved in matters of international significance, most of our everyday activities are regulated by private law. Note that in this chapter and the next we examine private law as it applies in Canada's common law provinces and in the territories. In Quebec, private law is largely regulated according to the civil law system and its rules are predominantly based on provisions found in the *Civil Code of Quebec*. (See Chapters 2 and 3 for more on the civil law system, civil law in Quebec specifically and Canada as a bijural nation.)

Generally, being involved in a private (or civil) law dispute is considered less of a social concern than being the subject of a public law matter—in particular, being charged with a crime, which in most cases has a moral stigma attached to it and can result in jail time. This is reflected in the different standards of proof in civil claims and criminal cases. In civil claims, litigants only need prove their cases on a *balance of probabilities* (that is, prove that their allegations are more likely to be true than not). In criminal cases, on the other hand, the prosecution must adduce evidence proving that the person charged has committed the crime *beyond a reasonable doubt* (which requires a high degree of certainty).

This chapter covers two key areas of private law—tort law and contract law—as well as some areas related to these two. Chapter 10 covers property law and family law, and concludes with a brief summary of other areas of private law. Business and consumer law are covered in Chapter 11.

Dividing the law into separate subject areas is an aid to learning. But it is important to keep in mind that many legal problems involve more than one area of law. For example, the outcome of a torts claim for a skiing injury may depend on whether the injured skier contractually agreed to absolve the ski-hill operator of liability. For the purposes of teaching, we speak of specific areas of law, but you will find that, in the actual practice of law, these areas overlap.

Constitutional Basis of Private Law

Most private law falls under the jurisdiction of the provincial and territorial legislatures. This is because the provinces have jurisdiction over "Property and Civil Rights" under section 92(13) of the *Constitution Act, 1867*. The territories have a similar jurisdiction assigned to them, by other legislation. However, there are areas of private law where Parliament's role is more significant. For example, under sections 91(22) and 91(23) of the *Constitution Act, 1867*, intellectual property is regulated federally. In the area of family law, marriage and divorce are federally regulated (section 91(26)), whereas family property rights are under the jurisdiction of the provinces and territories. (See Chapter 5 for an examination of constitutional areas of jurisdiction generally.) In the following discussion of specific subject areas, jurisdictional issues are covered as they arise.

Figure 9.1 shows the main subdivisions of private law. (To see private law in a broader context—that is, in relation to other areas of law—see Figure 1.1 on page 27 of this text.)

FIGURE 9.1 Private law and its subdivisions

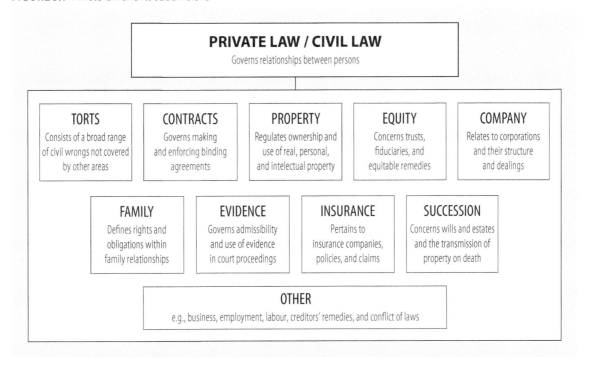

Tort Law

Tort law is an area of private law that deals with certain types of wrongful conduct, and the remedies available to those affected by that conduct. It covers a wide range of behaviours and is primarily concerned with providing a means of compensation (see Chapter 1 under Corrective Justice Today). However, depending on the conduct in question, it can serve other purposes, such as deterrence and punishment. A **tort**, therefore, is a type of civil wrong for which the person wronged can obtain damages or some other remedy (the English word *tort* derives from the Latin *tortum*, meaning "something twisted" or "something crooked."). A **civil wrong** is a wrong defined by private law, which covers the relationships between persons.

Tort law is often seen as a "residuary" category within private law—in other words, a catch-all or miscellaneous category that includes all those civil wrongs that are not covered by other areas of private law, such as contract law, property law, family law, or equity.

Modern tort law can be divided into four categories, based on the type of fault involved:

1. intentional torts,
2. negligence,
3. strict liability torts, and
4. a miscellaneous group of torts, with unique principles of liability.

These four categories are described below. Because of space restrictions, we cannot discuss all torts, just the most commonly litigated ones.

Intentional Torts

The defendant's intentional behaviour defines these torts. In other words, the defendant intended to bring about the consequences of his actions or at least knew that the consequences were likely to result. It is the intentional nature of the conduct that makes these torts the most serious ones. In fact, many of the torts in this category are also crimes for which the defendant could find himself facing criminal charges.[1]

The intentional torts can be roughly divided into two categories:

1. intentional interferences with persons or property, and
2. intentional interferences with other interests.

Interferences with Persons or Property

The main intentional torts in this category are

---

1   There have been many famous cases in Canada with both a criminal and a civil component: for example, cases involving on-ice violence in hockey, such as the Todd Bertuzzi and Steve Moore cases (criminal assault and related civil actions); and, more recently, the Colonel Russell Williams case (murders, sexual assaults, and related civil actions). Usually, the criminal proceedings are completed first, before any civil actions move forward. This can be an advantage to the victim: if there is a conviction in the criminal case, the underlying facts can be taken as proven in the civil case. Even if there is an acquittal in the criminal case, most civil cases still proceed because the standard of proof the plaintiff must meet in such cases (balance of probabilities) is more easily met than the standard of proof that must be met in criminal ones (beyond a reasonable doubt).

- trespass to person,
- trespass to land, and
- trespass to goods (also referred to as "trespass to chattels").

In Canada, the conduct involved in these torts is *presumed* to be intentional or careless; it is up to the defendant to prove otherwise. Other common law jurisdictions, such as the United Kingdom and the United States, require the plaintiff to prove intent as an element of the tort. It is customary in all common law jurisdictions to refer to these torts as "intentional," regardless of whether intent must be proved or whether fault is presumed.

These torts all involve forms of direct interference, such as hitting, walking on, or moving. They don't require actual damage (although, without actual damage, any monetary award is likely to be small).

TRESPASS TO PERSON

Three actions qualify as **trespass to person**: (1) assault, (2) battery, and (3) false imprisonment. **Assault** is a kind of psychological tort, not requiring actual physical contact. If the plaintiff is threatened and apprehends harmful physical contact from the defendant, and if the defendant has the means to carry out the threat in the near future, an assault has occurred. For example, threatening to hit, shoot, stab, or sexually interfere with someone is an assault if the victim believes the threat will soon materialize, even if the assailant stops short of actual physical contact.

The intentional tort of **battery** requires the actual occurrence of harmful or offensive physical contact. Many trespass-to-person claims have both an assault and a battery component. For instance, if a threat creates an apprehension of harm and then the threatened physical contact occurs, there has been an assault prior to contact and a battery once it occurs. Note also that, in criminal law, there is no distinction between assault and battery; both actions are covered by the crime of assault.[2]

The kind of trespass-to-person offence classified as **false imprisonment** occurs when one person totally restrains the movement of another person. The defining element here is the presence of an enclosed boundary around the person being restrained, so that there is no reasonable means of escape. The boundary can be physical (for example, a locked jail cell) or psychological (for example, someone with a gun telling the plaintiff not to move). This tort is sometimes referred to as "false arrest" in cases where a police officer or security guard is the person being sued. But *false imprisonment* and *false arrest* are, legally speaking, the same action. In both cases, the word "false" is a bit misleading. The plaintiff is not required to prove that his imprisonment was "false" (that is, unjustified), only that he was imprisoned. Once that is established, the onus is on the defendant to establish that the imprisonment was authorized. If the defendant is a police officer, this authority usually comes from a statutory power of arrest.

---

2   Concerning wrongful sexual conduct, it is criminal and may be prosecuted as a sexual assault under the *Criminal Code* (in other words, in the sphere of public law), but there are also a number of potential tort claims based on sexual wrongdoing. Such actions are not based on a stand-alone tort, however; in other words, there is no tort known as "sexual wrongdoing." Rather, these actions are founded on established torts, such as assault, battery (often referred to in this context as "sexual battery"), or intentional infliction of mental suffering.

TRESPASS TO LAND

Trespass to land involves the physical intrusion by one person onto land occupied by another. This may take the form of a bodily intrusion, or it may involve an object propelled by one person onto another person's land. There are also criteria as to height and depth. Intruding on another person's airspace—that is, the space above that person's piece of land—up to a reasonably usable height (for example, by an overhanging sign) may qualify as a trespass. So may the intrusion on another person's subsoil down to a reasonably usable depth—for example, in a case where one person, to secure a structure on her own land, has inserted anchor rods into the plaintiff's land.

TRESPASS TO GOODS

Trespass to goods (or **trespass to chattels**) is a tort whereby one person intentionally interferes with another's possession of movable property, such as a motor vehicle—by, for example, moving it.

There are other torts besides trespass to goods that concern movable property. *Conversion* is the civil law equivalent of theft in criminal law. It involves one person substantially interfering with—including stealing or destroying—another person's goods. Another tort in this category is *detinue*, which involves the wrongful withholding of the owner's goods (even if the defendant initially came into possession of the goods lawfully, as in a case where the goods were loaned to the defendant by the owner).

OTHER INTENTIONAL INTERFERENCES WITH PERSONS OR PROPERTY

The torts of trespass are the most established of the torts involving intentional interferences with persons or property. But there are many others, including the following:

- invasion of privacy (covering all manner of intrusions such as surveillance, eavesdropping, and publishing private communications);
- expropriation of personality (a special form of invasion of privacy whereby the defendant uses the plaintiff's name or likeness to promote the defendant's business without the plaintiff's consent); and
- harassment (which could involve sexual or non-sexual behaviour that is persistent and offensive).

These torts are relatively new and have not been fully considered and clearly defined by the Supreme Court of Canada (SCC). So we might say they are "under development" in the courts of the territories and common law provinces. In the case of the first of them, however—that is, the invasion of privacy—the provinces of British Columbia, Manitoba, Newfoundland and Labrador, and Saskatchewan have bypassed the development of the common law and have enacted legislation clearly making the invasion of privacy a tort.[3]

Intentional infliction of nervous shock is another example of a tort that is not considered a "trespass" tort but that does involve intentional interference with a person. This tort involves one person's intentionally inflicting mental suffering on another person. It is, like assault, a psychological tort, and a long-established one. But it is extremely difficult to prove. Its defining elements are extreme, flagrant, or outrageous conduct by the defendant, and consequent

---

3 See *Privacy Act*, RSBC 1996, c 373; *The Privacy Act*, RSM 1987, c P125; *Privacy Act*, RSN 1990, c P-22; and *The Privacy Act*, RSS 1978, c P-24.

injury to the plaintiff in the form of a psychological disorder—typically, a disorder recognized in the *Diagnostic and Statistical Manual of Mental Disorders* (DSM-5).[4]

Intentional Interferences with Other Interests

The torts in this category all involve indirect forms of injury, and they generally have more to do with purely financial losses than with physical or psychological losses.

Misuse of court proceedings by a defendant can be tortious. The two most important torts in this area are *malicious prosecution* and *abuse of process*. Malicious prosecution is based on an earlier misuse of *criminal* (as opposed to civil) proceedings. In this case, the defendant is sued for having had groundless charges laid against the plaintiff—charges of which the plaintiff was later acquitted—while knowing they were groundless. Abuse of process is based on an earlier misuse of *civil* proceedings. In this case, the defendant commenced proceedings against the plaintiff for purposes unrelated to the claim itself—for example, in order to embarrass the plaintiff or put him out of business. These two torts are difficult to establish because they require proof of bad faith on the part of the defendant. Such proof is often lacking.

Other torts in this category—that is, torts involving intentional interferences with other interests—are certain "business torts." Most of these involve some form of intentional behaviour that has led to purely financial or economic loss by the plaintiff. Some commonly litigated examples are

- deceit (or fraud),
- passing off (that is, where one person misrepresents his goods or services as those of another person),
- inducing breach of contract,
- intimidation, and
- abuse of power.

DECEIT

The tort of *deceit* occurs when the defendant intentionally misleads the plaintiff into taking a course of action that results in damage to the plaintiff. In a common example of this tort, the plaintiff invests in a doomed venture based on false information provided by the defendant, who knows the information is false. Deceit claims can also be based on physical or personal injury losses. For example, deliberately misleading someone about how to use dangerous equipment could support a deceit claim if personal injury resulted.

PASSING OFF

Passing off is related to expropriation of personality, except that it is not the plaintiff's name or likeness that the defendant is trading on, but the plaintiff's superior goods or services. This tort covers "knock-offs"—inferior products that the defendant passes off as having been produced by the plaintiff. The damage here consists in the fact that the plaintiff's brand can lose market share and consumer goodwill through being associated with an inferior product.

---

4   American Psychiatric Association, *Diagnostic and Statistical Manual of Mental Disorders*, 5th ed (Arlington, Va: American Psychiatric Association, 2013). The DSM has been a standard reference in non-legal and legal matters involving mental disorders since it was first published in 1952. This latest edition follows the DSM-IV, which was published in 1994 (and slightly revised in 2000).

INDUCING BREACH OF CONTRACT

It is a tort to intentionally and unlawfully interfere with the contracts of others. The tort of inducing breach of contract (also known as interference with contractual relations) occurs as follows: one party, in pursuit of its own interests, deliberately pressures a second party to break its contractual obligations to a third party. The third party, if damaged by the broken contract, can sue the meddling first party.

INTIMIDATION

Intimidation, as the name suggests, is a tort involving threats. The plaintiff in an intimidation case must show that the defendant unlawfully threatened the plaintiff or a third party and that the plaintiff has suffered a loss as a result of the threat. In a labour dispute, for example, if a group of striking workers threatened to harm a worker who was planning to go to work, the latter could make an intimidation claim if she stayed away from work on the basis of the threat and lost wages as a result.

ABUSE OF POWER

Related to the tort of intimidation is a tort involving misuse of public office by a public official—in particular, the abuse of power involving the misuse of discretion. For example, if a public official gives a political appointment to a family member rather than to the person best qualified for the job, he is misusing discretion in this way. In another example, a public official might use her power to create economic hardship for a political opponent. The *Roncarelli* case is the most famous example of this tort.[5] (See Box 1.8 in Chapter 1 for a discussion of this case.)

Defences to Intentional Torts

There are many defences to the intentional torts. Some of these defences are specific to the particular torts. The defences argued most frequently—consent, self-defence, and legal authority—typically arise in the context of intentional interferences with persons or property. *Consent* occurs where a claimant agrees to the interference in question. For example, inviting someone onto your land would negate your trespass-to-land claim. Consent can be given expressly (for example, in a written release) or implicitly (for example, by voluntarily participating in the activity). Consent issues often arise in cases involving medical procedures and sporting injuries.

Self-defence applies if the defendant can show that she committed the tort, such as assault or battery, to protect herself. Two important requirements in this case are that the defendant

1. honestly and reasonably believed that she was going to be attacked, and
2. responded in a way that was reasonable in the circumstances.

With respect to the first requirement, the defendant's belief need not have been correct; it must simply have been a belief, reasonable under the circumstances, that force was necessary to prevent immediate harm to herself. With respect to the second requirement for this defence, what is reasonable will depend on the facts of each case. If the force used is beyond what is reasonable, then it is excessive and the defence will not apply. Deadly force may be seen as having been reasonable if the person was required to protect herself from death or

---

5   *Roncarelli v Duplessis*, [1959] SCR 121.

serious physical injury. Similar rules apply in cases where the defendant was defending third parties and property.

With the intentional torts, the *legal authority* governing defences is not one cohesive defence but a collection of defences based on various statutory rules, each of which allows for intentional interferences with persons or property in specified circumstances. Some consistent principles seem to inform the legislation setting out these circumstances. The legislation generally provides, for example, that there must be reasonable grounds for the interference (for example, because a crime was being or was about to be committed) and that any force used must be reasonable.

Finally, it's important to note that *lack of capacity* is sometimes raised as a defence in the case of intentional torts, usually on behalf of infants (that is, people under the age of majority) or of mentally incompetent adults. Technically, capacity is a required *element* in all of the intentional torts. However, it is presumed that the defendant had the capacity to commit the tort in question unless the defendant challenges this presumption. There is no fixed age when children begin to be held responsible for intentionally inflicted injury; it depends on the intelligence and cognitive ability of the child in question. For both children and mentally incompetent adults, the key question is whether they have the mental ability to understand and appreciate the nature and consequences of their actions. If they do, then they have the capacity to be sued.

Torts Involving Negligence

The largest area of tort law is the law of negligence. It covers almost every type of human activity. Personal injury cases, especially those resulting from motor vehicle accidents, are the most commonly litigated negligence cases. Unlike intentional tortious behaviour, which is made up of numerous individual torts with their own names and special rules, the tort of negligence has one set of rules, developed by the courts, that cover most instances of *carelessly* inflicted injury.

What Is Negligence?

The word **negligence** can have at least two legal meanings. In its broadest sense, negligence refers to the tort itself, meaning the entire cause of action or claim in negligence, including all its constituent elements. In its narrowest sense, it refers to just one element in the claim, the standard of care or more specifically *breach* of the standard of care (a defendant who falls below the required standard of care for the activity in question is said to be *negligent*, or careless in a legal sense). The elements of a basic negligence claim are described in Box 9.1.

Types of Negligence: Misfeasance and Nonfeasance

Negligence liability usually applies to conduct that involves positive "doing." Such conduct might involve, for example,

- driving too fast or driving while impaired,
- operating on a patient and taking out the wrong kidney, or
- designing a bridge and miscalculating the stress points.

Doing something carelessly in this way is referred to as **misfeasance**. However, in special cases, the law imposes liability for injuries resulting from a failure to act—in other words, from "not doing." Examples of this would include situations where, for example,

BOX 9.1

The Elements of a Negligence Claim

The required elements of a negligence claim have been variously named, described, and numbered. There is still no consensus on terminology, although the courts in Canada today consistently refer to the five elements outlined below. The plaintiff has the burden of proof with respect to all of these elements, although in most cases the defendant will concede some of them and the litigation will focus on just one or two (most often, breach of the standard of care, and damages).

1. Duty

In order for the law of negligence to apply, the law must recognize that the defendant had an obligation or duty to take care to avoid injuring the plaintiff, given the relationship between the parties and the activity in question. If the law has recognized a similar duty in the past, this element will be easy to establish.

If the situation is new and unprecedented, however, the court will engage in a detailed analysis to determine whether to recognize a new duty; it will consider, among other things,

- whether the defendant could have foreseen the injury while engaged in the activity,
- the nature of the relationship between the defendant and the plaintiff, and
- whether others would be deterred from behaving like the defendant if a duty were recognized (as well as other policy considerations).

See Box 9.2 for an example involving the alleged duty of a mother to her child for injuries caused to the child while the mother was pregnant.

2. Standard of Care and Breach

If a duty is recognized, the question then arises whether the defendant has acted in accordance with that duty. This tends to be the most frequently disputed element in a negligence case.

Standard of Care

In ordinary cases, the test for standard of care is the following question: How would a reasonable person have acted in the same circumstances? In professional malpractice cases, the test is modified to the following: How would a reasonable professional in the same field (for example, doctor, lawyer, or engineer) have acted in the same circumstances? Where the defendant is a child, the question posed is the following: How would a child of like age, intelligence, and experience have acted in the circumstances?

Breach

It must be determined whether the defendant, measured by the applicable standard, fell below or breached that standard. To make this determination, the court will consider all the circumstances of the case, including factors such as

- the risk of injury inherent in the activity,
- the existence of any social benefits flowing from the activity,
- the extent to which others have acted similarly (that is, was the behaviour customary for someone in the defendant's position?), and
- the existence of legislative rules governing the activity and whether they have been followed or ignored.

For example, in one famous case, the court had to consider whether a municipality was liable for injuries caused to one of its firefighters when a jack in the back of a fire truck rolled on to the firefighter while the truck was responding to a fire. The jack was needed for the fire but couldn't be properly secured on this particular truck, which was the only one available at the time. In weighing the risk of injury by deploying the truck with an improperly secured jack against the benefit of saving "life and limb" in responding to the fire, the court concluded that in all the circumstances, the standard of care had not been breached (see *Watt v Hertfordshire County Council*, [1945] 2 All ER 368 (CA)).

3. Factual Causation

Often simply referred to as "causation," this element concerns whether the defendant's negligent conduct has actually caused the loss. Two tests are commonly used here:

1. the "but for" test, which asks whether the loss would not have occurred *but for* (that is, *in the absence of*) the defendant's conduct; and
2. the "material contribution" test, which asks whether the defendant's conduct materially contributed to the loss.

Recall, again, the sample case in Chapter 7, *Matthews v MacLaren*. This case illustrates the duty and standard of care elements above, but was in fact decided against Matthews' estate on the basis of this third element, factual causation. Matthews would not likely have survived even if the defendant MacLaren had exercised proper care in rescuing him. Lake Ontario was very cold at the time and the evidence was that Matthews probably died shortly after hitting the water.

4. Legal Causation

Because negligence liability concerns *carelessness* rather than *intentional wrongdoing*, the law places a limit on the extent of the defendant's liability. For defendants to be liable, there must be a sufficiently close connection between their conduct and the loss. The question here is whether the defendant's conduct was a "proximate cause" of the loss; it concerns the conduct's "remoteness"—or, more precisely, *lack* of remoteness—as a causal factor in the loss.

The test used to limit liability is the "reasonable foreseeability" test; a defendant is only responsible for losses that are a reasonably foreseeable consequence of his behaviour.

In 2008, the SCC had to decide whether a supplier of bottled water was responsible for a serious psychological illness suffered by a consumer who witnessed a dead fly in an unopened bottle. The SCC held that all of the elements of the negligence cause of action were met on these facts, except legal causation. The injury in this case was too remote to be compensable; it was not reasonably foreseeable that a person of ordinary fortitude would suffer serious injury from seeing a dead fly in a bottle of water (see *Mustapha v Culligan of Canada Ltd*, 2008 SCC 27).

5. Damages

The plaintiff has to show that she has suffered, or will suffer, a loss or injury that the court recognizes as worthy of compensation, such as personal injury, serious psychological injury, property damage, or financial loss. "Ordinary" inconvenience, stress, or aggravation resulting from a careless defendant's behaviour is not compensable.

- the driver of a motor vehicle fails to properly secure a child passenger,
- a bar owner fails to ensure that a drunken patron has a safe ride home, or
- a manufacturer omits to warn consumers about the risks associated with its product.

Not doing something you have an obligation to do is referred to as **nonfeasance**. See the sample case *Matthews v MacLaren* in Chapter 7, Appendix 7.1, which concerned a duty to rescue in the context of a boating mishap.

COMMON AREAS OF NEGLIGENCE

The following events and contexts typically produce a great number of negligence claims:

- *Motor vehicle accidents*. The largest number of negligence cases are a consequence of speeding, impairment by drugs or alcohol, or some other failure to exercise reasonable care when driving a motor vehicle.
- *Sports*. Participants in athletic activities can expect varying degrees of physicality depending on the sport and on whether they play professionally, at the amateur level, or in pick-up games with friends. Sometimes, the degree of violence exceeds what is expected in the given context. Aggressive behaviour can lead to intentional tort claims such as battery. Excessively careless behaviour can similarly lead to negligence claims.
- *Manufacture of defective products*. Product liability cases arise where manufacturers negligently design or produce goods.
- *Substandard construction*. Architects, engineers, and builders can be liable for negligently designing or constructing buildings.

BOX 9.2

Does a Mother Owe a Duty to Her Unborn Child?

In *Dobson (Litigation Guardian of) v Dobson*, [1999] 2 SCR 753, the SCC dealt with a case involving a pregnant woman who was driving her vehicle carelessly when it collided with another vehicle. Her child was born with permanent mental and physical disabilities as a result of the prenatal injuries sustained in the accident.

There was no precedent for this, and the Court had to decide for the first time whether a mother owes a duty to her child with respect to her behaviour while pregnant. The Court had to consider the law's role in regulating the lifestyle choices of pregnant women. It was clear that injury is foreseeable if a pregnant woman drives without care and attention, and that the relationship between mother and child is a close one.

However, after weighing various policy considerations—in particular, the concern over imposing additional burdens on pregnant women, and the possible psychological consequences of liability for a new mother and the family—the Court concluded that imposing a duty on women in these circumstances was not appropriate.

Note that the child was suing his mother (through a representative) because she was covered by insurance. The insurance money would have been used to offset the extra expenses his disability brought to his upbringing. Courts do not generally consider the existence of insurance in making their decisions about liability.

- *Professional malpractice.* Professionals such as doctors, lawyers, architects, engineers, and accountants are liable if they are negligent in the services they provide to their clients.

- *Careless words* (or *negligent misrepresentation*). In situations where a special relationship exists between the defendant and the plaintiff (for example, where it is reasonable for the plaintiff to rely on the defendant because of the latter's expertise and position of trust), the court will impose an obligation on the defendant to exercise care in providing information to the plaintiff.

- *Careless inspections.* Government agencies, particularly municipalities, perform many kinds of inspections—for example, approving new construction, and checking roads and highways for hazards. Negligently performed inspections resulting in loss can be actionable.

Different activities can lead to different types of harm. The following forms of loss or injury can be the basis of a negligence tort claim:

- *Personal injury.* Bodily injuries, ranging from broken bones to soft tissue injuries, including brain damage, occur as a result of many activities. In assessing the awards for such losses, courts refer to awards in similar cases. The SCC has set an upper limit for non-pecuniary losses (that is, losses like pain and suffering that are not financial in nature): $100,000, in 1978 dollars. With inflation factored in, the maximum award is now over $300,000. Psychological injuries often accompany these bodily injuries and make up another element of the plaintiff's claim. So do financial losses—for example, loss of earnings, and care costs. Financial losses are not subject to the SCC's upper limit and, in serious cases, such as those involving paralysis, can be in the millions of dollars.

- *Psychological injury.* When psychological injury alone is claimed (that is, where there is no accompanying physical injury), the injured party must prove that the injury is a recognized mental disorder—for example, the clinical depression or post-traumatic stress disorder that a person might suffer after witnessing a horrific accident. Financial losses may accompany such claims.

- *Property damage*. Negligent conduct resulting in damage to property—for example, when motor vehicles are damaged in accidents or buildings are flooded—can lead to liability. Again, any accompanying financial losses (such as the cost of replacement transportation while a damaged vehicle is repaired) may be part of the claim.

- *Pure economic loss*. A pure economic loss is one that is not connected to any of the previous three types of loss. In limited circumstances, such losses can be recovered. Common examples are investment losses—a case where a financial advisor negligently advises a client about an investment—or a loss resulting from an accountant or lawyer's carelessly structuring a business transaction.

Defences to Negligence

There are a number of defences available to a person sued in negligence. The onus is on the defendant to raise and prove these defences. There are three main ones:

1. contributory negligence,
2. consent, and
3. illegality.

Contributory negligence applies in a case where the plaintiff has negligently contributed to her own losses. It is not a complete defence, however; where the court finds contributory negligence, it will apportion liability between the plaintiff and the defendant. Where it is not clear that one party is more at fault than the other (or others, if there are multiple defendants), the court will apportion liability equally.[6]

Consent and illegality are complete defences. This means that, if the court finds these defences applicable to the case, the plaintiff recovers nothing. **Consent** (also referred to as "voluntary assumption of risk," or by its Latin name *volenti non fit injuria*, or *volenti* for short) applies if, prior to engaging in the activity that led to injury, the plaintiff consented to the physical risks associated with it (for example, a sporting event) *and* expressly or implicitly agreed to give up the right to sue the defendant in the event of injury. Releases and exclusion clauses on the backs of tickets can be used as evidence of such an agreement.

The defence of **illegality** (sometimes referred to by its Latin name *ex turpi causa non oritur action*, or *ex turpi* for short) historically applied only if the plaintiff and defendant had been involved in criminal or immoral activity at the time of the injury. More recently, this defence has been all but abolished by the SCC. It may now be used only in very limited situations—for example, in a case where the plaintiff is trying to use the negligence action to avoid a criminal penalty, such as a fine. For example, if the plaintiff had to pay a criminal fine and sued the defendant (an accomplice in the crime) for damages to help pay the fine, the defendant might use the defence of illegality.

Lack of capacity is sometimes used as a defence in negligence cases, as it is in intentional tort cases. As with the latter, however, the defendant's capacity is technically an element of the tort and is taken for granted unless the defendant challenges this presumption. There is no fixed age when children begin to be held responsible for negligence. For both children and mentally incompetent adults, the issue is whether the defendant has the mental ability to appreciate the nature of the duty imposed on him and to fulfill the duty by adhering to the requisite standard of care.

---

6   All provinces and the Yukon have enacted legislation setting rules regarding apportionment of liability under this defence. See, for example, *The Tortfeasors and Contributory Negligence Act*, RSM 1987, c T90; *Negligence Act*, RSO 1990, c N.1; and *The Contributory Negligence Act*, RSS 1978, c C-31.

A Tort Related to Negligence: Occupiers' Liability

An area of liability closely related to negligence but with its own set of rules is **occupiers' liability**. It concerns the liability of occupiers of land for injuries that visitors (that is, entrants) sustain while on the property. At common law, the occupier's duty or obligation varies according to the type of entrant. The four main categories of entrant are

1. trespasser,
2. licensee (a person on the property with permission),
3. invitee (a person on the property for a business purpose—for example, a customer in a store), and
4. contractual entrant (someone who has a contract with the occupier allowing him to be there, such as a patron at a hotel, a movie theatre, or a fitness club).

The required level of care increases incrementally with each category. In the case of a burglar (a kind of trespasser), an occupier of land has a duty to act with "common humanity." But in the case of a contractual entrant, the level of required care increases; there is a duty to ensure that the property is "reasonably safe" to use.

In most provinces, legislation has modified the common law concerning occupiers' liability, simplifying the rules. This legislation has abolished the formal categories of entrants and imposed one general statutory duty that can be adjusted to cover different circumstances. Typically, the new statutory duty requires occupiers "to take such care as in all the circumstances of the case is reasonable to ensure that each person entering the premises and his belongings are reasonably safe while on the premises."[7] Given that the duty is to take such care as is reasonable "in all the circumstances of the case," the level of care will vary depending on whether the visitor is a violent intruder, a friend over for dinner, or a person bidding at an auction.

The same defences apply to occupiers' liability (at common law and under legislation) as to negligence generally.

Strict Liability Torts

Much of tort law is focused on the fault of the defendant. For the intentional torts, the defendant must have intended to bring about the consequences of his actions. With the tort of negligence, it is necessary to prove that the defendant's conduct fell below a reasonable standard of care. However, some forms of tort liability are not based on either intention or negligence. Under certain conditions, a defendant can be held responsible even if the consequences of his tortious actions were not intended and even if he were not negligent. Such actions are known as **strict liability torts**. Strict liability torts in Canada most often involve the following three activities:

1. the use of dangerous substances,
2. the ownership of animals, and
3. the employment of agents (vicarious liability).

---

7 For example, see the following: *Occupiers' Liability Act*, RSA 2000, c O-4, s 5; *Occupiers' Liability Act*, RSBC 1996, c 337, s 3; *Occupiers' Liability Act*, SNS 1996, c 27, s 4; and *Occupiers' Liability Act*, RSO 1990, c O.2, s 3. Saskatchewan, Newfoundland and Labrador, and the territories still apply the common law in this area. New Brunswick has abolished all specialized occupiers' liability rules and relies on other tort law rules, particular those relating to negligence, to regulate occupiers' liability disputes.

Dangerous Substances

Strict liability involving dangerous substances is based on the so-called **rule in *Rylands v Fletcher***.[8] The rule here is that a person who brings a dangerous substance (or uses in a dangerous way a substance that is not ordinarily dangerous) onto his property is answerable for the damage it causes if it should escape.

The property-owner's strict liability under *Rylands v Fletcher* is subject to two conditions. These conditions are that

1. the substance brought onto the defendant's land must *escape* to a neighbouring property and cause property damage or personal injury there, and
2. the use of the substance must be a *non-natural use*, meaning that it is unusual, extraordinary, or unsuitable, and that it increases the risk of danger to others.

The main defences to *Rylands v Fletcher* claims are the following:

- the plaintiff consented to the use of the escaping substance;
- the escape was caused by an "act of God" (an unforeseeable natural disaster, such as a violent storm);
- the substance escaped through the deliberate act of a third party (for whom the defendant is not responsible); and
- legislative authority (where legislation shields the defendant from this form of liability).

Animals

Strict liability principles can also apply to owners of animals. Unlike dangerous substances, strict liability for damage caused by animals, whether they are wild or domestic, is generally not predicated on their escape from the defendant's property. Wild animals (for example, bears, lions, chimpanzees, and alligators) are always presumed to be dangerous, and their owners are strictly liable for the damage they cause.

For domestic animals that cause injury or damage, liability is only strict if the following conditions are met:

1. the animal had previously manifested a vicious or mischievous propensity to cause the type of harm in question, and
2. the owner knew of this propensity.

The second condition—the owner's knowledge of the animal's dangerous nature—is the most contentious point in actions involving domestic animals (usually dogs). The legal word for this knowledge is *scienter* (from the Latin for "knowingly"), and a plaintiff's action for damage caused by a domestic animal is often called a ***scienter* action**.

Another type of animal liability is **cattle trespass**. Strict liability for damage caused by straying cattle or other farm animals, unlike liability for domestic (or wild) animals generally, does require escape onto a neighbour's property. (Damage caused by animals that stray

_____

8   *Rylands v Fletcher* (1868), LR 3 HL 330.

onto highways is governed by ordinary rules of negligence.) In that respect, cattle trespass is related to liability for dangerous substances.

The defence of consent is one of the very few defences available in actions based on strict liability for animals. For example, this defence would be available if the plaintiff had entered the defendant's property despite a "Beware of Dog" sign, then was mauled by the defendant's pit bull.

Vicarious Liability

The final type of strict liability tort is the kind involving **vicarious liability**. It is an important one. Vicarious liability involves the liability of one party for the fault of another, due to the special relationship between them. A special relationship of this kind exists, for example, between a car owner and the people who drive the owner's car with her permission. When such people commit a tort in the course of driving the owner's car, she is generally held vicariously responsible, under provincial and territorial motor vehicle legislation.

Parents are generally *not* vicariously liable for torts committed by their children; however, a few provinces (for example, British Columbia, Manitoba, and Ontario) have enacted legislation making them responsible for their children's actions in limited situations. Parents can also be found primarily responsible in negligence if they have failed to properly supervise their children, and this has resulted in injury to others.

The relationship to which vicarious liability most often applies is the principal–agent relationship. And the most commonly litigated principal–agent relationship is that of employer–employee. The general rationale for vicarious liability is as follows: even though the employee rather than the employer has caused the damage, the employer should bear the responsibility for the damage because the employer's enterprise has put the risk into the community. The plaintiff can still sue the employee as the primary tortfeasor (that is, the person who commits the wrong), but vicarious liability gives the injured party an additional and typically "deeper pocket" to claim from.

Two conditions must be met before an employer will be found vicariously liable for the actions of an employee:

1. An employer–employee relationship, as opposed to a business–contractor relationship, must be established. The more control exercised over a person's work, the more likely the person will be classed as an employee.
2. The tort must have been committed in the course of employment. Employers are not responsible for torts committed by their employees on the latter's own time.

There are no specific defences to vicarious liability, although the employer can argue any of the defences that the employee can. If found liable, the employer can always choose to seek indemnity (that is, compensation) from the employee. Generally speaking, however, employers don't pursue this avenue.

Miscellaneous Torts

Two important torts that do not fit neatly into the three categories discussed above (intentional torts, negligence torts, and strict liability torts) are *nuisance* and *defamation*. These torts have their own special rules. Arguably, they could both be considered forms of strict liability torts because the focus in assessing them, as with strict liability torts, is on the *effect* of the defendant's actions on others, not on whether the defendant intentionally or negligently brought about the damaging consequences.

TABLE 9.1   Public Nuisance and Private Nuisance

PUBLIC NUISANCE	PRIVATE NUISANCE
• Unreasonable interference with public interests, such as obstructions of highways and pollution of waterways • If a crime has been committed, charges may be laid • Generally, the attorney gerneral has to bring any civil actions for damages or an injunction • A private citizen can bring an action for a public nuisance only if she has suffered special damage, such as personal injury, interference with private property interests, or economic losses that are substantially different from others also affected by the nuisance	• Unreasonable interference with plaintiff's use and enjoyment of his land • If the plaintiff has suffered material damage, an unreasonable interference is presumed • Where the damage is intangible , such as personal inconvenience or injury to the "senses or nerves" caused by noise or smell, whether the interference is unreasonable will depend on the court's assessment of the following factors: (1) nature, severity, and duration of interference; (2) character of the neighbourhood; (3) utility of the defendant's conduct; and (4) whether the plaintiff displayed abnormal sensitivity

Nuisance

In law, **nuisance** can be one of two kinds: public nuisance or private nuisance (see Table 9.1). A **public nuisance** occurs when a public interest is interfered with, such as when a highway is obstructed or a river is polluted through the defendant's actions. Generally, it is up to the government to seek redress for public nuisances—private citizens can only sue for public nuisances if they have suffered "special" damage that distinguishes them from the public at large.

A **private nuisance** occurs when the defendant has interfered with a person's reasonable use and enjoyment of his land. Trespass and/or physical damage may be involved—for example, where the defendant neighbour's felled tree lands on the plaintiff's house. But neither trespass nor physical injury is required. Interferences may involve foul odours or loud noises.

The main defences to nuisance claims are the same as for claims based on *Rylands v Fletcher*—namely:

- the plaintiff consented to the activity causing the nuisance;
- the nuisance has come about by an act of God (that is, an unforeseeable natural disaster);
- the nuisance has come about through the deliberate act of a third party (for whom the defendant is not responsible); and
- legislative authority (where legislation shields the defendant from liability for nuisance).[9]

Defamation

Defamation is concerned with published allegations of impropriety that injure a person's reputation. The word *published*, in this context, simply means "communicated to others"; it doesn't necessarily mean these allegations have appeared in print. The rules relating to defamation attempt to balance individual rights with broader rights relating to free speech and

---

9   Municipalities, for instance, are protected by legislation in most provinces and territories from being sued in nuisance by citizens for damages caused by blocked storm drains and sewers. The same legislation also usually protects municipalities from strict liability under *Rylands v Fletcher*.

access to information. The two main types of defamation are **libel** and **slander**. Libel deals with defamatory language that is written—for example, in a newspaper article or a book, whether in print or online. Slander deals with oral communications as well as other transitory kinds of communications (for example, looks or gestures). The common law considers libel a more serious form of defamation than slander; it doesn't require proof of damage for libel but it does, in most cases, for slander.

The distinction between libel and slander has been abolished in a number of provinces—Alberta, Manitoba, New Brunswick, Newfoundland and Labrador, Nova Scotia, and Prince Edward Island—and in the territories. In these jurisdictions, libel and slander are treated equally and damage is presumed or not required to support an action for either.

DEFENCES TO DEFAMATION

It is frequently said that, where defamation actions are concerned, "truth is a defence." This defence is also referred to as *justification*. The defendant's own belief in the truth of the information is not a sufficient defence. Likewise, accurately repeating what someone else has said to you is still defamatory if what was said is untrue. That is why, especially for publishers, it is important that sources be checked.

Other important defences against a claim of defamation are the following: (1) *privilege*, which can be absolute or qualified; (2) *responsible communication on matters of public interest*; and (3) *fair comment*. These defences apply even if the statements are untrue.

Examples of statements protected by absolute privilege are statements by high-ranking government officials made in the course of official duties, and statements made during parliamentary proceedings. Such statements cannot be sued as defamatory even if they are made maliciously. The rationale for this defence is simply that public officials need absolute protection for their on-the-job defamatory words, so that they can aggressively pursue the public good without fear of private actions against them.

The defence of qualified privilege applies to a variety of situations. It could apply to information published by a journalist if that information is in the public interest—for example, information related to public meetings or to public bodies such as the police or fire department. Also, this defence is available to a defendant who made the defamatory statements in the course of trying to protect her own interests or those of third parties. Such privilege is "qualified" in the sense that, unlike absolute privilege, it no longer applies if the plaintiff can show that the defendant was motivated by malice in making the statements. For example, a newspaper reporter who maliciously publishes false information about a public figure against whom she bears a personal grudge would not be able to claim privilege.

Until recently, the Canadian courts had never clearly defined, in the context of media reporting, the exact extent of the qualified privilege defence with respect to matters of public interest. In 2009, the SCC recognized a new defence to clear up the confusion.[10] *Responsible communication on matters of public interest* (commonly known by its shorter, less accurate name: *responsible journalism*) is available as a defence to any person who reports responsibly on matters of public interest, even if the some of the facts turn out to be untrue. Under this defence, matters of public interest can include anything that invites public attention, affects public welfare, or concerns matters of notoriety or controversy. The reporter must be responsible, however, in the sense of having been diligent in trying to verify the accuracy of the allegations.

---

10   *Grant v Torstar Corp*, 2009 SCC 61, [2009] 3 SCR 640.

BOX 9.3

Hyperlinking and Defamation

In *Crookes v Newton*, 2011 SCC 47, [2011] 3 SCR 269, new information practices ran up against old law. The SCC had to determine whether placing a link to a defamatory article on a website was the same as reproducing the article on the website. In other words, was the website owner liable for defamation? Newspapers and other publishers are responsible for checking the accuracy of the information they publish and print. Are website owners similarly responsible if they provide a hyperlink to defamatory material?

The plaintiff, Crookes, owned a business and commenced a number of lawsuits against various persons, including Newton, whom he felt had defamed him. Crookes claimed to be the victim of a smear campaign. Newton owned a website that contained commentary on political matters, including

free speech, and that included a hyperlink to another site that allegedly contained information that was defamatory of Crookes.

The narrow issue in this case was whether hyperlinking is publishing. A majority of the SCC concluded that it was not. They concluded that placing the burden of defamation lawsuits on website owners who had done no more than link to other sites that were defamatory would unduly restrict the free flow of information on the Internet. There was nothing on Newton's site itself that was defamatory. A site's providing a link to a second site is not the same thing as the first site's publishing that information itself, and the victim of defamation can always go after the owner of the site that actually contains the defamatory words.

Fair comment is a defence to defamation if the false statements are made in the context of commentary on matters of public interest, provided certain conditions are met—for example, provided that the statement is clearly recognizable as commentary or opinion (rather than put forward as a statement of fact) and provided that it amounts to an opinion someone could honestly and reasonably hold. Strictly speaking, such commentary cannot be false because it is an opinion and does not claim to be factual in nature.

Tort Remedies

Among the remedies available to victims of torts are damages, injunctions, and extrajudicial remedies.

Damages

The main remedy available to the victim of a tort is damages. There are many different ways to classify damage awards. One way is to classify them according to the purpose the award serves. By this classification scheme, there are three main types of damages:

1. compensatory,
2. nominal, and
3. punitive.

Compensatory damages compensate the plaintiff for proven and recognized types of losses. These are what most plaintiffs are seeking in most tort actions. Sometimes the losses are easy to quantify—for example, where there have been out-of-pocket expenses necessitated by the tort, and receipts can be entered into evidence. These are often referred to as *special damages*. In other cases, the calculation is less exact—for example, where the court is attempting to compensate the plaintiff for pain and suffering or for future lost earnings. These are called *general damages*.

Nominal damages refer to damages that reflect the breach of a right where no actual loss has been sustained. While many torts—negligence, most notably—require the plaintiff to prove an actual *compensable* loss in order to bring an action in the first place, some torts allow an action to be brought without proof of loss (such torts are said to be *actionable per se*). Torts in this latter category include trespass to land, trespass to person, invasion of privacy, and libel. Where no actual loss has been sustained as a result of one of these torts, an award of nominal damages is possible. The word "nominal" in this context does not mean small, and such awards are not required to be small; however, unless the tortious behaviour in question is particularly extreme, nominal damage awards do tend to be relatively small.

Punitive damages are granted in situations where the court wishes to punish the defendant for socially objectionable behaviour. Such damage awards are in a sense a windfall to the plaintiff because they are over and above any amount needed for compensation or for acknowledging the infringement of rights. The intentional torts more than other torts result in this kind of award. In extreme cases of negligence and defamation, however, punitive damages have been awarded.

Other Remedies

After damages, the next most important remedy for the victim of a tort is the *injunction*. Injunctive relief is most commonly prohibitory (that is, it takes the form of an order to stop doing something—for example, to stop using the plaintiff's backyard as a short cut). But injunctive relief can in some cases be mandatory (that is, it may take the form of an order to do something, such as removing an obstruction blocking the plaintiff's access to his property). Claims concerning the tort of nuisance, more frequently than any other tort, include requests for injunctions.

A class of remedy that is rarely used but is available in limited circumstances is the extra-judicial remedy. Two examples of this are *abatement of nuisance* and *recapture of goods*. The abatement of nuisance remedy allows the claimant to bring an end to the nuisance himself, without waiting to go to court. An example of this kind of remedy would be allowing the claimant to cut down a branch from a neighbour's tree if the branch is overhanging the claimant's property. The remedy of recapture allows a plaintiff to recover goods that have been wrongfully removed or withheld. The law is not entirely clear on the limits of these remedies. Whenever the plaintiff's recovery of her goods involves an application of force or a trespass to land, there is a risk that the court may find the bounds of "reasonableness" have been exceeded, leaving the plaintiff open to counterclaims. The fine line here is between self-help and vigilantism.

Contract Law

Contract law is a special area of the law. It empowers us to enter into agreements with others and thereby create a legal relationship based on our own set of rules. For the most part, we choose the rules that define our contractual relationships. This makes contract law different from many other areas of the law—for example, torts and criminal law—where the rules are *imposed* by the common law or by legislation.

There are some limits, however, on our freedom to make contracts according to our own rules. These limits have to do with accepted community standards. For instance, many types of contracts or contractual terms are subject to judge-made or statutory rules dealing with illegality, human rights, employment standards, business practices, and consumer protection. These contracts or terms will be unenforceable if they do not follow those rules.

Pervasiveness of Contracts

Contracts are everywhere. Most of us enter into multiple contractual arrangements every day, without realizing it. We enter into contracts when we

- purchase gasoline for our vehicles (contract with a gasoline retailer),
- take public transit or hire a taxi (common-carrier contracts), or
- purchase food for immediate consumption (contract with a fast-food business).

Then there are all our contracts for non-food items (for example, clothing); for personal services (for example, haircuts) and home services (for example, cable and Internet access); and for entertainment (movie rentals, for example, or tickets to sporting events). The list is long.

And even when we're not making new contracts, we're living by the terms of old ones—meeting our continuing service obligations (for example, making monthly payments on a gym membership), and requiring that the goods we purchase meet the contractual terms concerning their fitness for their stated purpose. If your newspaper was not delivered on a day when it should have been, the newspaper publisher may be in breach of its contract with you. If your new condominium begins to leak soon after you purchase it, you may have a claim in contract against the developer who sold it to you. If your smoke alarm fails to sound during a fire, you may have a contract claim against the home supply store that sold it to you.

Contracts not only play a key role in many activities in everyday life but, not surprisingly, they inform many separate areas in the *study* of law. Some legal subjects—for example, insurance, employment, labour, and landlord and tenant—are about one particular type of contract. Other areas of law—for example, trusts, corporate law, securities, commercial transactions, consumer law, real property, and natural resources—feature contracts of various types.

Even areas of law that do not feature contracts in a major way touch upon them in some way. In torts, for example, claims for financial losses based on negligent misrepresentation or deceit almost always arise in the context of a contractual relationship, and the tort of inducing breach of contract always does. In family law, marriage contracts, separation agreements, and cohabitation agreements can affect the parties' rights to property and support during and upon termination of the relationship. And in criminal law, the outcome of charges dealing with theft and fraud may turn on the interpretation of contracts the accused had or believed he had concerning the property or money in question. During sentencing, "plea bargains"—a type of contract—will bind the Crown to the agreed-upon punishment for the convicted person.

Formation of a Contract

It is generally accepted that up to six elements are required to make a valid contract: offer, acceptance, consideration, certainty of terms, intention to contract, and (in some cases) formal requirements. Similarly to tort law, capacity to contract is a required element but is presumed unless the defendant raises the issue (see the Excuses That Protect Weaker Parties heading later in this section). Figure 9.2, at the end of this section, summarizes the components of an enforceable contract.

Offer

An offer is a statement by one person (offeror) to another (offeree) indicating a willingness to commit to a binding arrangement. The test of whether this element is present is the following question: Did the alleged offeror display an intention to be bound by the terms of the proposal should it be accepted? If the answer to this question is *yes*, an offer has been made. It should be noted that in contract law, the courts often resort to an intention test, as here, to determine the will of the parties. The intention that the court is almost always concerned with is an *objective intention*. This is determined by asking what a "reasonable person" would think was intended by the parties based on what they said and did, and the surrounding circumstances. This can be contrasted to a *subjective intention*, which is based on what the parties actually believed in their own minds, and with which the court is generally not concerned.

The following should be noted with regard to offers:

- Precise words or formalized language are not necessary in the offer.
- Statements that do not qualify as offers are considered negotiating statements, often referred to as "invitations to treat" or "invitations to deal." Negotiating statements generally do not have much legal significance unless they are false and induced the other party to enter into the contract.
- For most contracts, offers can be made either orally, in writing (for example, by letter or brochure, by posting a reward notice, or by means of a newspaper advertisement), electronically (for example, by email, fax, or on a website), by conduct (for example, by gesture or by providing a service), or through a combination of these.
- Offers must be deliberately communicated to the offeree or offerees before they can be accepted.
- Offers can be revoked at any time prior to acceptance.

Acceptance

Acceptance is the signification by the offeree of her willingness to enter into an agreement with the offeror on the offeror's terms. The test of whether this element is present is the following question: Did the offeree absolutely and unequivocally agree with the terms of the offer? If the answer to this question is *yes*, there has been an acceptance.

The following should be noted with regard to acceptance:

- Precise words or formalized language are not needed for an acceptance.
- Responses to an offer that do not qualify as acceptances can fall into a number of categories:
  - *A mere inquiry or simple request to modify terms.* Here, the offeree indicates a willingness to accept on the offeror's terms but wishes to know if there is room for "movement" by the offeror in modifying the proposed terms. Such an inquiry or request does not "kill" the original offer; it remains open for acceptance.
  - *A counteroffer.* Here, the response includes a material change to the offer, such as modifying the price. A counteroffer kills the offer and requires an acceptance of its terms before a contract will be formed.
  - *An outright rejection of the offer.* This brings the negotiation to an end unless a new offer is made by one of the parties.
- Like offers, acceptances can generally be made either orally, in writing, electronically, by conduct, or by a combination of these.
- If the offeror requires a particular method of acceptance (for example, a special form, or a precise time or place of acceptance), then this requirement must be met before the acceptance will be effective and the offeror bound to the contract.

- As a general rule, acceptances must be communicated to the offeror to be effective. The principal exceptions to this rule are
  - when the "postal acceptance rule" applies (if it is reasonable in the circumstances to use the post, it is presumed that a mailed acceptance is effective as soon as it is posted, even if the acceptance is lost in the mail and is never received by the offeror), and
  - when the offeror has dispensed with the need for communication (see discussion of unilateral contracts below).
- After acceptance, a contract is formed (assuming all other elements are present) and the parties are bound. At this point, it is too late for the parties to withdraw.

Consideration

At common law, contracts require an *exchange*, or a *bargain*. Consideration is something of value given by one party (the promisee) in return for the promise or obligation of the other party (the promisor). Consideration is crucial to making the contract binding.

A contractual promise must be supported by a requested consideration coming from the other party (promisee) which is a benefit to the promisor (for instance, a promise to sell something could by supported by payment or a reciprocal promise to pay) and/or a loss to the promisee (using the same example, the loss of the purchase moneys to obtain what is being sold).

An exception to consideration relates to promises made under seal. A seal is a mark, placed on a document, that indicates a degree of formality and is acknowledged by the promisor as his own. Types of seal include impression seals, wax seals, or common stationers' red wafer seals. Such promises are binding without consideration. For example, when a person guarantees a bank loan to another person, the bank will often require the guarantor to sign *and seal* the guarantee. In most cases, the bank will not have provided any consideration to the guarantor for his promisor, but the guarantee will still be binding because of the seal.

Certainty of Terms

If important terms—for example, those relating to the price or the nature of the property or service in question—are so vaguely expressed or uncertain in the contract that the court cannot ascribe any reasonable meaning to them, then the whole contract will be struck down as void on the grounds of uncertainty. The same applies if important terms are omitted altogether or if they are left open to be negotiated at a later date.

If the uncertainty relates to less important terms, such as times and places of delivery, the court will usually infer terms based on what is reasonable in the circumstances.

Intention to Contract

For a contract to be valid, the parties must intend to be *legally* bound by the terms of their arrangement.

In commercial settings, it is presumed that the parties did intend a legally binding relationship. This presumption can be rebutted by clear language to the contrary, if the parties want the arrangement to be in "honour" only and not binding.

In family and social settings, it is presumed that the parties did *not* intend a legally binding relationship. (This presumption, too, can be rebutted by clear language to the contrary.) And this presumption does not apply in the case of marriage contracts and separation agreements, where the intention is always to bind.

FIGURE 9.2 Summary of contract elements

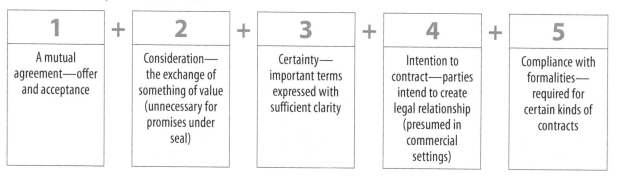

Formal Requirements

All provinces and territories have legislation requiring certain kinds of contracts, such as land contracts or specific types of consumer contracts (for example, direct sales contracts—contracts entered into away from a seller's regular place of business), to be in writing and to contain certain information. The legislation in this area can be complicated and must be read carefully to determine the precise requirements and consequences of failing to meet them.

General Forms of Contracts

Important types or forms of contract include *unilateral* and *bilateral contracts, executed* and *executory contracts, contingent agreements, standard form contracts, options, deeds,* and *electronic contracts.* These types of contracts are not mutually exclusive. For instance, it is possible to have a bilateral, standard form contact that is entered into electronically and is to be performed in the future. (For more information on electronic contracts and e-commerce, see Box 9.4.)

Unilateral and Bilateral Contracts

Unilateral contracts are contracts in the form of a "promise for an action," and they are sometimes referred to as "if" contracts because the offeror promises something (usually payment) *if* the offeree accepts by performing a requested action. Service contracts and renovation contracts are frequently in this form. Such a contract might say, for example, "If you paint my house, I will pay you $5,000."

Bilateral contracts are in the form of a "promise for a promise." Here, the offeror promises something in exchange for a reciprocal promise. She might say explicitly, for example, "I promise to sell you my car in exchange for your promise to pay me $5,000." Or she might simply say, "I offer to sell you my car for $5,000." Such an offer will usually be interpreted as a promise that impliedly calls for a reciprocal promise; simply by accepting the offer, the offeree will be seen to have "promised" to pay in return.

The important difference between unilateral and bilateral contracts is that bilateral contracts become binding as soon as the offeree accepts the offer, even though the promised actions (for example, transfer of ownership and payment) may not have occurred yet. With unilateral contracts, the parties are not bound to each other until the act of acceptance commences (for example, the offeree starts to paint the house). Up to that point, either party can change his mind and walk away from the deal (by revoking or rejecting the offer).

Electronic Contracts and E-Commerce

Contracts can be formed by means of electronic media. As mentioned above, offers and acceptances can be made electronically through, for example, faxes, emails, text messages, website forms, or combinations of these methods. Virtually any contract, regardless of its subject matter, can be electronic.

All Canadian jurisdictions have now enacted legislation providing that contracts may be made by electronic means, and that clicking on computer icons, touching computer screens, or even speaking to computers are effective means of communicating contractual intentions.* This legislation is modelled on a law for electronic transactions adopted in 1996 by the United Nations Commission on International Trade (UNCITRAL), supplemented by further work on the law by the Uniform Law Conference of Canada, a body dedicated to the harmonization of provincial and territorial laws (and federal laws, where appropriate).

Different terms are gaining acceptance to describe the precise method by which e-contracts are entered into, such as "shrink-wrap," "click-wrap," and "browse-wrap" agreements:

- A *shrink-wrap agreement* usually relates to software and gets its name from the fact that some software is sold in a box enclosed in shrink wrap, but when the software is loaded, often from a CD or DVD, a further agreement presents itself on the computer, this time between the software creator and the user as opposed to retailer and user. Such agreements are usually licences restricting the user's ability to copy the software.

- A *click-wrap agreement* refers to a purchase contract made over the Internet, including but not restricted to software purchases; it gets its name from the fact that the user of the website is required to read an online contract and click an "I agree" icon or something similar.
- A *browse-wrap agreement*, like a click wrap agreement, refers to Internet purchases. It is distinguished by the fact that the user indicates assent or agreement simply by using the product after having been made aware of the product's terms of use.†

E-commerce is responsible for a larger percentage of overall consumer sales each year, and by some estimates now accounts for 50 percent of such sales. And decisions about 80 percent of all purchases, whether or not they are actually made online, are influenced by online research. M-commerce, which refers to purchases using mobile communication devices like cellphones, although still a relatively small segment of total e-commerce, has been identified as a rapidly growing area.

*   For example, see Ontario's *Electronic Commerce Act, 2000*, SO 2000, c 17 and BC's *Electronic Transactions Act*, SBC 2001, c 10.

†   For a discussion of these kinds of agreements, see *Century 21 Canada v Rogers Communications*, 2011 BCSC 1196.

In many cases, it is not clear how the parties intended to structure their contract. When faced with this kind of ambiguity, courts tend to interpret the contract as bilateral. The courts presume the parties must have intended a bilateral contract because of the certainty and security that come from having a binding arrangement at the outset.

Executed and Executory Contracts

Another way to characterize the structure of contracts is based on the timing of their performance. Contracts that are fully performed are said to be *executed contracts*. If they are fully performed at the time (or shortly after) they are entered into, they are also *immediately* performed. Such contacts can be termed *immediate performance contracts*, although there is no generally accepted name for such contracts. Other contracts, however, delay performance for, or are continuously performed over, a period of time (sometimes for days, months, or even years). These contracts are referred to as *executory contracts*, or, more frequently nowadays, as *future performance contracts*. An example of an immediate performance contract would be one where you pay for and receive goods or a service contemporaneously, such as when you buy your coffee at a coffee shop or go for a haircut. Future performance contracts, which are binding at the outset, are used whenever the promised actions take place in the future and sometimes over a period of time. They cover the full spectrum of planned arrangements from gym memberships to home purchases to ongoing business relations.

Contingent Agreements

Related to future performance arrangements are *contingent agreements*, sometimes called delayed performance or defeasible contracts. Contingent agreements include special terms called *conditions precedent* and/or *conditions subsequent*. A condition precedent delays the start of performance of the contract until a defined event occurs. A "subject to financing" clause in a home purchase contract is an example of a condition precedent; until financing is obtained by the purchaser, the contract does not take effect. In other words, if no financing is obtained, the contract simply fizzles out before it begins. A condition subsequent makes a contract "defeasible," meaning that at some point *after* performance has started the contract can be brought to a premature end if a defined event occurs. For example, an ongoing supply contract could include a condition subsequent that protects the supplier and terminates the contract should something happen that makes the product no longer profitable to supply.

Standard Form Contracts

Contracts also differ structurally depending on whether they are individually negotiated or are in a standard form. Individually negotiated contracts are tailored to the specific circumstances of a situation. They are time-consuming to draft and tend to be used when the transaction is complex and involves something valuable. Standard form contracts tend to be used for predictable, uniform, common transactions—situations where individual negotiation would be impractical. Examples of standard form contracts include the tickets you receive when using public transit or going to movies. More complex transactions, such as car rental agreements, also involve standard form contracts.

Options and Deeds

An option contract is an "offer" in the form of a contract, whereby an offeror makes a binding promise to keep an offer open for a fixed period of time during which, at any point, the option holder can accept the offer. In order to be bound, the person granting the option must have received consideration from the option holder or have made the promise under seal. Stock options and options to purchase real property are common examples of this form of contract. A deed is technically not a contract but a promise that has been "signed, sealed and delivered." It is the traditional instrument for conveying ownership of real property, and it operates much like a contract, except that consideration is not required in order for the promise to be binding. The seal acts as a substitute for consideration (see the discussion, above, under "Consideration").

Contract Terminology and Terms

An examination of different contracts will reveal an assortment of arrangements and obligations and terms. Some of these are specific and individual; they will not be found in any other contract. Other elements are common to many agreements. The more common ones are briefly described in Box 9.5.

BOX 9.5

Words for Terms

Many different words are used to describe contract terms in a general sense, words such as "term," "clause," "representation," "condition," "provision," "stipulation," and "rider." Sometimes these words can have specific and even multiple meanings, and close attention to context is required. For instance, the word *condition* can refer to any general stipulation or term in a contract. But, as we have seen, it may also refer, more specifically, to a *condition precedent* or a *condition subsequent* or to an important term which, if not followed, triggers a right of termination.

In lengthier contracts, it is not unusual to find a definition clause that defines specific words and phrases used in the contract. Such clauses are like definition sections at the beginning of statutes (see Chapter 5). Because certainty of terms is a required element of contractual validity, the definition clause is important, especially if the subject matter of the agreement is complex or technical.

Contracts that bind the parties over a long period of time usually include a termination clause that gives the parties the right to end the arrangement, usually by providing some kind of notice or by providing a reason. If the reason is one party's dissatisfaction with the other's performance, the termination clause will typically provide for an opportunity to correct the problem before termination can occur. Conditions precedent and conditions subsequent can also result in the termination of a contract, as noted above.

Exclusion clauses can be found in all kinds of contracts, but are often associated with standard form contracts. They typically limit the liability of one of the parties either to a fixed dollar amount or—for certain types of breaches—altogether. For example, a ski-hill ticket may limit the liability of the resort operator for any injuries the patron sustains while on the ski hill, even if these injuries are caused by the operator's negligence in grooming or marking the runs. There are many different ways of referring to exclusion clauses. In addition to "exclusion," the following adjectives are used: "exclusionary," "exculpatory," "exemption," "exempting," "limitation," "limiting," and "disclaimer."

Terms in a contract can be simple representations of fact ("This car I'm selling you has 100,000 kilometres on it"), or they can be promised actions ("I promise to cut your lawn next Tuesday"). With respect to liability, there is no difference between the two. If a representation is untrue, the party who made it can be sued for breach of contract. Similarly, if a promised event does not come to pass, the party who promised that it would come to pass will be liable (unless he has a recognized excuse or defence).

Express Terms and Implied Terms

Another common distinction, where contracts are concerned, is between *express terms* and *implied terms*. An **express term** is one that the parties have put their minds to and deliberately included in the contract. In an oral contract, for instance, an express term is something the parties have specifically discussed. In a written contract, an express term will be spelled out in the text of the document.

Implied terms are terms the parties have not expressed in their contract, but are nonetheless part of the deal. The SCC has held that there are three kinds of implied terms that *may* be included in a contract, depending on the circumstances. The three kinds are as follows:

1. *Terms implied in fact.* These are terms that, in the court's view, the parties would have agreed to if they had put their minds to it. The test of whether a term is implied in fact is whether it is needed to give "business efficacy" to the contract. In other words, is this term necessary for the efficient performance of the contract?

2. *Terms implied in law.* These terms are automatically part of the contract owing to the nature of the contract and the laws regulating the area in question. Terms implied in law are based on what the court feels is necessary for the "fair functioning" of the agreement. Also included in this category are terms that legislation makes part of the contract. For example, sale of goods acts in all provinces and territories make it an implied term of any sale of goods contract that the goods sold will be "reasonably fit for the purpose" for which they were intended.

3. *Terms implied by custom or usage.* These terms are based on industry standards for similar types of contracts. It is assumed that the parties intended similar terms to be part of their own deal. Generally, the parties can exclude any of these implied terms, if they choose to, by doing so expressly in their agreement. In some cases, legislation may prevent them from such exclusion.

Conditions and Warranties

Terms in a contract can also be differentiated according to their level of importance to the parties. *Conditions* and *warranties* are two such terms; a breach of condition is much more serious than a breach of warranty, and the remedies required differ accordingly. All that an innocent party can recover for the breach of a warranty is damages. The word *condition*, by contrast, refers to the most important type of contract term—for example, payment of the purchase price or delivery of the promised goods. In the event that a condition is not met, the innocent party can not only sue for damages (as she can for a breach of warranty) but can terminate the contract if she so chooses.

The parties' particular intentions determine which elements in the contract are conditions and which are warranties. For example, a definition clause could make it clear how the parties wanted the various terms to be characterized. However, if the contract does not make the parties' intentions clear, the court will make the determination for them based on its assessment of the relative importance of the various terms.

Note that the words *warranty* and *condition* can mean different things in different contexts. For instance, the word *warranty* as we've been using it above is not the same thing as a manufacturer's "warranty," which refers to a guarantee of quality, usually for a limited period of time. And, as we have seen, the word "condition" has multiple meanings, including a generic reference to any term in a contract.

Excuses for Non-Performance of Contracts

After a contract has been entered into, information may come to light or new circumstances may arise that make the agreement unfair or even impossible to fulfill as originally made. With contracts, we talk not of "defences" but of "excuses" for not having to perform one's contractual obligations. The more common excuses are described below.

Misrepresentation

During the course of negotiations, one party may falsely represent a state of affairs, usually a fact relating to the contract—for instance, stating that a house for sale has just had a new roof put on it when it fact it hasn't. This is called a **misrepresentation**. Misrepresentations may be

- *innocent* (made without knowing the information was untrue),
- *negligent* (made without knowing the information was untrue, but made under circumstances where the party ought to have known the information was untrue), or
- *fraudulent* (made while knowing the information was untrue or at least while knowing there was a serious risk it was untrue).

All three types of misrepresentation may provide an excuse for terminating the contract if the misrepresentation was material—in other words, if it was significant enough to induce a reasonable person to enter into a contract she would not have entered otherwise. What usually happens is that, once the innocent party discovers the misrepresentation, she refuses to complete the contract—for example, by not paying the balance owing on the contract. The other party then sues and the innocent party offers up the misrepresentation as an excuse for not paying. She may even get back any money already paid by claiming rescission. (For an explanation of rescission, see the discussion of remedies, below).

Mistake and Frustration

Mistake and frustration are also excuses for not performing. There are two main kinds of mistake:

1. where the parties are confused about the terms they have agreed to (this usually occurs where the contract's terminology is ambiguous); and
2. where both parties have mistaken assumptions about matters that are fundamental or essential to the operation of the contract (for example, a construction contract where the parties assumed the land was zoned for the project when it wasn't).

In both situations, once the mistake is discovered, it may provide an excuse for discontinuing further performance.

Frustration, as an excuse for non-performance of a contract, is similar to the mistaken assumption excuse, but the timing involved is different. In the case of mistake, the problem exists at the time of the contract. With frustration, the problem develops *after* the contract has been entered into and during performance, and it comes about because of a change of circumstances. The changed circumstances must be significant enough to make continued performance impossible or at least to change the fundamental nature of the agreement. Consider the zoning example again. If a construction contract is based on existing zoning, and the municipality, during performance, changes the zoning rules so as to make it impossible to complete the contract, the contract may become frustrated, thereby excusing the parties. Generally, the parties will be required to share the cost of any losses incurred up to the point where the contract became frustrated.

Excuses That Protect Weaker Parties

Some excuses for non-performance of a contract are intended to protect weaker parties. The main excuses of this type are duress, undue influence, unconscionability, and lack of capacity.

DURESS

Duress applies when one of the parties entered into the agreement against his will. It is a common law doctrine and does not apply unless the will of the victim is taken away. If someone holds a gun to your head to make you sign a contract, the agreement can be set aside. Traditionally, there had to be a threat of physical violence for duress to apply. More recently, the courts have started to recognize "economic duress" as an excuse, too. For economic duress to qualify as an excuse, however, the financial pressure has to be so extreme that it deprives the party experiencing it of his freedom to exercise his will. Simple commercial pressure is not enough.

UNDUE INFLUENCE

Undue influence can be thought of as "duress light." Undue influence is an equitable doctrine; that is, it was developed by the courts of equity (see Chapter 2). It qualifies as an excuse for non-performance of a contract when one party has exerted unconscionable use of power over another and has thereby influenced the weaker party to enter the contract. This influence may fall short of depriving the weaker party of his will. Undue influence may be established in one of two ways:

1. proving *actual* undue influence (for example, where one party threatens to sue or prosecute a relative of the other party unless the other enters into a contract); and
2. proving that a recognized "special relationship" exists between the parties (for example, a doctor–patient or lawyer–client relationship), in which case the court may *presume* undue influence unless the stronger party proves otherwise.

UNCONSCIONABILITY

Unconscionability, like undue influence, is an equitable doctrine; it applies where there is a power imbalance between the two parties. The difference is that unconscionability doesn't necessarily involve the application of actual or presumed pressure. As an excuse for non-performance of a contract, it applies when one party takes advantage of another. To establish it, two elements are required:

1. inequality of bargaining power (such as might exist between a young, fit person and a seriously ill or mentally incompetent relative), and
2. an unfair bargain (meaning the stronger party obtains property or some other benefit for less than its fair market value by taking advantage of the weaker party).

INCAPACITY

Incapacity may also be raised as an excuse by weaker parties. Technically, capacity to contract is a required "element" of a valid contract. In contract law as in tort law, capacity is presumed; the onus is on the party seeking to escape responsibility to prove *lack* of capacity. The majority of persons in Canada have the capacity to enter into contractual arrangements. The two main exceptions today are

1. infants, and
2. individuals who are deemed to be mentally incompetent.

An infant is someone under the age of majority, which has been fixed by legislation in all provinces and territories at either 18 or 19. Despite the legal view that infants lack the capacity to contract, common law and legislated rules grant them limited capacity to enter certain kinds of contracts—for example, contracts for necessities such as food and clothing, contracts for student loans, and contracts for property settlements in the event they are getting married. (In the latter case, the contract would usually be overseen by a public trustee of the court).

Incapacity based on mental incompetence applies where one party's mental incapacity prevents her from appreciating the nature of the contact entered into. The incompetence may be a matter of permanent mental disability or a matter of temporary impairment by drugs or alcohol. Apparently (the case law is uncertain in this respect), mental incompetence only qualifies as an excuse for non-performance of a contract in cases where the plaintiff—that is, the person trying to enforce the contract—was aware of the other party's incompetence at the time the contract was made.

Illegality

Finally, contracts that are contrary to public policy at common law or are illegal under legislation may be unenforceable. In such cases, the parties have an excuse for not adhering to the agreed-to terms. For example, contracts to commit criminal or tortious acts are contrary to public policy and are not enforceable; parties may in fact face criminal charges for such agreements.

Contracts with restraint-of-trade provisions generate the most litigation on the grounds of illegality. Non-competition arrangements in contracts of employment often include these kinds of provisions, whose purpose is to prevent employees from competing against their former employers. Restraint-of-trade provisions are also included in contracts for the sale of businesses; they are intended to prevent former business owners (the sellers) from competing with the purchasers. The courts will strike down such provisions and sometimes the whole contract if the restraint-of-trade provision is unreasonably restrictive, especially with respect to its duration and the geographical area it is supposed to cover.

Other kinds of contracts that may prove unenforceable owing to illegality include

- contracts for unregulated medical services,
- surrogacy contracts,
- contracts with a sexual services component, and
- gaming and wagering contracts.

Gaming and wagering contracts are illegal under most provincial and territorial insurance statutes, although specific exceptions apply to government-sanctioned gambling.

Contract Remedies

Remedies are available if one party fails to perform his obligations under a contract or makes representations that are untrue. Representations may either be contractual (if incorporated into the contract as a term) or pre-contractual (if made during negotiations and not intended to be part of the contract). If a representation is contractual and turns out to be untrue, that amounts to a breach of contract for which damages will be recoverable (unless an exclusion clause prevents such a claim). If a representation is pre-contractual and turns out to be untrue, the innocent party may be able to sue for *rescission* (see below).

If a party to a contract makes untrue representations or does not fulfill his contractual obligations, the other party[11] may be able resort to a number of remedies, including the following:

- damages,
- lawful repudiation of contract,
- specific performance,
- injunctive relief,
- rescission, or
- rectification.

Damages and Lawful Repudiation

As in tort law, the most important remedy in contract law is damages. Contract damages are classified differently, though. The three main categories in contract law are

1. expectation damages,
2. reliance damages, and
3. restitution damages.

Expectation damages attempt to place the innocent party in the position she would have been in if the contract had been performed as promised and all the contractual representations were true. This method of assessing damages is the standard method used to calculate damages in contract disputes. Expectation damages typically claimed include out-of-pocket expenses to correct defective performance (for example, where construction work is shoddy and has to be fixed) and loss of profits (for example, where a commodity was not delivered and the purchaser was unable to resell for a profit as planned).

Expectation damages sometimes have alternate names depending on what they represent or how they are calculated. For instance, out-of-pocket expenses, just referred to, can also be called *special damages* because they have already been incurred and are certain. The term *general damages* can be used to describe the value of a lost expectation that is not specifically quantifiable, such as the enjoyment the plaintiff hoped to experience on a vacation (where a vacation planner failed to deliver as promised). *Liquidated damages*, which are another type of expectation claim, refer to damages that the parties have calculated in advance. They can only be claimed, however, where the parties have put a clause in the contract setting out what the damages are to be, and where the amount represents a genuine pre-estimate of the loss expected to be suffered in the event of breach. Liquidated damages clauses can save the parties the trouble of arguing about what the damages are if the contract is broken.

Reliance and restitution damages can be claimed as alternatives to expectation damages in cases where there is no expectation loss or it can't be proved. **Reliance damages** are intended to cover expenses incurred *preparing for* contractual obligations (for example, the cost of special materials purchased by a building contractor that become wasted when the other party cancels the contract). **Restitution damages** generally cover moneys—deposits

---

11 Generally, only parties to a contract acquire rights under it. This is known as the "privity rule." Privity of contract—that is, being a party to it—is generally required in order to maintain an action for damages or other remedy. Some exceptions apply, however, in the case of "third-party beneficiaries." A third-party beneficiary is someone mentioned in the contract who benefits in some way from it.

BOX 9.7

Damages for Wrongful Dismissal: A Special Case

Generally speaking, the measurement of expectation losses in breach of contract cases is "open." In other words, there is no fixed formula for calculating the damages. However, in wrongful dismissal cases, the courts have developed a unique approach.

This special approach applies specifically to open-ended employment contracts, which cover most employment arrangements. An open-ended employment contract is one that is *not* for a fixed term or based on a collective agreement negotiated on behalf of the employee by a union. Employees covered by open-ended employment contracts can be let go *immediately* for cause (for stealing or serious insubordination, for example). This is not surprising. More surprising is that employees covered by these kinds of contracts can also be dismissed at any time *without cause* and for almost any reason or even for no reason.* The only difference is that, if an employee is dismissed without cause, *the employer must give the employee reasonable notice or salary in lieu.* Open-ended employment contracts include an implied term that employers must provide reasonable notice or equivalent pay in the case of without-cause dismissals.

If an employer dismisses an employee without cause and without notice or pay, the implied term dealing with termination will have been breached; in other words, there will have been a wrongful dismissal. How much notice is reasonable notice? Employment-standards legislation, federally and in the provinces and territories, sets basic statutory minimums; they work out to roughly one week of notice for every year of service. However, the common law "formula" is almost always more generous. The legislation doesn't prevent pursuing a claim at common law, and in the event of a dispute, a dismissed employee will most often choose the common law remedy over the legislation. This is not only because of the potential for a larger award, but because the legislation usually makes the statutory award final and precludes any further claims for compensation.

The common law formula is based on a "factors test." Most courts in Canada use as a starting point the test set out in the 1960 case of *Bardal v Globe & Mail Ltd.* The test is as follows:

There can be no catalogue laid down as to what is reasonable notice in particular classes of cases. The reasonableness of the notice must be decided with reference to each particular case, having regard to the character of the employment, the length of service of the servant, the age of the servant and the availability of similar employment, having regard to the experience, training and qualifications of the servant.[†]

The factors mentioned in this test are sometimes referred to as the "*Bardal* factors."[‡] They are still applied today, although sometimes courts consider other factors as well—for example, whether the employer induced the employee to leave his previous place of employment or whether promises of job security were made. Although no single factor takes precedence, the "character of the employment" and "length of service" factors are important ones.

The more responsibility and seniority an employee has, the longer the notice will be, and sometimes it will be far in excess of the statutory minimums. For example, in a recent Ontario Court of Appeal decision, *Love v Acuity Investment Management Inc*, a 50-year-old senior vice-president with only two-and-a-half-years' service, who had been dismissed without cause or notice, was awarded nine months' salary.[§] The statutory minimum was just two weeks.

---

*   There are a few exceptions, though. Dismissing an employee for discriminatory reasons, for instance, is prohibited by human rights legislation, federally and in all provinces and territories.

†   *Bardal v Globe & Mail Ltd* (1960), 24 DLR (2d) 140 at 145 (Ont HCJ).

‡   The Supreme Court of Canada recently approved of the continued use of the *Bardal* factors in making "reasonable notice" determinations: see *Keays v Honda Canada Inc*, 2008 SCC 39, [2008] 2 SCR 362.

§   *Love v Acuity Investment Management Inc*, 2011 ONCA 130.

and part payments, for example—that the innocent party paid over to the other party. By recovering such expenses and moneys paid, the innocent party at least breaks even and doesn't suffer a loss as a result of the other party's breach.

A party may be able to claim *punitive damages* in addition to either expectation, reliance, or restitution damages. As in tort claims, punitive damages are designed to punish the defendant for socially objectionable behaviour. Again, they represent a windfall to the plaintiff because they are over and above what is needed for compensation.

If the breach of contract was particularly serious, as when there is a breach of condition, the innocent party, besides being able to claim for damages, may also choose to terminate the contract. This is formally known as a *lawful repudiation of the contract*. The innocent party may decline to do this, however. If the contract is still of some benefit to her, she may choose to keep it alive and merely sue for damages.

Other Remedies for Contract Disputes

Besides damages and lawful repudiation, a number of other remedies are sometimes available in contract disputes. Four of these are the following:

1. specific performance,
2. injunctive relief,
3. rescission, and
4. rectification.

These four remedies are all equitable remedies and, as such, the court will not grant them unless the plaintiff has come to court "with clean hands" (in other words, has been fair and reasonable in bringing the proceedings). Other equitable bars can apply to these remedies as well (such as where the plaintiff has misrepresented some fact in connection with the transaction). Also, the court will not order this remedy if it would negatively affect an innocent third party (see the example in connection with specific performance referred to next).

Specific performance is a remedy whereby the court orders the party in breach to perform his obligations as promised by transferring the property or—more rarely—by performing the service agreed to. Besides the other equitable defences, the rights of third parties can be significant in this context. For example, the court would not order a party to transfer a residence if that party's ex-spouse were still living on the property.

When courts grant *injunctions* in contract claims, it is usually to prevent a party from ignoring a contractual provision intended to prevent that party from engaging in certain behaviour, such as selling competing products or stealing customers.

Rescission is a special remedy whereby the contract is cancelled and the parties are returned to the positions they were in just before the contract was entered into. Usually this involves returning anything received under the contract, such as money or property, up to the point of cancellation. Rescission is not available as a remedy for breach of contract; it is meant for problems that arose prior to contract formation. It is most often claimed for material misrepresentations that were made before the contract was entered into. If the misrepresentations were also negligent or fraudulent, they may support a separate claim for damages *in tort*.

As a remedy, rescission is subject to a number of limitations. One of these is the practical impossibility of returning any property in precisely the same form in which it was received; for instance, a car may be in an accident, and a building may be substantially renovated or torn down altogether.

Rectification is an unusual and limited remedy that applies where the parties have made a mistake in recording the terms of their contract in a written document. This remedy involves an order that the contract be rewritten so as to correct the mistake. What usually happens in rectification cases is the following: a mistake comes to light, and the party benefiting from the mistake tries to enforce the contact as written. The other party, in order to obtain the remedy, must prove, among other things,

- what terms were actually and clearly agreed to orally,
- that a mistake was made in recording the agreement, and
- that the mistake can be corrected easily by the substitution of a few words.

Related Areas of Private Law

There are many areas of private law, and many of them overlap. Some even cross the divide into public domestic law and some, even further, into international law. The following is an overview of certain areas of private law that are related to torts and contracts but that are increasingly treated as their own distinct areas.

Areas Related to Torts

Two areas with a torts connection that can be considered distinct subjects are sports law and professional malpractice.

Sports law deals with the law as it relates to professional and amateur sports. Many of the injuries that occur in sporting activities produce claims in negligence and even the intentional torts. Of course, sports law touches on other areas of law as well, including, for example, the following:

- contracts (agreements between professional athletes and their agents and teams, as well as waivers and releases),
- criminal law (in the case of recklessly or deliberately caused injuries),
- labour law (player associations),
- civil liberties (equal opportunity and drug testing), and
- other areas.

Professional malpractice concerns the liability of professionals to their clients for a wide range of misdealings, from incompetence to fraud. Tort law features prominently with claims in negligence and deceit, but contract claims (for example, breach of obligations to exercise reasonable care), claims in equity (for example, breach of fiduciary duties), and occasionally criminal charges play a role, too.

Areas Related to Contracts

Contract law is its own area, but it also informs many areas of law that we think of as distinct, including employment law, insurance law, and corporate and commercial law.

Employment law is largely focused on the contractual relationship between employer and employee in a non-unionized environment. Employment law also has a legislative component, from employment standards and workers' compensation legislation to human rights legislation concerning (for example) discrimination in the workplace. *Labour law* deals primarily with unionized work environments and the collective bargaining process. Federal, provincial, and territorial labour legislation determines rights to strike, picket, and lock out workers, among other things. Administrative law issues concerning civil liberties are also part of this area. *Workers' compensation* is sometimes considered as a separate area of law. It covers a special government-run insurance scheme for injuries caused at work.

Insurance law is based on the contract between an insured person and the insurer (usually, a large insurance company). It covers risk planning for businesses and individuals, handling of claims, interpretation of contract clauses, fiduciary obligations, and many other topics. Different legal issues can arise depending on the type of insurance involved. These types include property insurance, motor vehicle insurance, life insurance, fire insurance, or business-interruption insurance. They vary in their contractual provisions, and the legislation regulating the different types of insurance also varies.

Corporate and commercial law has a number of subcategories that we can address individually; all have a significant contracts component. *Company law* (or corporate law) concerns the law of business associations with respect to the formation, structure, and management of corporations. This law covers shareholders' rights and remedies as well as the duties and obligations of corporate managers. Legislation (federal, provincial and territorial) heavily regulates the area of business corporations. *Close corporations* (small companies that are not publicly traded), *corporate transactions* (for example, mergers and acquisitions), and *corporate finance* (raising funds for corporate purposes) generate particular issues and are often treated as discrete subject areas.

Securities law regulates the public trading of shares and other corporate instruments. It is a complex area with elaborate public disclosure requirements (which involve prospectuses and other documents) and liability rules, all designed to protect members of the public when they are investing in the market. The requirements of securities commissions, stock exchanges, and other organizations have to be satisfied, often in multiple jurisdictions if the shares are sold across provincial and/or international boundaries. *Business and consumer law*, described in Chapter 11, overlaps with some of these areas.

When company law is examined in a broader context along with other forms of business organization and together with various types of business transactions, the area is commonly referred to as *business law*. Finally, *consumer protection law*, also referred to simply as *consumer law*, has developed from the increasing attention paid by lawmakers to the protection of consumers who are on the "demand" side of business and economics. (See Chapter 11 for an overview of these areas.)

CHAPTER SUMMARY

Private law regulates the relationships between persons in many areas. Two of these areas are torts and contracts.

Tort law covers more claims than any other area of private law. Its scope is large because it is not a unified area but rather a diverse one that addresses civil wrongs not covered by other areas of law. Tort claims can be classified according to whether they involve intentional or negligent wrongdoing, or whether they are based on strict liability principles. Classic examples of intentional torts are assault and battery. Torts involving negligence include many situations, from car accidents to professional malpractice. Strict liability torts cover relatively few situations: using dangerous substances, owning dangerous animals, and vicarious liability. A few miscellaneous torts, such as nuisance and defamation, defy easy classification but are similar to strict liability torts insofar as they are focused on the effects of an action rather than the intention behind it.

Contract law is one of the few areas of law where parties can create their own rules and define the terms of their own relationship. Contracts apply to many aspects of our daily routines. The main elements of contract formation are offer, acceptance, and consideration (the parties' reciprocal exchange of something of value). Contract disputes often centre on the interpretation of terms and on whether excuses are available for non-performance of the contract. Excuses for one party's non-performance might be, for example, misrepresentations by the other party during negotiations, or mistakes made about the nature of the contract agreed to. Breach of contract occurs where one party fails to live up to the terms of the agreement. The most common remedies in contract disputes are damages to compensate the innocent party for her lost expectation or a court order forcing the party in breach to specifically perform his obligations.

KEY TERMS

assault psychological tort involving one person's apprehension of harmful physical contact from another person *(p. 247)*

battery tort requiring actual occurrence of harmful or offensive physical contact *(p. 247)*

bilateral contract contracts in the form of a "promise for a promise" whereby the offeror promises something in exchange for a reciprocal promise *(p. 266)*

cattle trespass a strict liability tort involving damage caused by straying cattle or other farm animals *(p. 257)*

civil wrong a wrong that occurs in the context of relationships between persons and is addressed by one of the areas of private law *(p. 246)*

compensatory damages damages in a tort claim that compensate the plaintiff for proven and recognized types of losses *(p. 261)*

consent (defence of) a defence against a variety of tort claims that is based on the idea that the plaintiff was aware of the risks associated with the activity that led to damages and agreed to participate in the activity anyway *(p. 255)*

contributory negligence (defence of) a defence against negligent tort claims that is based on the idea that the plaintiff negligently contributed to her losses *(p. 255)*

defamation a tort involving allegations of impropriety that injure a person's reputation *(p. 259)*

exclusion clause clause in a contract limiting the liability of one of the parties to a fixed dollar amount or (for certain types of breaches of contract) completely *(p. 269)*

expectation damages a remedy for contract disputes that attempts to place the innocent party in the position she would have been in if the contract had been performed as promised and all the contractual representations had been true *(p. 274)*

express terms contract terms that the parties have considered and deliberately included in the contract *(p. 269)*

false imprisonment tort whereby one person totally restrains the movement of another person *(p. 247)*

illegality (defence of) a defence to negligence claims that used to be applied when the plaintiff and defendant were involved in criminal or immoral activity at the time of the injury, but is now applied mainly when the plaintiff is trying to use the negligence action to avoid a criminal penalty *(p. 255)*

implied terms contract terms that the parties have not explicitly included in the contract, but that are nonetheless part of the agreement *(p. 269)*

libel a kind of defamation that involves defamatory language in writing, such as in a newspaper article or book, whether in print or online *(p. 260)*

misfeasance negligent tort that involves doing something carelessly (as opposed to omitting to do something) *(p. 251)*

misrepresentations false representations made during contract negotiations *(p. 271)*

negligence area of tort law that addresses harm caused by *carelessness*, not intentional harm *(p. 251)*

nominal damages damages in a tort claim that reflect the breach of a plaintiff's right where no actual loss has been sustained *(p. 262)*

nonfeasance negligent tort that involves omitting to do something the law requires you to do *(p. 253)*

nuisance in law, either public or private nuisance *(p. 259)*

occupiers' liability the liability of occupiers of land for injuries that visitors sustain while on the occupiers' property *(p. 256)*

private nuisance a tort that involves one person's using her property in such a way as to substantially interfere with another person's enjoyment or use of his property, but without any actual trespass occurring *(p. 259)*

public nuisance occurs when a public interest is interfered with—for example, when a highway is obstructed or a river is polluted through the defendant's actions *(p. 259)*

punitive damages damages in a tort claim that are granted in situations where the court wishes to punish the defendant for socially objectionable behaviour *(p. 262)*

rectification for contract disputes based on errors in the written contract, a remedy whereby the court orders that the contract be rewritten to correct the mistake *(p. 277)*

reliance damages a remedy for contract disputes that compensates the innocent party for expenses he incurred preparing for the performance of contractual obligations *(p. 274)*

rescission a remedy for contract disputes whereby the contract is cancelled and the parties are returned to the positions they were in just before the contract was entered into *(p. 276)*

restitution damages a remedy for contract disputes that compensates the innocent party for moneys usually paid over to the other party (deposits and part payments, for example) *(p. 274)*

rule in *Rylands v Fletcher* the strict liability rule that the person who brings a dangerous substance onto his property is answerable for the damage it causes if it should escape *(p. 257)*

***scienter* action** a strict liability tort claim concerning damage caused by a domestic animal; based on the idea that the defendant (the owner) had knowledge the animal was dangerous *(p. 257)*

slander a kind of defamation transmitted via oral or other transitory forms of communication *(p. 260)*

specific performance a remedy for contract disputes whereby the court orders the party in breach to perform his obligations as promised *(p. 276)*

strict liability tort a tort for which the defendant is held responsible even if the damaging action was neither intentional nor a result of negligence *(p. 256)*

tort a type of civil wrong for which damages can be obtained by the person wronged *(p. 246)*

trespass to goods (or trespass to chattels) a tort whereby one person intentionally interferes with another's rightful possession of movable property *(p. 248)*

trespass to land tort involving the physical intrusion by one person onto land occupied by another *(p. 248)*

trespass to person an intentional tort encompassing three subcategories of tort: assault, battery, and false imprisonment *(p. 247)*

unilateral contract contracts that are in the form of a "promise for an action," the offeror promising something (usually payment) if the offeree accepts by performing a requested action *(p. 266)*

vicarious liability the strict liability of one party for the fault of another due to the special relationship between them (typically, an employer–employee relationship) *(p. 258)*

FURTHER READING

BOOKS

Atkinson, Paul. *The Canadian Justice System: An Overview*, 2d ed (Markham, Ont: LexisNexis, 2010).

Duxbury, Robert. *Nutshells: Contract Law*, 8th ed (London: Sweet & Maxwell, 2009).

Fitzgerald, Patrick, Barry Wright & Vincent Kazmierski. *Looking at Law: Canada's Legal System*, 6th ed (Markham, Ont: LexisNexis, 2010).

Fridman, GHL. *An Introduction to the Law of Torts*, 2d ed (Markham, Ont: LexisNexis, 2003).

Rock, Nora, Laurence M Olivo & Jean Fitzgerald. *Contract and Tort Law for Paralegals* (Toronto: Emond Montgomery, 2013).

WEBSITES

Canadian Intellectual Property Office (CIPO): <http://www.cipo.ic.gc.ca>.

World Intellectual Property Organization: <http://www.wipo.int>.

REVIEW QUESTIONS

1. List three intentional torts.

2. Of the three main defences to negligence liability, which one allows for the apportionment of liability between the parties?

3. Explain the law relating to defamation, and describe the varieties of this tort.

4. Identify the most common defences to intentional torts, and explain these defences.

5. List the elements of a negligence claim.

6. How have the provinces modified the common law concerning occupiers' liability and simplified the rules concerning this tort?

7. List the elements of a valid contract.

8. Describe the difference between unilateral and bilateral contracts.

9. Explain the concept of an implied term in a contract, and explain the different kinds of implied terms according to the SCC definition.

10. What are standard form contracts and what kinds of transactions are they appropriate for?

11. What are the *Bardal* factors?

EXERCISES

1. Consent is a common defence to the intentional torts. In the case of *Norberg v Wynrib*, [1992] 2 SCR 226, a young woman had sex with an elderly doctor in order to get prescription painkillers. Locate and read La Forest J's judgment in the *Norberg* case and answer the following questions:

   a. Why was the defence of consent not applicable on these facts?

   b. On the basis of what tort was the doctor found liable?

   c. Why do you agree or disagree with this decision?

2. First, refer to Box 9.1 and the summary of the duty principles for negligence. Then:

   a. Locate and read the SCC case of *Childs v Desormeaux*, 2006 SCC 18, in which the SCC had to decide whether a social host owed a duty of care to third parties injured by an intoxicated guest. Describe the reasoning of the Court in reaching its decision that, generally, no such duty exists.

   b. Consider the following problem. A psychiatrist has a patient who says he's going to kill his wife. The psychiatrist tells no one, and the patient does attempt to murder his wife. Although his attempt fails, the attack causes her serious injury. She now wants to sue the psychiatrist for not warning her. Assume that no duty to warn a potential victim of a patient has ever been imposed on a doctor. Prepare an argument explaining why you think such a duty should, or should not, be recognized.

3. Imagine that you have started a new job and only have two weeks' vacation time in your first year. As the end of this year approaches, you start to look forward to your first chance to relax and unwind since you started the job. You have just ended a relationship, and you book a holiday to a Caribbean island through a local tour operator, who promises luxurious five-star accommodations at a small boutique hotel that caters to "singles." The owner is described as a charming person who speaks fluent English, and you are told there will beach parties, snorkeling and scuba diving in crystal-clear waters, local entertainment, and lots of other singles to meet. When you arrive you find a decrepit, run-down hotel. The owner is bad-tempered and speaks almost no English (the only language you speak). There are two couples and an older single person already there, but they all leave after a few days. You are all by yourself and no one else comes. There is no equipment for snorkeling or scuba diving on the premises, although there is an inflatable inner tube to use. There is no entertainment (except when the owner's cousin drops by to play Auld Lang Syne on the steel drums for five minutes), the food is bad, and there are bugs in your room. Finally, you decide to book an early flight home, thoroughly disappointed and extremely depressed by the experience. You now have to wait another year for a holiday. Assume that you paid $2,500 for this vacation. Based on the types of damages available for breach of contract, how do you think your damages should be assessed? See *Jarvis v Swan Tours*, [1973] 1 QB 233 (Eng CA).

4. A general principle that underlies Canadian contract law is freedom of contract, meaning that parties *generally* have the freedom to enter into binding agreements according to the terms they choose. Based on the overview of contract law in this chapter, detail three scenarios where the law would impose limits on that freedom and explain which specific rule imposes the limit in each case.

10 Private Law II: Property Law, Family Law, and Other Areas

LEARNING OUTCOMES

After reading this chapter, you will understand:

- The different types of property (real, personal, and intellectual), and the different forms of property ownership and control
- The basic rights and obligations attached to land ownership, and the different systems of land registration
- How real estate transactions work
- The constitutional basis of family law
- The basic requirements of essential validity for marriage, and the basic requirements of formal validity for marriage

- The role of family law in relation to divorce, common law relationships, family property, support obligations, and the rights of children
- The range of other areas of private law, including those related to property and family law, and some distinct areas such as equity, creditors' remedies, and transnational law subjects
- The scope of comprehensive areas such as legal process and ethics that apply beyond the boundaries of private law

Private law is a pervasive phenomenon of our social life, a silent but ubiquitous participant in our most common transactions. It regulates the property we own and use, the injuries we inflict or avoid inflicting, the contracts we make or break. It is the public repository of our most deeply embedded intuitions about justice and personal responsibility.

Ernest J Weinrib, *The Idea of Private Law*, revised ed
(Oxford: Oxford University Press, 2012) at 1

Introduction

Having considered torts and contracts in Chapter 9, we now turn to two other key areas of private law—property law and family law.

The law divides property into two broad categories: real property and personal property. **Real property** (or **real estate**) refers to land, and also includes anything attached to land—buildings, for example, as well as resources beneath the land, such as minerals. A house is not owned separately from the land on which it is located; the owner of the land owns the house, too. She also owns the natural resources beneath the land, unless they belong to the Crown by virtue of the original grant or according to legislation. (In Canada, the Crown owns the natural resources in most areas of the country.)

Personal property includes not only tangible, movable objects like computers and cars, but also intangible interests like shares in a company. A third form of property, **intellectual property**, has gained prominence in recent years; it refers to property derived from the intellect, or mind—works of art, musical creations, books, inventions, and designs. It is an intangible form of property, but it is usually classed separately from other forms of intangible personal property such as shares in a company.

The laws that regulate family relations are a fundamental part of the private law of any country. Family law intersects with religion more often than most other areas of law. In many parts of the world, religion regulates family matters. In Chapter 2, we saw how some countries insist on the separation of church and state, while others accept a strong connection between the two. When the connection between the state and its religion is close, it tends to be expressed in the regulation of families. In countries that recognize Muslim law (that is, sharia), family relations are strictly governed by religious rules. In Israel, while civil or state law applies for the most part, religious law (that is, Halacha), applies to Jews exclusively in matters of marriage and divorce. And in India, Hindu law regulates family matters for the Hindu members of the population.

In Canada, the situation is different. The separation of religion and state in this country means that our courts and legislatures define the laws relating to families. Religious rules may influence those laws, but it is those laws, not religious rules, that ultimately define our legal rights and obligations in family matters (see Box 2.2). For instance, religious marriage ceremonies are not by themselves "official"; a legal marriage requires that a civil procedure (such as obtaining a licence) also occur.

Property law and family law are the main topics of this chapter, but we also survey other areas of private law, such as equity, creditors' remedies, and transnational subjects like conflict of laws. We conclude by reviewing some areas that play a significant role in private law but extend beyond, such as legal process and legal ethics. See also the beginning of Chapter 9 for a general discussion of the constitutional basis of private law. Where special constitutional issues arise in connection with the areas of private law described in this chapter, they are highlighted in context.

Property Law

As noted in the introduction, the law recognizes two main kinds of property: real property and personal property.

Real Property

In most of Canada, the law relating to real property is based on concepts of ownership that evolved in Norman England 1,000 years ago. The exception is Quebec, where property law is also based on concepts derived from France and from continental Europe. After the Norman Conquest in 1066, William I became the owner of all land in England, and he gradually imposed the feudal system on the country. This meant that the whole country was divided into approximately 1,500 parcels of land over which—except for the portions the King kept for himself—the King's barons were given rights. These rights were conditional. The barons' control over their lands was dependent on their giving the King continued support (fealty) and military service. In other words, these feudal lords were not absolute owners but tenants of a kind. And they, in turn, assigned subtenancy rights to subordinates of their own in exchange for loyalty and service.

In countries such as Canada, where the British Crown remains the formal head of state, the feudal era has left a legacy—namely, the notion that the Crown owns all the land and that landowners below this station are, in a sense, tenants who hold a lesser interest or estate in the land (see below).

The Crown owns all the land in Quebec, too, and the subordinate landowners' estates and interests are generally the same there as in the rest of Canada. There are slight differences in Quebec property law, owing to the influence of the French civil law tradition. One difference is the terminology. Mortgages, for example, are called *hypothecs* in Quebec.

Interests in Land and Types of Ownership

When we use the term **interest** in the context of real estate law, we mean any right, claim, or privilege that an individual has with respect to real or personal property. In theory, the Queen is the ultimate owner of all land in Canada. In reality, the executive authority here

BOX 10.1

Aboriginal Title

For a complete picture of land ownership in Canada, we must take into account Aboriginal title. Aboriginal rights, including Aboriginal title, are constitutionally recognized and protected under section 35 of the *Constitution Act, 1982* (see Chapter 4). As defined by court decisions, some Aboriginal rights, such as the right to hunt and fish, are not based upon exclusive occupancy of the land. In contrast, Aboriginal title (while associated with traditional uses) *is* based on exclusive occupancy. Claims to land and resources by Aboriginal peoples began to occur with increasing frequency in the 20th century (see Box 4.3).

When Europeans first settled and occupied Canada, their encounters with First Nations peoples were not governed by a legal protocol. After the Seven Years War, King George III issued the Royal Proclamation of 1763 claiming territory in North America for Great Britain. Part of the Royal Proclamation dealt with relations with First Nations, and included a general proscription against purchasing or otherwise acquiring land from them—only the Crown could do this. The Proclamation is a key instrument in the history of Aboriginal title. Today, it is generally accepted that Aboriginal title can only be extinguished through surrender of lands to the Crown by treaty or, since 1982 and the constitutional protection of Aboriginal rights, by constitutional amendment (from the time of Confederation until 1982, title could be extinguished by ordinary federal legislation).

Historically, many treaties were entered into and land was surrendered to the Crown. Not all of these treaties were clear or fair, however, and in many instances the two sides have interpreted them differently. Disputes still arise concerning their interpretation. Most of Canada is covered by these old treaties, but not all of it—for example, in parts of Quebec, Labrador, and the territories, and in almost all of British Columbia, no treaties were entered into and the land was never formally surrendered to the Crown. With respect to claims to land that has not been formally surrendered, the two main mechanisms by which claims are established are: (1) court challenge, or (2) participation in a land claims process leading to a treaty.

In recent court cases—*Delgamuukw v British Columbia*, [1997] 3 SCR 1010 and *R v Marshall; R v Bernard*, 2005 SCC 43, [2005] 2 SCR 220, in particular—the SCC has examined the concept of Aboriginal title more closely. In general terms, the Court has recognized that Aboriginal title is *sui generis* (that is, in its own class, or unique) and is not based on "traditional

real property rules." It is also, as noted, included within the broader conception of Aboriginal rights and is constitutionally protected. The following key principles have emerged concerning Aboriginal title:

1. Aboriginal title derives from the *exclusive occupation* of land, and that occupation must have existed at the time the Crown asserted sovereignty over the land. There can be breaks in the continuity of the occupation, provided that a substantial connection to the land has been maintained.
2. While the occupation of the land is determined by reference to particular uses (or activities) that create an attachment to the land, those *uses can change over time* provided they are not inconsistent with the uses that form the basis of the attachment. For example, resource development might be a new use, but if it would necessarily destroy habitat and negatively affect hunting, it would not be a permissible use (assuming hunting was a basis of the group's attachment to the land).
3. It is a *communal title* that inheres in a particular group in relation to a particular area. Aboriginal title does not recognize rights of individual ownership in parcels of land the way the common law does, for example.
4. Aboriginal lands are *inalienable*, except to the Crown. In order for third parties to acquire Aboriginal lands, the lands must first be surrendered to the Crown and then transferred to the third parties.

Not all Aboriginal peoples agree that these principles are accurate markers of their title, and some believe they are still rooted in non-Aboriginal ideas of land ownership. Concerning the requirement of traditional occupancy, this has been difficult to establish in some cases. At the time of writing, no First Nation has proven Aboriginal title in the courts—however, the recognition of Aboriginal title has informed the modern treaty process. Most modern claims to Aboriginal lands are being asserted through a formalized land claims negotiation process (for example, the BC treaty process or the comprehensive claims process), with settlement and a treaty the desired end. And the greatest success in establishing rights to and control over land by Aboriginal peoples has come through such processes (for example, the Nisga'a Treaty entered into with the federal government in 2000).

in Canada—that is, the federal and provincial governments, which we refer to as "the Crown"—holds the underlying title to all the land. Practically speaking, that underlying ownership only manifests itself if a person dies *intestate*—that is, without having made a will—and has no relatives who can inherit the land on an intestacy. The land, in that case, will revert back to the Crown and become "government" property. The technical phrase in this situation is that the Crown will take the land by *escheat*.

The Crown's underlying title to the land makes all other forms of ownership in Canada conditional and subordinate. These subordinate interests in the land come in many types; there are too many to list comprehensively here. The most common types are the following:

- fee simple ownership
- life estates
- leasehold interests
- mortgages and other charges against land.[1]

It is possible for more than one person to own an estate or interest in land. Also, in our system of law, ownership can be "legal" or "equitable." These interests and types of ownership are described next.

FEE SIMPLE OWNERSHIP

Owning land in fee simple is the closest a person can come to absolute ownership in Canada. The "bundle of rights" attached to the estate in fee simple gives the owner more power and flexibility to deal with the land than any other form of ownership. The **fee simple** owner has the right to possess the land and to build on it. She also has full power to transfer the estate to others while she is alive (a process known as *inter vivos* transfer) and to transfer the property in a will once she dies (a process known as testamentary transfer). Should the owner die intestate, the property will pass to her relatives according to statutory intestacy rules.

The fee simple owner also has the right to carve less permanent estates, such as life estates or leases (described below), out of the fee simple whole. When these lesser estates expire, they revert back to the fee simple owner, making her estate whole again. The fee simple owner's interest, when it is subject to one of these lesser estates, is referred to as a "reversionary interest," and the fee simple owner is technically referred to as a "remainderman."

LIFE ESTATES

If the fee simple owner transfers title to land to someone (the transferee) for the life of the latter, a form of ownership called a **life estate** is created. The life estate holder is sometimes called a "life tenant." A life estate cannot be inherited, but the life tenant can transfer it to another person *inter vivos*—that is, while the life estate holder is alive. But the life estate will end with the passing of the original life tenant and revert to the fee simple owner (or remainderman).

---

1 Other interests in property confer a right to use property without transferring an interest *in* the property. For example, a licence creates a right to use property for a defined purpose; a person who has a hot dog concession in a shopping mall will in most cases have a licence from the mall owner to use the space. Another common example of a non-possessory interest is an easement, which typically provides a nearby owner with a right of way across the property or allows for water, sewer, or electrical lines to cross the property.

Uncommon today, the life estate is mostly used in a case where a deceased spouse leaves the surviving spouse (a second wife, say, who is step-mother to the deceased's children from a first marriage) a life estate, with the remainder going to the children or other relatives. This ensures that the surviving spouse has a place to live for life but that the children get the property eventually.

The life estate carries with it a right of exclusive possession. However, it is subject to the "doctrine of waste." This means that the fee simple owner can hold the life tenant responsible for any damage the latter does to the property, though not for ordinary wear and tear or deterioration owing purely to the passage of time. The life tenant can also make improvements to the property. The rules associated with exclusive possession can be modified by express terms in the transfer documents or in a contract, if there is one.

Sometimes life estates are made **defeasible**. This means that they can be terminated if certain conditions are not met or if certain defined events occur. Such events could include changes in the use of the property. For example, if a life tenant held property subject to a condition that it be used for charitable purposes and began to use the property for commercial purposes, the fee simple owner could terminate the life estate.

LEASEHOLD INTERESTS

Leasehold interests are distinguishable from freehold interests. **Freehold interests** are a form of ownership that does not involve an obligation to pay rent. Fee simple and life estates are freehold estates. **Leasehold interests** imply an obligation to pay rent.

When an owner leases her property to someone, she creates a landlord–tenant relationship. The owner is the landlord, or *lessor*, and the renter is the tenant, or *lessee*. A leasehold interest can be residential (renting a place to live) or commercial (renting a place to do business). It can also be in one of two main forms, fixed term or periodic. A fixed term tenancy is for a defined period of time (one year or two years, for example), after which it automatically comes to an end. There may or may not be a right of renewal. A periodic tenancy (for example, week-to-week or month-to-month) *automatically* renews itself at the end of each period, unless either party gives notice.

The rights and obligations of landlord and tenant can be varied and sometimes complicated. They are based on the terms and conditions in the lease, as well as on the relevant provincial or territorial tenancy legislation. The main obligation of the tenant is to pay rent in exchange for the right to occupy and use the property. The landlord generally assumes primary responsibility for repairs. With commercial tenancies, this responsibility for repairs may be shifted to the tenant under the terms of the lease. In the case of residential tenancies, legislation typically *requires* landlords to accept responsibility for maintaining the property in accordance with health and safety regulations, and doesn't allow them to contract out of this obligation. The same legislation also usually requires tenants to maintain the property according to reasonable standards of health and cleanliness, and to repair any damage they cause.

MORTGAGES AND OTHER CHARGES AGAINST LAND

Some interests in land (again, an interest in this context is any right, claim, or privilege that a person has in relation to property) are not for the purpose of possessing or using the property, but for securing a debt or right. This type of interest includes charges and encumbrances. **Charges and encumbrances** are any claim on a parcel of real property—for example, mortgages or rights of way (allowing access to the property for specified purposes).

In simplified terms, a **mortgage** is a kind of charge against land that secures a debt owed by the landowner. The modern concept of a mortgage differs from the traditional concept.

Traditionally, a mortgage involved transferring the landowner's title to the land to the lender. The lender would hold this title as security against the loan, with a promise to transfer title back to the owner once the latter had repaid the mortgage loan in full. If the owner/borrower (the mortgagor) missed a payment or otherwise went into default, the lender (the mortgagee, often a bank) was entitled to keep the land unconditionally. However, in equity, the mortgagor was given a period of time to come up with the balance—in other words, a redemption period (see the discussion of the Court of Chancery, in Chapter 2). The owner's right to redeem his property came to be known as the mortgagor's "equity of redemption"; it was valued at the worth of the property minus the amount of the mortgage debt still owing. Hence we now refer to a property owner's "equity" in the property, which refers to the net market value of his unencumbered interest in the property.

After a mortgagor went into default, the mortgagee would have to bring proceedings to "foreclose" the mortgagor's right to redeem the property. These proceedings were called **foreclosure proceedings**. If the redemption period expired without the mortgagor's coming up with the balance owing, the mortgagee could take absolute title to the property.

In many jurisdictions today, mortgages have been simplified by legislation and no longer involve the actual transfer of title to the creditor. In other respects, they operate the same way as before. Mortgagors are still given redemption periods, and mortgagees are still required to bring foreclosure proceedings if they wish to take over the property.

There are other charges against land that creditors use to secure property owners' debts. One of these is a **builders' lien**, which builders use to secure amounts owed them for work done on landowners' property. Another charge of this type is a *registered judgment*, which can be used to secure any judgment debt the landowner may owe. A judgment debt is an award granted in judicial proceedings. In the case of both the builder's lien and the registered judgment, the creditor can eventually force the sale of the property to recover the debt if the landowner doesn't repay it otherwise.

One charge that operates much like a mortgage is the **agreement for sale**. It is only used in real estate purchase situations. With an agreement for sale, a person who wants to sell her property agrees to finance the purchase herself, because the purchaser can't pay the full amount. The seller keeps title to the property but lets the purchaser take possession of it. The agreement for sale provides that once the balance of the purchase price is paid, the seller will transfer title to the purchaser. If the purchaser misses a payment or otherwise goes into default, the seller can begin a process called cancellation proceedings, which are similar to foreclosure proceedings. By this process, she can retake control of the property. An agreement for sale allows for vendor financing in much the same way as a *vendor takeback mortgage*; with the latter, the vendor sells the property outright to the purchaser at the time of purchase but immediately takes back a mortgage to secure the unpaid portion of the purchase price.

Other charges against property are concerned with securing not a debt but a right. These charges include the following:

- an *option to purchase*, which secures a right to purchase at the discretion of the option holder;
- a *right of first refusal*, which secures a right to purchase the property *if* it is offered for sale;
- a *caveat*, which prevents the owner from selling the property temporarily to allow the caveat holder to pursue its claim against the property; and
- a *right of way*, which, as mentioned above, allows limited access to the property (such as a right to cross over it).

CO-OWNERSHIP

It is possible for more than one person to own an estate in land. All co-owners have equal rights of possession and use of the property. Most often, it is the fee simple estate that is co-owned.

The two principal forms of co-ownership are *joint tenancy* and *tenancy in common*. In order for a **joint tenancy** arrangement to exist, four "unities" must be present:

1. *Possession.* Each co-owner must have equal right to possess the entire property.
2. *Interest.* The interest of each co-owner must be identical in terms of nature, extent, and duration. The extent will depend on the number of joint tenants. For example, with two owners, each owns 50 percent. With three owners, each owns 33⅓ percent.
3. *Time.* The co-owners must each receive their interests at the same time.
4. *Title.* The co-owners must each receive their interests under the same instrument, such as a will or a transfer document.

The main feature of the joint tenancy is the **right of survivorship**, or *jus accrescendi*. This means that on the death of one co-owner the remaining co-owner(s) automatically inherit the deceased owner's share. The last remaining co-owner becomes the sole owner.

Joint tenants are not allowed to leave their share in a will because of the right of survivorship. They can, however, transfer their interest *inter vivos*—that is, during their lifetime—but this has the effect of severing the unities of time and title, and thereby converts the co-ownership into a tenancy in common.

A **tenancy in common** is similar to a joint tenancy insofar as possession is equally shared. But the unities of interest, time, and title are not required for this kind of ownership. Tenants in common can own different percentage interests in the property, and they can become co-owners at different times and by different means. Also, there is no right of survivorship with this kind of ownership; tenants in common can leave their interests in their wills or transfer them to others *inter vivos* without destroying the tenancy in common.

Another special form of co-ownership exists when a "strata lot" (that is, a condominium or townhouse) is purchased. Ownership of a strata unit combines individual ownership with shared or common ownership. The individual ownership relates to the actual unit. The shared ownership relates to the common areas such as hallways, elevators, foyers, and exercise rooms. This form of co-ownership is relatively recent (first introduced in Australia in the 1960s) and is purely a creation of legislation; it requires a strata corporation to manage the property, and it requires the passage of bylaws to set the rules for this form of community living.

LEGAL AND EQUITABLE TITLE

A unique aspect of property ownership is the idea of "legal" and "equitable" ownership. This evolved out of the split jurisdiction between the royal courts and the courts of equity (see Chapter 2).

Title to estates in land can be split between a legal owner, called a **trustee**, and a **beneficial owner**, sometimes called an equitable owner. The legal owner's name will appear on any title documents, usually with an indication that the land is held "in trust" (or words to that effect), but this person (the trustee) will have to own and manage the property for the benefit of the equitable owner. The trustee may be required to ensure that the land and any buildings on it are cared for adequately and that any rents or profits are kept for or passed on to the beneficial owner. This split form of ownership is most common in connection with land, but it can apply to all forms of property, not just real property.

Split ownership of this kind is not recognized in Quebec, where ownership of property is "exclusive"; the civil law does not recognize a split between legal and equitable title.

Rights and Obligations Attached to Land Ownership

The most basic rights and obligations attached to land ownership have been described above. In what follows, we mention some other rights and obligations. These ones relate to support, use of water resources, and land use generally.

A property owner is entitled to rely on the physical **support** that a neighbour's property provides to his or her own property. This obligation between neighbours is reciprocal, and it becomes a matter of legal significance when, for example, one party is having his property excavated as part of a construction project. Excavation on or close to the property line may cause the neighbour's soil to subside and thereby cause damage to her buildings. In this situation, the property owner who is doing such work must ensure that adequate steps are taken to shore up the neighbouring property. Otherwise, he may face a damage claim (see Box 10.2). Liability in this case is strict, and negligence or intent to cause damage does not have to be established.

Properties next to lakes or rivers may have something called **riparian rights** attached to them. Riparian rights include the right to make reasonable use of the water for activities such as swimming, fishing, and boating, and even the right to divert some of the water for drinking, washing, and irrigation. However, these rights are qualified by the obligation not to interfere unfairly with the riparian rights of others. A property owner would not be meeting this obligation, for example, if he diverted so much river water to irrigate his fields that the flow downstream was compromised, or if the discharge of effluent from his agricultural concern made the water unsafe for others to use.

Every jurisdiction has particular legislation relating to support and to the use of water. Property owners must carefully consider these rules when working close to their property lines or exercising their riparian rights.

Generally speaking, property ownership comes with many responsibilities and restrictions concerning use. The federal, provincial, and municipal (or local) governments all regulate it. Property owners must be aware of the relevant restrictions, which concern such matters as type of use (for example, single-family, multi-family, commercial use), allowable construction, cutting down trees, and pollution.

BOX 10.2

Digging Holes and Collapsing Buildings: The Right to Lateral Support

In *Rytter v Schmitz* (1974), 47 DLR (3d) 445 (BCSC), the plaintiffs and the defendant owned adjoining properties. There was a concrete-block building on the Rytters' property. Schmitz began to excavate his property with a view to constructing a building on his lot. His workmen excavated along the property line to a depth of 10 feet but didn't properly shore up the property. As a result, the subsoil on the Rytters' property fell away and caused the property to subside. Part of the Rytters' concrete-block building also collapsed and fell into the excavation.

The court held, among other things, that the plaintiff landowners were entitled to the lateral support of their land by their neighbour's property and that this right was a strict one—that is, it was not necessary to show that the defendant was negligent or intended to cause the damage.

Systems of Land Registration: Deed Registry and Land Titles

The common law procedure for transferring land, which evolved centuries ago, relied entirely on deeds. **Deeds** are formal documents showing evidence of ownership. They have always involved a certain amount of risk. After successive transfers and generations of owners, there was always the possibility that mistakes would be made, frauds committed, or deeds missed when tracing the line of ownership. There was always a risk that someone with a superior title to the property might pop up and, on the grounds of the *nemo dat* principle, challenge the current owner's rights over it.

What is the *nemo dat* principle? The full Latin expression is *nemo dat quod non habet*, which means "one cannot give what one does not have." According to this principle, the purchase of a possession from someone who has no ownership right to it also denies the purchaser any ownership title. This usually applies even if the purchaser does not know that the seller is not a true owner.

To increase the certainty related to property ownership, registration systems were devised. Two main systems emerged, both used in Canada today: (1) the deed registration system, and (2) the Torrens system. The deed registration system uses the traditional idea of transfer by deed. But it provides some certainty by requiring deeds to be registered, and it creates a deed repository to help with the tracing process. Mistakes can still be made, however, and *nemo dat* is still the guiding principle with this system.

The **Torrens system** is named after Robert Torrens, the Australian who first devised and implemented the system in 1858. The Torrens system and systems modelled on it eliminate the transfer of title by deeds, replacing them with statutory transfer forms. Title for all land within the jurisdiction must be registered, and anyone purchasing property can rely on the state of the register. Registered title is **indefeasible**. This means that the legislation essentially guarantees that "what you see is what you get" when you look at the registry entries for a particular piece of property. The true owner's name will appear on title, and any charges relating to the property—for example, mortgages or liens—must be registered against the title to be effective. An assurance fund, set up under the legislation, is there to protect any innocent parties in the event that a fraud is perpetrated and someone gets on the title improperly. In 1870, British Columbia became the first jurisdiction in North America to adopt the Torrens system.

In Canada, deed registration systems are employed in southern Ontario (which is in the process of converting to a Torrens system at the time of writing) and the Atlantic provinces. Quebec uses a system similar to the deed registry system. In northern Ontario and the four western provinces, the land titles or Torrens system is used. The uncertainty over true title is less common than it used to be, but it still exists to some extent in the deed registration system. There is a much greater demand for "title insurance" in jurisdictions that use the older system than there is in jurisdictions that use the newer Torrens system.

Real Estate Transactions

The law relating to the purchase and sale of real estate is often treated as its own subject because of the number of issues and the volume of litigation arising from such transactions. The following is no more than a brief outline of this area.

The transaction starts with property that is made available or listed for sale by a seller (sometimes referred to as the "vendor"). How exactly the sale proceeds depends on:

- whether the property is residential (and on whether it is a single lot with or without a house on it, or a strata unit),

- whether the property is commercial (and on what type of business is involved), or
- whether the property is for investment (and on what the particular tax implications are).

In most cases, the seller will hire a real estate agent to assist with the sale. The real estate agent will also frequently help prospective purchasers, although she has to be careful because of the potential for conflict of interest. Such a conflict would exist, for example, if the agent promoted certain bidders favoured by the agent and discouraged others at the expense of the seller, or if the agent took a secret commission from the successful purchaser. In a case where the seller has hired the agent, agency rules dictate that her primary responsibility and loyalty must be to the seller. In cases where purchasers have their own agents, this potential conflict is avoided.

The relationship between the real estate agents and other parties in the real estate transaction involves many contractual and fiduciary obligations, so the potential for litigation is great. For example, a real estate agent has to disclose to the parties any interest he may have in the property or any secret profits he may stand to gain as a result of the sale. Also, the agent can be responsible in tort for any negligent or fraudulent misrepresentations relating to the property (for example, telling a purchaser the property is zoned for a basement suite when it is not). It should be noted as well that real estate agents are regulated by real estate legislation in all provinces and territories and are subject to disciplinary action. They can lose their licences if they fail to follow required codes of conduct.

Disagreements concerning the terms in the contract of purchase and sale (sometimes called an interim agreement, because it precedes the actual transfer of title) can arise directly between the seller and the purchaser. This contract is frequently a standard form contract. Differences of interpretation may arise over particular terms in the contract—for example, terms dealing with the time for completing the contract and with conditions precedent (that is, terms defining events that must occur, such as financing or inspection, before the contract can move forward).

After the contract is entered into (sometimes months after negotiations begin), the actual transfer of title, or conveyance, occurs. **Conveyancing** is a very specialized process, and is sometimes treated separately from the rest of the real estate transaction. The exact process varies according to the usual variables:

- whether a deed system or land titles system is involved;
- whether the transaction relates to single lot, strata lot, or a commercial or investment property; and
- the relevant legislative requirements concerning registration and other matters.

Financing matters are another prominent feature of real estate transactions. Financing can be managed in a variety of ways, including the following:

1. vendor financing (for instance, through the use of an agreement for sale or mortgage back to the vendor);
2. third-party financing (from a bank or other lender, through the use of a mortgage); and
3. multiple investors, all participating in the purchase.

Which financing method is chosen will affect the whole process, including the legalities involved, from the start of the transaction through to the conveyance and completion.

Personal Property

As mentioned at the beginning of this chapter, personal property includes not only tangible, movable objects, but also intangible interests such as corporate securities.

The sale of personal property is regulated by legislation in most situations. Some of that legislation—legislation dealing with sales of goods, consumer protection, and business transactions—is discussed in Chapter 11.

Tangible Personal Property

Tangible, movable objects such as furniture, equipment, and cars are sometimes referred to as **chattels**. Interests in them are referred to as *corporeal interests*.

Under certain circumstances, property that would ordinarily be considered personal property comes under the law relating to **fixtures**, or things that are attached to the land. The principle discussed at the beginning of this chapter—that is, the notion that anything that is attached to land becomes part of the land—influences these situations. For instance, a seller of equipment on credit may assume that the equipment sold can be retaken under the terms of the sale—for example, in the case of non-payment. But if, in the meantime, the equipment has become affixed to the buyer's land, recovering it may not be possible. Also, if there is a mortgagee (a lender) who has not been paid by the owner of the real property, priority issues could arise between the mortgagee and the seller who wants to recover his equipment. The mortgagee will likely want to recover his equipment to help satisfy the mortgage debt.

Determining whether goods have become affixed to the land requires looking at the *degree* of annexation and the *object* of annexation. The more easily the goods can be removed (for example, if they're attached merely by a few hooks, screws, or nails), the less likely they are to be classed as fixtures. On the other hand, if the object or purpose in attaching them was to improve the value or utility of the property, they are likely to be classed as fixtures (see Box 10.3). Each case is individual.

BOX 10.3

Is Wall-to-Wall Carpeting Personal Property?

In *La Salle Recreations Ltd v Canadian Camdex Investments Ltd* (1969), 68 WWR 339 (BCCA), the British Columbia Court of Appeal had to decide whether wall-to-wall carpeting in a hotel was affixed to the building and therefore also to the land. The owner of the property had defaulted on his credit arrangement with the carpet seller as well as on his mortgage loan.

The carpet seller wanted to repossess the carpet. The mortgagee wanted it left in place because it would increase the value of the hotel. The legislation in place at the time dictated that if the carpet had become affixed to the land, priority over the carpet would be given to the mortgagee (whose charge covered the land).

The carpet had been attached to the floors by small nails or pins protruding upward around the perimeter of the unfinished plywood floors. The carpeting could be easily removed, causing little damage to the floors or the carpeting. On the other hand, the colour of the carpeting matched the colour scheme of the walls around it. The court applied the *degree* of annexation and the *object* of annexation tests, and held that while the carpet was only lightly affixed (degree of annexation) the purpose of the carpeting was for the "better and more effectual use of the building as a hotel" (object of annexation), and therefore the carpet was a fixture. As a result, the mortgagee was successful and able to keep the carpeting.

We have seen that there are many kinds of estates or interests in real property. The case is different with personal property. In most cases, ownership in goods is absolute. However, goods can be leased (for example, cars), and liens and charges can be placed against goods to secure debts. Goods can also be held in trust, so that ownership is divided between the trustee (the legal owner) and the beneficiary (the equitable owner).

There are a couple of well-known expressions concerning physical possession and ownership. One of these is "possession is nine-tenths of the law"; the other is "finders, keepers; losers, weepers." The principle expressed here—the idea that physically possessing property is somehow proof of ownership—is not necessarily accurate, however. Possession may be *evidence* of ownership, but it is not *conclusive*. If it were, this would be very good news for thieves. All evidence of ownership needs to be considered, including any bills of sale or agreements of sale relating to the property.

Intangible Interests

Intangible interests are sometimes called *incorporeal interests*. The classic examples of these interests are corporate securities (for example, shares and bonds), as already noted. A **chose in action** is another example of an intangible personal property right. A chose (pronounced "shows") in action is the right to sue someone for an unpaid debt or other liability. For example, if a business owner had the right to sue a customer for property delivered but not paid for, the business owner could transfer that right, or chose in action, to a collection agency. In this situation, the collection agency often "purchases" the debt from the business owner at a discount.

As with goods, ownership of intangible interests is usually absolute, although liens and charges are possible, as are trust arrangements. Special legislative rules sometimes apply to the transfer of such interests, including notice requirements (for instance, effectively assigning or transferring a debt or chose in action may require notice to the debtor, depending on the type of debt).

Personal Property Security Legislation

Whenever a creditor (such as a seller or a lender) is owed money that is secured by personal property the debtor controls, there is a risk that the debtor will sell the personal property or further encumber it. This can lead to complex disputes over priority between the creditor and innocent third parties who dealt with the debtor in good faith, believing the property was not subject to any competing interests.

Personal property security legislation provides for the registration of a creditor's interest in personal property that the debtor controls or possesses. This enables others to check the state of the property in question before entering into dealings with the debtor. The common expression for this kind of background search is "checking for liens."

In the 1970s, Ontario adopted a new personal property security regime with the enactment of the *Personal Property Security Act*. Since then, all common law provinces and the territories have adopted similar legislation by the same name. Quebec, too, has legislation based on civil law principles that protect creditors through a system of registration. These provincial statutes are complicated. Among their key features are the following:

1. coverage of almost all forms of personal property, both tangible (for example, cars, equipment, and other goods) and intangible (for example, corporate securities);
2. provisions that protect a creditor with respect to the debtor's personal property;

3. a special interest called a "purchase money security interest," or PMSI, which can be granted to a lender who enables a debtor to acquire goods (for example, where a finance company lends money to a purchaser of a motor vehicle at the point of purchase);

4. the protection of creditors through the registration of their security interests; and

5. the creation of a system of priorities and "superpriorities," which starts from the principle that priority is given to creditors whose security interests in a debtor's property are registered earliest.

All provinces and territories have registries that can be checked electronically for security interests against personal property. If a check reveals no charge against the property, prospective creditors or lenders can be confident that when they register their security it will take priority over the securities of others who register later. For example, if a bank lends money to a client and registers the first security interest in the client's personal property, the bank knows that when the property is sold it will have first priority over the sale proceeds, which it can apply to the loan if it is not repaid by the client. If a second lender is approached by the client for another loan, the second lender will be able to see the bank's prior registered security interest. This will help the second lender decide whether loaning the client more money is too risky. The value of the property and the total value of the two loans will be important considerations.

Intellectual Property

Intellectual property (IP) is an area of private law that is, for the most part, regulated at the federal level (see sections 91(22)–(23) of the *Constitution Act, 1867*). In this it differs from real and personal property, which are predominantly under provincial and territorial control.

The reason our Constitution provides for federal regulation of IP is that, nationwide, certainty and consistency are needed in the laws concerning this creative and sometimes challenging form of intangible property, whose geographical location can be difficult to define. Also, the federal government is best equipped to negotiate international agreements in this area. IP is increasingly traded—some would say *stolen*—across national boundaries, becoming part of the intellectual "human" commons. Federal regulators are better able to respond effectively to international changes and pressures than local regulators would be.

The Canadian Intellectual Property Office (CIPO) is the central registry for Canadian intellectual property. International cooperation and agreements have led to the creation of the World Intellectual Property Organization (WIPO), which is an agency of the United Nations. Its headquarters are in Geneva, Switzerland. Registration with WIPO can assist with the protection of IP rights on the international stage.

Table 10.1 summarizes four key areas of IP and their associated federal statutes.

TABLE 10.1   Types of Intellectual Property

CATEGORY	DESCRIPTION	SOURCE
Copyright	Copyright refers to the right to copy, which only belongs to the copyright owner, who is usually the creator of the work or a person assigned ownership by the creator. Copyright exists as soon as the work is created and does not need to be registered to be enforceable. However, registration with CIPO provides evidence of ownership that can be used in court. Copyright protection lasts for the life of the creator plus 50 years, and applies in respect of • original dramatic, musical, artistic, and literary works (including computer programs); and • performances, communication signals, and sound recordings.	*Copyright Act*, RSC 1985, c C-42
Industrial Design	An industrial design is a design used in making an object by hand, tool, or machine. Industrial designs can be protected for up to 10 years if registered with CIPO. Without registration, a person cannot claim ownership of the design and thereby prevent others from using it to make articles. To qualify for registration, the design must be an original design with unique visual features that is used to make objects (e.g., a unique design for an ordinary object, such as a chair).	*Industrial Design Act*, RSC 1985, c I-9
Patents	A patent is a right that the government grants to an inventor to prevent others from using his or her invention. Patent holders are protected for up to 20 years after the patent application is filed with the Patent Office, which is part of CIPO. If the patent has not been filed, the inventor has no protection. Patents cover only the following: • new inventions (which can be processes, machines, or compositions of matter), and new improvements in an existing invention; and • inventions that satisfy the three basic criteria of novelty, utility, and ingenuity.	*Patent Act*, RSC 1985, c P-4
Trademarks	A trademark distinguishes the goods or services of a person, business, or organization from those of others in the marketplace. Trademark registration provides evidence of ownership but, as with copyrights, it is not conclusive. A registered trademark gives its holder an exclusive right to use the trademark throughout Canada for 15 years, and it is renewable after that. A trademark, to be registrable, must be a word, symbol, or design (alone or in combination) used to distinguish goods or services.	*Trade-marks Act*, RSC 1985, c T-13

Family Law

The last area of private law we single out for detailed consideration is family law.

Constitutional Basis

Constitutional jurisdiction over families is split between the federal and provincial governments. Section 91(26) of the *Constitution Act, 1867* gives the federal Parliament jurisdiction over "Marriage and Divorce," and sections 92(12) and 92(13) assign the provinces power over "Solemnization of Marriage" and "Property and Civil Rights."

The result of this division of responsibilities is that the federal government has exclusive jurisdiction over the definition of a valid marriage (that is, over defining its *substantive requirements*) and over the grounds for divorce. The provincial and territorial governments have exclusive jurisdiction over the procedure or manner in which marriages must take place (in other words, their solemnization), over the division of family assets when relationships break down, and over the adoption of children (property and civil rights). (See

Box 10.5.) Support obligations and child custody matters are areas of shared jurisdiction. (See Chapter 5, and the discussion of the legislative power of Parliament and the provinces under the Constitution.)

Marriage

Canadian law recognizes a difference between the *essential* validity and the *formal* validity of a marriage. **Essential validity** concerns a person's capacity to marry and the substantive requirements of a valid marriage. Questions of this kind, as mentioned above, are under federal jurisdiction. **Formal validity** refers to the formalities or ceremonial requirements of a marriage, and these matters come under provincial jurisdiction.

Essential Validity

Despite the federal government's power to regulate essential validity, there is no comprehensive legislation in this area. There are just two statutes dealing with specific aspects of a person's capacity to marry (the *Civil Marriage Act* and the *Marriage (Prohibited Degrees) Act*, discussed below). In this area, courts have relied heavily on common law rules, which are strongly influenced by English canon (or church) law, which in turn relies on the Christian Bible and on other sources such as the Anglican *Book of Common Prayer*. It is an area where religious rules have clearly shaped the law, as mentioned above.

A marriage that has essential validity must meet the following six requirements:

1. two persons must be involved;
2. both parties must have the ability to consummate the marriage;
3. there must not be too close a degree of consanguinity or affinity between the two parties (for example, the marriage of a brother and sister is not valid);
4. the parties involved must be unmarried;
5. both parties must have given consent; and
6. both must be old enough to marry.

If it becomes apparent, after a marriage ceremony, that one or more of these requirements has not been met, the union can be set aside or annulled. Depending on which requirement is not satisfied and on the exact nature of the problem, the marriage will be either void from the beginning (regardless of whether it is challenged), referred to as being void *ab initio*, or voidable (that is, it will only be set aside if challenged; otherwise it will stand). The rules about the void/voidable distinction and about which party can challenge the validity of the marriage are complicated and not always clearly or consistently applied.

TWO PERSONS

This requirement used to be the common law "opposite-sex" rule. But in 2005, after a number of constitutional court challenges to this requirement, Parliament passed the *Civil Marriage Act*. Section 2 of this Act provides that "marriage, for civil purposes, is the lawful union of two persons to the exclusion of all others," and section 4 provides that "a marriage is not void or voidable by reason only that the spouses are of the same sex."[2]

---

2 *Civil Marriage Act*, SC 2005, c 33.

In Canada, then, same-sex marriages are now recognized. What used to be the "opposite-sex" element of essential validity can be restated as the *two individuals* (or *two persons*) requirement. The requirement that marriages be a union of two people clearly also concerns the *number* of individuals involved. It means that polygamous marriages, for example—marriages involving more than two persons—are not legally recognized. In fact, polygamy is an offence under the *Criminal Code*.[3] Some religious and other groups have challenged the constitutional validity of limiting marriage to just two people and of specifically criminalizing polygamy (see Box 10.4).

ABILITY TO CONSUMMATE

For a marriage to be valid, both parties must have the ability to consummate it. The common law test for the consummation of an opposite-sex marriage is whether both parties are capable of having sexual intercourse at the outset of the marriage.[4] If one or both parties are impotent (that is, incapable of consummation) due to some *incurable* physical or mental disability, then the marriage may be annulled. Curable defects must be remedied and will not support an **annulment**. Note also that sterility—the inability to have children—is not the same thing as impotence and will also not support an annulment.

If a spouse is capable of consummating the marriage but simply refuses, or has a curable defect but refuses to fix it, the other party will not be able to obtain an annulment.

A marriage only needs to be consummated once for the consummation requirement to be satisfied. Once consummated, the marriage is always consummated. Lack of capacity or impotence that develops later is not grounds for annulment.

DEGREE OF CONSANGUINITY OR AFFINITY

Consanguinity refers to a blood relationship between relatives (that is, the relationship of people who descend from the same ancestor) and **affinity** refers to the relationship that a person has to the blood relatives of his or her spouse. Early in its development, the common law, adopting canon law rules, prohibited a wide range of relatives from marrying. The prohibited degrees of consanguinity and affinity extended up to and included the third degree of relationship. This means that third cousins and those lineally above and below them were prohibited from marrying. Later, these rules were relaxed—a gradual relaxation at common law over time.

In 1990, federal legislation was passed that clarified and simplified the rules. The *Marriage (Prohibited Degrees) Act* states that marriage between relatives is generally permissible unless they are lineal relatives (parents, grandparents, children, grandchildren) directly up or down, or brothers or sisters (or half-brothers and half-sisters), including by adoption.[5] Section 2 provides as follows:

> 2(1) Subject to subsection (2), persons related by consanguinity, affinity or adoption are not prohibited from marrying each other by reason only of their relationship.
> (2) No person shall marry another person if they are related lineally, or as brother or sister or half-brother or half-sister, including by adoption.

---

3 *Criminal Code*, RSC 1985, c C-46, s 293.

4 So far, the courts have not defined the consummation requirements for gay and lesbian couples.

5 *Marriage (Prohibited Degrees) Act*, SC 1990, c 46.

First cousins are permissible marriage partners in Canada, and nephews and nieces may marry their aunts and uncles.

UNMARRIED

Being married to one person, even if separated and apart from that person, is a bar to marrying a second person. Marrying one person while still married to another is bigamy, and it is an offence under the *Criminal Code*.

If one of the parties to a proposed marriage was previously married, the officiant or minister at the new marriage will need documentary evidence to prove that the prior marriage ended, either by annulment, divorce, or the death of the other spouse.

CONSENT

Both parties must consent to marry, freely and voluntarily. If one party consents to a marriage but lacks the capacity to understand the nature of its duties and responsibilities, the consent is invalid. This lack of capacity may be temporary—a matter of impairment due to drugs or alcohol—or it may be the effect of a permanent mental disability.

BOX 10.4

Polygamy and Canadian Law

The town of Bountiful, in southeastern British Columbia (pictured), is the home of a fundamentalist Mormon community that believes in polygamy. Its population is around 1,000. The first member of this Mormon group bought property there in 1946, and most of the town's residents today have descended from just six men.

In the wake of media attention and a police investigation into allegations of abuse involving Bountiful's young women and underaged girls, a special prosecutor was appointed to decide whether criminal charges should be laid. He concluded that there was little evidence of sexual abuse and exploitation in the community, and recommended instead that a reference question be placed before the court concerning the constitutionality of the rarely used section of the *Criminal Code* dealing with polygamy, section 293.*

In a 335-page decision handed down by the chief justice of the BC Supreme Court in November 2011, the court concluded that while section 293 of the *Criminal Code* infringed the constitutional right to religious freedom (under section 2 of the Charter) and to fundamental justice (under section 7 of the Charter), a criminal prohibition against polygamy was a "reasonable limit" on that freedom under section 1 of the Charter, which states that the rights and freedoms are subject "to such reasonable limits prescribed by law as can be demonstrably justified in a free and democratic society." The court found section 293's prohibition against polygamy justified because of the demonstrable "harm to women, to children, to society and to the institution of monogamous marriage" caused by the practice. In other words, the harms associated with polygamy outweigh any claims to religious freedom.

* *Reference re: Section 293 of the Criminal Code of Canada*, 2011 BCSC 1588.

When one party enters a marriage under duress, compelled by fear of harm to herself or to a third person, the marriage will not be considered consensual and will not be valid. The expression "shotgun wedding" is based on this idea.

Fraud or mistake can invalidate apparent consent. However, the misunderstanding must concern the nature of the ceremony or the actual identity of one of the parties. One party's misrepresentation of his wealth or status, for example, will not invalidate the other party's consent—though it might support a tort claim for deceit.

Finally, sham marriages that people enter into for immigration or other purposes, with no intention of living as a married couple, are considered not to involve real consent and are therefore invalid.

AGE

The common law age requirements for marriage are 12 for females and 14 for males. No federal legislation has changed these minimums. They are somewhat incongruous, for the following reason: depending on the exact ages and age differences between two young people getting married, the act of consummation necessary to validate the marriage could amount to a sexual offence under the *Criminal Code*.[6]

However, the issue of sexual offences in the context of marriages between infants (that is, people under the age of majority) has not been a problem in Canada. This is because the *Criminal Code* recognizes close-in-age and marriage defences starting at ages 12 and 14 respectively. Also, not many infants are able to obtain the necessary consents or approvals to get married in the first place. That is because provincial and territorial legislation requires parental (or guardian) consent to the solemnization of a marriage between young people under the age of majority. And infants under the age of 16 generally cannot be married even with the consent of parents or guardians. In very limited situations, however, courts are authorized under the legislation to order the solemnization of a marriage involving a person under 16. The usual test is that the marriage must be "in the interests of the parties." In making its decision, a court could consider such factors as cultural expectations or the pregnancy of one of the parties. Such marriages are rarely authorized, however.[7]

Formal Validity

The provinces and territories have jurisdiction over solemnization procedures or formalities that must occur for a marriage to be valid. The provincial and territorial marriage acts set the requirements, which typically include the following:

1. a marriage licence (some jurisdictions, such as Ontario, allow the **banns of marriage**—the public announcement in church of an impending marriage—to be used in place of licences);
2. a public marriage ceremony (religious or civil) before at least two witnesses;
3. a presiding official (religious or civil) who is authorized under the legislation to perform marriage ceremonies; and
4. registration of the marriage with the vital statistics office for the province or territory in question.

---

6 *Criminal Code*, RSC 1985, c C-46, ss 150-153.

7 Given that age is a matter of essential validity, there is at least an argument that these provincial and territorial age minimums are unconstitutional because they are higher than the ages set by the common law (in an area of federal jurisdiction). However, Canadian social norms today support barriers to marriage between youths, so it is unlikely any challenges will occur.

Basic Rights and Responsibilities in Marriage

During the marriage, the parties to the marriage have basic rights and obligations to each other and to their children.

At common law, and now as set out in provincial and territorial family law legislation, spouses are expected to financially support each other. The level of support is usually based on a test of what is reasonable in the circumstances, with regard to such things as the role of each spouse in the family, express or implied agreements on the matter, care-giving obligations for any children, and economic status.

Similarly, spouses within a marriage have an obligation to do what is reasonable and necessary to maintain and support their children, including providing for their education.

Matrimonial Property

Historically, the common law viewed marriage as creating a "unity of personality." This idea can be traced to the Christian belief that, upon marriage, the couple became one. What this meant in a patriarchal society, practically speaking, was that, upon marrying, the wife came under the husband's control. The husband assumed control over everything related to the family, including family property (even property that the wife brought into the marriage).

Manitoba was the first province, in 1871, to pass legislation enabling a woman to hold property in her own name and to control it free of her husband's influence and debts. Separate legislation was later passed in Manitoba to ensure that women's earnings during marriage were their own. By the early 1900s, most other provinces had followed suit, with similar legislation.[8] Legislation has since given women in Canada the same power as men to own and control property in their own right during marriage. In other words, the *unity* of personality concept has been replaced by a *separation* of personality concept.

Marriage Breakdown and Divorce

Marriage breakdown is usually a gradual process that begins while the parties are still together and moves next to separation and then divorce, although some parties may choose to stay separated without divorce. On marriage breakdown, support and other obligations are triggered under provincial legislation, whether or not there is a divorce.

Individuals in the midst of family breakdown are facing significant life decisions and are usually more emotionally fragile than are people involved in other kinds of legal conflicts. Dealing with individuals in such situations requires sensitivity from family law professionals. The special nature of disputes in this area is the reason that lawmakers in almost every Canadian jurisdiction have introduced unique measures for their resolution. These measures typically include:

- encouraging or requiring the parties to use alternative dispute resolution mechanisms (for example, collaborative law or negotiation-based approaches) before resorting to the courts; and
- creating unified family courts to simplify the process, should the courts be needed (see Chapter 7).

---

8   For examples of current legislation, see the following: *The Married Women's Property Act*, RSM 1987, c M70; *Married Women's Property Act*, RSNWT 1988, c M-5; *Married Women's Property Act*, RSNS 1989, c 272; and *Family Law Act*, RSO 1990, c F.3, s 64.

Grounds for Divorce

Divorce in Canada is federally regulated and the governing statute is the *Divorce Act*. When it was first passed in 1968, the *Divorce Act* simplified the rules of divorce and introduced the idea of "no-fault" divorce.

For couples who want to formally end their relationship, there is just one ground of divorce under the *Divorce Act*—namely, marriage breakdown. Marriage breakdown can be established in one of three ways:

1. living separate and apart for one year (the no-fault basis),
2. adultery by the other party, or
3. physical or mental cruelty by the other spouse "of such a kind as to render intolerable the continued cohabitation of the spouses."[9]

The vast majority of divorces in Canada proceed under the first ground, with the couple first living separate and apart for one year. It is not necessary to actually go to court to get a divorce decree if the parties consent to the order. It can simply be filed in the appropriate court registry.

Spousal and Child Support

As mentioned, support obligations exist prior to marriage breakdown under provincial and territorial legislation. However, it is on marriage breakdown that they are most often disputed. Sometimes, different terms are used to describe the obligations. "Maintenance" and "alimony" are synonyms for payments one spouse makes to another once marriage breakdown has occurred, whether or not there has been divorce. The word "support" is more general and can refer to pre- and post-breakdown obligations, and can apply to both spousal and child payment obligations.

The parties can agree between themselves, by way of a separation agreement, who will support whom and for how long and what the payments will be, or they can go to court and have a judge make the determination for them. If they settle out of court, they may still file a consent order along with the agreement in court, which will make the settlement easier to enforce and can be adjusted if circumstances change.

Support orders, consent or otherwise, are made under provincial and territorial family law legislation until the parties proceed to divorce. If the parties proceed to divorce, support orders are made under the federal *Divorce Act*.

There are federal guidelines for spousal and child support obligations. In practice, these federal guidelines are followed in negotiated settlements involving legal professionals, as well as in court-ordered resolutions, and they are followed regardless of whether the support orders are made under provincial/territorial legislation or under the federal *Divorce Act*. Support orders can be changed at a later date if there is a significant change in circumstances.

Children: Custody and Access

When spouses who are separating have children, the main issue concerning the children is whether there will be joint custody, or whether there will be sole custody for one parent with (or without) access rights for the non-custodial parent.

As with support, if there is no divorce, any non-negotiated resolution will have to be made under provincial or territorial family law legislation. And if there is a divorce, any custody and

---

9 *Divorce Act*, RSC 1985, c 3 (2d Supp), s 8.

access orders will be under the *Divorce Act*. Regardless of which route is taken, the test for determining custody and access rights is essentially the same under all legislation, and that is to determine what is in the "best interests of the child" in light of all the circumstances.

Division of Family Assets

The provinces and territories have exclusive jurisdiction over the division of matrimonial property upon the breakdown of marriage. When the marriage collapses, family law legislation in all jurisdictions triggers rights to share in the marital possessions.

The legislation defines what constitutes family property, and the definitions vary depending on the province or territory. Typically, houses, pensions, retirement savings plans (RSPs), and bank accounts are included, while business assets are excluded. Inheritances are sometimes included and sometimes excluded, depending on the circumstances.

In general, this legislation creates a presumption that family assets should be split 50/50 between the parties. However, the court has the power to reapportion the division—that is, to split the assets otherwise than 50/50—in cases where an even split would be unfair or unconscionable. In choosing to reapportion, the court will consider various factors—for example, the length of the marriage, how much property each spouse brought into the marriage, the extent of each party's personal debts, and the economic self-sufficiency of each spouse. Marriage agreements and separation agreements that provide for a split other than 50/50 will also be considered by the courts, but they are not conclusive. The courts may choose to disregard such agreements.

Common Law Marriages

When two people live together in an intimate, marriage-like relationship but without going through a formal marriage ceremony, they take on some of the rights and some of the obligations of a married couple. There are various names for such relationships: common law marriages (or common law relationships), domestic partnerships, and civil unions.

Each province and territory defines what constitutes a common law marriage in its family law legislation and its financial legislation (for example, statutes dealing with taxes, pensions, and income supplements). The federal government does this, too, in its financial legislation.

In general, couples, including same-sex couples, living together in a marriage-like relationship for two years will take on some of the same rights and obligations as legally married couples. However, the applicable legislation must be read carefully. For example, under federal tax legislation, two people qualify as a common law couple if they cohabit in a conjugal relationship for just one year or if they have a child together. In Ontario, on the other hand, support obligations apply only to couples who have been together for three years or who have a child in common.

Assuming a couple satisfies the relevant legislative definition for common law marriage, the rights and obligations concerning spousal support and government financial matters will generally be the same as if they were married. Quebec is an exception and does not recognize support obligations between partners in common law relationships. Support obligations apply only to Quebec couples who are legally married or who are in a special type of civil union, not found elsewhere in Canada, that involves certain ceremonial formalities and a registration process similar to the process used for marriages.

Child support obligations are the same for common law couples as for married couples because they are based on parenthood, not marriage.

One area where a significant difference exists between common law marriages and conventional marriages has to do with the division of family property in the event of breakup. Most provinces and territories require couples to be legally married before the presumption of a 50/50 split will apply.[10] This means that a person living in a common law relationship whose partner owns most or all of the family property will be at risk of receiving little or no property if the couple breaks up.

Where no division-of-property rights exist, the main way common law partners can protect themselves in the event of breakup is through a cohabitation agreement—in other words, an agreement between unmarried couples that deals with property rights. They may also insist on co-ownership of family property—for example, owning the matrimonial home as joint tenants or tenants in common. It is possible that if a common law spouse who is not on title has contributed in some way to the acquisition of property owned by the other spouse, a trust argument could be made that the contributing spouse is entitled to a share of the property. Such arguments are complicated and can be expensive to litigate. Generally, they are a last resort.

Protection of Children

The protection of children—that is, child welfare—is entrusted in all provinces and territories to government officials, who have the power to intervene in situations where children are in need of protection.

Statutes in every jurisdiction impose duties on everyone—not just on family members, but also on friends, teachers, or social workers—to inform authorities about children who need protection from abuse or neglect.[11] Even in situations where the information is second-hand and is received in confidence, or in situations where privilege normally applies, as with communications between spouses (lawyer–client privilege is an exception to this), the legislation requires the person to report the matter and makes it an offence not to do so. It is also an offence to file a false report.

A child is in need of protection where there has been physical, sexual, or emotional abuse. Intervention is also required in cases where parents or guardians have neglected to care for or supervise the child, and harm to the child has occurred or is likely to occur because of this neglect.

After reports are received and assessed, childcare officials will respond according to the circumstances. They can offer support services to the family and meet with them; they can investigate the matter further and involve the police or courts; and, in extreme cases, they can remove the child from the home and make arrangements for alternative care, either temporarily or permanently. As a safeguard, child protection statutes allow the actions of the authorities to be challenged and reviewed in court at the request of the child and other affected family members.

The primary goals of the legislation are as follows:

- to protect children from harm;
- to keep immediate families together if possible;

---

10 So far, only British Columbia has extended division-of-property rights to common law couples: see *Family Law Act*, SBC 2011, c 25.

11 See, for example, the *Child, Youth and Family Enhancement Act*, RSA 2000, c C-12, s 4; *Family Services Act*, SNB 1980, c F-2.2, s 30; and *Child and Family Services Act*, RSO 1990, c C.1, s 72.

BOX 10.5

Regulating the Adoption of Children

Each province and territory has legislation regulating the adoption of children.

Generally, there are two processes for adopting children: public adoption and private adoption. Public adoption involves applying to adopt a child through a government agency. While it also involves a screening process, the waitlists are generally much longer. Private adoption is done through a private agency. While it does involve a screening process, the waitlists are much shorter. Private adoptions also offer more opportunities for the adoptive parents to deal directly with the birth mother while she is pregnant or shortly after birth. Public adoptions are generally free, whereas private adoptions can cost $10,000 or more. Despite this, most adoptions are done through private agencies. To be approved by the court, as is required in most jurisdictions, the adoption must pass the "best interests of the child" test.

International adoptions—that is, adoptions involving a child from another country—are more complicated than domestic adoptions. They must follow the rules in place for adoption and emigration in the country of birth, and they must also follow Canada's immigration rules. They are also more expensive.

An adopted child is legally the same as if she were the couple's biological child.

- to maintain kinship ties (where care by the extended family is possible);
- in cases involving Aboriginal children, to preserve their cultural identity; and
- to do what is generally in the best interests of the child in all the circumstances.

Support for Parents

Do adult children have an obligation to support their parents once the latter become elderly and unable to care for themselves? The answers to this question vary depending on the upbringing of the children and factors such as culture and religious beliefs.

With respect to the law in Canada, the *Criminal Code* imposes an obligation on adult children to care for their elderly parents if the parents are under their charge. The parents are most clearly under their charge if the children are living with them.[12] However, allegations and convictions for failing to live up to this obligation are rare.[13]

In some provinces and territories, family law legislation imposes civil obligations on adult children to support their parents. As with criminal charges, however, claims based on these obligations are rare. These civil obligations, where they exist, do not necessarily depend on whether the parent is under the charge of the child but on a number of factors, including the following:

- whether the parent had cared for and supported the adult child as a youth,
- the parent's current needs, and
- the adult child's current ability to support the parent.[14]

---

12 See s 215(1)(c) of the *Criminal Code*, RSC 1985, c C-46.

13 One such case is *R v Peterson* (2005), 201 CCC (3d) 220 (Ont CA), which involved an adult son who was living in the family home with his 84-year-old father, who was suffering from Alzheimer's. The son, who failed to care for his father, was convicted and sentenced to six months in jail.

14 For example, see Ontario's *Family Law Act*, RSO 1990, c F.3, s 32. Some jurisdictions are moving away from such obligations, however. Alberta repealed its child–parent support requirements in 2003 and British Columbia did so in 2011.

Other Areas of Private Law

There are many areas of private law, and many of them overlap. Some even cross the divide into public domestic law and some, even further, into international law. In this chapter, we have considered two significant areas of private law: property law and family law. Other areas of law are closely related to these two areas and could be seen as subcategories of them. At the same time, they are substantial enough to constitute their own categories of private law. We briefly discuss these areas below. We then consider various other areas of private law. Equity subjects—trusts, fiduciary duties, and equitable remedies—constitute one such area, as do some transnational law subjects like conflict of laws and admiralty law.

Areas Related to Property Law

As we mentioned earlier in this chapter, *real estate transactions*, *conveyancing*, and *landlord and tenant law* can be thought of as subcategories of real property law. Other subcategories within property law in general are *commercial transactions* and *secured transactions*. The law concerned with commercial transactions covers all goods transactions, from the point of manufacture through supply and retail to final purchase by consumers or businesses. It is concerned with the transfer of property rights.

The area of secured transactions covers the use of personal property as security for obligations, usually consumer or business debt. The focus of this area of law is the relatively uniform personal property security legislation in force in all jurisdictions across Canada, briefly described above.

Areas Related to Family Law

Elder law, as the name suggests, deals with the various legal issues facing the elderly. It has emerged in recent years, with an aging population, as a separate area of study and practice. While elder law is obviously related to family law, it touches on other legal areas; in fact, it could be described as a collection of the legal areas most often related to elders' lives. Elder law comprises the following, for example:

- torts and criminal law (to address, for example, the various forms of physical, emotional, and financial abuse suffered by the elderly);
- contracts (for example, to address the validity of contracts that the elderly negotiate under duress or undue influence, and to consider the need for powers of attorney or representation agreements authorizing representatives to make financial and personal care decisions for the elderly);
- property and succession (to address the validity of wills executed under pressure); and
- family law (to address, for example, the obligations owed to parents by adult children).

Other topics addressed by elder law include assisted-living opportunities, the loss of driving privileges, powers of attorney, and issues to do with end of life and palliative care.

Succession law is also related to family law. However, it also has a strong connection to property law. The law of succession covers issues to do with wills and estates and the transmission of property upon death. Most often, the property goes to family members. Legally speaking, however, there is nothing to prevent a person from leaving everything to a favourite charity instead. Specifically, succession law concerns the following:

- estate planning (sometimes viewed as a specialized field by itself);
- wills (drafting them, interpreting them, and challenging them based on, for example, a lack of testamentary capacity);
- succession legislation (including rules relating to the limited power of the court to vary wills and a testator's wishes on the basis of fairness; rules in connection with the transmission of property in the event that someone dies intestate [that is, without a will]; and rules relating to the rights and responsibilities of personal representatives [for example, executors and administrators] who manage the estate pending the transfer of the deceased's property to beneficiaries and others); and
- other estate matters, such as applicable taxes and fees.

Equity

The Courts of Chancery were courts authorized to apply principles of equity (rather than common law) to cases brought before them (see Chapter 2). For the most part, equity served to modify, soften, or put a gloss on the common law—for example, in setting rules for the interpretation of contract clauses or provisions in property transfers. Many of the rules developed according to these principles are still with us today, and modern courts continue to refine and expand upon some of them. Generally speaking, the discussion of equity and its modifications comes up in the context of the areas of law to which these modifications apply—contracts or property transfers, for example. Occasionally, however, equity went further and created stand-alone actions or claims for remedies. These actions or remedies can be treated as separate areas of private law.

Three discrete "equity" subjects stand out:

1. trusts,
2. fiduciary duties, and
3. equitable remedies.

The law of *trusts* deals with how trusts are created, the relationship between the legal owner of property (the trustee) and the equitable owner (or beneficiary), the regulation of trust relationships by legislation, and the remedies for breach of trust.

The study of *fiduciary duties* examines the obligations that arise in certain kinds of relationships—for example, between lawyers and clients, between banks and customers, and between financial advisors and investors. This area of law concerns such aspects of fiduciary duty as obligations of good faith, openness, and accountability (for example, with respect to any secret profits).

The area of law concerned with *equitable remedies* looks in detail at the various remedies developed by the courts of equity. These remedies include injunctions, specific performance, rescission, rectification, equitable damages, and equitable compensation. (Some of these were described in Chapter 9, in connection with contract remedies.)

Creditors' Remedies

During the pursuit of a civil claim and after its resolution, either by court judgment or through settlement, the successful party may have to concern herself with collecting what is owed. If the debtor pays willingly, then all is well. If he does not, then the area of *creditors' remedies* becomes important.

Creditors have a large arsenal of available techniques to collect their debts, including pre-judgment garnishment of bank accounts, post-judgment garnishment of wages, seizure and sales of motor vehicles, and the registration of judgments against real property. The exact number of techniques varies according to the nature of the claim or debt (for example, builders' liens are only available to building contractors), and additional options are available to secured creditors (that is, those with security against a particular asset). In all cases, however, "collections" rules tend to be fairly strict and the requirements of the relevant legislation must be carefully followed.

Transnational Law Subjects

As discussed in Chapter 2, the world is increasingly interconnected. An awareness of legal frameworks other than our own helps us with transactions that involve an interprovincial, intercultural, or international component. The term *transnational law* refers broadly to all areas of law dealing with issues that cross national boundaries. *Comparative law* is the name for one such area; it was the subject of Chapter 2. *Public international law* (or *international law*) deals primarily with the relationship between states, and is considered in Chapter 12 along with other subjects connected to public international law. Transnational law subjects rooted in private law include conflict of laws and admiralty law.

Conflict of laws, also referred to as *private international law* (to distinguish it from public international law), is an area of law that covers private law disputes that have an interprovincial or an international component. These disputes could include, for example,

- product liability disputes where the goods were manufactured abroad,
- contracts between parties residing in two different countries,
- marriages and divorces involving two people from outside the country or people with different citizenships, and
- succession cases involving foreign property.

Conflict of laws is always relevant to international trade and international business transactions. Within this general context, some of the specific topics covered are jurisdiction (which jurisdiction's courts can hear the dispute), applicable law (which jurisdiction's laws govern the dispute), and the enforcement of foreign judgments.

Admiralty (or maritime) law concerns maritime trade and commerce and the rules for resolving maritime disputes. It has a private international law component. Some of the issues it addresses are wages and conditions for seamen, shipowners' obligations toward people injured on board, responsibility for injuries, rights of salvage (in other words, reward for recovering the property of others lost at sea), and rules relating to piracy. Admiralty law is not the same as the *law of the sea*. The latter is a branch of public international law described in Chapter 12 and it defines, among other things, the rights and responsibilities of nations in their use of the world's oceans.

Procedure and Practice Areas

There are some areas in the study of law that defy easy classification and apply in both private law and public law contexts. They are not hybrid subjects but overarching subjects applicable regardless of the substantive nature of the legal matter in question. One such area can be referred to by the compendious title "procedural law" (see Figure 1.1 on page 27); another important one is legal ethics. Both are described briefly here because, while they are not confined to private law, arguably they do "more work" on this side of the divide.

Legal Process

Legal process (or *legal procedures* or *procedural law*) refers generally to the processes or procedures involved in proceedings before courts or tribunals. Different processes apply depending on the subject matter of the hearing and the court in question. While international and transnational courts also have defined processes, we are concerned here with the procedures applicable to our domestic courts.

Legal representatives must be knowledgeable about the relevant process for a given dispute if the matter is to proceed smoothly though the court system. However, it is also important to keep in mind that approximately 90 percent of legal disputes are in fact settled out of court, either before any court process commences or at some point during the process. Three important reasons for this, particularly relevant in the context of private law disputes, are:

1. *Expense.* A few days in court with the legal fees and all of the associated disbursements can easily eat away at any expected award.
2. *Time.* It can take years to proceed through all levels of court if decisions are appealed.
3. *Uncertainty.* If a dispute gets as far as court, there is likely some uncertainty about what the law is or how it should be applied.

These three reasons provide a significant incentive to settle disputes outside of court if at all possible. Negotiation, mediation, collaborative law (more and more common in family law matters), and arbitration (often used for long-term business relationships) are examples of an increasingly important area known as *alternative dispute resolution* (ADR). Access-to-justice issues are driving this field, and many legal professionals are being trained specifically in ADR. See Chapters 16 and 13, and Box 13.3 (in connection with alternative dispute resolution systems in criminal matters).

Where cases do proceed to court, the subject name used to describe the process in private law disputes is *civil procedure* (or *civil litigation*). Civil procedure is a very specialized area and deals with the conduct of civil actions before various courts from the provincial or territorial court level all the way up to the SCC. Each court has its own set of rules governing procedure. Among other things, these rules cover:

- the steps involved in starting an action,
- the notice requirements for opposing parties,
- time limitations,
- the security required for the costs involved in the action, and
- the discovery processes.

These rules must be followed carefully; otherwise, litigants run the risk of having their claims or defences rejected on technical grounds.

There are also specialized processes when public law matters are dealt with before the courts. An important and specialized area here is *criminal procedure*. As with civil procedure, the rules vary depending on the subject matter (in this context, the crime in question) and the various courts that may be involved (which, again, can be from the provincial or territorial court level all the way up to the SCC). For more on the criminal trial process, see Chapter 13.

Once in court, it is essential to be aware of the law of *evidence*. Evidentiary rules govern everything from tests of relevancy and privilege to special issues relating to the admission of documentary proof, oral testimony of witnesses, and expert evidence (for example, evidence of medical professionals about the nature of injuries or in connection with a mental disorder defence in a criminal case). *Advocacy*, another in-court subject, assumes a knowledge of evidence and is about the effective presentation of evidence, examination of witnesses, and use of argumentation.

Legal Ethics

In the legal field generally, one of the most important subjects of all is **legal ethics** (sometimes referred to as *professional responsibility*). The basic relationship between law and ethics in a theoretical sense was discussed briefly in Chapter 1. As a subject, it deals with the ethical issues facing legal professionals in all facets of their practice and, in particular, in connection with their duties to their clients, the courts, and the public. Legal ethics issues are most often highlighted when legal professionals are sued or disciplined for *professional misconduct*. In Chapter 15, legal codes of ethics and the specific types of ethical issues arising in the practice of law are described.

CHAPTER SUMMARY

The ownership of real and personal property has been a source of power in Western society since ancient times, and the laws concerning real property, or land, are among our oldest. The closest a person can come to absolute ownership of land is with the fee simple estate, which allows an owner full power to dispose of her land as she wishes during her life and on her death. Various lesser estates and charges against property come with specific rights and obligations and with more limited powers of control. In Canada, interests in land are registered either in a deed registry or a land title system, depending on the province in which the land is located. Land title systems, such as the Torrens system, are used in parts of Ontario and western Canada, and they provide more security of ownership than deed registry systems do.

Personal property refers to tangible goods and to some intangible interests such as corporate securities. Ownership rules for personal property are simpler than the ownership rules for land. Personal property securities legislation that is in force in all provinces and territories governs the process by which one party takes another's personal property as security. Intellectual property (that is, property that is created through intellectual effort) has become a more important form of property in recent years and is regulated exclusively at the federal level. The principle forms of IP protection relate to copyright, industrial designs, patents, and trademarks.

Certain aspects of marriage and divorce—for example, the substantive requirements of a valid marriage—are federally regulated. Other aspects, such as the formal and ceremonial requirements of a marriage, are under provincial jurisdiction.

New laws concerning same-sex marriage and permissible degrees of consanguinity (blood relation) and affinity have expanded the range of marriageable couples. When marriages end, most couples get divorced, and most divorces in Canada are based on the no-fault one-year separation rule set out in the federal *Divorce Act*. Issues relating to support and care of children become important on the breakdown of marriage. Spousal support focuses on what is reasonable for both parties in the circumstances. Child support and custody and access determinations are based on what is in the best interests of the child. Division-of-property rules, which are regulated by the provinces and territories, favour a 50/50 split of family property unless good reasons exist to adjust this division—a process known as reapportionment. Regulation of common law relationships is very similar to that of traditional marriages. Family law also covers other matters such as adoption, child welfare, and support of parents.

Besides the four main areas of private law discussed in Chapters 9 and 10—torts, contracts, property, and family—there are many others. Some are closely related to these four main areas. Employment and insurance law, for example, are specialized areas of contract law. Other areas of private law are distinct, such as claims in equity, creditors' remedies, and private international law, which deals with transborder differences in laws relating to civil matters. Finally, some areas test the limits of classification. For example, procedural law (in its broadest sense) and legal ethics concern the legal system more generally and can apply in either private law or public law settings.

KEY TERMS

admiralty (or maritime) law area of law that concerns maritime trade and commerce and that has a private international law component *(p. 309)*

affinity the relationship that a person has to the blood relatives of his or her spouse *(p. 299)*

agreement for sale agreement by which a person selling his property agrees to finance the purchase himself, keeping the title to the property while allowing the purchaser to take possession of it, and then transferring the title to the purchaser once the balance of the purchase price is paid *(p. 289)*

annulment the legal cancellation or invalidation of a marriage *(p. 299)*

banns of marriage the public announcement in church of an impending marriage *(p. 301)*

beneficial owner also called an equitable owner, the person on whose behalf and for whose benefit the trustee holds and manages the property *(p. 290)*

builders' lien charge against land that builders use to secure amounts owed them for work done on landowners' property *(p. 289)*

charges and encumbrances any claim on a parcel of real property—for example, mortgages, property taxes, or water rights *(p. 288)*

chattels tangible, movable objects such as furniture, equipment, and cars *(p. 294)*

chose in action the right to sue someone for an unpaid debt or liability; an intangible personal property right *(p. 295)*

conflict of laws area of law—also referred to as *private international law*—that covers private law disputes that have an interprovincial or international component *(p. 309)*

consanguinity a blood relationship between relatives *(p. 299)*

conveyancing the part of the real estate transaction that begins after the contract is entered into and that involves the actual transfer of title, or conveyance *(p. 293)*

deeds formal documents showing ownership of property *(p. 292)*

defeasible term used for life estates that can be terminated by the fee simple owner if certain conditions are not met or certain defined events occur *(p. 288)*

elder law area of private law that covers the various legal issues facing the elderly *(p. 307)*

essential validity concerns a person's capacity to marry and the substantive requirements of a valid marriage *(p. 298)*

fee simple ownership the most absolute form of private ownership, entitling the owner to possess the property, to build on it, and to transfer it to others during her lifetime or in a will at her death *(p. 287)*

fixtures things that are attached to the land *(p. 294)*

foreclosure proceedings proceedings that the mortgagee (the lender) brings against the defaulting mortgagor (borrower) in order to foreclose the mortgagor's right to redeem her property *(p. 289)*

formal validity concerns the formalities or ceremonial requirements of a marriage *(p. 298)*

freehold interests form of property ownership that does not imply an obligation to pay rent *(p. 288)*

indefeasible not able to be annulled, made void, or overturned *(p. 292)*

intellectual property property derived from the intellect, or mind—works of art, inventions, and designs *(p. 284)*

interest any right, claim, or privilege that an individual has with respect to real or personal property *(p. 285)*

joint tenancy a form of co-ownership that features the right of survivorship as well as the "four unities" of *possession* (each co-owner has an equal right to possess the entire property), *interest* (each co-owner has an identical interest in the property), *time* (the co-owners receive their interests at the same time), and *title* (the co-owners receive their interests under the same instrument, such as a will) *(p. 290)*

leasehold interests form of property ownership that implies an obligation to pay rent *(p. 288)*

legal ethics area of law that deals with the ethical issues facing legal professionals in all facets of their practice *(p. 311)*

life estate ownership type of ownership whereby the fee simple owner grants a person (the life tenant) exclusive possession of a property for that person's lifetime, with the condition that the estate reverts to the fee simple owner at the life tenant's death *(p. 287)*

mortgage a kind of charge against land that secures a debt owed by the landowner *(p. 288)*

personal property tangible, movable objects as well as intangible interests such as shares in a company *(p. 284)*

personal property security creditor's security based on the debtor's personal property *(p. 295)*

real property (or real estate) land and anything attached to the land, such as buildings and resources *(p. 284)*

right of survivorship a main condition of joint tenancy whereby the surviving co-owners automatically inherit a deceased owner's share *(p. 290)*

riparian rights rights that are attached to property fronting lakes or rivers and that include the right to make use of the water for certain activities and the obligation not to interfere with the riparian rights of others *(p. 291)*

succession law area of private law that covers issues to do with wills and estates and the transmission of property upon death *(p. 307)*

support property owner's obligation to consider how changes made to his property may affect his neighbour's property *(p. 291)*

tenancy in common a form of co-ownership that does not involve the four unities or the right of survivorship, so that a co-owner can transfer her interest to others during her lifetime or leave it to others in her will *(p. 290)*

Torrens system system for registering property ownership that eliminates the transfer of title by deeds and replaces them with statutory transfer forms, so that the title is guaranteed (or *indefeasible*) *(p. 292)*

trustee someone who has legal title to the property, but holds it for another and has the fiduciary responsibility to make decisions for the benefit of the other party *(p. 290)*

FURTHER READING

BOOKS

Fitzgerald, Patrick, Barry Wright & Vincent Kazmierski. *Looking at Law: Canada's Legal System*, 6th ed (Markham, Ont: LexisNexis, 2010).

Kurtz, JoAnn. *Family Law: Practice and Procedure*, 3d ed (Toronto: Emond Montgomery, 2010).

Sinclair, Alan M & Margaret E McCallum. *An Introduction to Real Property Law*, 5th ed (Markham, Ont: LexisNexis, 2005).

WEBSITES

Canadian Intellectual Property Office (CIPO): <http://www.cipo.ic.gc.ca>.

World Intellectual Property Organization: <http://www.wipo.int>.

REVIEW QUESTIONS

1. What are the distinguishing features of the fee simple estate?

2. Define life estate ownership, and outline its rights and obligations.

3. Explain how mortgages work, and describe how the modern concept of a mortgage differs from the traditional concept.

4. What is the difference between joint tenancy and tenancy in common?

5. What does the term "support" mean in the context of property ownership?

6. What is the purpose of registration systems for property ownership, and what are the registry systems currently used in Canada?

7. What is the test for determining whether formerly movable property has become affixed to land and therefore part of the realty?

8. What are the six basic requirements of essential validity for marriage?

9. What is the difference between the annulment of a marriage and a divorce?

10. In terms of ownership and control of matrimonial property, what is the "unity of personality" principle, and does it apply today? Explain.

11. Name three specific situations in the area of family law where the courts consider the "best interests of the child."

12. What is the private law area known as "conflict of laws" concerned with?

EXERCISES

1. Using the legislation website for your province or territory (see the list of Further Reading in Chapter 5), locate the statute that regulates residential tenancies and review the provisions dealing with termination. For a month-to-month tenancy, name three no-fault reasons that will support a decision by a landlord to end the lease, and describe the specific notice requirements.

2. You have just written a script for an animated film that you believe has the potential to be Disney's next big hit. You want to send it around for others to read and critique but are concerned about its being plagiarized. Go to the CIPO website listed above and review the information about copyrights. What steps must be taken to register your original script? Once registered, does CIPO guarantee protection for your work? Explain.

3. In your opinion, should couples who choose not to get married but who live in a committed marriage-like relationship be treated the same way as married couples when it comes to division of family assets? Provide reasons for your answer.

11 Business and Consumer Law

After reading this chapter, you will understand:

- The most common ways of carrying on a business in Canada—sole proprietorships, partnerships, and corporations—and the advantages and disadvantages of each
- The importance of sale of goods acts in Canada
- How consumers are protected under the federal *Competition Act*

- The role of the federal *Food and Drugs Act* and the *Canada Consumer Product Safety Act* in protecting the health and safety of Canadian consumers
- Selected areas covered by provincial consumer protection legislation
- How the Canadian advertising industry attempts to protect consumers

> Modern technology has placed at the disposal of the Canadian consumer a bewildering variety of highly complex products, consumable and non-consumable, many of which were unknown before the war. The notion of the consumer bargaining from a position of equal strength has become a fiction in any but the most attenuated sense.
>
> JS Ziegel, "The Future of Canadian Consumerism"
> in MH Ogilvie, ed, *Consumer Law: Cases and Materials*, 3d ed
> (Toronto: Captus Press, 2007) 2 at 2

Introduction

There are many different ways of carrying on a business. In Canada, the three most common business structures are the sole proprietorship, the partnership, and the corporation.

No matter which business structure is chosen, people running the business need to be aware of legislation—both provincial and federal—regulating the products or services that they are manufacturing and selling to the public. Both levels of government have enacted key legislation that sets standards and defines rights and responsibilities with regard to these products and services, in order to protect the rights and safety of Canadian consumers.

This chapter will give a general overview of sole proprietorships, partnerships, and corporations and note the main legal differences among them. It will consider sales purchases and some implied conditions in such transactions under provincial sale of goods acts. It will also discuss the federal *Competition Act*, the *Food and Drugs Act*, and the *Canada Consumer Product Safety Act*, along with a selected provincial act, showing how changes in the marketplace and growing concern over consumer safety have led to increased government regulation of sales to consumers. Lastly, it will consider a code of standards administered by Advertising Standards Canada to protect consumers.

Sole Proprietorships

The simplest form of business structure in Canada is the **sole proprietorship**. The business, in this case, is owned and operated by one person—the sole proprietor. For example, a sole proprietorship might be a neighbourhood dog-grooming business, a street vendor, or a business selling products on the Internet. With sole proprietorships, besides the owner there are generally few (if any) employees, and it is not unusual for the business to be based in the sole proprietor's home; however, depending on the size and type of business (and this applies regardless of how the business is structured), it could be in a retail store, warehouse, or office building, or even be a mobile business. Legal requirements for starting up a sole proprietorship are minimal, but still must be followed.

Depending on particular laws in each province, a sole proprietor may conduct her business under her own personal name. If the sole proprietor chooses to do otherwise—if she wishes to give her business a name different from her own name—she may (depending again on the province) be required to register that different name with the provincial government. There may be further restrictions in this regard. In Saskatchewan, for example, section 8(1) of *The Business Names Registration Act* states that no business name shall be registered if, in the opinion of the Registrar, it is the same as or similar to an existing corporation's name and would likely cause confusion; or if the name suggests or implies a connection with the Crown, the government, a political party, a professional association, or a university.[1]

With a sole proprietorship, there are federal and provincial laws and taxes that may also apply to its operation. There is the federal goods and services tax (GST), provincial sales tax (PST), and, in some provinces, including Ontario and the Atlantic provinces, a combined harmonized sales tax (HST) that is collected by the Canada Revenue Agency, which then remits a portion back to the participating provinces. Municipal bylaws may also apply to facets of the business, such as land use, zoning, parking, noise, and the location of advertising signs. Business permits and other licences may also be needed—for example, for electricians—depending on the type of business. Indeed, all of the business structures reviewed in this part are subject to taxes and other obligations under federal, provincial, and municipal laws.

Advantages and Disadvantages

A sole proprietorship is relatively easy to start up and operate. Income from the business is considered taxable income for the sole proprietor, but an income tax deduction based on a percentage of the costs of operating the business at home may be available.

The main disadvantage of a sole proprietorship is that it is not a separate legal business structure apart from its owner. Sole proprietors are legally liable for all of the business's debts and obligations. Such business debts may also put the sole proprietor's personal assets at risk.

Partnerships

Business owners may choose to change their business structure as their circumstances change. For example, a sole proprietor might wish to expand her home-based dog-grooming business. In order to raise capital to rent a storefront office and buy more equipment, she might convert her business into a partnership, with a co-owner. This partnership structure could reduce business costs per person and increase business opportunities; the partners

---

1 *The Business Names Registration Act*, RSS 1978, c B-11.

could share costs and work together to attract new customers. The three types of partnerships available in Canada are the general partnership, the limited partnership, and the limited liability partnership. Table 11.1 on page 322 provides a comparison of the three types.

General Partnership

The nature of a general partnership is defined in law. Ontario's *Partnerships Act*, for example, defines it as "the relation that subsists between persons carrying on a business in common with a view to profit."[2] The Act also lists a number of rules in section 3 for determining the existence of a partnership and states that a partnership is called, collectively, a firm. In a **general partnership**, the partners manage the business together and share profits, as well as debts and obligations, that may arise.

Though it is not compulsory, these general partners could, by consent, have a partnership agreement to vary their mutual rights and duties. However, if a partnership has no such partnership agreement of its own, partnership acts govern the relationship among the general partners themselves and their relationship to third parties. Partners also owe a **fiduciary duty** to each other, which requires them to act in good faith and to share profits and opportunities; they are also required to act carefully and reasonably in their partnership dealings. As with a sole proprietorship, a general partnership is not legally separate from the partners themselves.

Advantages and Disadvantages

A general partnership, like a sole proprietorship, can be established with minimal expense. It can reduce business costs on an individual basis and increase business opportunities through the pooling of resources. A major disadvantage of this business structure is that the individual partners have *joint and several liability* for the actions of the business (see Figure 11.1). This means that every partner is liable with the other partners for any debts or liabilities incurred by the firm. This liability again places the partners' personal assets at risk of a creditor suing to collect money owing to them by the partnership.

Limited Partnership

The main difference between a **limited partnership** and a general partnership is that, in a limited partnership, not all partners participate in the business. A limited partnership consists of one or more general partners and one or more limited partners. The general partners are the ones who operate the partnership and are liable for any partnership liabilities. A limited partner, on the other hand, contributes money or property to the partnership, but does not operate the partnership or take part in managing its business. The limited partner has the right to a share in the partnership profits but, unlike the general partners, is not liable for any partnership obligations. The liability of limited partners is restricted only to the value of money and other property they contributed to the partnership.

In Ontario, for example, a limited partnership is formed when a declaration is filed with the provincial government in accordance with the province's *Limited Partnerships Act*.[3]

---

2 *Partnerships Act*, RSO 1990, c P.5, s 2.

3 RSO 1990, c L.16, s 3(1).

FIGURE 11.1 Joint and several liability

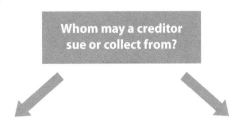

Source: Margaret Buchan et al, *Canadian Business Law*, 2d ed (Toronto: Emond Montgomery, 2012) at 208.

Advantages and Disadvantages

An advantage here is that a limited partnership enables the partners to raise needed money by attracting new investors who can share in the partnership profits but limit risks involved in their investment to no more than the money or property they have contributed. Not all investors in a partnership want to assume all its risks.

One difficulty involved in a limited partnership is that the distinction between general and limited partners may become blurred. A limited partner who takes part in managing and controlling the partnership can, by section 13(1) of Ontario's *Limited Partnerships Act*, for example, run the risk of losing his limited partner status and being held liable as a general partner.

Limited Liability Partnership

Traditionally, many professionals, such as lawyers and accountants, have been attracted to the business structure of a general partnership. It enables them to share office costs, work in a collegial environment, and, with two or more people generating business, it increases the firm's potential to attract new clients. However, one problem with this business structure is that all partners in the firm are liable for the professional negligence of any one partner. An alternative partnership structure that provides a solution to this concern is the **limited liability partnership**, in which partners are *not* liable for each other's professional negligence.

Limited liability partnerships (LLPs) are available across Canada—for lawyers and accountants in all provinces except PEI, and in the Northwest Territories. The governing legislation in each jurisdiction where they are permitted sets out the rules for creating LLPs, and the attendant rights and responsibilities attaching to this business structure. In Ontario, for example, the legislation regulating lawyers allows them to carry on their business using the LLP business structure, and the province's *Partnerships Act* provides that an LLP is formed when two or more persons sign a written agreement that designates their partnership as an LLP and states that the *Partnerships Act* governs the agreement. Under this Act

TABLE 11.1   Comparison of the Three Types of Partnerships

	GENERAL PARTNERSHIP	LIMITED PARTNERSHIP	LIMITED LIABILITY PARTNERSHIP
Typical example	Two friends go into business together; they share capital costs, debts, work, profit, and liability.	A sole proprietor needs capital and finds investors who become limited partners; they provide capital, share debts, and are entitled to profit, but they do not work in the business and have limited liability. The sole proprietor becomes a general partner.	A group of accountants form a partnership; they share capital costs, debts, work, and profit; and they are not liable for each other's professional negligence.
Liability	All partners are jointly and severally liable for each other's debts and negligence, including professional negligence. Liability is unlimited.	At least one general partner must be fully liable for the debts of the firm and any negligence of the other partners. Liability of general partners is limitless. Limited liability partners are liable for the debts of the firm and any negligence of the other partners only to the extent provided in the partnership agreement (usually to the extent of their capital investment).	Some or all partners may be limited liability partners, who are liable only for the general debts of the firm and not for the professional negligence of the other partners.
Decision making and profit taking	Partners often make decisions and share profit equally. A partnership agreement may provide that some partners have more decision-making power and are entitled to more profit (usually because of a larger initial investment) than others.	Limited partners have no decision-making powers. If they become involved in business decisions, they risk losing their limited liability status. Limited partners are entitled to profit according to the terms of the partnership agreement.	Limited liability partners may have decision-making powers and are entitled to profit according to the terms of the partnership agreement.

Source: Margaret Buchan et al, *Canadian Business Law*, 2d ed (Toronto: Emond Montgomery, 2012) at 215.

(sections 44.1-44.3), the firm name of the LLP must be registered under Ontario's *Business Names Act*, and the firm name must also contain the words "limited liability partnership" or the abbreviation "LLP" as the last words or letters of the firm name.[4] At the time of writing, British Columbia is the only province that allows LLPs for other professions, besides law and accounting, and for businesses generally.

Advantages and Disadvantages

The main advantage of the limited liability partnership is that one partner is not liable for the professional negligence of another partner, though the negligent partner himself cannot hide behind limited liability protection. One limitation on this form of business structure is that, even where it is recognized, it is generally not available to all professions or businesses.

---

4 *Partnerships Act, supra* note 2.

Corporations

As noted, two main concerns for those operating a sole proprietorship or a partnership are

1. raising new money for the business, and
2. being personally liable for the business debts and obligations of the sole proprietorship or partnership.

A **corporation** is a legal entity separate from those who create it. Because it is independent from its owners (the shareholders) and those who manage it (the directors and officers or their appointees), these individuals are in most cases not personally and legally liable for the company's debts and obligations. When first incorporating a company, one must consider who will provide the initial investment and be its shareholders, and who will be its directors and officers. Often in the initial stages of a corporation's existence, the owners, or shareholders, will also be the directors and officers—its first managers.

It is also necessary to consider where the head office will be located, and whether to incorporate federally or provincially. Incorporating under the federal *Canada Business Corporations Act* ensures a right to carry on business anywhere in Canada and provides increased name protection. If a company plans to carry on business locally, however, incorporation under the relevant provincial or territorial statute is common. These companies can still carry on business in other provinces and territories if they wish, provided that they register as required in those jurisdictions. (Federal companies have to register in jurisdictions in which they do business, too, but the process is simpler.)

A corporation is created when its incorporators file with the appropriate government office a document known either as (depending on the province) letters patent, memorandum of association, or—in the case of federal incorporation—articles of incorporation.[5] These are standard-form documents containing certain information the government requires, such as the company name, the location of its head office, the names and addresses of its first directors, and the number and types of company shares.

In addition, the application for incorporation must also include a NUANS (Newly Updated Automated Name Search) report. This is a report confirming that the government names database has been searched and that there are no existing corporations already using the proposed name. If the name is similar to that of an existing corporation, and the similarity is likely to cause confusion, the proposed new name may not be accepted. If the name proves problematic in this way and the incorporators want to get their new company up and running quickly, a company can be created using a number instead of a name. Once all the required paperwork is submitted and the submission fee is paid, the company comes into existence.

Corporations have the ability to raise capital by issuing and selling shares to the public, something not possible for a sole proprietor or partnership. Deciding whether to offer shares to the public, thereby creating a *public company*, or limiting the number of shareholders and operating as a *private company*, is one of many important matters to review with legal advisers when structuring or expanding a company. Public companies, whose shares can be sold on stock exchanges, are much more heavily regulated than private companies. *Securities regulation* is a very complex and detailed area of the law.

---

5   See Margaret Buchan et al, *Canadian Business Law*, 2d ed (Toronto: Emond Montgomery, 2012).

Application of Charter Protections and Criminal Law to Corporations

What other implications flow from the special legal status of corporations? What treatment do corporations receive under statutes—such as the *Canadian Charter of Rights and Freedoms* or the *Criminal Code* that were primarily designed to apply to people? Generally, whether the special legal status of corporations entitles them to the protections of the Charter depends on the type of right or freedom under consideration. For example, freedom of expression has been interpreted as extending to corporations in the case of *Irwin Toy Ltd v Quebec (Attorney General),* but the right to equality and the freedom of religion have been restricted to human beings.

Does criminal law apply to corporations? A corporation cannot be sent to jail for criminal acts, but governments are more and more willing to create criminal offences (such as environmental offences) for which corporations can be found guilty and punished through substantial fines. In some cases, the directors of a corporation may be jailed for serious criminal offences perpetrated by the corporation.

Source: Reproduced from Margaret Buchan et al, *Canadian Business Law*, 2d ed (Toronto: Emond Montgomery, 2012) at 222.

Advantages and Disadvantages

One legal advantage of this business structure is that the owners and directors of a company are not personally liable for its debts and obligations. Another advantage, for public companies, is that the corporation can sell shares to raise new capital. Disadvantages for public companies include the cost and complexity of running them because of the detailed securities regulations that apply, and because of the increased costs that are associated with those regulations.

Product Sales and Consumer Protection Legislation

No matter what business structure someone chooses, going into business on your own is not for everyone. Many responsibilities, risks, and liabilities come along with the possibility of making large profits. A business that sells products to the public must also comply with sale of goods acts in each province and territory. Contracts have to be carefully executed. Selling a defective product that might injure someone is a major concern. Here, consumer protection legislation establishes product standards and responsibilities that manufacturers and suppliers must be careful to meet.

When common law rules relating to sales of goods were first codified in the *Sale of Goods Act* in England in 1893, the marketplace was of course very different than it is now. Gerald Fridman notes the following in his seminal work, *Sale of Goods in Canada*:

> When the 1893 Act was framed it was based upon common law that had been formulated in a less developed economic, less consumer-conscious age. It was designed for seller–buyer relationships of a very different order from those that are the norm today. At that time there was less buying on credit: goods were bought at shops much more than by catalogues, mass-production had not emerged, which made the then operative common law and statutory provisions relating to quality and fitness of goods more pointed and meaningful. Similarly, the more personal

relationships of those bygone days highlighted the provisions of the Sale of Goods Act and the Factors Act dealing with transfer of title by a non-owner.[6]

In these earlier times described by Fridman, a prevailing common law doctrine pertaining to the marketplace was ***caveat emptor***—let the buyer beware when purchasing a new product. It was expected that a buyer would check the quality of goods prior to purchasing them. This was an easier task then than it is now.

Generally speaking, the marketplace has changed tremendously since 1893. Like the products themselves, it has gotten more complex. Many consumers today do not have a personal relationship with a retailer. Many buy on credit, online, or from a catalogue. Owing to extensive shrink-wrap packaging and store security concerns, it is often not possible for consumers to inspect products before buying them. Many products today are mass-produced, often in overseas factories, and in some cases are so technically complicated that inspecting them adequately prior to purchase is difficult. Also, buying products today (and services, too) often means to agreeing to use pre-printed standard-form contracts that offer little chance of negotiating terms.[7]

As Jacob Ziegel observed (see the quotation at the beginning of this chapter): "The notion of the consumer bargaining from a position of equal strength has become a fiction in any but the most attenuated sense." The response of legislators in the last 100-plus years has been as varied and complex as the change in the marketplace itself. Some of the key responses, including the enactment of sale of goods acts mentioned above, are briefly described next.

Sale of Goods Acts

As noted, the English *Sale of Goods Act* was passed in 1893. It was the first attempt to codify laws about buying and selling goods, and to add some basic safeguards respecting the rights of buyers and sellers. All common law provinces and territories in Canada have passed similar acts based on this English statute. Quebec's *Civil Code* likewise includes protections for sales transactions.[8] These acts modernize sale of goods law for the benefit of purchasers. In doing so, they help counter the traditional harshness of *caveat emptor*. One instance of this modernization is the introduction of some conditions implied to be in every contract of sale. We will use British Columbia's *Sale of Goods Act* as an example in discussing these implied conditions.[9]

Implied Conditions: Character and Quality of Goods Sold

Five major implied conditions listed in BC's *Sale of Goods Act* are the following:

1. *Seller's title and right to sell.* There is an implied condition under section 16 of the Act that a seller has a right to sell or lease the goods.
2. *Sale by description.* If goods are sold by description, there is an implied condition under section 17 that the goods correspond with that description.
3. *Fitness for purpose.* If a buyer expressly or by implication indicates to a seller his particular purpose requiring a product, and is relying on the seller's skill or

---

6 GHL Fridman, *Sale of Goods in Canada*, 5th ed (Toronto: Thomson, 2004) at 2.

7 See, for example, SN Spetz & GS Spetz, *The Rule of Law: Canadian Business Law*, 2d ed (Toronto: Copp Clark, 1995) at 276-77.

8 Articles 1726-1731 CCQ.

9 *Sale of Goods Act*, RSBC 1996, c 410.

judgment, and the seller is in the business of selling that product, then there is, under section 18(a) of the Act, an implied condition that the goods sold are reasonably fit for the purpose for which the product was bought.

4. *Goods of merchantable quality*. If goods are bought by description from a seller who deals in goods of that description, there is an implied condition, under section 18(b) of the Act, that the goods are of merchantable quality—that is, fit to be used for the ordinary purposes for which products of its kind are manufactured and sold.

5. *Sale by sample*. If goods are sold by sample, there is an implied condition under section 19 of the Act that the goods in bulk correspond to that sample in type and quality.

While this legislation protects consumers to a degree, as these five implied conditions illustrate, it is important to note that sale of goods acts are primarily about contractual rights and responsibilities generally and not consumer protection per se. These codified rules apply to all sales of goods transactions, whether they are between businesses (for example, one commercial enterprise selling machinery to another), between private individuals (such as a sale of goods at a garage sale), or between businesses and consumers (for example, a retail business selling clothing to a customer).

Federal Consumer Protection Legislation

Although provincial sale of goods acts assist purchasers by imposing implied conditions—along with additional safeguards—on commercial sale transactions, these statutes do not cover all areas affecting consumers who buy an item for their own personal use rather than for business reasons. Increasingly, both the federal and provincial/territorial governments have enacted numerous other pieces of legislation more comprehensive in scope than sale of goods acts to help protect consumers from changing marketplace concerns, such as:

- anti-competitive and dishonest business tactics,
- false and misleading advertising,
- deceptive marketing practices, and
- products that may jeopardize the safety of consumers.

Three examples of this additional federal legislation are discussed below.

The Competition Act

In Canada today, the *Competition Act* is the principal federal statute regulating trade and commerce with respect to conspiracies, trade practices, and mergers that affect competition.[10] Its purpose is defined in section 1.1, as follows:

> 1.1 The purpose of this Act is to maintain and encourage competition in Canada in order to promote the efficiency and adaptability of the Canadian economy, in order to expand opportunities for Canadian participation in world markets while at the same time recognizing the role of foreign competition in Canada, in order to ensure that small and medium-sized enterprises have an

---

10 RSC 1985, c C-34.

equitable opportunity to participate in the Canadian economy, and in order to provide consumers with competitive prices and product choices.

The Act authorizes the federal government to take action in several ways against those who it alleges violate its provisions, either through criminal proceedings or by reviewing less serious matters by the Competition Bureau and the Competition Tribunal (see Box 11.2). The Commissioner of Competition is responsible for the administration and enforcement of this Act. Below, we list selected examples of both types of actions covered under this Act.

OFFENCES IN RELATION TO COMPETITION: A CRIMINAL MATTER

One serious criminal offence under the *Competition Act* is conspiracy in relation to competition. The offence of **conspiracy** is identified in section 45 of the Act. It applies to persons who conspire with competitors to lessen competition—and thereby exploit consumers—in ways outlined in the section. The section states the following:

> 45(1) Every person commits an offence who, with a competitor of that person with respect to a product, conspires, agrees or arranges
>
>> (a) to fix, maintain, increase or control the price for the supply of the product;
>>
>> (b) to allocate sales, territories, customers or markets for the production or supply of the product; or
>>
>> (c) to fix, maintain, control, prevent, lessen or eliminate the production or supply of the product.

Criminal proceedings are carried out in criminal court by the federal Department of Justice.

BOX 11.2

Media Monopoly

Because of their significance as vehicles for airing diverse points of view, the news media are businesses in which healthy competition is extremely important. Although the case described below is a case that merely concerned an advertising supplement, it has wider implications.

In *Canada (Director of Investigation and Research) v Southam Inc*, 1991 CanLII 1702 (CT), the defendant corporation, a media giant, purchased two British Columbia newspapers, the *North Shore News* and the *Real Estate Weekly*. The *North Shore News*, a profitable and widely read newspaper, contained a weekly real estate supplement. Before the defendant corporation purchased the papers, this supplement and the *Real Estate Weekly* were the only two real estate advertising papers distributed on the North Shore.

The Competition Tribunal's director of investigation and research brought an application asking the tribunal to order that the corporation sell one or the other of the two papers, alleging that the defendant's ownership of both papers eliminated competition in the real estate market in the area. The

defendant proposed, as an alternative remedy, that the *North Shore News* begin to carry, as an insert, an independent real estate supplement referred to as "HOMES."

The tribunal found that the corporation's ownership of both the *Real Estate Weekly* and the *North Shore News* eliminated competition in the real estate advertising sales market in the region. It was unconvinced that an independent HOMES supplement would be as attractive to advertisers or as financially viable as the existing *North Shore News* supplement (which at the time of the merger was slightly outperforming the *Real Estate Weekly*). The tribunal also believed that it lacked the power to make the order the defendant requested.

The tribunal ordered the corporation to sell either the *North Shore News* or the *Real Estate Weekly* to restore competition in the marketplace.

Source: Reproduced from Margaret Buchan et al, *Canadian Business Law*, 2d ed (Toronto: Emond Montgomery, 2012) at 182.

DECEPTIVE MARKETING PRACTICES: A CIVIL REVIEWABLE MATTER

"Reviewable conduct" is mentioned in section 74.01(1) of the Act and occurs when a person who is promoting the supply or use of a product makes a false or misleading representation to the public not based on an adequate and proper test or makes a misleading guarantee or warranty about it. This civil reviewable matter goes before the Competition Tribunal, which investigates the matter. An example of reviewable conduct follows:

- *Sale above the advertised price.* Described in section 74.05(1), this reviewable conduct occurs when a person advertises a product as being on sale and during this time supplies the product at a higher price than advertised.

The Food and Drugs Act

Canada's *Food and Drugs Act* is another key piece of federal legislation protecting consumers.[11] It protects the health and safety of Canadians in connection with the sale of food, drugs, cosmetics, and medical devices manufactured and sold in Canada.

Section 4(1) of the Act covers food safety and food adulteration. It states the following:

4(1) No person shall sell an article of food that
(a) has in or on it any poisonous or harmful substance;
(b) is unfit for human consumption;
(c) consists in whole or in part of any filthy, putrid, disgusting, rotten, decomposed or diseased animal or vegetable substance;
(d) is adulterated; or
(e) was manufactured, prepared, preserved, packaged or stored under unsanitary conditions.

Section 5 addresses deception in selling, packaging, labelling, advertising, treating, and processing any food, while section 7 covers manufacturing (and storing) food under unsanitary conditions.

The Act also contains provisions concerning drugs. Section 8 states the following:

8. No person shall sell any drug that
(a) was manufactured, prepared, preserved, packaged or stored under unsanitary conditions; or
(b) is adulterated.

Section 9 covers deception in the labelling, packaging, treating, processing, advertising, and selling of drugs, and section 11 applies to their manufacture and storage under unsanitary conditions.

Cosmetics are covered in section 16, as follows:

16. No person shall sell any cosmetic that
(a) has in or on it any substance that may cause injury to the health of the user when the cosmetic is used,
(i) according to the directions on the label or accompanying the cosmetic, or
(ii) for such purposes and by such methods of use as are customary or usual therefor;

---

11 RSC 1985, c F-27.

> (b) consists in whole or in part of any filthy or decomposed substance or of any foreign matter; or
>
> (c) was manufactured, prepared, preserved, packaged or stored under unsanitary conditions.

This last provision is supplemented by section 18, which repeats the prohibition against the manufacture and storage of cosmetics under unsanitary conditions.

Lastly, medical devices are covered in section 19, which states the following:

> 19. No person shall sell any device that, when used according to directions or under such conditions as are customary or usual, may cause injury to the health of the purchaser or user thereof.

Section 20 concerns misleading or deceptive labelling, packaging, treatment, selling, processing, and advertising of such devices.

The Canada Consumer Product Safety Act

In 2011, the *Canada Consumer Product Safety Act*[12] (CCPSA) came into force, bringing Canada's consumer protection laws in line with the new realities of international manufacturing and the marketplace, and responding to the desire of consumers for more information about the products they use. The Act is administered by Health Canada.

The purpose of the CCPSA, as set out in section 3, is to protect the public by addressing or preventing dangers to human health or safety that are posed by consumer products in Canada, including imported products. The Act applies to consumer products that individuals may use for non-commercial purposes—such as domestic, recreational, and sports purposes—as well as to their parts, accessories, and packaging. A wide range of products is thus covered, from children's toys to household products and sporting goods, to name a few. The Act does not apply to goods that are governed by other specific legislation, such as food, cosmetics, medical devices, natural health products, drugs, and vehicles.

Sections 7(a) and 8(a) of the CCPSA contain what is known as the general prohibition. Section 7(a) prohibits manufacturers and importers from manufacturing, importing, advertising, or selling consumer products that constitute a danger to human health or safety, and section 8(a) prohibits anyone from advertising or selling a consumer product they know is a danger to human health or safety. Under the Act, the minister of health has the authority to order a manufacturer, importer, or seller to recall any product that the minister believes is a danger to human health or safety. Industry is expected to undertake recalls voluntarily when necessary.

Other key provisions of the Act include the following:

- Industry must provide Health Canada and suppliers of products with information related to safety incidents or product defects that could result in death or harmful health effects.
- Packaging, labelling, and advertising must not mislead or deceive consumers as to the safety of a product.
- Certain records must be kept by manufacturers, importers, advertisers, vendors, and testers of consumer products in order to make it possible to trace unsafe products back to their source.

---

12   SC 2010, c 21.

- Manufacturers or importers may be required to provide or obtain information about their products (including studies) so that Health Canada can verify that a product is in compliance with the requirements of the CCPSA.

Provincial and Territorial Areas of Consumer Protection

The federal government is not alone in protecting consumers. The provinces and territories are also involved in this area, and have enacted legislation specifically focused on the protection of consumers. Typically, this legislation defines a consumer as someone who has entered into a transaction "for personal, family or household purposes" and excludes from its application business or commercial transactions. This is different from sale of goods acts, which apply generally to all transactions. In other respects, though, consumer protection legislation is broader than sale of goods acts, because it applies to sales of goods *and services*, and in some jurisdictions, even to the sale of real property.

One example of this legislation is Ontario's *Consumer Protection Act, 2002*, which applies to all Ontario consumer transactions.[13] For example, it covers consumer rights and warranties, credit agreements, leasing and procedures for consumer remedies. The Act lists a number of "unfair practices," such as making a "false, misleading or deceptive representation" (section 14(1)) or pressuring a consumer to renegotiate a transaction by keeping custody or control of their goods (section 16). As well, the Act contains additional rights and obligations for some specific consumer agreements, such as those involving time shares, personal development services, and Internet agreements.

As illustrated in Box 11.3, businesses that are aware of serious defects in their products but fail to take swift action to resolve them may have punitive damages awarded against them by the courts.

Another specific area the Act covers is motor vehicle repairs, a major concern for all consumers who drive. Part VI of the Act helps to protect drivers against inflated bills for car repairs. Among its provisions are the following:

- No repairer shall charge consumers for any work or repairs without first giving them an estimate (section 56(1)).
- A repairer cannot charge a fee for giving the estimate unless the consumer is told in advance that a fee will be charged (section 57(1)).
- Repairers cannot charge for any work or repairs unless the work and repairs have been authorized by the consumer (section 58(1)).
- A repairer shall be deemed to warrant all new and reconditioned parts and labour for a minimum of 90 days or 5,000 kilometres, whichever comes first (section 63(1)).

Advertising Standards

To supplement federal and provincial consumer legislation, major stakeholders in the advertising and marketing industries have formed industry associations that also help protect consumers. These associations have established self-regulating and industry-approved

---

13 SO 2002, c 30, Schedule A.

BOX 11.3

Punitive Damages for Failure to Protect Consumers

In the Supreme Court case *Prebushewski v Dodge City Auto (1984) Ltd*, 2005 SCC 28, [2005] 1 SCR 649, the consumer bought a brand new Dodge Ram half-ton truck from a dealership. She and her husband drove the truck without incident for 16 months until, one day, the husband's employer noticed a fire outside the office. The husband ran outside to discover the truck in flames. It was completely destroyed.

Both the dealer and the manufacturer denied liability, referring the consumer and her husband to their insurer. After some investigation, it was determined that the fire was caused by a defect in the daytime running light system. A representative of the manufacturer eventually testified that the manufacturer had known of this defect for several years without issuing a recall.

The trial court found a breach of a statutory warranty under the Saskatchewan *Consumer Protection Act*. In addition to ordering regular damages of about $40,000, the trial judge ordered exemplary (punitive) damages of $25,000 against the manufacturer and dealer. The manufacturer and dealer appealed to the Court of Appeal and were successful in having the exemplary damage award struck out. The consumer appealed to the Supreme Court of Canada.

The SCC restored the order of exemplary damages, finding that the consumer protection legislation had increased the accessibility of exemplary damages (under the common law, it is very difficult to win damages of this kind). (The Ontario *Consumer Protection Act, 2002* also permits awards of exemplary damages under section 18(11).)

Source: Reproduced from Margaret Buchan et al, *Canadian Business Law*, 2d ed (Toronto: Emond Montgomery, 2012) at 172.

---

codes of standards and policy guidelines. Advertising Standards Canada (ASC), created in 1957, is one such body; it administers the Canadian Code of Advertising Standards, first published in 1963. The Code is widely endorsed by Canadian advertisers and sets out standards for advertising that is truthful, fair, and accurate in the following 14 areas:

1. accuracy and clarity,
2. disguised advertising techniques,
3. price claims,
4. bait and switch,
5. guarantees,
6. comparative advertising,
7. testimonials,
8. professional or scientific claims,
9. imitation,
10. safety,
11. superstition and fears,
12. advertising to children,
13. advertising to minors, and
14. unacceptable depictions and portrayals.

ASC updates the Code regularly to ensure that it keeps pace with consumer and societal expectations. It also administers it: the clauses above form the basis for the review of consumer and special interest group complaints, and trade disputes. As part of its commitment to a transparent consumer complaint process, ASC compiles reports of the complaints it receives and the decisions of its council on each one. The reports are listed by year on ASC's website. The following are several examples:[14]

- In 2009, an advertisement in a Punjabi-language newspaper in Ontario assured readers that, through black magic, the advertiser could eliminate all of their personal worries, fulfill all of their desires, remove all of the obstacles in the way of

---

14   Advertising Standards Canada, online: Ad Complaints Reports <http://www.adstandards.com/en/Standards/report.aspx>.

their marrying a loved one, and eliminate their lottery problems and business worries. The ad stated that results were 100 percent guaranteed. Council found that the ad exploited superstitions and played upon fears to mislead consumers, contrary to clause 11.

- In 2010, a manufacturer in the food/supermarkets industry in Quebec released a commercial in which a man shown in a deserted area was suddenly surrounded by a group of people who hit him repeatedly until he fell to his knees on the ground. Council considered a complaint that the commercial encouraged violence and found that, despite its humorous elements, the scenario did seem to condone violence, contrary to clause 14(b).

- In 2013, a popular Canadian clothing retailer advertised that all fall merchandise was being offered at a discount of 20–50 percent off the regular price. The complainant alleged that the discount was less than 20 percent off on many items. Council found that the ad contained a misleading savings claim contrary to clauses 1(a) and 3(a), and the advertiser agreed that the ad should have stated that only *select* items were being offered at 20–50 percent off.

CHAPTER SUMMARY

There are many ways to carry on a business in Canada. The three most common business structures are the sole proprietorship, the partnership, and the corporation. Each one has its advantages and disadvantages. Sole proprietorships are relatively easy and inexpensive to set up and operate, but they are not a separate legal structure from their owners, who are liable for all debts and obligations that their businesses may incur and whose personal assets are thus put at risk.

There are several kinds of partnership structure—the general partnership, the limited partnership, and the limited liability partnership—each with advantages and disadvantages. The general partnership structure is the standard one. It offers the advantage of being relatively inexpensive to create, and it provides the business with a collegial environment, an extended pool of capital based on cost-sharing, and a group of members from which to attract new clients. Its main disadvantage is that each partner is personally liable for all of the firm's debts and liabilities, which may put the partners' personal assets at risk.

A limited partnership has one or more general partners and one or more limited partners. A limited partner contributes money and property, and shares in partnership profits, but is not liable for partnership obligations so long as they take no part in managing the partnership.

A limited liability partnership, if it meets certain criteria, has one key advantage: one partner is not liable for the professional negligence of another partner.

A corporation is a legal entity separate from those who create it. The owners and directors are not personally liable for the company's debts and obligations, but the incorporation process can be expensive, and running a corporation can be a complicated undertaking.

If a business is selling goods to other businesses and consumers, sale of goods acts apply. These laws are now mainly contained in provincial sale of goods statutes in all common law provinces and territories and in Quebec's *Civil Code*.

Legislation protecting consumers has greatly expanded in recent times. Both the federal and provincial governments have enacted consumer protection statutes that are wider in scope than sale of goods acts. The federal *Competition Act* and *Food and Drugs Act*, for example, ensure that consumers have competitive prices and product choices, as well as have laws protecting their health and safety respecting food, drugs, cosmetics, and medical devices manufactured and sold in Canada. Provincial consumer protection legislation, such as Ontario's *Consumer Protection Act, 2002*, protects consumers in a variety of other areas, including motor vehicle repairs.

KEY TERMS

caveat emptor principle that the buyer alone is responsible for ensuring the fitness of the goods he or she is purchasing (Latin: "Let the buyer beware") *(p. 325)*

conspiracy arranging with other sellers to lessen competition and thereby exploit consumers *(p. 327)*

corporation company or group of people authorized by statute to act as a single entity (legally a person) and recognized as such in law *(p. 323)*

fiduciary duty in the context of a partnership, the responsibility to act carefully and reasonably in the best interest of the firm *(p. 320)*

general partnership business structure in which two or more persons carry on business in common with a view to profit *(p. 320)*

limited liability partnership partnership structure used by certain professions in Canada (accountants and lawyers, for the most part) whereby partners are not liable for the professional negligence of other partners *(p. 321)*

limited partnership partnership structure involving at least one general partner, who operates the partnership and is liable for any partnership debts, and at least one limited partner, who invests in the partnership but does not operate it or take part in managing its business and is not personally liable for its debts and obligations *(p. 320)*

sole proprietorship business that is owned and operated by an individual and that is not a legal entity separate from the owner *(p. 318)*

FURTHER READING

BOOKS

Buchan, Margaret, et al. *Canadian Business Law*, 2d ed (Toronto: Emond Montgomery, 2012).

DuPlessis, Dorothy, Steve Enman & Shannon O'Byrne. *Canadian Business and the Law*, 4th ed (Toronto: Nelson, 2011).

Ogilvie, Margaret, ed. *Consumer Law: Cases and Materials*, 3d ed (Toronto: Captus Press, 2007).

Pritchard, Brenda & Susan Vogt. *Advertising and Marketing Law in Canada*, 2d ed (Markham, Ont: LexisNexis, 2006).

Waddams, SM. *Products Liability*, 5th ed (Toronto: Carswell, 2011).

Weir, JD. *Critical Concepts of Canadian Business Law*, 5th ed (Boston: Pearson, 2010).

Yates, Richard, T Bereznicki-Korol & T Clarke, *Business Law in Canada*, 9th ed (Toronto: Pearson, 2011).

WEBSITES

Advertising Standards Canada: <http://www.adstandards.com>.

Canadian Cosmetic, Toiletry and Fragrance Association: <http://cctfa.ca>.

Competition Bureau: <http://www.competitionbureau.gc.ca>.

Health Canada: <http://www.hc-sc.gc.ca>.

Industry Canada: <http://strategis.ic.gc.ca>.

REVIEW QUESTIONS

1. List two advantages of a sole proprietorship.

2. Explain the meaning of the term "fiduciary duty."

3. What is the advantage of a limited partnership for an investor?

4. What must be included in the name of a limited liability partnership?

5. List two main advantages to be gained by incorporating a company.

6. List five implied conditions of sale under provincial sale of goods acts.

7. List four areas covered by the federal *Food and Drugs Act*.

8. What are two ways the marketplace today causes difficulties for consumers who want to know more about a product before they buy it?

EXERCISES

1. Four architects decide to form a partnership and to work out of one office suite. List three advantages these architects could gain from such an arrangement, and list some potential problems that could arise from their partnership.

2. Why is the law providing ever more legislative protections for consumers? Is it a trend that you expect to continue? Why or why not?

3. Section 3(1) of the *Food and Drugs Act* states that "[n]o person shall advertise any food, drug, cosmetic or device to the general public as a treatment, preventative or cure for any of the diseases, disorders or abnormal physical states referred to in Schedule A." Look at Schedule A to this Act, and discuss conditions that you think ought or ought not to be included on the list.

12 Public Law

The European Parliament in Strasbourg, France is the only directly elected EU institution. In addition to its official powers, the Parliament works closely with the national parliaments of EU countries.

After reading this chapter, you will understand:

- The meaning of the term public law
- The distinction between public domestic law and public international law, and the main subdivisions and branches of these two broad categories
- The role of administrative agencies in society, the functions they perform, the legal framework in which they operate, and the grounds and processes for challenging their decisions

- The basic principles of international law, as well as its history and its main sources
- The relationship between international law and domestic law
- How international law is enforced
- The wide range of public law regulation

Public law: 1) the area of law that deals with the relations of individuals with the state and regulates the organization and conduct of government and 2) international law regulating the relations among sovereign states or nations as distinguished from private international law.

Merriam-Webster's Dictionary of Law, sub verbo "public law"

Introduction

The term "public law" has two meanings. It can refer either to public *domestic* law or to public *international* law. It usually refers to the former—public domestic law. In this chapter, we examine both of these types of public law.

Public law at the domestic level—that is, within a nation—governs the relationship between persons and the state. It is one of the three main categories of domestic law, the other two being private law (see Chapters 9, 10, and 11), and military law. Public domestic law, like private law, covers many subject areas.

This chapter begins by discussing an important subcategory of public domestic law known as administrative law, which regulates the way in which governments interact with persons through administrative agencies such as boards, commissions, and tribunals.[1] We then move on to public international law (or international law), and we consider the basic concepts and principles concerning the legal relationship between states. We also discuss other areas of public law, such as municipal, immigration, and tax law, along with some hybrid public–private law areas. In the chapter's final section, we describe some important branches of international law as well as some hybrid areas that touch on both international and domestic law.

---

1   Other key areas of public law are covered elsewhere in the book: constitutional law, in Chapters 5–8; and criminal law, in Chapter 13.

Constitutional Basis of Public Law

The constitutional basis of public law is complex. Constitutional law itself is an area of public law and applies to both federal and provincial governments. Some areas of public law are primarily federally regulated (for example, criminal, Aboriginal, and immigration law); some are provincially regulated (for example, municipal law); and others are areas of split jurisdiction (for example, administrative law and tax law).

The issue of overlap applies in public law, both domestic and international, as it does in private law. Many legal problems transcend subject classifications. For example, a single case could involve elements of immigration law, administrative law, constitutional law, and even international law.

Figure 12.1 shows the relationship between public domestic law and public international law, as well as the main subdivisions and branches of these two areas of law. (To see public law in a broader context—that is, in relation to other areas of law—see Figure 1.1 on page 27 of this text.)

FIGURE 12.1 The divisions of public domestic law and public international law

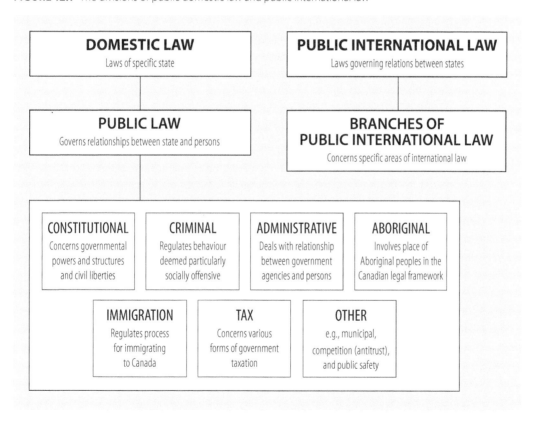

Administrative Law

Administrative agencies[2] are government bodies created under various federal, provincial, and territorial statutes. Their purpose is to administer the legislative schemes set out in these statutes. Below, we give an overview of the *legal* framework within which these agencies operate.

What Is Administrative Law?

Administrative law is a subcategory of public domestic law, and its objective, as Guy Régimbald has remarked, "is to regulate the relationships between the government and governed—the population."[3] Administrative agencies are central to these relationships.

Because of the complexity of modern societies and the amount of regulation applicable to most activities involving the public, elected officials cannot participate directly in all aspects of such regulation. The government delegates certain of these responsibilities to administrative agencies. The word *agency* in this context simply refers to any person, institution, body, board, or tribunal that has been assigned governance powers under legislation.

Delegating government tasks to administrative agencies offers a number of advantages. First, it speeds things up. Having more decision-makers on the ground enables the government to respond more quickly and efficiently to the needs of the public. A second advantage is specialization; agency officials are likely to be appointed on the basis of their familiarity with the area of regulation. Such expertise produces better decisions, which can, in turn, enhance the credibility of government.

The range of agencies to which administrative law applies is extensive. These agencies include not only traditional government entities such as licensing bodies, securities commissions, and labour boards, but also hospitals, universities, self-regulating professions, and certain trade associations that have been delegated regulatory authority under legislation.

Administrative law, then, is about the regulation of government agencies that have been delegated the task of carrying out government functions. The scope of this area of law is broad and covers the following:

- how these delegated entities are structured;
- the manner in which they interact with "the governed";
- the extent of their jurisdiction—that is, the types of activities they can engage in and the types of decisions they can make; and
- the means by which their actions and decisions can be challenged.

In short, administrative law is about "rules for rulers."

---

2 Administrative agencies are referred to in various ways. Generically speaking, they are known as "bodies," "entities," or "agencies." Their actual names or titles commonly include, if not the word "agency," one of the following terms: "board," "commission," "council," "institution," "office," "organization," "service," or "tribunal." Generally speaking, an agency's name tells us little about its particular delegated function. There is one exception to this. An administrative body that is referred to as a "tribunal" usually performs quasi-judicial functions.

3 Guy Régimbald, *Canadian Administrative Law* (Markham, Ont: LexisNexis, 2008) at 1.

Constitutional Basis of Administrative Law

How do we determine whether the constitutional authority to create an administrative agency comes from the federal government or from the provincial government? We look to the *Constitution Act, 1867*, which tells us which level of government has jurisdiction over the subject matter of the agency's enabling statute. To take one example, section 91(23) of the *Constitution Act, 1867* gives the federal government jurisdiction over copyrights. Thus empowered, the federal government has enacted legislation creating the Copyright Board, a federal administrative tribunal that makes decisions about copyright.

The provinces have jurisdiction over other areas. Section 92(8) of the *Constitution Act, 1867*, for example, gives the provinces power over "Municipal Institutions." With this power, the provinces have enacted legislation under which cities, towns, and other municipal organizations are created. The territories have a parallel jurisdiction assigned to them.

There are several constitutional provisions that are specifically relevant to administrative law. For instance, the federal government's power to appoint and to pay delegated officials to sit on administrative agencies is specifically reinforced under sections 91(8) of the *Constitution Act, 1867*. The provincial government's power in this regard is spelled out in section 92(4).

Constitutional Limitations on Administrative Tribunals

As explained below, administrative agencies may be assigned different functions. Sometimes they are given the power to resolve disputes and exercise court-like (or quasi-judicial) functions. For example, a labour board may hear a dispute between an employer and a union about the right to picket. When court-like functions are assigned to an agency in this way, it is acting like a tribunal. One significant constitutional limitation on a government's ability to delegate court-like powers to administrative agencies is that the agency thus created must not be too close in operation to a section 96 court—that is, a provincial superior court (see Chapter 7).

If the constitutionality of an administrative agency's powers is challenged in court on the basis of this limitation, the court has to make a determination, based on three questions:

1. whether the subject matter of the dispute is one that had been historically assigned (that is, by common law at the time of Confederation) to superior courts;
2. whether the tribunal is exercising a judicial function by applying recognized rules in an impartial manner to resolve disputes; and
3. whether the judicial function is part of a wider institutional framework or whether, as with a section 96 court, the adjudicative role is its sole or primary function.

If the tribunal is exercising a power similar to that of a traditional superior court and is resolving disputes as a court does (that is, applying recognized rules), it may still be acceptable as an administrative agency if the decision-making aspect of its jurisdiction is merely *part* of what it does.

If the tribunal resembles a provincial superior court in all three ways, then it will be deemed to be a section 96 court and will be required, like other superior courts, to have federally appointed judges. Without federally appointed judges, the agency will be declared unconstitutional. This is a problem for provincial boards (and provincial inferior courts) that have been delegated too much power and too many responsibilities.

The requirement that only federally appointed judges can hear matters at the superior court level can be problematic for federal administrative tribunals as well as for provincial ones. It is not uncommon for some panellists on administrative tribunals to be lay appointees without formal legal training. Their qualifications and the process by which they are appointed are not necessarily the same as those for superior court judges.

Delegated Power and Functions of Administrative Agencies

Administrative agencies can only exercise power that has been delegated to them by the federal government or by provincial (or territorial) governments. They are charged with administering the legislative regime set out in the legislation that created (or enabled) them.

The government functions that can be delegated to these agencies reflect the three branches of government itself:

1. *legislative* functions (for example, passing bylaws or rules of procedure for appearing before a tribunal),
2. *administrative* or executive functions (for example, issuing business licences), and
3. *quasi-judicial* functions (for example, rendering decisions in labour disputes, as noted above).

A single administrative body may exercise more than one function. When an administrative action or decision is challenged, the available remedies vary according to function. For example, there are fewer opportunities to challenge legislative actions than administrative ones. (Challenging administrative decisions is discussed later in this section.)

With most administrative agencies, a single level of government—federal or provincial (or territorial)—creates an agency and delegates to it all the power it needs (basic delegation). But it is sometimes the case, depending on the area of regulation for which the agency is responsible, that an agency will require powers from more than one level of government.

Under the Constitution, *cross-delegation*—that is, the process whereby one level of government delegates power directly to the other level—is not permitted.[4] However, the Supreme Court of Canada (SCC) has recognized that *inter-delegation*, whereby one level of government creates an agency and the agency subsequently receives some of its power from the other level of government, *is* permissible.[5] For instance, a provincial agency that normally licenses trade within the province (*intra*provincial trade) may wish to license a business to do some trade outside the province (*inter*provincial trade). Interprovincial trade, however, is under federal jurisdiction. In this case, the federal government could delegate some power to that provincial agency. A final type of delegation arrangement is *subdelegation* (or redelegation), whereby an agency attempts to further delegate some of the power it has already received. Subdelegation is generally not permitted unless the enabling legislation authorizes it. This is the *delegatus non potest delegare* principle described in Chapter 5 in connection with subordinate legislation. For example, municipalities—which themselves exercise delegated power—are not able to delegate the power to make bylaws to a subordinate body they create, such as a planning committee. Figure 12.2 illustrates these delegation principles.

Administrative agencies, regardless of the delegation arrangement they involve or the particular functions they have been delegated, operate as part of the executive branch of government and are controlled by it, with the legislative branch authorizing the executive branch's power in this regard.

---

4 *Attorney General of Nova Scotia v Attorney General of Canada*, [1951] SCR 31.

5 *Coughlin v The Ontario Highway Transport Board*, [1968] SCR 569.

FIGURE 12.2 Basic rules of delegation

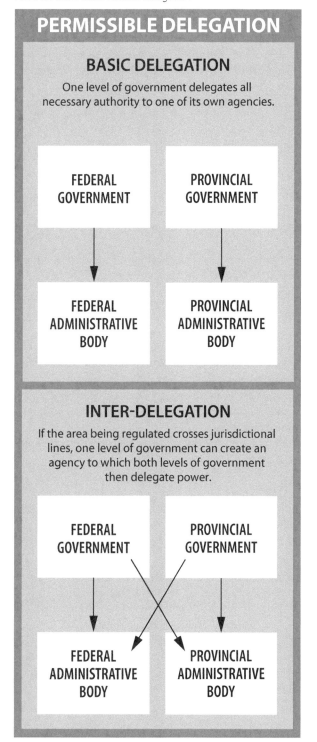

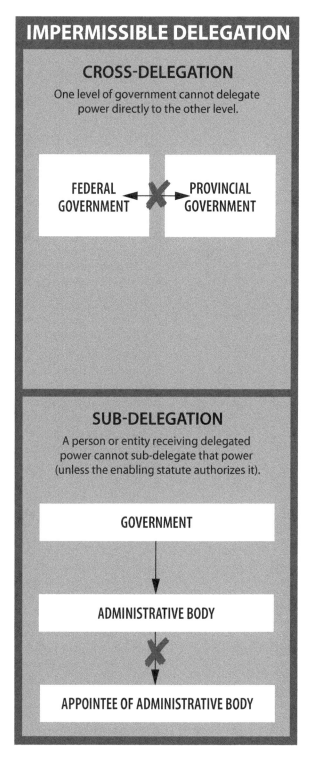

Legislative Functions

Administrative agencies fulfill legislative functions in two main areas: (1) municipal institutions making bylaws, and (2) quasi-judicial tribunals creating rules of procedure.

In the case of municipalities, the delegation of legislative authority to administrative agencies works in the following way. The provincial or territorial legislation that provides for the incorporation of local governments delegates to these governments the power to pass bylaws. These bylaws concern a wide range of municipal matters, including the following:

- raising taxes for schools and utilities,
- setting zoning requirements, and
- city planning and land use.

The provincial or territorial legislation sets out procedures for passing bylaws, and these procedures usually parallel those for enacting primary legislation (see Chapter 5). As with primary legislation, for example, the enacting of bylaws usually requires three readings and the opportunity for public input.

Administrative tribunals with quasi-judicial powers can also fulfill legislative functions insofar as they are frequently empowered to make their own rules governing how they hold hearings and how they resolve disputes.

Administrative Functions

Many executive or administrative functions are commonly delegated to administrative bodies. The issuing of licences and permits is one such function. In Canada, licences are mandatory for numerous activities. This country requires, for example, driver's licences, fishing and hunting licences, business licences, liquor licences, broadcasting licences, special event permits, building permits, and pollution permits. All of these licences and permits require applications to administrative agencies.

Administrative agencies perform many other functions, too, in their decision-making capacity. Among these functions are the following:

- ordering expropriations of property,
- authorizing adoptions,
- issuing discipline orders (in the case of administrative bodies that regulate trades or professions),
- granting passports,
- making dispensations or deportation orders in immigration cases, and
- granting pardons.

Administrative decision making—for example, dealing with applications of various kinds, or deciding who will be granted a licence and who will not—involves an element of discretion. The enabling legislation will offer guidelines about the exercise of delegated power. In the end, however, an official in an administrative agency has considerable discretion regarding his or her decisions. This can lead to abuse of power.

Quasi-Judicial Functions

Many administrative agencies exercise quasi-judicial functions by resolving disputes between opposing parties. In this capacity, these bodies are **administrative tribunals**, although, like all administrative agencies, they are still considered part of the executive branch of government. When administrative agencies are acting in a court-like capacity, they can be thought of as cousins to the inferior courts. (As we have discussed, one important constitutional limitation relating to such tribunals is that they cannot too closely resemble section 96 courts—that is, provincial superior courts—in their operation.)

The difference between administrative tribunals and inferior courts is that the former function more quickly and less formally than the latter. This is in keeping with their relatively limited jurisdiction in comparison to the courts' jurisdiction. (See Figure 7.1 on page 175 for the position of administrative tribunals in the overall Canadian court system.)

Generally speaking, administrative tribunals reduce the pressure on an overburdened court system and, in some areas, help alleviate concerns about access to justice. Human rights tribunals play an integral role in the protection of civil liberties in the private sector (see Chapter 8). In Canada, tribunals play an important role in adjudicating disputes in other areas too. Table 12.1 lists a few of the many Canadian tribunals.

It is sometimes asked whether judicial independence—that is, the principle that judges should be free to make decisions based on the law, without threat of negative consequences should their decisions be unpopular (see Chapter 7)—applies to administrative tribunals. The answer varies according to the tribunal. Generally speaking, tribunal members do not have the same kind of salary and tenure protection as judges do. The tribunal's enabling statute will specify what protections, if any, have been afforded the tribunal's members. Apart from the enabling statutes, there are also—in some jurisdictions in Canada—certain "general" statutes regulating administrative tribunals, and these may provide for some form of institutional independence. In British Columbia, for instance, the *Administrative Tribunals Act* gives administrative tribunals in that province "the power to control [their] own processes and [to] may make rules respecting practice and procedure to facilitate the just and timely resolution of the matters before [them]."[6] It is necessary to review these statutes to determine a tribunal's degree of judicial independence.

The Public's Interaction with Administrative Bodies

Most interactions between the public and administrative agencies occur in connection with the latter's exercise of administrative or quasi-judicial functions. But tribunals' legislative functions can be particularly significant where the public is concerned. These legislative activities are the source, for example, of proposed municipal bylaws that may affect the public interest, and the process may allow for members of the public to consult with the tribunals about such bylaws.

Generally speaking, there are two sets of rules for the public to be aware of when dealing with administrative bodies: substantive rules and procedural rules.

Substantive Rules

Substantive rules are the public's fundamental rights and obligations with respect to an administrative regime. For the most part, these rules will be found in the relevant legislation. For example, if a person were applying for a broadcasting licence from the Canadian Radio-television and Telecommunications Commission (CRTC), the substantive rules of which the applicant needs to be aware—for example, Canadian-content restrictions and the various media delivery limitations—are located in the *Canadian Radio-television and Telecommunications Commission Act*, the *Broadcasting Act*, and a few other statutes, along with the

---

6   SBC 2004, c 45, s 11. See also Alberta's *Administrative Procedures and Jurisdiction Act*, RSA 2000, c A-3; and Ontario's *Statutory Powers Procedure Act*, RSO 1990, c S.22.

TABLE 12.1   Administrative Tribunals by Subject and Jurisdiction

SUBJECT	JURISDICTION	ADMINISTRATIVE TRIBUNALS
Access to Information	British Columbia	Information and Privacy Commissioner
	Ontario	Information and Privacy Commissioner
Aeronautics	Federal	Canada Civil Aviation Tribunal
Corporate, Commercial Law	Federal	Competition Tribunal
	British Columbia	BC Securities Commission, Commercial Appeals Commission, Liquor Appeal Board
	Ontario	Securities Commission
Energy	Federal	National Energy Board
	Alberta	Energy Resources Conservation Board
	British Columbia	BC Utilities Commission
	Ontario	Energy Board
Environmental Law	Alberta	Environmental Appeal Board
	Ontario	Environmental Review Tribunal
Forestry Law	British Columbia	Forest Practices Board
Human Rights	Federal	Canadian Human Rights Tribunal
	British Columbia	BC Human Rights Tribunal
	Nova Scotia	Human Rights Commission
	Ontario	Human Rights Tribunal of Ontario
Immigration	Federal	Immigration and Refugee Board of Canada
Intellectual Property	Federal	Copyright Board, Patent Appeal Board, Trade-marks Opposition Board
Labour and Employment Law	Federal	Canada Industrial Relations Council, Public Service Relations Board, Canadian Artists and Producers Professional Relations Tribunal, Umpires under the *Employment Insurance Act*, Pension Appeals Board
	Alberta	Workers' Compensation Appeals Commission
	British Columbia	Labour Relations Board, Employment Standards Tribunal, Workers' Compensation Board
	Manitoba	Labour Board
	Ontario	Workplace Safety and Insurance Appeals Tribunal
Telecommunications	Federal	Canadian Radio-television and Telecommunications Commission
Trade	Federal	Canadian International Trade Tribunal
Transportation	Federal	Canadian Transportation Agency

regulations passed pursuant to them. The substantive rules will also include any CRTC and judicial interpretations of the legislation.

Occasionally, substantive rules may be found in the common law as well, such as in the area of civil liberties (for example, the right of free speech).

A review of all the relevant substantive rules is the first step in dealing successfully with administrative agencies.

Procedural Rules

Many administrative agencies have established their own rules of practice and procedure that members of the public must follow in order to move forward with applications and hearings. These rules concern such things as what documents need to be filed with the agency, who else needs to receive copies, what the timelines are, and whether legal representation is allowed. Generally, the procedural rules for administrative agencies are less formal or rigid than those for court proceedings.

When trying to determine what the procedural rules are, you begin by checking the enabling legislation, then proceed to the administrative agency itself. Checking agency websites and contacting agency personnel are generally the best ways to obtain information about procedural rules.

In addition to considering the legislated rules that are in place for a particular administrative agency, you must also consider common law rules. Common law rules concerning procedural fairness and natural justice in relation to administrative bodies are well established (see below). They must be followed unless they have been abrogated by the legislation.

Challenging Administrative Decisions

A party negatively affected by an administrative decision (or action) may wish to challenge it. There are various means of doing so. The following discussion primarily concerns decisions involving administrative and quasi-judicial functions.

Internal Means of Challenge

As a first step, a party wishing to contest an administrative decision should exhaust all internal means of challenge. The agency structure may have mechanisms providing for this. Once these options have been exhausted, it may be necessary to consider intervention by the courts.

Challenging in the Courts

There are two ways in which an administrative decision can be challenged in the courts: on appeal or by judicial review. Note that the expression "judicial review" in this context refers to the review of the decisions of administrative bodies and is not the same as judicial review of provincial and federal legislation on constitutional grounds as discussed earlier in Chapter 4.

The process of appealing an administrative decision is generally similar to the process of appealing a court decision. The difference has to do with the scope of the appeal available and the available remedies. When a court decision is appealed, the court engages in a full substantive reconsideration of the merits of the decision, corrects any errors that were made, and makes orders as it normally would. With an administrative decision, the scope of the appeal and the available remedies are always subject to the enabling legislation. Generally speaking, *any right to appeal only exists if the enabling legislation expressly provides for it*. There is no inherent, common law right to appeal an administrative decision. Where the enabling legislation does provide for such a right, the person contesting the administrative decision must go this route before mounting a challenge by the other possible means—namely, judicial review.

Judicial review, as a means of challenging an administrative decision, is a final option. Sara Blake has made this point as follows:

> Application to the court for review of a decision of an inferior tribunal should be made only as a last resort. Parties should take advantage of internal procedures available to a tribunal to correct its errors and of rights of appeal granted by statute. Only when those routes are unavailable, or have been tried without success, should parties resort to judicial review.[7]

Judicial review of an administrative decision tends to be more limited in scope than proceeding by way of an appeal (when such a right is granted by statute). Substantive reviews are possible, but they are not typical. When it comes to procedural reviews, for example, the courts are confined to reviewing the "process" by which decisions have been reached.

Jurisdiction of Superior Courts to Review

The provincial superior courts have an inherent, common law power to oversee and review the decisions of both inferior courts and administrative boards and tribunals. This jurisdiction has been modified by legislation. The *Federal Courts Act* assigns exclusive jurisdiction to review federal tribunals to the Federal Court and to the Federal Court of Appeal.[8]

Sections 18 and 18.1 of the *Federal Courts Act* combine to give the Federal Court exclusive power to review federal agencies in general. The exceptions are set out in section 28 of the Act; it gives the Federal Court of Appeal exclusive jurisdiction to review the decisions of certain federal agencies, which are specifically identified. Section 28 provides in part:

> 28(1) The Federal Court of Appeal has jurisdiction to hear and determine applications for judicial review made in respect of any of the following federal boards, commissions or other tribunals:
>
> (a) the Board of Arbitration established by the *Canada Agricultural Products Act*;
>
> (b) the Review Tribunal established by the *Canada Agricultural Products Act*;
>
> (b.1) the Conflict of Interest and Ethics Commissioner appointed under section 81 of the *Parliament of Canada Act*;
>
> (c) the Canadian Radio-television and Telecommunications Commission established by the *Canadian Radio-television and Telecommunications Commission Act*;
>
> (d) the Pension Appeals Board established by the *Canada Pension Plan*;
>
> (e) the Canadian International Trade Tribunal established by the *Canadian International Trade Tribunal Act*;
>
> (f) the National Energy Board established by the *National Energy Board Act*.

---

7 Sara Blake, *Administrative Law in Canada*, 4th ed (Markham, Ont: LexisNexis, 2006) at 172.

8 *Federal Courts Act*, RSC 1985, c F-7.

Section 28 goes on to list other tribunals over which the Federal Court of Appeal has the power of review. These include the following:

- the Canada Industrial Relations Board,
- the Public Service Labour Relations Board,
- the Copyright Board,
- the Canadian Transportation Agency,
- the Canadian Artists and Producers Professional Relations Tribunal,
- the Competition Tribunal,
- the Public Servants Disclosure Protection Tribunal, and
- the Specific Claims Tribunal.

To summarize, the *Federal Courts Act* gives the Federal Court of Appeal exclusive jurisdiction over the certain federal agencies and the Federal Court exclusive jurisdiction over all the others. The provincial superior courts, based on what remains of their inherent common law jurisdiction, have exclusive jurisdiction over provincial agencies, but have no general power of review over federal ones. Review of territorial tribunals is assigned by federal legislation to the territorial superior courts.

Privative Clauses

A privative clause is a statutory provision that restricts or prevents altogether the judicial review of an administrative agency's decision. Legislatures sometimes include such provisions because they want a particular administrative process to be final. There can be a variety of reasons for their wanting this finality—for example, the special expertise of the tribunal officials may make judicial review of their decision especially difficult.

The specific terms of the statutory provision will determine the limits of judicial review. Judicial review is always a possibility, however, whatever the legislation says. Even where a privative clause states that the administrative agency's decision is "final and conclusive" or states that the tribunal has "exclusive jurisdiction" in the matter or states—even more strongly—that judicial review is prohibited, the court has the jurisdiction to review. Any attempt by a legislature to enact a privative clause so strong as to exclude review in all cases—even in a case, for example, where a tribunal has exceeded its jurisdiction—would likely be declared unconstitutional.

This is not to say that the privative clause has no function. The strength of the privative clause is one of the factors the court will consider in determining how much deference it will pay to the administrative decision. The clearer and stronger the privative clause, the more the court will defer to the administrative agency's decision. In the end, however, the courts always have the right to review an administrative agency's decision. Let's say, for example—to take an extreme case—a labour board passed a decision ordering a union official to assassinate the head of a multinational corporation. In such a case, even a privative clause clearly prohibiting review by the court under any circumstances would not prevent the judicial review of the board's decision.

Grounds for Review

There are several possible bases for challenging administrative decisions by review. They are variously named in federal, provincial, and territorial legislation as well as in the academic literature on the subject. Recent case law emphasizes three broad grounds: (1) substantive review, (2) review of discretionary decisions, and (3) procedural review. These grounds are distinct, but, in a given case, more than one ground may be cited (see Box 12.1).

SUBSTANTIVE REVIEW

Substantive review refers to a review that considers both the legal and factual bases of the tribunal's analysis. When conducting a review of this kind, the courts have first to decide what **standard of review** is applicable. The standard of review defines the level of deference the court pays to the tribunal. The SCC has recently simplified this decision-making area, stating that there are only two standards of review: (1) correctness, and (2) reasonableness.[9]

When, in the course of a substantive review, the court is reviewing the legal basis of an administrative decision, it applies the correctness standard and pays no deference to the tribunal. It simply substitutes its decision for the tribunal's. The legality of a decision is in issue when the court is reviewing fundamental questions of law—for example, whether the tribunal had the jurisdiction to make the particular decision being reviewed. When a tribunal has made a decision it had no authority to make under the enabling legislation, it has exceeded its jurisdiction. Such a decision is said to be *ultra vires*, or without jurisdiction. (A decision by a tribunal that is within its jurisdiction is *intra vires*.) Jurisdictional questions usually turn on statutory interpretation and the intended scope of delegated power under the legislation. For example, a provincial human rights tribunal would clearly have no jurisdiction to issue a federal patent for a new type of cellphone. The courts would review such a decision according to the correctness standard.

When reviewing decisions with regard to less fundamental questions of law, or to fact, discretion, or policy, the court applies the reasonableness standard. Here, instead of simply substituting its own decision for the tribunal's, the court pays deference to the tribunal. It does so in the following way. First, it will determine if any previous cases have already defined the level of deference owed the tribunal. If such cases exist and a level of deference has been established, the court will generally follow the established level. If there are no precedents of this kind, the court will determine the level of deference by referring to a number of factors, including the following:

- whether the enabling legislation contains a privative clause, and
- whether the agency adjudicator possesses expertise in relation to the matter in question.

If the legislation contains a privative clause and the adjudicator who made the decision possesses expertise in the area, the decision under review will have to be clearly unreasonable before the court will overturn it.

It is the reference to different standards of review that distinguishes judicial review of an administrative decision from substantive review based on a statutory right of appeal. In the latter case, the standard is always correctness in the opinion of the court.

REVIEW OF DISCRETIONARY DECISIONS

Review of discretionary decisions is hard to categorize. Depending on how discretion is exercised, it can have aspects of either a substantive error or a procedural one (as described next).

Administrative officials must exercise any discretion delegated to them under legislation with a view to furthering the legislative objectives. The granting of licences, for example,

---

9   *Dunsmuir v New Brunswick*, 2008 SCC 9, [2008] 1 SCR 190.

involves a discretionary element (that is, the agency *may* grant a licence to someone who applies for one). In exercising discretion, administrative officials must not act arbitrarily or capriciously or be influenced by factors that are unconnected with advancing the legislative purposes—for example, by considerations related to personal gain, religious beliefs, or political leanings (see Box 1.8). Conversely, they must not omit to consider relevant factors under the legislation (see Box 12.1).

PROCEDURAL REVIEW

Arguments concerning process or procedure generate the most litigation. Even if there are no substantive issues surrounding a decision and no problems with the exercise of discretion, there may still be procedural grounds for review.

At common law, administrative officials are required to adhere to standards of **fairness**, also referred to as **procedural fairness** or **natural justice**, when making decisions that affect a person's interests. Natural justice dictates that certain "rights" will be accorded to persons engaged with an administrative process, regardless of whether the process involved is administrative or quasi-judicial. Some of these rights include the following:

- the right to notice (in other words, the right to know what the opposing case is),
- the right to be heard and to respond,
- the right to representation,
- the right to cross-examine,
- the right to reasons, and
- the right to an adjudicator who is free from bias or an appearance of bias.

BOX 12.1

Discretion and Procedural Fairness in Administrative Decisions

In 1992, Mavis Baker was ordered to be deported to Jamaica. She came to Canada in 1981, as a visitor, but never received permanent resident status. When her visitor's visa expired, she stayed in Canada and worked illegally as a live-in domestic worker. During her time in Canada she had four children, all Canadian citizens. She also suffered from mental illness for which she was receiving treatment.

The deportation order required her to apply for permanent residency status from outside Canada. She argued that she should be exempted from this requirement on humanitarian and compassionate grounds; the order would cause her to be separated from her children, and treatment for her mental condition might not be available in Jamaica.

The senior immigration officer handling her file gave her the opportunity to make written submissions, but not to appear in person and make oral sub-

missions. She argued that this infringed her right to procedural fairness. Her case eventually made it to the SCC.* The SCC held that procedural fairness was a flexible and variable concept. She had been given the opportunity to respond fully and completely in writing, and this was sufficient in the circumstances. The Court deemed that there was no violation of the requirement of procedural fairness.

However, the Court went on to hold that the immigration officer, in exercising his discretion, had failed to consider important factors relevant under the legislation, such as the impact of the decision on Ms. Baker's children. The order was overturned on this basis.

* *Baker v Canada (Ministry of Citizenship and Immigration)*, [1999] 2 SCR 817.

The degree of fairness and the number of these "rights" that natural justice requires in a particular case will vary according to a number of factors, including the following:

1. the nature of the decision to be made by the administrative body,
2. the relationship existing between that body and the individual, and
3. the effect of that decision on the individual's rights.

Legislation may also dictate that certain procedural standards be adhered to in a given situation. Generally, the more significant the decision's impact, the more procedural safeguards will be required.[10] For instance, a decision that resulted in a person losing her job or means of livelihood would trigger more procedural protection than a decision denying a person the right to light fireworks in her backyard on her birthday.

Remedies on Review

A number of special common law remedies are available to those who have suffered as a result of substantive or procedural errors made by administrative bodies. These remedies, called **prerogative writs**, are granted following an application to the superior courts. There are various kinds of prerogative writs (see Box 12.2). Historically, subjects would apply to the Crown, which could issue these writs as part of the monarch's royal prerogative power (see Chapter 6). Control over these writs has long since passed into the hands of the courts.

In addition to prerogative writs, the courts also have the power to grant injunctive relief (that is, ordering someone to do something) as well as declaratory relief (that is, simply declaring what the legal position is). Most provinces and territories have now enacted legislation simplifying the procedure for applying for prerogative writs and for these other remedies. At one time, a separate application was required for each prerogative writ. Ontario and British Columbia have the simplest application procedure. In these provinces, one statutory application for judicial review serves as an application for all available remedies (except damages).[11]

In addition to any rights of appeal or review, a person challenging an administrative decision may also have a private law claim, depending on the circumstances.[12]

Public International Law

In recent years, the following global issues have highlighted the importance of **public international law (or international law)**:

- terrorism and state responses to it,
- continuing regional and ethnic conflicts around the world,

---

10 See *Knight v Indian Head School Division No 19*, [1990] 1 SCR 653, the leading case in Canada on procedural fairness.

11 See the *Judicial Review Procedure Act*, RSBC 1996, c 241; and *Judicial Review Procedure Act*, RSO 1990, c J.1.

12 Sometimes it is possible to sue agencies in negligence, if they have been careless in carrying out their duties under legislation. A number of cases involving negligent inspections have resulted in successful claims for damages. For example, see *Just v British Columbia*, [1989] 2 SCR 1228. And if a government official abuses his discretionary power, damages in tort based on a claim of "abuse of power" may be recoverable (see Box 1.8).

Prerogative Writs

The main prerogative writs are the following:

- Writ of *certiorari*: In the context of Canadian judicial review proceedings, this kind of writ is used to "quash" or overturn an administrative body's decision in cases where there have been substantive errors, abuse of discretion, or procedural unfairness.
- Writ of prohibition: This writ is an order, issued by the superior court, requiring the administrative body not to proceed with a planned action.
- Writ of *mandamus*: This writ is the reverse of a writ of prohibition. It is an order by the superior court requiring the administrative body to proceed with an action it wouldn't have proceeded with otherwise (for example, the court might order the administrative body to issue a permit).

- Writ of *quo warranto*: With this remedy, a public official is ordered to give up his office because he has not been validly appointed. Such an order would of course prevent the official from making any official decisions.
- Writ of *habeas corpus*: This most ancient of the prerogative writs is mentioned in the *Magna Carta* of 1215. It concerns the lawfulness of individuals' being detained by government authorities. Today it is most significant in connection with the detention of immigrants (by immigration officials), of prisoners (by prison officials), of children (by child protection agencies), and of the mentally handicapped (by mental health facilities).

- the fragility of the global economy,
- a growing awareness of the economic interdependence of nations, and
- major changes to the environment.

The following is a general overview of the basic concepts and principles of international law, its sources, and its methods of enforcement. For a history of international law, see Box 12.3.

What Is International Law?

In simple terms, international law is the law that is primarily concerned with regulating the relationship between independent states. Generally speaking, it is a type of public law (see the two-part definition at the beginning of this chapter). But that definition provides little insight into its depth or range of influence. International law is a vast, complex, and developing field of regulation that concerns all of humankind. John Currie has described it as follows:

> Public international law is not so much an area or topic of the law as it is an entire legal system that is conceptually distinct from the national legal systems that regulate daily life within states.[13]

The following question is frequently posed: Is international law about "law" at all, or is it about other types of norms? International law lacks a number of the elements that characterize most domestic legal systems. It lacks, for example, a centralized law-making structure, and it lacks executive and judicial branches that administer and apply the law. It also lacks an effective enforcement mechanism. Despite this, there is a general respect for the system of international law that is in place; its rules are followed more than they are broken.

---

13   John Currie, *Public International Law*, 2d ed (Markham, Ont: LexisNexis, 2008) at 1.

BOX 12.3

History of International Law

Scholars recognize three distinct periods in the history of international law: (1) the so-called primitive period; (2) the classical, or traditional, period; and (3) the modern period.

Primitive Period: Before 1648

In the period leading up to the mid-1600s, relations between states in Europe were marked by a tension between two opposing ideas or premises:

1. States are free to do as they please in the international arena based on the "might is right" principle.
2. In both international and domestic affairs, states are subject to overarching natural law principles—that is, principles derived from a higher power or source that guides our behaviour and offers us an ideal standard.

Notions of what those natural law principles were precisely and the degree of control they ought to have over a state's actions varied according to the writer. A natural law thinker, Hugo Grotius, whose writings on international relations culminated in *On the Law of War and Peace* (1625), is generally regarded as the father of modern international law, and this work as the seminal international law treatise. He espoused a natural law system based on "reason" and asserted the notion of the interdependence of states.

Classical or Traditional Period: 1648–1919

The Peace of Westphalia was a series of treaties made in 1648 that marked the end of two long-standing wars: the Thirty Years' War between France and the Habsburg rulers of the Holy Roman Empire, and the Eighty Years' War between Spain and the Dutch. These treaties were significant because they clearly gave the principle of state sovereignty priority over other considerations such as religious and dynastic allegiances. State sovereignty focuses on the right of a state to control itself. Religious and dynastic allegiances recognize controls from outside.

The Peace of Westphalia marks the beginning of the classical or traditional period of international law. In the centuries that followed it, secularism in state affairs grew and religious influences declined. There was a rise in nationalism, and the independence of sovereign states in international dealings became entrenched. Grotius's idea of interdependence manifested itself primarily through treaty making.

In the 1800s, positivistic thinking, which was based on empiricism (or knowledge from experience), looked at state conduct as a possible basis of laws between states. In other words, the theory that custom—the established conduct of states in their international relations—could be a source of international law began to take hold. Most of this thinking arose in Europe, but eventually Middle Eastern and Oriental states also started to accept these general principles concerning state sovereignty, treaty making, and custom.

Modern Period: 1919–Present

Modern international law dates from the end of the First World War and the Paris Peace Conference of 1919, which led to the creation of the League of Nations in the same year. The League was an intergovernmental organization consisting of 42 member states whose main purpose was to maintain world peace. It sought to resolve international disputes through negotiation, and when these negotiation failed, it relied heavily on its strongest members to enforce its resolutions. Though US president Woodrow Wilson was a driving force behind the League's founding, the United States never joined it, and it was ineffective in stopping the Axis powers in the leadup to the Second World War. It was officially disbanded in 1946.

In 1945, the UN was formed as the successor organization to the League of Nations. Today, it has 193 member nations. The UN and the UN Charter are at the centre of the modern system of international law. The guiding principles of international law have never been so clearly expressed and actively developed as they are today. Nor have they ever been so widely accepted as binding.

There are over 190 independent countries in the world today, and even with the cultural, religious, ethnic, political, and economic differences that exist among these countries, most of them recognize the need for a stable framework of agreed-upon rules that can help them peacefully coexist.

It is important to keep in mind that not all legal relationships that involve an *international* component are the province of public international law. Private law relationships may have transnational aspects to them—for example, in cases where individuals or corporations residing in different countries do business together. This is the province of *private* international law (or *conflict of laws*), as noted in the brief discussion of this area in Chapter 10.

Subjects and Objects in International Law

International law recognizes a loose distinction between "subjects" and "objects." A **"subject" of international law** has an "international legal personality" and is capable of possessing international rights and obligations. An *object* is the focus of a subject's rights and obligations, and it can be a person, an entity, a geographical area, or a resource.

The main subjects are states. However, there are no clear limitations either on who or what can be a subject or on who or what can be an object. States can, by agreement or recognition, confer statehood on new members. Furthermore, a state can be a subject in one context and an object in another. So can an individual person. For example, a country as subject might owe an individual as object certain human rights obligations, and an individual as subject might owe a country as object an obligation not to perpetrate or orchestrate war crimes. The entities in the following list are "objects" in some contexts but have limited "subject" status in others:

- countries such as Taiwan, Palestine, and Tibet, which are not fully recognized as "states" internationally;
- peoples seeking self-determination (ethnic groups or indigenous peoples within countries who don't fully accept state control), such as the Basques of Spain, the Chechens of Russia, the Kurdish people of the Middle East, or the Québécois separatists of Canada;
- International or intergovernmental organizations (IGOs), such as the North Atlantic Treaty Organization (NATO) or the European Union;
- Non-governmental organizations (NGOs), such as Oxfam and Greenpeace;
- individuals; and
- corporations (multinational or otherwise).

State Sovereignty and State Jurisdiction

Two key and related concepts in international law are *state sovereignty* and *state jurisdiction*. **State sovereignty** refers to the state's exclusive power in certain areas—for example, the power to make, administer, and adjudicate its own laws in relation to itself and its own citizens and residents. It is also clear that sovereign states can enter into relations with other states—for example, to make treaties. **State jurisdiction** is the area of control within which a state's sovereignty can be exercised. The area can be physical or territorial, or it can be conceptual—related, for example, to a subject matter such as civil or criminal liability. States have jurisdiction over almost all matters within their territorial limits.

States have restricted jurisdiction over matters outside their territorial limits. For nations bordering oceans and seas, their jurisdiction over the area off the coast is based on a complex system of customs and conventions; there are rules for 12-mile limits (exclusive control over virtually all matters), 200-mile limits (exclusive economic control), and other limits. With respect to its own nationals or citizens, a state may exercise jurisdiction over them outside its territorial limits if they "injure" the state there—for example, by threatening its security. (The term "nationals" usually refers to individual citizens, but it can also include corporations and ships that fly the state's flag.)

A state can also exercise jurisdiction over non-nationals—citizens of a different country—outside its territorial limits for conduct that affects or has affected the state and amounts to a crime against humanity.[14] (See the discussion of international criminal law in the next section.) Whether a state's extraterritorial jurisdiction can involve the use of force in another state to apprehend or punish a person (regardless of whether the conduct was committed territorially or extraterritorially) is another issue. Claiming jurisdiction over someone or something extraterritorially is one thing. Using force in another country is another. There are peaceful methods of exercising jurisdiction, such as diplomacy and international court processes. It is generally accepted that the use of such force requires the consent of the other state.

State Responsibility and State Immunity

Another important idea in international law is that of **state responsibility**. This refers to the state's accountability for breaches of international obligations. The equivalent of responsibility, in domestic law, is a person's being required to pay damages for breach of contract, or being sent to jail for committing a serious crime. Until recently, this area was unclear with respect to international law. In 2001, however, the International Law Commission adopted a draft set of articles which, while not yet officially adopted by the United Nations or by individual states at the time of writing, is gaining wide acceptance. The International Court of Justice (ICJ)—the main judicial arm of the United Nations—has already cited this set of articles with approval. It should pave the way for much greater certainty in the area of accountability.[15]

State immunity can be thought of as the flip side of state responsibility, although it is not precisely that. Based on customary international law, state immunity generally applies where one state, its representatives (mainly diplomats and consuls), or their property have been made subject to judicial proceedings in another state. This immunity, when claimed, prevents the judicial proceedings from progressing any further.

There are questions about how absolute this immunity is and what exceptions to it there might be. In 1982, Canada passed the *State Immunity Act*, which clearly sets out a number of exceptions. Under this legislation, states and their representatives do not enjoy immunity in Canada either in relation to commercial activities—for example, buying and selling—or when they cause death, personal injury, or property damage in this country. There could be contractual, tortious or criminal liability arising from such activities, depending on the circumstances.

The exceptions set out in Canada's *State Immunity Act* appear to be broader than the exceptions established by international custom. This disparity could prove problematic: for example, if Canadian courts were to permit judicial proceedings against a foreign official based on the exceptions set out in the Act, these proceedings could be contrary to international law.

---

14 See *Attorney-General of Israel v Eichmann*, judgment of the District Court of Jerusalem (1961), translated and reprinted in (1962) 56 Am J Int'l L 805.

15 *Draft Articles on the Responsibility of States for Internationally Wrongful Acts* (International Law Commission, 2001).

Finally, state immunity does not apply in international settings or venues—the ICJ, for example, which is not under the control of a single state. State immunity is territorially based. When it does apply, it is confined to protecting one state or its representatives from having to submit to judicial proceedings in another state.

The UN Charter: Core Principles of International Law

The United Nations (UN) is at the centre of the modern system of international law, and its principles are expressed in its constitution, the *Charter of the United Nations* (UN Charter). These are core principles of international law and serve as guides for state behaviour, treaties, and policy making.

Article 1 of the UN Charter sets out the *purposes* of the UN. The following is a summary of them:

1. to maintain international peace and security, and to resolve international disputes in conformity with the principles of justice and international law;
2. to develop friendly relations among nations based on a respect for equal rights and self-determination of peoples;
3. to solve economic, social, cultural, or humanitarian problems of an international character, and to promote respect for human rights through cooperation; and
4. to be a centre for harmonizing the actions of nations in the attainment of these common ends.

Article 2 describes the *principles* that the UN and its members are to follow in pursuing the purposes identified in the Charter. The following is a summary of these principles:

1. recognizing sovereign equality of members,
2. fulfilling obligations in good faith,
3. settling international disputes peacefully,
4. not threatening or using force against other states,
5. assisting the UN as necessary,
6. respecting non-member states, and
7. not intervening in the domestic affairs of a state except to maintain or restore international peace, or in self-defence.

Sources of International Law

The principal sources of international law are set out in article 38 of the Statute of the International Court of Justice (ICJ Statute).[16] They are as follows:

> a. international conventions, whether general or particular, establishing rules expressly recognized by the contesting states [that is, *treaties*],
> b. international custom, as evidence of a general practice accepted as law [that is, *international custom*],
> c. general principles of law recognized by civilized nations [that is, *general principles of law*], and

---

16   The ICJ Statute, which constitutes the ICJ, is annexed to the UN Charter and can only be changed by a two-thirds majority of the General Assembly of the UN.

    d. subject to the provisions of Article 59, judicial decisions and the teachings
of the most highly qualified publicists of the various nations, as subsidiary means
for the determination of rules of law [that is, *domestic judgments and commentary*].

According to article 38, then, the main sources of international law are (1) treaties, (2) international custom, (3) general principles of law, and (4) domestic judgments and commentary. Other sources of international law include resolutions by international organizations, such as the UN, and self-imposed obligations by states.

Treaties

Treaties are agreements between states concerning their legal rights and obligations in relation to specific matters. As noted above, they can be bilateral (between two states) or multilateral (between three or more states—for example, the UN Charter). There are hundreds of current treaties in the world today covering a multitude of topics, including state privileges and immunities, human rights, refugees and stateless persons, drugs, human trafficking, health, international trade, oceans, outer space, disarmament, and the environment.

    Making treaties is governed by another treaty: the Vienna Convention on the Law of Treaties (1980) (VCLT). The VCLT essentially codifies the customary rules concerning treaty making, rules that were already in place in 1980. As of 2010, the VCLT has been ratified by 111 nations, and even states that have not formally signed on to it recognize it as an authoritative guide. It applies only to treaties between states, not to agreements between states and non-state entities such as IGOs (public or governmental organizations created by treaty or agreement between states, such as the European Union or the Arab League) or NGOs (organizations established by individuals or associations of individuals, such as Greenpeace or Amnesty International). Nor does it apply to agreements between IGOs and NGOs.

    The VCLT contains rules about a number of issues related to treaties, including their form, validity, interpretation, and dispute resolution. Regarding the latter, for example, the VCLT prescribes that any dispute involving *jus cogens*—that is, important international customs that have achieved a special status, as described below—must go before the ICJ.

International Custom

An international custom is a settled, general practice between states that has been accepted as law. Such customs develop over time. They begin as limited practices that states engage in not with a view to making law but to protecting their own interests, such as customs prohibiting genocide and torture. Some of the criteria defining a custom are the following:

1. *Duration.* The longer the practice has existed, the more likely it is to have evolved into a custom. However, no particular amount of time is required to have elapsed before a practice qualifies as a custom, and the ICJ does not emphasize this element.

2. *Consistency and uniformity of practice.* The practice must be one that has not varied substantially during its existence.

3. *Generality of practice.* For a practice to be considered a custom, there must be "substantial universality" in its use by world states. Absolute universality is not required.

4. *Opinio juris.* This term (Latin for "opinion of law") refers to the *belief* that an action is carried out because there is a legal obligation to do so; it is sometimes described as the "psychological" element of custom. States' official declarations of their motivations for some action could be evidence of *opinio juris*. In other words,

a state may believe it has an obligation to do something, declare that it does have this obligation, and that becomes *opinio juris*. The more evidence of this kind exists, the more likely a practice will be held to be custom.[17]

The criterion of "substantial universality" means that not all states need to engage in or accept a practice that other states regard as a custom. If a state has persistently refrained from or rejected a practice that has developed into a custom for other states, that state is not considered subject to it.

As described below, some important customs reach the status of *jus cogens*, and have a special status in international law. They take precedence over treaties that conflict with them. Apart from customs that have this *jus cogens* status, the interrelation between custom and treaties is a complex and somewhat unclear area.

General Principles of Law

Article 38 of the ICJ Statute lists "general principles of law" as another one of the sources of international law. This provision is not clear and has been the subject of much debate. It appears to refer to principles of general application commonly found in domestic legal systems—for example, the principle of *res judicata*, which prevents the relitigation of an already fully litigated matter; and equitable principles such as estoppel, which requires a party to act consistently with previous actions or declarations of intention.

Domestic Judgments and Commentary

Article 38 categorizes this last-listed source of international law as a "subsidiary means for the determination of rules of law." This phrasing suggests that domestic judgments and commentary are not true sources at all, but rather secondary sources to help evidence or buttress the other formal sources. Not all jurists agree, and some believe that these domestic sources should be considered binding.

Other Sources of International Law

UN Security Council resolutions are binding sources of international law. The Security Council is set up under the UN Charter and is charged with the primary responsibility of maintaining international peace and security. It is composed of 15 member states, some of which have permanent places on the Council; other states are elected for two-year periods. Its resolutions are made binding by virtue of article 25 of the UN Charter: "The Members of the United Nations agree to accept and carry out the decisions of the Security Council in accordance with the present Charter."

Resolutions of the UN General Assembly—which is made up of all the members of the UN—are recommendations only and are not a source of international law. The contents of these resolutions, however, may evidence other sources of international law, such as customs.

Unilateral declarations by states about their obligations can also amount to sources of international law. However, they are only binding on the state making the declaration.

---

17   Ian Brownlie, *Principles of Public International Law*, 7th ed (Oxford: Oxford University Press, 2008) at 7-10.

Hierarchy of Sources

Is there a hierarchy among the sources of international law listed above? If the sources disagree, which takes precedence? In the Canadian domestic system, when there is a conflict between legislation and common law, the doctrine of parliamentary sovereignty dictates that the legislation takes precedence. Is there a similar kind of doctrine in international law?

The short answer is a qualified "yes." Absolute certainty in this regard is not possible, however, because there is no formal, binding international constitution. The ordering in article 38 does not appear to be determinative, and it is the following hierarchy that has the support of most jurists:

1. *Jus cogens.* Latin for "compelling law," **jus cogens** are overriding or peremptory principles of international law based on custom. They cannot be changed by treaty, only replaced by new customary rules. Examples of such fundamental custom-based principles in international law include the prohibitions against the aggressive use of force, against genocide, against racial discrimination, and against slavery and piracy.[18] Some customs, though compelling, are not considered overriding or peremptory and do not qualify as *jus cogens.* Where there is a conflict between treaties and these kinds of customs (that is, customs that are not *jus cogens*), the relationship is not clear.

2. *Law-making treaties.* Not all treaties make law in the sense of creating or evidencing general norms of international behaviour. When one does, usually in the form of a multilateral treaty, it becomes a principal source of international law. Examples of these kinds of law-making treaties include treaties about international human rights and the Geneva Conventions dealing with the humanitarian treatment of non-combatants during times of war. Not all treaties have this status, however; not all provide evidence of general norms of international behaviour. Some may simply be bilateral arrangements for limited purposes (for example, sharing a water source or a trade agreement). These types of treaties are sometimes referred to as "contract treaties" and are not a source of international law.

   The UN Charter provides that UN obligations take precedence over all other treaty obligations. Article 103 states: "In the event of a conflict between the obligations of the Members of the United Nations under the present Charter and their obligations under any other international agreement, their obligations under the present Charter shall prevail." The Charter is itself a treaty and contains obligations. According to article 103, then, these obligations would clearly take priority over all other treaty obligations. Article 103 also suggests that UN Security Council resolutions that are passed under the UN Charter and that create obligations would take priority over other treaty obligations.

3. *Other sources.* There does not appear to be any consensus about the relative authority of other sources of international law except insofar as they are all subordinate to custom and treaties.

In terms of the hierarchical ordering of the sources of international law, it is clear the *jus cogens* customs are first and that law-making treaties are second. Beyond that, there is no consensus.

---

18 *Ibid* at 510-11.

Relationship Between International Law and Domestic Law

It may appear that the UN Charter is the international equivalent of a nation's constitution and that the UN General Assembly is the equivalent of a legislature. The Secretariat—headed by the secretary-general, who is elected by the members—seems comparable to an executive branch of government. And the ICJ seems analogous to a nation's judiciary. The appearance, however, is not the reality.

This analogy breaks down on closer examination, for the simple reason that the UN is a voluntary organization. The General Assembly does not have the power to make binding laws, and the treaties that its members enter into are a matter of choice, not obligation. It is closer to a contract-facilitating organization than to a law-making power. The Secretariat has no laws to administer, and the ICJ's judgments have no precedential value the way decisions in common law jurisdictions do. Article 59 of the ICJ Statute expressly states the following: "The decision of the Court has no binding force except between the parties and in respect of that particular case." UN enforcement powers are also limited, as we discuss below. In short, the UN and its agencies do not have the same power on an international scale that parallel institutions have at the national level.

Reception of International Law into Canada

International law is not precisely analogous to domestic law. Nonetheless, it does exist, and there are increasingly well-defined sources for determining its content. In terms of how international laws are relevant at the state level, it is important to understand that there is a distinction between states' obligations to each other, and the binding force of international law *within* a state.

The principle of state sovereignty means that international law, in order to be binding within a state, needs to be implemented or adopted using that state's law-making machinery. With respect to treaties, article 26 of the VCLT requires parties to perform their treaty obligations in good faith, and article 27 states that parties cannot use their own internal legal systems as an excuse for not performing their treaty obligations. Countries must *implement* treaties before they become binding within their territories. This means they must enact legislation making the treaties part of their domestic law.

In Canada, this process is slightly complicated by the fact that our country is a federal state. Some treaties deal with areas that, under section 92 of the *Constitution Act, 1867*, are provincial areas of jurisdiction. These treaties require the provincial legislatures to pass statutes implementing them.[19] If the treaty covers a purely federal matter, such as criminal law, Parliament can implement the treaty by itself, with federal legislation.

International customs, unlike treaties, are presumptively *adopted* by the common law in Canada. However, such customs can be changed by clearly worded legislation passed by the appropriate level of government (see Box 12.4).

---

19 Section 132 of the *Constitution Act, 1867* appears to give the federal government the power to implement treaties by passing all necessary legislation, but it has been interpreted narrowly. The decision of the Privy Council in *Attorney-General of Canada v Attorney-General of Ontario (Labour Conventions)*, [1937] AC 326 established that treaties dealing with provincial subject matters require provincial legislation to implement them. For instance, when the federal government ratified the *United Nations Convention on Contracts for the International Sale of Goods* (1980), each province was required to pass legislation implementing it before it was binding within Canada. Sales of goods transactions generally fall within the "Property and Civil Rights" power belonging to the provinces (s 92(13)).

BOX 12.4

Does International Custom Apply *Inside* Canada?

In 1943, there was an international custom according to which a state was prohibited from taxing property within its own territory if the property was owned by a foreign state or by officials of the foreign state. That year, the province of Ontario delegated to the city of Ottawa and to another municipality the power, under municipal legislation, to raise money for municipal purposes by taxing property based on ownership. The wording of the legislation was general and did not restrict the municipality's power to tax property or qualify that power according to who owned the property. Under the authority of this legislation, Ottawa and the other municipality taxed property owned by foreign officials. These officials objected to being taxed on the grounds that it was contrary to international law.

In a reference that year,* Duff CJC followed the English position regarding international custom. He held that *international custom is presumed to be part of the common law in Canada* unless it has been expressly changed by competent legislative authority. This is sometimes known as the presumption rule. However, Duff CJC went on to hold that the Ontario legislation didn't clearly abrogate the international custom in question—that is, the prohibition against taxing property owned by a foreign state or by its officials. Therefore, the legislation had to be interpreted as qualified and as not applying to foreign officials.

The other judges in the case were not as clear about whether the presumption rule applied. Nevertheless, Duff CJC's position is generally accepted as being correct, and the SCC has not had occasion to reconsider this issue.

---

*   Reference as to Powers to Levy Rates on Foreign Legations, [1943] SCR 208.

Enforcement of International Law

One of the major weaknesses of the UN and of international law generally is that there is no strong, consistently used machinery for enforcing breaches of international law.

Non-Violent Infractions

In 2001, as we mentioned above, the International Law Commission adopted a draft set of articles concerning states' accountability for breaches of their international obligations. This set of articles, which has gained the approval of the ICJ, is gaining wide acceptance. However, it has not been officially adopted by the UN. As it stands now, there is no enforceable requirement that states submit to the jurisdiction of the ICJ to resolve non-violent disputes, such as those arising from trade-agreement violations. Settling such disputes or accepting the ICJ's jurisdiction over them is essentially voluntary. The ICJ resolves disputes submitted to it by states ("contentious jurisdiction") and also provides advisory opinions on legal questions submitted to it by the UN Assembly and international organizations ("advisory jurisdiction"). States that submit their disputes to the ICJ must always consent to the ICJ's jurisdiction in the particular case.[20]

Breaches of International Peace and Security

There is no global police force or army. When breaches of international peace and security occur, the response usually comes from one of the following: ad hoc groups of nations directed by the UN Security Council; other organizations, such as the NATO; or individual nations.

---

20   Thomas Buergenthal & Sean D Murphy, *Public International Law in a Nutshell*, 4th ed (St Paul, Minn: West Publishing, 2007) at 79.

COLLECTIVE RESPONSES

The UN Security Council is charged with maintaining international peace and security. Under article 42 of the UN Charter, this responsibility can involve armed responses. Armed responses depend on the Security Council's being able to negotiate an agreement or agreements with UN members for the supply of air, sea, and land forces, as described in article 43 of the Charter. So far, no such agreements have been negotiated, and collective responses have usually depended on ad hoc responses of states that—while acting in support of a Security Council resolution—are under national command.[21]

Article 52 of the UN Charter also provides for "regional arrangements" to be made for maintaining peace and security as long as these arrangements are "consistent with the Purposes and Principles of the United Nations." This has been the basis for NATO responses to aggressive behaviour, such as the 2011 NATO-led armed support of rebels in Libya that resulted in the fall of the Gadhafi regime. This response was sanctioned by UN Security Council Resolution 1973.

RESPONSES BY INDIVIDUAL STATES

Generally, an individual state's right of enforcement in relation to a breach of international law is confined to breaches directly affecting the state itself. Article 2 of the UN Charter requires the peaceful settlement of disputes and prohibits the use of force against other states. However, article 51 provides that individual states have the inherent right to defend themselves in the event of an armed attack until the Security Council takes measures to maintain peace.

Whether pre-emptive self-defence is permissible under customary law has been a subject of debate for many years. Most of the evidence of custom in this area comes from the 1800s and is less than clear. To the extent that such a right exists, it must be based on a credible threat of attack. Until there is a ruling by an international tribunal, it is likely the debate will continue.

Other Areas of Public Law

Major areas of public law are discussed elsewhere in this book: constitutional law in Chapters 5–8, and criminal law in Chapter 13. Earlier in this chapter, we discussed administrative law and public international law. Now we provide an overview of the following:

- other areas of public domestic law;
- hybrids of public law and private law;
- particular branches of public international law; and
- hybrids of international law and domestic law.

Public Domestic Law

Other areas of public domestic law include municipal law, immigration law, taxation law, and certain subareas of criminal law.

---

21   *Ibid* at 342.

Municipal Law

Among the areas of public law we have not yet discussed is *municipal law*, which concerns the powers and activities of local governments. Municipal law is generally classed by itself as a separate subarea of administrative law because of the special nature of the issues it addresses and because of the size, power, and complexity of municipalities. Often referred to as local governments, municipal governments are the third level of government after the federal and provincial (and territorial) governments. They are incorporated under provincial and territorial legislation, which delegates to them legislative, administrative, and quasi-judicial powers to govern at the local level. They have the power to raise taxes, and they often own and control assets of substantial value. Many of the issues that arise in this area of law are related to the following:

- the extent of the local government's delegated power,
- judicial review of the local government's actions,
- conflicts of interest,
- municipal regulation of business activities,
- land use and planning by local governments, and
- private law liability in tort and for breach of contract (see footnote 12).

Immigration Law

Immigration law is another area of public domestic law. It is under federal jurisdiction and covers a wide range of matters that arise under the *Immigration and Refugee Protection Act* and other legislation. These matters include the following: the procedure for immigrating to Canada; the various visas and other documents that are required; sponsorship rules for family members and others; provincial nominee programs; criteria for eligibility (or ineligibility, for reasons related to criminality or health), and removals and deportation orders (see Box 12.1).

Taxation Law

Taxation law is a complex, wide-ranging area of public domestic law. It encompasses federal, provincial, and municipal taxation laws applicable to personal, property, and business income; capital gains; property ownership; and sales transactions. Adding to the complexity of this area is that its rules are frequently changing, perhaps more quickly than in any other area of law. Income tax is the largest source of revenue for governments and an important area of taxation law. It concerns the taxation of various types of income, allowable kinds of deductions, and the calculation of gains and losses. Income tax law is largely focused on the statutory interpretation of the federal *Income Tax Act* and of other tax statutes.

Subareas of Criminal Law

Criminal law includes a number of subareas that could be classed as separate subjects or areas of public law. (See Chapter 13 for a discussion of criminal law generally.) For example, *competition law* (in the United States, referred to as *antitrust law*) deals with unfair competition in the marketplace; *proceeds-of-crime law* covers dealings with assets illegally obtained through or used in the commission of crimes; and *public safety law* concerns laws that are in place to combat serious risks to public safety (including anti-terrorism measures).

Hybrids of Public Domestic Law and Private Law

Some areas of the law cross the line between public and private law. Among these are the following: insolvency law, environmental law, natural resources law, and entertainment law.

Insolvency law deals with legal responses to unmanageable debt incurred by businesses and individuals. Some of the issues debtors and creditors face relate to debt restructuring, settlements with other creditors, collection of secured debts, the priority between tax debts and business or personal debts, and bankruptcy options. While there are some common law insolvency rules, this area is mainly governed by federal legislation. Two of the key statutes are the *Bankruptcy and Insolvency Act* and the *Companies' Creditors Arrangement Act*.

Environmental law has a large regulatory component. It involves governments' defining such matters as the following: their obligations concerning land, air, and water pollution; the requirements for environmental impact studies; property reclamation; and environment-related First Nations' issues. Private law issues can arise in the context of land transfers when responsibility for pollution is unclear. Transnational law issues can arise when pollution crosses borders and thereby violates treaties or other international rules.

The matters dealt with by *natural resources law* include: (1) transactions and royalties involved in the extraction of natural resources (for example, purchase and sale of oil and gas leases, under which the freehold natural resources owner—either the owner of the surface rights or the government if natural resources have been reserved—transfers rights to a resource company to remove the resource); and (2) the regulatory structure for the particular resource being developed. The nature of the transactions, royalties, and regulatory structure vary according to whether the resource is oil and gas, minerals, coal, water, forests, or wildlife and fisheries.

Entertainment law touches many areas, including taxation, intellectual property, and broadcasting and telecommunications regulatory issues. It covers rules regarding marketing and advertising, the financing of films and other entertainment ventures, and the negotiation and performance of production contracts as well as contracts with actors, musicians, writers, and composers. The legal framework for the area spreads across all jurisdictions, and it bridges the divide between private and public law.

Branches of Public International Law

Earlier in this chapter, we approached the subject of international law from a conceptual perspective, discussing the key principles involved in this legal area. But international law is not only about concepts; it is also about specific areas of regulation. There are many branches of international law. Each of these branches has its own subject-specific sources, which can include treaties, customs, general principles of law, and other sources. A few of the main branches are the following:

- law of war,
- international criminal law,
- international human rights law,
- international environmental law, and
- law of the sea (and related areas).

The Law of War

International law came about largely to promote peace and security among nations. The *law of war* deals with justifications for war, acceptable conduct during war, and reparations following war. It has been the subject of legal philosophers, and the basis of international customs and treaties, for hundreds of years. The Geneva Convention, which the nations of the world agreed to in the wake of the Second World War, still forms the basis of modern humanitarian rules for dealing with prisoners of war, for helping the sick and injured during war, and for protecting civilians. Other international conventions include the following:

- the Hague Convention for the Protection of Cultural Property (1954), which, as its name suggests, covers the protection of cultural property;
- the UN Convention against Torture and Other Cruel, Inhuman or Degrading Treatment or Punishment (CAT) (1987), which prohibits torture and has 150 signatory states; and
- the Ottawa Treaty (1990), which bans land mines.

The complete catalogue of conventions concerned with the law of war is extensive.

International Criminal Law

International criminal law deals with atrocities often committed in the course of armed conflict—for example, genocide, crimes against humanity, and war crimes. These are extremely serious offences that transcend national boundaries and are defined in treaties. As a branch of international law, international criminal law is somewhat unique because it focuses on individual responsibility as opposed to state responsibility. After World War II, for example, the Nuremberg trials—which brought international criminal law fully into public attention—prosecuted Nazi war criminals individually. There have been numerous tribunals and treaties in this area over the years. There remain in place multiple courts and conventions dedicated to this area of law.

The *Rome Statute* is the governing statute for the International Criminal Court (ICC).[22] It defines "crimes against humanity" as acts such as murder, extermination, torture, or rape, when "committed as part of a widespread or systematic attack directed against any civilian population, with knowledge of the attack." These serious crimes also amount to crimes in domestic legal systems, and perpetrators can face charges in national courts as well as in the ICC.

International Human Rights Law

The internationalization of human rights has led to the development of *international human rights law* as a separate branch of international law. It concerns the advancement of human rights at all levels—international, regional, and domestic. A major document in the field is the Universal Declaration of Human Rights (1948), a UN General Assembly document that is not officially binding but that arguably enshrines customary law, and that has formed the basis of subsequent conventions, including the following: CAT (generally considered a human rights instrument), the Convention on the Rights of the Child (1990), and the Convention on the Rights of Persons with Disabilities (2008).

---

22 The *Rome Statute* came into force in 2002. The ICC, unlike the ICJ, is independent of the UN. It is currently the most important international criminal court; as of 2011 there were approximately 120 states that were parties to the *Rome Statute*.

International Environmental Law

International environmental law deals with the same issues as environmental law (see above), except that it addresses them in the international context. There are numerous treaties, protocols and conventions, customary laws, and judicial decisions from international tribunals in this area. The Kyoto Protocol, for example, dealing with greenhouse gas emissions and global warming, has received a lot of attention in recent years, though it has had limited success. (Canada, for example, withdrew from the Protocol in 2010.)

Law of the Sea and Related Areas

The *law of the sea*, like the law of war, has a long history. Part of the reason for its early development had to do with power imbalances on the seas; some states, such as England and Spain, had strong naval forces that allowed them to control the seas. The law of the sea attempts, in part, to provide a balance of power in this regard. Some of the main legal questions that the law of the sea addresses today concern the territorial boundaries of coastal nations, the ownership and development of mineral resources at sea, the protection of fisheries, and pollution. This area of law is based on many conventions, customs, and judicial decisions, as well as copious literature. Other branches of international law, like the law of the sea, address stateless, "common" areas such as the polar regions, outer space, and cyberspace. Hence there are *polar regions law*, *space law*, and the *law of cyberspace*.

Hybrids of Public International Law and Domestic Law

International trade law and *international business transactions* are areas that are part international law and part domestic law. International trade law focuses on how trade between countries is regulated; it addresses treaties (for example, the North American Free Trade Agreement), customs rules, and organizations such as the World Trade Organization (WTO). International business transactions law in Canada focuses on specific types of transactions, such as international sales of goods, cross-border financing arrangements, the regulatory frameworks in other countries, as well as some of the non-legal subtleties of cross-cultural business dealings.

Aviation law is another hybrid area. It concerns business rules and regulations both in the airline's home state and in destination states. Domestic laws and foreign laws are involved, potentially also giving rise to private international law issues (see conflict of laws under Transnational Law Subjects in Chapter 10). It also involves public international law issues insofar as the airline must adhere to international conventions relating to air travel.

CHAPTER SUMMARY

Public law in the domestic context regulates the relationships between the state and persons. One particularly important area of public law is administrative law, governing the agencies through which governments regulate individuals and businesses in a multitude of contexts. Because of the degree and complexity of regulation in developed societies today, it is necessary for governments to delegate many governmental tasks to specialized agencies. The functions they perform range from making rules and regulations to administering the law and adjudicating disputes. Regulatory agencies are created under specific statutes—federal, provincial, or territorial—that contain many of the rules governing how the public interacts with them.

There are different methods by which the public can challenge administrative decisions, and these methods vary according to the particular agency and the legislation involved. A statutory right of appeal, if available, is the most effective route to take. If that is not an option, judicial review is another way to challenge an administrative decision. Review of regulatory decisions is based on one of three broad grounds: (1) substantive review of the merits of the decision; (2) review of discretionary decisions; and (3) procedural review, which concerns the fairness of the process by which the decision was reached.

Public international law is a system of law regulating the relations between countries. Its basic concepts and principles have been evolving for hundreds of years; the modern system began with the peace process at the end of the First World War. Some of the fundamental principles guiding nations since then have been the sovereign equality of states, the peaceful settlement of disputes, and non-intervention in the domestic affairs of other nations. The two main sources of international law are (1) treaties—that is, agreements between states; and (2) customs, which are established, settled practices between countries. Countries generally resolve their disputes by negotiation, but they can also submit the matter to the International Court of Justice.

With respect to the application of international law principles within individual states, the rules must be brought into the domestic legal system either through the passage of legislation (in the case of treaty rules) or through adoption by the courts (in the case of custom). The weakness of the current international law system is the lack of an effective enforcement mechanism. The whole institutional infrastructure at the international level is based on consent. In cases of serious disturbances of international peace, enforcement depends on the will and financial support of a few of the most powerful nations in the world. The international system continues to evolve, however, and generally there is a desire worldwide to see it become stronger and more effective.

Besides these areas, there are many other divisions of public domestic law and of public international law. There are also hybrid areas that span public law and private law, and international law and domestic law. Here, as elsewhere, many legal problems cross subject boundaries, and multiple areas of law may apply to their resolution.

KEY TERMS

administrative agency government bodies created under various federal, provincial, and territorial statutes with the purpose of administering particular statutory regimes *(p. 338)*

administrative tribunal administrative agency that fulfills quasi-judicial functions as part of its mandate *(p. 342)*

fairness (also procedural fairness or natural justice) principle that fairness requires that certain "rights" be accorded to persons engaged with an administrative process, such as the right to notice, the right to be heard and to respond, the right to representation, and the right to an adjudicator who is free from bias or an appearance of bias *(p. 349)*

judicial review process by which a superior court can review the decision of an administrative body or inferior court on a number of grounds, including: substantive review (review of the merits of the decision), review of discretionary decisions, and procedural review (review of the "process" followed in making the decision) *(p. 346)*

jus cogens principles of international law, based on custom, that are overriding or peremptory and that cannot be changed by treaty *(p. 358)*

prerogative writs special common law remedies for administrative infractions *(p. 350)*

public international law (or international law) the law relating to international treaties and customs, to inter-state relationships, and to the relationship between states and non-nationals *(p. 350)*

standard of review defines the level of deference the court pays to the tribunal when conducting a judicial review *(p. 348)*

state immunity immunity that a state or its officials have in the event they become the subject of judicial proceedings in another state *(p. 354)*

state jurisdiction area of control within which a state's sovereignty can be exercised *(p. 353)*

state responsibility principle that a state should be held accountable for breaches of international obligations *(p. 354)*

state sovereignty principle that a state has exclusive power in certain areas, such as the power to make, administer, and adjudicate its own laws in relation to itself and its own citizens and residents *(p. 353)*

"subject" of international law usually a state that has as an "international legal personality" and is capable of possessing international rights and obligations *(p. 353)*

substantive review review of an administrative decision's merits that considers both the legal and factual bases of the tribunal's analysis *(p. 348)*

FURTHER READING

BOOKS

Blake, Sara. *Administrative Law in Canada*, 4th ed (Markham, Ont: LexisNexis, 2006).

Brownlie, Ian. *Principles of Public International Law*, 7th ed (Oxford: Oxford University Press, 2008).

Buergenthal, Thomas & Sean D Murphy. *Public International Law*, 4th ed (St Paul, Minn: West Publishing, 2007).

Currie, John. *Public International Law*, 2d ed (Markham, Ont: LexisNexis, 2008).

Jones, David P & Anne S de Villars. *Principles of Administrative Law*, 5th ed (Toronto: Carswell, 2009).

Madsen, Chris. *Military Law and Operations*, loose-leaf (Toronto: Canada Law Book, 2011).

Régimbald, Guy. *Canadian Administrative Law* (Markham, Ont: LexisNexis, 2008).

WEBSITES

Research Guide for Canadian Administrative Boards & Tribunal Decisions: <http://guides.library.ubc.ca/cases/can>.

United Nations: <http://www.un.org/en>.

United Nations Treaty Collection: <http://treaties.un.org>.

International Court of Justice: <http://www.icj-cij.org>.

International Criminal Court: <http://www.icj-cij.org>.

Court Martial Appeal Court of Canada. *Overview of Canadian Military Law and Courts*: <http://www.cmac-cacm.ca/business/military_law_e.shtml>.

REVIEW QUESTIONS

1. Name three specific areas of public domestic law and three specific branches of public international law.

2. What three factors do the courts consider in determining whether an administrative tribunal is too close in operation to a section 96 court?

3. What does inter-delegation refer to in relation to an administrative body's power?

4. Explain the difference between substantive and procedural rules as they relate to dealings with administrative agencies.

5. Which court has exclusive jurisdiction to review Copyright Board decisions?

6. Explain the idea of state responsibility in international law, and provide two examples of a state's being responsible to another state.

7. What was significant about the Peace of Westphalia in the development of international law?

8. What is *opinio juris*, and what is its significance in international law?

9. How are treaties that the Canadian government enters into made part of our domestic law?

10. What is international criminal law concerned with?

EXERCISES

1. Using the Canadian Administrative Boards & Tribunal Decisions database link provided above, select a board or tribunal (human rights, labour, or employment standards, for example) and then choose a decision listed in the database. Read the decision and prepare a short summary of it.

2. In your own words, explain how the "standard of review" concept limits the judicial review of administrative decisions in comparison with a full appeal of such a decision.

3. Review the general principles of international law set out in article 2 of the UN Charter and then the basic principles relating to the enforcement of international rules. Prepare an argument based on these principles demonstrating why you think the US-led invasion of Iraq in 2003 was either justified or not justified.

4. Review the institutional framework of the UN and compare it with Canadian government branches. On the assumption that having a strong and effective UN is a desirable objective, do you think the UN could be improved by changing its infrastructure? How? Explain what changes you would recommend and how those changes could be implemented.

5. For the province or territory in which you live, locate the general provincial or territorial statute (variously named as municipal or local government acts, or community charters) delegating powers to municipalities. Try to locate the specific section that authorizes making bylaws respecting animals. Use the "laws" website for your jurisdiction. (See the list under Further Reading in Chapter 5.)

13 Canada's Criminal Justice System

After reading this chapter, you will understand:

- The division of responsibility between federal and provincial governments regarding criminal justice in Canada
- The primary sources of Canadian criminal law
- How criminal offences are classified and how offenders are prosecuted under Canada's *Criminal Code*
- Police powers to investigate crime
- Constitutional safeguards in the *Charter of Rights and Freedoms* applicable to criminal justice in Canada

- Procedures for conducting a criminal trial, and the principles that apply to the sentencing of offenders
- How correctional jurisdiction is divided in Canada
- The application of the *Youth Criminal Justice Act* to young offenders and its key provisions
- Aboriginal perspectives on criminal justice
- Factors contributing to Aboriginal overrepresentation in the criminal justice system

Criminal laws are primarily designed to denounce and to punish inherently wrongful behaviour, and to deter people from committing crimes or engaging in behaviour that presents a serious risk of harm.

K Roach, *Criminal Law* (Concord, Ont: Irwin Law, 1996) at 2

Introduction

In addition to providing a continuous source of news headlines and heated political debates, the criminal justice system is a critical component of Canadian society. Unlike private law matters, in which private citizens take legal action against one another, criminal law concerns the state itself: criminal offences are seen as transgressions against society as a whole, and are prosecuted by lawyers known as **Crown attorneys** or Crown prosecutors, so-named because they represent the official head of government in Canada, the reigning British (and Canadian) monarch.[1]

Canada's criminal justice system works to determine whether or not persons charged with criminal offences are guilty according to the law and, if they are, what measures should be taken to punish, deter, and/or rehabilitate them, and to protect the rest of society from further harm. Our criminal justice system is jurisdictionally complex. Substantive criminal law and the procedures involved in the system—namely, police investigation of a crime, bringing the accused to court, trying the accused, and sentencing accused persons who are found guilty—are carried out within a constitutional framework that involves both the federal and provincial governments. Since the advent of the *Canadian Charter of Rights and Freedoms*, constitutional safeguards protect an accused person's rights throughout the criminal process.

---

1 This is reflected in the style of cause of criminal cases, which invariably begin with the letter "R," standing for "Regina," the Latin word for queen. The letter can also stand for "Rex," meaning king.

This chapter presents an overview of the criminal justice system in Canada. We will examine criminal law in relation to the division of federal and provincial powers under the Constitution, explain the classification of offences, and outline how a criminal offence is investigated by police, including a review of the Charter rights of persons who are detained or arrested and the limits on police powers of search and seizure. We will consider criminal pretrial matters and the conduct of a criminal trial, as well as sentencing. Lastly, we will briefly examine the correctional system in Canada, the *Youth Criminal Justice Act*, and the relationship between Aboriginal people and the Canadian criminal justice system.

Figure 13.1 illustrates both the larger context of Canada's criminal justice system and the individual elements that comprise it.

Sources of Canadian Criminal Law

When Canada was created as a modern nation in 1867, the framers of our Constitution assigned jurisdiction over criminal law and criminal procedure to the federal Parliament. In the debates leading up to Confederation in 1867, John A. Macdonald stated that "[i]t is one of the defects in the United States system, that each separate state has or may have a criminal code of its own—that what may be a capital offence in one state, may be a venial offence, punishable slightly, in another."[2]

Macdonald believed this potential for variance among state criminal codes produced confusion, and he argued that criminal law in Canada should be assigned to the general (that is, federal) government so that it would be the same throughout the country. Under our Constitution, said Macdonald:

> [W]e shall have one body of criminal law, based on the criminal law of England, and operating equally throughout British America, so that a British American, belonging to what province he may, or going to any other part of the Confederation, knows what his rights are in that respect, and what his punishment will be if an offender against the criminal laws of the land.[3]

Macdonald's view carried, and section 91(27) of the *Constitution Act, 1867* gave the Parliament of Canada exclusive jurisdiction over criminal law and procedure in criminal matters. This means that criminal law and criminal procedure are *national* in scope. They apply throughout Canada.

Two major sources of criminal law in Canada today are statute law and common (or case) law. Originally, criminal law in Canada was largely judge-made law, as it was in England—there was no central criminal law statute. Our *Criminal Code*[4] was enacted in 1892, and today it is the main source of Canadian criminal law. Since its inception, it has been extensively amended. The *Criminal Code* is a lengthy and complex statute that defines and classifies criminal offences, and describes the procedures for prosecuting them. It also provides directions for sentencing. The Code is composed of 28 parts, each concerned with a specific subject area.

---

2   Quoted in PB Waite, ed, *The Confederation Debates in the Province of Canada, 1865* (Toronto: McClelland & Stewart, 1963) at 46.

3   *Ibid* at 46.

4   RSC 1985, c C-46.

FIGURE 13.1 Overview of Canada's criminal justice system

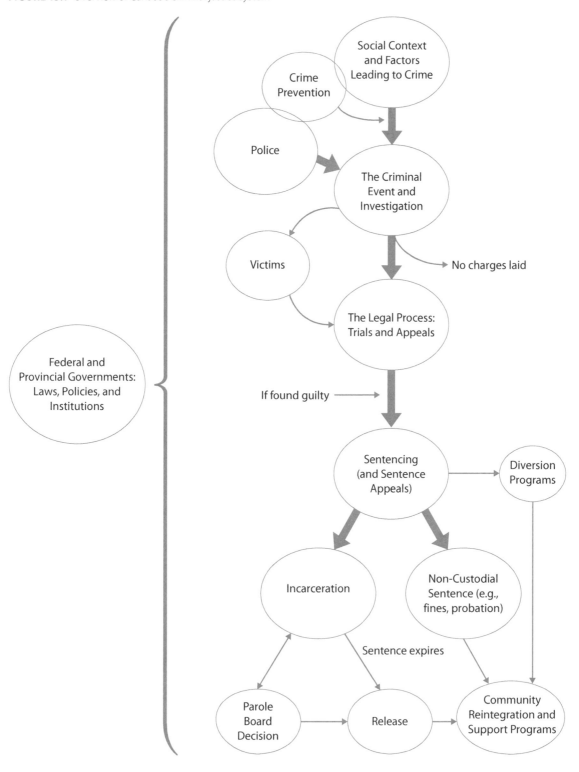

Source: K O'Reagan & S Reid, eds, *Thinking About Criminal Justice in Canada* (Toronto: Emond Montgomery, 2013) at xiv.

The common law, too, continues to be another primary source of our criminal law, and there is much case law pertaining to the *Criminal Code*. For this reason, many lawyers practising criminal law in Canada use annotated versions and easy-to-carry books of the Code and related statutes, to use in court, produced by commercial publishers. A well-known annotated version is *Martin's Annual Criminal Code* and a useful small companion book is *Martin's Pocket Criminal Code*, both published by Carswell.[5] Besides the *Criminal Code*, there are other important federal statutes that relate to the criminal law field, including:

- the *Canada Evidence Act*, RSC 1985, c C-5;
- the *Controlled Drugs and Substances Act*, SC 1996, c 19; and
- the *Youth Criminal Justice Act*, SC 2002, c 1.

The *Canada Evidence Act* covers witnesses and evidence law. Section 2 in Part I, for example, provides that Part I applies to "all criminal proceedings and to all civil proceedings and other matters whatever respecting which Parliament has jurisdiction."

The *Controlled Drugs and Substances Act* regulates certain kinds of dangerous drugs and narcotics in Canada, called "controlled substances." Search, seizure, and detention are covered in Part II of the Act, which concerns enforcement, while Part III covers the disposal of controlled substances.

The *Youth Criminal Justice Act* (YCJA) is a federal statute that deals with young persons who commit crimes in this country. It came into force on April 1, 2003, replacing the *Young Offenders Act*. The YCJA applies to young persons who are between the ages of 12 and 17 when they commit a criminal offence. The Act outlines procedures for trying young persons separately from adult offenders, in youth justice courts. We will look at youth justice later in this chapter.

Although our federal Parliament has sole jurisdiction over criminal law and criminal procedure, section 92(14) of the *Constitution Act, 1867* gives the provinces jurisdiction over "[t]he Administration of Justice in the Province, including the Constitution, Maintenance, and Organization of Provincial Courts, both of Civil and of Criminal Jurisdiction, and including Procedure in Civil Matters in those Courts." In addition, section 92(15) of this Act gives provinces jurisdiction over "[t]he Imposition of Punishment by Fine, Penalty, or Imprisonment for enforcing any Law of the Province made in relation to any Matter coming within any of the Classes of Subjects enumerated in this Section." This means that provinces can make statutes and enforce laws for matters that fall under their own jurisdiction, such as highway traffic acts regulating, for example, speeding on provincial roads, by imposing punishments listed in section 92(15). Such offences are known as **quasi-criminal offences** or provincial offences, and they do not result in a criminal record (see Box 13.1).

Basic Principles of Criminal Law

Because the consequences of being convicted of a criminal offence are so serious and can result in individuals being deprived of their liberty, the Crown attorney's burden in proving that an accused committed a crime is very high. In this section, we will look at *what* the Crown must prove and *how* they must prove it.

---

5   *Martin's Annual Criminal Code 2013* (Toronto: Canada Law Book, 2012); *Martin's Pocket Criminal Code 2013* (Toronto: Canada Law Book, 2012).

BOX 13.1

Quasi-Criminal Offences

"True" criminal offences are crimes over which the federal government has jurisdiction pursuant to its power under section 91(27) of the *Constitution Act, 1867*. These federal crimes are typically serious in nature and are often thought of as being inherently wrong. They generally have a *mens rea*, or guilty mind, element. In addition to receiving penalties that can be severe, being convicted of a crime carries with it a criminal record and a social stigma. Quasi-criminal offences, on the other hand, are less serious offences and do not fall under the federal criminal law power. They are sometimes referred to as regulatory offences and deal with the regulation of conduct in the public interest. They may have a *mens rea* component, but are more frequently strict liability offences (that is, offences without a mental element but where due diligence is a defence—for example, pollution offences) or absolute liability offences (offences based solely on the commission of the proscribed act—such as driving over the speed limit—and without a mental element or possible defence of due diligence).

Quasi-criminal offences can be federal, provincial, territorial, or municipal, but most of these offences are creatures of provincial legislation (provincial quasi-criminal offences are often simply referred to as "provincial offences"). Section 92(15) of the *Constitution Act, 1867* states that the provinces have jurisdiction over: "[t]he Imposition of Punishment by Fine, Penalty, or Imprisonment for enforcing any Law of the Province made in relation to any Matter coming within any of the Classes of Subjects enumerated in this Section." The territories have an analogous power to create quasi-criminal offences in relation to the areas over which they have legislative jurisdiction (as devolved to them by the federal Parliament). Municipalities (or local governments) have a similar power delegated to them by the provinces. And the federal government can always pass legislation creating quasi-criminal offences under a power other than its criminal law power. (See Chapter 5 for a discussion of the areas or "subjects" over which Parliament, the provinces, and territories have legislative jurisdiction.)

There are a vast number of quasi-criminal, or regulatory, offences in Canada, of which the following are a small sampling:

- Motor vehicle offences, such as careless driving and parking offences (for example, under Ontario's *Highway Traffic Act*, RSO 1990, c H.8);
- Offences related to the selling or supplying of liquor (for example, under New Brunswick's *Liquor Control Act*, RSNB 1973, c L-10);
- Offences related to workplace safety covering a range of violations, such as an employer's failure to provide a safe work environment or to immediately report accidents causing critical injury or death (for example, under BC's *Workers Compensation Act*, RSBC 1996, c 492).
- Pollution offences covering land, air, or water (for example, under the federal *Fisheries Act*, RSC 1985, c F-14); and
- Offences relating to the sale and distribution of securities (for example, under Yukon's *Securities Act*, RY 2007, c 16).

Quasi-criminal offences are prosecuted according to the procedures set out in the relevant Act—for example, provincial offences in Ontario are prosecuted under the *Provincial Offences Act*. Punishment for these types of offences is usually a fine (though it can involve imprisonment) and may also include other penalties, such as demerit points on a convicted person's driver's licence or the loss of the licence itself. Because quasi-criminal offences are not true criminal offences, they do not result in a criminal record.

The Elements of a Criminal Offence

Criminal offences in Canada are set out in the *Criminal Code* and several other statutes. We saw in Chapter 11, for example, that conspiracy in relation to competition is a crime under the *Competition Act*. Generally speaking, criminal offences are composed of an objective physical element, known as the **actus reus** or "guilty act," and a mental element, known as **mens rea** or "guilty mind."

In committing the guilty act component of an offence, an individual must engage in a proscribed action, conduct, or behavior. In addition, the *actus reus* may involve the accused being found in particular circumstances; failing to act when required to do so by a legal duty; or causing particular consequences. An important feature of the *actus reus* is that, for criminal consequences to apply, it must be carried out consciously and voluntarily. Some defences go to these elements—for example, duress (see the discussion of defences later in this chapter).

For persons to be found guilty of a criminal offence, not only must they commit a particular criminal act, they must do so with a blameworthy guilty mind or with a particular intention. For example, section 265(1)(a) of the *Criminal Code* states that a person commits an assault when "without the consent of another person, he applies force intentionally to that other person, directly or indirectly." Such force might be applied in a variety ways—intentionally in a fight or during a robbery, or unintentionally in a crowded public area due to factors beyond their control. While some of these acts are blameworthy and could attract criminal consequences, others might not.

Burden of Proof and Standard of Proof

A key principle of our criminal justice system that has existed for centuries is the *presumption of innocence*. This common law safeguard is now a Charter legal right: section 11(d) states that any person charged with an offence has the right "to be presumed innocent until proven guilty according to law in a fair and public hearing by an independent and impartial tribunal." In addition, section 6(1)(a) of the *Criminal Code* prescribes that a person shall be deemed not to be guilty until he is convicted or discharged of the offence. In other words, the state has the *burden* or the *onus of proof* to establish its case, and an accused is presumed innocent until proven guilty in court.

In contrast to civil matters, which require proof on a balance of probabilities, the criminal *standard of proof* is a much higher standard of proof "beyond a reasonable doubt." This means that the Crown must also prove *all* of the elements of the offence beyond a reasonable doubt for the accused to be found guilty. If the defence is able to raise a reasonable doubt in the minds of the judge or jury as to whether the accused committed the offence, the accused must be found not guilty.

Organization and Classification of Criminal Code Offences

In this section, we will look first at how criminal offences are organized in the *Criminal Code*, and then review its three categories of offences. These are:

1. summary conviction offences,
2. indictable offences, and
3. hybrid offences.

How an offence is classified largely determines, for example, the scope of investigatory powers granted to the police, the terms of the accused's pretrial release, how the offence is prosecuted, which court hears the matter, which punishments can apply on a conviction, and the process for an appeal.[6]

---

6   R Barnhorst & S Barnhorst, *Criminal Law and the Canadian Criminal Code*, 5th ed (Toronto: McGraw-Hill Ryerson, 2009); Kent Roach, *Criminal Law* (Concord, Ont: Irwin Law, 1996); Nora Rock & Dayna E Simon, *Foundations of Criminal and Civil Law in Canada* (Toronto: Emond Montgomery, 2000); Mary Ann Kelly, "Criminal Procedure" in Laurence Olivo, ed, *Introduction to Law in Canada*, Ont ed (Toronto: Captus Press, 1995-2009) at 245; Joel E Pink & David C Perrier, eds, *From*

Organization of Criminal Code Offences

The *Criminal Code* organizes specific offences into general subject matter categories, as follows:

- Part II covers offences against public order—for example, treason, sedition, unlawful assemblies and riots, duels, piracy, and offences against air or maritime safety.
- Part II.1 covers terrorism.
- Part III covers offences involving firearms and other weapons.
- Part IV covers offences against the administration of law and justice, including corruption and disobedience, and misleading justice.
- Part V covers sexual offences, public morals, and disorderly conduct.
- Part VI covers invasion of privacy.
- Part VII covers disorderly houses, gaming, and betting.
- Part VIII covers offences against the person and reputation—for example, criminal negligence, homicide, murder, suicide, assault, kidnapping, defamatory libel, and hate propaganda.
- Part IX covers property offences—for example theft, robbery, breaking and entering, and forgery.
- Part X covers fraudulent transactions relating to contracts and trade.
- Part XI covers wilful and forbidden acts in respect of certain property, including mischief and arson.
- Part XII covers offences relating to currency, while Part XII.1 covers instruments and literature for illicit drug use and Part XII.2 covers proceeds of crime.
- Part XIII covers attempts, conspiracies, and accessories.

There has been and continues to be much discussion and debate regarding the kind of behaviour that society should criminalize. Arguments in favour of decriminalizing certain acts—such as possession of small amounts of marijuana for personal use—have arisen that many people today consider persuasive, which may result in future changes to the *Criminal Code*. These arguments often have their basis in the rights guaranteed by the Charter (see Box 13.2).

Summary Conviction Offences

Summary conviction offences are the least serious offences in the *Criminal Code* and are dealt with under Part XXVII. Such offences include, for example, making an indecent telephone call, and public nudity. Trials for summary conviction offences are held before a provincial court judge; no jury is permitted and there is no preliminary hearing. **Limitation periods** apply to summary offences—in general, summary offence charges must be laid within six months from the time the offence was committed.

Crime to Punishment: An Introduction to the Criminal Law System, 6th ed (Toronto: Thomson, 2007); Michael Gulycz & Mary Ann Kelly, *Criminal Law for Legal Professionals* (Toronto: Emond Montgomery, 2014).

BOX 13.2

Canada's Prostitution Laws: Unconstitutional

In 2010, three former and current Ontario sex workers, Terri-Jean Bedford, Amy Lebovitch, and Valerie Scott, challenged the constitutionality of Canada's prostitution laws in the Ontario Superior Court. Their challenge made its way to the Ontario Court of Appeal, and finally, to the SCC.*

The women argued that certain provisions in the *Criminal Code* needlessly endangered them, violating their right to security of the person under section 7 of the Charter. The provisions in question were:

1. section 210, which prevented sex workers from working in a "bawdy house" (fixed indoor location) and limited them instead to street prostitution or outcalls (that is, meeting clients in different locations);
2. section 212(1)(j), which criminalized "living on the avails" of prostitution and made it illegal for sex workers to hire drivers, security, and so on, to protect themselves against some of the risks inherent in prostitution under the regime in force at the time; and
3. section 213(1)(c), which prohibited communicating in public for the purposes of prostitution, effectively making it illegal for sex workers to negotiate terms related to their activities with clients.

In December 2013, the Supreme Court delivered its landmark ruling on the prostitution provisions in the *Criminal Code*. Setting out the issue before the Court, Chief Justice McLachlin stated that the appeals and cross-appeal were not about whether prostitution should be legal or not, but "about whether the laws Parliament has enacted on how prostitution may be carried out pass constitutional muster" (at para 2). In a unanimous 9–0 ruling, the Court declared that the sections in question were inconsistent with the Charter and therefore void. In the words of Chief Justice McLachlin (at para 60):

> The prohibitions at issue do not merely impose conditions on how prostitutes operate. They go a critical step further, by imposing *dangerous*

conditions on prostitution; they prevent people engaged in a risky—but legal—activity from taking steps to protect themselves from the risks.

The bawdy-house and communication offences (sections 210 and 213(1)(c)) had as their main purpose the control of nuisances, but the Court held that the outright ban against keeping a bawdy-house or communicating in public for the purpose of prostitution was a grossly disproportionate response in pursuing this objective (in many cases, these activities would not create a nuisance); further, the outright ban made prostitution more dangerous because it took away opportunities for prostitutes to increase their safety. Concerning the offence of "living on the avails" (section 212(1)(j)), while the control of exploitive relationships was its objective, the Court held that, as worded, it was an overbroad response because it also punished those who were not in exploitive relationships, including those who could increase the safety of prostitutes, such as drivers and bodyguards. All three provisions were therefore held to be contrary to section 7 of the Charter.

Although the Court declared the challenged provisions invalid, it acknowledged Parliament's right to impose limits on how prostitution may be conducted and noted that its regulation is a "complex and delicate matter." Parliament would have the opportunity to redraft Canada's prostitution laws, but how long should the existing provisions remain in effect?

The Court had to decide whether the declaration of invalidity should take effect immediately (leaving prostitution "totally unregulated" while Parliament decided how to redraft the provisions) or should be suspended, and if so, for how long (leaving sex workers at increased risk and continuing to violate their constitutional right to security of the person for the duration of the suspension period). With regard to all the interests at stake, the Court decided to suspend the declaration of invalidity for one year.

* *Canada (Attorney General) v Bedford*, 2013 SCC 72.

If convicted of a summary conviction offence, a person is liable, under section 787(1) of the Code, to "a fine of not more than five thousand dollars or to a term of imprisonment not exceeding six months or to both." The maximum penalty for a number of offences, known as "super summary conviction offences," exceeds the general penalty. For example, the offences of assault with a weapon and sexual assault both carry a maximum summary conviction sentence of 18 months.

Indictable Offences

Indictable offences are the most serious offences in the *Criminal Code*, and the procedure by which they are prosecuted is more involved than the process for summary conviction offences. Limitation periods do not apply to indictable offences, and a person can be charged at any time. Being convicted of them also brings more severe penalties, to a maximum of life imprisonment. The seriousness of an indictable offence determines what court has jurisdiction to hear it. One of the most serious indictable offences is murder, along with some others listed under section 469 of the Code, such as treason and piracy. These offences must be tried before a judge and jury in a province's **superior court of criminal jurisdiction**,[7] unless both the accused and the attorney general consent to a trial before a superior court judge alone under section 473 of the Code. The least serious types of indictable offences are those listed in section 553 of the Code—for example, theft (other than theft of cattle), obtaining money or property by false pretenses, and failure to comply with a probation order. These offences are under the absolute jurisdiction of a provincial court judge, without a jury.

If charged with an indictable offence *not* listed in either section 469 or section 553, an accused may choose or elect his or her mode of trial. The accused can choose to be tried either before a provincial court judge alone, a superior court of justice judge alone, or a superior court of justice judge with a jury. Section 536 of the Code outlines the election procedure.

Hybrid Offences

A **hybrid offence** is also called a *dual procedure offence* or a *Crown election offence*. This means that the Crown attorney has the option of choosing whether to prosecute it as a summary conviction offence or as an indictable offence. The offence of assault causing bodily harm is an example of a hybrid offence; the procedure and potential penalties are different depending on whether the Crown decides to proceed by indictment or summarily. Factors that will affect the Crown's decision include the accused's prior criminal record, the specific circumstances involved, and the time since the offence (limitation period). A hybrid offence is deemed to be an indictable offence by default unless the Crown attorney chooses to prosecute it as a summary offence.

Police Investigation of Crime

When a crime is committed and this fact becomes known to authorities in the criminal justice system, the first step is an investigation by the police. The police gather evidence and attempt to determine who is responsible for the offence; they may then arrest and charge the person or persons they believe to be responsible.

There are three levels of police forces in Canada: federal, provincial, and municipal. The federal police force is the Royal Canadian Mounted Police (RCMP). Not all provinces and territories have their own provincial/territorial police forces, and in such cases the RCMP

---

7   Section 2 of the Code provides the names of the superior court of criminal jurisdiction in each province and territory. For example, in Nova Scotia, British Columbia, and Newfoundland and Labrador, the superior court of criminal jurisdiction is the Supreme Court or the Court of Appeal, while in Ontario it is the Court of Appeal or the Superior Court of Justice, and in Nunavut it is the Nunavut Court of Justice.

is responsible for policing in that province or territory. The majority of police officers in Canada are members of municipal police forces.

Police do not have unlimited powers to investigate crime. The *Criminal Code*, the common law, and the Charter all place limits on the investigatory powers of police and safeguard the rights of individuals with whom police interact. Failure on the part of police to abide by the law in this regard may result in evidence against an accused being excluded in a criminal trial. As described in Chapter 8, section 24(2) of the Charter requires courts to exclude evidence whose admission "would bring the administration of justice into disrepute" when an application is made under section 24(1). (See Box 8.4.)

In the following sections, we will look more closely at the law related to the detention and arrest of persons suspected of committing crimes, and the law governing the search and seizure of evidence by police.

Detention and Arrest

The Charter sets out further legal requirements with which police must comply whenever they are dealing with persons whom they detain or **arrest**. For example, section 10 of the Charter states:

> 10. Everyone has the right on arrest or detention
>   (a) to be informed promptly of the reasons therefor;
>   (b) to retain and instruct counsel without delay and to be informed of that
>   right; and
>   (c) to have the validity of the detention determined by way of *habeas corpus* and to be released if the detention is not lawful.

With respect to reasons, section 29(2)(b) of the *Criminal Code* states that it is the duty of everyone who arrests a person to give notice to that person of the reason for the arrest; the common law requires this, too. Sections 7 and 11(c) of the Charter provide an accused person with the right to remain silent while being questioned by police and during his or her trial.

If an accused decides to waive his right to silence and give a statement, before the statement can be admissible against the accused the court must determine whether it was given *voluntarily*; this is usually established in a *voir dire*, or a trial within a trial. The common law confessions rule aims to prevent wrongful convictions by requiring the Crown to prove that any statement made by an accused person to a person in authority was given voluntarily, for the statement to be admissible against the accused (see Box 13.3).

Search and Seizure

Police investigation can involve searching people and places, as well as seizing physical evidence that is related to the crime. Prior to a criminal trial, the Crown has a legal duty to provide the accused with all relevant information in its possession that relates to the investigation (in the absence of any legal restrictions) so that the accused can better understand and prepare a defence to the charge(s) against him or her—in other words, make "full answer and defence." This duty, known as the **duty of disclosure**, exists at common law and is guaranteed by section 7 of the Charter. In the Supreme Court of Canada case of *R v Stinchcombe*,[8] the Court framed the duty as follows:

---

8   *R v Stinchcombe*, [1991] 3 SCR 326.

Voluntariness and *Oickle*

In *R v Oickle*, 2000 SCC 38, [2000] 2 SCR 3, the Court noted that false confessions are "rarely the product of proper police techniques" (para 45) and stated that, if a confession is produced in certain situations or under certain circumstances, the voluntariness of the confession is difficult to determine. Judges must look carefully at *all* of the circumstances surrounding a confession and how it was obtained and consider the degree to which the following four factors were present:

1. threats or promises [for example, the promise of preferential treatment, or the threat of physical violence/torture],
2. an atmosphere of oppression [contributing actions include prolonged interrogations, fabricated evidence, and disregard for the dignity/well-being of the accused],
3. an operating mind [the accused must have the cognitive ability to understand what it being said to her, what she is saying, and the consequences of saying it to police; the presence of an operating mind may be affected by shock, intoxication, presence of a mental disorder, etc.], and

4. police trickery [unacceptable trickery is determined by the "community shock test"—for example, an officer pretending to be a chaplain and extracting a confession].

The first three factors are connected with the voluntariness of a statement; depending on the context in which the statement was made, the presence of just one of these three factors to a sufficient degree, or a combination of all three, may be enough to render the statement involuntary. The presence of the fourth factor to a sufficient degree may be enough to exclude a statement on the basis of the fact that the actions of the police reflect negatively on the justice system and have the potential to bring the administration of justice into disrepute.

Source: Reproduced from Kerry Watkins, Gail Anderson & Vincenzo Rondinelli, *Evidence and Investigation: From the Crime Scene to the Courtroom* (Toronto: Emond Montgomery, 2012) at 300.

[T]here is a general duty on the part of the Crown to disclose all materials it proposes to use at trial and especially all evidence which may assist the accused even if the Crown does not propose to adduce it.[9]

The Court also explained the proper use to which the information gathered by the Crown should be put:

The fruits of the investigation which are in its possession are not the property of the Crown for use in securing a conviction but the property of the public to be used to ensure that justice is done.[10]

The Crown's duty of disclosure places a corollary duty on police to disclose the "fruits of the investigation" to the Crown, and to ensure that the evidence they collect is not contaminated, lost, or destroyed, and that the chain of continuity is not broken (that is, it must be possible to account for the whereabouts of any piece of physical evidence from the time of its collection to the time it is entered as an exhibit in the trial record).

The Charter places further limits on the ability of police to search for and seize evidence. Section 8 states that everyone "has the right to be secure against unreasonable search

---

9 *Ibid* at 338, adopting as correct law this statement from McEachern CJBC in *R v C (MH)* (1988), 46 CCC (3d) 142 (BCCA).

10 *Supra* note 8 at 333.

or seizure," and court decisions have determined what constitutes a reasonable or an unreasonable search. For a search to be considered reasonable, it must meet the following test as stated by the SCC in *R v Collins*:

1. it must be authorized by law;
2. the law itself must be reasonable (that is, the law that authorizes the search); and
3. the search must be conducted in a reasonable manner.[11]

Section 487(5) of the *Criminal Code* authorizes a justice to issue a police officer a **search warrant**, which provides police with the legal authority to conduct a search. Once authorized to conduct a search, the police must then, as noted in *Collins* and following section 8 of the Charter, conduct the search in a reasonable manner. This normally requires them to have the search warrant with them and show it if asked; use reasonable force when executing the warrant; request voluntary admittance before making a forcible entry; and search premises only during the daytime, unless the search warrant authorizes execution at night.[12]

There are a limited number of exceptions to the general rule requiring police to obtain a warrant before conducting a search and seizure. For example, section 487.11 of the *Criminal Code* permits a peace officer to conduct a search without a warrant "if the conditions for obtaining a warrant exist but by reason of exigent circumstances it would be impracticable to obtain a warrant."[13]

The Criminal Trial Process

In this section, we will examine pretrial procedures, the trial itself, and sentencing.

Pretrial Procedures

A number of procedures occur prior to a criminal trial.[14] Once the police have finished investigating a crime and have gathered and assessed their evidence, they may lay a criminal charge against a suspect. They must also ensure that the accused person comes before a court. Part XVI of the Code sets out several ways police may do this. (See also Box 13.4.)

First, if the offence is an indictable type mentioned in section 553 (the least serious indictable offences), a hybrid offence, or a summary conviction offence, the police officer may issue an **appearance notice** to the accused person. The appearance notice is a document given to a person, usually at the scene of the offence, requiring that person to come to court on a certain date and time to answer to a charge. The accused must sign the appearance notice, and then may leave. Having issued an appearance notice, the police officer must then swear an information before a justice that the accused person has committed an offence. The officer must do this as soon as practicable, before the date and time prescribed in the appearance notice for the accused's future court appearance.

---

11   *R v Collins*, [1987] 1 SCR 265. See also Gulycz & Kelly, *supra* note 6 at 142.

12   Kelly, "Criminal Procedure," *supra* note 6 at 252-54.

13   For a detailed discussion of police investigatory powers, see Kerry Watkins, Gail Anderson & Vincenzo Rondinelli, *Evidence and Investigation: From the Crime Scene to the Courtroom* (Toronto: Emond Montgomery, 2012) ch 6; and Gulycz & Kelly, *supra* note 6 at 142-54.

14   For more information on pretrial procedures, see Gulycz & Kelly, *supra* note 6, ch 17.

BOX 13.4

Specialized Courts

In Canada, a number of specialized courts have been created outside of the regular court system. They aim to achieve better long-term outcomes for offenders in certain circumstances and for society as a whole.

Gladue Courts

The first Gladue court was established in Toronto in 2001. Named for the Supreme Court decision *R v Gladue* (see the discussion on page 387), Gladue courts hear criminal matters involving Aboriginal persons. At the time of writing, Gladue courts are operating in several cities in Ontario and are being considered for a number of others. Like regular courts, Gladue courts include a judge, duty counsel, Crown, and defence lawyers, but most of the individuals involved are trained in the issues pertinent to the offenders who appear before them. Caseworkers prepare reports on offenders' life circumstances, which are used to determine an appropriate sentence. In some other provinces, such as British Columbia, partnerships exist between courts and non-governmental organizations to ensure that Gladue-type information is systematically incorporated into sentencing procedures for Aboriginal offenders.

Domestic Violence Court

Created in 1997, Ontario's Domestic Violence Court (DVC) Program deals with criminal cases that involve allegations of domestic abuse. The DVC Program aims to facilitate the prosecution of such cases, provide early intervention and better support to victims, and increase offender accountability. It is the most extensive such program in Canada, and includes specialized teams made up of police, Crown attorneys, community agencies, victim/witness assistance program staff, and others who aim to make the safety and needs of victims of domestic violence and their children a priority. One component of the DVC Program is the Partner Assault Response (PAR) program that offenders are ordered to attend. The 16-week-long program, which consists of counselling and educational services, aims to teach non-violent strategies for handling conflict and provide offenders with an opportunity to examine their attitudes toward domestic violence. Staff also work with offenders' partners to provide referrals to resources in the community, help with safety planning, and provide information about the offender's progress.

Toronto Mental Health Court

The Toronto Mental Health Court (MHC) opened in 1998 in response to the growing number of accused suffering from mental disorders who were appearing before the courts. The Toronto MHC, which was the first court of its kind in Canada, is a non-adversarial court available to individuals suffering from mental illness who are charged with non-violent criminal offences. Ideally, arrested persons who meet the criteria for diversion will be sent to the MHC, where they will be seen by psychiatrists, legal aid, and social workers; they will then have a fitness hearing and a bail hearing. The goals of the court, whose underlying philosophy is that the justice system should aim to heal as well as to protect, include "to expedite case processing, create effective interactions between the mental health and criminal justice system, increase access to mental health services, reduce recidivism, improve public safety and reduce the length of confinement in jails for mentally disordered offenders."[*] The MHC aims to help those whose contact with the criminal justice system stems from mental illness regain a normal life, while avoiding unnecessary incarceration and a criminal record.[†] Court-employed social workers help accused persons access community support programs and treatment, find shelter, and so on. While on bail, offenders must report back to the court while they become stabilized on their medications and attend programs. Often, the Crown will stay the charges, or agree to a custodial sentence, where offenders comply with the court's requirements.

Drug Treatment Courts

At the time of writing, six Drug Treatment Courts (DTCs) are operating across Canada, in Toronto (since 1998); Vancouver (since 2001); and Edmonton (since 2005); and in Winnipeg, Ottawa, and Regina (since 2006).[‡] Participation is open to non-violent offenders with addictions who have been charged with possession or trafficking of small quantities of drugs such as crack, cocaine, and heroin; minor property crimes; or prostitution. The aim of DTCs is to reduce the amount of crime committed due to substance abuse by a combination of court-monitored treatment and community support for offenders; the larger aim is to reduce the costs stemming from addiction to Canadian law enforcement, and to the legal and corrections systems. Participation in the courts is voluntary, but participants are required to appear in court regularly, attend counselling sessions, receive medical attention as needed (e.g., methadone treatment), and undergo random drug tests. Through partnerships with community agencies and organizations, court staff also seek to meet the other needs of participants, such as job training, employment, and safe housing. Successful completion of the court's requirements usually results in criminal charges being stayed or in a non-custodial sentence. Offenders who do not meet the requirements of the court are sentenced according to the regular court process.

[*]   Edward F Ormston, "Mental Health Court in Ontario" (2005) 2:8 Visions: BC's Mental Health and Addictions Journal 31.

[†]   Sheldon Gordon, "Out of the Darkness" (Winter 2005) Network, online: <http://ontario.cmha.ca/network/out-of-the-darkness/>.

[‡]   See <http://nationalantidrugstrategy.gc.ca/dtc-ttt.html>.

Second, sometimes the accused will be brought to court by a **summons**. To start this process, the police officer goes before a justice and swears an information that there are reasonable grounds to believe an accused has committed an offence. If the justice is satisfied that an arrest warrant is not necessary, a summons is issued, following the requirements set out in section 509 of the Code. The summons requires the accused to attend court on a certain date and time to answer to the charge. It is served personally on the accused.

The third way of bringing an accused before the court is for a justice to issue a warrant for the person's arrest, directing the police to take the accused into custody and bring him or her to court. As always, police actions in compelling the accused to appear in court are subject to the rights everyone has under the Charter.

Generally, a considerable amount of time elapses between the date an accused is charged with an offence and the date the actual trial takes place. Note that section 11(b) of the Charter states that any person charged with an offence has the right "to be tried within a reasonable time." Given that an accused's trial may be some time in the future, the *Criminal Code* outlines procedures by which a police officer, a justice of the peace, or a judge may release an accused prior to her trial. Here, again, the Charter applies. Section 11(e) states that any person charged with an offence has the right "not to be denied reasonable bail without just cause."

Pretrial release of the accused, often called *bail*, is formally known in the *Criminal Code* as **judicial interim release**. If the accused is still in custody, the pretrial release of that person is determined at a bail hearing. The bail hearing follows different procedures depending on the seriousness of the charge. For less serious offences—that is, for offences not listed in section 469—the accused must be taken before a justice for his bail hearing within 24 hours of arrest and detention.

At this regular bail hearing, the Crown attorney has the onus to "show cause" why the accused should *not* be released or should be released with certain conditions attached. If the Crown does not show cause, the justice must release the accused on an **undertaking** without conditions or "with such conditions as the justice directs" (the conditions that may be applied are set out in section 515(2) of the Code). However, the onus is not always on the Crown. There are a number of situations, set out in section 515(6) of the Code, in which the onus is on the accused to show why he should *not* be detained in custody prior to the trial. Such a reverse onus could happen if, for example, the accused were charged with an indictable offence while already out on bail for another indictable offence.

For an accused charged with a more serious section 469 indictable offence (for example, murder or treason), more stringent considerations apply. The accused must apply for a bail hearing before a judge in a superior court of criminal jurisdiction, under section 522 of the Code. In this case, due to the seriousness of the offence, the accused has the onus to show cause why her detention is not justified. If the judge is not persuaded, the accused will be detained until her trial.

Before the trial begins, the accused and his lawyer have a number of important matters to consider, including the following:

- Obtaining disclosure of all the Crown's relevant evidence against the accused. Such disclosure is required by common law, as per *Stinchcombe*, as well as the Charter.
- Having a pretrial hearing conference, as set out in section 625.1 of the Code. Such conferences are mandatory for jury trials.
- Discussing how to **plead** to the offence. Under section 606 of the Code, permitted pleas are either guilty or not guilty, or one of the special pleas authorized under section 607 of the Code. These are:
  - *autrefois acquit* (available when the person charged has been previously acquitted with respect to the charge),

- *autrefois convict* (available when the person charged has been previously convicted with respect to the charge), and
- pardon (the offence and the penalty are forgiven, usually by a head of state or Parliament).

• Considering whether a **plea bargain** should be negotiated with the Crown. A plea bargain comes about when the Crown attorney and the defence counsel negotiate an agreement on matters such as how the accused will plead to the offence and what sentence the Crown will ask for in court if the accused pleads guilty. For example, the accused may plead guilty to a lesser offence and receive a reduced sentence.

• Electing the mode of trial. This consideration is relevant if the accused is charged with an indictable offence that is not listed in either section 469 or section 553 of the Code. The options are trial by a judge of the superior court of justice with a jury, trial by a judge of the superior court of justice without a jury, and trial by a provincial court judge without a jury.

• Considering (in a case where the accused chooses to have the trial in the superior court) whether to have a **preliminary inquiry**. The procedure for a preliminary inquiry is described in Part XVIII of the Code. It is conducted before a provincial court judge, who determines whether there is sufficient evidence to require the accused to stand trial for the offence.

• Deciding whether the accused will testify at his or her own trial. (There is no requirement that the accused do so.) This right is also protected under section 11(c) of the Charter.

The Trial

In Canada, trials are open to the public. If the trial is in a provincial court, the charging document describing the offence(s) with which the accused is charged is called an **information**. If the trial is in superior court, the charging document describing the offence(s) is called an **indictment**. The nature of a criminal trial is complex, and various sections of the *Criminal Code* outline how the trial proceeds. The trial itself starts with the **arraignment,** whereby the charge is read to the accused in open court and the accused is asked how he or she wishes to plead. If the accused pleads guilty to the offence, the Crown will read a summary of the facts to the judge, and the defence will admit to them. If the trial judge agrees, he or she finds the accused guilty and enters a **conviction**. The accused will then be sentenced (see the discussion below).

If the accused pleads not guilty to the offence, the Crown attorney presents its case first. The Crown then attempts to prove its case with evidence against the accused. Evidence may take a number of forms, including oral evidence (spoken evidence given by a witness under affirmation or oath); physical evidence (actual objects, such as DNA, photographs, or a weapon); and documentary evidence (any documents produced mechanically or by hand, such as medical records or transcripts). For a discussion of admissibility of evidence, see Box 13.5.

As mentioned above, the Crown must prove all the elements of the offence beyond a reasonable doubt. Following the Crown's own examination-in-chief of their witness, the defence counsel may conduct a cross-examination, which the Crown may then follow with a re-examination. The judge may also question the witness, and then the next witness may be called. After the Crown has finished calling all of its witnesses and presenting all of its evidence, the Crown closes its case. If the defence believes the Crown has not provided any

Admissibility of Evidence

In general, any evidence that is relevant to a material issue in a trial should be admitted, *unless* a policy or rule of evidence requires that it be excluded. Exclusionary rules are found both at common law and in statutes [including the Charter].

The judge may decide not to admit a piece of evidence for the following reasons:

1. *The evidence is irrelevant.* If the evidence does not help prove facts that need to be proved or is immaterial to the issues, it may be excluded.
2. *The evidence is unreliable.* Certain kinds of evidence are unreliable due to their nature. For example, hearsay evidence is generally inadmissible for this reason.
3. *The evidence is more prejudicial than probative.* If the evidence would be more likely to influence decision-makers in a way that would be unfair or undeserved to the accused than to prove or disprove a certain fact ("probative value"), then the judge will likely exclude the evidence. Character evidence falls into this category. As an example, in general the Crown may not provide evidence as to the accused's poor character or reputation.
4. *The evidence was obtained unfairly.* Evidence [may] be excluded if the way in which it was obtained violated the accused's rights under the Charter ... . [See Box 8.4 under "Section 24(2): Exclusion of Evidence."]
5. *Admitting the evidence would be unfair to the defence, would waste time, or would confuse issues.* Other reasons that evidence may be excluded include procedural rules and reasons. For example, the Crown may not call evidence after the defence has finished calling its evidence (a practice known as splitting the case).

Source: Kerry Watkins, Gail Anderson & Vincenzo Rondinelli, *Evidence and Investigation: From the Crime Scene to the Courtroom* (Toronto: Emond Montgomery, 2012) at 6.

evidence on an essential element of the offence, the defence may make a motion to the trial judge for a directed verdict of acquittal. If the motion is allowed, the accused will be acquitted; if it is dismissed, the trial will continue, with the defence then opening its case and calling its evidence. At this stage of the trial, the defence conducts the examination-in-chief of their own witnesses; the Crown then cross-examines the witness(es) and the defence re-examines them. As stated, the accused is not obligated to testify at his or her own trial.

A number of defences are set out in the *Criminal Code*. (These are discussed briefly in the following section.) When the defence has finished presenting all of its evidence, it closes its case. The Crown and the defence then both make closing submissions to the judge. If the trial is before a judge alone, the judge decides if the accused is guilty or not guilty. If the trial is before a judge and jury, the judge reviews the evidence and each side's case for the jury and instructs or charges them on how to apply the law to the facts of the case in order to reach their decision. The jury then retires to a jury room to deliberate and determine a **verdict** of guilty or not guilty. Jurors do not need to give reasons for their verdict, but their verdict must be unanimous. If they find the accused guilty, the trial judge imposes the sentence (see the discussion below).

Defences

Prior to the enactment of the *Criminal Code*, defences to criminal offences were derived from case law. Today, they are found in the *Criminal Code* and, by section 8(3) of the Code, at common law. The following are some examples of defences:[15]

---

15 For more information on defences, see Gulycz & Kelly, *supra* note 6, ch 10.

- *Self-defence.* The defence of self-defence is set out in section 34 of the *Criminal Code*. It states that a person is not guilty of an offence if (a) he believes on reasonable grounds that force is being used against him or another person or that a threat of force is being made against him or another person; (b) the act that constitutes the offence is committed for the purpose of defending or protecting himself or the other person from that use or threat of force; and (c) the act committed is reasonable in the circumstances. In determining whether the act committed is "reasonable in the circumstances," the court will consider factors including but not limited to the nature of the force or threat; the extent to which the use of force was imminent and whether there were other means available to respond to the potential use of force; whether any party to the incident used or threatened to use a weapon; and the size, age, gender, and physical capabilities of the parties to the incident.

- *Consent.* To rely on the defence of consent, the accused must prove that the alleged victim freely consented to the acts carried out by the accused. Assault is an offence to which the defence of consent may apply—for example, in sporting matches involving physical contact. Certain offences exclude the defence of consent—for example, the infliction of death.

- *Provocation.* This defence is only available where the accused is charged with murder. It is a partial defence, which, if established, does not result in the acquittal of the accused but rather in the accused being convicted of the lesser offence of manslaughter. The provocation may take various forms (such as words or gestures), but the result must be that the accused suddenly lost self-control and did not have time to take into account the consequences of her actions.

- *Duress.* The defence of duress exists at common law and in section 17 of the *Criminal Code*. It is a complex defence when the accused was compelled to commit a criminal offence as a result of threats of immediate death or bodily harm from a person present when the offence was committed. Section 17 does not apply to some specific offences, such as murder, sexual assault, or robbery.

- *Mental disorder.* Section 16 states that no person is criminally responsible for a criminal act or omission made "while suffering from a mental disorder that rendered the person incapable of appreciating the nature and quality of the act or omission or of knowing that it was wrong." Furthermore, the presence of such a disorder must be proved on the balance of probabilities. The burden of proof that an accused was suffering from a mental disorder that exempts him or her from criminal responsibility is on the party who raises the issue.

Other defences include necessity, automatism, intoxication, mistake of fact, and mistake of law.

Sentencing

A **sentence** is the punishment imposed by a trial judge on someone found guilty of a criminal offence. The sentence aims to protect society, as well as to punish the offender and deter others from committing crimes. Sentencing is dealt with in Part XXIII of the *Criminal Code*.[16] The purpose and objectives are set out in section 718 as follows:

---

16 A detailed description of sentencing is outside the scope of this text. Interested readers should consult Gulycz & Kelly, *supra* note 6, ch 20.

718. The fundamental purpose of sentencing is to contribute, along with crime prevention initiatives, to respect for the law and the maintenance of a just, peaceful and safe society by imposing just sanctions that have one or more of the following objectives:

> (a) to denounce unlawful conduct;
>
> (b) to deter the offender and other persons from committing offences;
>
> (c) to separate offenders from society, where necessary;
>
> (d) to assist in rehabilitating offenders;
>
> (e) to provide reparations for harm done to victims or to the community;

and

> (f) to promote a sense of responsibility in offenders, and acknowledgment

of the harm done to victims and to the community.

The fundamental principle of sentencing is expressed in section 718.1 of the Code, which states: "A sentence must be proportionate to the gravity of the offence and the degree of responsibility of the offender." In determining the appropriate sentence, section 718.2 provides other sentencing principles. For example, section 718.2(b) states that a sentence "should be similar to sentences imposed on similar offenders for similar offences committed in similar circumstances," while section 718.2(c) states that "where consecutive sentences are imposed, the combined sentence should not be unduly long or harsh."

Note that there is a particular sentencing principle in the Code that applies specifically to Aboriginal offenders, whose overrepresentation has been called "one of the most documented trends in the Canadian criminal justice system."[17] Section 718.2(e) states that "all available sanctions other than imprisonment that are reasonable in the circumstances should be considered for *all* offenders, *with particular attention to the circumstances of aboriginal offenders*" (emphasis added). This principle, which was added to the *Criminal Code* in 1996, represents among other things an attempt to redress Aboriginal overrepresentation in the criminal justice system. In the seminal case *R v Gladue*,[18] the Supreme Court first articulated the rules and principles applicable to this section when imposing sentences on Aboriginal offenders. Particular background factors that judges must consider are the following:

> (A) The unique systemic or background factors which may have played a part in bringing the particular aboriginal offender before the courts; and
>
> (B) The types of sentencing procedures and sanctions which may be appropriate in the circumstances for the offender because of his or her particular aboriginal heritage or connection.[19]

The Court elaborated on these further, as follows:

> The background factors which figure prominently in the causation of crime by aboriginal offenders are by now well known. Years of dislocation and economic

---

17   Brian R Pfefferle, "Gladue Sentencing: Uneasy Answers to the Hard Problem of Aboriginal Over-Incarceration" (2009) 32:2 Man LJ 113.

18   [1999] 1 SCR 688. The case involved an Aboriginal woman from British Columbia, Jamie Tanis Gladue, who pled guilty to manslaughter for killing her common law husband. For more information on the case and Gladue rights, see Jay Istvanffy's *Gladue Primer* under Further Reading at the end of this chapter.

19   *R v Gladue, supra* note 18 at para 66.

development have translated, for many aboriginal peoples, into low incomes, high unemployment, lack of opportunities and options, lack or irrelevance of education, substance abuse, loneliness, and community fragmentation. These and other factors contribute to a higher incidence of crime and incarceration.[20]

The Court also noted some differences between traditional Aboriginal sentencing ideals and those of Canada's criminal justice system, highlighting their importance to the analysis:

> A significant problem experienced by aboriginal people who come into contact with the criminal justice system is that the traditional sentencing ideals of deterrence, separation, and denunciation are often far removed from the understanding of sentencing held by these offenders and their community … most traditional aboriginal conceptions of sentencing place a *primary* emphasis upon the ideals of restorative justice. This tradition is extremely important to the analysis under s. 718.2(e).[21]

Unfortunately, more than a decade after the precedent-setting *Gladue* decision, the Supreme Court observed that—according to statistics, and due in part to "a fundamental misunderstanding and misapplication of both s. 718.2(e) and this Court's decision in *Gladue*"—section 718.2(e) has not had a "discernible impact" on Aboriginal overrepresentation in the criminal justice system to date.[22]

Under section 718.2, a judge must also consider possible aggravating circumstances before imposing a sentence. An **aggravating circumstance** is any circumstance related to the offence or the offender that increases the seriousness of the offence and which may result in an increased sentence. Section 718.2(a) sets out a number of circumstances that may be considered aggravating—for example, evidence that the offence was motivated by bias, prejudice, or hate based on a prohibited ground of discrimination; that the offender abused someone under the age of 18; that the offender, in committing the offence, abused a position of trust or authority in relation to the victim; and that the offence was a terrorism offence. A **mitigating circumstance** is any circumstance associated with the offence or the offender that decreases the seriousness of the offence, and which may result in a reduced sentence. Although section 718.2 does not provide examples, some could include whether the offender cooperated with police, the offender's age and absence of a criminal record, whether the offender showed remorse, or whether the offender committed the offence as a result of having been provoked.

To help them decide on an appropriate sentence, particularly in the case of a first-time offender, judges may also request a **pre-sentence report**, prepared by a probation officer, to learn more about the background and character of the offender. In addition to the pre-sentence report, the victim and relatives of the victim may prepare and file a victim impact statement, describing the impact the crime has had on their lives. At the sentencing hearing, both the Crown and defence counsel have an opportunity to make submissions; they may also make a joint submission. Possible sentences include an absolute or conditional discharge, a fine, a suspended sentence and probation, or imprisonment. If either the Crown or accused person decides to appeal, Part XXI of the *Criminal Code* governs appeals for indictable offences, while Part XXVII governs appeals for summary conviction offences.[23]

---

20 *Ibid* at para 67.

21 *Ibid* at para 70 (emphasis in original).

22 *R v Ipeelee*, 2012 SCC 13, [2012] 1 SCR 433 at para 63.

23 For more information on appeals, see Gulycz & Kelly, *supra* note 6, ch 21.

Canada's Correctional System

In Canada, correctional jurisdiction is divided between the provinces/territories and the federal government. Adults who receive a custodial sentence of less than two years serve their sentence in a provincial or territorial correctional facility operated by the province/territory under relevant provincial/territorial legislation—in Ontario, for example, corrections are administered under the *Ministry of Correctional Services Act* by the Ontario Ministry of Community Safety and Correctional Services. Adults who receive a custodial sentence of two years or more serve their sentence in federal institutions, referred to as penitentiaries, which are operated by the Correctional Service of Canada (CSC) under the *Corrections and Conditional Release Act*.

Depending on the assessment and classification of a particular offender by correctional officials, the offender may serve his sentence in a maximum, medium, or minimum security facility, or in a multi-level institution. Offenders may be released once their entire sentence has been served, or by parole granted prior to completion of the sentence by either the Parole Board of Canada or by various provincial/territorial parole boards established by some provinces/territories for inmates serving time in provincial/territorial correctional facilities. In addition to the provincial/territorial and federal correctional systems, the third correctional system in Canada is the youth criminal justice system for young persons (see below).

Another way in which someone convicted of an offence can serve their sentence in the community and remain out of custody is through a suspended sentence and probation. Under section 731(1)(a) of the *Criminal Code*, provided that no minimum punishment is prescribed by law, a judge can, having regard to the offender's age and character, the nature of the offence, and the circumstances surrounding it, suspend the sentence and release the offender on probation. This order prescribes certain mandatory conditions and permits the court to prescribe "additional conditions" listed in section 732.1(3). If, however, the offender fails or refuses to comply with the order without a reasonable excuse, he may be charged with an additional offence of breach of probation under section 733.1 of the *Criminal Code*.

Youth Criminal Justice Act

In Canada today, young people who commit criminal offences set out in the *Criminal Code* are treated differently from adults. Young persons 12 years of age or older but less than 18 years of age do not have their offence dealt with in adult criminal court, but rather are tried in a youth justice court established under the provisions of the *Youth Criminal Justice Act* (YCJA), which came into force in 2003.

The YCJA has a declaration of principle in section 3 that contains the policy in Canada for dealing with young persons. The Act is structured to process young persons charged with *Criminal Code* offences from their first contact with police through to (if applicable) their trial and sentence with this policy in mind. Special procedures aim to ensure the fair treatment of young persons and the protection of their rights.

Among the Act's features are the use of "extrajudicial measures," requiring a police officer to consider, for example, giving a warning to a young person or making a referral to a community program before starting judicial proceedings (section 6); giving young persons the right to retain and instruct counsel without delay at *any* stage of the proceedings (section 25); requiring parental notice of their child's arrest (section 26); and provisions relating to the sentencing, custody, and supervision of young persons in parts 4 and 5 of the Act. The sentencing principles in section 38(1) state that

[t]he purpose of sentencing under section 42 (youth sentences) is to hold a young person accountable for an offence through the imposition of just sanctions that have meaningful consequences for the young person and that promote his or her rehabilitation and reintegration into society, thereby contributing to the long-term protection of the public.

Sentences may include a judicial reprimand, a fine, compensation or restitution, or a community service order. Custody and supervision orders are also possible.

Youth sentences are generally less severe than adult sentences, but in some cases the Crown can apply to the court to have the youth sentenced as an adult. An adult sentence may be appropriate where the youth is convicted of a serious violent crime (such as murder, manslaughter, or aggravated sexual assault) or where the offence is part of a pattern of violent offences. Youths receiving adult sentences serve their sentences in youth facilities; however, if they turn 20 in a youth facility, they may be transferred to an adult facility (sections 64-81).

Aboriginal People and the Criminal Justice System

In recent decades, the overrepresentation of Aboriginal people in Canada's criminal justice system, especially corrections, has reached alarming proportions.[24] The Office of the Correctional Investigator now estimates that the incarceration rate for Aboriginal adults (that is, those who self-identify as First Nations, Inuit, or Métis) is as much as 10 times higher than for non-Aboriginal adults. As of 2013, although Aboriginal people made up only approximately 4 percent of Canada's population, they accounted for over 23 percent of the federal inmate population.[25]

A range of studies, task forces, royal commissions, conferences, and inquiries have highlighted the adverse impact of the enforcement and administration of criminal law on Aboriginal people, and put forth suggestions for intervention. The Office of the Correctional Investigator noted recently that, compared with non-Aboriginal inmates, Aboriginal inmates are:

- classified as higher risk and higher need in areas such as community reintegration, family supports, and unemployment;
- released later in their sentences, with most leaving prison at the statutory release or warrant expiry date;
- overrepresented in segregation and maximum security populations;
- disproportionately involved in self-injury and use-of-force interventions while incarcerated; and
- more likely to return to prison on revocation of parole for administrative reasons rather than criminal violations.[26]

---

24 For a detailed discussion, see Darion Boyington in John Roberts, Darion Boyington & Shahé S Kazarian, *Diversity and First Nations Issues in Canada*, 2d ed (Toronto: Emond Montgomery, 2012) ch 11.

25 "Backgrounder: Aboriginal Offenders—A Critical Situation," online: Office of the Correctional Investigator <http://www.oci-bec.gc.ca/cnt/rpt/oth-aut/oth-aut20121022info-eng.aspx>.

26 *Ibid.*

In addition to the background factors described by the Supreme Court in *Gladue*, the fundamental differences between Euro-Canadian and traditional Aboriginal notions of justice has been suggested as another contributing factor to the higher incidence of Aboriginal crime and incarceration (see Table 13.1). Manitoba Justice Murray Sinclair, who served as the chair of the Truth and Reconciliation Commission, explains:

> The starting point is a difficult one for people raised with the liberal ideals of "civil rights" and "equality"; it requires one to accept the possibility that being Aboriginal and being non-Aboriginal involve being different. It requires one to come to terms with the concept that the Aboriginal Peoples of North America, for the most part, hold world views and life philosophies fundamentally different from those of the dominant Euro-Canadian society, and that these ... are so fundamentally different as to be inherently in conflict. ...
>
> There are areas of thought and belief that are substantially shared by both Aboriginal and non-Aboriginal peoples. Nevertheless, the differences are broad enough and general enough to make many Euro-Canadian institutions incompatible with the moral and ethical value systems and approaches of Aboriginal Canadians.[27]

The modern instruments of criminal justice—jails, police officers, and courts—were unknown to Aboriginal peoples prior to European contact. Mediation was used to resolve disputes and restore the offender to a harmonious relationship with the rest of the community, through the acceptance of responsibility and through making the necessary amends, both to the the victim and the larger community. All community members, and elders in particular, played an important role.[28] Given all that has occurred over the past few hundred years, however, as Mary Ellen Turpel suggests in the Royal Commission on Aboriginal Peoples report on justice issues, it would be fruitless to attempt simply to return to pre-colonial ways:

> Can the pre-colonial regime ever be reconstructed? My own view is no, not except as a relic of the past. It cannot be resurrected because we have all been touched by imperialism and colonialism, and there is no simplistic escape to some pre-colonial history except a rhetorical one. In my view, we [Aboriginal people] need to regain control over criminal justice, indeed all justice matters, but in a thoroughly post-colonial fashion. ... One cannot erase the history of colonialism, but we must, as an imperative, undo it in a contemporary context. ... We have to accept that there are profound social and economic problems in Aboriginal communities today that never existed pre-colonization and even in the first few hundred years of interaction. Problems of alcohol and solvent abuse, family violence and sexual abuse, and youth crime—these are indications of a fundamental breakdown in the social order in Aboriginal communities of a magnitude never known before. A reform dialogue or proposals in the criminal justice field have to come to grips with this contemporary reality and not just retreat into a pre-colonial situation.[29]

---

27 Murray Sinclair, "Aboriginal Peoples, Justice and the Law" in Richard Gosse, James Youngblood Henderson & Roger Carter, eds, *Continuing Poundmaker and Riel's Quest: Presentations Made at a Conference on Aboriginal Peoples and Justice* (Saskatoon: Purich, 1994), 173-84 at 175-76.

28 Roberts, Boyington & Kazarian, *supra* note 24 at 329. These were the broad principles of Aboriginal justice. Different moral codes, religious beliefs, and life philosophies existed among different Aboriginal peoples.

29 Royal Commission on Aboriginal Peoples, *Bridging the Cultural Divide: A Report on Aboriginal People and Criminal Justice in Canada* (Ottawa: Supply and Services Canada, 1996) at 65-66.

TABLE 13.1   Anglo–Canadian Versus Traditional Aboriginal Justice

ANGLO–CANADIAN JUSTICE	TRADITIONAL ABORIGINAL JUSTICE
Laws formulated by elected representatives	Laws formulated by the community through tradition and consensus
Laws tied to man-made economy	Laws tied to the natural environment, only a few universally condemned actions
Protestant ethic and Christianity the moral foundation of law	Traditional Indian religions the foundations of codes of behavior
Personal offences seen as transgressions against the state as represented by the monarch	Personal offences seen as transgressions against the victim and his/her family; community threatened only when the public peace is threatened
Law administered by representatives of the state in the form of officially recognized or operated social institutions	Laws usually administered by the offended party, i.e., family, clan
Force and punishment used as methods of social control	Arbitration and ostracism usual peacekeeping methods
Individualistic basis for society and the use of the law to protect private property	Communal basis for society; no legal protection for private property; land held in trust by an individual and protected by the group

Source: JS Frideres & RR Gadacz, *Aboriginal Peoples in Canada: Contemporary Conflicts,* 7th ed (Toronto: Pearson, 2005) at 136.

The Royal Commission on Aboriginal Peoples recommended that the federal, provincial, and territorial governments "recognize the right of Aboriginal nations to establish and administer their own systems of justice,"[30] and others, such as the Aboriginal Justice Implementation Commission of Manitoba, have recommended an autonomous Aboriginal justice system to address the failure of the current criminal justice system for Aboriginal people. Other possibilities include "indigenizing" the current criminal justice system through increased Aboriginal representation among police officers, lawyers, judges, and correctional officers; creating autonomous Aboriginal agencies to work within the existing system; and the continued implementation of the Correctional Service of Canada strategic plan for Aboriginal Corrections, which aims to provide culturally appropriate programming and services in custody facilities.[31]

Despite some positive developments—for example, the eight healing lodges currently operating across the country, and the Aboriginal-specific In Search of Your Warrior Violent Offender Healing Program—success has been limited. Many bridges still need to be built to cross the cultural divide between mainstream and Aboriginal concepts of law and justice, and to address the underlying causes of Aboriginal overrepresentation in the criminal justice system.

---

30   *Ibid* at 312.

31   Roberts, Boyington & Kazarian, *supra* note 24 at 330-31.

CHAPTER SUMMARY

Canada's *Constitution Act, 1867* gives the Parliament of Canada exclusive jurisdiction over criminal law and procedure in criminal matters. Pursuant to this power, the federal government enacted a *Criminal Code* in 1892, which, since then, has been the primary source of Canadian criminal law. The *Criminal Code* contains key principles of our criminal law, including elements making up an offence and the burden and standard of proof in criminal cases. It organizes specific offences into general subject matter categories and classifies offences into three categories: summary, indictable, and hybrid. It also contains law relating to the criminal trial process, defences, sentencing, and appeals.

In addition to the *Criminal Code*, other federal statutes and the Charter play an important role in this area. As well, decisions of the courts—especially SCC decisions interpreting criminal law statutes and the Charter—are an integral part of our criminal law.

The larger field of criminal justice also involves policing, corrections, and youth justice. Police investigation of crime may lead police to charge an individual with a criminal offence. If, after their trial, individuals are found guilty, then depending on their offence they may be sentenced to incarceration in either a provincial or a federal correctional institution. In Canada today, young persons who commit criminal offences are treated differently than adults and are tried separately in a youth justice court.

KEY TERMS

actus reus the objective part of a criminal offence; the actual criminal act *(p. 374)*

aggravating circumstance a factor in the case that causes the judge to impose a harsher sentence on the convicted person than he or she otherwise would *(p. 388)*

appearance notice a document given to a person, usually at the scene of the crime, requiring that person to come to court on a certain date and time to answer to a charge *(p. 381)*

arraignment procedure by which the charge is read to the accused in open court and the accused is asked how he or she wishes to plead *(p. 384)*

arrest detaining or holding a person by legal authority *(p. 379)*

conviction a judge or jury's finding an accused person guilty of an offence *(p. 384)*

Crown attorney a lawyer, also known as a Crown prosecutor, who is an agent of the attorney general and who represents the Crown in court, particularly in criminal matters *(p. 370)*

duty of disclosure the Crown's mandatory disclosure to the accused, before the trial, of the evidence against him or her *(p. 379)*

hybrid offence a dual procedure offence, meaning that the Crown attorney has the option of choosing whether to prosecute it as a summary conviction offence or as an indictable offence *(p. 378)*

indictable offence the most serious type of offence in the *Criminal Code* (for example, murder), carrying the most serious sentences *(p. 378)*

indictment written document, used in superior court, describing the offences with which the accused is charged *(p. 384)*

information written document, used in provincial court, describing the offences with which the accused is charged. *(p. 384)*

judicial interim release formal name for bail; the release of an accused prior to his or her trial *(p. 383)*

limitation period the period of time in which a legal action must be taken or the ability to do so is lost *(p. 376)*

mens rea the subjective part of a criminal offence; the intention or knowledge of wrongdoing *(p. 374)*

mitigating circumstance a factor in the case that causes the judge to impose a milder sentence on the convicted person than he or she would otherwise *(p. 388)*

plea bargain agreement between the Crown and the defence on how the accused will plead in court and on the sentence he or she will receive *(p. 384)*

plead to answer to a criminal charge in ways permitted by the *Criminal Code* *(p. 383)*

preliminary inquiry hearing before a Provincial Court judge to determine whether the Crown has sufficient evidence for the accused to stand trial for the offence *(p. 384)*

pre-sentence report a report, prepared by a probation officer that provides information about the background and character of the offender, to assist a judge in sentencing *(p. 388)*

quasi-criminal offences offences that are created by provinces and municipalities and that fall within provincial jurisdiction—for example, health, education, and highway traffic laws *(p. 373)*

search warrant a warrant, issued by a justice of the peace or a provincial court judge, authorizing police to conduct a search *(p. 381)*

sentence the punishment the judge imposes on a person convicted of a criminal offence *(p. 386)*

summary conviction offence the least serious type of offence in the *Criminal Code* (for example, trespassing or disturbing the peace), tried only in provincial court and subject to the lightest sentences *(p. 376)*

summons a document served personally on an accused person requiring him or her to be in court at a certain date and time *(p. 383)*

superior court of criminal jurisdiction the highest court in each province and territory to hear criminal matters, sometimes with a jury, its designation varying by province and territory *(p. 378)*

undertaking a promise to appear in court at a certain date and time *(p. 383)*

verdict the finding of a jury on the matter before it—for example, whether the accused is guilty or not guilty *(p. 385)*

FURTHER READING

Barnhorst, R & S Barnhorst. *Criminal Law and the Canadian Criminal Code*, 5th ed (Toronto: McGraw-Hill Ryerson, 2009).

Bell, Sandra J. *Young Offenders and Youth Justice: A Century After the Fact*, 3d ed (Toronto: Nelson, 2007).

Gulycz, Michael & Mary Ann Kelly. *Criminal Law for Legal Professionals* (Toronto: Emond Montgomery, 2014).

Hamilton, AC. *A Feather Not a Gavel: Working Towards Aboriginal Justice* (Winnipeg: Great Plains Publications, 2001).

Ismaili, Karim, Jane B Sprott & Kim Varma, eds. *Canadian Criminal Justice Policy: Contemporary Perspectives* (Toronto: Oxford University Press, 2012).

Hennessy, P. *Canada's Big House: The Dark History of the Kingston Penitentiary* (Toronto: Dundurn, 1999).

Istvanffy, Jay. *Gladue Primer* (British Columbia: Legal Services Society, 2011): <http://resources.lss.bc.ca/pdfs/pubs/Gladue-Primer-eng.pdf>.

Martin's Pocket Criminal Code 2013 (Toronto: Canada Law Book, 2012).

O'Regan, Karla & Susan Reid. *Thinking About Criminal Justice in Canada* (Toronto: Emond Montgomery, 2012).

Pink, Joel E & David C Perrier, eds. *From Crime to Punishment: An Introduction to the Criminal Law System*, 6th ed (Toronto: Thomson, 2007).

Watkins, Kerry, Gail Anderson & Vincenzo Rondinelli. *Evidence and Investigation: From the Crime Scene to the Courtroom* (Toronto: Emond Montgomery, 2012).

REVIEW QUESTIONS

1. What did John A. Macdonald dislike about the American system of criminal law and how did he prevent it from happening in Canada?

2. List four federal statutes that are sources of Canadian criminal law.

3. List and describe the two elements of a criminal offence in the *Criminal Code*.

4. Explain the criminal standard of proof "beyond a reasonable doubt." To whom does this standard apply?

5. What are the three classifications of criminal offences in the *Criminal Code*?

6. Why is disclosure so important to an accused person?

7. What is an aggravating circumstance? Give three examples.

8. List five important matters for an accused to consider before his or her trial begins.

EXERCISES

1. Do you think a specialized court like Ontario's Domestic Violence Court is a good idea? Why or why not?

2. Read the SCC decision in *Bedford* (see Box 13.2). Assume that you are responsible for redrafting one of the provisions that the SCC declared unconstitutional. Choose one—the bawdy-house, living on the avails, or communication offence—and redraft it. Try to go no further than is necessary to achieve the purpose of the offence (controlling nuisances or exploitive relationships), and try to ensure that there is no increased risk to sex workers in pursuing their livelihood.

    Next, research whether Parliament has redrafted the particular *Criminal Code* provision you have chosen. If it has, compare the new provision with your version, and explain why you think it is a better or a worse attempt to make the law constitutional.

3. Examine the first paragraph in the preamble to the *Youth Criminal Justice Act*. What do you think are the "developmental challenges and the needs of young persons"? What members of society are best placed to guide young persons into adulthood, and why?

4. In recent decades, changes to the way Canada's criminal justice system deals with Aboriginal people accused and convicted of crimes have sought to improve treatment and outcomes for Aboriginal offenders. What do you think of these solutions and their potential for reform? Depending on your answer, should Aboriginal people have jurisdiction to operate their own criminal justice system? Defend your answer.

PART IV
Working with the Law

14 The Legal Profession

After reading this chapter, you will understand:

- Educational requirements for lawyers and paralegals in common law provinces
- How the practice of law has changed in Canada
- Various career possibilities in the legal profession for lawyers and paralegals
- The role of law societies as governing bodies for lawyers

> Any attempt to offer a comprehensive portrait of Canadian lawyers is fraught with difficulty. No one knows very much about them, but there is a great deal to know.
>
> HW Arthurs, R Weisman & FH Zemans, "The Canadian Legal Profession"
> (1986) 11:3 Am Bar Found Res J 447 at 448

Introduction

The legal profession itself is, of course, an essential component within the whole system of Canadian law. Lawyers are prominent in public life, and they play a large role in our three branches of government. Judges in the judicial branch are appointed from the legal profession. Many members of Parliament, the legislative branch, have been lawyers, and so have many prime ministers. In the executive branch, lawyers play a key role in the civil service formulating government policies, drafting new legislation, and serving on administrative boards, agencies, commissions, and tribunals.

This chapter presents a historical overview of the legal profession in Canada. It shows, first, how the educational requirements for common law lawyers and paralegals have changed over the years. The chapter then reviews how the practice of law itself has changed over time, with sole practitioners and small partnerships giving way to today's large corporate law firms in major urban centres. We then identify various career possibilities open to lawyers and paralegals in the legal field. The chapter focuses specifically on lawyers and paralegals. Legal ethics applicable to them, and to other kinds of legal practitioners who provide legal services to the public, such as notaries, patent and trademark agents, and immigration consultants, are covered in Chapter 15. The chapter concludes by examining how provincial law societies regulate the practice of law in Canada.

Legal Education for Common Law Lawyers

In Canada, there has been a long-standing debate in common law provinces over rival methods for teaching the law. Some members of the legal community have adhered to the belief that traditional English vocational methods for training lawyers should be followed. These methods were based on an apprenticeship model whereby law students served "under **articles**." In doing so, they obtained practical experience and direct knowledge of the law by working in the office of a supervising practising lawyer. This training could also be supplemented with law society lectures. Ontario, for example, followed this apprenticeship, or articling, model for a long time.

On the other side of the legal education debate were those who favoured the idea of someone attending a university law school where professors rather than practising lawyers taught the law. Those in Canada who supported this rival academic approach had American law schools, most notably Harvard University, and university law schools in Canada, such as McGill in Quebec and Dalhousie in Nova Scotia, as examples to follow.[1]

The first Canadian common law province to teach future lawyers at a university law school was Nova Scotia, in 1883, at Dalhousie University law school in Halifax.[2] There, law students studied full-time and then articled for a period of time, as prescribed by that province's law society (the Barristers' Society of Nova Scotia), before becoming lawyers.

This debate over how best to train lawyers continued in other common law provinces as they were formed, especially in Western Canada.[3] The model currently in place in the common law provinces, which combines academic coursework with articling requirements, is now the generally accepted one.[4]

Prospective lawyers in common law provinces must now generally meet the following educational requirements:

- an undergraduate bachelor's degree with a high grade-point average (though many applicants have more advanced degrees, such as master's degrees, and some law schools may take incoming students with a minimum of two years at a university);
- a high score on the Law School Admission Test (LSAT);
- three years of full-time study at law school completing an LLB or JD degree;
- a period of articling as determined by their province's law society; and
- completion of a bar admission course, consisting of a series of lectures and examinations established by a province's law society.

Once all these educational and placement requirements are met, law students are then **called to the bar**, a formal ceremony whereby they are admitted to the law society of their province and may begin to practise law. In Canada they are usually called lawyers, and formally called barristers and solicitors.

---

1   See Ian C Pilarczyk, *A Noble Roster: One Hundred and Fifty Years of Law at McGill* (Montreal: McGill University Faculty of Law, 1999); Léon Lortie, "The Early Teaching of Law in French Canada" (1976) 2 Dal LJ 521; C Ian Kyer & Jerome Bickenbach, *The Fiercest Debate: Cecil A Wright, the Benchers and Legal Education in Ontario, 1923-1957* (Toronto: University of Toronto Press, 1987); JPS McLaren, "The History of Legal Education in Common Law Canada" in RJ Matas & DJ McCawley, eds, *Legal Education in Canada* (Montreal: Federation of Law Societies of Canada, 1987) 111.

2   John Willis, *A History of Dalhousie Law School* (Toronto: University of Toronto Press, 1979).

3   JR London, "The Admissions and Education Committee: A Perspective on Legal Education and Admission to Practice in the Province of Manitoba, Past, Present and Future" in C Harvey, ed, *The Law Society of Manitoba, 1877-1977* (Winnipeg: Peguis, 1977) 74 at 75; W Wesley Pue, *Law School: The Story of Legal Education in British Columbia* (Vancouver: University of British Columbia Faculty of Law, 1995).

4   William H Hurlburt, *The Self-Regulation of the Legal Profession in Canada and in England and Wales* (Calgary and Edmonton: Law Society of Alberta/Alberta Law Reform Institute, 2000) 69-78.

Legal Education for Paralegals

Paralegals are not lawyers but they are qualified in education and experience to work in a legal environment such as a law firm or a government ministry like the federal Department of Justice or provincial Ministry of the Attorney General (or Ministry of Justice). Paralegals work under lawyers' supervision and assist them in various practice areas. Generally, they are not permitted to give legal advice and do not represent anyone in court matters. Paralegals in Ontario are a special exception (see Box 15.2 in Chapter 15). In Ontario, licensed paralegals may represent people in some lower-level courts and before administrative bodies.

In the past, no formal education was needed to become a paralegal, but this has now changed significantly. Most paralegals today are graduates of a specialized certificate or diploma program at a college or university. There are many variants in terms of whether the programs are part-time, full-time, onsite, or online, and in terms of the admission requirements (some require work or post-secondary education experience, and some allow admission directly from high school). As well, some academic institutions now offer a four-year degree program in paralegal education. Currently, the Law Society of Upper Canada (LSUC) is the only law society to regulate paralegals, requiring them to be graduates of an accredited paralegal program and to pass a licensing exam. Other law societies are considering a similar approach.

The Changing Practice of Law in Canada

When we view the current practice of law in this country from a historical perspective, we can see how much it has changed. As legal historian Carol Wilton has written, "law firms are not islands unto themselves. On the contrary, their work, organization, and culture are intimately tied to the economies and societies of which they are a part."[5] Ged Baldwin, a lawyer who established his law practice in the Peace River district of Alberta in the early 1900s, wrote a book about his career that illustrates Wilton's point and gives us some idea of how much the legal profession has changed in the past century. The following passage, for example, describes Baldwin's early start in the town of Berwyn:

> For my legal services on behalf of the town and my hockey-playing skills on behalf of the town team, they would pay me a small salary. I accepted. I opened a little law office in Berwyn. One by one other clients began to trickle in. Some even managed to pay for my services in coin of the realm. More often, my recompense was stove wood, or lumber, or crop produce, even livestock sometimes. These were, after all, the Depression years.[6]

Prior to Confederation in 1867, Canada was largely a pre-industrial, rural country. Cities were small. A transportation infrastructure composed of canals, roads, bridges, and railways was just getting started. Natural resources such as furs, timber, minerals, and fish were key staples of the economy. Commercial life was expanding with the rise of banks, insurance

---

5   C Wilton, "Introduction: Inside the Law—Canadian Law Firms in Historical Perspective" in C Wilton, ed, *Essays in the History of Canadian Law: Inside the Law—Canadian Law Firms in Historical Perspective*, vol 8 (Toronto: University of Toronto Press, 1996) 3 at 4.

6   Ged Baldwin, *Frontier Justice: The Reminiscences of Ged Baldwin* (Edmonton: University of Alberta Press, 1987) at 3.

companies, and corporations, but these institutions were not as developed as they are today. Legal practice was intimately tied to the economy and society of this era. Lawyers had a general practice doing land conveyancing and mortgages, drafting wills and contracts, and doing debtor–creditor and litigation work. Most lawyers worked as sole practitioners or in small, two-person partnerships.[7]

However, as social and economic change came to Canada after Confederation, the practice of law started to change. It was becoming an era of railway-building, for example. As the railway business grew in importance, so did the lawyers involved with it. Aemilius Irving of Ontario, for example, became in-house corporate counsel for the Great Western Railway—one of the first lawyers in Canada to hold this new kind of in-house corporate position.[8] As the country's economy further developed, there were more and more positions of this kind. Lawyers with corporate clients in the country's business community could go on to hold high positions in government. The legal career of John A. Macdonald exemplifies this direction (see Box 14.1).

Other economic developments in Canada after Confederation affected the nature and practice of law. Electricity began to power new factories, and people moved from farms to the cities in greater numbers. New industries arose during this period—iron and steel, for example, and, in Western Canada, wheat, pulp and paper, as well as oil and gas. Inventions such as the car, the airplane, and the telephone continued to further transform society.[9] Every change created new roles and opportunities for lawyers.

Law firms grew larger during this new post-Confederation commercial and industrial era. Corporate law was becoming more complex, with more mergers and regulatory requirements, and some Canadian companies were becoming international. Lawyers in large firms began to specialize in corporate law and act for the growing financial services sector, for mortgage and loan companies, and for new municipal utilities such as hydro. With the rise of unions, labour law was also becoming important, along with other areas such as litigation, insurance work, securities, taxation, and administrative law. Even newer fields were developing, such as condominium law, environmental law, intellectual property law, and consumer law.[10]

By the second half of the 20th century, the Canadian government, both at the provincial and the federal levels, was intervening more in the economy, and regulatory compliance became another important legal area, along with Charter litigation after 1982. Today, the structure of the legal profession, as well as its range of legal activities, is very different from what it was a century ago. Sole practitioners with a general practice still exist, as do small partnerships, but the rise of large corporate law firms servicing large commerical and industrial clients have brought some key transformations to the profession. The following changes, in particular, are noticeable in today's legal environment:

---

7   Wilton, *supra* note 5. See also Philip Girard, *Lawyers and Legal Culture in British North America: Beamish Murdoch of Halifax* (Toronto: University of Toronto Press, 2011).

8   Jamie Benidickson, "Aemilius Irving: Solicitor to the Great Western Railway" in Wilton, *supra* note 5 at 100.

9   Carol Wilton, "Introduction: Beyond the Law—Lawyers and Business in Canada, 1830 to 1930" in Carol Wilton, ed, *Essays in the History of Canadian Law: Beyond the Law—Lawyers and Business in Canada, 1830 to 1930* (Toronto: Butterworths, 1990) 3.

10 See Ronald J Daniels, "Growing Pains: The Why and How of Law Firm Expansion" (1993) 43:2 UTLJ 147; Christopher Moore, *McCarthy Tetrault: Building Canada's Premier Law Firm, 1855-2005* (Vancouver/Toronto: Douglas & McIntyre, 2005); Christopher Moore, "Megafirm: A Chronology for the Large Law Firm in Canada" in Constance Backhouse & W Wesley Pue, eds, *The Promise and Perils of Law: Lawyers in Canadian History* (Toronto: Irwin Law, 2009) 103.

BOX 14.1

John A. Macdonald: Corporate Lawyer

Much is known about Sir John A. Macdonald as Canada's first prime minister. Less is known about him as a leading corporate lawyer acting for business and commercial clients in Kingston and elsewhere both before and during his career in federal politics.

As a corporate lawyer, according to historian J.K. Johnson, Macdonald held the following positions:

- a director of the Commercial Bank of the Midland District, Kingston's main financial institution;
- member of the board of directors for two British firms, the Trust and Loan Company of Upper Canada and the Times and Beacon Assurance Company of London; and
- president of the St. Lawrence Warehouse Dock and Wharfage Company of Quebec City, from 1864 to 1889.

Macdonald was also involved with railways, steamships, road companies, and real estate speculation across southern Ontario.

Johnson wonders if Macdonald's extensive business background helped facilitate economic activity in Canada. In his opinion, it did, and he cites as evidence Macdonald's later support of a "National Policy" for a high tariff to protect domestic Canadian manufacturers, a policy favoured by a majority of urban Canadian business leaders.

Sources: JK Johnson, "John A Macdonald, the Young Non-Politician" (1971) 6:1 Canadian Historical Association Historical Papers 138; JK Johnson, "John A Macdonald and the Kingston Business Community" in G Tulchinsky, ed, *To Preserve and Defend: Essays on Kingston in the Nineteenth Century* (Montreal and London: McGill-Queen's University Press, 1976) 141.

- *Recruitment.* Today, with so many law students seeking jobs in the legal profession, high academic excellence and achievement are critical assets. Law firms seek to recruit and hire the best and the brightest new lawyers.
- *Rise of the megafirm.* These large law firms have come about through mergers and alliances, giving them national, North American, and even international reach.
- *Collaborative teams.* It is common, especially in large corporate law firms, to use collaborative teams of lawyers, associates, juniors, paralegals, and clerical support staff to serve the complex needs of law firm clients. Other collaborations can be with non-legal professionals such as accountants, financial services professionals, health-care professionals, engineers, and architects (commonly referred to as multi-disciplinary practices, or MDPs).
- *Work–life balance.* Like many occupations today, practising law is very demanding. Long hours are expected, and there is great pressure to bill clients. Stress is common. It is not easy to change or modify this work environment.[11]

---

11 See HW Arthurs, "Lawyering in Canada in the 21st Century" (1996) 15 Windsor YB Access Just 202; RA Macdonald, "Let Our Future Not Be Behind Us: The Legal Profession in Changing Times" (2001) 64:1 Sask L Rev 1; D Stager & H Arthurs, *Lawyers in Canada* (Toronto: University of Toronto Press, 1990).

Career Possibilities for Lawyers and Paralegals

A legal education opens many doors. Lawyers can and do change jobs, and the demand for lawyers in many areas is expanding. The following are some related career possibilities within the legal services market available to lawyers:

- *Government.* Many lawyers in Canada work for municipal, provincial, and federal governments. Lawyers are particularly important for developing government policies in many areas, handling litigation matters, and for drafting new legislation for Parliament. Many lawyers are politicians themselves at all three levels of government.

- *Legal aid.* For people who are unable to afford a lawyer, provincial governments have publicly financed a legal aid fund. Part of this goes to community legal aid clinics, where lawyers and paralegals assist lower-income Canadians (see Chapter 16).

- *In-house counsel.* Many large Canadian companies now have their own legal departments, where lawyers are on staff and do legal work exclusively for the company.

- *Administrative boards, commissions, agencies, and tribunals.* Many lawyers serve as adjudicators on these various bodies, which play an increasingly large part in regulating economic activity in Canada.

- *Public interest advocacy organizations.* Many lawyers are attracted to work in such organizations, which are becoming more numerous in Canada. Examples are the Women's Legal Education and Action Fund (LEAF) and the Canadian Civil Liberties Association. Such organizations are involved in litigating specific matters that concern them, often using the Charter, and they are also involved in public education, lobbying governments, and in appearing as intervenors before courts, in particular the Supreme Court of Canada.

- *The judiciary.* Some lawyers, during or at the end of their legal careers, may serve as judges on provincial or federal courts.

- *Legal publishing.* The legal publishing industry is a significant one in both the United States and Canada. It produces academic textbooks, practitioner manuals, law journals, and legal reference books for those in related occupations such as policing, social work, and medicine. Materials to help with legal research, as well as specialized legal research software, are an increasingly important part of this industry. Many lawyers are authors and editors of such works.

- *Mediation, arbitration, and negotiation.* Owing to high legal costs, long trial delays, complex legal procedures, lack of privacy in court, and the court's use of the adversary system, many people are turning to alternative dispute resolution (ADR) mechanisms to settle their disputes. Mediation is one such method. Using this method, the disputing parties try to reach a settlement with the assistance of a third party. Lawyers can sometimes serve in this mediator role. (See Chapter 16 for a discussion of ADR more generally.)

- *Teaching.* Lawyers are employed as professors in many academic institutions—not only in university law schools, but also in paralegal programs in colleges and universities.

BOX 14.2

Hamilton's "United Nations" Law Firm

The small firm of Millar, Alexander, Tokiwa, and Isaacs, which existed from 1962 to 1993, nicknamed Hamilton's "United Nations law firm," was a leader and an inspiration in addressing the issue of race and the practice of law. The firm's four partners were Irish, Black, Japanese, and Aboriginal lawyers, respectively, at a time when multiracial law firms were rare in Canada.

Over time it became one of the most prominent and successful law firms in Hamilton. Its underlying success was partly owing to political, social, and economic forces that were reshaping Canadian society in the era following the Second World War. These forces began to change how—and by whom—law was practised in this country. The postwar era in Hamilton saw a broad transition away from a predominantly white male and Anglo-Celtic bar to one that included more visible minorities and women. Under these changing circumstances, the firm of Millar, Alexander, Tokiwa, and Isaacs was able to transform what would have been a disadvantage in an earlier era—its multiracial character—into an advantage.

The firm's multiracial character kept it in touch with the changing times. Many immigrants who settled in Hamilton after the war were anxious to buy their first home and sought out this multiracial firm to meet their legal needs in this regard. Paul Tokiwa, for example, could speak to the firm's new Japanese-Canadian clients in their own language.

There were other reasons for the firm's success. Lincoln Alexander's rise to political prominence as the first black member of Parliament in 1968 brought the firm national goodwill and further recognition. Moreover, all of the firm's members were excellent lawyers, whose reputations for doing good legal work brought in many new clients. As a small law firm, it also had the advantage of being able to service these new clients on a one-to-one basis.

The success of Millar, Alexander, Tokiwa, and Isaacs showed that in a modern Canadian multicultural society, diversity within a law firm could be a benefit. Indeed, this benefit is becoming more apparent as Canada grows ever more multicultural and multiracial, and business becomes more global.

Source: P Sworden, "'A Small United Nations': The Hamilton Firm of Millar, Alexander, Tokiwa, and Isaacs, 1962-1993" in C Wilton, ed, *Essays in the History of Canadian Law*, vol 7, *Inside the Law: Canadian Law Firms in Historical Perspective* (Toronto: University of Toronto Press, 1996) 469.

As with lawyers, the demand for paralegals in many areas is expanding. Some related career possibilities for paralegals include:

- court administration (such as a court clerk, reporter, or trial coordinator);
- legal research (such as a law librarian);
- legal recruitment;
- corporate compliance officer;
- private investigation;
- policing and corrections (such as a probation and parole officer);
- legal publishing (such as an editor, legal software developer, or technical writer);
- insurance (such as a claims adjuster, broker, or insurance agent); and
- human resources and office management.

Law Societies

In Canada, the legal profession is under provincial jurisdiction, is self-regulated, and is under the supervision and direction of the **law society** of each province or territory—in other words, its governing body of lawyers. The names of these law societies vary from province to province. For example, the law society in Nova Scotia is known as the Barristers'

Society; in Ontario, it is called the Law Society of Upper Canada. In Quebec, the law society has two divisions—the *Barreau du Québec* and the Board of Notaries. Law societies are responsible for, among other things,

- establishing requirements relating to the admission of lawyers to the province's bar,
- administering a code of professional conduct for lawyers,
- handling public complaints about lawyers,
- maintaining lawyer discipline and professional competence, and
- providing continuing legal education.

Law societies are composed of a small executive group of elected lawyers known in most jurisdictions as **benchers**, and might have some government appointed non-lawyers known as lay benchers. One of the benchers, called the president or treasurer, acts as the head. All of the benchers meet in convocation and form committees—the discipline committee, for example—to regulate and supervise the legal profession in the province.[12] See Chapter 15 for an examination of lawyers' duties to the profession and their law societies, and for a discussion of the disciplinary process.

---

12   FC DeCoste, *On Coming to Law: An Introduction to Law in Liberal Societies*, 2d ed (Markham, Ont: LexisNexis, 2007) at 36-39; Hurlburt, *supra* note 4.

CHAPTER SUMMARY

Lawyers play major roles in the legislative, judicial, and executive branches of government. Their education is rigorous, and their profession increasingly complex and demanding. The practice of law has changed dramatically over the past 150 years, from a profession made up largely of sole practitioners and small partnerships to one that is increasingly dominated by large law firms employing many paralegals in addition to lawyers.

Legal education in Canada has evolved, too. The old English apprenticeship model was one where law students were taught by a practising lawyer while serving "under articles." While it was favoured by some, it was opposed by supporters of a rival academic model, where future lawyers received their education at university law schools. The model currently in place in the common law provinces, which combines academic coursework with articling requirements, is now the generally accepted one. Education requirements for

paralegals have changed significantly, too. Whereas previously no formal education was required, most paralegals today are graduates of a college diploma program or a degree program in paralegal studies.

A range of opportunities exist for lawyers outside of the traditional law firm or courtroom settings, including work at all levels of government, in community legal aid clinics, and as in-house counsel for companies, and with administrative agencies and tribunals, public interest advocacy organizations, and legal publishers. Paralegals may work as court administrators and in private investigation, legal research, policing, insurance, and human resources.

In every province and territory, law societies composed of elected lawyers regulate and supervise the practice of law. Their functions include administering a code of conduct for lawyers, handling public complaints, providing continuing legal education, and disciplining lawyers.

KEY TERMS

article to serve an apprenticeship with a practising lawyer *(p. 400)*

bencher lawyers (and some non-lawyers) who are responsible for administering and governing the work of a provincial law society *(p. 407)*

call to the bar formal ceremony whereby a law student becomes entitled to practise law *(p. 401)*

law society the governing body of lawyers in a province *(p. 406)*

FURTHER READING

Alexander, Lincoln M. *"Go to School, You're a Little Black Boy": The Honourable Lincoln M Alexander—A Memoir* (Toronto: Dundurn Press, 2006).

Backhouse, Constance & W Wesley Pue, eds. *The Promise and Perils of Law: Lawyers in Canadian History* (Toronto: Irwin Law, 2009).

Brockman, Joan. *Gender in the Legal Profession: Fitting or Breaking the Mould* (Vancouver: University of British Columbia Press, 2001).

Collis, Diana & Cynthia Forget. *Working in a Legal Environment*, 2d ed (Toronto: Emond Montgomery, 2011).

Friedland, Martin. *My Life in Crime and Other Academic Adventures* (Toronto: University of Toronto Press, 2007).

Moore, Christopher. *McCarthy Tétrault: Building Canada's Premier Law Firm, 1855-2005* (Vancouver/Toronto: Douglas & McIntyre, 2005).

Sheehy, Elizabeth & Sheila McIntyre, eds. *Calling for Change: Women, Law, and the Legal Profession* (Ottawa: University of Ottawa Press, 2006).

Williams, David Ricardo. *Just Lawyers: Seven Portraits* (Toronto: University of Toronto Press, 1995).

PROVINCIAL LAW SOCIETY WEBSITES

Alberta: <http://www.lawsocietyalberta.com>.

British Columbia: <http://www.lawsociety.bc.ca>.

Manitoba: <http://www.lawsociety.mb.ca>.

New Brunswick: <http://www.lawsociety-barreau.nb.ca>.

Newfoundland and Labrador:
   <http://www.lawsociety.nf.ca>

Northwest Territories: <http://www.lawsociety.nt.ca>.

Nova Scotia: <http://www.nsbs.org>.

Nunavut: <http://www.lawsociety.nu.ca>.

Ontario: <http://www.lsuc.ca>.

Prince Edward Island: <http://www.lspei.pe.ca>.

Quebec: <http://www.barreau.qc.ca>.

Saskatchewan: <http://www.lawsociety.sk.ca>.

Yukon: <http://www.lawsocietyyukon.com>.

REVIEW QUESTIONS

1. In what ways do lawyers play a key role in the executive branch of government?

2. What were the two sides in the debate in Canada's common law provinces over how best to train new lawyers?

3. What is the significance of Dalhousie Law School for legal education in Canada?

4. In Canada's common law provinces today, what are the educational requirements a prospective lawyer must meet for admission to practise law?

5. Explain the role of paralegals.

6. What were some of the economic developments in post-Confederation Canada, and how did they affect the legal profession?

7. List four responsibilities of a provincial (or territorial) law society.

EXERCISES

1. Visit the website for your province's law society. Comment on how effectively the website provides information concerning how to find a lawyer in your area of interest.

2. Assume you are in high school and are thinking of becoming a lawyer. List the academic requirements you will likely need to complete in order to become a lawyer in your province.

3. Why did Canadian law firms grow larger in the decades after 1867?

4. Do you think that Canada's increasingly aging population will have an impact on the future practice of law? Discuss.

5. Why do you think an institutional client like a bank or large corporation is so valuable to a law firm?

6. Do you believe that lawyers should be self-governed by their own professional body or regulated directly by their provincial government? Discuss.

15 Legal Ethics

After reading this chapter, you will understand:

- The nature of legal ethics, codes of conduct, and the specific types of ethical obligations that legislation and law society rules impose on legal practitioners
- Legal practitioners' duty to the state, including the responsibility to uphold the law and not to advise or assist in its violation
- Legal practitioners' duty to the court, including the obligation to act with courtesy and in good faith
- The ethics of advocacy, and how legal practitioners are expected to deal with difficult clients and cases

- Legal practitioners' duty to the profession and to the public, including their obligations with respect to undertakings, advertising, and solicitation of clients
- Legal practitioners' duty to the client, including their primary obligations of competence, confidentiality, and loyalty
- The regulatory framework for monitoring ethical behaviour in the legal profession and the process for disciplining ethical breaches

I ntegrity without knowledge is weak and useless, and knowledge without integrity is dangerous and dreadful.

Samuel Johnson (1709–1784) from *Rasselas*, ch 41

Introduction

In Chapter 1, we compared law with other rules or norms, including moral and ethical obligations. We noted that, though there is no generally accepted distinction between morality and ethics, the two terms have slightly different connotations. We tend to associate ethical norms with specific social contexts, such as acceptable standards of behaviour within certain professions. The purpose of this chapter is to provide an overview of the ethics of the legal profession.

The popular media—films and television dramas, for example—often like to characterize legal professionals, especially lawyers, as lacking in integrity. But most legal professionals are in fact extremely ethical in their practice of the law. The profession is tightly regulated by its governing bodies, whose foremost concern is to protect the public. The consequences of ethical lapses in the practice of law can be very serious.

This chapter begins with an overview of legal ethics and of the main codes of conduct that guide the legal profession in Canada. It then covers the various duties that form the standard of ethical behaviour expected of legal practitioners. These include the duties to the state, the court, the profession, the public, and the client. The final section deals with disciplinary consequences of ethical breaches.

Origins of the Legal Profession

The legal profession in western society can be traced to ancient Greece. In that ancient society, people with legal problems used orators—that is, skilled speakers—to argue legal points on their behalf. These orators were not formally recognized as belonging to a legal profession.

Athenian law, for example, forbade their charging fees. (*Public* advocates, appointed to prosecute important criminal cases, were, however, paid a small fee.)[1]

The situation was similar for many years in ancient Rome, where orators or advocates would plead cases for others without remuneration. Over time, Rome saw the emergence of a class of legal specialists, called jurisprudents, who had a recognized expertise in the law, acquired through study.[2] Like the unpaid orators before them, however, they were amateurs and worked for free. It was not until the reign of Emperor Claudius (41–54 CE) that the practice of law was "professionalized," and legal representatives in Roman society could charge fees for their services up to a maximum of 10,000 sesterces (probably around $5,000 dollars in today's currency).[3]

By the time the Byzantine Empire was founded in the fourth century CE, the legal profession was firmly established, with clear rules of practice. In many respects, it resembled the legal profession of today. There were lawyers who specialized in arguing cases before the courts—the equivalent of today's litigators—and there were others, similar to the solicitors or notaries of today, who specialized in drafting documents and performing a range of administrative duties. With the fall of the Western Roman Empire and the onset of the Dark Ages, the legal profession essentially disappeared. The church became the dominant force, and ecclesiastical or canon law provided the basis of social regulation. Ecclesiastical law was for the most part interpreted and enforced by priests and by other members of the religious establishment.

In the Middle Ages, with the rise of civil government, a separate legal profession re-emerged. Initially, these legal practitioners were thought of narrowly as "canonists"—that is, experts in ecclesiastical law. During the 1200s, however, throughout Europe and in England, paid jurists again established themselves as part of the state's regulatory structure.

The early history of the English legal profession is complicated because of the wide variety of practitioner classes. There were many kinds or classes of lawyers, each with its own set of responsibilities. This complexity diminished over time, until two main types of lawyers remained: barristers and solicitors. This distinction between barristers (that is, litigators) and solicitors is still observed in England today, though it is less pronounced than it once was. In North America, by comparison, the profession has always been simplified in this regard; Canadian and American lawyers can practise as both barristers and solicitors. That said, most lawyers in North America specialize either in pleading cases before courts and tribunals (barrister work) or in representing and serving clients in non-litigious matters (solicitor work). See Chapter 14 for a general discussion of the legal profession in Canada today.

Ethical standards have always been involved in the practice of law. They were reflected in the oaths that lawyers were required to swear before civil and ecclesiastical courts throughout Europe, after the legal profession's re-emergence in the Middle Ages. They were reflected in England's first *Statute of Westminster*, enacted in 1275, which made it an offence to perpetrate a fraud before the court. And they are reflected in the codes and rules that govern the profession today.

---

1   Robert J Bonner, *Lawyers and Litigants in Ancient Athens: The Genesis of the Legal Profession* (New York: Benjamin Blom, 1927) at 201.

2   John A Crook, *Legal Advocacy in the Roman World* (London: Duckworth, 1995) at 40.

3   *Ibid* at 129-30.

What Are Legal Ethics?

Legal ethics are the rules of conduct that govern the legal profession. They encompass more than the civil wrongs or criminal behaviour for which any person can be held accountable. Their primary purpose is the protection of the public. Why does the public need to be protected from lawyers? Legal professionals exercise considerable power. Generally speaking, they have expertise in the workings of the machinery of state, and they must be required to use that expertise responsibly. Practically speaking, they have access to personal and financial information that could be damaging to their clients and others, and they are often dealing, in their professional capacity, with individuals who are vulnerable or unsophisticated. Holding legal professionals to high ethical standards is necessary for the protection of those persons who may be affected by their conduct.

Written codes of conduct for lawyers are a relatively recent development in common law jurisdictions. In the past, there was some statute law and case law defining inappropriate conduct in the practice of law. But the profession resisted adopting anything more comprehensive than that. The common assumption seems to have been that the legal profession was, after all, an ancient, noble, and learned profession; it went without saying that honour and integrity governed its practice. This professional aplomb persisted until the 19th century.

Our discussion of legal ethics in this chapter is generally focused on lawyers. But legal ethics also apply to other kinds of legal professionals—notaries and paralegals, for example—who have begun to play an increasing role in the practice of law. Ethical obligations apply to them either directly, through their own licensure obligations, or indirectly, in cases where they act under the supervision of others, usually lawyers, who are licensed.

Codes of Conduct

In the late 1800s, the governing bodies for lawyers in common law jurisdictions began developing written **codes of conduct** to guide their members. Generally speaking, these codes are not enforceable by the courts. It is the profession itself, in the form of law societies, that takes disciplinary action against those of its members who breach the codes of conduct.

Lawyers are the primary actors in the history of the legal profession. But in the modern era, as we have seen, other kinds of legal practitioners such as paralegals have joined lawyers in ever-increasing numbers to deliver legal services to the public. Some of these newer practitioners have their own sets of ethical codes. The following is an overview of the ethical codes in Canada that are applicable to the country's legal practitioners, whom we may divide into four broad categories:

1. lawyers,
2. notaries,
3. paralegals, and
4. other legal practitioners.

Lawyers

The Canadian Bar Association (CBA) is a federal organization, membership in which is voluntary for lawyers in some provinces but mandatory in others. It developed and adopted its first code of conduct in 1920—Canada's first code for lawyers. The Canons of Legal Ethics (CBA Canons), as it was called, borrowed in part from the Canons of Professional Ethics, adopted in 1908 by the American Bar Association. The CBA Canons was revised and replaced in 1974 with the Code of Professional Conduct. This latter Code has been revised a number of times, most recently in 2009. The CBA Code of Professional Conduct is currently known as the CBA Code.

Legislation in every province and territory in Canada has empowered law societies to discipline their members and to set the standards of practice for the profession. Almost every law society in Canada has passed its own code of conduct, similar to the CBA Code if not identical to it. (Prince Edward Island, the Northwest Territories, and Nunavut have simply adopted the CBA Code.)

In 2009, the Federation of Law Societies of Canada (FLSC), working with the law societies from all Canadian provinces and territories, adopted the Model Code of Professional Conduct (FLSC Model Code). It is drawn in part from the CBA Code. Membership in provincial/territorial law societies is mandatory for lawyers practising in a particular jurisdiction, as is following the law society's particular code. One of the consequences of living in a federal state is a multiplicity of rules. Uniformity is valuable in this context, however; hence the move to create the FLSC Model Code. New rules dealing with conflicts of interest and confidentiality were added to the FLSC Model Code in 2011. Some law societies have adopted, or are in the process of adopting, new codes based on the FSLC Model Code. (See Box 15.1.) For example, the Law Society of Manitoba adopted a new code based on the FLSC Model Code in 2011, and the Law Society of British Columbia did the same in 2013.

Notaries

Notaries (or notaries public) perform work that is defined as "solicitor" work in some provincial or territorial legislation. Whether notaries can act independently of lawyers, as a separate branch of the legal profession, depends on the legislative rules within their particular jurisdiction. Examples of typical notarial work include the following:

- witnessing affidavits (used as evidence in court proceedings) and statutory declarations (generally used for purposes other than court proceedings);
- preparing contracts; and

BOX 15.1

The FLSC Model Code

The preface to the FLSC Model Code emphasizes the importance of legal ethics in relation to the public interest. It includes the following provision:

> Rules of conduct should assist, not hinder, lawyers in providing legal services to the public in a way that ensures the public interest is protected. This calls for a framework based on ethical principles that, at the highest level, are immutable, and a profession that dedicates itself to practise according to the standards of competence, honesty and loyalty.

The seven chapters of the FLSC Model Code are as follows:

- Chapter 1: Interpretation and Definition
- Chapter 2: Standards of the Legal Profession
- Chapter 3: Relationship to Clients
- Chapter 4: Marketing of Legal Services
- Chapter 5: Relationship to the Administration of Justice
- Chapter 6: Relationship to Students, Employees, and Others
- Chapter 7: Relationship to the Society and Other Lawyers

- preparing real estate documentation (for example, transfers, mortgages, easements, and rezoning applications), estate planning, assisting with passport documentation, and preparing powers of attorney and representation agreements.

In most jurisdictions, lawyers are *automatically* notaries. Non-lawyers can become notaries after passing a prescribed examination. Non-lawyer notaries are generally appointed by the attorney general or the minister of justice of the province or territory in which they reside. The ethical rules of conduct governing their behaviour are the same as those imposed on public servants generally. British Columbia is an exception in this regard. Notaries in British Columbia have their own governing body, the Society of Notaries Public of British Columbia. This body has adopted its own ethical code, the Principles for Ethical & Professional Conduct Guideline, and it is responsible for disciplining its members for professional misconduct.[4] Also, it should be noted that notaries in Quebec are not the same as in other parts of Canada. Civil law notaries in Quebec are in fact lawyers and are required to have a civil law degree—their practice is roughly equivalent to a solicitor's practice in common law jurisdictions.

Paralegals

At the time of writing and as described in Chapter 14, in most jurisdictions in North America other than Ontario, the term "paralegal" refers to a person who is qualified by education and experience to perform specifically delegated substantive and procedural legal work while working *under the supervision of a lawyer*. Paralegals are employed by law firms, federal and provincial/territorial government departments and agencies, and corporations and non-profit organizations. They are not independently regulated or certified. The stature they enjoy comes from the particular education they have received and the experience they have gained through employment in the legal field. Box 15.2 describes the paralegal profession in Ontario.

In most jurisdictions, then, paralegals can provide the same legal services as lawyers can (and at a reduced cost to the client or employer), subject to the limitations set out in the legislation regulating the legal profession and law society rules. Their work typically includes the following:

- file management;
- interviewing clients and witnesses;
- drafting pleadings, contracts, wills, intellectual property, conveyancing, and corporate documents;
- legal research (case law, legislative, and secondary source research); and
- assisting with trials.

Paralegals are typically restricted from doing the following:

- giving legal advice directly to clients,
- providing undertakings to third parties, and
- appearing in courts and tribunals by themselves, as advocates.

These restrictions are not rigid, however, and may not apply if the relevant rules of practice and rules of procedure before courts and tribunals permit such activities.

---

4 *Notaries Act*, RSBC 1996, c 334.

BOX 15.2

Paralegals in Ontario

In Ontario, the term "paralegal" refers to a person with a unique classification. In that province alone, paralegals are permitted to practise independently of lawyers. In most common law jurisdictions in Canada, lawyers have long had a virtual monopoly over the practice of law. Historically, Ontario was the one jurisdiction where lawyers did not have this kind of monopoly. The Ontario legislation used to define specific areas of practice that were reserved for lawyers, and it left all other areas unregulated. One consequence of this was the emergence of an unregulated "paralegal" profession. Since 2007, however, the legislative framework in Ontario has changed. Lawyers in Ontario, as in other jurisdictions, are now given a virtual monopoly over the practice of law except in certain broad areas where paralegals, now regulated, are allowed to practice.

Paralegals in Ontario, then, licensed by the Law Society of Upper Canada (LSUC), are authorized to provide certain legal services *independently* of lawyers—that is, the work need not be delegated—within the limits set out in the relevant legislation and rules (bylaws) of the LSUC.

To become a paralegal in Ontario, a person must have graduated from a law society–accredited paralegal education program and have passed a prescribed licensing examination and met a good-character requirement. Work that licensed

paralegals in Ontario can perform independently of lawyers includes the following:

- representing clients in Small Claims Court, in the Ontario Court of Justice in respect of provincial offences, on summary conviction offences where the maximum penalty does not exceed six months' imprisonment, and before administrative tribunals;
- giving legal advice concerning rights and responsibilities in connection with the subject matter of a proceeding;
- drafting court documents for use in a proceeding; and
- negotiating on behalf of a client who is a party to a proceeding.*

In 2007, the LSUC approved an ethical code of conduct for paralegals practising in Ontario: the *Paralegal Rules of Conduct*. The LSUC is responsible for handling complaints against paralegals and for disciplinary decisions concerning their professional misconduct.

* For a history of the legal profession in Ontario and the process, beginning in 2007, that led to the regulation of paralegals in that province, see S Patricia Knight, *Ethics and Professional Practice for Paralegals*, 2d ed (Toronto: Emond Montgomery, 2010) ch 1. See also the Law Society of Upper Canada, online: <http://www.lsuc.on.ca>.

Law society rules and ethical codes address the relationship between lawyers and their employees, including paralegals. For example, rule 6.1-1 of chapter 6 of the FLSC Model Code provides as follows:

> 6.1-1 A lawyer has complete professional responsibility for all business entrusted to him or her and must directly supervise staff and assistants to whom the lawyer delegates particular tasks and functions.

By implication, therefore, lawyers' ethical obligations with respect to their work apply to the paralegals—or law clerks, in the case of Ontario—to whom they delegate that work. Lawyers have complete professional responsibility for all business entrusted to them, so their employees' ethical lapses could subject the supervising lawyers to discipline. Other employees of lawyers, such as students-at-law (or articling students) and legal assistants (or legal administrative assistants),[5] likewise take on the ethical obligations of the lawyers who have delegated them the work. It is the lawyers' responsibility to ensure that their employees are aware of the high ethical standards that must guide them in their work.

5 Job titles can be confusing in this area. Legal administrative assistants used to be called legal secretaries. Paralegals used to be called legal assistants in many jurisdictions, though not in Ontario. Increasingly, legal administrative assistants are now being called legal assistants.

Other Legal Practitioners

Other legal practitioners who can work independently of lawyers include patent and trademark agents, immigration consultants, commissioners for taking affidavits, and court agents.

Patent and trademark agents are federally licensed through the Canadian Intellectual Property Office (CIPO), after passing licensure examinations. The Intellectual Property Institute of Canada has a set of ethical guidelines that its members are required to follow: the Intellectual Property Institute of Canada Code of Ethics.

Immigration consultants are federally licensed through Citizenship and Immigration Canada. In 2011, the Immigration Consultants of Canada Regulatory Council (ICCRC) became the designated regulator for immigration consultants. Immigration consultants must take an accredited practitioner program and pass the required examinations. They are subject to discipline for professional misconduct and must follow the ICCRC's ethical guidelines as set out in the Code of Ethical Conduct.

Commissioners for taking affidavits (sometimes referred to as *commissioners of oaths*) are usually limited, in terms of their range of practice, to administering oaths and witnessing affidavits and statutory declarations. Lawyers, notaries, and other designated individuals—for example, government officials—are automatically commissioners. Non-designated individuals, however, can apply under the relevant legislation to become commissioners. Usually, the legislation will provide that certain kinds of employment qualify a person to act as a commissioner. Because commissioners play a limited role, there are no separate ethical codes of conduct applicable to them, beyond the code connected with the person's main source of employment.

In some provinces, courts permit lay practitioners, known as *court agents*, to appear before them as advocates for individuals who would otherwise go unrepresented due to the unavailability of trained professionals. This is something that happens, for example, in sparsely populated areas where lawyers are scarce. Courts do not have to permit these lay agents to appear. Although there are no separate codes applicable to such agents, they are held to a high standard of behaviour. The court may refuse to allow them to appear if it is not satisfied regarding the agent's professionalism. In British Columbia, for example, the legislation provides that the court has the right to refuse audience to a court agent and "has the same control over an unprofessional person practising in the court or before the justice as the court or justice would have over a qualified practitioner practising in there."[6]

Professionalism and Integrity

Underlying all the more specific ethical obligations imposed on legal professionals is the general obligation to act honourably, in good faith, and with integrity when dealing with others.

The preface to the CBA Code states the following:

> The essence of professional responsibility is that the lawyer must act at all times *uberrimae fidei*, with utmost good faith to the court, to the client, to other lawyers, and to members of the public.

---

6 *Court Agent Act*, RSBC 1996, c 76, s 2.

BOX 15.3

A Question of Integrity

Ryan was a lawyer hired by clients to pursue a possible wrongful dismissal claim against their employer. For over six years, he did nothing to further their claim. In response to their inquiries about the progress of the claim, he "spun an elaborate web of deceit." He told them that others were responsible for the delays, including other members of the bar; that discoveries had been cancelled; that he was pursuing a contempt motion against the defendants for failing to appear; and that a new precedent would require them to start the entire process over again. He even went so far as to forge a decision of the Court of Appeal. Finally, he admitted to his clients that he had done nothing and that all of his excuses were lies.

His clients filed a complaint with the Law Society of New Brunswick. Ryan was "apologetic and contrite and admitted his fault." In his defence, he argued that he was suffering from physical and emotional problems after separating from his wife, and that he was abusing alcohol and taking medication for panic attacks. Ryan had been disciplined twice before for failing to carry out services for his clients. The decision of the Discipline Committee was that Ryan should be disbarred. They reasoned that, given all the circumstances, his "unethical behaviour" was very serious and that "his honesty, trustworthiness, and fitness as a lawyer were irreparably compromised." When the case finally made it to the Supreme Court of Canada, the decision of the Discipline Committee was affirmed.*

Do you think that Ryan's excuses for failing to pursue his client's claim mitigate the lack of integrity demonstrated by his lies and by the forged court document? Was his lack of integrity so serious as to justify disbarment?

*   *Law Society of New Brunswick v Ryan*, 2003 SCC 20, [2003] 1 SCR 247.

Chapter I of the CBA Code, entitled "Integrity," states the following:

> The lawyer must discharge with integrity all duties owed to clients, the court or tribunal or other members of the profession and the public.

Rule 2.1 of chapter 2 of the FLSC Model Code, also entitled "Integrity," provides as follows:

> 2.1-1 A lawyer has a duty to carry on the practice of law and discharge all responsibilities to clients, tribunals, the public and other members of the profession honourably and with integrity.
>
> 2.1-2 A lawyer has a duty to uphold the standards and reputation of the legal profession and to assist in the advancement of its goals, organizations and institutions.

The commentary following these provisions states that integrity is the "fundamental quality of any person who seeks to practise as a member of the legal profession." The commentary goes on to state that while dishonourable conduct in a lawyer's private life can be so serious as to call into question the lawyer's professional integrity, law societies will not, generally speaking, be concerned with a lawyer's purely private activities.

Lawyers' Ethical Duties/Obligations

The following discussion focuses on ethical obligations that apply specifically to lawyers. Similar obligations will apply to other legal practitioners depending on the area of practice and the jurisdiction.

Duty to the State

The legal profession occupies a special position in society. This is owing to the knowledge lawyers have concerning the machinery of state, including how laws are made, unmade, and enforced. With this knowledge comes power and a corresponding obligation to respect social order. The old CBA Canon and some older provincial codes provide that a "lawyer owes a duty to the State, to maintain its integrity and its law." The notions of "duty to the state" and "integrity" are flexible ones, changing with the times (see Box 15.4). The modern codes do not expressly refer to a duty to the state, but they do cite an obligation to "encourage public respect for and try to improve the administration of justice."[7]

It might seem common sense that lawyers must not break the law or promote its breach. That is the ideal, of course, but the reality is bound to be different. Numerous *practising* lawyers have broken the law. Their offences have ranged from impaired driving, to possession of narcotics, to theft, to violent crimes. The disciplinary consequences have varied depending on the circumstances, from reprimands, to fines, to disbarment. There is a difference, of course, between, on the one hand, breaking the law or advocating that it should be broken and, on the other hand, using legal means to argue that the law should be changed or challenged. Unjust or unconstitutional laws can be questioned by appropriate methods, such as court challenges or fighting for political or legislative change.

Advising or assisting in the violation of the law—aiding and abetting—can be illegal in itself. Just as breaking the law directly will attract disciplinary consequences, so too will advising or assisting in the violation of the law.

Duty to the Court

Lawyers are "officers of the court" in Canada, a status now confirmed by legislation in most provinces and territories.[8] As officers of the court, lawyers are subject to the summary jurisdiction of the court and can be held liable for civil or criminal contempt for misconduct.

Courtesy and Respect

As noted earlier, the Preface to the CBA Code states that the lawyer must act "with utmost good faith to the court." Chapter IX states the following:

> When acting as an advocate, the lawyer must treat the court or tribunal with courtesy and respect and must represent the client resolutely, honourably and within the limits of the law.

Rule 5.1 of chapter 5 of the FLSC Model Code is entitled "The Lawyer as Advocate." Rule 5.1-1 is similar to the CBA Code rule regarding courtesy and respect. It provides as follows:

> 5.1-1 When acting as an advocate, a lawyer must represent the client resolutely and honourably within the limits of the law, while treating the tribunal with candour, fairness, courtesy and respect.

---

7 See CBA Code, ch XIII and FLSC Model Code, ch 5, r 5.6-1. The provincial and territorial codes all contain similar provisions. See Mark M Orkin, *Legal Ethics*, 2d ed (Toronto: Canada Law Book, 2011) ch 2 ("Duty to the State").

8 See, for example, *Legal Profession Act*, RSA 2000, c L-8, s 102(2); *Legal Profession Act*, RSBC 1998, c 9, s 14(2); *Legal Profession Act*, RSNWT (Nu) 1988, c L-2, s 64; and *Law Society Act*, RSO 1990, c L.8, s 29.

BOX 15.4

A Person of Good Repute

In the mid-20th century, W.J. Gordon Martin, a Canadian citizen who happened to be a communist, was not allowed to become a lawyer in British Columbia. Despite his successful completion of the educational requirements for practising law, Martin's support for communist doctrine, which prescribes the abolition of private property and the forcible overthrow of the existing social order, led the Benchers of the Law Society to conclude that he was not a person of good repute. They refused to call him to the bar or admit him to the province's Supreme Court. Their decision was upheld on appeal, first to the BC Supreme Court and then to the Court of Appeal.* The case arose at the height of the Cold War and against the backdrop of McCarthyism—that is, the campaign against alleged communists in the US government and other institutions carried out under Senator Joseph McCarthy. It is unlikely that the Martin case would be decided the same way today.

*   *Martin v Law Society of British Columbia*, [1950] 3 DLR 173 (BCCA).

The commentary following this last provision states that maintaining decorum and dignity in the courtroom is not an "empty formality." This statement is based on the principle that, "unless order is maintained, rights cannot be protected." This requirement that lawyers behave with courtesy and respect extends beyond court proceedings to "proceedings before boards, administrative tribunals, arbitrators, mediators and others who resolve disputes, regardless of their function or the informality of their procedures."

Abuse of Process

Rule 5.1-2(a) of chapter 5 of the FLSC Model Code states the following:

> 5.1-2(a)   When acting as an advocate, a lawyer must not abuse the process of the tribunal by instituting or prosecuting proceedings that, although legal in themselves, are clearly motivated by malice on the part of the client and are brought solely for the purpose of injuring the other party.

A lawyer has two strong reasons not to abuse the process in the way prohibited by this provision. First, the lawyer would be potentially liable for misconduct. Second, the client would be at risk of facing a later tort claim by the defendant for abuse of process or for malicious prosecution.

Other Obligations to the Court

Lawyers' responsibility to act in good faith and with courtesy and respect when appearing before the courts involves a number of specific obligations. Among them are the following:

- they must not knowingly mislead the tribunal by using false evidence (such as a false affidavit), and they must not misstate the facts;
- they must not fail to inform the court of binding authority that is directly on point, if that binding authority is not otherwise before the court; and
- they must not publicly criticize the tribunal or the adjudicator if they are on the wrong end of a ruling.

422 Part IV Working with the Law

Ethics of Advocacy

The ethics of advocacy overlap with lawyers' duty to the court. We may distinguish the two on the following grounds: the duty to the court deals with responsibilities that affect the court process, whereas the ethics of advocacy are more concerned with lawyers' need to balance their obligations to the court and their obligations to others.

Conflicting Obligations to the Court, to the Client, and to Others

Lawyers are required to treat tribunals with "candour, fairness, courtesy and respect," but at the same time to represent their clients "resolutely." As an advocate, a lawyer "has a duty to the client to raise fearlessly every issue, advance every argument, and ask every question, however distasteful, that the lawyer thinks will help the client's case."[9] It is hardly surprising, then, that lawyers sometimes have difficulty knowing when the pursuit of one objective infringes the other. The line between decorum and the pursuit of justice can become blurred. For example, a lawyer who aggressively cross-examines a witness—attempting to illicit favourable evidence for her client—may be seen as failing in her responsibility to be "courteous and civil and act in good faith" with others.[10] Conflicting loyalties of this kind can give rise to complicated ethical issues for lawyers.

Problems That Arise in Litigation

Lawyers face many situations during the litigation process that give rise to ethical questions. A few of the more common ones are discussed below.

PARTICULAR CLIENTS: ORGANIZATIONS AND ACCUSED PERSONS

Generally, a lawyer should conduct litigation the same way for all clients. Special considerations can apply when lawyers are dealing with organizations or when defending accused persons.

When representing an organization, the lawyer may discover that the organization has perpetrated a fraud—has falsified evidence, for example. The lawyer must disclose the fraudulent or illegal activity not only to the person in the organization from whom the lawyer is taking instructions but also to the chief legal officer and, in some cases, to the chief executive officer. The lawyer must also advise that the activity should be stopped. If this advice is not followed, the lawyer must withdraw from representing the client. This requirement applies when the lawyer is providing any kind of legal service, not just services related to litigation.

When representing an accused person, the lawyer must do his utmost to ensure that his client is not convicted unless it is on sound legal evidence before a competent tribunal. In his efforts to ensure this, he should rely on technicalities, so long as he knows them not to be false or groundless. The lawyer must do this regardless of what he believes about his client's credibility or the merits of the case. However, if the accused is competent and clearly admits to committing the crime, there will be limitations on what the lawyer can do. The lawyer will not be able to "set up an affirmative case inconsistent with the admission."[11] The client should be made aware of this restriction at the outset.

---

9   See the commentary following FLSC Model Code, ch 5, r 5.1-1.

10   See, for example, FLSC Model Code, ch 7, r 7.2-1.

11   See the commentary following FLSC Model Code, ch 5, r 5.1-1.

PARTICULAR CASES: CRIMINAL PROSECUTIONS AND FAMILY LAW MATTERS

Criminal cases tend to give rise to particular ethical problems for lawyers. Defence counsel face special problems (as described above), but so do prosecutors. Crown attorneys (also referred to as Crown prosecutors) in criminal cases are in a unique position compared with other advocates. Because they represent the public interest and the administration of justice, their primary duty is not to convict but to see that justice is done. This means that the Crown attorney cannot do anything to hinder the accused's ability to obtain representation or to communicate with counsel. Also, the Crown attorney must make timely disclosure to defence counsel (or to the accused directly, if he is unrepresented) of relevant facts and witnesses, regardless of whether these facts and witnesses support the accused's guilt or his innocence.

Family law cases also pose particular ethical problems for lawyers. In these cases, the adversarial process will not always lead to the best outcome. This is particularly so if the custody and support of children are involved. Representing a client "resolutely" in these cases will most often mean *not* pursuing every litigation tactic available to win a judgment for the client. For example, in divorce proceedings a client may instruct his legal representative to argue for exclusive custody of his child. Such an outcome, however, may not be in the best interests of the child. In family law cases, negotiation and mediation have been shown to result in better long-term outcomes than the adversarial system does (see the discussion of alternative dispute resolution more generally in Chapter 16 and in Chapter 10).

WITHDRAWING FROM CASES

Lawyers must not withdraw from representing a client without good reason. This applies whether or not the client's file is before the courts. During litigation, however, withdrawal can be particularly damaging to the client's interests. If there is a serious breakdown in the relationship—for example, if the client is not paying his fees or is engaging in criminal behaviour that is affecting the litigation—the lawyer can withdraw his services. If the lawyer is withdrawing from a criminal defence case and the trial date is close, he must try to obtain an adjournment.

In all cases, the lawyer must withdraw her services if she has been discharged by the client, if the client continually requests that she violate professional ethics, or if the lawyer finds herself not competent to handle the file.

DELAYING TACTICS

Lawyers may use the rules of the court—for example, by taking full advantage of all the time available—to advance their clients' interests. However, tactics that are designed solely to delay or to embarrass the other side and are not directly related to the client's case are considered unethical.

DUTY TO SETTLE

Most cases that begin as lawsuits settle out of court. There is no guarantee of winning a large judgment by going to court. There is always the risk of winning nothing. If a fair and reasonable result is possible through agreement, the lawyers on both sides should encourage the parties to take that route.

Rule 3.2-4 of chapter 3 of the FLSC Model Code states the following in this regard:

BOX 15.5

What Would You Do?

Assume you are a lawyer. The client you are representing in a case is a young child who has been seriously and permanently disabled by the negligence of a doctor—the defendant in the case. The claim is centered on the cost of future care for the child. At the time your firm was retained, the child was in an expensive facility that cares 24 hours a day for patients with your client's type of disability.

You win a favourable award at trial, an award that will cover the cost of the care facility for the rest of the child's life. The case is appealed. During argument on appeal, a judge asks you if the child is still in the facility. You answer truthfully that, as far as you are aware, the child is still in the facility. On a break in the proceedings, you contact the parents of the child, who tell you that they couldn't stand being apart from their child and that he is now back at home with them and that they are caring for him at a much reduced cost.

What would you do? When the proceedings resume, will you inform the court of this new information, knowing that it could affect the quantum (that is, amount) of the award for your client's future care?

Now assume that you are a paralegal assisting the lawyer in this case and that it is you who phones the parents during the break and becomes aware of this new information. Do you tell the lawyer—your employer? What if you tell the lawyer and she fails to pass this information on to the court. What do you do then?

3.2-4 A lawyer must advise and encourage a client to compromise or settle a dispute whenever it is possible to do so on a reasonable basis and must discourage the client from commencing or continuing useless legal proceedings.[12]

USE OF EVIDENCE

Lawyers must not mislead the court with false evidence, no matter how strongly they believe in the overall merits of a client's case and want the client to win. This line must never be crossed. Lying to the court directly is wrong, and so is failing to enlighten the court about any falsehood with respect to evidence in the case. For a lawyer knowingly to allow false evidence to go before the court is clearly a breach of this obligation. So is not correcting a mistake or falsehood discovered after evidence has been entered.

Where witnesses are concerned, a number of rules apply. For example, supporting witnesses can be interviewed and "prepared" for proceedings, but they must not be counselled to give false evidence or to suppress evidence. Similarly, lawyers cannot, without the leave of the court, communicate with their supporting witnesses while the opposing side is cross-examining them. And lawyers must not unduly harass or abuse adverse witnesses during examination.

OTHER ISSUES

During the pretrial discovery process, no adjudicator is present, and there is a potential for lawyers to abuse the opposition. They must not do this. Lawyers at this early stage in the process should not engage in, for instance, "the dogged pursuit of irrelevant details, and questioning that is calculated to exhaust or intimidate the opponent."[13]

---

12 See also CBA Code, ch III, commentary 6.

13 Gavin MacKenzie, *Lawyers and Ethics: Professional Responsibility and Discipline*, 5th ed (Toronto: Carswell, 2009) ch 4.6.

In jury trials, lawyers can evaluate potential jurors but must not communicate with them during or after trials.[14]

In the heat of battle, lawyers may be tempted to publicly criticize opposing counsel. This is unprofessional and encourages disrespect for the system.

Duties to the Profession and to the General Public

Along with the duties they owe to the state and to the court, lawyers owe duties to their governing bodies, to other legal professionals, and to members of the public.

Duty to the Legal Profession: Integrity

Chapter XV of the CBA Code, entitled "Responsibility to the Profession Generally," states the following: "The lawyer should assist in maintaining the integrity of the profession and should participate in its activities." The commentary on this provision gives some specific examples of what is being referred to. Lawyers must respond promptly to communications from the governing body (that is, the law society), and they must report ethical breaches by other lawyers, particularly if these breaches involve serious matters such as misappropriation of client funds or criminal activity related to the lawyer's practice.

Rule 7.1 of chapter 7 of the FLSC Model Code has the following heading: "Responsibility to the Society and the Profession Generally." It is similar to the CBA Code requirement regarding integrity except that it takes what is commentary in the CBA Code and makes it part of the rule.

Both codes emphasize the importance of effectively communicating with the law society and of reporting malpractice. These things are important because of the potentially serious consequences to clients and to the public if professional misconduct is left unchecked.

Duty to Legal Professionals and to Others: Courtesy and Good Faith

Chapter XVI of the CBA Code, entitled "Responsibility to the Profession Generally," states the following:

> The lawyer's conduct toward all persons with whom the lawyer comes into contact in practice should be characterized by courtesy and good faith.

Rule 7.2-1 of chapter 7 of the FLSC Model Code is similar in what it prescribes:

> 7.2-1 A lawyer must be courteous and civil and act in good faith with all persons with whom the lawyer has dealings in the course of his or her practice.

These rules provide that everyone with whom a lawyer has dealings—other legal professionals, clients, and the public—should be treated fairly and with deference. The rationale for these rules is that the legal profession plays an important role in society and that its representatives must positively reflect the system of justice they serve.

---

14 See CBA Code, ch IX, commentary 21 and FLSC Model Code, ch 5, r 5.5.

Specific Issues in Practice

Lawyers have a number of specific obligations based on these general duties regarding integrity, courtesy, and good faith. Among the more important of these obligations are those concerned with undertakings and advertising.

UNDERTAKINGS

Practising lawyers are frequently called upon to give undertakings. An **undertaking** is a clear statement of intention by one person that another person may reasonably rely on. Most lawyers' undertakings are made to further clients' interests. For instance, a lawyer representing a purchaser in a real estate transaction might receive a title transfer document from the seller on an undertaking by the lawyer to the seller not to register the transfer until the lawyer's client, the purchaser, has paid the lawyer the purchase price so that the lawyer can in turn pay the seller.

Undertakings by lawyers are solemn promises and are crucial to many legal transactions. Any lawyer who fails to live up to an undertaking has committed a serious ethical breach and will be liable for professional misconduct.

ADVERTISING

Historically, advertising by lawyers was considered undignified or worse. Governing bodies treated it as conduct that warranted disciplinary action. In 1982, for example, just before the Charter came into effect, the Supreme Court of Canada (SCC) affirmed a law society ruling disciplining a lawyer for advertising his services, which the law society held to be "conduct unbecoming" a lawyer.[15]

Times have changed. The Charter in effect guarantees "freedom of expression" under section 2. In consequence, there is general acceptance by the profession and by the public that advertising legal services is acceptable if done within reasonable bounds (that is, if it is not misleading or untruthful, meets a public need, and is done with integrity).[16] Television ads and full page listings in directories promoting legal services are now common.

OTHER MATTERS: SHARP PRACTICE AND PUBLIC CRITICISM

Engaging in so-called sharp practices—issuing misleading statements to opposing counsel or to the court, breaking agreements with other lawyers, issuing threats, making improper use of process, or using tricky means that are barely within the law—and taking advantage of "slips, irregularities or mistakes" by other lawyers are not considered fair play.[17] Public criticism by lawyers of other lawyers is unacceptable. Soliciting clients in order to take them away from other lawyers is also regarded as unethical. The practice of law is not like other businesses, which have fewer restrictions on competition.

Duty to the Client

Lawyers have a general right to refuse to take a particular client or case if they don't want to. It is this right that enables lawyers to specialize in certain areas if they so choose. For instance,

---

15 *AG Can v Law Society of BC*, [1982] 2 SCR 307.

16 See CBA Code, ch XIV (and the 2009 supplement, "Guidelines for Ethical Marketing Practices Using New Information Technologies") and FLSC Model Code, ch 4, r 4.2.

17 See Orkin, *supra* note 7 at 131.

a lawyer may choose to do only criminal cases or family disputes cases or wills and estates cases. Or a lawyer may choose to define her practice area more broadly—for example, "all types of civil cases" or "all types of civil cases except family disputes," or "all cases except criminal cases."

The right to refuse a client is a right that lawyers must exercise carefully, however, particularly if the would-be client will have difficulty obtaining legal services elsewhere. And there is one clear exception to the general principle that lawyers have the right to refuse a client: lawyers must take a client if the client has been assigned to the lawyer by a court or tribunal. Another exception is that a lawyer cannot refuse a client on discriminatory grounds. The ethics codes make it clear that lawyers have a general duty of non-discrimination.

Once a lawyer takes on a client, the parties are in a contractual relationship. It is a special kind of contractual relationship, however. It is one of confidence and one that has attached to it certain **fiduciary obligations** that require the lawyer to be open and honest, to be loyal, and to treat the client with good faith. The contractual relationship also involves an implied term that the lawyer must be competent and must exercise reasonable care in the delivery of the agreed-upon services.

In addition to contractual obligations, lawyers are subject to a duty in negligence. In other words, a lawyer can be liable for his negligent performance of services and for his careless words if the client's reliance on them results in damage to the client. In such a case, the degree of the lawyer's liability depends on the closeness of the lawyer–client relationship and on the "neighbour principle"—that is, every person's obligation to take reasonable care to avoid acts or omissions that might injure his or her neighbour. (For more in-depth discussion of this principle and of torts generally, see Chapters 1 and 9).

In addition to these contractual and tortious obligations where their clients are concerned, lawyers have related *ethical* duties of competence, confidence, and loyalty. What distinguishes these ethical duties from most others is that they coincide with legal or fiduciary obligations in contract and tort, as described above. Clients can clearly sue for their breach. For example, if a lawyer represents a purchaser in a real estate transaction and stands to profit from the sale because of his relationship with the seller, he has to disclose this conflict of interest to his client—the purchaser. If he fails to do so, he will not only be in breach of his ethical obligations to his client but also his contractual and fiduciary obligations, and can be sued.

As discussed, lawyers are permitted to incorporate their law practices to limit liability for ordinary operational risks (see the discussion of limited liability partnerships and corporations in Chapter 11). However, legislation prevents lawyers from using the corporate shield to avoid personal liability for failing to satisfy contractual, tortious, or other private law obligations.[18]

With respect to legal ethics, the duty to the client is the one that concerns most lawyers in day-to-day practice.

Duty of Competence

Lawyers have an obligation to provide services competently. The **duty of competence** does not require the lawyer to meet a standard of perfection, but it does require her to meet the standard of a reasonably skilled lawyer. If a matter is outside a lawyer's competence, the lawyer has a number of options: she may decline to act, she may request permission to

---

18 See, for example, *Legal Profession Act*, SBC 1998, c 9, s 84; *The Legal Profession Act*, SM 2002, c 44, s 36(1); *Legal Profession Act*, SNS 2004, c 28, s 23(1); *Law Society Act*, RSO 1990, c L.8, s 61.0.5(1).

bring in skilled co-counsel, or she may seek extra time to become competent in the matter (so long as this does involve added risk or expense for the client).

Duty of Confidentiality

Lawyers have an obligation not to divulge information concerning a client's affairs that is acquired in the course of the "professional relationship," unless they are authorized to do so by the client. However, information acquired in informal settings, outside of a professional relationship, is not protected.

The rationale for this **duty of confidentiality** is that it is required for the proper administration of justice. If clients had no assurance of the full confidentiality of their communications, many would only partially disclose relevant information to their lawyers, and this would hinder the lawyer's ability to provide appropriate and effective legal services.

This duty of confidentiality applies to all information concerning a client, subject to a few exceptions. One notable exception is a case where the lawyer reasonably believes, on the basis of information disclosed by the client, that there is an imminent risk of serious harm to someone. Also, while the codes are silent on this point, we may assume that the duty of confidentiality doesn't apply to "criminal communications"—in other words, to communications that are criminal in themselves (for example, a threat of physical harm to the lawyer or to her employees) or to communications made with a view to furthering a criminal scheme.[19]

The duty of confidentiality survives the professional relationship. The lawyer cannot subsequently use information about the client for personal benefit or for the benefit of others. This duty also applies to the lawyer's colleagues (for example, articling students and other lawyers) and staff (for example, paralegals, legal administrative assistants, and human resources personnel).

The duty of confidentiality is distinguishable from the related rule concerning **lawyer–client privilege**, also known as solicitor–client privilege. The latter is a rule of evidence and is slightly narrower in application than the duty of confidentiality. Lawyer–client privilege applies to confidential information that meets the following two criteria:

1. it is connected to the giving or receiving of legal advice; and
2. it is in the form of a communication between lawyer and client.

The duty of confidentiality applies to all client information regardless of whether it is connected with legal advice and regardless of the source of the information. The difference between the duty of confidentiality and lawyer–client privilege is not important to most clients. What is not covered by the privilege is covered by the duty.

Duty of Loyalty

A lawyer's **duty of loyalty** applies both to conflicts of interest between clients, and to conflicts of interest between the lawyer and her client.

CONFLICTS OF INTEREST BETWEEN CLIENTS

Lawyers owe a duty of loyalty to their clients. One of the consequences of this duty is that they cannot represent two clients who are opposing each other in a dispute or who are on

---

19 Alice Woolley, *Understanding Lawyers' Ethics in Canada* (Markham, Ont: LexisNexis, 2011) at 112-15.

opposite sides of certain kinds of financial transactions. The reason is that there might be a conflict of interest; it could be difficult for the lawyer to avoid advancing one client's interests at the expense of the other's interests. The duty-of-loyalty obligation extends beyond current clients. Lawyers cannot represent a new client whose interests conflict with those of a former client.

In certain situations, where the conflict of interest is minimal, lawyers might be permitted to represent both sides. In order to do so, however, they must inform both parties of the conflict, and the parties must give consent.

Conflicts of interests between clients are especially a problem for large law firms that have many lawyers and many clients (with the rise of megafirms and multinational mergers, clients of one firm could number in the thousands). Difficulties in this regard also arise from the fact that lawyers are very mobile, often moving from one firm to another. For example, a lawyer may work for a period of time in a firm that represents a client on one side of a dispute. Then, subsequently, this lawyer may leave that firm and go to work for the firm that represents the other party in the dispute. Law firms are required to be diligent in this regard and to have systems in place to ensure that any conflicts are discovered and dealt with appropriately.

Concerning *former clients*, the SCC has recognized that, even without client disclosure and consent, it might be possible for members of a law firm to represent a client in a dispute despite the fact that another member of the firm has formerly represented the other party (a former client) and has confidential information that could be used against that former client. The SCC identified two conditions that must be present for this to be possible:

1. the members of the law firm representing the client have not received any confidential information about the other side from the colleague that formerly represented the other side; and
2. the law firm has implemented effective institutional mechanisms securing confidential information, in order to rebut the presumption that the information has been shared between lawyers working at the same firm. These institutional mechanisms are sometimes called **cones of silence**. (The expression "Chinese wall," referring to the Great Wall of China, is also sometimes used to describe an institutional barrier to the sharing of confidential information.)

Concerning *current clients*, the SCC set out the **bright line rule** in 2002. This rule provides that a lawyer may not represent one client whose interests are directly adverse to the immediate interests of another current client, and that it is not just the individual lawyer but the lawyer's firm that is subject to this rule.[20] (See Box 15.6.)

CONFLICTS OF INTEREST BETWEEN LEGAL PROFESSIONAL AND CLIENT

The duty of loyalty applies also to conflicts between lawyer and client. A conflict can arise not only where a lawyer has business dealings directly with a client but also where the lawyer has dealings with others, and these dealings might prejudice the client's interests. This kind of conflict also arises where an associate or relative of the lawyer has dealings that could hurt the client's interests.

---

20 For recent applications of the "bright line" rule, see *Strother v 3464920 Canada Inc*, 2007 SCC 24, [2007] 2 SCR 177 and *Wallace v Canadian Pacific Railway*, 2011 SKCA 108, [2012] 1 WWR 251.

BOX 15.6

"Bright Line" Rule

In *R v Neil*, 2002 SCC 70, [2002] 3 SCR 631, the accused was a paralegal in Alberta who had been working independently and providing legal advice. In doing so, he was acting contrary to the province's *Legal Profession Act*. After an investigation, he faced criminal charges on two grounds:

* advising a client in a divorce case to forge documents, and
* scheming to defraud a financial institution.

Neil was represented by a law firm under a general retainer, advising him on legal matters generally. The firm gave Neil some initial advice relating to the charges, but did not go on to represent him before the courts in these criminal matters. (It is not clear who represented Neil before the courts; he may have represented himself.) It turned out that one of the lawyers working at the firm was currently representing other clients whose interests were opposed to Neil's. One of these clients was a co-accused in the fraud indictment. No confidential information was in fact used against Neil in the criminal proceedings. Nonetheless, Neil argued that his criminal charges should be stayed because his law firm had a conflict of interest representing two clients opposed in interest.

The SCC held that the criminal proceedings were not tainted by the conflict and that there was no reason to stay the charges. However, concerning the law firm's ethical obligations, the Court stated the following (at para 29):

> [I]t is the firm, not just the individual lawyer, that owes a fiduciary duty to its clients, and a bright line is required. The bright line is provided by the general rule that a lawyer may not represent one client whose interests are directly adverse to the immediate interests of another current client—*even if the two mandates are unrelated*—unless both clients consent after receiving full disclosure (and preferably independent legal advice), and the lawyer reasonably believes that he or she is able to represent each client without adversely affecting the other.

Therefore, although Neil was unsuccessful in having his criminal charges stayed, he had the option of suing his law firm civilly for breach of their duty of loyalty. And the law firm representing Neil was answerable to the law society for professional misconduct.

Such a conflict impairs the lawyer's ability to provide the best advice. Facing such a conflict, the lawyer must decline to enter into the offending transaction or must obtain the consent of the client after full disclosure (and preferably after the client has received independent legal advice). A lawyer proceeding with the transaction after disclosure and consent should also ensure that doing so is fair and reasonable in the circumstances.

Other Obligations

Among the other important ethical obligations lawyers owe their clients are the obligations

1. to maintain client property entrusted to the lawyer,[21]
2. not to withdraw services without good cause, and
3. to avoid close personal or sexual relationships with clients.

These other ethical obligations may or may not coincide with legal or fiduciary obligations in contract or tort. For example, the second and third obligations listed will in most cases not. The lawyer's facing civil liability for breaching them is unlikely, although she may face discipline for professional misconduct. Regarding the last obligation—to avoid close personal or sexual relationships with clients—there is no absolute rule in this regard where

---

21 Typically, this will involve money held by the lawyer in a trust account. See CBA Code, ch VIII and commentaries and FLSC Model Code, ch 3, r 3.5 and commentaries.

lawyers are concerned. However, there is a risk that such relationships may affect the lawyer's ability to act with integrity and good faith, to maintain confidences, and to avoid conflicts of interest. (See FLSC Model Code and the commentary following chapter 3, rule 3.4-2.) Codes of ethics for some other professions, particularly in the medical field, are more strict in this area and absolutely ban sexual relationships.

Disciplinary Proceedings

Lawyers are the principal legal practitioners in all jurisdictions in Canada, and legislation in all provinces and territories defines who can practise law within each jurisdiction. The legislation also creates law societies to which lawyers must belong in order to practise law. The administration of these law societies is entrusted to executives or governors, called "benchers" in most jurisdictions, who are elected from and by the membership to oversee the profession and the disciplinary process for misconduct.

As noted earlier, other regulated legal professionals—federal immigration consultants, Ontario's paralegals, and BC's notaries, for example—have their own disciplinary processes, similar to those of lawyers.

Purposes and Grounds for Disciplinary Action

We hold lawyers and other legal professionals to high standards of conduct because we want an effective system of justice and because we want to protect the public. As we mentioned at the beginning of this chapter, the public sometimes takes a jaded view of lawyers and the legal profession generally. The reality, however, is that this self-regulating profession is very responsive to complaints against its members.

With respect to lawyers, the governing legislation sets a threshold for what will trigger disciplinary action. The threshold is usually defined as conduct that amounts to

1. professional misconduct,
2. conduct unbecoming a lawyer,
3. professional incompetence, or
4. breach of the governing legislation itself.

Disciplinary Process and Sanctions for Disciplinary Conduct

The benchers are generally delegated power under the legislation to create a discipline committee or panel to handle discipline issues. Legislation or the law society rules will determine the composition of the committee, typically made up of benchers, non-elected lawyers, and at least one non-lawyer.

Lawyers' misconduct usually comes to the attention of the discipline committee through complaints from the public, from other lawyers, or from the courts. Occasionally, the committee is alerted by media reports or by a lawyer admitting his own misconduct. To qualify as misconduct, the lawyer's actions must have breached the profession's ethical code of conduct. In some cases, these actions may amount to more than professional misconduct; they may amount to civil or criminal wrongdoing.

After an investigation and a hearing (if the process moves to that stage), the discipline committee will determine whether the lawyer's action qualifies as misconduct on one of the grounds identified above.

If the committee concludes that discipline is appropriate in all the circumstances, a number of sanctions are possible. These include one or more of the following: reprimands, fines, practice conditions, suspension, retraining, and disbarment. Misconduct that is isolated and not on the serious end of the scale might only result in a reprimand (for example, lack of civility in dealing with a particular client or lawyer), whereas misconduct that is far-reaching and with serious consequences will often result in disbarment (see, for example, the *Ryan* case, described in Box 15.3). Figure 15.1 shows how complaints received by the BC Law Society are processed. As can be seen, the majority of complaints turn out to be unsubstantiated.

FIGURE 15.1 Complaints process in British Columbia

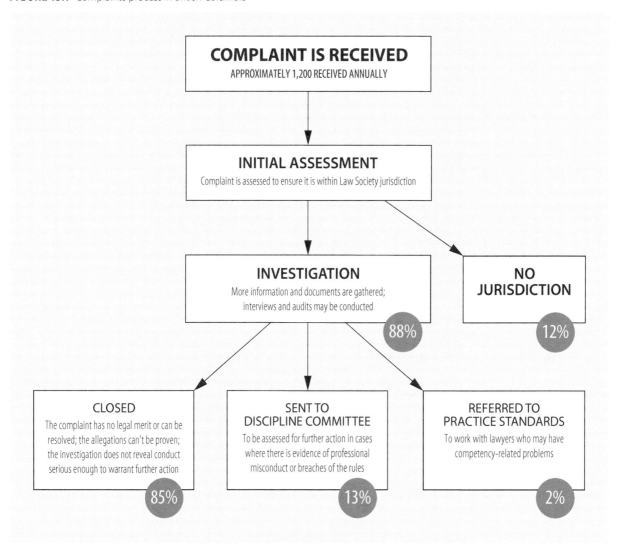

Source: Law Society of British Columbia.

CHAPTER SUMMARY

High ethical standards have always been expected of the legal profession. An effective system of justice needs such high standards, which help protect the public. Historically, these high standards were taken for granted, at least within the profession itself. In the modern era, codes of conduct are the main ethical guides for lawyers and other legal professionals. For lawyers in particular, these codes define various duties, including their duties to the state (or administration of justice), to the courts, to the profession and public, and to clients.

Integrity and good faith underlie the notion of professional responsibility. A lawyer's duty to the state involves, at the very least, his upholding the law and not advising or assisting in its violation. A lawyer's duty to the court involves showing courtesy and respect, respecting the established process, and not misleading the court or unfairly criticizing judges. The ethics of advocacy, which overlap with the duty to the court, often involve balancing obligations to the client with obligations to others. Lawyers sometimes find it difficult to pursue a client's case resolutely, as they are

obliged to do, while maintaining courtesy to the courts and witnesses.

Lawyers' duties to the profession include providing prompt and accurate communications to the law society and reporting malpractice. Duties that lawyers owe to others are courtesy and good faith. Lawyers observe these duties through the absolute reliability of their undertakings and through professionalism in advertising.

The lawyer's ethical duty to the client has three main aspects: (1) providing competent services, (2) keeping client information confidential, and (3) avoiding conflicts of interest between clients and between lawyer and client. Frequently, breaches of ethics in this area will also involve civil liability based on contractual, fiduciary, or tortious duties.

Law societies are responsible for disciplining lawyers. Discipline committees treat complaints against lawyers seriously, and they investigate these complaints. A finding of professional misconduct and conduct unbecoming a lawyer, based on breaches of ethical and other duties, can result in fines, suspension, or disbarment, among other sanctions.

KEY TERMS

bright line rule strict rule that a lawyer or law firm cannot represent two current clients whose interests are directly adverse to each other unless both clients consent after receiving full disclosure from the lawyer *(p. 429)*

codes of conduct written sets of rules regulating the ethical behaviour of professionals *(p. 414)*

cones of silence institutional mechanisms used by law firms to secure confidential information so that lawyers working at the same law firm are prevented from accessing information that could prejudice a former client; sometimes also called Chinese walls *(p. 429)*

duty of competence lawyer's obligation to provide services that meet the standard of a reasonably skilled lawyer *(p. 427)*

duty of confidentiality lawyer's obligation not to divulge information concerning a client's affairs that has been acquired in the course of the professional relationship, unless the client authorizes the lawyer to divulge this information *(p. 428)*

duty of loyalty lawyer's obligation to avoid conflicts of interest between clients and between lawyer and client *(p. 428)*

fiduciary obligations trust-like obligations, such as loyalty and good faith, that apply in certain contexts, including lawyer–client dealings *(p. 427)*

lawyer–client privilege lawyer's obligation not to divulge confidential information concerning a client's affairs that has been communicated to the lawyer by the client and is connected to the giving or receiving of legal advice *(p. 428)*

undertaking clear statement of intention by one person that is reasonably relied on by another, amounting to a solemn promise that must be kept or the person who has given the undertaking will be liable for misconduct *(p. 426)*

FURTHER READING

BOOKS

Graham, Randal NM. *Legal Ethics: Theories, Cases, and Professional Regulation*, 2d ed (Toronto: Emond Montgomery, 2011).

Hutchinson, Allan. *Legal Ethics and Professional Responsibility*, 2d ed (Toronto: Irwin Law, 2006).

Knight, S Patricia. *Ethics and Professional Practice for Paralegals*, 2d ed (Toronto: Emond Montgomery, 2010).

MacKenzie, Gavin. *Lawyers and Ethics: Professional Responsibility and Discipline*, 5th ed (Toronto: Carswell, 2009).

MacNair, M Deborah. *Conflicts of Interest: Principles for the Legal Profession* (Toronto: Canada Law Book, 2011).

Orkin, Mark M. *Legal Ethics*, 2d ed (Toronto: Canada Law Book, 2011).

Woolley, Alice. *Understanding Lawyers' Ethics in Canada* (Markham, Ont: LexisNexis, 2011).

WEBSITES

Lawyers

CBA Code 2009, Code of Professional Conduct, Canadian Bar Association: <http://www.cba.org/cba/activities/pdf/codeofconduct.pdf>.

FLSC Model Code, Model Code of Professional Conduct, Federation of Law Societies of Canada: <http://www.flsc.ca/en/model-code-of-professional-conduct>.

Notaries

BC Notaries, Principles for Ethical & Professional Conduct Guideline: <http://www.notaries.bc.ca/resources> (see under Society Standards).

Paralegals

Paralegal Rules of Conduct, Law Society of Upper Canada: <http://www.lsuc.on.ca/with.aspx?id=1072>.

Patent and Trademark Agents

Intellectual Property Institute of Canada Code of Ethics: <http://www.ipic.ca> (search for Code of Ethics).

REVIEW QUESTIONS

1. Briefly define legal ethics.

2. Name two ethical codes of conduct for Canadian lawyers that are national in scope.

3. A number of legal paraprofessional groups are permitted to practise independently in Canada. Name three that have their own ethical codes of conduct.

4. In the practice of law, what core ethical principle underlies professional responsibility?

5. Define the duty of lawyers in relation to the administration of justice.

6. Describe three specific obligations involved in a lawyer's duty to the court.

7. How is a Crown attorney's duty in a criminal case different from a lawyer's duty in a civil case?

8. What is an undertaking and what obligations does it entail for lawyers?

9. Explain the difference between a lawyer's duty of confidentiality and lawyer–client privilege.

10. What are "cones of silence"?

11. What is the "bright line" rule?

12. Name three grounds for disciplinary action against a lawyer.

EXERCISES

1. Imagine a Canadian justice system in which legal professionals are no longer held to any particular ethical standards and the legal profession is treated like any other business. Using specific arguments and examples, describe how you think these altered expectations and standards would change the Canadian justice system as we know it.

2. Research the law society website for your province or territory and find the code of conduct for lawyers. Identify and record the specific rule that deals with a lawyer's duty of competence.

3. A lawyer has recently received a judgment in a court action in which a piece of real property was sold. The court ordered that the proceeds of the sale be paid out by the lawyer to various parties, in specified amounts. A paralegal (or a law clerk, in Ontario), working under the supervision of the lawyer, was delegated the task of arranging payment to the various parties. By mistake, the paralegal neglected to pay one of the parties. When the party contacted the lawyer's firm, the paralegal was asked to deal with the inquiry. He realized his mistake but refused to admit what had happened. It was not until the supervising lawyer reviewed the whole affair that the mistake was discovered and the money paid out as required.

   Name and describe at least two specific ethical rules that have been breached here.

4. A husband and wife are both practising lawyers who do not work together and who specialize in different areas of the law. When either one has a legal problem that relates to the other's expertise, they employ each other as counsel. What ethical problems arise, if any, when they provide each other with advice in this way?

5. Research the law society website for your province or territory and locate the record of disciplinary hearings. Find cases involving lawyers who have been cited for professional misconduct that involved criminal activity (for example, impaired driving, possession of illegal drugs, domestic violence, or fraud). From among these cases, choose one that interests you and describe which ethical obligations were violated in the case.

6. Do you think the "bright line" rule goes too far, especially in an age of megafirms that have offices around the world and thousands of clients? Assuming that confidential information is being adequately protected by the lawyers involved, should a law firm always be prohibited from representing two clients with opposing interests at the same time unless the clients give the firm their consent? Why or why not?

16 Access to Justice and Law Reform

Demonstration in support of Indigenous rights,
Parliament Hill, Ottawa.

After reading this chapter, you will understand:

- What lawyers in Canada have accomplished to provide affordable legal services to the public
- How alternative dispute resolution mechanisms function in comparison with courts
- Selected measures that have been taken to make the law and legal knowledge more accessible to the public
- Some law reform initiatives that governments have introduced
- How public interest groups and their legal strategies influence law reform

> Surely it is time for the law to be available to those it is meant to govern.
>
> ML Friedland, *Access to the Law: A Study Conducted for the Law Reform Commission of Canada* (Toronto: Carswell/Methuen, 1975) at 9

Introduction

As the foregoing chapters in this text have shown, Canadian law has seen many changes since colonial times, when French civil law and English common law were first received into this country. For example, Canada's becoming a federal state in 1867 brought significant changes to our legal system, as did the *Canadian Charter of Rights and Freedoms* in 1982.

Canada's laws have changed as our country has changed. We have seen, for example, how a heightened awareness of human rights in the aftermath of the Second World War, in combination with the influence of the American Civil Rights movement in the 1950s and 1960s, helped motivate the provinces to introduce human rights codes (see Chapter 8). We have also seen a movement for greater consumer protection in today's marketplace (see Chapter 11).

This chapter looks at elements of the multifaceted access-to-justice movement and discusses some modern law reform initiatives undertaken by governments, lawyers, courts, and the public that help change (and improve) Canadian law.

Access to Legal Services

A general legal trend in Canada, beginning prior to the Second World War, has been toward increased access to legal services for *all* Canadians, regardless of their socioeconomic level, or their status as a minority or person with a disability. A number of developments in the criminal justice system and the legal profession illustrate this trend.

Legal Aid Plans

It has been an increasing concern of lawyers and the public in Canada that lower-income and otherwise disadvantaged individuals have better access to legal services. A movement based on this concern began in the decades before the Second World War and continued to grow after the war. Lawyers in Ontario and lawyers belonging to the national Canadian Bar Association (CBA) began to acknowledge a social responsibility as a group regarding the legal needs of *all* Canadians, especially those who could not afford to pay for the services of a lawyer.[1] Lawyers also became aware that the legal needs of indigent persons were different from those of wealthier clients capable of paying lawyers' fees. People living on a lower income—including those living on a pension or on social assistance—were more likely to need legal help with matters such as rental accommodation, welfare, employment assistance, discrimination, debt, worker's compensation, education expenses, and accessing government services in general.[2] Increasingly conscious of the barriers faced by lower-income Canadians, lawyers all across Canada began working with their respective law societies and provincial governments to affect change. Their efforts resulted in formalized publically funded **legal aid** programs that began in the 1960s.

Today, legal aid services for designated matters, criminal and non-criminal, are provided to lower-income Canadians across Canada either free of charge or for a modest fee. Legal aid plans vary from province to province. Generally speaking, they help those in need in the following ways:

- Lawyers in private practice can do legal aid work based on a judicare or fee-for-service delivery system. The process works in the following way. A person who needs legal help attends his local legal aid office, which determines whether he is qualified to receive legal aid on the basis of his particular legal need and a financial means test. If qualified, this person takes a legal aid certificate to a lawyer of his choice who is on a legal aid panel. The lawyer then performs the legal work and bills for it in accordance with the rates set by the legal aid tariff. The lawyer is paid by legal aid, not by the client.

- Many people coming to court for the first time do so without legal representation, and many lack an understanding of the courtroom process. Legal aid plans help these individuals by directing them to a lawyer known as "duty counsel," who typically can help with criminal, immigration, or family law matters (exact eligibility rules vary depending on the province or territory). Duty counsel lawyers in criminal court might, for example, speak to the judge on their clients' behalf and arrange an adjournment so that an accused can apply for legal aid.

- Legal aid plans in some jurisdictions have also established community legal clinics. These are an alternative form of delivering legal services. Their salaried staff—lawyers and community legal workers—help low-income Canadians with legal matters concerning such areas as landlord and tenant obligations, social welfare assistance, job search, immigration, debt collection, and human rights.[3] In Ontario, for example, specialty legal clinics help Canadians from ethnically diverse communities, as well as people with disabilities, with their unique needs. These legal clinics also tend to have offices that are easily accessible.

---

1 Mary P Reilly, "The Origins and Development of Legal Aid in Ontario" (1988) 8 Windsor YB Access Just 81; N Larsen, "Legal Aid in Manitoba" in C Harvey, ed, *The Law Society of Manitoba, 1877-1977* (Winnipeg: Peguis, 1977) 158.

2 James E Lockyer, QC, "The Roles and Responsibilities of the Legal Profession in Furthering Access to Justice" (1992) 12 Windsor YB Access Just 356; I Cotler & H Marx, eds, *The Law and the Poor in Canada* (Montreal: Black Rose Books, 1977).

3 Mary Jane Mossman, "Community Legal Clinics in Ontario" (1983) 3 Windsor YB Access Just 375.

In addition to provincial legal aid plans, other measures that lawyers in Canada have taken to help make this country's justice system less costly and more accessible to the public are as follows:[4]

- offering pro bono legal services,
- increasing the use of paralegals,
- offering prepaid legal services plans, and
- producing legal scholarship on access-to-justice matters.

Pro Bono Legal Services

Many lawyers may not be involved with legal aid work but may still want to help lower-income Canadians, charities, and disadvantaged persons with their legal needs. These lawyers can choose to offer assistance to the public **pro bono**, or without charge (from the Latin *pro bono publico*, meaning "for the public good"). They can do this, for example, by

- providing justice education in high schools and participating in school "law days";
- providing legal talks at neighbourhood community centres on selected topics, such as making a will;
- helping people on social assistance; or
- giving free legal advice to new immigrants to Canada.

Pro bono organizations have been established in many provinces (see Box 16.1).

Increased Use of Law Clerks and Paralegals

Legal services are becoming increasingly expensive. Another way that lawyers in law firms have sought to reduce expenses and make their legal services more financially affordable to the public is by using more paralegals.[5] Lawyers can use these persons as support staff, who can do assigned work in the law firm at a lower rate than the lawyers, and pass cost savings on to the firm's clients.

Paralegals are not lawyers, but they are trained to do legal tasks under the supervision of a lawyer (in Ontario, "paralegals" who work exclusively under the supervision of lawyers are called "law clerks"). Many paralegals nowadays do some of the routine legal tasks previously done by lawyers. Their office duties may include, for example, drafting pleadings for court, searching titles, doing legal research for an upcoming trial, and preparing legal documents using specialized legal software.

Paralegals are also now used increasingly by law firms and by government departments such as the federal Department of Justice. And paralegals in Ontario have a special status allowing them to represent clients in some lower-level courts and before administrative bodies. (In Ontario, as discussed in Chapters 14 and 15, paralegals may provide legal services in some designated areas independently of lawyers, and are regulated by the Law Society of

---

4 See Roderick A Macdonald, "Access to Justice in Canada Today: Scope, Scale and Ambitions" in Julia Bass, WA Bogart & Frederick Zemans, eds, *Access to Justice for a New Century: The Way Forward* (Toronto: Law Society of Upper Canada, 2004) at 19.

5 Frederick H Zemans, "The Non-Lawyer as a Means of Providing Legal Services" in Robert G Evans & Michael J Trebilcock, eds, *Lawyers and the Consumer Interest: Regulating the Market for Legal Services* (Toronto: Butterworths, 1982) 263.

BOX 16.1

Pro Bono Law Ontario

Pro Bono Law Ontario is a charity founded in 2001 to bridge the justice gap between lawyers who want to give back and the many Ontarians who can't afford legal services and have a legal problem not covered by government funding. PBLO creates and manages volunteer programs that connect these lawyers with low-income Ontarians—either directly or in partnership with charitable organizations working in the local community. Through this work, PBLO has emerged as the legal profession's only organized volunteer response to unmet legal needs. The result is that PBLO serves over 13,000 clients each year who have nowhere else to turn. The demand for these services increases each year.

Programs for the Public

PBLO manages a variety of programs in-house and creates several others that are managed externally. PBLO's in-house programs focus on:

- people suing or being sued in the civil courts and who are unable to afford a lawyer
- children who face barriers to their health, wellbeing, and educational progress and who might benefit from assistance of a lawyer
- charities and nonprofits that do not have the resources to address their legal needs.

As much as possible we "go to where our clients are," embedding programs in court houses, children's hospitals, and community organizations. This means that individuals trying to navigate the court system, children and families with legal issues that affect health outcomes, and other individuals in the community have access to legal help at the very time and place they need it.

Source: Reproduced from Pro Bono Law Ontario <http://www.pblo.org>.

Upper Canada.) Other jurisdictions are considering moving in the direction of the Ontario model as they try to improve access to justice. Implementing the necessary changes will depend on rules set by provincial or territorial legislation for the jurisdiction in question, by the relevant courts and tribunals, and by the province's or territory's law society. At the time of writing, in British Columbia, for example, "designated paralegals" have been given a limited right to appear before the courts on behalf of clients; however, they still work under the supervision of a lawyer.

Prepaid Legal Services Plans

Another new delivery method for legal services—and a model that is particularly attractive to middle-income Canadians—is a prepaid legal services benefits plan. Such plans arose in Canada in the 1980s, under the leadership of the Canadian Auto Workers. Members of this union make individual contributions to the plan, which helps pay for a lawyer who does prescribed legal services under the plan for members at a reasonable cost.[6]

Legal Scholarship

Canada's legal community includes many legal academics who support law reform. They write books and articles on this subject, and such scholarship can be influential in affecting changes in the law. The *Windsor Yearbook of Access to Justice* is an example of a specialized law journal that publishes learned articles in this area.

---

6   C Wydrzynski, K Hildebrandt & D Blonde, "The CAW Prepaid Legal Services Plan: A Case Study of an Alternative Funding and Delivery Method for Legal Services" (1990) 10 Windsor YB Access Just 22.

Courts and Alternative Dispute Resolution Mechanisms

The traditional adjudicative process of resolving legal disputes in courts has come under increasing criticism in Canada. Many people worry about the cost of a lawyer. Long trial delays, complex legal procedures, lack of privacy, unfamiliar legal terminology and rules of evidence, and an expensive appeal process are further concerns about the court process held by many middle-income Canadians. Many are also intimidated by the adversarial system used in civil court, whereby one side tries to win outright, with the loser paying the winner's costs.

As a result, a growing number of people are favouring **alternative dispute resolution (ADR)** mechanisms instead of courts. There are three main ADR mechanisms: (1) negotiation, (2) mediation, and (3) arbitration.

Negotiation

Negotiation is the simplest method of resolving disputes and is conducted by the parties themselves. Both sides talk to each other, usually informally, to determine the possibility of finding a mutually acceptable solution to their dispute. Because both sides must agree to the solution for it to be binding, both parties need to cooperate, be flexible, and be willing to compromise for a negotiation to be successful.

Mediation

Mediation takes negotiation one step further. A neutral and impartial third party, called a mediator, assists the parties in their efforts to resolve their dispute. It may be a dispute, for example, between two neighbours over pets in the backyard. It may also involve a dispute between two tenants over loud noise, or a business dispute between a franchisor and franchisee. The mediator, who is picked by the parties beforehand, helps both sides find a solution to their problem. This person does not necessarily have to be a lawyer. The mediator's role is to keep both sides talking, clarify issues, help uncover sources behind the conflict, and suggest compromises and solutions that both sides can accept. The mediator meets often with both sides, individually as well as together, and can do so at their own homes. Sessions are confidential, informal, and may be flexible in terms of timing. For example, the meetings might take place in the evenings or on weekends. However, as with negotiation, a mediator can only *recommend* a solution, which is not binding on the parties unless both sides agree to it.

When we compare the traditional court process of resolving disputes with this alternative approach, we can see why many people are attracted to mediation. In the court system, the parties cannot pick their judge. The judge will not come to the parties' home or meet with them on weekends. Nor will a judge meet with one side in the absence of the other. In the traditional court system, the judge's decision must be obeyed, even if one side does not like it, and the costs for legal representation there can be expensive.

Arbitration

In the case of **arbitration**, as with mediation, the parties consent beforehand to the appointment of an impartial third party, here called an arbitrator, to help resolve their dispute.

They also agree to assume the costs involved. However, unlike mediation, the parties can also decide beforehand to accept binding or non-binding arbitration. In binding arbitration, the decision of the arbitrator must be followed. In non-binding arbitration, the arbitrator's decision is only advisory. The advantages of using arbitration are the following:

- the parties can pick their own arbitrator, often someone with experience in the area;
- sessions can be informal and confidential; and
- the process can proceed at the parties' own pace.

One difficulty with arbitration is that the process can become quite legalistic and formal, particularly if the arbitrator is a lawyer and both sides are represented by a lawyer as well.[7]

Table 16.1 shows a comparison of adjudication (the traditional adversarial court process), arbitration, and mediation.

TABLE 16.1   Comparison of Adjudication, Arbitration, and Mediation as Third-Party Conflict Resolution Techniques

	ADJUDICATION	ARBITRATION	MEDIATION
Nature of process	Rights-based	Rights-based	Interest-based
Appointment of third party	Appointed by the state	Selected by the parties	Selected by the parties
Mode of participation	Indirect—parties are represented by legal advisers	Indirect—parties are normally represented by an agent or lawyer	Direct—parties participate directly in the process
Degree of formality of the process	Process is adversarial—with formal rules of procedure and evidence	Process is adversarial—with informal rules of procedure	Process is non-adversarial—ground rules are informal and consensual
Mode of communication between parties	Closed—issues are narrowly defined, and information is presented in the form of facts and arguments	Closed—issues are somewhat less narrowly defined, but information is presented in the form of facts and arguments	Open-ended—parties define the issues that are relevant and need to be discussed
Role of third party	Authoritative—third party is responsible for the outcome	Authoritative—third party is responsible for the outcome	Facilitative—parties are responsible for the outcome
Outcome	Coercive—outcome is binding, regardless of parties' consent	Neutral—parties determine in advance whether outcome shall be binding or non-binding	Consensual—no agreement without parties' consent

Source: Cheryl Picard et al, *The Art and Science of Mediation* (Toronto: Emond Montgomery, 2004) at 53.

---

7   Cheryl Picard et al, *The Art and Science of Mediation* (Toronto: Emond Montgomery, 2004); EG Tannis, *Alternative Dispute Resolution That Works* (Toronto: Captus Press, 1989); W Estey, "Who Needs Courts?" (1981) 1 Windsor YB Access Just 263.

Public Access to Legal Information

Even if ADR mechanisms become more widely used, courts are still central to the administration of justice and are not likely to be replaced anytime soon. Canadians who are unable to afford a lawyer or who do not qualify for legal aid face some difficult problems when going to court. Among their most pressing concerns are how and where they can obtain legal information about these matters:

- how the formal legal system works,
- what the law is concerning their legal matter, and
- what their rights are in court.

Many such people have to be self-reliant and find answers to these questions on their own. For this reason, they want the law demystified and they want technology to help them gain knowledge about the law.

This topic—public access to legal information—was examined by professor Martin Friedland in a groundbreaking 1975 study he conducted for the Law Reform Commission of Canada.[8] Friedland noted that many people did not know where to go for accurate and complete legal information, and had trouble using and understanding legal materials such as cases, statutes, and regulations. He identified four ways of providing the public with better access to law:

- improving the clarity of existing legal materials;
- doing more to educate the public about law;
- improving the quality of legal information that intermediary facilities, such as community information centres and public libraries, provide to the public; and
- developing a new reference source, such as an encyclopedia of law for non-lawyers, that could be regularly updated and made available in public libraries, schools, and government offices.

Many technological measures for improving public access to legal information have been taken since Friedland's 1975 study. These measures include, for example, telephone access to legal information providers such as the Legal Information Society of Nova Scotia; a lawyer referral service administered by provincial law societies; dial-a-law programs for taped legal information; online legal research websites such as that created by the Canadian Legal Information Institute (CanLII); and having federal, provincial, and territorial governments place government statutes, regulations, and other legal information online on official government websites.[9]

---

8 ML Friedland, *Access to the Law: A Study Conducted for the Law Reform Commission of Canada* (Toronto: Carswell/Methuen, 1975).

9 T Gregory Kane & Edward R Myers, "The Role of Self-Help in the Provision of Legal Services" in Evans & Trebilcock, *supra* note 5 at 439.

Government Measures to Enhance Access to Justice

The access-to-justice movement has influenced federal and provincial governments to make further reforms that increase public access to government institutions and policies. The use of collaborative law models is being encouraged in some jurisdictions, particularly in the resolution of family law matters. Other reforms introduced by federal and provincial governments to make the court process more accessible include the following:

- unified family courts (UFCs), where family matters—which are under the jurisdiction of both the federal and provincial governments—are heard in one convenient place;
- raising the monetary limits of small claims courts (where non-lawyers can appear), so that matters need not go to a higher court where only lawyers can appear;
- creating specialized courts, such as domestic violence and drug treatment courts, which aim to achieve better long-term outcomes for some types of offenders and for society as a whole (see Box 13.3 in Chapter 13);
- case management, where a designated court official, such as a judge or a master, is responsible for supervising the flow of cases going through the courts, so that delays are minimized; and
- the establishment of administrative bodies to address areas of law more efficiently dealt with outside of the court process. (See the discussion of administrative agencies in Chapter 12.)

Public access to government records is another area related to access to justice. In the 1960s, a determined campaign began in Canada for greater public access to information contained in government records. Influenced by a similar movement in the United States and led by lawyers, academics, the press, and some members of Parliament, proponents argued that increased access would make governments more accountable to the public.

Today, access-to-information legislation exists at the provincial, territorial, and federal levels. The Supreme Court of Canada has characterized the overarching purpose of this legislation as facilitating democracy "by helping to ensure that citizens have the information to participate meaningfully in the democratic process and that politicians and bureaucrats remain accountable to the citizenry."[10] The federal *Access to Information Act*[11] came into effect in July 1983, making Canada one of the first countries in the world to protect this right. The Act gives Canadian citizens and permanent residents the right to access information contained in government records. Section 2(1) sets out the three principles that underpin the Act:

1. Government information should be available to the public,
2. Necessary exceptions to the right of access should be limited and specific, and
3. Decisions on the disclosure of government information should be reviewed independently of government.

---

10   *Dagg v Canada (Minister of Finance)*, [1997] 2 SCR 403.

11   RSC 1985, c A-1.

Although the Act requires the head of a government institution to make reasonable efforts to assist individuals with their requests and to respond to requests accurately, completely, and in a timely way, in reality insufficient resources and a large increase in the volume of requests create barriers to access; between 2002–3 and 2011–12, the number of requests increased by 88 percent.[12] Many have expressed concerns that the Act, which has changed little in the three decades since its passage, has not kept pace with technological advances and other developments, and that the right to access is being undermined in critical ways.

In addition to information acts, in many provinces the office of the ombudsman has helped improve access to justice for Canadians by drawing public attention and scrutiny to problems people have with the government—for example, government waste or inaction. The ombudsman (called an ombudsperson in certain provinces, such as British Columbia) is an official with powers to investigate alleged government abuses or maladministration at the request of citizens. The ombudsman acts independently of the legislature and reports to it. Alberta was the first province to introduce this office, in 1967, and other provinces and territories have followed suit. The ombudsman does not have unlimited jurisdiction to investigate maladministration in all government departments, ministries, agencies, and institutions. It is also an office whose powers vary from province to province. In all cases, the ombudsperson's services are provided free of charge. (See Box 16.2.)

Law Reform

Both the federal and provincial governments, as well as citizens working alone or in organized groups, can try to change laws. Law reform may be initiated by law reform commissions, public inquiries, political demonstrations, lobbying by national organizations, or by public interest groups appearing as intervenors before the Supreme Court of Canada (SCC).

Law Reform Commissions

Law reform commissions are independent bodies set up by either the provincial or federal government to study selected areas of law and recommend ways to improve, modernize, and reform them. Members of the commission publish reports recommending how laws in that area could be improved. (Martin Friedland's 1975 report on access to justice, mentioned above, was one of these reports.) Though the government is not bound to accept and implement all (or any) of the commission's recommendations, its reports are considered important contributions to legal scholarship and can be cited in courts.

The Law Reform Commission of Canada, which existed from 1971 to 1993 and again from 1997 to 2006 (as the Law Commission of Canada), was set up to make recommendations regarding areas of law under federal jurisdiction—for example, criminal law and criminal procedure. It also considered bijural aspects regarding our law, which, as we have seen, uses both the common law and civil law legal systems.

At the provincial level, most of Canada's provinces have established provincial law reform commissions at one time or another (though most have now ceased operation as a result of funding cuts). Law reform commissions recommend measures to improve and reform laws

---

12   Office of the Information Commissioner of Canada, "The Access to Information Act in Canada: Taking Stock of 30 Years" (Presentation to the Library of Parliament, 5 December 2013), online: <http://www.oic-ci.gc.ca/eng/media-room-salle-media_speeches-discours_2013_9.aspx>.

BOX 16.2

What Kinds of Matters Can an Ombudsman Help Resolve?

A provincial or territorial ombudsman may help resolve a range of problems or misunderstandings, subject to certain exceptions. Ombudsmen oversee provincial or territorial ministries; Crown corporations; and administrative tribunals, agencies, boards, and commissions—for example, in Ontario, the Ministry of Aboriginal Affairs, the Ministry of the Attorney General, the Ministry of Community Safety and Correctional Services, the Liquor Control Board of Ontario, and Small Business and Consumer Services. They may deal with thousands of complaints each year. Ombudsmen *cannot* investigate matters between individuals and private companies, individuals and other individuals (for example, judges, doctors, or lawyers), or individuals and the federal government.

The case summaries below illustrate just two of the many situations an ombudsperson may help resolve.

BC Ombudsperson Case Summary

We received a complaint from Ms. G that the Ministry of Small Business and Revenue would not return her phone calls. She told us that she had left numerous messages for someone at the Ministry to discuss what she needed to provide in order to demonstrate that she was eligible for an exemption from social services tax on a transfer in the ownership of a motor vehicle.

When we contacted the Ministry we learned that the employee she was trying to contact was no longer employed there. We also learned that the employee had left his position without changing his personal voice mail message to indicate that he was no longer available. This meant Ms. G's concerns went unanswered, while she continued to leave messages on a government telephone line that was no longer being used.

Shortly after we notified the Ministry of this problem, Ms. G was contacted by a manager from the Ministry to discuss her situation. The manager received enough information from Ms. G to cancel over $1,500 in taxes, penalties and interest that the Ministry had been seeking from her. The Ministry issued her a written apology and advised her that steps had been taken to update the voice mail of its former employee.[*]

Ontario Ombudsman Case Summary

A mother of two turned to the Ombudsman for help because she was not receiving child support payments from her ex-husband. She had a court order, registered with the Family Responsibility Office (FRO), that said her ex could be jailed for 10 days if he failed to pay. Despite this, she had only received one payment and was owed more than $35,000. She had complained to the FRO numerous times over the past three years and was extremely frustrated.

An Ombudsman investigator followed up with FRO staff, who said some steps had been taken to enforce the court order, including reporting the ex-husband to a collection agency, suspending his driver's licence and garnishing any federal monies he might receive, such as an income tax refund. There was also a writ of seizure and sale placed on his property. In response to the Ombudsman's inquiries, the FRO also obtained an address for the ex-husband's employer and made arrangements to garnish his pay.

As a result, the woman began receiving payments for support of the children, and accumulated arrears. The FRO promised to report the ex-husband to the regulatory body of his profession, which could revoke his licence if he stopped payments again.[†]

[*]   Office of the Ombudsperson, Province of British Columbia, online: "Investigations" <http://www.ombudsman.bc.ca>.

[†]   Ombudsman Ontario, online: "Investigations" <http://www.ombudsman.on.ca>.

under provincial jurisdiction, such as the administration of justice in a province. They generally operate with a small number of lawyers, academics, and judges on their board of governors, and utilize research staff to conduct research into areas considered in need of reform. This scholarly analysis of the law found in background and discussion papers, and in final reports published by commissions, provides an excellent source of well-researched information about many areas of law.

Canada-wide, the Federation of Law Reform Agencies of Canada is also involved in promoting cooperation between Canada's law reform agencies on the broad topic of law reform. As well, the Uniform Law Conference of Canada, in existence since 1918, works to improve harmony between laws of the provinces and territories across Canada.

Public Inquiries

Public inquires into matters of national and public concern, formerly known as royal commissions, have played an important role in the development of law and policy in Canada. They may be tasked with finding facts and reporting on those facts, with making recommendations aimed at developing public policy, or with a combination of these two functions.[13] Either the federal government or a provincial government may call an inquiry; legislation provides the executive with the authority to appoint a commission, and provides the commission with the authority it needs to carry out its mandate.[14]

Fact-finding inquiries (and inquiries that combine fact-finding and policy recommendations) are often established in response to an event, such as a high-profile scandal or a tragedy, that negatively affects the public's trust in or perception of public institutions—for example, miscarriages of justice such as wrongful convictions, deaths in hospitals, and tainted water scandals. The goal of such inquiries is often to address failings and restore the public's confidence in the system. High-profile inquiries include the Air India Inquiry into the terrorist bombing of Air India Flight 182; the Braidwood Inquiry into the tasering death of Robert Dziekanski; and the Missing Women Commission of Inquiry into the disappearance of women from Vancouver's Downtown East Side.

Inquiries with a focus on policy analyze issues and make recommendations for policies in the future. For example, an inquiry conducted by Justice Emmett Hall in the 1960s was instrumental in the creation of the national medicare system, and the Royal Commission on Bilingualism and Biculturalism was responsible for some of the policies that exist in these areas today (see Box 16.3).

Political Demonstrations

People upset with a particular government law or policy, and who also want laws reformed, have traditionally participated in public protest marches and political demonstrations, which might end up before a city hall, a provincial legislature, or before Parliament Hill in Ottawa. The widespread use of social media today has made it easier for people to organize and coordinate such events. The problem with demonstrations, as a political tactic, is that not all Canadians support them, and they can also attract negative publicity, depending on the tactics used. Another disadvantage is that they tend to be one-off events, with momentum and publicity often—though not always—subsiding at their conclusion. As well, the government may not support the change requested.

---

13 Hon Associate Chief Justice Dennis R O'Connor and Freya Kristjanson, "Some Observations on Public Inquiries" (Canadian Institute for the Administration of Justice, Annual Conference, 10 October 2007, Halifax), online: <http://www.ontariocourts.ca/coa/en/ps/speeches/publicinquiries.htm>.

14 The federal legislation is the *Inquiries* Act, RSC 1985, c I-11; an example of provincial legislation is Ontario's *Public Inquiries Act, 2009*, SO 2009, c 33, Schedule 6.

BOX 16.3

Royal Commission on Bilingualism and Biculturalism

The Royal Commission on Bilingualism and Biculturalism (pictured), also known as the B and B Commission and the Laurendeau–Dunton Commission, was convened by Lester B. Pearson's government in 1963 in response to tensions between Canada's French and English populations. Francophones, who represent a majority in Quebec but are a minority in the other Canadian provinces, believed their French language was in need of protection: not only was English the predominant language in Canada, but government services, they argued, were offered only in English and only a small percentage of the federal public service was bilingual.

The Commission's mandate was to recommend "what steps should be taken to develop the Canadian Confederation on the basis of an equal partnership between the two founding races, taking into account the contribution made by the other ethnic groups to the cultural enrichment of Canada." * To this end, ten commissioners, all of whom were bilingual, held nation-wide consultations with citizens, researchers, and provincial premiers over a six-year period. In its preliminary report, the Commission noted the inequality between the two languages and warned of "a crisis, in the sense that Canada has come to a time when decisions must be taken and developments must occur leading either to its break-up, or to a new set of conditions for its future existence."† In its six-volume final report, published in 1969, the Commission recommended that English and French be declared the official languages of the federal Parliament, and of the federal administration and federal courts.

The *Official Languages Act*, passed in 1969, was one of the Commission's most important legacies. The Act declares French and English to be the official languages of Canada and requires all federal institutions to provide their services in both English and French.

* Office of the Commissioner of Official Languages, "A Defining Moment: The Royal Commission on Bilingualism and Biculturalism" (Fall 2009) 5 Beyond Words: Canada's Official Languages Newsletter at para 3, online: <http://www.ocol-clo.gc.ca/newsletter_cyberbulletin/commission_bb_e.htm>.

† *Ibid* at para 5.

National Organizations and Lobbying

Many professional and occupational groups across Canada have established national organizations that meet annually to discuss issues important to their members. Examples of such national organizations are

- the Canadian Bar Association,
- the Assembly of First Nations, and
- the Canadian Labour Congress.

These associations also try to influence governments to introduce law reforms or policies that favour their group's interests. Many of these national organizations have full-time staff and offices in provincial capitals or in Ottawa. They submit briefs to the government and meet with members of Parliament and with key bureaucrats in the civil service to further their association's goals. Many also seek to influence government action by **lobbying**.

Lobbying is an organized effort to try and influence legislators and bureaucrats with respect to laws and government policies. For example, lobbying can be done to obtain material benefits from the government such as favourable tax breaks, research grants, subsidies, or government supply contracts. Lobbying may not result in as high a public profile as demonstrating in the streets. It is perhaps more effective, however; lobby groups can retain a law firm or the services of skilled public relations professionals and former politicians who have direct knowledge of the political process and previous familiarity with the legislators.[15]

Public Interest Groups as Intervenors

Another way public interest groups can try to influence and change Canadian law or government policy is to participate as **intervenors** in cases before the SCC.[16] (For more on intervenors, see Chapter 8.) If granted intervenor status, which is given at the Court's discretion, an interest group may be entitled to give further evidence to supplement the record or be authorized to present an oral argument at the hearing.[17] They have to demonstrate sufficient interest in the court case, have submissions that are useful and different from the other parties' submissions, and be a credible organization. Examples of public interest groups who have participated as intervenors this way are LEAF (the Women's Legal Education and Action Fund) and the Canadian Civil Liberties Association. The SCC is now increasingly receptive to hearing from public interest intervenors; the judges on the Court realize that many matters facing them are complex and that their decisions will have far-reaching implications for Canadian law. An interest group may influence the Court to take a broader perspective on a matter under consideration and increase its awareness of the issues, or change, it is intervening to support.

---

15   Rand Dyck, *Canadian Politics: Critical Approaches* (Toronto: Nelson, 2012) 425-53; Keith Archer et al, *Parameters of Power: Canada's Political Institutions*, 2d ed (Toronto: Nelson, 1999).

16   See Sharon Lavine, "Advocating Values: Public Interest Intervention in Charter Litigation" (1993) 2 NJCL 27; Ian Brodie, *Friends of the Court: The Privileging of Interest Group Litigants in Canada* (Albany, NY: State University of New York Press, 2002).

17   Under the Rules of the Supreme Court of Canada (SOR/2002-156), a Motion for Intervention is rule 55. Adding and Substituting Parties is rule 18. See also I Brodie, "Lobbying the Supreme Court" in H Mellon & M Westmacott, eds, *Political Dispute and Judicial Review: Assessing the Work of the Supreme Court of Canada* (Toronto: Nelson, 2000) 195.

CHAPTER SUMMARY

The issue of access to justice has become increasingly important to Canadians as court costs rise, court delays grow longer, and the court process becomes harder for many low- and middle-income Canadians to navigate. A multi-faceted reform movement, exploring alternative dispute resolution mechanisms such as mediation and arbitration, is gaining acceptance. The benefits of these alternative forms of dispute resolution are many. They offer reduced court costs, less time in court, and more personal control over the process. Other benefits of ADR are confidentiality, and the opportunity for the parties to craft solutions they feel are best suited to their problem.

Canadian law has changed over time in response to broad shifts in our society. As outlined in this chapter, one desire for change is increasingly focused on making the law more accessible and affordable to the public. Many people today want or need to access legal information on their own, and want this legal information to be understandable. As for specific initiatives to reform the law, law reform commissions and institutes have researched various areas of the law and made recommendations for improvement (and some of these recommendations have been implemented through legislative change). Sometimes, individual Canadians try to change the law on their own, while others pursue collective action. Such action can take a variety of forms, including political demonstrations, national organizations, lobbying, and applying to participate as intervenors in court cases.

KEY TERMS

alternative dispute resolution (ADR) process used instead of a court trial to help settle a dispute *(p. 442)*

arbitration dispute resolution process whereby the parties agree beforehand on an arbitrator to assist them, and they agree on whether the arbitrator's decision will be advisory or binding *(p. 442)*

intervenor a party, other than the original parties to a court proceeding, who does not have a substantial and direct interest in the proceeding but has interests and perspectives helpful to the judicial determination and whose input is accepted by the court *(p. 450)*

legal aid government funding of lawyers who provide legal assistance to persons with low income *(p. 439)*

lobbying organized effort to influence legislators on behalf of a particular interest *(p. 449)*

mediation dispute resolution process whereby the parties try to reach a settlement with the assistance of a third party *(p. 442)*

negotiation dispute resolution process whereby the parties talk to each other directly and seek a mutually acceptable solution to their problem *(p. 442)*

pro bono term applied to legal work that lawyers do at no charge to help the public (from the Latin *pro bono publico*: "for the public good") *(p. 440)*

FURTHER READING

Brodie, Ian. *Friends of the Court: The Privileging of Interest Group Litigants in Canada* (Albany, NY: State University of New York, 2002).

Hanycz, Colleen M, Trevor CW Farrow & Frederick H Zemans. *The Theory and Practice of Representative Negotiation* (Toronto: Emond Montgomery, 2008).

Jhappen, Radha, ed. *Women's Legal Strategies in Canada* (Toronto: University of Toronto Press, 2002).

Morton, FL & Avril Allen. "Feminists and the Courts: Measuring Success in Interest Group Litigation in Canada" (2001) 34 Can J Poli Sci 55.

Rowat, Donald Cameron, ed. *The Making of the Federal Access Act: A Case Study of Policy-Making in Canada* (Ottawa: Carleton University, 1985).

Trebilcock, Michael, Anthony J Duggan & Lorne Sossin. *Middle Income Access to Justice* (Toronto: University of Toronto Press, 2012).

Windsor Yearbook of Access to Justice (Windsor, Ont: University of WIndsor Faculty of Law), online: <http://www1.uwindsor.ca/law/wyaj/>.

Young, Margot, et al, eds. *Poverty: Rights, Social Citizenship, and Legal Activism* (Vancouver: UBC Press, 2007).

REVIEW QUESTIONS

1. How do legal aid plans help lower-income people in need of legal services? List three main ways.

2. List three measures that lawyers in Canada have taken to increase access to justice for disadvantaged Canadians.

3. List five common criticisms of the traditional court adjudicative process for resolving disputes.

4. What is a main difference between negotiation and mediation?

5. How does arbitration differ from mediation?

6. When two parties are using arbitration to resolve their disputes, what can they decide beforehand regarding the arbitrator's decision?

7. What four measures did Martin Friedland propose for improving Canadians' access to legal information?

8. List three measures the government has taken to increase the Canadian public's access to justice.

EXERCISES

1. Do you think enough is being done in this country to increase access to justice for lower-income and disadvantaged Canadians? Explain. Suggest another measure that you think might be introduced.

2. Look up the legal term *in forma pauperis*. Would the Canadian legal system be improved by lawyers adopting this concept? Why or why not?

3. Using the Internet, look up the website for the Canadian Federation of Students. List and discuss ways that this association tries to help post-secondary students.

4. Describe the qualities you think a good mediator would possess. Give reasons for your choices.

Appendixes

Note: To view the complete versions of the *Constitution Act, 1867* and the *Constitution Act, 1982*, with full explanatory footnotes, visit www.emp.ca/ilc.

A Constitution Act, 1867

30 & 31 Victoria, c. 3 (U.K.)

TABLE OF CONTENTS

An Act for the Union of Canada, Nova Scotia, and New Brunswick, and the Government thereof; and for Purposes connected
therewith

(29th March 1867)

Whereas the Provinces of Canada, Nova Scotia, and New
Brunswick have expressed their Desire to be federally united
into One Dominion under the Crown of the United Kingdom
of Great Britain and Ireland, with a Constitution similar in
Principle to that of the United Kingdom:

And whereas such a Union would conduce to the Welfare
of the Provinces and promote the Interests of the British
Empire:

And whereas on the Establishment of the Union by Authority of Parliament it is expedient, not only that the Constitution of the Legislative Authority in the Dominion be
provided for, but also that the Nature of the Executive Government therein be declared:

And whereas it is expedient that Provision be made for the
eventual Admission into the Union of other Parts of British
North America:

I. PRELIMINARY

Short title

1. This Act may be cited as the *Constitution Act, 1867.*

2. Repealed.

II. UNION

Declaration of Union

3. It shall be lawful for the Queen, by and with the Advice
of Her Majesty's Most Honourable Privy Council, to declare by
Proclamation that, on and after a Day therein appointed, not
being more than Six Months after the passing of this Act, the
Provinces of Canada, Nova Scotia, and New Brunswick shall
form and be One Dominion under the Name of Canada; and
on and after that Day those Three Provinces shall form and be
One Dominion under that Name accordingly.

Construction of subsequent Provisions of Act

4. Unless it is otherwise expressed or implied, the Name
Canada shall be taken to mean Canada as constituted under
this Act.

Four Provinces

5. Canada shall be divided into Four Provinces, named
Ontario, Quebec, Nova Scotia, and New Brunswick.

Provinces of Ontario and Quebec

6. The Parts of the Province of Canada (as it exists at the
passing of this Act) which formerly constituted respectively
the Provinces of Upper Canada and Lower Canada shall be
deemed to be severed, and shall form Two separate Provinces.
The Part which formerly constituted the Province of Upper
Canada shall constitute the Province of Ontario; and the Part
which formerly constituted the Province of Lower Canada
shall constitute the Province of Quebec.

Provinces of Nova Scotia and New Brunswick

7. The Provinces of Nova Scotia and New Brunswick shall
have the same Limits as at the passing of this Act.

Decennial Census

8. In the general Census of the Population of Canada
which is hereby required to be taken in the Year One thousand
eight hundred and seventy-one, and in every Tenth Year thereafter, the respective Populations of the Four Provinces shall be
distinguished.

III. EXECUTIVE POWER

Declaration of Executive Power in the Queen

9. The Executive Government and Authority of and over
Canada is hereby declared to continue and be vested in the
Queen.

Application of Provisions referring to Governor General

10. The Provisions of this Act referring to the Governor
General extend and apply to the Governor General for the
Time being of Canada, or other the Chief Executive Officer or
Administrator for the Time being carrying on the Govern-
ment of Canada on behalf and in the Name of the Queen, by
whatever Title he is designated.

Constitution of Privy Council for Canada

11. There shall be a Council to aid and advise in the Gov-
ernment of Canada, to be styled the Queen's Privy Council for
Canada; and the Persons who are to be Members of that Coun-
cil shall be from Time to Time chosen and summoned by the
Governor General and sworn in as Privy Councillors, and
Members thereof may be from Time to Time removed by the
Governor General.

All Powers under Acts to be exercised by Governor General with Advice of Privy Council, or alone

12. All Powers, Authorities, and Functions which under
any Act of the Parliament of Great Britain, or of the Parliament
of the United Kingdom of Great Britain and Ireland, or of the

Legislature of Upper Canada, Lower Canada, Canada, Nova Scotia, or New Brunswick, are at the Union vested in or exerciseable by the respective Governors or Lieutenant Governors of those Provinces, with the Advice, or with the Advice and Consent, of the respective Executive Councils thereof, or in conjunction with those Councils, or with any Number of Members thereof, or by those Governors or Lieutenant Governors individually, shall, as far as the same continue in existence and capable of being exercised after the Union in relation to the Government of Canada, be vested in and exerciseable by the Governor General, with the Advice or with the Advice and Consent of or in conjunction with the Queen's Privy Council for Canada, or any Members thereof, or by the Governor General individually, as the Case requires, subject nevertheless (except with respect to such as exist under Acts of the Parliament of Great Britain or of the Parliament of the United Kingdom of Great Britain and Ireland) to be abolished or altered by the Parliament of Canada.

Application of Provisions referring to Governor General in Council

13. The Provisions of this Act referring to the Governor General in Council shall be construed as referring to the Governor General acting by and with the Advice of the Queen's Privy Council for Canada.

Power to Her Majesty to authorize Governor General to appoint Deputies

14. It shall be lawful for the Queen, if Her Majesty thinks fit, to authorize the Governor General from Time to Time to appoint any Person or any Persons jointly or severally to be his Deputy or Deputies within any Part or Parts of Canada, and in that Capacity to exercise during the Pleasure of the Governor General such of the Powers, Authorities, and Functions of the Governor General as the Governor General deems it necessary or expedient to assign to him or them, subject to any Limitations or Directions expressed or given by the Queen; but the Appointment of such a Deputy or Deputies shall not affect the Exercise by the Governor General himself of any Power, Authority, or Function.

Command of Armed Forces to continue to be vested in the Queen

15. The Command-in-Chief of the Land and Naval Militia, and of all Naval and Military Forces, of and in Canada, is hereby declared to continue and be vested in the Queen.

Seat of Government of Canada

16. Until the Queen otherwise directs, the Seat of Government of Canada shall be Ottawa.

IV. LEGISLATIVE POWER

Constitution of Parliament of Canada

17. There shall be One Parliament for Canada, consisting of the Queen, an Upper House styled the Senate, and the House of Commons.

Privileges, etc., of Houses

18. The privileges, immunities, and powers to be held, enjoyed, and exercised by the Senate and by the House of Commons, and by the members thereof respectively, shall be such as are from time to time defined by Act of the Parliament of Canada, but so that any Act of the Parliament of Canada defining such privileges, immunities, and powers shall not confer any privileges, immunities, or powers exceeding those at the passing of such Act held, enjoyed, and exercised by the Commons House of Parliament of the United Kingdom of Great Britain and Ireland, and by the members thereof.

First Session of the Parliament of Canada

19. The Parliament of Canada shall be called together not later than Six Months after the Union.

20. Repealed.

THE SENATE

Number of Senators

21. The Senate shall, subject to the Provisions of this Act, consist of One Hundred and five Members, who shall be styled Senators.

Representation of Provinces in Senate

22. In relation to the Constitution of the Senate Canada shall be deemed to consist of Four Divisions:

1. Ontario;
2. Quebec;
3. The Maritime Provinces, Nova Scotia and New Brunswick, and Prince Edward Island;
4. The Western Provinces of Manitoba, British Columbia, Saskatchewan, and Alberta;

which Four Divisions shall (subject to the Provisions of this Act) be equally represented in the Senate as follows: Ontario by twenty-four senators; Quebec by twenty-four senators; the Maritime Provinces and Prince Edward Island by twenty-four senators, ten thereof representing Nova Scotia, ten thereof representing New Brunswick, and four thereof representing Prince Edward Island; the Western Provinces by twenty-four senators, six thereof representing Manitoba, six thereof representing British Columbia, six thereof representing Saskatchewan, and six thereof representing Alberta; Newfoundland shall be entitled to be represented in the Senate by six members; the Yukon Territory, the Northwest Territories and Nunavut shall be entitled to be represented in the Senate by one member each.

In the Case of Quebec each of the Twenty-four Senators representing that Province shall be appointed for One of the Twenty-four Electoral Divisions of Lower Canada specified in Schedule A. to Chapter One of the Consolidated Statutes of Canada.

Qualifications of Senator

23. The Qualifications of a Senator shall be as follows:

(1) He shall be of the full age of Thirty Years;

(2) He shall be either a natural-born Subject of the Queen, or a Subject of the Queen naturalized by an Act of the Parliament of Great Britain, or of the Parliament of the United Kingdom of Great Britain and Ireland, or of the Legislature of One of the Provinces of Upper Canada, Lower Canada, Canada, Nova Scotia, or New Brunswick, before the Union, or of the Parliament of Canada after the Union;

(3) He shall be legally or equitably seised as of Freehold for his own Use and Benefit of Lands or Tenements held in Free and Common Socage, or seised or possessed for his own Use and Benefit of Lands or Tenements held in Franc-alleu or in Roture, within the Province for which he is appointed, of the Value of Four thousand Dollars, over and above all Rents, Dues, Debts, Charges, Mortgages, and Incumbrances due or payable out of or charged on or affecting the same;

(4) His Real and Personal Property shall be together worth Four thousand Dollars over and above his Debts and Liabilities;

(5) He shall be resident in the Province for which he is appointed;

(6) In the Case of Quebec he shall have his Real Property Qualification in the Electoral Division for which he is appointed, or shall be resident in that Division.

Summons of Senator

24. The Governor General shall from Time to Time, in the Queen's Name, by Instrument under the Great Seal of Canada, summon qualified Persons to the Senate; and, subject to the Provisions of this Act, every Person so summoned shall become and be a Member of the Senate and a Senator.

25. Repealed.

Addition of Senators in certain cases

26. If at any Time on the Recommendation of the Governor General the Queen thinks fit to direct that Four or Eight Members be added to the Senate, the Governor General may by Summons to Four or Eight qualified Persons (as the Case may be), representing equally the Four Divisions of Canada, add to the Senate accordingly.

Reduction of Senate to normal Number

27. In case of such Addition being at any Time made, the Governor General shall not summon any Person to the Senate, except on a further like Direction by the Queen on the like Recommendation, to represent one of the Four Divisions until such Division is represented by Twenty-four Senators and no more.

Maximum Number of Senators

28. The Number of Senators shall not at any Time exceed One Hundred and thirteen.

Tenure of Place in Senate

29. (1) Subject to subsection (2), a Senator shall, subject to the provisions of this Act, hold his place in the Senate for life.

Retirement upon attaining age of seventy-five years

(2) A Senator who is summoned to the Senate after the coming into force of this subsection shall, subject to this Act, hold his place in the Senate until he attains the age of seventy-five years.

[Sections 30–36 omitted.]

THE HOUSE OF COMMONS

Constitution of House of Commons in Canada

37. The House of Commons shall, subject to the Provisions of this Act, consist of three hundred and eight members of whom one hundred and six shall be elected for Ontario, seventy-five for Quebec, eleven for Nova Scotia, ten for New Brunswick, fourteen for Manitoba, thirty-six for British Columbia, four for Prince Edward Island, twenty-eight for Alberta, fourteen for Saskatchewan, seven for Newfoundland, one for the Yukon Territory, one for the Northwest Territories and one for Nunavut.

Summoning of House of Commons

38. The Governor General shall from Time to Time, in the Queen's Name, by Instrument under the Great Seal of Canada, summon and call together the House of Commons.

Senators not to sit in House of Commons

39. A Senator shall not be capable of being elected or of sitting or voting as a Member of the House of Commons.

[Sections 40–49 omitted.]

Duration of House of Commons

50. Every House of Commons shall continue for Five Years from the Day of the Return of the Writs for choosing the House (subject to be sooner dissolved by the Governor General), and no longer.

[Section 51 omitted.]

Constitution of House of Commons

51A. Notwithstanding anything in this Act a province shall always be entitled to a number of members in the House of Commons not less than the number of senators representing such province.

Increase of Number of House of Commons

52. The Number of Members of the House of Commons may be from Time to Time increased by the Parliament of Canada, provided the proportionate Representation of the Provinces prescribed by this Act is not thereby disturbed.

Money Votes; Royal Assent

Appropriation and Tax Bills

53. Bills for appropriating any Part of the Public Revenue, or for imposing any Tax or Impost, shall originate in the House of Commons.

Recommendation of Money Votes

54. It shall not be lawful for the House of Commons to adopt or pass any Vote, Resolution, Address, or Bill for the Appropriation of any Part of the Public Revenue, or of any Tax or Impost, to any Purpose that has not been first recommended to that House by Message of the Governor General in the Session in which such Vote, Resolution, Address, or Bill is proposed.

Royal Assent to Bills, etc.

55. Where a Bill passed by the Houses of the Parliament is presented to the Governor General for the Queen's Assent, he shall declare, according to his Discretion, but subject to the Provisions of this Act and to Her Majesty's Instructions, either that he assents thereto in the Queen's Name, or that he withholds the Queen's Assent, or that he reserves the Bill for the Signification of the Queen's Pleasure.

Disallowance by Order in Council of Act assented to by Governor General

56. Where the Governor General assents to a Bill in the Queen's Name, he shall by the first convenient Opportunity send an authentic Copy of the Act to One of Her Majesty's Principal Secretaries of State, and if the Queen in Council within Two Years after Receipt thereof by the Secretary of State thinks fit to disallow the Act, such Disallowance (with a Certificate of the Secretary of State of the Day on which the Act was received by him) being signified by the Governor General, by Speech or Message to each of the Houses of the Parliament or by Proclamation, shall annul the Act from and after the Day of such Signification.

Signification of Queen's Pleasure on Bill reserved

57. A Bill reserved for the Signification of the Queen's Pleasure shall not have any Force unless and until, within Two Years from the Day on which it was presented to the Governor General for the Queen's Assent, the Governor General signifies, by Speech or Message to each of the Houses of the Parliament or by Proclamation, that it has received the Assent of the Queen in Council.

An Entry of every such Speech, Message, or Proclamation shall be made in the Journal of each House, and a Duplicate thereof duly attested shall be delivered to the proper Officer to be kept among the Records of Canada.

V. PROVINCIAL CONSTITUTIONS

Executive Power

Appointment of Lieutenant Governors of Provinces

58. For each Province there shall be an Officer, styled the Lieutenant Governor, appointed by the Governor General in Council by Instrument under the Great Seal of Canada.

Tenure of Office of Lieutenant Governor

59. A Lieutenant Governor shall hold Office during the Pleasure of the Governor General; but any Lieutenant Governor appointed after the Commencement of the First Session of the Parliament of Canada shall not be removeable within Five Years from his Appointment, except for Cause assigned, which shall be communicated to him in Writing within One Month after the Order for his Removal is made, and shall be communicated by Message to the Senate and to the House of Commons within One Week thereafter if the Parliament is then sitting, and if not then within One Week after the Commencement of the next Session of the Parliament.

Salaries of Lieutenant Governors

60. The Salaries of the Lieutenant Governors shall be fixed and provided by the Parliament of Canada.

Oaths, etc., of Lieutenant Governor

61. Every Lieutenant Governor shall, before assuming the Duties of his Office, make and subscribe before the Governor General or some Person authorized by him Oaths of Allegiance and Office similar to those taken by the Governor General.

Application of Provisions referring to Lieutenant Governor

62. The Provisions of this Act referring to the Lieutenant Governor extend and apply to the Lieutenant Governor for the Time being of each Province, or other the Chief Executive Officer or Administrator for the Time being carrying on the Government of the Province, by whatever Title he is designated.

Appointment of Executive Officers for Ontario and Quebec

63. The Executive Council of Ontario and of Quebec shall be composed of such Persons as the Lieutenant Governor from Time to Time thinks fit, and in the first instance of the following Officers, namely,—the Attorney General, the Secretary and Registrar of the Province, the Treasurer of the Province, the Commissioner of Crown Lands, and the Commissioner of Agriculture and Public Works, with in Quebec the Speaker of the Legislative Council and the Solicitor General.

Executive Government of Nova Scotia and New Brunswick

64. The Constitution of the Executive Authority in each of the Provinces of Nova Scotia and New Brunswick shall, subject to the Provisions of this Act, continue as it exists at the Union until altered under the Authority of this Act.

Powers to be exercised by Lieutenant Governor of Ontario or Quebec with Advice, or alone

65. All Powers, Authorities, and Functions which under any Act of the Parliament of Great Britain, or of the Parliament of the United Kingdom of Great Britain and Ireland, or of the Legislature of Upper Canada, Lower Canada, or Canada, were or are before or at the Union vested in or exerciseable by the respective Governors or Lieutenant Governors of those Provinces, with the Advice or with the Advice and Consent of the respective Executive Councils thereof, or in conjunction with those Councils, or with any Number of Members thereof, or by those Governors or Lieutenant Governors individually, shall, as far as the same are capable of being exercised after the Union in relation to the Government of Ontario and Quebec respectively, be vested in and shall or may be exercised by the Lieutenant Governor of Ontario and Quebec respectively, with the Advice or with the Advice and Consent of or in conjunction with the respective Executive Councils, or any Members thereof, or by the Lieutenant Governor individually, as the Case requires, subject nevertheless (except with respect to such as exist under Acts of the Parliament of Great Britain, or of the Parliament of the United Kingdom of Great Britain and Ireland,) to be abolished or altered by the respective Legislatures of Ontario and Quebec.

Application of Provisions referring to Lieutenant Governor in Council

66. The Provisions of this Act referring to the Lieutenant Governor in Council shall be construed as referring to the Lieutenant Governor of the Province acting by and with the Advice of the Executive Council thereof.

Administration in Absence, etc., of Lieutenant Governor

67. The Governor General in Council may from Time to Time appoint an Administrator to execute the Office and Functions of Lieutenant Governor during his Absence, Illness, or other Inability.

Seats of Provincial Governments

68. Unless and until the Executive Government of any Province otherwise directs with respect to that Province, the Seats of Government of the Provinces shall be as follows, namely,—of Ontario, the City of Toronto; of Quebec, the City of Quebec; of Nova Scotia, the City of Halifax; and of New Brunswick, the City of Fredericton.

LEGISLATIVE POWER

1. Ontario

Legislature for Ontario

69. There shall be a Legislature for Ontario consisting of the Lieutenant Governor and of One House, styled the Legislative Assembly of Ontario.

[Section 70 omitted.]

2. Quebec

Legislature for Quebec

71. There shall be a Legislature for Quebec consisting of the Lieutenant Governor and of Two Houses, styled the Legislative Council of Quebec and the Legislative Assembly of Quebec.

[Sections 72–80 omitted.]

3. Ontario and Quebec

[Sections 81–85 omitted.]

Yearly Session of Legislature

86. There shall be a Session of the Legislature of Ontario and of that of Quebec once at least in every Year, so that Twelve Months shall not intervene between the last Sitting of the Legislature in each Province in one Session and its first Sitting in the next Session.

[Section 87 omitted.]

4. Nova Scotia and New Brunswick

Constitutions of Legislatures of Nova Scotia and New Brunswick

88. The Constitution of the Legislature of each of the Provinces of Nova Scotia and New Brunswick shall, subject to the Provisions of this Act, continue as it exists at the Union until altered under the Authority of this Act.

5. Ontario, Quebec, and Nova Scotia

89. Repealed.

6. The Four Provinces

Application to Legislatures of Provisions respecting Money Votes, etc.

90. The following Provisions of this Act respecting the Parliament of Canada, namely,—the Provisions relating to Appropriation and Tax Bills, the Recommendation of Money Votes, the Assent to Bills, the Disallowance of Acts, and the Signification of Pleasure on Bills reserved,—shall extend and apply to the Legislatures of the several Provinces as if those Provisions were here re-enacted and made applicable in Terms to the respective Provinces and the Legislatures thereof, with the Substitution of the Lieutenant Governor of the Province for the Governor General, of the Governor General for the Queen and for a Secretary of State, of One Year for Two Years, and of the Province for Canada.

VI. DISTRIBUTION OF LEGISLATIVE POWERS

POWERS OF THE PARLIAMENT

Legislative Authority of Parliament of Canada

91. It shall be lawful for the Queen, by and with the Advice and Consent of the Senate and House of Commons, to make Laws for the Peace, Order, and good Government of Canada, in relation to all Matters not coming within the Classes of Subjects by this Act assigned exclusively to the Legislatures of the Provinces; and for greater Certainty, but not so as to restrict the Generality of the foregoing Terms of this Section, it is hereby declared that (notwithstanding anything in this Act) the exclusive Legislative Authority of the Parliament of Canada extends to all Matters coming within the Classes of Subjects next hereinafter enumerated; that is to say,

1. Repealed.
1A. The Public Debt and Property.
2. The Regulation of Trade and Commerce.
2A. Unemployment insurance.
3. The raising of Money by any Mode or System of Taxation.
4. The borrowing of Money on the Public Credit.
5. Postal Service.
6. The Census and Statistics.
7. Militia, Military and Naval Service, and Defence.
8. The fixing of and providing for the Salaries and Allowances of Civil and other Officers of the Government of Canada.
9. Beacons, Buoys, Lighthouses, and Sable Island.
10. Navigation and Shipping.
11. Quarantine and the Establishment and Maintenance of Marine Hospitals.
12. Sea Coast and Inland Fisheries.
13. Ferries between a Province and any British or Foreign Country or between Two Provinces.
14. Currency and Coinage.
15. Banking, Incorporation of Banks, and the Issue of Paper Money.
16. Savings Banks.
17. Weights and Measures.
18. Bills of Exchange and Promissory Notes.
19. Interest.
20. Legal Tender.
21. Bankruptcy and Insolvency.
22. Patents of Invention and Discovery.
23. Copyrights.
24. Indians, and Lands reserved for the Indians.
25. Naturalization and Aliens.
26. Marriage and Divorce.

27. The Criminal Law, except the Constitution of Courts of Criminal Jurisdiction, but including the Procedure in Criminal Matters.
28. The Establishment, Maintenance, and Management of Penitentiaries.
29. Such Classes of Subjects as are expressly excepted in the Enumeration of the Classes of Subjects by this Act assigned exclusively to the Legislatures of the Provinces.

And any Matter coming within any of the Classes of Subjects enumerated in this Section shall not be deemed to come within the Class of Matters of a local or private Nature comprised in the Enumeration of the Classes of Subjects by this Act assigned exclusively to the Legislatures of the Provinces.

Exclusive Powers of Provincial Legislatures

Subjects of exclusive Provincial Legislation

92. In each Province the Legislature may exclusively make Laws in relation to Matters coming within the Classes of Subjects next hereinafter enumerated; that is to say,

1. Repealed.
2. Direct Taxation within the Province in order to the raising of a Revenue for Provincial Purposes.
3. The borrowing of Money on the sole Credit of the Province.
4. The Establishment and Tenure of Provincial Offices and the Appointment and Payment of Provincial Officers.
5. The Management and Sale of the Public Lands belonging to the Province and of the Timber and Wood thereon.
6. The Establishment, Maintenance, and Management of Public and Reformatory Prisons in and for the Province.
7. The Establishment, Maintenance, and Management of Hospitals, Asylums, Charities, and Eleemosynary Institutions in and for the Province, other than Marine Hospitals.
8. Municipal Institutions in the Province.
9. Shop, Saloon, Tavern, Auctioneer, and other Licences in order to the raising of a Revenue for Provincial, Local, or Municipal Purposes.
10. Local Works and Undertakings other than such as are of the following Classes:
    (*a*) Lines of Steam or other Ships, Railways, Canals, Telegraphs, and other Works and Undertakings connecting the Province with any other or others of the Provinces, or extending beyond the Limits of the Province:
    (*b*) Lines of Steam Ships between the Province and any British or Foreign Country:
    (*c*) Such Works as, although wholly situate within the Province, are before or after their Execution declared by the Parliament of Canada to be for the general Advantage of Canada or for the Advantage of Two or more of the Provinces.
11. The Incorporation of Companies with Provincial Objects.
12. The Solemnization of Marriage in the Province.
13. Property and Civil Rights in the Province.
14. The Administration of Justice in the Province, including the Constitution, Maintenance, and Organization of Provincial Courts, both of Civil and of Criminal Jurisdiction, and including Procedure in Civil Matters in those Courts.
15. The Imposition of Punishment by Fine, Penalty, or Imprisonment for enforcing any Law of the Province made in relation to any Matter coming within any of the Classes of Subjects enumerated in this Section.
16. Generally all Matters of a merely local or private Nature in the Province.

Non-Renewable Natural Resources, Forestry Resources and Electrical Energy

Laws respecting non-renewable natural resources, forestry resources and electrical energy

92A. (1) In each province, the legislature may exclusively make laws in relation to
    (*a*) exploration for non-renewable natural resources in the province;
    (*b*) development, conservation and management of non-renewable natural resources and forestry resources in the province, including laws in relation to the rate of primary production therefrom; and
    (*c*) development, conservation and management of sites and facilities in the province for the generation and production of electrical energy.

Export from provinces of resources

(2) In each province, the legislature may make laws in relation to the export from the province to another part of Canada of the primary production from non-renewable natural resources and forestry resources in the province and the production from facilities in the province for the generation of electrical energy, but such laws may not authorize or provide for discrimination in prices or in supplies exported to another part of Canada.

Authority of Parliament

(3) Nothing in subsection (2) derogates from the authority of Parliament to enact laws in relation to the matters referred to in that subsection and, where such a law of Parliament and a law of a province conflict, the law of Parliament prevails to the extent of the conflict.

Taxation of resources

(4) In each province, the legislature may make laws in relation to the raising of money by any mode or system of taxation in respect of

    (*a*) non-renewable natural resources and forestry resources in the province and the primary production therefrom, and

    (*b*) sites and facilities in the province for the generation of electrical energy and the production therefrom,

whether or not such production is exported in whole or in part from the province, but such laws may not authorize or provide for taxation that differentiates between production exported to another part of Canada and production not exported from the province.

"Primary production"

(5) The expression "primary production" has the meaning assigned by the Sixth Schedule.

Existing powers or rights

(6) Nothing in subsections (1) to (5) derogates from any powers or rights that a legislature or government of a province had immediately before the coming into force of this section.

EDUCATION

Legislation respecting Education

93. In and for each Province the Legislature may exclusively make Laws in relation to Education, subject and according to the following Provisions:

    (1) Nothing in any such Law shall prejudicially affect any Right or Privilege with respect to Denominational Schools which any Class of Persons have by Law in the Province at the Union;

    (2) All the Powers, Privileges, and Duties at the Union by Law conferred and imposed in Upper Canada on the Separate Schools and School Trustees of the Queen's Roman Catholic Subjects shall be and the same are hereby extended to the Dissentient Schools of the Queen's Protestant and Roman Catholic Subjects in Quebec;

    (3) Where in any Province a System of Separate or Dissentient Schools exists by Law at the Union or is thereafter established by the Legislature of the Province, an Appeal shall lie to the Governor General in Council from any Act or Decision of any Provincial Authority affecting any Right or Privilege of the Protestant or Roman Catholic Minority of the Queen's Subjects in relation to Education;

    (4) In case any such Provincial Law as from Time to Time seems to the Governor General in Council requisite for the due Execution of the Provisions of this Section is not made, or in case any Decision of the Governor General in Council on any Appeal under this Section is not duly executed by the proper Provincial Authority in that Behalf, then and in every such Case, and as far only as the Circumstances of each Case require, the Parliament of Canada may make remedial Laws for the due Execution of the Provisions of this Section and of any Decision of the Governor General in Council under this Section.

Quebec

93A. Paragraphs (1) to (4) of section 93 do not apply to Quebec.

UNIFORMITY OF LAWS IN ONTARIO, NOVA SCOTIA, AND NEW BRUNSWICK

Legislation for Uniformity of Laws in Three Provinces

94. Notwithstanding anything in this Act, the Parliament of Canada may make Provision for the Uniformity of all or any of the Laws relative to Property and Civil Rights in Ontario, Nova Scotia, and New Brunswick, and of the Procedure of all or any of the Courts in those Three Provinces, and from and after the passing of any Act in that Behalf the Power of the Parliament of Canada to make Laws in relation to any Matter comprised in any such Act shall, notwithstanding anything in this Act, be unrestricted; but any Act of the Parliament of Canada making Provision for such Uniformity shall not have effect in any Province unless and until it is adopted and enacted as Law by the Legislature thereof.

OLD AGE PENSIONS

Legislation respecting old age pensions and supplementary benefits

94A. The Parliament of Canada may make laws in relation to old age pensions and supplementary benefits, including survivors' and disability benefits irrespective of age, but no such law shall affect the operation of any law present or future of a provincial legislature in relation to any such matter.

Concurrent Powers of Legislation respecting Agriculture, etc.

95. In each Province the Legislature may make Laws in relation to Agriculture in the Province, and to Immigration into the Province; and it is hereby declared that the Parliament of Canada may from Time to Time make Laws in relation to Agriculture in all or any of the Provinces, and to Immigration into all or any of the Provinces; and any Law of the Legislature of a Province relative to Agriculture or to Immigration shall have effect in and for the Province as long and as far only as it is not repugnant to any Act of the Parliament of Canada.

VII. JUDICATURE

Appointment of Judges

96. The Governor General shall appoint the Judges of the Superior, District, and County Courts in each Province, except those of the Courts of Probate in Nova Scotia and New Brunswick.

Selection of Judges in Ontario, etc.

97. Until the Laws relative to Property and Civil Rights in Ontario, Nova Scotia, and New Brunswick, and the Procedure of the Courts in those Provinces, are made uniform, the Judges of the Courts of those Provinces appointed by the Governor General shall be selected from the respective Bars of those Provinces.

Selection of Judges in Quebec

98. The Judges of the Courts of Quebec shall be selected from the Bar of that Province.

Tenure of office of Judges

99. (1) Subject to subsection (2) of this section, the judges of the superior courts shall hold office during good behaviour, but shall be removable by the Governor General on address of the Senate and House of Commons.

Termination at age 75

(2) A judge of a superior court, whether appointed before or after the coming into force of this section, shall cease to hold office upon attaining the age of seventy-five years, or upon the coming into force of this section if at that time he has already attained that age.

Salaries, etc., of Judges

100. The Salaries, Allowances, and Pensions of the Judges of the Superior, District, and County Courts (except the Courts of Probate in Nova Scotia and New Brunswick), and of the Admiralty Courts in Cases where the Judges thereof are for the Time being paid by Salary, shall be fixed and provided by the Parliament of Canada.

General Court of Appeal, etc.

101. The Parliament of Canada may, notwithstanding anything in this Act, from Time to Time provide for the Constitution, Maintenance, and Organization of a General Court of Appeal for Canada, and for the Establishment of any additional Courts for the better Administration of the Laws of Canada.

VIII. REVENUES; DEBTS; ASSETS; TAXATION

[Sections 102–104 omitted.]

Salary of Governor General

105. Unless altered by the Parliament of Canada, the Salary of the Governor General shall be Ten thousand Pounds Sterling Money of the United Kingdom of Great Britain and Ireland, payable out of the Consolidated Revenue Fund of Canada, and the same shall form the Third Charge thereon.

[Sections 106–107 omitted.]

Transfer of Property in Schedule

108. The Public Works and Property of each Province, enumerated in the Third Schedule to this Act, shall be the Property of Canada.

Property in Lands, Mines, etc.

109. All Lands, Mines, Minerals, and Royalties belonging to the several Provinces of Canada, Nova Scotia, and New Brunswick at the Union, and all Sums then due or payable for such Lands, Mines, Minerals, or Royalties, shall belong to the several Provinces of Ontario, Quebec, Nova Scotia, and New Brunswick in which the same are situate or arise, subject to any Trusts existing in respect thereof, and to any Interest other than that of the Province in the same.

[Sections 110–116 omitted.]

Provincial Public Property

117. The several Provinces shall retain all their respective Public Property not otherwise disposed of in this Act, subject to the Right of Canada to assume any Lands or Public Property required for Fortifications or for the Defence of the Country.

[Sections 118–120 omitted.]

Canadian Manufactures, etc.

121. All Articles of the Growth, Produce, or Manufacture of any one of the Provinces shall, from and after the Union, be admitted free into each of the other Provinces.

Continuance of Customs and Excise Laws

122. The Customs and Excise Laws of each Province shall, subject to the Provisions of this Act, continue in force until altered by the Parliament of Canada.

[Sections 123–124 omitted.]

Exemption of Public Lands, etc.

125. No Lands or Property belonging to Canada or any Province shall be liable to Taxation.

[Section 126 omitted.]

IX. MISCELLANEOUS PROVISIONS

General

127. Repealed.

Oath of Allegiance, etc.

128. Every Member of the Senate or House of Commons of Canada shall before taking his Seat therein take and subscribe before the Governor General or some Person authorized by him, and every Member of a Legislative Council or Legislative Assembly of any Province shall before taking his Seat therein take and subscribe before the Lieutenant Governor of the Province or some Person authorized by him, the Oath of Allegiance contained in the Fifth Schedule to this Act; and every Member of the Senate of Canada and every Member of the Legislative Council of Quebec shall also, before taking his Seat therein, take and subscribe before the Governor General, or some Person authorized by him, the Declaration of Qualification contained in the same Schedule.

Continuance of existing Laws, Courts, Officers, etc.

129. Except as otherwise provided by this Act, all Laws in force in Canada, Nova Scotia, or New Brunswick at the Union, and all Courts of Civil and Criminal Jurisdiction, and all legal Commissions, Powers, and Authorities, and all Officers, Judicial, Administrative, and Ministerial, existing therein at the Union, shall continue in Ontario, Quebec, Nova Scotia, and New Brunswick respectively, as if the Union had not been made; subject nevertheless (except with respect to such as are enacted by or exist under Acts of the Parliament of Great Britain or of the Parliament of the United Kingdom of Great Britain and Ireland,) to be repealed, abolished, or altered by the Parliament of Canada, or by the Legislature of the respective Province, according to the Authority of the Parliament or of that Legislature under this Act.

[Sections 130–131 omitted.]

Treaty Obligations

132. The Parliament and Government of Canada shall have all Powers necessary or proper for performing the Obligations of Canada or of any Province thereof, as Part of the British Empire, towards Foreign Countries, arising under Treaties between the Empire and such Foreign Countries.

Use of English and French Languages

133. Either the English or the French Language may be used by any Person in the Debates of the Houses of the Parliament of Canada and of the Houses of the Legislature of Quebec; and both those Languages shall be used in the respective Records and Journals of those Houses; and either of those Languages may be used by any Person or in any Pleading or Process in or issuing from any Court of Canada established under this Act, and in or from all or any of the Courts of Quebec.

The Acts of the Parliament of Canada and of the Legislature of Quebec shall be printed and published in both those Languages.

[Sections 134–144 omitted.]

X. INTERCOLONIAL RAILWAY

145. Repealed.

XI. ADMISSION OF OTHER COLONIES

Power to admit Newfoundland, etc., into the Union

146. It shall be lawful for the Queen, by and with the Advice of Her Majesty's Most Honourable Privy Council, on Addresses from the Houses of the Parliament of Canada, and from the Houses of the respective Legislatures of the Colonies or Provinces of Newfoundland, Prince Edward Island, and British Columbia, to admit those Colonies or Provinces, or any of them, into the Union, and on Address from the Houses of the Parliament of Canada to admit Rupert's Land and the North-western Territory, or either of them, into the Union, on such Terms and Conditions in each Case as are in the Addresses expressed and as the Queen thinks fit to approve, subject to the Provisions of this Act; and the Provisions of any Order in Council in that Behalf shall have effect as if they had been enacted by the Parliament of the United Kingdom of Great Britain and Ireland.

[Section 147 omitted.]

[The First and Second Schedules omitted.]

THE THIRD SCHEDULE

PROVINCIAL PUBLIC WORKS AND PROPERTY TO BE THE PROPERTY OF CANADA

1. Canals, with Lands and Water Power connected therewith.
2. Public Harbours.
3. Lighthouses and Piers, and Sable Island.
4. Steamboats, Dredges, and public Vessels.
5. Rivers and Lake Improvements.
6. Railways and Railway Stocks, Mortgages, and other Debts due by Railway Companies.
7. Military Roads.
8. Custom Houses, Post Offices, and all other Public Buildings, except such as the Government of Canada appropriate for the Use of the Provincial Legislatures and Governments.
9. Property transferred by the Imperial Government, and known as Ordnance Property.
10. Armouries, Drill Sheds, Military Clothing, and Munitions of War, and Lands set apart for general Public Purposes.

[The Fourth Schedule omitted.]

THE FIFTH SCHEDULE

OATH OF ALLEGIANCE

I *A.B.* do swear, That I will be faithful and bear true Allegiance to Her Majesty Queen Victoria.

Note.—The Name of the King or Queen of the United Kingdom of Great Britain and Ireland for the Time being is to be substituted from Time to Time, with proper Terms of Reference thereto.

Declaration of Qualification

I *A.B.* do declare and testify, That I am by Law duly qualified to be appointed a Member of the Senate of Canada [*or as the Case may be*], and that I am legally or equitably seised as of Freehold for my own Use and Benefit of Lands or Tenements held in Free and Common Socage [*or seised or possessed for my own Use and Benefit of Lands or Tenements held in Francalleu or in Roture (as the Case may be*),] in the Province of Nova Scotia [*or as the Case may be*] of the Value of Four thousand Dollars over and above all Rents, Dues, Debts, Mortgages, Charges, and Incumbrances due or payable out of or charged on or affecting the same, and that I have not collusively or colourably obtained a Title to or become possessed of the said Lands and Tenements or any Part thereof for the Purpose of enabling me to become a Member of the Senate of Canada [*or as the Case may be*], and that my Real and Personal Property are together worth Four thousand Dollars over and above my Debts and Liabilities.

THE SIXTH SCHEDULE

PRIMARY PRODUCTION FROM NON-RENEWABLE NATURAL RESOURCES AND FORESTRY RESOURCES

1. For the purposes of section 92A of this Act,

(*a*) production from a non-renewable natural resource is primary production therefrom if

(i) it is in the form in which it exists upon its recovery or severance from its natural state, or

(ii) it is a product resulting from processing or refining the resource, and is not a manufactured product or a product resulting from refining crude oil, refining upgraded heavy crude oil, refining gases or liquids derived from coal or refining a synthetic equivalent of crude oil; and

(*b*) production from a forestry resource is primary production therefrom if it consists of sawlogs, poles, lumber, wood chips, sawdust or any other primary wood product, or wood pulp, and is not a product manufactured from wood.

B Constitution Act, 1982

TABLE OF CONTENTS

PART I

CANADIAN CHARTER OF RIGHTS AND FREEDOMS

Whereas Canada is founded upon principles that recognize the supremacy of God and the rule of law:

Guarantee of Rights and Freedoms

Rights and freedoms in Canada

1. The *Canadian Charter of Rights and Freedoms* guarantees the rights and freedoms set out in it subject only to such reasonable limits prescribed by law as can be demonstrably justified in a free and democratic society.

Fundamental Freedoms

Fundamental freedoms

2. Everyone has the following fundamental freedoms:
(*a*) freedom of conscience and religion;
(*b*) freedom of thought, belief, opinion and expression, including freedom of the press and other media of communication;
(*c*) freedom of peaceful assembly; and
(*d*) freedom of association.

Democratic Rights

Democratic rights of citizens

3. Every citizen of Canada has the right to vote in an election of members of the House of Commons or of a legislative assembly and to be qualified for membership therein.

Maximum duration of legislative bodies

4. (1) No House of Commons and no legislative assembly shall continue for longer than five years from the date fixed for the return of the writs at a general election of its members.

Continuation in special circumstances

(2) In time of real or apprehended war, invasion or insurrection, a House of Commons may be continued by Parliament and a legislative assembly may be continued by the legislature beyond five years if such continuation is not opposed by the votes of more than one-third of the members of the House of Commons or the legislative assembly, as the case may be.

Annual sitting of legislative bodies

5. There shall be a sitting of Parliament and of each legislature at least once every twelve months.

Mobility Rights

Mobility of citizens

6. (1) Every citizen of Canada has the right to enter, remain in and leave Canada.

Rights to move and gain livelihood

(2) Every citizen of Canada and every person who has the status of a permanent resident of Canada has the right
(*a*) to move to and take up residence in any province; and
(*b*) to pursue the gaining of a livelihood in any province.

Limitation

(3) The rights specified in subsection (2) are subject to
(*a*) any laws or practices of general application in force in a province other than those that discriminate among persons primarily on the basis of province of present or previous residence; and
(*b*) any laws providing for reasonable residency requirements as a qualification for the receipt of publicly provided social services.

Affirmative action programs

(4) Subsections (2) and (3) do not preclude any law, program or activity that has as its object the amelioration in a province of conditions of individuals in that province who are socially or economically disadvantaged if the rate of employment in that province is below the rate of employment in Canada.

Legal Rights

Life, liberty and security of person

7. Everyone has the right to life, liberty and security of the person and the right not to be deprived thereof except in accordance with the principles of fundamental justice.

Search or seizure

8. Everyone has the right to be secure against unreasonable search or seizure.

Detention or imprisonment

9. Everyone has the right not to be arbitrarily detained or imprisoned.

Arrest or detention

10. Everyone has the right on arrest or detention
(*a*) to be informed promptly of the reasons therefor;

(*b*) to retain and instruct counsel without delay and to be informed of that right; and

(*c*) to have the validity of the detention determined by way of *habeas corpus* and to be released if the detention is not lawful.

Proceedings in criminal and penal matters

11. Any person charged with an offence has the right

(*a*) to be informed without unreasonable delay of the specific offence;

(*b*) to be tried within a reasonable time;

(*c*) not to be compelled to be a witness in proceedings against that person in respect of the offence;

(*d*) to be presumed innocent until proven guilty according to law in a fair and public hearing by an independent and impartial tribunal;

(*e*) not to be denied reasonable bail without just cause;

(*f*) except in the case of an offence under military law tried before a military tribunal, to the benefit of trial by jury where the maximum punishment for the offence is imprisonment for five years or a more severe punishment;

(*g*) not to be found guilty on account of any act or omission unless, at the time of the act or omission, it constituted an offence under Canadian or international law or was criminal according to the general principles of law recognized by the community of nations;

(*h*) if finally acquitted of the offence, not to be tried for it again and, if finally found guilty and punished for the offence, not to be tried or punished for it again; and

(*i*) if found guilty of the offence and if the punishment for the offence has been varied between the time of commission and the time of sentencing, to the benefit of the lesser punishment.

Treatment or punishment

12. Everyone has the right not to be subjected to any cruel and unusual treatment or punishment.

Self-crimination

13. A witness who testifies in any proceedings has the right not to have any incriminating evidence so given used to incriminate that witness in any other proceedings, except in a prosecution for perjury or for the giving of contradictory evidence.

Interpreter

14. A party or witness in any proceedings who does not understand or speak the language in which the proceedings are conducted or who is deaf has the right to the assistance of an interpreter.

EQUALITY RIGHTS

Equality before and under law and equal protection and benefit of law

15. (1) Every individual is equal before and under the law and has the right to the equal protection and equal benefit of the law without discrimination and, in particular, without discrimination based on race, national or ethnic origin, colour, religion, sex, age or mental or physical disability.

Affirmative action programs

(2) Subsection (1) does not preclude any law, program or activity that has as its object the amelioration of conditions of disadvantaged individuals or groups including those that are disadvantaged because of race, national or ethnic origin, colour, religion, sex, age or mental or physical disability.

OFFICIAL LANGUAGES OF CANADA

Official languages of Canada

16. (1) English and French are the official languages of Canada and have equality of status and equal rights and privileges as to their use in all institutions of the Parliament and government of Canada.

Official languages of New Brunswick

(2) English and French are the official languages of New Brunswick and have equality of status and equal rights and privileges as to their use in all institutions of the legislature and government of New Brunswick.

Advancement of status and use

(3) Nothing in this Charter limits the authority of Parliament or a legislature to advance the equality of status or use of English and French.

English and French linguistic communities in New Brunswick

16.1 (1) The English linguistic community and the French linguistic community in New Brunswick have equality of status and equal rights and privileges, including the right to distinct educational institutions and such distinct cultural institutions as are necessary for the preservation and promotion of those communities.

Role of the legislature and government of New Brunswick

(2) The role of the legislature and government of New Brunswick to preserve and promote the status, rights and privileges referred to in subsection (1) is affirmed.

Proceedings of Parliament

17. (1) Everyone has the right to use English or French in any debates and other proceedings of Parliament.

Proceedings of New Brunswick legislature

(2) Everyone has the right to use English or French in any debates and other proceedings of the legislature of New Brunswick.

Parliamentary statutes and records

18. (1) The statutes, records and journals of Parliament shall be printed and published in English and French and both language versions are equally authoritative.

New Brunswick statutes and records

(2) The statutes, records and journals of the legislature of New Brunswick shall be printed and published in English and French and both language versions are equally authoritative.

Proceedings in courts established by Parliament

19. (1) Either English or French may be used by any person in, or in any pleading in or process issuing from, any court established by Parliament.

Proceedings in New Brunswick courts

(2) Either English or French may be used by any person in, or in any pleading in or process issuing from, any court of New Brunswick.

Communications by public with federal institutions

20. (1) Any member of the public in Canada has the right to communicate with, and to receive available services from, any head or central office of an institution of the Parliament or government of Canada in English or French, and has the same right with respect to any other office of any such institution where

(*a*) there is a significant demand for communications with and services from that office in such language; or

(*b*) due to the nature of the office, it is reasonable that communications with and services from that office be available in both English and French.

Communications by public with New Brunswick institutions

(2) Any member of the public in New Brunswick has the right to communicate with, and to receive available services from, any office of an institution of the legislature or government of New Brunswick in English or French.

Continuation of existing constitutional provisions

21. Nothing in sections 16 to 20 abrogates or derogates from any right, privilege or obligation with respect to the English and French languages, or either of them, that exists or is continued by virtue of any other provision of the Constitution of Canada.

Rights and privileges preserved

22. Nothing in sections 16 to 20 abrogates or derogates from any legal or customary right or privilege acquired or enjoyed either before or after the coming into force of this Charter with respect to any language that is not English or French.

MINORITY LANGUAGE EDUCATIONAL RIGHTS

Language of instruction

23. (1) Citizens of Canada

(*a*) whose first language learned and still understood is that of the English or French linguistic minority population of the province in which they reside, or

(*b*) who have received their primary school instruction in Canada in English or French and reside in a province where the language in which they received that instruction is the language of the English or French linguistic minority population of the province,

have the right to have their children receive primary and secondary school instruction in that language in that province.

Continuity of language instruction

(2) Citizens of Canada of whom any child has received or is receiving primary or secondary school instruction in English or French in Canada, have the right to have all their children receive primary and secondary school instruction in the same language.

Application where numbers warrant

(3) The right of citizens of Canada under subsections (1) and (2) to have their children receive primary and secondary school instruction in the language of the English or French linguistic minority population of a province

(*a*) applies wherever in the province the number of children of citizens who have such a right is sufficient to warrant the provision to them out of public funds of minority language instruction; and

(*b*) includes, where the number of those children so warrants, the right to have them receive that instruction in minority language educational facilities provided out of public funds.

ENFORCEMENT

Enforcement of guaranteed rights and freedoms

24. (1) Anyone whose rights or freedoms, as guaranteed by this Charter, have been infringed or denied may apply to a court of competent jurisdiction to obtain such remedy as the court considers appropriate and just in the circumstances.

Exclusion of evidence bringing administration of justice into disrepute

(2) Where, in proceedings under subsection (1), a court concludes that evidence was obtained in a manner that infringed or denied any rights or freedoms guaranteed by this Charter, the evidence shall be excluded if it is established that, having regard to all the circumstances, the admission of it in the proceedings would bring the administration of justice into disrepute.

GENERAL

Aboriginal rights and freedoms not affected by Charter

25. The guarantee in this Charter of certain rights and freedoms shall not be construed so as to abrogate or derogate from any aboriginal, treaty or other rights or freedoms that pertain to the aboriginal peoples of Canada including

(*a*) any rights or freedoms that have been recognized by the Royal Proclamation of October 7, 1763; and

(*b*) any rights or freedoms that now exist by way of land claims agreements or may be so acquired.

Other rights and freedoms not affected by Charter

26. The guarantee in this Charter of certain rights and freedoms shall not be construed as denying the existence of any other rights or freedoms that exist in Canada.

Multicultural heritage

27. This Charter shall be interpreted in a manner consistent with the preservation and enhancement of the multicultural heritage of Canadians.

Rights guaranteed equally to both sexes

28. Notwithstanding anything in this Charter, the rights and freedoms referred to in it are guaranteed equally to male and female persons.

Rights respecting certain schools preserved

29. Nothing in this Charter abrogates or derogates from any rights or privileges guaranteed by or under the Constitution of Canada in respect of denominational, separate or dissentient schools.

Application to territories and territorial authorities

30. A reference in this Charter to a province or to the legislative assembly or legislature of a province shall be deemed to include a reference to the Yukon Territory and the Northwest Territories, or to the appropriate legislative authority thereof, as the case may be.

Legislative powers not extended

31. Nothing in this Charter extends the legislative powers of any body or authority.

APPLICATION OF CHARTER

Application of Charter

32. (1) This Charter applies

(*a*) to the Parliament and government of Canada in respect of all matters within the authority of Parliament including all matters relating to the Yukon Territory and Northwest Territories; and

(*b*) to the legislature and government of each province in respect of all matters within the authority of the legislature of each province.

Exception

(2) Notwithstanding subsection (1), section 15 shall not have effect until three years after this section comes into force.

Exception where express declaration

33. (1) Parliament or the legislature of a province may expressly declare in an Act of Parliament or of the legislature, as the case may be, that the Act or a provision thereof shall operate notwithstanding a provision included in section 2 or sections 7 to 15 of this Charter.

Operation of exception

(2) An Act or a provision of an Act in respect of which a declaration made under this section is in effect shall have such operation as it would have but for the provision of this Charter referred to in the declaration.

Five year limitation

(3) A declaration made under subsection (1) shall cease to have effect five years after it comes into force or on such earlier date as may be specified in the declaration.

Re-enactment

(4) Parliament or the legislature of a province may re-enact a declaration made under subsection (1).

Five year limitation

(5) Subsection (3) applies in respect of a re-enactment made under subsection (4).

CITATION

Citation

34. This Part may be cited as the *Canadian Charter of Rights and Freedoms.*

PART II

RIGHTS OF THE ABORIGINAL PEOPLES OF CANADA

Recognition of existing aboriginal and treaty rights

35. (1) The existing aboriginal and treaty rights of the aboriginal peoples of Canada are hereby recognized and affirmed.

Definition of "aboriginal peoples of Canada"

(2) In this Act, "aboriginal peoples of Canada" includes the Indian, Inuit and Métis peoples of Canada.

Land claims agreements

(3) For greater certainty, in subsection (1) "treaty rights" includes rights that now exist by way of land claims agreements or may be so acquired.

Aboriginal and treaty rights are guaranteed equally to both sexes

(4) Notwithstanding any other provision of this Act, the aboriginal and treaty rights referred to in subsection (1) are guaranteed equally to male and female persons.

Commitment to participation in constitutional conference

35.1 The government of Canada and the provincial governments are committed to the principle that, before any amendment is made to Class 24 of section 91 of the "*Constitution Act, 1867*", to section 25 of this Act or to this Part,

(*a*) a constitutional conference that includes in its agenda an item relating to the proposed amendment, composed of the Prime Minister of Canada and the first ministers of the provinces, will be convened by the Prime Minister of Canada; and

(*b*) the Prime Minister of Canada will invite representatives of the aboriginal peoples of Canada to participate in the discussions on that item.

PART III

EQUALIZATION AND REGIONAL DISPARITIES

Commitment to promote equal opportunities

36. (1) Without altering the legislative authority of Parliament or of the provincial legislatures, or the rights of any of them with respect to the exercise of their legislative authority, Parliament and the legislatures, together with the government of Canada and the provincial governments, are committed to

(*a*) promoting equal opportunities for the well-being of Canadians;

(*b*) furthering economic development to reduce disparity in opportunities; and

(*c*) providing essential public services of reasonable quality to all Canadians.

Commitment respecting public services

(2) Parliament and the government of Canada are committed to the principle of making equalization payments to ensure that provincial governments have sufficient revenues to provide reasonably comparable levels of public services at reasonably comparable levels of taxation.

PART IV

CONSTITUTIONAL CONFERENCE

37. Repealed.

PART IV.I

CONSTITUTIONAL CONFERENCES

37.1 Repealed.

PART V

PROCEDURE FOR AMENDING CONSTITUTION OF CANADA

General procedure for amending Constitution of Canada

38. (1) An amendment to the Constitution of Canada may be made by proclamation issued by the Governor General under the Great Seal of Canada where so authorized by

    (*a*) resolutions of the Senate and House of Commons; and

    (*b*) resolutions of the legislative assemblies of at least two-thirds of the provinces that have, in the aggregate, according to the then latest general census, at least fifty per cent of the population of all the provinces.

Majority of members

(2) An amendment made under subsection (1) that derogates from the legislative powers, the proprietary rights or any other rights or privileges of the legislature or government of a province shall require a resolution supported by a majority of the members of each of the Senate, the House of Commons and the legislative assemblies required under subsection (1).

Expression of dissent

(3) An amendment referred to in subsection (2) shall not have effect in a province the legislative assembly of which has expressed its dissent thereto by resolution supported by a majority of its members prior to the issue of the proclamation to which the amendment relates unless that legislative assembly, subsequently, by resolution supported by a majority of its members, revokes its dissent and authorizes the amendment.

Revocation of dissent

(4) A resolution of dissent made for the purposes of subsection (3) may be revoked at any time before or after the issue of the proclamation to which it relates.

Restriction on proclamation

39. (1) A proclamation shall not be issued under subsection 38(1) before the expiration of one year from the adoption of the resolution initiating the amendment procedure thereunder, unless the legislative assembly of each province has previously adopted a resolution of assent or dissent.

Idem

(2) A proclamation shall not be issued under subsection 38(1) after the expiration of three years from the adoption of the resolution initiating the amendment procedure thereunder.

Compensation

40. Where an amendment is made under subsection 38(1) that transfers provincial legislative powers relating to education or other cultural matters from provincial legislatures to Parliament, Canada shall provide reasonable compensation to any province to which the amendment does not apply.

Amendment by unanimous consent

41. An amendment to the Constitution of Canada in relation to the following matters may be made by proclamation issued by the Governor General under the Great Seal of Canada only where authorized by resolutions of the Senate and House of Commons and of the legislative assembly of each province:

    (*a*) the office of the Queen, the Governor General and the Lieutenant Governor of a province;

    (*b*) the right of a province to a number of members in the House of Commons not less than the number of Senators by which the province is entitled to be represented at the time this Part comes into force;

    (*c*) subject to section 43, the use of the English or the French language;

    (*d*) the composition of the Supreme Court of Canada; and

    (*e*) an amendment to this Part.

Amendment by general procedure

42. (1) An amendment to the Constitution of Canada in relation to the following matters may be made only in accordance with subsection 38(1):

    (*a*) the principle of proportionate representation of the provinces in the House of Commons prescribed by the Constitution of Canada;

    (*b*) the powers of the Senate and the method of selecting Senators;

    (*c*) the number of members by which a province is entitled to be represented in the Senate and the residence qualifications of Senators;

    (*d*) subject to paragraph 41(*d*), the Supreme Court of Canada;

    (*e*) the extension of existing provinces into the territories; and

    (*f*) notwithstanding any other law or practice, the establishment of new provinces.

Exception

(2) Subsections 38(2) to (4) do not apply in respect of amendments in relation to matters referred to in subsection (1).

Amendment of provisions relating to some but not all provinces

43. An amendment to the Constitution of Canada in relation to any provision that applies to one or more, but not all, provinces, including

(*a*) any alteration to boundaries between provinces, and

(*b*) any amendment to any provision that relates to the use of the English or the French language within a province,

may be made by proclamation issued by the Governor General under the Great Seal of Canada only where so authorized by resolutions of the Senate and House of Commons and of the legislative assembly of each province to which the amendment applies.

Amendments by Parliament

44. Subject to sections 41 and 42, Parliament may exclusively make laws amending the Constitution of Canada in relation to the executive government of Canada or the Senate and House of Commons.

Amendments by provincial legislatures

45. Subject to section 41, the legislature of each province may exclusively make laws amending the constitution of the province.

Initiation of amendment procedures

46. (1) The procedures for amendment under sections 38, 41, 42 and 43 may be initiated either by the Senate or the House of Commons or by the legislative assembly of a province.

Revocation of authorization

(2) A resolution of assent made for the purposes of this Part may be revoked at any time before the issue of a proclamation authorized by it.

Amendments without Senate resolution

47. (1) An amendment to the Constitution of Canada made by proclamation under section 38, 41, 42 or 43 may be made without a resolution of the Senate authorizing the issue of the proclamation if, within one hundred and eighty days after the adoption by the House of Commons of a resolution authorizing its issue, the Senate has not adopted such a resolution and if, at any time after the expiration of that period, the House of Commons again adopts the resolution.

Computation of period

(2) Any period when Parliament is prorogued or dissolved shall not be counted in computing the one hundred and eighty day period referred to in subsection (1).

Advice to issue proclamation

48. The Queen's Privy Council for Canada shall advise the Governor General to issue a proclamation under this Part forthwith on the adoption of the resolutions required for an amendment made by proclamation under this Part.

Constitutional conference

49. A constitutional conference composed of the Prime Minister of Canada and the first ministers of the provinces shall be convened by the Prime Minister of Canada within fifteen years after this Part comes into force to review the provisions of this Part.

PART VI

AMENDMENT TO THE CONSTITUTION ACT, 1867

50.

51.

PART VII

GENERAL

Primacy of Constitution of Canada

52. (1) The Constitution of Canada is the supreme law of Canada, and any law that is inconsistent with the provisions of the Constitution is, to the extent of the inconsistency, of no force or effect.

Constitution of Canada

(2) The Constitution of Canada includes

(*a*) the *Canada Act 1982*, including this Act;

(*b*) the Acts and orders referred to in the schedule; and

(*c*) any amendment to any Act or order referred to in paragraph (*a*) or (*b*).

Amendments to Constitution of Canada

(3) Amendments to the Constitution of Canada shall be made only in accordance with the authority contained in the Constitution of Canada.

Repeals and new names

53. (1) The enactments referred to in Column I of the schedule are hereby repealed or amended to the extent indicated in Column II thereof and, unless repealed, shall continue as law in Canada under the names set out in Column III thereof.

Consequential amendments

(2) Every enactment, except the *Canada Act 1982*, that refers to an enactment referred to in the schedule by the name in Column I thereof is hereby amended by substituting for that name the corresponding name in Column III thereof, and any British North America Act not referred to in the schedule may be cited as the *Constitution Act* followed by the year and number, if any, of its enactment.

Repeal and consequential amendments

54. Part IV is repealed on the day that is one year after this Part comes into force and this section may be repealed and this Act renumbered, consequentially upon the repeal of Part IV and this section, by proclamation issued by the Governor General under the Great Seal of Canada.

54.1 Repealed.

French version of Constitution of Canada

55. A French version of the portions of the Constitution of Canada referred to in the schedule shall be prepared by the Minister of Justice of Canada as expeditiously as possible and, when any portion thereof sufficient to warrant action being taken has been so prepared, it shall be put forward for enactment by proclamation issued by the Governor General under the Great Seal of Canada pursuant to the procedure then applicable to an amendment of the same provisions of the Constitution of Canada.

English and French versions of certain constitutional texts

56. Where any portion of the Constitution of Canada has been or is enacted in English and French or where a French version of any portion of the Constitution is enacted pursuant to section 55, the English and French versions of that portion of the Constitution are equally authoritative.

English and French versions of this Act

57. The English and French versions of this Act are equally authoritative.

Commencement

58. Subject to section 59, this Act shall come into force on a day to be fixed by proclamation issued by the Queen or the Governor General under the Great Seal of Canada.

Commencement of paragraph 23(1)(*a*) in respect of Quebec

59. (1) Paragraph 23(1)(*a*) shall come into force in respect of Quebec on a day to be fixed by proclamation issued by the Queen or the Governor General under the Great Seal of Canada.

Authorization of Quebec

(2) A proclamation under subsection (1) shall be issued only where authorized by the legislative assembly or government of Quebec.

Repeal of this section

(3) This section may be repealed on the day paragraph 23(1)(*a*) comes into force in respect of Quebec and this Act amended and renumbered, consequentially upon the repeal of this section, by proclamation issued by the Queen or the Governor General under the Great Seal of Canada.

Short title and citations

60. This Act may be cited as the *Constitution Act, 1982*, and the Constitution Acts 1867 to 1975 (No. 2) and this Act may be cited together as the *Constitution Acts, 1867 to 1982*.

References

61. A reference to the "*Constitution Acts, 1867 to 1982*" shall be deemed to include a reference to the "*Constitution Amendment Proclamation, 1983*".

SCHEDULE TO THE CONSTITUTION ACT, 1982

(Section 53)

MODERNIZATION OF THE CONSTITUTION

Item	Column I Act Affected	Column II Amendment	Column III New Name
1.	British North America Act, 1867, 30-31 Vict., c. 3 (U.K.)	(1) Section 1 is repealed and the following substituted therefor: "1. This Act may be cited as the *Constitution Act, 1867.*" (2) Section 20 is repealed. (3) Class 1 of section 91 is repealed. (4) Class 1 of section 92 is repealed.	Constitution Act, 1867
2.	An Act to amend and continue the Act 32-33 Victoria chapter 3; and to establish and provide for the Government of the Province of Manitoba, 1870, 33 Vict., c. 3 (Can.)	(1) The long title is repealed and the following substituted therefor: "*Manitoba Act, 1870.*" (2) Section 20 is repealed.	Manitoba Act, 1870
3.	Order of Her Majesty in Council admitting Rupert's Land and the North-Western Territory into the union, dated the 23rd day of June, 1870		Rupert's Land and North-Western Territory Order
4.	Order of Her Majesty in Council admitting British Columbia into the Union, dated the 16th day of May, 1871.		British Columbia Terms of Union
5.	British North America Act, 1871, 34-35 Vict., c. 28 (U.K.)	Section 1 is repealed and the following substituted therefor: "1. This Act may be cited as the *Constitution Act, 1871.*"	Constitution Act, 1871
6.	Order of Her Majesty in Council admitting Prince Edward Island into the Union, dated the 26th day of June, 1873.		Prince Edward Island Terms of Union
7.	Parliament of Canada Act, 1875, 38-39 Vict., c. 38 (U.K.)		Parliament of Canada Act, 1875
8.	Order of Her Majesty in Council admitting all British possessions and Territories in North America and islands adjacent thereto into the Union, dated the 31st day of July, 1880.		Adjacent Territories Order

Item	Column I Act Affected	Column II Amendment	Column III New Name
9.	British North America Act, 1886, 49-50 Vict., c. 35 (U.K.)	Section 3 is repealed and the following substituted therefor: "3. This Act may be cited as the *Constitution Act, 1886*."	Constitution Act, 1886
10.	Canada (Ontario Boundary) Act, 1889, 52-53 Vict., c. 28 (U.K.)		Canada (Ontario Boundary) Act, 1889
11.	Canadian Speaker (Appointment of Deputy) Act, 1895, 2nd Sess., 59 Vict., c. 3 (U.K.)	The Act is repealed.	
12.	The Alberta Act, 1905, 4-5 Edw. VII, c. 3 (Can.)		Alberta Act
13.	The Saskatchewan Act, 1905, 4-5 Edw. VII, c. 42 (Can.)		Saskatchewan Act
14.	British North America Act, 1907, 7 Edw. VII, c. 11 (U.K.)	Section 2 is repealed and the following substituted therefor: "2. This Act may be cited as the *Constitution Act, 1907*."	Constitution Act, 1907
15.	British North America Act, 1915, 5-6 Geo. V, c. 45 (U.K.)	Section 3 is repealed and the following substituted therefor: "3. This Act may be cited as the *Constitution Act, 1915*."	Constitution Act, 1915
16.	British North America Act, 1930, 20-21 Geo. V, c. 26 (U.K.)	Section 3 is repealed and the following substituted therefor: "3. This Act may be cited as the Constitution Act, 1930."	Constitution Act, 1930
17.	Statute of Westminster, 1931, 22 Geo. V, c. 4 (U.K.)	In so far as they apply to Canada, (*a*) section 4 is repealed; and (*b*) subsection 7(1) is repealed.	Statute of Westminster, 1931
18.	British North America Act, 1940, 3-4 Geo. VI, c. 36 (U.K.)	Section 2 is repealed and the following substituted therefor: "2. This Act may be cited as the *Constitution Act, 1940*."	Constitution Act, 1940
19.	British North America Act, 1943, 6-7 Geo. VI, c. 30 (U.K.)	The Act is repealed.	
20.	British North America Act, 1946, 9-10 Geo. VI, c. 63 (U.K.)	The Act is repealed.	
21.	British North America Act, 1949, 12-13 Geo. VI, c. 22 (U.K.)	Section 3 is repealed and the following substituted therefor: "3. This Act may be cited as the *Newfoundland Act*."	Newfoundland Act
22.	British North America (No. 2) Act, 1949, 13 Geo. VI, c. 81 (U.K.)	The Act is repealed.	
23.	British North America Act, 1951, 14-15 Geo. VI, c. 32 (U.K.)	The Act is repealed.	

Item	Column I Act Affected	Column II Amendment	Column III New Name
24.	British North America Act, 1952, 1 Eliz. II, c. 15 (Can.)	The Act is repealed.	
25.	British North America Act, 1960, 9 Eliz. II, c. 2 (U.K.)	Section 2 is repealed and the following substituted therefor: "2. This Act may be cited as the *Constitution Act, 1960.*"	Constitution Act, 1960
26.	British North America Act, 1964, 12-13 Eliz. II, c. 73 (U.K.)	Section 2 is repealed and the following substituted therefor: "2. This Act may be cited as the *Constitution Act, 1964.*"	Constitution Act, 1964
27.	British North America Act, 1965, 14 Eliz. II, c. 4, Part I (Can.)	Section 2 is repealed and the following substituted therefor: "2. This Part may be cited as the *Constitution Act, 1965.*"	Constitution Act, 1965
28.	British North America Act, 1974, 23 Eliz. II, c. 13, Part I (Can.)	Section 3, as amended by 25-26 Eliz. II, c. 28, s. 38(1) (Can.), is repealed and the following substituted therefor: "3. This Part may be cited as the *Constitution Act, 1974.*"	Constitution Act, 1974
29.	British North America Act, 1975, 23-24 Eliz. II, c. 28, Part I (Can.)	Section 3, as amended by 25-26 Eliz. II, c. 28, s. 31 (Can.), is repealed and the following substituted therefor: "3. This Part may be cited as the *Constitution Act (No. 1), 1975.*"	Constitution Act (No. 1), 1975
30.	British North America Act (No. 2), 1975, 23-24 Eliz. II, c. 53 (Can.)	Section 3 is repealed and the following substituted therefor: "3. This Act may be cited as the *Constitution Act (No. 2), 1975.*"	Constitution Act (No. 2), 1975

Glossary

actus reus the objective part of a criminal offence; the actual criminal act *(p. 374)*

administrative agency government bodies created under various federal, provincial, and territorial statutes with the purpose of administering particular statutory regimes *(p. 338)*

administrative tribunal administrative agency that fulfills quasi-judicial functions as part of its mandate *(p. 342)*

admiralty (or maritime) law area of law that concerns maritime trade and commerce and that has a private international law component *(p. 309)*

adversarial system system, used in common law courts, whereby the primary responsibility for the presentation of cases lies with the opposing litigants and their counsel, not with the judge presiding over the case *(p. 41)*

affinity the relationship that a person has to the blood relatives of his or her spouse *(p. 299)*

affirmative action policy, particularly in relation to education or employment, intended to assist groups who have suffered past discrimination *(p. 224)*

aggravating circumstance a factor in the case that causes the judge to impose a harsher sentence on the convicted person than he or she otherwise would *(p. 388)*

agreement for sale agreement by which a person selling his property agrees to finance the purchase himself, keeping the title to the property while allowing the purchaser to take possession of it, and then transferring the title to the purchaser once the balance of the purchase price is paid *(p. 289)*

alternative dispute resolution (ADR) process used instead of a court trial to help settle a dispute *(p. 442)*

annulment the legal cancellation or invalidation of a marriage *(p. 299)*

appearance notice a document given to a person, usually at the scene of the crime, requiring that person to come to court on a certain date and time to answer to a charge *(p. 381)*

appellant individual, corporation, or other entity who lost at trial and who initiates an appeal to a higher court *(p. 193)*

arbitration dispute resolution process whereby the parties agree beforehand on an arbitrator to assist them, and they agree on whether the arbitrator's decision will be advisory or binding *(p. 442)*

arraignment procedure by which the charge is read to the accused in open court and the accused is asked how he or she wishes to plead *(p. 384)*

arrest detaining or holding a person by legal authority *(p. 379)*

article to serve an apprenticeship with a practising lawyer *(p. 400)*

assault psychological tort involving one person's apprehension of harmful physical contact from another person *(p. 247)*

banns of marriage the public announcement in church of an impending marriage *(p. 301)*

battery tort requiring actual occurrence of harmful or offensive physical contact *(p. 247)*

bencher lawyers (and some non-lawyers) who are responsible for administering and governing the work of a provincial law society *(p. 407)*

beneficial owner also called an equitable owner, the person on whose behalf and for whose benefit the trustee holds and manages the property *(p. 290)*

bicameral legislature with two houses involved in the passage of legislation *(p. 104)*

bijural nation a country, usually a federal state, having two different legal systems *(p. 60)*

bijuralism the operation of two legal systems in one jurisdiction, such as the common law and civil law systems in Canada *(p. 53)*

bilateral contract contracts in the form of a "promise for a promise" whereby the offeror promises something in exchange for a reciprocal promise *(p. 266)*

Bill of Rights (1689) English statute that formally ended the power of the Crown to legislate without the consent of Parliament *(p. 41)*

bill the draft version of a proposed new statute *(p. 117)*

binding term used to describe a higher court decision that a lower court in the same jurisdiction must follow according to the principle of *stare decisis* *(pp. 38, 186)*

bona fide occupational requirement in the context of employment, a bona fide (Latin for "in good faith") requirement is one that exists for a legitimate reason—for example, safety—and that cannot be removed without undue hardship on the employer *(p. 224)*

bright line rule strict rule that a lawyer or law firm cannot represent two current clients whose interests are directly adverse to each other unless both clients consent after receiving full disclosure from the lawyer *(p. 429)*

builders' lien charge against land that builders use to secure amounts owed them for work done on landowners' property *(p. 289)*

call to the bar formal ceremony whereby a law student becomes entitled to practise law *(p. 401)*

case depending on context, refers to the reasons for judgment (where the court provides them), to the court process more generally, or to the entire dispute from beginning to end *(p. 193)*

case brief summary of a case, with the constituent parts of the court's reasons for judgment arranged in a set order *(p. 199)*

cattle trespass a strict liability tort involving damage caused by straying cattle or other farm animals *(p. 257)*

caveat emptor principle that the buyer alone is responsible for ensuring the fitness of the goods he or she is purchasing (Latin: "Let the buyer beware") *(p. 325)*

cession the transfer of a colony from one country to another *(p. 62)*

Chancery department of state established by English monarchs to assist with legal matters and to issue writs *(p. 36)*

chapter number the number assigned to a statute when it is first passed or when it is republished in a statutory revision—refers to the chronological position of the statute within a particular legislative session, year, or revision *(p. 125)*

charges and encumbrances any claim on a parcel of real property—for example, mortgages, property taxes, or water rights *(p. 288)*

chattels tangible, movable objects such as furniture, equipment, and cars *(p. 294)*

chose in action the right to sue someone for an unpaid debt or liability; an intangible personal property right *(p. 295)*

civil code authoritative legislative encoding of a country's private law *(p. 42)*

Civil Code of Quebec (*Code Civil du Québec*) Quebec's current civil code, which came into effect on January 1, 1994, and which replaced the *Civil Code of Lower Canada* that had been in force since 1866 *(pp. 45, 68)*

civil law system of law based on codified rules; may also refer to private law *(p. 34)*

civil liberties rights and freedoms protected by the Charter *(p. 219)*

civil wrong a wrong that occurs in the context of relationships between persons and is addressed by one of the areas of private law *(p. 246)*

codes of conduct written sets of rules regulating the ethical behaviour of professionals *(p. 414)*

commencement (or coming into force) section section that details when or how a statute comes into effect *(p. 127)*

commissioner federally appointed official who is the formal head of the territorial executive government *(p. 154)*

Commissioner in Executive Council official name for a territorial Cabinet *(p. 154)*

common law system of law based on the English legal tradition, which relies on precedent rather than on codified rules; may also refer to (1) decisions by courts exercising their "common law" jurisdiction as opposed to their "equitable" jurisdiction based on broad principles of fairness, or to (2) case law generally as opposed to legislation *(p. 34)*

compensatory damages damages in a tort claim that compensate the plaintiff for proven and recognized types of losses *(p. 261)*

cones of silence institutional mechanisms used by law firms to secure confidential information so that lawyers working at the same law firm are prevented from accessing information that could prejudice a former client; sometimes also called Chinese walls *(p. 429)*

Confederation the coming together of the three British North American colonies of Nova Scotia, New Brunswick, and the Province of Canada (Ontario and Quebec) to form the Dominion of Canada in 1867. The term later included all the provinces and territories that have joined Canada since that date *(p. 64)*

confidence convention convention requiring the government to resign if it loses the support of the majority of the elected representatives in the House of Commons and, if a new government cannot be formed, to call an election *(p. 154)*

conflict of laws area of law—also referred to as *private international law*—that covers private law disputes that have an interprovincial or international component *(p. 309)*

consanguinity a blood relationship between relatives *(p. 299)*

consent (defence of) a defence against a variety of tort claims that is based on the idea that the plaintiff was aware of the risks associated with the activity that led to damages and agreed to participate in the activity anyway *(p. 255)*

consequential amendment section section in a new statute that amends existing legislation to make it consistent with the new statute *(p. 127)*

conspiracy arranging with other sellers to lessen competition and thereby exploit consumers *(p. 327)*

constitutional law law dealing with the distribution of governmental powers under Canada's Constitution *(p. 96)*

constitutionally entrenched describes a statute that falls within the definition of the Constitution of Canada as set out in section 52 of the *Constitution Act, 1982* *(p. 106)*

contributory negligence (defence of) a defence against negligent tort claims that is based on the idea that the plaintiff negligently contributed to her losses *(p. 255)*

convention established and traditional "rules" on which our system of responsible government is based and which qualify many of the rules of government set out in constitutional legislation such as the *Constitution Act, 1867*, but which are not, technically, legally binding *(p. 152)*

conveyancing the part of the real estate transaction that begins after the contract is entered into and that involves the actual transfer of title, or conveyance *(p. 293)*

conviction a judge or jury's finding an accused person guilty of an offence *(p. 384)*

corporation company or group of people authorized by statute to act as a single entity (legally a person) and recognized as such in law *(p. 323)*

Corpus Juris Civilis comprehensive codification of Roman civil law, compiled by the Emperor Justinian (483–565 CE) *(p. 44)*

corrective justice theory of justice according to which (1) a person has a moral responsibility for harm caused to another, and (2) the latter's loss must be rectified or corrected *(p. 8)*

court state-sanctioned forum where disputes between opposing litigants are formally adjudicated *(p. 170)*

Court of Chancery English court, existing separate from common law courts, established to provide equity *(p. 37)*

Court of King's (or Queen's) Bench English court that decided criminal matters *(p. 36)*

critical legal studies theory of law largely concerned with exposing law as an instrument of the rich and powerful *(p. 20)*

critical race theory theory of law that focuses on race-based inequities; an offshoot of critical legal studies *(p. 21)*

Crown the sovereign (currently the Queen), whose authority in Canada has been formally delegated to the governor general (federally) and to the lieutenant governor (provincially), but is actually exercised by the executive branch of government *(p. 148)*

Crown attorney a lawyer, also known as a Crown prosecutor, who is an agent of the attorney general and who represents the Crown in court, particularly in criminal matters *(p. 370)*

Crown immunity covering term for the various protections afforded the Crown, including Crown privilege, the presumptions of legislation not applying to the Crown, and (formerly) immunity from tortious liability *(p. 158)*

Crown privilege aspect of Crown immunity that permits the Crown to claim that evidence is privileged on the ground that its disclosure would adversely affect some matter of public interest *(p. 159)*

customary law system of law based on rules of conduct considered binding either at a local or an international level, with no formalized process in place for making, changing, or recording them *(p. 50)*

decision depending on context, refers to the outcome or disposition of a case, to the holding in the case, or (where the court provides them) to the entire set of reasons the court gives for its judgment *(p. 193)*

deeds formal documents showing ownership of property *(p. 292)*

defamation a tort involving allegations of impropriety that injure a person's reputation *(p. 259)*

defeasible term used for life estates that can be terminated by the fee simple owner if certain conditions are not met or certain defined events occur *(p. 288)*

defendant individual, corporation, or other entity who defends a non-criminal lawsuit initiated by the plaintiff *(p. 192)*

definition section a statute section that defines words that have a specific meaning in the statute *(p. 127)*

delegates non potest delegare principle that a person or body to whom power is delegated cannot subdelegate that power (Latin: "one to whom power is delegated cannot himself further delegate that power") *(p. 135)*

deontological theories that focus on the inherent rightness or wrongness of behaviour, without regard to the behaviour's consequences or outcomes *(p. 7)*

devolution the legislative arrangement whereby a central authority grants power to regional authorities that are subordinate to the central authority *(p. 123)*

discrimination prejudicial treatment of people on the ground of race, age, or sex; prohibited by human rights legislation *(p. 223)*

dissent refers (in the context of a split decision on appeal) to the judgment of one or more justices in the minority *(p. 179)*

distinguishable term given to a precedent from a higher court that a lower court decides not to follow, usually on the grounds that the facts in the cases differ *(p. 39)*

distributive justice theory of justice concerned with appropriate distributions of entitlements, such as wealth and power, in a society *(p. 12)*

division of powers refers to the divided jurisdiction—between Parliament, on one hand, and the provinces, on the other hand—to make legislation in a federal state such as Canada *(p. 110)*

domestic law the law of a particular state or society *(p. 26)*

double-aspect law a law whose subject matter falls within a federal subject area *and* a provincial one *(p. 116)*

duty of competence lawyer's obligation to provide services that meet the standard of a reasonably skilled lawyer *(p. 427)*

duty of confidentiality lawyer's obligation not to divulge information concerning a client's affairs that has been acquired in the course of the professional relationship, unless the client authorizes the lawyer to divulge this information *(p. 428)*

duty of disclosure the Crown's mandatory disclosure to the accused, before the trial, of the evidence against him or her *(p. 379)*

duty of loyalty lawyer's obligation to avoid conflicts of interest between clients and between lawyer and client *(p. 428)*

elder law area of private law that covers the various legal issues facing the elderly *(p. 307)*

enabling section section that delegates authority to make regulations to another person or body *(p. 127)*

entrenched in the Canadian context, law that is enshrined in the Constitution and cannot be changed unilaterally by the federal government or by any province, and cannot be changed except according to formal amending procedures set out in the Constitution *(p. 84)*

equity discretionary legal decisions offered by judges in the Court of Chancery, based on fairness and providing relief from the rigid procedures that had evolved under common law courts *(p. 37)*

essential validity concerns a person's capacity to marry and the substantive requirements of a valid marriage *(p. 298)*

ethics standards of right and wrong often applied to specific groups—for example, professions *(p. 7)*

exclusion clause clause in a contract limiting the liability of one of the parties to a fixed dollar amount or (for certain types of breaches of contract) completely *(p. 269)*

executive the branch of government that is responsible for administering or implementing the laws in Canada and whose authority, in this country, is divided between the federal, provincial, and territorial governments based on the division of legislative authority under the Constitution *(p. 148)*

expectation damages a remedy for contract disputes that attempts to place the innocent party in the position she would have been in if the contract had been performed as promised and all the contractual representations had been true *(p. 274)*

express terms contract terms that the parties have considered and deliberately included in the contract *(p. 269)*

facta (sing. factum) written legal arguments to be presented on an appeal *(p. 178)*

fairness (also procedural fairness or natural justice) principle that fairness requires that certain "rights" be accorded to persons engaged with an administrative process, such as the right to notice, the right to be heard and to respond, the right to representation, and the right to an adjudicator who is free from bias or an appearance of bias *(p. 349)*

false imprisonment tort whereby one person totally restrains the movement of another person *(p. 247)*

federal paramountcy doctrine doctrine according to which, in the event of conflict between a federal law and a provincial law in an area over which both levels of government have jurisdiction, the federal law governs and overrides the provincial one *(p. 117)*

federal superior courts (or federal courts) the Federal Court, the Federal Court of Appeal, the Tax Court of Canada, and the Court Martial Appeal Court *(p. 174)*

federalism in Canada, the division of state powers between the federal Parliament in Ottawa and the legislatures of the provinces and territories *(p. 81)*

fee simple ownership the most absolute form of private ownership, entitling the owner to possess the property, to build on it, and to transfer it to others during her lifetime or in a will at her death *(p. 287)*

feminist theories of law theories of law that generally concern the legal, social, and economic rights and opportunities of women *(p. 20)*

feudalism socio-political system in medieval Europe based on relationships of obligation and allegiance among king, nobles, and subjects, with land given to subordinates in return for loyalty and military support *(p. 35)*

fiduciary duty in the context of a partnership, the responsibility to act carefully and reasonably in the best interest of the firm *(p. 320)*

fiduciary obligations trust-like obligations, such as loyalty and good faith, that apply in certain contexts, including lawyer–client dealings *(p. 427)*

fixtures things that are attached to the land *(p. 294)*

foreclosure proceedings proceedings that the mortgagee (the lender) brings against the defaulting mortgagor (borrower) in order to foreclose the mortgagor's right to redeem her property *(p. 289)*

formal validity concerns the formalities or ceremonial requirements of a marriage *(p. 298)*

freehold interests form of property ownership that does not imply an obligation to pay rent *(p. 288)*

general partnership business structure in which two or more persons carry on business in common with a view to profit *(p. 320)*

governor general Queen's representative in Canada, formally authorized to exercise her powers as head of the executive government in Canada, but who, by convention, exercises these powers only on the advice of the prime minister and federal Cabinet *(p. 151)*

Governor in Council official name for the federal Cabinet *(p. 151)*

headnote (case) concise summary of reasons for judgment, located near the beginning of a reported version of the case *(p. 193)*

headnotes (statute) notes immediately above a section briefly summarizing its contents, serving the same purpose as marginal notes *(p. 128)*

human rights rights that respect the dignity and worth of an individual *(p. 222)*

hybrid offence a dual procedure offence, meaning that the Crown attorney has the option of choosing whether to prosecute it as a summary conviction offence or as an indictable offence *(p. 378)*

illegality (defence of) a defence to negligence claims that used to be applied when the plaintiff and defendant were involved in criminal or immoral activity at the time of the injury, but is now applied mainly when the plaintiff is trying to use the negligence action to avoid a criminal penalty *(p. 255)*

imperial statute law passed by the English Parliament applying specifically to an overseas English colony *(p. 62)*

implied terms contract terms that the parties have not explicitly included in the contract, but that are nonetheless part of the agreement *(p. 269)*

indefeasible not able to be annulled, made void, or overturned *(p. 292)*

indictable offence the most serious type of offence in the *Criminal Code* (for example, murder), carrying the most serious sentences *(p. 378)*

indictment written document, used in superior court, describing the offences with which the accused is charged *(p. 384)*

inferior courts provincial and territorial courts whose jurisdiction is limited to the less serious criminal matters, family and youth matters, and small claims disputes; the federal courts martial, part of the military court system, are also inferior courts *(p. 172)*

information written document, used in provincial court, describing the offences with which the accused is charged. *(p. 384)*

Inns of Court professional associations for lawyers in England and Wales, with supervisory and disciplinary functions over their members and authority to call law students to the bar; the four Inns of Court today are Inner Temple, Middle Temple, Lincoln's Inn, and Gray's Inn *(p. 38)*

inquisitorial system a feature of civil law proceedings whereby trial judges actively assist lawyers in presenting their cases and are free to call and question witnesses and to order investigations into other evidentiary matters; contrasts with the adversarial system used in common law courts *(p. 45)*

instrumentalist theories that focus on something—for example, justice or the law—as a means to an end *(p. 7)*

intellectual property property derived from the intellect, or mind—works of art, inventions, and designs *(p. 284)*

interest any right, claim, or privilege that an individual has with respect to real or personal property *(p. 285)*

intervenor a party, other than the original parties to a court proceeding, who does not have a substantial and direct interest in the proceeding but has interests and perspectives helpful to the judicial determination and whose input is accepted by the court *(pp. 236, 450)*

joint tenancy a form of co-ownership that features the right of survivorship as well as the "four unities" of *possession* (each co-owner has an equal right to possess the entire property), *interest* (each co-owner has an identical interest in the property), *time* (the co-owners receive their interests at the same time), and *title* (the co-owners receive their interests under the same instrument, such as a will) *(p. 290)*

judgment final outcome or disposition of the dispute heard before the court, or, when the court provides reasons for its judgment, the entire set of reasons *(p. 171)*

Judicial Committee of the Privy Council the highest appeal authority for colonies in the British Empire; exercised final appeal for Canada until 1949 *(p. 85)*

judicial independence principle that judges should be free to make decisions based on the law and free from outside interference *(p. 189)*

judicial interim release formal name for bail; the release of an accused prior to his or her trial *(p. 383)*

judicial review (of decisions by administrative bodies) process by which a superior court can review the decision of an administrative body or inferior court on a number of grounds, including: substantive review (review of the merits of the decision), review of discretionary decisions, and procedural review (review of the "process" followed in making the decision) *(p. 346)*

judicial review (of government power on constitutional grounds) process by which a court reviews the exercise of government power to ensure that it is constitutionally valid *(p. 86)*

jurisdiction refers (in the context of legislative power under the Constitution) to the specific subject areas over which the federal Parliament and the provincial legislatures have been assigned authority *(p. 107)*

jurisprudence also known as "philosophy of law" or "science of law"; concerns theories that are used to describe, explain, or criticize the law *(p. 14)*

jus cogens principles of international law, based on custom, that are overriding or peremptory and that cannot be changed by treaty *(p. 358)*

king's peace the ideal peace and well-being of a nation that the English monarch was obliged to uphold and protect *(p. 36)*

law and society a kind of legal study that looks at law from a broadly social, interdisciplinary perspective *(p. 20)*

law society the governing body of lawyers in a province *(p. 406)*

lawyer–client privilege lawyer's obligation not to divulge confidential information concerning a client's affairs that has been communicated to the lawyer by the client and is connected to the giving or receiving of legal advice *(p. 428)*

leasehold interests form of property ownership that implies an obligation to pay rent *(p. 288)*

legal aid government funding of lawyers who provide legal assistance to persons with low income *(p. 439)*

legal ethics area of law that deals with the ethical issues facing legal professionals in all facets of their practice *(p. 311)*

legal positivism theory that the only valid source of law is the principles, rules, and regulations expressly enacted by the institutions or persons within a society that are generally recognized as having the power to enact them *(p. 17)*

legal realism a theory, developed in the US and Scandinavian countries, that encouraged a more thoroughly empirical study of the process by which laws are made and applied *(p. 18)*

legislation written laws made by legislative assemblies *(p. 105)*

legislative intent a legislature's express or implied intent in passing a statute *(p. 128)*

legislature representative assembly charged under a constitution with making laws for a particular region or state *(p. 104)*

letters patent orders, based on royal prerogative, that establish rights, titles, or offices of particular persons or corporations *(p. 155)*

libel a kind of defamation that involves defamatory language in writing, such as in a newspaper article or book, whether in print or online *(p. 260)*

lieutenant governor formal head of the provincial executive government who, by convention, exercises executive power on the advice of the provincial premier and Cabinet *(p. 151)*

Lieutenant Governor in Council official name for a provincial Cabinet *(p. 154)*

life estate ownership type of ownership whereby the fee simple owner grants a person (the life tenant) exclusive possession of a property for that person's lifetime, with the condition that the estate reverts to the fee simple owner at the life tenant's death *(p. 287)*

limitation period the period of time in which a legal action must be taken or the ability to do so is lost *(p. 376)*

limited liability partnership partnership structure used by certain professions in Canada (accountants and lawyers, for the most part) whereby partners are not liable for the professional negligence of other partners *(p. 321)*

limited partnership partnership structure involving at least one general partner, who operates the partnership and is liable for any partnership debts, and at least one limited partner, who invests in the partnership but does not operate it or take part in managing its business and is not personally liable for its debts and obligations *(p. 320)*

lobbying organized effort to influence legislators on behalf of a particular interest *(p. 449)*

majority refers (in the context of a split decision on appeal) to the group of justices who form the majority and whose decision becomes the decision of the court *(p. 179)*

marginal notes notes in the margin beside a section briefly summarizing its contents *(p. 128)*

Marxist theories of law legal theories, based on the writing of the communist philosopher Karl Marx, that are concerned with the distribution of wealth in a society; related to distributive justice theories *(p. 20)*

mediation dispute resolution process whereby the parties try to reach a settlement with the assistance of a third party *(p. 442)*

mens rea the subjective part of a criminal offence; the intention or knowledge of wrongdoing *(p. 374)*

military law a constitutionally separate and relatively self-contained system of law regulating the Canadian Forces *(p. 26)*

misfeasance negligent tort that involves doing something carelessly (as opposed to omitting to do something) *(p. 251)*

misrepresentations false representations made during contract negotiations *(p. 271)*

mitigating circumstance a factor in the case that causes the judge to impose a milder sentence on the convicted person than he or she would otherwise *(p. 388)*

morality standards of right and wrong, often associated with personal character *(p. 6)*

mortgage a kind of charge against land that secures a debt owed by the landowner *(p. 288)*

municipal bylaws form of subordinate legislation passed by municipalities *(p. 136)*

natural law theory that there is a source of law that is higher than man-made law, with which man-made law must try to comply *(p. 14)*

negligence area of tort law that addresses harm caused by *carelessness*, not intentional harm *(p. 251)*

negotiation dispute resolution process whereby the parties talk to each other directly and seek a mutually acceptable solution to their problem *(p. 442)*

neutral citation unique citation protocol, recognized internationally and in all Canadian courts, according to which courts number each of their judgments consecutively for the year in question, as well as the paragraphs within judgments *(p. 209)*

nominal damages damages in a tort claim that reflect the breach of a plaintiff's right where no actual loss has been sustained *(p. 262)*

nonfeasance negligent tort that involves omitting to do something the law requires you to do *(p. 253)*

nuisance in law, either public or private nuisance *(p. 259)*

obiter dicta or obiter (sing. obiter dictum) statements made by the court in its reasons for judgment that may be of interest but that are inessential to the decision and therefore have no binding authority *(p. 198)*

occupiers' liability the liability of occupiers of land for injuries that visitors sustain while on the occupiers' property *(p. 256)*

open court principle principle that judicial proceedings should be administered in public *(p. 189)*

parliamentary sovereignty doctrine that Parliament has ultimate and complete power to pass any law *(p. 138)*

patriate remove a nation's legislation or constitution from the control of the mother country and bring it under the control of the nation itself *(p. 87)*

personal property tangible, movable objects as well as intangible interests such as shares in a company *(p. 284)*

personal property security creditor's security based on the debtor's personal property *(p. 295)*

persuasive describes a precedent that a court is persuaded to give some weight to but is not bound to follow, because the precedent is from another jurisdiction or is otherwise not binding *(pp. 39, 186)*

plaintiff individual, corporation, or other entity who initiates a non-criminal lawsuit *(pp. 37, 192)*

plea bargain agreement between the Crown and the defence on how the accused will plead in court and on the sentence he or she will receive *(p. 384)*

plead to answer to a criminal charge in ways permitted by the *Criminal Code* *(p. 383)*

POGG power the general *residuary power* given to Parliament—in other words, the power to fill in the gaps left by the specifically enumerated areas of jurisdiction assigned to the two levels of government *(p. 112)*

positive law man-made law, as opposed to a higher law (natural law) that transcends persons or institutions *(p. 18)*

pre-sentence report a report, prepared by a probation officer that provides information about the background and character of the offender, to assist a judge in sentencing *(p. 388)*

preamble an introductory sentence or two at the beginning of a statute that succinctly states the statute's key philosophical aspect or purpose *(p. 126)*

precedent court decision that, under the doctrine of *stare decisis*, is binding on lower courts in the same jurisdiction *(pp. 38, 185)*

preliminary inquiry hearing before a Provincial Court judge to determine whether the Crown has sufficient evidence for the accused to stand trial for the offence *(p. 384)*

premier the political head of a provincial or territorial government who leads the party with control of the majority in the Legislative Assembly (in Nunavut, there are no political parties but the premier must command the support of the majority in the Assembly) *(p. 154)*

prerogative writs special common law remedies for administrative infractions *(p. 350)*

prime minister the political head of state in Canada who leads the party with control of the majority of in the House of Commons *(p. 153)*

principle of non-interference the convention prohibiting direct interference by politicians with court proceedings *(p. 161)*

private bill a bill dealing with a private matter that relates, for example, to a particular individual, corporation, or charity *(p. 117)*

private law law that concerns the relationships between persons *(p. 26)*

private nuisance a tort that involves one person's using her property in such a way as to substantially interfere with another person's enjoyment or use of his property, but without any actual trespass occurring *(p. 259)*

pro bono term applied to legal work that lawyers do at no charge to help the public (from the Latin *pro bono publico*: "for the public good") *(p. 440)*

procedural law law relating to the process by which core rights and obligations are determined and enforced *(p. 26)*

proclamation a special government order bringing a statute into force *(p. 119)*

prorogued the formal closing of a legislative session *(p. 112)*

provincial superior courts provincially constituted courts with inherent jurisdiction to hear all matters (unless taken away by legislation) with two levels, a trial level and an appeal level—sometimes refers just to the trial level *(p. 173)*

public bill a bill dealing with a matter of public policy *(p. 117)*

public international law (or international law) the law relating to international treaties and customs, to inter-state relationships, and to the relationship between states and non-nationals *(pp. 26, 350)*

public law law dealing with the legal relationship between a state and individual members of the state *(p. 26)*

public nuisance occurs when a public interest is interfered with—for example, when a highway is obstructed or a river is polluted through the defendant's actions *(p. 259)*

puisne term applied to describe judges who rank below another judge or judges on the same court—for example, the judges below the chief justice on an appeal court *(p. 176)*

punitive damages damages in a tort claim that are granted in situations where the court wishes to punish the defendant for socially objectionable behaviour *(p. 262)*

quasi-criminal offences offences that are created by provinces and municipalities and that fall within provincial jurisdiction—for example, health, education, and highway traffic laws *(p. 373)*

quasi-legislative materials non-legislated written rules that relate to and affect a legal process *(p. 137)*

Queen's Privy Council for Canada formal advisory council of the governor general, the active portion of which consists of the federal Cabinet *(p. 154)*

ratio or **ratio decidendi** Latin phrase ("the reason for the decision") referring to the governing rule in a case or the way it was applied to the facts *(pp. 38, 185)*

reading a bill's formal presentation to the legislature before it becomes a statute *(p. 118)*

real property (or real estate) land and anything attached to the land, such as buildings and resources *(p. 284)*

rectification for contract disputes based on errors in the written contract, a remedy whereby the court orders that the contract be rewritten to correct the mistake *(p. 277)*

reference special case in which the executive branch of government refers a question of law to a court of appeal, usually a question concerning the constitutionality of a statute or course of action the government is considering *(p. 178)*

regulations form of subordinate legislation passed by a person or body (frequently the government Cabinet) to expand on or fill out a statute's legislative scheme *(p. 136)*

reliance damages a remedy for contract disputes that compensates the innocent party for expenses he incurred preparing for the performance of contractual obligations *(p. 274)*

rescission a remedy for contract disputes whereby the contract is cancelled and the parties are returned to the positions they were in just before the contract was entered into *(p. 276)*

reserve postpone rendering its decision, after a hearing has concluded, so the court can carefully prepare the reasons for its judgment *(p. 179)*

respondent individual, corporation, or other entity who won at trial and who is responding to the appellant on an appeal to a higher court *(p. 193)*

responsible (or parliamentary) government system of government in which the members of the executive branch are drawn from the elected members of the legislative branch and in which their power continues only so long as they enjoy the support of the majority in the legislature *(p. 148)*

restitution damages a remedy for contract disputes that compensates the innocent party for moneys usually paid over to the other party (deposits and part payments, for example) *(p. 274)*

retributive justice theory of justice based on *lex talionis*, or the law of retaliation *(p. 10)*

revised statutes republished, revised collection of all public statutes for a jurisdiction, providing a comprehensive statutory "snapshot" as of the revision date *(p. 140)*

right of survivorship a main condition of joint tenancy whereby the surviving co-owners automatically inherit a deceased owner's share *(p. 290)*

riparian rights rights that are attached to property fronting lakes or rivers and that include the right to make use of the water for certain activities and the obligation not to interfere with the riparian rights of others *(p. 291)*

royal assent formal approval of a bill by the Queen's representative *(p. 118)*

royal prerogative powers and privileges given by the common law to the Crown; a source of limited executive power *(p. 155)*

royal proclamation public announcement of a formal order concerning some executive action based on royal prerogative, such as a declaration of war *(p. 155)*

rule in *Rylands v Fletcher* the strict liability rule that the person who brings a dangerous substance onto his property is answerable for the damage it causes if it should escape *(p. 257)*

rule of law a key legal concept whose central tenets are that everyone is equal before the law and that power under the law should not be used arbitrarily *(p. 21)*

***scienter* action** a strict liability tort claim concerning damage caused by a domestic animal; based on the idea that the defendant (the owner) had knowledge the animal was dangerous *(p. 257)*

search warrant a warrant, issued by a justice of the peace or a provincial court judge, authorizing police to conduct a search *(p. 381)*

section 96 courts provincial superior courts, so called because their judges are federally appointed under section 96 of the *Constitution Act, 1867* *(p. 173)*

section the basic unit of a statute *(p. 127)*

sentence the punishment the judge imposes on a person convicted of a criminal offence *(p. 386)*

separation-of-powers doctrine doctrine according to which separate powers are assigned to the legislative, executive, and judicial branches of government *(p. 104)*

short title abbreviated version of the full statute title *(p. 125)*

slander a kind of defamation transmitted via oral or other transitory forms of communication *(p. 260)*

sociology of law a kind of sociological study that looks at law from a broadly social, interdisciplinary perspective *(p. 20)*

sole proprietorship business that is owned and operated by an individual and that is not a legal entity separate from the owner *(p. 318)*

specific performance a remedy for contract disputes whereby the court orders the party in breach to perform his obligations as promised *(p. 276)*

standard of review defines the level of deference the court pays to the tribunal when conducting a judicial review *(p. 348)*

stare decisis Latin phrase ("to stand by decided matters") referring to the common law principle that a precedent is binding on lower courts in the same jurisdiction *(pp. 38, 185)*

state immunity immunity that a state or its officials have in the event they become the subject of judicial proceedings in another state *(p. 354)*

state jurisdiction area of control within which a state's sovereignty can be exercised *(p. 353)*

state responsibility principle that a state should be held accountable for breaches of international obligations *(p. 354)*

state sovereignty principle that a state has exclusive power in certain areas, such as the power to make, administer, and adjudicate its own laws in relation to itself and its own citizens and residents *(p. 353)*

statutes the primary form of legislation *(p. 105)*

statutory interpretation process of interpreting legislation to resolve any ambiguities regarding its meaning or effect *(p. 128)*

strict liability tort a tort for which the defendant is held responsible even if the damaging action was neither intentional nor a result of negligence *(p. 256)*

style of cause the name of the case or title of the proceeding, consisting of the names of the parties to the dispute *(p. 209)*

"subject" of international law usually a state that has as an "international legal personality" and is capable of possessing international rights and obligations *(p. 353)*

subordinate (or delegated) legislation legislation passed pursuant to a statute, whereby the principal lawmaking power has *delegated* authority to another body to make laws *(p. 135)*

substantive laws laws that deal with core rights and obligations *(p. 26)*

substantive review review of an administrative decision's merits that considers both the legal and factual bases of the tribunal's analysis *(p. 348)*

succession law area of private law that covers issues to do with wills and estates and the transmission of property upon death *(p. 307)*

summary conviction offence the least serious type of offence in the *Criminal Code* (for example, trespassing or disturbing the peace), tried only in provincial court and subject to the lightest sentences *(p. 376)*

summons a document served personally on an accused person requiring him or her to be in court at a certain date and time *(p. 383)*

superior court of criminal jurisdiction the highest court in each province and territory to hear criminal matters, sometimes with a jury, its designation varying by province and territory *(p. 378)*

support property owner's obligation to consider how changes made to his property may affect his neighbour's property *(p. 291)*

supremacy clause section 52(1) of the *Constitution Act, 1982*, which provides that the Constitution is the supreme law of Canada and empowers the courts to find that laws that are inconsistent with the Constitution are of no force and effect *(p. 109)*

Supreme Court of Canada Canada's highest court and final court of appeal *(p. 174)*

tenancy in common a form of co-ownership that does not involve the four unities or the right of survivorship, so that a co-owner can transfer her interest to others during her lifetime or leave it to others in her will *(p. 290)*

territorial superior courts federally constituted superior courts with jurisdiction in the territories *(p. 174)*

Torrens system system for registering property ownership that eliminates the transfer of title by deeds and replaces them with statutory transfer forms, so that the title is guaranteed (or *indefeasible*) *(p. 292)*

tort a type of civil wrong for which damages can be obtained by the person wronged *(p. 246)*

trespass to goods (or trespass to chattels) a tort whereby one person intentionally interferes with another's rightful possession of movable property *(p. 248)*

trespass to land tort involving the physical intrusion by one person onto land occupied by another *(p. 248)*

trespass to person an intentional tort encompassing three subcategories of tort: assault, battery, and false imprisonment *(p. 247)*

trustee someone who has legal title to the property, but holds it for another and has the fiduciary responsibility to make decisions for the benefit of the other party *(p. 290)*

ultra vires outside the jurisdiction of the enacting authority *(p. 110)*

undertaking (1) a promise to appear in court at a certain date and time *(p. 383)*; (2) clear statement of intention by one person that is reasonably relied on by another, amounting to a solemn promise that must be kept or the person who has given the undertaking will be liable for misconduct *(p. 426)*

unicameral legislature with one house involved in the passage of legislation *(p. 104)*

unified family courts special divisions of the trial level of a provincial superior court with complete jurisdiction over family law matters, including matters that would otherwise be heard in a provincial inferior court *(p. 181)*

unilateral contract contracts that are in the form of a "promise for an action," the offeror promising something (usually payment) if the offeree accepts by performing a requested action *(p. 266)*

unitary government a form of government whereby one supreme authority governs the whole country *(p. 81)*

verdict the finding of a jury on the matter before it—for example, whether the accused is guilty or not guilty *(p. 385)*

vicarious liability the strict liability of one party for the fault of another due to the special relationship between them (typically, an employer–employee relationship) *(p. 258)*

writ court document, obtained by a plaintiff, by which the defendant was informed that a particular type of action had been started against him or her *(p. 37)*

Index

Image Credits

CHAPTER 1

Page 3: © Anthony Baggett | Dreamstime.com.

Page 10: © duncan1890/iStock.

Page 13: Chiloa/Wikipedia Commons.

Page 22: Photos.com/Thinkstock.

CHAPTER 2

Page 33: © TommL/iStock.

Page 43: © EmmePi Images/Alamy.

Pages 54-55: With permission of JuriGlobe.

CHAPTER 3

Page 59: Law Society of Upper Canada Archives, Archives Department collection, "Toronto. Osgoode Hall.", S1156.

Page 62: C.W. Robinson, Life of Sir John Beverley Robinson (Toronto, 1904), 66.

Page 65: Collections of the Nova Scotia Historical Society. Volume XVIII. Printed for the Society by WM MacNab & Son, Halifax, N.S. 1914

Page 67: The Death of General Wolfe, 1770, Benjamin West. American, British, 1738–1820, oil on canvas, 152.6 x 214.5 cm. Transfer from the Canadian War Memorials, 1921 (Gift of the 2nd Duke of Westminster, England, 1918). National Gallery of Canada (no. 8007).

Page 68: MP-0000.1815.2 | Photograph | Commission to codify the laws of Lower Canada in civil matters, Quebec City, QC, about 1865 © McCord Museum.

Pages 70-71: Canadian Geographic.

Page 72: M993X.5.1010 | Print | The East welcomes the West. Presentation of B.C. representatives to Sir John A. © McCord Museum.

CHAPTER 4

Page 75: Ron Poling/CP Photo.

Page 80: G.P. Roberts/Library and Archives Canada, C-000733.

Page 95: John McNeill/The Globe and Mail/CP Photo.

CHAPTER 5

Page 103: Keith Binns/iStock/Thinkstock.

Page 107: jiawangkun/Shutterstock.

Page 109: © Wangkun Jia | Dreamstime.com.

CHAPTER 6

Page 147: Library and Archives Canada/C-9060.

Page 150: © All rights reserved. Queen Elizabeth RCMP Inspection—Regina, May 2005. Reproduced with the permission of the Minister of Canadian Heritage, 2013.

Page 152: Speech from the Throne: Turning a New Leaf, Privy Council Office, 2013. Reproduced with the permission of the Minister of Public Works and Government Services, 2013.

CHAPTER 7

Page 169: Keith Binns/iStock/Thinkstock.

Page 179: © Supreme Court of Canada. Photographer: Philippe Landreville.

Page 180: Michael Bedford, Ottawa.

CHAPTER 8

Page 217: Canadian Charter of Rights and Freedoms, © Government of Canada. Reproduced with the permission of the Minister of Public Works and Government Services Canada (2013). Source: Library and Archives Canada/Robert Stacey fonds/e010758222.

Page 221: DPA/Landov.

Page 230: Tom Hanson/CP Photo.

CHAPTER 9
Page 243: © wragg/iStock.

CHAPTER 10
Page 283: © teekid/iStock.

Page 299: Ric Ernst/The Province/PNG.

CHAPTER 11
Page 317: Alexander Novikov/iStock/Thinkstock.

CHAPTER 12
Page 335: © Silver11 | Dreamstime.com.

CHAPTER 13
Page 369: © MivPiv/iStock.

CHAPTER 14
Page 399: Kzenon/Shutterstock.

Page 404: Library and Archives Canada/PA-12848.

CHAPTER 15
Page 411: © pixhook/iStock.

CHAPTER 16
Page 429: CHRIS WATTIE/Reuters/Landov.

Page 449: Library and Archives Canada/PA-37463/
With permission from the Estate of Duncan Cameron.